"With remarkable clarity and helpful analysis, Brian Rosner provides a template for understanding the expressive individualism so prevalent in the West. Rosner does so in an irenic way that makes this book approachable to those caught up in individualist approaches. It will be a helpful primer to some of the more important conversations people have *at* each other today—and it can help us to start talking *with* one another instead."

Ed Stetzer, Professor and Dean, Wheaton College

"What a solid and needed book! *How to Find Yourself* is about locating yourself not in the privatized world of your own self-constructed identity but in the social and divine contexts in which people live, made as they are in the image of God. In a modern world filled with loneliness and dislocation, this book connects you with life as it was designed to be lived with others. It sees life in the world for the challenge it often is, including the faults of what we do to one another, but it does not hide from the responsibility we all have for making it that way and from the opportunity that a connection to God and care for others has for making it better."

Darrell L. Bock, Executive Director of Cultural Engagement, The Hendricks Center, Dallas Theological Seminary

"*How to Find Yourself* gives readers a roadmap to the stories that compete for our affections. And Brian Rosner reveals the gospel as the compass that shows the way home. If you want to understand this cultural moment, pay close attention to this book."

Collin Hansen, Vice President for Content and Editor in Chief, The Gospel Coalition; Host, *Gospelbound* podcast

"How do I 'find myself'? For many today, this question is both puzzling and provocative. How does it involve my sexuality, my ethnicity, my family, my country, and my very soul? For Brian Rosner, this is not merely academic but deeply personal. As he exposes the shortcomings of looking only inward, he answers these questions from sociology and, above all, the Bible. This volume is a countercultural but profoundly helpful contribution to the topic of identity."

Richard Chin, National Director, Australian Fellowship of Evangelical Students; author, *Captivated by Christ*

"*How to Find Yourself* powerfully confronts one of the most pertinent cultural issues of our time—namely, personal identity. Rosner writes with clarity and verve, synthesizing the best current research and scholarship. The book reveals the numerous shortcomings of the dominant cultural narrative of expressive individualism, which encourages us to 'find ourselves' through looking inward and becoming who we 'really are.' Powerful though it is, there is a deep poverty to this idea, which leaves people—particularly younger generations—profoundly dissatisfied. *How to Find Yourself* turns to an alternative and far richer story. Paradoxically, rather than belonging to ourselves, it is precisely in losing ourselves that we can find our identity, by belonging to the story of God's people, based on the life of Jesus Christ. Providing insights from his own deeply moving story, Rosner shows that this countercultural path offers a way of finding ourselves that gives meaning to our suffering and is a call to serve others. *How to Find Yourself* will challenge you to assess your most foundational assumptions about who you are."

Sarah Irving-Stonebraker, Senior Lecturer in Modern European History, Western Sydney University

"The personal restlessness, dissatisfaction, and cultural mayhem produced by our attempts to find and identify ourselves from within, without external reference points, is deeply saddening. Once, we assumed that our identity related to the greater purposes of a higher being. Increasingly now, we favor starting with the idea that we can be our own gods, providing our own morality, reason for being, purpose, and direction in life, only to find that we are grievously inadequate to the task. Brian Rosner writes with the quiet authority of a deeply informed mind, keen observation of the human condition, and the warm understanding of personal experience of that condition. The result is a highly valuable book that offers wise counsel on combining a right personal reflectiveness with the wisdom of the ages as a better way."

John Anderson, Former Deputy Prime Minister of Australia

How to Find Yourself

How to Find Yourself

Why Looking Inward Is Not the Answer

Brian Rosner

Foreword by Carl R. Trueman

WHEATON, ILLINOIS

How to Find Yourself: Why Looking Inward Is Not the Answer

Copyright © 2022 by Brian Rosner

Published by Crossway
         1300 Crescent Street
         Wheaton, Illinois 60187

Cover design: Spencer Fuller, Faceout Studios

First printing 2022

Printed in the United States of America

Some content in the introduction and chapters 1, 4, 8, 11, and 13 are taken from *Known by God: A Biblical Theology of Personal Identity* by Brian S. Rosner. Copyright © 2017 by Brian S. Rosner. Used by permission of Zondervan. www.zondervan.com.

Some content in chapter 10 is take from Brian Rosner, "Justice," in *NIV Biblical Theology Study Bible* edited by D. A. Carson. Copyright © 2018 by Zondervan. Used by permission of Zondervan. www.zondervan.com.

Some content in the introduction and chapters 2, 10, 11, and 12 is adapted from Brian S. Rosner, "Identity Angst: Narrative Identity and Anglican Liturgy," in *Making the Word of God Fully Known: Essays on Church, Culture, and Mission in Honor of Archbishop Philip Freier* edited by Paul A. Barker and Bradley S. Billings. Used by permission of Wipf and Stock Publishers, www.wipfandstock.com.

Trade paperback ISBN: 978-1-4335-7815-1
ePub ISBN: 978-1-4335-7818-2
PDF ISBN: 978-1-4335-7816-8
Mobipocket ISBN: 978-1-4335-7817-5

Library of Congress Cataloging-in-Publication Data

Names: Rosner, Brian S., author. | Trueman, Carl R, other.
Title: How to find yourself : why looking inward is not the answer / Brian Rosner ; foreword by Carl R Trueman.
Description: Wheaton, Illinois : Crossway, 2022. | Includes bibliographical references and index.
Identifiers: LCCN 2021045822 (print) | LCCN 2021045823 (ebook) | ISBN 9781433578151 (trade paperback) | ISBN 9781433578168 (pdf) | ISBN 9781433578175 (mobipocket) | ISBN 9781433578182 (epub)
Subjects: LCSH: Identity (Psychology)—Religious aspects—Christianity. | Self—Religious aspects—Christianity. | Individualism—Religious aspects—Christianity.
Classification: LCC BV4509.5 .R6635 2022 (print) | LCC BV4509.5 (ebook) | DDC 248.4—dc23
LC record available at https://lccn.loc.gov/2021045822
LC ebook record available at https://lccn.loc.gov/2021045823

Crossway is a publishing ministry of Good News Publishers.

VP			31	30	29	28	27	26	25	24	23	22
15	14	13	12	11	10	9	8	7	6	5	4	3	2	1

To my children, their partners, and my grandchildren:
Elizabeth, Emily, William, Toby, Phil, Gabbie, Eloise, and Ivy.

Contents

PART 4: THE NEW YOU

Foreword

TODAY, THERE IS perhaps no more pressing a topic than identity. Whether we are speaking about race, ethnicity, or sexuality and how they shape political discourse, or about our own personal sense of self and how that informs our day-to-day lives, the question of identity is omnipresent, all-pervasive, and deeply influential. And yet this is historically unusual: one can look long and hard in literature prior to the 1960s and find little or no discussion of identity in the manner in which we think of it today. And that in itself is significant for it is only when something can no longer be assumed, when it becomes something about which we imagine we have some power of choice, that it becomes a source of reflection and debate.

So it is with identity. In times past, a relative static social order and comparatively stable institutions—for example, nation, church, family—meant that personal identity was something we were given, something over which we had little or no choice. But in a world of flux and change, such as that which we now inhabit, such solid external markers of identity no longer provide us with the framework for understanding ourselves. At the same time, and perhaps in part as a response to this, the question of identity has been further complicated by the prioritizing of feelings and psychology as determinative of who we are. To the question, Who are you?, there now seems for so many people no easy or straightforward answer.

This is particularly pressing for Christians. Not only are we Christians called to maintain that human identity is ultimately rooted in the fact that we are made in God's image; we are also called to relativize any competing claims to offer identity in light of that fact. In a world where so many identities now set themselves in direct opposition to traditional Christianity, that makes our situation even more complicated.

Any Christian response must address, first, the nature of contemporary thinking about identity and the self. Then, second, it needs to look at how identities are actually formed. Yes, we tend to think of identity as a monologue: I am exactly who I tell myself I am, and I make the choices that contribute to that. But in reality, identity is always a dialogue: the choices I make are shaped by the people and the institutions with which I have connections; I, like you, am a relational being whose identity cannot be isolated from the network of social relationships in which I exist. And third, it needs to set these two dimensions—the monologic and the dialogic—in the context of biblical teaching. Clearly, the Bible contains introspection—look at many of the Psalms—and also places a premium on interpersonal human relationships, but it also sets both within the context of the great, objective existence of God and the truth of the gospel story. The key is to see how that story should inform how we think about selfhood and identity today.

In this volume, Brian Rosner does just that. Even as he critiques many aspects of modern identity, he seeks to build connections between how we think and how the Bible indicates we should think. This is not polemical, but it is not soft on what is wrong in our era. Nor is it heavy sociology or theology, but rather it is substantial and engaging, pressing on an issue— perhaps *the* issue—of our day in a clear and thoughtful manner. And Brian has that rare gift of being able to communicate deep biblical insight in prose that does not drag or confuse but rather engages the reader and helps us to see ourselves more clearly. This is a fine volume that punches far above its weight. Pastors, teachers, youth leaders, parents, and thoughtful Christians everywhere will find it a worthwhile and edifying read.

Carl R. Trueman
Grove City College

Preface

THIS BOOK IS ABOUT your favorite subject: you! Personal identity is a subject of unprecedented interest in our day. It has never been more important to know who you are. It has also never been more difficult. That conundrum lies at the heart of this book. My interest in the subject of personal identity goes back to my own crisis of identity in the mid-1990s. It is an intensely personal book, both for the author and the readers.

This is my second book on personal identity. *Known by God: A Biblical Theology of Personal Identity* (Grand Rapids, MI: Zondervan, 2017) concentrates on the Bible's teaching about the subject. This book looks more directly at our cultural moment and the identity angst that seems to have engulfed our age. It was written with two convictions: many people find personal identity to be a subject that is confusing and confronting; and the gospel story offers a better way to find and be yourself than the one currently offered by modern society.

Every author knows that humans are social beings and that sole authorship is a ruse. This book began its life as the 2017 New College Lectures at the University of New South Wales. I am grateful to New College for the privilege of delivering the lectures and for an enjoyable week during which my ideas were challenged and revised.

Ridley College has been a great context in which to develop the ideas of this book. The gospel-shaped community of faculty, staff, and students is warm and cheerful, and it upholds the highest academic standards. I finished the book during a semester's study leave in the second half of 2019. I appreciate the board's generous support and encouragement of the increasingly scarce species of scholar principal.

I owe a debt of gratitude to many other people who helped in writing the book, too numerous to list in full. The standouts include Gina Denholm, whose keen eye helped me to knock off many of the rough edges, and the team at Crossway for their fellowship in the gospel and consummate professionalism. Kevin Emmert's work as editor was impeccable. My wife, Natalie, continues to be my most forthright critic and principal encourager.

Thanks are also due to Carl Trueman for writing the foreword. Having overlapped with me in the 1990s at the University of Aberdeen, Carl was around at the very beginning of my wrestling with questions of identity. His own book *The Rise and Triumph of the Modern Self: Cultural Amnesia, Expressive Individualism, and the Road to Sexual Revolution* (Wheaton, IL: Crossway, 2020) appeared too late for me to take into account in this book. Fortunately, our books explore different aspects of the subject. If Carl's is about the roots of the modern self, mine looks at the fruit and points to a better place to plant yourself.

My hope and prayer is that *How to Find Yourself* will help many people experience the joy and comfort of looking for their identity in the right places and discovering that their true "identity is hidden with Christ in God" (Col. 3:3, my translation).

Introduction

Stranger in the Mirror

"Be who you are and say what you feel."

DR. SEUSS'S EPONYMOUS CAT IN THE HAT

"Be true to yourself."

EVERYONE FROM OPRAH, ELLEN DEGENERES,
BEYONCÉ, AND MICHELLE OBAMA
TO STEPH CURRY, DONALD TRUMP,
AND EVERY STUDENT BODY PRESIDENT

"Who am I? Lonely questions mock me."

DIETRICH BONHOEFFER[1]

KNOWING WHO YOU ARE and being true to yourself have never been more important than in the twenty-first century West. They are seen as signs of good mental health and wellbeing, and the keys to authentic living and true happiness.

The topic of personal identity is of unprecedented interest. The terms "personal identity" and "identity formation" were barely in use before 1960; they now appear frequently in a wide range of disciplines and

---

1 Dietrich Bonhoeffer, *Widerstand und Ergebung: Briefe und Aufzeichnungen aus der Haft*, ed. E. Bethge (Muenchen: Christian Kaiser, 1964), 243; my translation.

literature. Whereas once the advice to "be yourself" was rarely heard, now it is commonplace.[2]

Of course, to be yourself, you have to know who you are. Most people today believe that there is only one place to look to find yourself, and that is inward. Personal identity is a do-it-yourself project. All forms of external authority are to be rejected, and everyone's quest for self-expression should be celebrated. This strategy of identity formation, sometimes labelled *expressive individualism*, is the view that you are who you feel yourself to be on the inside and that acting in accordance with this identity constitutes living authentically.

Yet, ironically, knowing who you are has also never been more difficult. Scores of people today feel anxious and uncertain about their identities. A myriad of factors weighs against having a stable and satisfying sense of self. Living our lives in the separate compartments of home, work, and leisure can produce superficial relationships. Multiple careers and relationship breakdowns can lead to confusion over some of the most basic of answers to the question of who we are. Questions over gender and sexuality have sprung up like never before. And defining ourselves via social media is fraught with dangers and can even lead to projecting an inauthentic self. Ours is a day of identity angst.

Perhaps the most disturbing aspect of our cultural moment is that the current approach to finding yourself doesn't appear to be working very well, either for individuals or for society as a whole. Many people in our day, including me, find questions about identity to be confusing and confronting. Anxiety, depression, narcissism, anger, and resentment are all on the rise. And happiness, by any measure, is actually in decline.

In this book, I do three things. First, in part 1, I investigate the issues surrounding questions about identity formation in our day. What is driving the move to look primarily inward to find yourself? How novel

2   These statistics are summaries of word searches using Google Ngram Viewer.

is this approach? What are the benefits of looking inward? Does it lead to the good life? Are there other directions in which to look?

Second, in parts 2 and 3, I consider some of the other places we look to form our identities—to the people around us and to the societal narratives we inhabit. Again, I look at these and ask, What are the benefits? Are there any downsides? Do they offer us what we are longing for? Do they lead to a good life?

And third, woven throughout the whole book and culminating in part 4, I present and commend an alternative way of developing personal identity, one that has been followed by millions of people for thousands of years. It's the one promoted by the Bible. Is this way now hopelessly obsolete? Is it a viable alternative to today's dominant identity formation strategy? Does it lead to a good life?

A book on personal identity is, by definition, deeply personal, both for the author and the reader. As it turns out, my own experience of a painful identity crisis some twenty-odd years ago caused me to think again about my own identity and led to me to dig deep into the subject.[3] I'll share my story throughout the book.

The big goal of this book is not just to think about a trend in Western culture but to help you think about yourself: Who are you? What defines you? What makes you, you? Most importantly, where are you looking to find yourself? If you are a Christian, I hope you'll learn to embrace your identity by looking in the right places. If you are not a Christian, I invite you to consider a different way to be yourself.

---

3 My first book on the subject, *Known by God: A Biblical Theology of Personal Identity*, Biblical Theology for Life (Grand Rapids, MI: Zondervan Academic, 2017), is a more technical book of biblical scholarship and less focused on our cultural moment. I recommend it to readers interested in further material on personal identity in the Bible.

PART 1

———

LOOKING FOR YOURSELF

1

Looking Inward

"[People today believe that] when you are figuring
out how to lead your life, the most important
answers are found deep inside yourself."

DAVID BROOKS[1]

"Modern freedom and autonomy centres us on
ourselves, and the ideal of authenticity requires that
we discover and articulate our own identity."

CHARLES TAYLOR[2]

NATALIE AND I were married in 2004, and we took our honeymoon on Mana Island, a Fijian island in the South Pacific. A tropical paradise, it was a great location for obvious reasons: sun, sand, beaches, hammocks, exotic food, water sports, tennis, fishing. What's more, coming from our own life in urban Australia, we found the cultural contrasts fascinating to experience. From the food and the local language to the means of transportation and the music and singing, everything was strikingly different. Two things in particular stood out to me: the attitude toward time and the pace of life. During that short stay, we shook off the Western obsession with "being on time." Our gaits also

1   David Brooks, *The Road to Character* (New York: Random House, 2015), 21.
2   Charles Taylor, *The Ethics of Authenticity* (London: Harvard University Press, 1991), 81.

slowed considerably, in part due to the warming sun and high humidity, but mostly by example and imitation. Returning home, it was difficult to readjust. I still miss walking at that Fijian island pace.

As this experience showed me, many aspects about who we are and how we behave are determined by the culture in which we are immersed. Culture is that invisible force that influences the ideas, customs, and social behaviors of a particular people or society. Often, it's only the visitors to a culture who notice its pervasive power. Or it is those members of a culture who after having spent time in another culture, come back to their own and see things in a whole new light. Some of those, like taste in food, music, games, and holidays, are consciously determined and easily changed. But many others are unconscious, difficult even to think about, let alone change.

Edward T. Hall likened the effects of culture to an iceberg.[3] Some aspects of a culture are overt, in clear view above the waterline, so to speak. But most are hidden deep below the surface, forming the bulk of the iceberg: our concepts of time, friendship, fairness, and justice; styles of nonverbal communication, facial expressions, eye contact, and gestures; approaches to raising children, decision making, and problem solving; and attitudes toward different age groups, competition, authority, work, and death. For most of these, we take our views and approaches entirely for granted and can scarcely imagine any alternative.

In this chapter, I want to look at the very bottom of the cultural iceberg: the way we "do identity" in the postmodern Western world.

The Self-Made Self

You don't need to look far today to notice that personal identity is a do-it-yourself project. A gym near where I live advertises itself with the slogan: "Be Fit. Be Well. Be You." A new apartment complex around

---

3   Edward T. Hall, *Beyond Culture* (New York: Random House, 1976).

the corner, offering high-end luxury design, carries the byline: "An Unlimited You." People think about themselves constantly, it seems, and with high expectations!

High schools are also in on the act. One school's marketing gave this advice to its current and prospective students: "Be Inspired. Be Challenged. Be Excellent. Be You." The goal for every pupil in our day, we might say, is to leave school singing the most popular song from *The Greatest Showman*: "Look out 'cause here I come." A veritable anthem for Millennials and Gen Z, the lyrics speak of unapologetically marching to your own drumbeat and proudly announcing to the world who you really are.

Popular culture regularly taps into this preoccupation with self-knowledge and self-expression. Think of the several decades-long success of Madonna—singer, songwriter, actress, and business woman—who embodies this approach to identity. Madonna is famous for regularly reinventing not only her music but also her image. Not surprisingly, her sixth major concert tour was styled the "Reinvention World Tour." Personal identity today is all about self-definition and self-expression.

"In the past, an individual's identity was more established and predictable than it is today. Many of the big questions in life were basically settled before you were born: where you'd live, what you'd do, the type of person you'd marry, your basic beliefs, and so on. It's not that there was no choice whatsoever. Rather, the shape of your life was molded by constraints that limited your choices."[4] Today, we are open to any and every possibility. We take for granted the obligation to find and define or even invent ourselves for ourselves.[5] The advice heard frequently in many contexts is to "be true to yourself," "follow your heart," "be yourself," and, the most recent and hippest version, "you do you."[6]

4   Brian Rosner, "Looking beyond ourselves to remain true to one's self," The Age (website), April 2, 2012, https://www.theage.com.au/.

5   Consider the title of Sarah-Jayne Blakemore's book on adolescence: *Inventing Ourselves: The Secret Life of the Teenage Brain* (London: Transworld, 2018).

6   The Urban Dictionary defines "you do you" as "just be yourself."

People today increasingly have what sociologists call the "buffered self," a self defined and shaped from within, to the exclusion of external roles and ties. We find our true selves by detaching ourselves from external influences like home, family, religion, and tradition, and thereby determine who we are for ourselves. The buffered self contrasts with the "porous self," which is the approach of most collectivist societies—in parts of Asia and Africa, for example—whereby external social ties and roles are determinative for identity. With the porous self, you find yourself as you move into your roles in family and community. Self-determination, rather than being a principle for nations at the end of the First World War, is now the responsibility of every individual.

Self-definition is thus the culturally endorsed route to identity formation in our day. Today, we have a do-it-yourself self or a self-made self, which looks only inward to find itself. Academics call this *expressive individualism*.

The major tenets of expressive individualism can be summarized in seven points:

- The best way to find yourself is to look inward.
- The highest goal in life is happiness.
- All moral judgements are merely expressions of feeling or personal preference.
- Forms of external authority are to be rejected.
- The world will improve dramatically as the scope of individual freedom grows.
- Everyone's quest for self-expression should be celebrated.
- Certain aspects of a person's identity—such as their gender, ethnicity, or sexuality—are of paramount importance.

The seven points form a coherent worldview, tell a compelling story, and, most importantly for our purposes, set out a strategy for forming personal identity.

The key point, and the one that gives the subtitle to this book, is the first one. A survey in 2015 found that 91 percent of adults in the United States agreed that the best way to find yourself is by looking within yourself.[7] Everything else flows from this conviction. The thinking is that to look anywhere else than inward would bring you under the control of those who wish to oppress you, would risk you not realizing your full potential, and, worst of all, would mean that you would not be true to yourself. That is the message coming loud and clear from every direction in our contemporary world. Francis Fukuyama writes, "Modern understandings of identity hold that we have deep interior spaces whose potentialities are not being realized, and that external society through its rules, roles, and expectations is responsible for holding us back."[8]

Philosopher Andrew Potter argues that "when it comes to personal fulfilment, many of us subscribe to the idea that the self is an act of artistic creation."[9] Sociologist Anthony Elliott agrees: "We respond to the instability of globalization . . . by reinventing ourselves."[10] And Dale Kuehne observes, "In the iWorld [meaning the individualistic postmodern world] identity is something we are instructed to select or create. If we don't like or aren't comfortable with who we are, we are encouraged to remake ourselves in whatever manner we are able and science will allow."[11]

One of the best-selling songs of all time is sung by Elsa, a character from the movie *Frozen*. It is something of an anthem for Generation Z,

7 David Kinnaman and Gabe Lyons, *Good Faith: Being a Christian When Society Thinks You're Irrelevant and Extreme* (Grand Rapids, MI: Baker, 2016), 58.

8 Francis Fukuyama, *Identity: The Demand for Dignity and the Politics of Resentment* (London: Profile Books, 2019), 103.

9 Andrew Potter, *The Authenticity Hoax: Why the "Real" Things We Seek Don't Make Us Happy* (New York: Harper, 2011), 3.

10 Reported by Bella Ellwood-Clayton, "Changing partners—Love actually," *Sun Herald*, June 28, 2009.

11 Dale S. Kuehen, *Sex and the iWorld: Rethinking Relationship Beyond an Age of Individualism* (Grand Rapids, MI: Baker, 2009), 139.

being viewed on YouTube over 1.5 billion times: "It's time to see what I can do / To test the limits and break through / No right, no wrong, no rules for me / I'm free!" As Tim Keller explains, the song's sentiment is

> a good example of expressive individualism. Identity is not realized, as in traditional societies, by sublimating our individual desires for the good of our family and people. Instead, we become ourselves only by asserting our individual desires against society, by expressing our feelings and fulfilling our dreams regardless of what anyone says.[12]

The corollary of knowing yourself is the advice to be true to yourself, which these days is about the most helpful thing you can say to someone. In 2008, filmmaker and photographer Andrew Zuckerman interviewed "some of the world's most eminent elders," the likes of Nelson Mandela, Madeline Albright, Billie Jean King, Judi Dench, the Dalai Lama, and Buzz Aldrin. A series of five books, entitled simply *Wisdom*, captured their images and their advice. When you open the first book, you find a distillation of their sage advice in large bold script on the first double page. It reads, "Nobody can teach me who I am."[13] When it comes to knowing and becoming who you are, the ball is squarely in your court.

A key driver of expressive individualism is the desire to live more authentic lives. To be true to yourself "captures the fullness of our commitment to authenticity as a moral ideal."[14] This is reflected in the way that personal autonomy is now the final word in almost every ethical debate. Whether the issue is gender, sexuality, abortion, or assisted dying, the preservation of individual choice is primary. As Leslie Cannold observes, "The central moral value in a modern multicultural

---

12 Timothy Keller, *Preaching: Communicating Faith in an Age of Scepticism* (London: Hodder & Stoughton, 2015), 134.
13 Chinua Achebe, quoted in Andrew Zuckerman, *Wisdom*, rev. ed. (New York: Harry N. Abrams, 2011).
14 Andrew Potter, *The Authenticity Hoax*, 18.

society is autonomy, the right of individuals to determine the course of their own lives according to their own needs and values."[15]

The Benefits of Looking Inward

Much of this book concentrates on the shortcomings of looking only inward to find yourself. However, it would be a mistake to critique the movement of expressive individualism without also understanding its appeal and the attractiveness of its basic values. As Charles Taylor puts it, when evaluating the movement, we must distinguish its "higher ideals" from its "debased practices."[16] My main objection to expressive individualism is the exclusivity it attaches to looking inward to find yourself; as I go on to argue in this book, there are other equally important places to look.

In principle, there is nothing wrong with looking inward. Personal exploration is commendable, and self-reflection acknowledges the gains of living an examined life. The alternative is far from attractive. Indeed, the movement of expressive individualism is, in part, a reaction against a 1950s culture of conformity, which is believed to have "crushed individuality and creativity, was too concerned with production and concrete results, repressed feeling and spontaneity, and exalted the mechanical over the organic."[17]

Expressive individualism is also driven by the admirable desire to see many marginalized groups in society affirmed as full members and given appropriate dignity. Many individuals with identity markers different from the mainstream, even in relatively harmonious multicultural societies, long for recognition and acceptance. Other groups are attracted to the movement for the freedom it offers them in terms of life choices. Many argue that expressive individualism has won some major social gains.

---

15 Leslie Cannold, "In the end, we should have faith in our right to choose," *Sun Herald*, September 26, 2010.

16 Charles Taylor, *The Ethics of Authenticity*, 72.

17 Charles Taylor, *A Secular Age* (Cambridge, MA: Harvard University Press, 2007), 476.

Authenticity as a moral ideal is also commendable, especially if the alternative is a blind conformity to external demands that can lead to hypocrisy when people fail to own key aspects of their life. It is much better for a person to inhabit an identity that they own and can fully appropriate for themselves; there is something to be said for feeling comfortable in your own skin. Psychologists generally regard authenticity as a basic requirement of mental health: "Authenticity is correlated with many aspects of psychological well-being, including vitality, self-esteem, and coping skills. Acting in accordance with one's core self—a trait called self-determination—is ranked by some experts as one of the three basic psychological needs."[18]

At the end of the book, I will return to these ideals and show how a Christian approach to identity formation can connect with them and deliver the desired benefits.

Evaluating the Self-Made Self

But whatever may be said about its strengths, the notion of people as discrete or buffered individuals is unusual in the history of ideas. And it's worth pausing to ask how well it's working.

How unique is this approach to identity? My answer is that it is close to unprecedented, a recent innovation in the sweep of human history—with one exception, which I will discuss in chapter 4. What is remarkable is the strength of commitment to expressive individualism across so many quarters of society and its unquestioned supremacy given that it is such an untested innovation.

Anthropologist Clifford Geertz puts it well, if a little abstrusely:

The Western conception of the person as a bounded, unique, more or less integrated motivational and cognitive universe, a dynamic center of awareness, emotion, judgment, and action organized into a distinctive

---

18   Karen Wright, "Dare to Be Yourself," *Psychology Today*, May 1, 2008, 72.

whole and set contrastively both against other such wholes and against its social and natural background, is, however incorrigible it may seem to us, a rather peculiar idea within the context of the world's cultures.[19]

Geertz's evaluation raises three pressing questions about personal identity. First, is the self-made self resilient? This idea of a buffered, bounded person may hold great appeal in our society and seem self-evident, but the jury is out on how enduring a path it is to lasting and meaningful identity formation.

Second, is the self-made self working? Doubtless, the buffered self has opened the door to endless choices and possibilities. But does expressive individualism actually lead to good outcomes for individuals? Does it lead to good outcomes for society as a whole? Does it lead to what we might call "the good life"?

Third, is the self-made self incorrigible? While expressive individualism, sitting as it does at the bottom of our cultural iceberg, beneath our awareness, may seem natural to us now, its peculiarity in human history begs the question: Is it really the obvious and true way to forge a sense of self?

The consequences for individuals and society of implementing an idea as foundational as the way we form our identities will take decades to uncover and assess. We've been on this path for at least twenty years now. In my view, it's time to step back and conduct an audit. That's where our next three chapters take us.

Questions for Reflection and Discussion

1. Think of a time when you've had an opportunity to step outside of your primary culture. What "bottom of the iceberg" aspects of your culture did you become aware of from that experience?

19 Clifford Geertz, "From the Native's Point of View: On the Nature of Anthropological Understanding," in *Culture Theory: Essays on Mind, Self and Emotion*, ed. Richard A. Shweder and Robert A. LeVine (Cambridge: Cambridge University Press, 1984), 126, cited in Jonathan Haidt, *The Righteous Mind: Why Good People are Divided by Politics and Religion* (London: Penguin, 2012), 16.

2. Read over the list of characteristics of expressive individualism as described on page 24. Do you subscribe to these beliefs? Do they all ring true for you? Just some of them? How strongly do you feel about them?

3. "Be true to yourself." What do you understand when you hear people use this sentiment or something similar? Is it good advice?

2

A Collective Identity Crisis

"Nothing is more unfathomable than ourselves, individually and collectively, at any given moment and from the earliest beginning of human time."

MARILYNNE ROBINSON[1]

"Confusion over identity arises as a condition of living in the modern world."

FRANCIS FUKUYAMA[2]

"The human race is suffering from a collective identity crisis."

KEVIN VANHOOZER[3]

MY OWN INTEREST in the topic of personal identity is not merely academic. Instead, it arose from something painfully personal.

Back in the mid-1990s, my life was pretty much on track. I was married with three children, and I held a good job as a lecturer at the University of Aberdeen in Scotland. I had a strong circle of friends and was involved in our local Baptist church. In 1996–1997, our family

1 Marilynne Robinson, *The Givenness of Things: Essays* (New York: Farrar, Straus and Giroux, 2015), 199.
2 Francis Fukuyama, *Identity: The Demand for Dignity and the Politics of Resentment* (London: Profile Books, 2019), 164.
3 Kevin Vanhoozer, "Human Being, Individual and Social," in *The Cambridge Companion to Christian Doctrine*, ed. Colin E. Gunton (Cambridge: Cambridge University Press, 1997), 158.

headed off to Germany for my twelve-month sabbatical. But when we returned to Scotland, I was confronted with something totally unexpected. My wife of thirteen years wanted to leave me and end our marriage. It was a big shock, and it rocked me to the core.

After about a year of turmoil and confusion, I moved with my children back to Australia, where I had grown up, and started a new job for which I had no official training. It felt like everything had changed. My past now seemed like it belonged to someone else, and making plans for the future was a luxury I couldn't afford. I suffered a bout of depression. A big part of the problem was my shaken sense of self. Who was I if much of what I thought defined me had disappeared? I went from having a stable sense of self, with things going pretty much according to plan, to being uncertain about who I really was.

Identity Angst

One thing I've learned in the last twenty-five years is that I am far from alone in experiencing serious uncertainty about my identity. I've had countless conversations with people of all ages in a variety of circumstances who are wondering who they really are: people who've been laid off; people whose parents have died; people whose online identity leaves them feeling like a phony; people who feel deflated by their aspirations for life not coming to fruition; people who feel diminished by all-consuming responsibilities for children or parents; people who feel lost at sea in our rapidly changing world. Identity angst is on the rise in the twenty-first century.

There are even some high-profile examples. In 2019, *The New York Times* ran a story about the acclaimed British actress Emma Thompson, titled "Emma Thompson Gets a Shock at 60":

> If anyone did not expect to have a midlife crisis, it was Emma Thompson. Being quite sure about things has been a central organiz-

ing principle of her life. It has informed most every character she has played. . . . All her life, she knew who she was. Now the roles she had embraced—mother, wife, performer—have her asking, "Am I any of those things? And if I'm not, who am I?"[4]

Being the same age as Emma Thompson, I was intrigued to learn that sixty is now classified as midlife! At the other end of the adult life cycle is *Game of Thrones* star Sophie Turner, who, despite having a stellar career and a celebrity husband, confessed at twenty-three, "I don't actually know who I really am."[5]

Popular culture is also increasingly picking up the theme of the tortuous search for identity. Movies starring Matt Damon, for example, often explore themes related to questions of personal identity and self-discovery, tapping into our fascination with inscrutable characters who need to find their identities. This is true of his roles to a greater or lesser extent in *Good Will Hunting*, *The Talented Mr. Ripley*, and *The Informant!* The clearest example is *The Bourne Identity*, where Damon's character is a riddle even to himself: "I know the best place to look for a gun is the cab or the gray truck outside, and at this altitude, I can run flat out for half a mile before my hands start shaking. How can I know that and not know who I am?"[6]

Whereas once identity formation almost took care of itself, nowadays everything about who you are is up for grabs. The midlife crisis notwithstanding, in the recent past most people's identities were set during their adolescence when they accepted, rejected, or adapted the identity handed to them by their parents in their childhood. These days, life-cycle dilemma experts believe that for many people, identity transitions occur earlier than midlife and much more often. The age of discontent can

4   Cara Buckley, "Emma Thompson Gets a Shock at 60," *New York Times*, May 23, 2019, https://www.nytimes.com/.

5   Josh Glancy, "I don't know who I really am," *The Australian*, June 1, 2019, https://www.theaustralian.com.au/.

6   *The Bourne Identity*, directed by Doug Liman (Universal City, CA: Universal Pictures, 2002).

happen at any and every age, the obligation to define or design yourself being always at hand. You don't have to wait for midlife to have doubts about how your life is tracking. The dreaded "thrisis" awaits those turning thirty, who, having climbed the ladder of success, are disillusioned to discover it's leaning against the wrong wall.[7] And those of us turning forty, fifty, sixty, or seventy years of age might experience "cuspiety," the anxiety associated with reaching the precipice of so-called cusp ages.

My view is that by advocating so strongly for looking only inward to find yourself, expressive individualism is a major contributor to the prevailing identity confusion and instability. The causes of our current identity angst related to expressive individualism include: (1) the elevation of certain identity markers to ultimate importance, and (2) the rise of social media.

Shifting Identity Markers

Who are you? If expressive individualism counsels you to look inward, what are you likely to find? What about you offers itself as an answer? How would you answer the question of your personal identity?

Let me use myself as an example. I am a white Australian straight able-bodied Christian male from a working-class background with an Austrian heritage on my father's side, married with four children, a mortgage-paying homeowner living in the Eastern suburbs of Melbourne, who works as a principal of a theological college, drives a Toyota Corolla, and is in his early sixties. My answer corresponds to ten traditional identity markers: my race, ethnicity and nationality; my gender and sexuality; my physical and mental capacity; my religion; my cultural background; my family of origin; my close relationships; my occupation; my possessions; and my age. All but one of these ten markers have been around forever.[8]

---

7   See Kasey Edwards, *30 Something and Over It: What Happens When You Wake Up and Don't Want to Work . . . Ever Again* (Edinburgh: Mainstream Publishing, 2009).

8   With reference to sexuality, Ed Shaw, *The Plausibility Problem: The Church and Same-Sex Attraction* (Nottingham, UK: IVP, 2015), 38, writes, "People only started being labelled as homosexuals back

The importance of such markers has always varied from culture to culture, from age to age, from place to place, and from one individual to another. One striking effect of expressive individualism, of looking inward to find yourself and defining yourself in those terms, is that some markers have been elevated over others. Markers that are in the minority will often be all-important to people's identities: things like ethnicity or nationality, sexuality, non-cis genders, disability, or being a certain age.

There are problems with this approach to identity. In chapter 10, I will look more closely at these identity markers and argue that in many cases, expressive individualism's elevation of certain markers carries with it a problematic narrative identity that can have the effect of pitting one group against another and producing considerable social discord. And the ill effects, along with damaging society as a whole, also affect individuals.

But even before looking at the markers themselves, we can see that another problem is that the negation of traditional markers and the elevation of some newer ones encourage us to place all our eggs in one or two identity baskets, so to speak. To settle on a single marker for your identity is unwise. While some markers are more set than others, many can change over time. If I look to my possessions or occupation for my identity, for example, what happens if I suffer a financial setback, lose my job, or retire? If my marital status is the main feature of who I am, what happens if that changes?

It is a mistake to reduce any human being's identity to one immutable marker. We are more complicated than that. British Pakistani novelist Mohsin Hamid writes,

It is worth bearing in mind a simple truth: no human being is only a Muslim and no human being is only an American. The people one might call Muslims, or Americans, are also women and men; mothers,

---

in the nineteenth century (philosopher Michel Foucault traced its first use to an article published in 1870)."

fathers, daughters, and sons; lovers and doctors and writers and schoolteachers; poor and wealthy; politically engaged and apathetic; sure in their beliefs and utterly uncertain. They are, in other words, complex, multidimensional, unique, and ever changing.[9]

Can we really learn much about a person simply by knowing their ethnicity, gender, sexuality, or occupation? In the past, we regarded such judgments to be stereotyping. The current tendency to be short-sighted in the way we approach identity labels and markers is a major contributor to the identity angst of our day.

The Self in the Spotlight

Meanwhile, we are not only encouraged to define ourselves by fewer and more specialized identity labels but invited to do so in a far more public way than ever before.

The digital age has added a new dimension to the question of personal identity. The web is now the platform on which many of us live our lives. With social media, the internet is the means through which you tell the world not just what you are up to and what you are thinking but who you are. Regular profile and status updates on media like Facebook, Instagram, and Snapchat have taken defining ourselves to a new level. Social media is a major factor in the rise of expressive individualism; many believe that the web has affected our very identity. As Peter Leithart notes, if humans have always worn "masks," "with the arrival of postmodern communication technologies the masks have become thicker and more concealing."[10]

Defining ourselves via social media raises many thorny issues. On one level, what we project of ourselves is firmly in our own hands. We get to curate our own photos, captions, and stories, and influence the way people

9   Mohsin Hamid, *Discontent and Its Civilizations: Dispatches from Lahore, New York and London* (London: Penguin, 2014), 111.

10   Peter J. Leithart, *Solomon among the Postmoderns* (Ada, MI: Brazos, 2008), 123.

see us. Yet numerous studies have raised questions about social media as a tool of identity formation. While choosing my own profile photo clearly empowers me to define myself, as one study concludes, "now that we can interact with hundreds—no, thousands—of people simultaneously, we've strengthened the impact that others have on our self-value."[11] It is ironic that social media appears to enable self-definition while in reality magnifying the influence of others on how you think about yourself. Social scientific research indicates that "increasingly, many young people are sourcing their identities from social media and advertising, and in the process losing their self-esteem."[12] Self-creation has become the responsibility of every young adult, and many experience anxiety as a result.

Other studies have found that what we think we are projecting with our profile pictures is often not what others perceive, with a low correlation between a profile owner's judgments of their own personality and the judgments of those viewing the photos. And the commonly posted selfie can also be problematic. Are selfies, of the shared variety, just an opportunity for self-expression? Are they a reclaiming of agency in how I am portrayed? Most shared selfies inevitably lead to comparison with others. And as Mia Freedman puts it, in many cases, "there is a blurred line between self-empowerment and self-objectification."[13] Many selfies belie an unhealthy thirst for likes and praise, an attempt to boost flagging and fragile self-esteem.

Social media provides unprecedented opportunities for self-definition. But excessive use can lead to an unhealthy thirst for the approval and validation of others, to the masking rather than expressing of identity, and, in the end, to loneliness[14] and self-doubt.

11 Philip Karahassan, "How Technology is Changing Dating," PsychAlive (website), accessed September 27, 2021, https://www.psychalive.org/.

12 Diocese of Gloucester, "Liedentity," Diocese of Gloucester (website), accessed September 27, 2021, https://www.gloucester.anglican.org/.

13 Mia Freedman, *Work, Strife, Balance* (Sydney: Macmillan, 2017), 114.

14 See Sherry Turkle, *Alone Together: Why We Expect More from Technology and Less from Each Other* (New York: Basic, 2017); and Hadiya Roderique, "I Have 1,605 Facebook Friends. Why Do I Feel So Alone?" *National Post*, February 14, 2018, https://nationalpost.com/.

The Fragile Self

Even though there have always been life experiences that can destabilize a person's identity, the rise of expressive individualism, aided by the powerful tools of social media, means that more people than ever are unsure who they really are and have a fragile sense of self. Along with the exciting opportunity to find yourself comes the daunting possibility of not succeeding, or of not liking what you find. The cruel irony is that while it's never been more important to know who you are, it's never been more difficult.

Many worrying social trends in Western countries around the world, including rising rates of anxiety and depression, as well as the breakdown in civil society, should at least give us reason to reflect. Is the recent move to a new approach to identity formation in part to blame for these trends?

In a scathing critique, David Brooks homes in on the fragility of character that our current approach to identity formation produces:

> We live in a culture that teaches us to promote and advertise ourselves and to master the skills required for success, but that gives little encouragement to humility, sympathy, and honest self-confrontation, which are necessary for building character. . . .
>
> Years pass and the deepest parts of yourself go unexplored and unstructured. You are busy, but you have a vague anxiety that your life has not achieved its ultimate meaning and significance. You live with an unconscious boredom, not really loving, not really attached to the moral purposes that give life its worth. You lack the internal criteria to make unshakeable commitments. You never develop inner constancy, the integrity that can withstand popular disapproval or a serious blow. You do not have a strategy to build character, and without that, not only your inner life but also your external life will eventually fall to pieces. . . .

A humiliating gap opens up between your actual self and your desired self.[15]

You don't have to agree with every aspect of Brooks's grim verdict about the self-made self to think that it might be worth taking a closer look at expressive individualism. Just how well is the current approach to identity formation working for us? What kind of self is it helping us to build? The next chapter will help us deepen this evaluation.

Questions for Reflection and Discussion

1. Have you experienced any crisis of identity in your own life? What identity markers were challenged, changed, or destabilized at that time?

2. How would you describe your "social media self"? In what ways does your online presentation of yourself reflect the reality of who you are? Are there any ways in which your social profiles substantially differ from the real-life you?

3. Reflect on the passage from David Brooks to conduct a mini audit of your own character. Ask yourself: Am I lacking in humility and sympathy? Do I have what it takes for honest self-confrontation? Do I have the inner constancy to withstand popular disapproval? Do I have a strategy for building my character? Is there a gap between who I want and expect to be and who I really am?

15 David Brooks, *The Road to Character* (New York: Random House, 2015), xiii, xiv.

3

Five Tests of the Good Life

"The unexamined life is not worth living."

SOCRATES[1]

*"It is emotionally unsettling for our deepest and unexamined
assumptions about life to be put to the test."*

TREVIN WAX[2]

*"The problem is that the inner selves we are celebrating
may be cruel, violent, narcissistic, or dishonest.
Or they may simply be lazy and shallow."*

FRANCIS FUKUYAMA[3]

ALL OF US WANT to live it. Everyone wants it for their children. But
what exactly is the good life? In the ancient world, the concept of the
good life was discussed at length by the likes of Socrates, Plato, Aristotle, and their followers. They debated whether the good life consists
primarily in things like health, wealth, and beauty or whether virtue

---

1   Quoted by Plato, *Euthyphro, Apology, Crito, Phaedo, Phaedrus*, trans. H. N. Fowler, vol. 1 of *Plato
in Twelve Volumes* (Cambridge, MA: Harvard University Press, 1966), 38a.
2   Trevin Wax, *Eschatological Discipleship: Leading Christians to Understand Their Historical and
Cultural Context* (Nashville: B&H Academic, 2018), 122.
3   Francis Fukuyama, *Identity: The Demand for Dignity and the Politics of Resentment* (London: Profile
Books, 2019), 95.

and character are more important. In our day, positive psychology has generated the happiness movement, which seeks to discover how to live a life filled with purpose, wellbeing, and joy.

In this chapter, we take our evaluation of expressive individualism a step further and ask where it is leading and what sort of personal identity it produces. To run the ruler over the self-made self, I have devised five tests of the good life. They build on some of the aforementioned discussions of the good life, both ancient and modern. They endeavor to face squarely the considerable challenges of the human condition in all its joys and sorrows. They also take seriously the fact that no life is lived in isolation; the best measures of a good life focus on the social nature of human existence and the way in which we respond to and treat others.[4] You can decide for yourself if you disagree with any of them or if you think I've left something out.

The five tests of the good life consider how well the self-made self deals with:

1. Suffering and disappointment
2. Pride and envy
3. The existence of weak and lowly people
4. Enemies and injustice
5. Happiness and pleasure

They refer respectively to what we might call the existential, ego, ethics, enemy, and enjoyment tests.

In each case, I'll cite some social trends that have been noticed by a range of commentators and sometimes bring a strand of teaching from the Bible to the table that offers some insights into the human condition. And we'll return to the five tests in later chapters as benchmarks against which to measure and compare a Christian approach to personal identity.

---

4   In chapter 6, I defend the notion that we are social beings.

I invite you to test yourself against the five measures. "Honest self-confrontation," to recall David Brooks's challenge, is no easy task and can be an uncomfortable experience. But given what's at stake—your own experience of the good life—it is worth the effort. Instead of asking, How is your "good self"?, I'm asking, How good is your self? How well do you deal with questions of existence, ego, ethics, enemies, and enjoyment?

1. The Existential Test: Suffering and Disappointments

We begin with the existential test of coping with life's setbacks. How does the self-made self deal with suffering and disappointment?

Every life is struck at one point or another with serious hardship. Some very early in life, some much later. From about the age of fifty, every one of my peers had experienced one or more burdens that left them feeling out of their depth. Despite the amazing advances in medical science in our lifetime, all human lives remain marked by things like serious illness, heartbreak, tragedy, loneliness, and grief.

My contention is that the self-made self is not suited to cope with such adversity, because expressive individualism typically cultivates unrealistic expectations for life. According to social researcher Hugh Mackay, many young people in the West today are in the grip of what he calls "the utopia complex, a world we dream of and think we are entitled to with outcomes that are always positive."[5] David Brooks reports that in a recent survey, "around 96% of eighteen- to twenty-nine-year old Americans agree with the statement 'I am certain that someday I will get where I want to be in life.' . . . In 1950 a personality test asked teenagers if they considered themselves an important person. Twelve percent said yes. By the late 1980s, 80 percent said yes."[6]

---

5   Cited in Simon Smart, "The generation brought up on self-esteem is struggling," *The Sydney Morning Herald*, April 13, 2017, http://www.smh.com.au/.

6   David Brooks, *The Social Animal: The Hidden Sources of Love, Character, and Achievement* (New York: Random House, 2012), 191.

A few years ago, my younger son, Toby, finished primary school. The school held a graduation of sorts where every student was introduced by his or her teacher as they walked across the stage, beaming with promise. In every case, the teacher gave a glowing description of the student's likely future. I was struck by how fortunate I was to be in the presence of so many forthcoming music and movie stars, world leaders and captains of industry! Interestingly, there was not a single office worker or tradesman in sight.

The stoking of such lofty aspirations is widespread. But are these high expectations likely to be realized for young people? It is hard to generalize, but it's worth noting that along with the rise in high expectations for life, some economists today see the rise of the "precariat": a social class formed by people suffering from a precarious existence, one without predictability or security. Forecasters predict five careers or more for young people entering the workforce. It might sound exciting, but the truth is that talk of multiple careers is spin for multiple layoffs and re-trainings. The stubborn trend of low job security and underemployment in many countries pushes back against thinking that we are all destined for a life full of positive outcomes.

In embracing such high expectations, we may well be setting ourselves up for a fall. Mira Adler-Gillies, pointing the finger at the self-improvement industry, alludes to the role of expressive individualism in this dilemma:

> The self-help books promise to orient the individual toward something that is meaningful. . . . The problem is that what is meaningful, according to the self-help industry, is always what is *within the individual*; so the person to must look within themselves, listen to their inner voice, find meaning within. This whole inward turn is only making us more unhappy.[7]

---

7   Mira Adler-Gillies, "Stand firm: Resisting the self-improvement craze," ABC Australia, May 22, 2017, https://www.abc.net.au/news/; emphasis added.

From childhood educators to psychologists, more experts are raising concerns about the lack of resilience in children today. Lenore Skenazy and Jonathan Haidt refer to those who grew up in the twenty-first century as "The Fragile Generation."[8]

As much as we might like to think that we are the authors of our lives, life's unscripted moments—loss of job, illness, bereavement, relationship breakdown, and the like—suggest that all of us belong to the precariat. Speaking personally, it was my own life going off the rails around the age of forty that alerted me to the fragility of my existence.

Since we exist precariously on this planet, in a world characterized by futility and frustration, then utopia is unattainable, and despite our fear of missing out, we all miss out in the end. The self-made self, formed by looking only inward and inflated by unrealistic expectations, is ill-equipped to cope with life's struggles and will likely be crushed under the weight of its disappointments.

2. The Egotism Test: Pride and Envy

Next, the egotism test. How well does the self-made self manage pride and envy?

If the utopia complex revealed the self-made self's unrealistic expectations in life, here we should note the widely reported rise in narcissism. A narcissist is someone who is preoccupied with himself and constantly craves the approval of others. In 2013, *Time* magazine reported that "the incidence of narcissistic personality disorder is nearly three times as high for people in their 20s as for the generation that's now 65 or older, according to the National Institutes of Health; 58% more college students scored higher on a narcissism scale in 2009 than in 1982."[9] Today, "Be your biggest fan" is actually a clothing

8   Jennifer Breheny Wallace, "How to Raise More Grateful Children," *The Wall Street Journal*, February 23, 2018, https://www.wsj.com/.

9   Joel Stein, "Millennials: The Me Me Me Generation," *Time*, May 20, 2013, https://time.com/.

brand, which unapologetically "pays homage to self love." And given the new profession of influencer, "self-promotion" coaches are not hard to find.[10]

Psychologist Ross King claims that "studies show those with [narcissistic] traits have jumped from about 3 per cent to 10 per cent of the population over the past three decades."[11] Indeed, some health professionals speak of an epidemic of narcissism in our society.[12] And in numerous studies psychologists warn that addiction to social media is strongly linked to narcissistic behavior and low self-esteem.[13]

Has the push to look within for our identities contributed to this rise in pathological self-centeredness? If the life of the buffered self is determined from within, against what are its accomplishments measured? The answer, of course, is other people. And in our day, there are unparalleled opportunities to make the comparisons, given that most of us participate in large social media networks. Among the social media platforms, Facebook alone has two billion users worldwide.

Clearly, it's possible to use social media and not be preoccupied with yourself, constantly craving the approval of others. However, according to many studies, the irony is that the more we focus on self-expression via social media, the lower our self-esteem. Excessive self-expression can lead to self-doubt and an unhealthy thirst for the validation of others. As one study concluded, Facebook users typically judge their attractiveness on the basis of their friends' comments on their photos. While the jury is still out on the impact of social media on the task of

10 Adeshola Ore, "Bragging rights: It's not cool to be humble and it's crazy to be modest according to this self-promotion coach," *The Australian*, May 23, 2020, https://www.theaustralian.com.au/.

11 Chloe Booker, "Narcissism is on the rise, but are you a narcissist? Take our quiz," *The Sydney Morning Herald*, July 1, 2017, http://www.smh.com.au/.

12 Jean M. Twenge and W. Keith Campbell, *Narcissism Epidemic: Living in the Age of Entitlement* (New York: Atria, 2010).

13 E.g., Sadia Malik and Maheen Khan, "Impact of facebook addiction on narcissistic behavior and self-esteem among students," *Journal of the Pakistan Medical Association* 65, no. 3 (March 2015): 260–63.

identity formation, there are reasons to think that the self-definition it fosters is naive and inadequate.

The message that each one of us is exceptional comes from many sides and can lead to an unhealthy pride, even arrogance. And it starts young. The advertising for many schools, especially the expensive private ones, is that our children can all be "exceptional"—a sample of five such schools in my city revealed that all five of them use the word in their marketing! The message is reinforced when people who are actually exceptional are interviewed in the media, be they high achievers in sports, business, or the arts. They typically attribute their success to working hard and following their dreams, with the sometimes-explicit message that you could achieve greatness if you did the same. But, by definition, we can't all be exceptional. After all, the people in question are being interviewed precisely because they are set apart from the rest of us!

Comedian Jane Caro puts it well when she says that the constant message that we all can be exceptional is a lie:

> You are not fabulous. Nor are the [men and] women—no matter how fabulous they may look or sound—who like to sprinkle such adjectives around. No one is. We are all flawed, insecure, tired, self-indulgent, often bewildered human beings who mostly struggle to stay on top of the demands of everyday life.[14]

Simon Smart is right that the widely reported rise in mental illness among young people suggests that "the generation brought up on an endless diet of their own specialness appears to be struggling with the hard truth that most of us are just ordinary." He notes that "according to a [recent] survey by the National Youth Mental Health Foundation, university and TAFE campuses [in Australia] are reporting epidemic

14 Jane Caro, "Why I am fine with being flawed and ordinary," *The Sydney Morning Herald*, July 28, 2017, http://www.smh.com.au/.

levels of mental health issues, with 70 per cent of students reporting high to very high levels of psychological distress."[15]

Is the self-made self, then, destined to have a robust ego? Not necessarily. The comparison with others can go the other way: instead of feeling superior, you end up feeling inferior, and envy takes over. The fact that viewing social media leads to envy is hardly surprising. What you see of your friends' lives is at best a curated highlight reel with heavy directorial cuts. And when it comes to personal identity, envy, like pride, also takes a toll. Envy does the envier considerable harm. Visual representations in the ancient world depict the envier with dry, lusterless eyes, sunken cheeks, contracted brows, and emaciated bodies, and some even have the envier with their hands around their own throats.

Pride and envy could be considered the consequences of an excessive attention to oneself, the very prerequisite of looking steadily inward to find yourself. Pride is not just thinking too much of yourself but also thinking too much about yourself. Correspondingly, humility is not about thinking poorly of yourself, but thinking about yourself less and more about the needs of others. The self-made self, in focusing too tightly on itself, is prone to puncture and distortion.

3. The Ethics Test: The Weak and Lowly

A third test of the good life is the ethics test: How does the self-made self respond to the weak and lowly?

This measure is hard to gauge, with contrary signals not hard to find. On the one hand, there is a rise in concern for those segments of society that experience prejudice, disadvantage, or discrimination, including women, migrants, gender and sexuality nonconformers, and so on. Who can deny the widespread and growing commitment of many young people to social justice issues?

15 Smart, "The generation brought up on self-esteem is struggling."

However, whether such concern actually translates into generous and compassionate action is the true measure of the ethics test. Some lay the cynical charge that many people engage in virtue signaling on social issues at no cost to themselves, supporting a politically correct cause simply to show how virtuous they are.

And while public gestures of social concern are clearly on the rise, it does appear that everyday kindness is a scarce commodity. In *On Kindness*, the psychoanalyst Adam Phillips and historian Barbara Taylor write, "We are a society where kindness is incidentally praised while being implicitly discouraged. Kindness—that is, the ability to bear the vulnerability of others, and therefore of oneself—has become a sign of weakness."[16]

If our day is ruled by a culture of self-interest and the pursuit of pleasure, built into a narrative of following your heart and achieving greatness, what room is there for the weak and lowly, those in need of kindness, generosity, and compassion? For what reasons might such people not be regarded simply as obstacles on your path to fulfilling your potential?

Taking authenticity to be the sole or chief criterion for human behavior and the main way to direct our lives raises significant concerns. On its own, the urge to be true to ourselves ignores the social fabric of our existence. Relationships can easily become disposable if they stand in the way of self-expression. As Charles Taylor contends, "Our ties to others, as well as external moral demands, can easily be in conflict with our personal development."[17]

Another problem with the ubiquitous advice to be true to yourself is that as well as having your identity drive your behavior, your behavior can also alter your identity. As C. S. Lewis observed, "Every time you make a choice you are turning the central part of you, the part of you that chooses, into something a little different from what it was

---

16 Adam Phillips and Barbara Taylor, *On Kindness* (London: Picador, 2010), 59.
17 Charles Taylor, *The Ethics of Authenticity* (London: Harvard University Press, 1991), 74.

before."[18] Authenticity is a two-way street: we act out of our identity, and our repeated acts alter that identity. Our character, which is formed by settled habits of action and feeling, is both fed by our identity and feeds that changing identity. Following your heart can turn you into a different person, and not necessarily for the better. The self-made self, in following its heart, can be prone to heartless behavior.

4. The Enemy Test: Adversaries and Injustice

Fourth, the enemy test. Does the self-made self, preoccupied with its own image, lack empathy for others? How does it respond when confronted with injustice?

Western society certainly seems to have taken a turn for the worse when it comes to anger management. Whereas once an ill-thought-out indiscretion could lead to being shunned at a party, nowadays one slip of the tongue on Twitter can lead to worldwide censure. As one commentator put it, especially in the online world, "hatred is everywhere; empathy and its cousin, civility, are nowhere. [We live in a] culture of reflexive outrage."[19] The phenomena of internet pile-ons and rabid twitch hunts—a campaign conducted on Twitter intended to destroy someone's reputation—would suggest that the self-made self is easily angered.

Callout culture is a related trend, whereby individuals or groups are held to account and shamed publicly for an unpopular view. Jamil Zaki, Psychology professor at Stanford University, believes the internet is undermining our natural human capacity for empathy because it provides endless opportunities for hateful abuse and toxic tribalism.[20] In what is known as "callout culture" and "ally theater" people demonstrate their commitment to a cause as allies of a marginalized population. This often incites online outrage that demands that a post or a tweet be taken down

18 C. S. Lewis, *Mere Christianity* (1952; repr., New York: Harper Collins, 2012), 86–87.

19 Michael Shammas, "Outrage Culture Kills Important Conversation," Huffington Post, January 27, 2017, http://www.huffingtonpost.com/.

20 Simon Caterson, "Trolls take toll on humanity," *The Australian*, August 10, 2019, https://www.the australian.com.au/.

or deleted. However, it's not just that the offensive opinion is deleted; the person who expressed it can also be removed from their place of influence or suffer some other consequences. In the worst cases, the people themselves are "cancelled," subject to termination of their employment or, in the case of some corporations, boycotted out of business.

To cite an offline example of a rise in levels of anger, road rage—angry and aggressive behavior behind the wheel—is on the rise, with responses to perceived offenses on the road ranging from long horn honks, swerving, and tailgating to attempts to fight the other driver. According to one survey, 86 percent of us feel aggressive behind the wheel, and 20 percent admit to chasing other cars while driving with aggressive intent. Perhaps sitting in a car alone with nothing but your own destination firmly in mind is a good illustration of the do-it-yourself identity formation strategy. If so, then resultant anger should be no surprise.

Digging more deeply, some have suggested that an ugly tribalism has replaced community in Western society. Whereas a community is bound together by mutual loves, a tribe is united by a common hatred—a common enemy intimacy, as some have called it. We live in a culture of contempt.[21] "There but by the grace of God go I" was once a common sentiment. But these days, even a comedian can be "cancelled" for having said something offensive twenty years ago. None of this is surprising, given that expressive individualism by definition entails resisting external influences in its quest for self-expression, "making your way through the world against opposition on all sides, finding and staying true to whoever it is you believe yourself to be."[22]

There are many dimensions to the problem. Globalization and the internet make judging others easier than ever before. To understand fully this harsh turn in Western societies, we will explore in chapters 9

21 Janet Albrechtsen, "Culture of contempt corrodes us," *The Australian*, August 10, 2019, https://www.theaustralian.com.au/.
22 Trevin Wax, "The Faithful Church in an Age of Expressive Individualism," *Kingdom People* (blog), The Gospel Coalition (website), October 22, 2018, https://www.thegospelcoalition.org/.

and 10 the narratives that, in my view, underly the problem. For now, I simply want to suggest that the rise in anger and outrage in society may be due in part to the turn to individuals assertively expressing their views and the related loss of community. When expressing an opinion becomes intrinsic to someone's identity, which can so easily happen with expressive individualism, it is not surprising for that person to respond with antagonism when that view is opposed. Small offenses can be exaggerated to the point where they seem like attacks on a person's identity.

Arthur C. Brooks explains that our culture of contempt is rooted in "motive attribution asymmetry—the assumption that your ideology is based in love, while your opponent's is based in hate." He believes that the sources of this widespread phenomenon are "divisive politicians, screaming heads on television, hateful columnists, angry campus activists and seemingly everything on the contempt machines of social media."[23] What is missing in this list is the rise of expressive individualism.

To explain the growing politics of resentment, Francis Fukuyama writes,

> Demand for recognition of one's identity is a master concept that unifies much of what is going on in world politics today. The universal recognition on which liberal democracy is based has been increasingly challenged by narrower forms of recognition based on nation, religion, sect, race, ethnicity, or gender.[24]

What unites the various shades of identity politics is a yearning for universal recognition and affirmation of one's identity. Any perceived disagreement with such identity markers is then taken as a personal attack and deemed an egregious offense to the dignity of the people

23 Arthur C. Brooks, "Our Culture of Contempt," *The New York Times*, March 2, 2019, https://www.nytimes.com/.
24 Fukuyama, *Identity*, 54.

involved and their many allies. Such reactions are justified by a powerful and compelling narrative of discrimination and prejudice, which cannot be tolerated (see chapter 10). Expressive individualism has a tendency to feed this culture of contempt, seen as a proportionate and justified response to perceived injustice.

How does the self-made self react when things don't go its way or when someone gets in the way? Arguably, the self-made self, fostered by expressive individualism, can be harsh and unforgiving when faced with opposition and adversity.

5. The Enjoyment Test: Happiness and Pleasure

How, then, does the self-made self do on the enjoyment test?

Even if expressive individualism could do better on our first four tests, with its emphasis on individual freedom and belief that the highest good is personal happiness, the self-made self is surely expected to perform well on the enjoyment test. After all, it is for the sake of individual freedom and pleasure that expressive individualism opposes such things as tradition, religion, received wisdom, regulations, and social ties. That is not to say that the self-made self is always an excuse for a shallow and selfish hedonism, but there is no doubt that happiness and pleasure are high on its agenda.

Yet, it depends what you mean by happiness. Martin Seligman, a pioneer of positive psychology, defines happiness in terms of three qualities: (1) positive emotion, the pleasant life; (2) positive character, the engaged life; and (3) positive institutions (clubs, churches, governments, and so on), the meaningful life. To Seligman, at least, happiness is more than subjective wellbeing but includes the experiences of having an absorbing purpose in life and living for something bigger than yourself. The concept of happiness, then, overlaps with notions of life satisfaction and contentment.[25]

---

25 Brian S. Rosner, "The Search for Happiness," Center for Public Christianity (website), May 18, 2008, https://www.publicchristianity.org/.

Most would agree that the greatest source of happiness consists in relationships, both family and friends. Clearly, close personal relationships are an essential element for human wellbeing and a major factor in the good life. Yet the turn to look inward to find yourself has brought the unintended consequence of diminishing us as social beings. Trevin Wax notes that "advanced stages of expressive individualism are characterized by isolation."[26] It has been reported that in the UK, more than nine million people often or always feel lonely, and in 2017 a Minister for Loneliness was appointed.[27] The link between self-definition and the breakdown of social obligation is clear:

> American cultural traditions define personality, achievement, and the purpose of human life in ways that leave the individual suspended in glorious, but terrifying, isolation. . . . This clear-sighted vision of each individual's ultimate self-reliance turns out to leave very little place for interdependence and to correspond to a fairly grim view of the individual's place in the social world.[28]

There is also what we might call the happiness paradox. The more you focus on being happy, the harder it seems to find it. A recent study conducted by the University of Melbourne showed that overemphasizing the importance of happiness actually results in an increase of unhappiness![29] The study highlighted the external pressure we feel to be happy: the more a participant felt pressured to not feel sad or anxious, the more likely they were to report an increase in depressive symptoms. It was amusingly entitled "(Don't) Always Look on the Bright Side of

26 Wax, "The Faithful Church in an Age of Expressive Individualism."

27 Ceylan Yeginsu, "UK Appoints a Minister for Loneliness," *The New York Times*, January 17, 2018, https://www.nytimes.com/.

28 Robert N. Bellah et al., *Habits of the Heart: Individualism and Commitment in American Life* (Berkeley, CA: University of California Press, 2007), 10.

29 Susanna Cornelius, "(Don't) always look on the bright side ff life," Pursuit (website), June 12, 2017, https://pursuit.unimelb.edu.au/.

Life: The pursuit of happiness at the expense of other emotions may, paradoxically, be making us sad." Maybe trying to be happy is like trying to get a good night's sleep. The harder you try, the more elusive the goal; both are by-products of doing something else.

It seems that the self-made self misses the mark when it comes to the enjoyment test by naively assuming a direct link between the satisfaction of desire and lasting pleasure and happiness.

Final Grade

Does looking only inward to find ourselves end well? The five tests considered in this chapter raise significant questions about the effectiveness of a do-it-yourself personal identity. Does it have the resources to withstand hardship and disappointment? Does it lead to the distortions of pride and resentment? Does it leave room for the weak and lowly? Does it respond to injustice with proportion? Does it lead to a life of joy and happiness? There are good reasons to think that the self-made self can easily end up crushed, deflated, mean, cranky, and unfulfilled.

People point in many directions for an explanation of the unfortunate societal trends that I've mentioned in this chapter: not enough mindfulness, technology addling our brains, crowd behavior, the failure of major institutions (politicians, churches, media, banks), loss of shared values, absence of community cohesion, and so on. However, some of these are symptoms rather than causes. I suggest that a shift in the way we do identity formation in our day is a big part of the problem.

While looking only inward to find ourselves is not the only cause of the utopia complex, the rise in narcissism, the absence of compassion in our society, our culture of reflexive outrage, and the fall in the happiness index, it would hardly be surprising for such an approach to not produce a personal identity that is self-deceived, self-absorbed, and self-centered.

The turn inward may well have been a wrong turn. As I'll argue in the next chapter, it's a bad move based on faulty foundations that were anticipated a long time ago.

Questions for Reflection and Discussion

1. What criteria would you devise to evaluate what makes a "good life"? How are these similar to or different from the five tests presented in this chapter?

2. "Authenticity is a two-way street: we act out of our identity, and our repeated acts alter that identity." What experience have you had, positive or negative, of your own patterns and habits forming your identity? What about your identity shaping your habits?

3. How does your own "self" stand up to examination when put to the existential, ego, ethics, enemy, and enjoyment tests? Revisit the questions at the end of each test. Do any of the five stand out to you as in need of deeper personal reflection?

4

Ancient Texts and
Modern Preoccupations

*"Christianity and Judaism are anthropologies,
whatever else."*

MARILYNNE ROBINSON[1]

"The Bible has the power to restore your true identity."

TIMOTHY KELLER[2]

IN THE PREVIOUS two chapters, I argued that the self-made self, the product of expressive individualism, is *fragile* and *failing*. Looking only inward to find oneself is not giving people a stable and satisfying sense of self, and it is leading to bad outcomes for both individuals and society as a whole.

In this chapter and the next, I will add a third F to our critique of expressive individualism, making the case that the buffered self is not only fragile and failing but also *faulty*. Looking only inward to find yourself neither is true to human experience nor acknowledges the truth of what it means to be a human being. The self-made self

---

1 Marilynne Robinson, "Can science solve life's mysteries?" *The Guardian*, June 5, 2010, https://www.theguardian.com/.

2 Timothy Keller with Kathy Keller, *The Songs of Jesus: A Year of Daily Devotions in the Psalms* (New York: Viking, 2015), 33.

is unstable and unsatisfying precisely because the very strategy of expressive individualism is unsound.

To make my case, I'm going to turn to the Bible. The Bible is what helped me most in my own experience of identity angst. There I found key characters like Moses and David asking, Who am I?, the same question of personal identity that had haunted me. There, too, I read answers to that question that brought me great comfort and reassurance. If I had looked in the mirror and failed to recognize myself, reading the Bible was like looking into a mirror and seeing myself afresh.[3] In the last ten years, I've shared the Bible's insights on identity in a variety of contexts, with everyone from college students and young people, to health professionals and economists, to prison chaplains and retirees, to city workers and missionaries, to the unemployed and academics. Each time, these ideas found positive reception. And in every group, I also heard back from a few people who were especially helped, often those in the midst of, or on the verge of, their own bout of identity angst.

I want to offer two reasons for looking at the Bible to solve the puzzle of personal identity: (1) The Bible addresses issues of personal identity, and (2) it describes and critiques an early version of expressive individualism, of looking only inward to find yourself.

Personal Identity in the Bible

Although no Hebrew word in the Old Testament or Greek word in the New Testament is typically translated into English as "identity," several words in the Bible have a wide range of meaning and include the notion of personal identity and the self.

In certain contexts, for example, words usually translated "soul" and "life" can be rendered "identity." When Jesus says in the Sermon on

---

3   See James 1:23–25: "For if anyone is a hearer of the word and not a doer, he is like a man who looks intently at his natural face in a mirror. For he looks at himself and goes away and at once forgets what he was like. But the one who looks into the perfect law, the law of liberty, and perseveres, being no hearer who forgets but a doer who acts, he will be blessed in his doing."

the Mount, "life is more than food, and the body more than clothing" (Matt. 6:25), we might translate, "your identity is more than food and clothing" pointing to his insistence on the limited role of material possessions in defining a person. When in Psalm 19:7 it says that "the law of the Lord refreshes the soul" (my translation), we can legitimately translate, "The law of the Lord refreshes your true identity," your very self.[4]

But we must not make the mistake of confusing terms for concepts; concepts are bigger than particular words. As I have explained elsewhere,

> A study of the biblical words for love, for example, does not fairly represent the Bible's teaching on love, since it ignores numerous narratives and parables, such as the Good Samaritan, which do not mention the word "love" but are nonetheless highly relevant. The word for "church" is rarely used in the Gospels, but they contain much significant material for a treatment of the topic of the church, including the notion of the kingdom as embodied in the lives of people on earth, the calling of the twelve disciples to be with Jesus, and the frequent use of communal language such as family, fraternity, little flock, and city. Furthermore, sometimes a biblical author will pursue the same concept as another author but with his own vocabulary. Concepts rather than words are a surer footing on which to gather the Bible's teaching on any topic.[5]

This is certainly the case with the concept of personal identity. Once you tune in, teaching relevant to personal identity is present on every page.

In terms of the history of ideas, Larry Siedentop's tour de force, *Inventing the Individual*, credits Christianity for the concept of ourselves as free agents, an essential notion for the very idea of a personal identity. According to Siedentop, in the apostle Paul's hands, "the identity of individuals is no

4   Keller and Keller, *The Songs of Jesus*, 33.
5   Brian S. Rosner, "Biblical Theology," in *New Dictionary of Biblical Theology*, ed. T. Desmond Alexander et al. (Downers Grove, IL: IVP Academic, 2000), 6.

longer exhausted [as it once was] by the social roles they happen to occupy."[6] The Bible had something to do with the very idea of the individual.

As it turns out, thinking about yourself is a thoroughly biblical thing to do. We find in the Bible the question, what is a human being? Many of the ways in which we refer to ourselves today in English overlap with and may even derive from terms used in the Bible, including words like "body," "soul," "spirit," "mind," and "heart." Many of the traditional markers of personal identity are treated at length, such as race, ethnicity, nationality, culture, gender, sexuality, family of origin, age, occupation, and possessions.[7] And the Bible actually includes the injunction to "think [about yourself] with sober judgment" (Rom. 12:3).

The Bible knows the human condition. It knows us inside out and from every angle: body, soul, spirit, mind, and heart. It addresses our deepest desires and yearnings, our frustrations and most painful sorrows. It includes instructions for every age group, condition, and circumstance, including young and old, happy and sad, rich and poor. And given that it was written in ancient times, its insights into modern human behavior are uncanny. The Bible, we might say, has "high emotional intelligence." The apostle Paul, for example, tells fathers not to exasperate their children, those undertaking deeds of mercy to do so with cheerfulness, those showing hospitality not to grumble, those in dispute not to judge or despise each other—all of which remains sound advice![8]

The Bible and the Self-Made Self

But there is more. Not only does the Bible address the subject of personal identity in general but, uncannily, it also discusses something

---

6   Larry Siedentop, *Inventing the Individual: The Origins of Western Liberalism* (Cambridge, MA: Belknap, 2014), 62.

7   See Brian Rosner, *Known by God: A Biblical Theology of Personal Identity*, Biblical Theology for Life (Grand Rapids, MI: Zondervan Academic, 2017), chapter 3.

8   Examples could easily be multiplied from other parts of the Bible. See especially the timeless wisdom of Proverbs.

approximating expressive individualism. Identity formation is actually a fundamental theme in the Bible. You could almost argue that the whole storyline of the Bible is set up in a way that describes, critiques, and replaces the self-made self.

The Bible depicts two ways of being human, both with representative prototypes to which the whole of humanity conforms. This can be seen most starkly in two passages: the temptations of Adam and Eve and Jesus Christ. Reading them side by side offers an intriguing ancient commentary on the postmodern search for do-it-yourself identity formation. And it suggests that however incorrigible the self-made self may be in our day, it is not a peculiar idea and actually dates back to ancient times. I will examine each episode separately before comparing and contrasting them.

The temptation of Adam and Eve concerned not only their continued obedience to God and happy existence in the garden of Eden but just as importantly their identity as God's children. Being made in the image of God signifies that human beings are God's offspring, relating to him as their parent and taking on the family likeness in certain ways. As Luke 3:38 puts it, Adam is "the son of God."

When the serpent tempted Eve in Genesis 3:1–5, he not only told her lies but also called God a liar:

> Now the serpent was more crafty than any other beast of the field that the Lord God had made.
>
> He said to the woman, "Did God actually say, 'You shall not eat of any tree in the garden'?" And the woman said to the serpent, "We may eat of the fruit of the trees in the garden, but God said, 'You shall not eat of the fruit of the tree that is in the midst of the garden, neither shall you touch it, lest you die.'" But the serpent said to the woman, "You will not surely die. For God knows that when you eat of it your eyes will be opened, and you will be like God, knowing good and evil." (Gen. 3:1–5)

God said not to eat of the fruit of one particular tree in the garden. According to Genesis 2:17, they must not eat from that tree for their own protection: if they eat, they will "surely die." Nothing in the narrative to this point had given Adam and Eve any reason to question God's motives for this prohibition. Their actions in disobeying God recall several of the tenets of expressive individualism. They reject an authority external to themselves, believe that their existence will improve dramatically as they assert their freedom, and they make moral judgments according to personal preference.

The serpent undermines God's word to Adam and Eve concerning the tree of knowledge of good and evil with three counterclaims, each of which tempts them to seek to establish their own autonomy and an identity independent of God: (1) you will not die; instead, (2) your eyes will be opened; and (3) you will be like God. Each of the three claims contains an element of truth and a tragic irony. Let's take them in reverse order.

First, in one sense Adam and Eve did become like God: in rebelling against him they asserted their personal autonomy and independence from God and usurped the place of authority in their lives that God had occupied. But ironically, as creatures made in the image and likeness of God, they were already "like God," in the best sense of being his children, made in his image and likeness. In disobeying God, they forfeited the privileges associated with that status, including being known by him intimately and personally in the Garden.

Second, Adam and Eve's eyes were actually opened, but not in a good way. They saw that they were naked, but ironically this realization led to fear and shame rather than liberation (Gen. 3:10–11). Prior to their transgression, "the man and his wife were both naked and were not ashamed" (Gen. 2:25).

And third, Adam and Eve did not die immediately. In fact, according to Genesis 5:5, Adam made it to 930 years of age before dying!

But in a more profound and dramatic sense, they did die, having cut themselves off from God.

The presence of God gave the garden its life-giving power (Gen. 2:7), an environment in which Adam and Eve experienced true life in knowing God and being known by him. But the serpent undermined their relationship with God by questioning God's motives: "God knows that when you eat of it your eyes will be opened, and you will be like God" (Gen. 3:5). As John Calvin states, Satan "charges God with malignity and envy, as wishing to deprive man of his highest perfection."[9] The serpent's lies were designed to undermine Adam and Eve's confidence in God and to tempt them to find their identity independent from him. In succumbing to the serpent's lies, they turned from their Father and became disobedient children.

Turning to the New Testament, it is indeed striking that the devil's three temptations of Jesus in the wilderness are also directly related to Jesus's identity as God's Son:

> Then Jesus was led up by the Spirit into the wilderness to be tempted by the devil. And after fasting forty days and forty nights, he was hungry. And the tempter came and said to him, "*If you are the Son of God*, command these stones to become loaves of bread." But he answered, "It is written,
>
> > "'Man shall not live by bread alone,
> >   but by every word that comes from the mouth of God.'"
>
> Then the devil took him to the holy city and set him on the pinnacle of the temple and said to him, "*If you are the Son of God*, throw yourself down, for it is written,

9   John Calvin, *Commentary on the First Book of Moses Called Genesis*, vol. 1, trans. John King (Bellingham, WA: Logos Bible Software, 2010), 149–50.

"'He will command his angels concerning you,'

and

"'On their hands they will bear you up,
    lest you strike your foot against a stone.'"

Jesus said to him, "Again it is written, 'You shall not put the Lord your God to the test.'" Again, the devil took him to a very high mountain and showed him all the kingdoms of the world and their glory. And he said to him, "All these I will give you, if you will fall down and worship me." Then Jesus said to him, "Be gone, Satan! For it is written,

"'You shall worship the Lord your God
    and him only shall you serve.'"

Then the devil left him, and behold, angels came and were ministering to him. (Matt. 4:1–11; see also Luke 4:1–13)

The first two of Satan's tests are prefaced with the taunt "If you are the Son of God . . ." (Matt. 4:3, 6). Satan's tests are designed to see whether Jesus will remain God's faithful and obedient Son. What does it mean to be the Son of God? What sort of Son is Jesus? All three temptations probe whether Jesus still trusts his Father in his weakened state. In response to the first temptation, to turn the stones into bread, Jesus quotes the Old Testament: "Man shall not live by bread alone, / but by every word that comes from the mouth of God." (Matt. 4:4; see also Deut. 8:3).

This same pattern is repeated with the second and third tests. In each case, Jesus quotes the Old Testament Scriptures to indicate that "listening to God is that which is life-sustaining."[10]

---

10 John Nolland, *The Gospel of Matthew: A Commentary on the Greek Text*, The New International Greek Testament Commentary (Grand Rapids, MI: Eerdmans, 2005), xvii; emphasis original.

The similarities and contrasts between Genesis 3 and Matthew 4 are striking:

- Both start with temptations to do with eating but occur in entirely different settings: one in the plenty of the garden, the other in the scarcity of the wilderness.
- Both scenes concern the truth and goodness of the word of God. If Adam and Eve deny what God said and succumb to temptation, Jesus affirms the sufficiency of God's word and stands firm.
- Both scenes reveal the identity of the ones being tempted. Adam and Eve are known by God intimately and personally as his children but doubt God's paternal goodness. Jesus, on the other hand, affirms his trust in his Father and proves himself to be God's faithful and obedient Son. Significantly, the scene immediately preceding the temptations of Jesus in Matthew is the baptism of Jesus, which climaxes with the voice from heaven saying, "This is my beloved Son, with whom I am well pleased" (Matt. 3:17).
- Both set the pattern for two different versions of what it means to be a human being. One, following Adam and Eve's example, the path of expressive individualism we might say, leading to death as God had warned; the other set the course for a new humanity, leading to life.

To sum up, in the garden, Adam and Eve believed the serpent and became rebellious children of God, suffering a symbolic death as a result. In the wilderness, Jesus passed the test and refused to believe Satan's lies; he was indeed the Son of God (see also Matt. 4:2, 6).

The Great Identity Deception

From a Christian perspective, these two biblical texts offer a disturbing critique of the self-made self of the postmodern West. With preacher's license, we might infer that Satan continues to tell lies about the identity of human beings in our day:

- God wants to keep your eyes closed and stop you from realizing your potential.
- Independence from God and personal autonomy is the path to life.
- Following the desires of your heart will lead to finding your true self.
- Shutting your ears to God, not looking up, is the key to authentic living.
- Becoming like God will open your eyes and lead to knowing who you really are.

The two archetypal episodes of temptation in the Bible were fought over the issue of personal identity. What is a human being? Who are Adam and Eve? Who is Jesus? Should they establish their identities independently of God? Will self-assertion lead to becoming like God? Does God their Father love them? Are Adam and Eve, as well as Jesus, truly children of God, and how should they behave?

In both cases, the lesson is that true freedom is found in knowing God as your Father, trusting his word, resisting satanic lies, and finding your identity in being known and loved by him. That's about as far from contemporary Western notions of freedom and fulfilment as you can get. And yet, given the novelty and mixed results of the do-it-yourself personal identity experiment, perhaps an ancient approach to identity formation, that has stood the test of time across a multitude of cultures, is worth considering.

The Bible addresses questions of personal identity and even describes something approximating expressive individualism. But it treats expressive individualism as faulty: a problem for forming the human person; perhaps even the root cause of all of our problems. Turning inward, according to this ancient text, is not the solution to identity angst. If not inward, where else should we look?

Questions for Reflection and Discussion

1. In your own questions around identity formation, has the Bible played a significant role? If so, in what way?

2. Having considered the stories of Adam and Eve and the story of Jesus's temptation in the desert, what do you make of the claim in this chapter that the whole storyline of the Bible is set up in a way that describes, critiques, and replaces the self-made self?

3. Consider the serpent's strategy for human identity formation as presented here. How familiar do any of these sound to you? Where do you hear them, or ideas like them, being promoted around you?

5

Looking Elsewhere

*"The self is too complexly configured to be accessible
to a single finite mind inquiring into itself by itself."*

DAVID JOPLING[1]

*"Personal identity cannot be anchored convincingly
without transcendence."*

PETER LEITHART[2]

MY MODEST CONTRIBUTION to social scientific research on personal
identity consists of a 2016 survey of the profile pictures of my eighteen
hundred so-called friends on Facebook. Social media platforms like
Facebook are the ultimate tool of self-definition. You choose which
photos you upload, the words in your profile description, and what you
post. What could be more self-made and authentic? It's the ultimate
"you do you."

So, in seeking to define themselves, what do my friends post as
their profile pictures? The biggest group, 46 percent, post pictures of
themselves alone. However, many friends, as many as 38 percent, post
pictures of themselves with or even just of significant others—defining
themselves in social terms—spouses, friends, parents, children. In other

---

1   David A. Jopling, *Self-Knowledge and the Self* (New York: Routledge, 2000), 137.
2   Peter J. Leithart, *Solomon Among the Postmoderns* (Grand Rapids, MI: Brazos, 2008), 131.

words, they look to others to define themselves. Still others, in the third statistically significant group, some 12 percent, post pictures that carry associations of experiences or accomplishments or passions that they believe somehow define them. So, these people look backward and forward, at their story and aspirations, to define themselves; they look to significant life events. (Smaller numbers post words, pictures of animals, famous people, or cartoon characters.)

Many of my friends on Facebook define themselves with reference to others or by looking at defining events in their lives. It is these dimensions of identity formation that expressive individualism fails to take sufficiently seriously. Like it or not, we humans instinctively look beyond our own navels when trying to figure out who we are. We find ourselves not only by looking inwardly but also by looking to others and at our life stories. It is a fallacy to think we can define ourselves with reference only to ourselves and our feelings in the present.

What kind of animal is the human being? To quote the titles of two significant books on the subject of human identity that I will discuss in later chapters, we are *social animals* and *storytelling animals*.[3] To find ourselves, we look around to others and we look backward and forward to our life stories. I'll introduce these two neglected dimensions of human identity formation briefly in this chapter and take them further in the following chapters. But I also want to look at a third dimension, which is just as instinctive and important—looking up.

We Look Around

The limitations of self-knowledge are impressed upon me every time I shop for clothes and the fitting room has more than one mirror. I'm used to seeing myself from just one angle—front on and in reverse. When confronted with the side and back views, I am always taken aback at what I see, even to the point of questioning the quality of the mirrors. The

---

3 The two books, by David Brooks and Jonathan Gottschall, are discussed in chapters 6 and 8, respectively.

self I know is far from a full and accurate picture. To cite another trivial experience, think too of what most of us find as an unpleasant surprise when hearing our own voice in a recording. You hear your voice through your skull. Those around you know your voice, and your appearance, better than you do. In response to the trend toward a buffered self, the social sciences are increasingly defining personhood in relational terms.

We Look Backward and Forward

To find ourselves, along with looking around to others, we look backward and forward to our life stories. Richard Bauckham observes that "the human self has no timeless existence outside of the temporal reality that we can only describe in narrative."[4]

We each have what Timothy Keller and many others call a narrative identity: "Everyone lives and operates out of some narrative identity, whether it is thought out and reflected upon or not."[5] Such narratives give meaning to our lives, sketch our character in outline and tell us what is important in life.

Your story is what connects you at different stages of your life. Your body is made up of between 50 and 75 trillion cells. It is sometimes said that every seven years, we become essentially new people, with every cell in our bodies having been replaced by a new cell. The thought might cross your mind: *Who am I, if I'm literally a different person from who I was seven years ago?* As it turns out, it's a bit of an urban myth. While sperm cells last three days and skin cells two or three weeks, your brain cells can last a lifetime (and hopefully do!).[6] But the point remains that the main thing that connects the older you to the younger you, let alone to you as a baby, is your story as recalled and recounted by you and others.

4 Richard Bauckham, *The Bible in the Contemporary World: Hermeneutical Ventures* (Grand Rapids, MI, Eerdmans, 2015), 138–39.
5 Timothy Keller, *The Reason for God: Belief in an Age of Skepticism* (London: Penguin, 2009), 15.
6 Benjamin Radford, "Does the Human Body Really Replace Itself Every 7 Years?" Live Science (website), April 5, 2011, https://www.livescience.com/.

We Look Upward

You are a social being, and you are your story. But there's more. I submit that we need to look not only around, and backward and forward, but also upward.

Some theologians insist that personal identity requires that you look well beyond yourself. Rowan Williams writes, "Without the transcendent we shall find ourselves unable, sooner or later, to make any sense of the full range of human self-awareness."[7] On the other side of the ledger, some have argued that Friedrich Nietzsche, often dubbed the first real atheist because of his fearless pursuit of the consequences of his antitheist stance, has no place for the notion of personal identity.[8] Does looking up have a role in identity formation?

You might think that religion, looking up, is on its way out; human beings are moving on from the need for the transcendent. It is true that religious adherence in most Western countries is in steady decline. But the picture is mixed. The common exception is migrant communities for whom religious identity remains a firm identity marker. And worldwide, the number of people who claim to be religious is actually increasing: presently, only one in six people have no religion, with a projected decrease to one in eight by 2060.[9]

In 2015, sociologist Rodney Stark reported that

of the world population 81 percent claim to belong to an organized religious faith, 74 percent say religion is an important part of their daily lives, and 50 percent have attended a place of worship in the past seven days. Russia has more occult healers than medical

7   Rowan Williams, *Why Study the Past? The Quest for the Historical Church* (Grand Rapids, MI: Eerdmans, 2018), 41.

8   See Helen Pluckrose, "How French 'Intellectuals' Ruined the West: Postmodernism and Its Impact, Explained," *Areo*, March 27, 2017, https://areomagazine.com/, who claims that Nietzsche and Heidegger rejected "the concept of the unified and coherent individual."

9   Matt Wade, "Australia might be losing its religion, but the world isn't," The Age (website), August 12, 2017, http://www.theage.com.au/.

doctors, 38 percent of the French believe in astrology, and 35 percent of the Swiss agree, 'Some fortune tellers can foresee the future.' Nearly everyone in Japan has their new car blessed by a Shinto priest.[10]

In Western countries, it can be misleading simply to look at the data on formal religious affiliation. Having no religion does not mean you are not spiritual in some sense. One report from the Pew Research Center in the United States indicated that more than a third of Americans between eighteen and thirty-five are now not affiliated to a religion; when asked on a survey what religious identity they hold, they answer "none of the above." However, the report goes on to say that "the overwhelming majority of those who claim to have no religion aren't necessarily atheists. Two-thirds believe in God or a universal spirit, and one in five even pray every day."[11]

Apparently, "millennial nones," those who claim to have no religion, are not abandoning religion to become secular humanists. Rather, "they are turning toward more individual forms of spiritualism, including yoga, meditation, healing stones, Wiccan spell casting and astrology."[12] In Australia, a McCrindle survey in 2012 found that nearly one-fifth of Australians identify as spiritual but not religious, more than ever before on any census. Even if looking up in traditional religious terms is on the wane, looking up in general is not.

Indeed, people are looking in all sorts of directions for some kind of spiritual experience. The decline of religion in the West does not mean that fewer people believe in the supernatural. In June 2019, about ten thousand people spontaneously gathered at Stonehenge in

---

10 Cited in Trevin Wax, *Eschatological Discipleship: Leading Christians to Understand Their Historical and Cultural Context* (Nashville: B&H Academic, 2018), 125.

11 Casper Ter Kuile, "Millennials haven't forgotten spirituality, they're just looking for new venues," PBS (website), March 3, 2017, https://www.pbs.org/.

12 Stephen Asma, "Religiously unaffiliated 'nones' are pursuing spirituality, but not community," *Los Angeles Times*, June 7, 2018, https://www.latimes.com/.

northern England to greet the summer solstice.[13] The gathering at the Neolithic monument at the start of the longest day of the year was described in reports as a spiritual experience and resembled an act of communal worship.

The best vantage point from which to look up—in every direction for that matter—was surely that afforded to those rare individuals who have walked on the Moon. The puniness of the earth and vastness of the universe is inescapable when viewed from the earth's only permanent natural satellite. Simon Smart reports that the experience in almost every case left a profound impression. One of the first, Buzz Aldrin, reports that "many of the astronauts involved in those early days of space walks and Moon visits embraced spirituality or religion. Some had existential crises and struggled to understand the meaning of their lives." Aldrin himself, just prior to his own short lunar walk, paused and took the Christian ritual of Communion. In his case, at least, it is striking that "in that moment of astonishing human achievement, perhaps the zenith of scientific endeavour to that point in time, [he] was reaching for something spiritual to make sense of the experience."[14]

A more subtle and subjective argument for the human attraction to the transcendent is the observation that each of us wants something more than simply the satisfaction of our most basic desires. Authors across a range of traditions, both religious and otherwise, have noted such yearnings. C. S. Lewis, for example, wrote of the human capacity for "an inconsolable longing for we know not what." In *The Pilgrim's Regress*, he describes the object of such longing as "that unnamable something, desire for which pierces us like a rapier at the smell of bonfire, the sound of wild ducks flying overhead, the title of *The Well at the World's End*, the morning cobwebs in late summer, or the noise of

13 "Stonehenge summer solstice: Thousands gather to cheer sunrise," BBC News, June 21, 2019, https://www.bbc.com/.

14 Simon Smart, "As the Moon landing unfolded, Buzz Aldrin took communion. Here's why," *ABC News* (Australia), July 19, 2019, https://www.abc.net.au/.

falling waves."[15] Such yearnings are, Lewis says, "good images of what we really desire; but they are not the thing itself; they are only the scent of a flower we have not found, the echo of a tune we have not heard, news from a country we have never yet visited."[16] Human beings are afflicted, or perhaps blessed, with a nostalgia for the garden, a painful yearning for our perfect past.

N. T. Wright suggests that there are at least four universal human longings of the heart that this world fails to satisfy: the yearning for justice, the hunger for relationships, the quest for spirituality, and the delight in beauty. Each theme, Wright suggests, can be heard "in the way that we might hear the echo of a voice, the elusive sound of someone speaking just around the corner, out of sight."[17] Such echoes raise the questions that only some form of spirituality or religion can answer. In Wright's view, "these 'echoes of a voice' are among the things which the postmodern, post-Christian, and now increasingly post-secular world cannot escape as questions, strange signposts pointing beyond the landscape of our contemporary culture and out into the unknown."[18]

The seventeenth-century French polymath and Christian apologist Blaise Pascal held that, when it comes to faith in God, "the heart has its reasons of which reason knows nothing: we know this in countless ways."[19] Analogous to knowing you are awake, we can be aware of God without mounting an argument from reason: "It is the heart which perceives God and not the reason. That is what faith is: God perceived by the heart, not by reason."[20] As to the reason why everyone

15 C. S. Lewis, *The Pilgrim's Regress: An Allegorical Apology for Christianity, Reason and Romanticism* (Grand Rapids, MI: Eerdmans, 1958), 204.
16 C. S. Lewis, *The Weight of Glory, and Other Addresses* (Macmillan, 1949), 102.
17 N. T. Wright, *Simply Christian: Why Christianity Makes Sense* (San Francisco, CA: HarperOne, 2010), ix.
18 Wright, *Simply Christian*, xi.
19 Blaise Pascal, *Pensées* (London: Penguin, 1995), 127.
20 Pascal, *Pensées*, 127. Pascal was not averse to the place of reason in supporting faith, but argued that it needs to be supplemented by reasons of the heart. In *Pensées*, for example, he defends the historical reliability of the Gospels and the resurrection of Jesus on rational grounds.

does not heed such yearnings and find faith in God, Pascal suggests many people drown them out by the white noise of busyness and by amusing themselves, an argument that might have even more traction today. Has there ever been a more distracted world than the one we live in today?

Speaking personally, I think both halves of my brain, the logical and analytical left part and the intuitive and creative right part, contribute to my being a Christian. I have both head reasons and heart reasons for faith, if you like. My head is convinced by the historical and philosophical grounds for Christian faith. My heart "is impressed by antiquity, searches for wisdom, yearns for justice, needs hope, loves beauty, senses my darkness, is appalled by evil, is repulsed by death and aches for the reassurance of a satisfying story to make sense of my existence."[21] The experience of such strong desires, unfulfilled by life on earth, are for me a strong motivation to look up and seek God.

Do you identify with such yearnings? Are you aware of C. S. Lewis's "inconsolable longings"? Can you hear N. T. Wright's "echoes of a voice"? Some people, of course, would write off the experience of such yearnings, pointing to our need of God as sentimental nonsense. But it is hard to deny the almost universal human experience of such deep emotions.

Looking up, one way or another, seems to be an irrepressible human urge. The idea that human beings have an incurable predilection to worship is certainly the Bible's view of human nature. An enigmatic verse in Ecclesiastes states that God has "put eternity in the human heart" (3:11, my translation). In striking fashion, this verse teaches that each of us has a God-given awareness that there is something more to life than what we experience on earth, something beyond the frustrating existence of life "under the sun."

---

21 Brian Rosner in "Interview with Alain De Botton," Centre for Public Christianity (website), May 11, 2012, www.publicchristianity.org/.

An intriguing Australian story in this connection is that of so-called Mr. Eternity, Arthur Stace.[22] As an illiterate alcoholic, Stace came to faith in 1930 in a Sydney church near the center of the city, St. Barnabas, on Broadway. Then for the next three decades, almost every day, he preached a famous one-word sermon, writing the word "eternity" in chalk on footpaths all over the city.

How did the increasingly godless city respond to this overtly religious message? What place has talk of eternity in its secular and irreligious soul? Oddly, there was plenty of room, it seems. To mark the new millennium, on January 1, 2000, the word "Eternity," without a squeak of complaint, was emblazoned on the iconic Sydney Harbour Bridge as Stace had written it more than half a million times. It was viewed, it is estimated, by some two billion people across the world. We might have expected a more accurate message for a predominantly secular humanist society like Sydney to be something like "Oblivion." Yet somehow the transcendent message of eternity struck a chord in human hearts around the globe.

Many agree that looking up in one form or another is thought to be good for you. Positive psychology guru Martin Seligman contends that human happiness depends in part on being committed to something bigger than yourself.[23] According to Einstein, we are as good as dead without it. Even atheist Richard Dawkins admits that awe is one of the highest experiences of the human psyche.[24]

But what of the atheist Christopher Hitchens's assertion that "religion poisons everything," the subtitle of his book *God Is Not Great*? Psychologist Michael Carr-Gregg, whose main interest is in child and

---

22 Tim Costello, "How an Illiterate Alcoholic Impacted a Whole City for Eternity," Eternity (website), July 20, 2017, https://www.eternitynews.com.au/. See Roy Williams and Elizabeth Meyers, *Mr Eternity: The Story of Arthur Stace* (Sydney: Acorn, 2017).

23 Martin Seligman, "Authentic Happiness," April 2011, https://www.authentichappiness.sas.upenn.edu/.

24 Sarah Berry, "The extraordinary influence of awe on humans," The Age (website), August 7, 2017, http://www.theage.com.au/.

adolescent development, has surveyed the literature on the subject of the effects of spirituality on human wellbeing and behavior:

> Spirituality, defined as a sense of connectedness or relatedness to something or someone that transcends the material world, is associated with better mental health. It can help increase self-esteem, aid in one's search for meaning in life, improve family and special relationships and decrease risk-taking behavior. It can also provide a moral compass to help navigate life.[25]

Academic psychiatrist Andrew Sims's summary of the voluminous studies on the subject of the effects of religious belief in the *American Journal of Public Health* comes to similar conclusions:

> Religious involvement correlates strongly with wellbeing, happiness, life satisfaction, hope and optimism, purpose and meaning in life, higher self-esteem, better adaptation to bereavement, greater social support, less loneliness, lower rates of depression, and faster rates of recovery from depression.[26]

Being Human

This chapter has set the agenda for the rest of the book by insisting that you cannot know who you are until you recognize what you are. The human species is classified as *homo sapiens*, from the Latin meaning "wise person." However, we are just as well, if not more accurately, categorized as:

1. *homo sociologicus*, social beings;
2. *homo narratus*, storytelling beings; and
3. *homo adorans*, worshiping beings.

25 Michael Carr-Gregg, "How to build happy and resilient children," in *Raising Resilient Kids* (Mt. Evelyn: Collective Wisdom, 2018), 7.

26 Cited by John C. Lennox, *Can Science Explain Everything?* (London: Good Book, 2019), 29.

We are profoundly social, deeply story-driven, and we have eternity in our hearts.

The biggest problem with looking only inward to find ourselves is that it is hopelessly reductionistic, ignoring crucial dimensions of what it means to be a human being. Human identity does not exist in isolation, it cannot be defined without reference to the narrative in which it finds itself, and it cannot help but look up.

In the rest of this book, I will seek to show that looking up is the key to both the social self and the story-telling self, and that the self that emerges when the three are aligned is better equipped than the self-made self to cope with life's setbacks and to respond well to the ordinariness, feebleness, and injustice that is the frustrating futility of human life under the sun.

Questions for Reflection and Discussion

1. Think about the idea that we look to others to know ourselves. How does being known affect your personal identity? How does it work in terms of identity formation? Does it change your character?

2. How does the fact that you are your story affect your personal identity? Are you in complete control of your story? Are you the sole author and narrator? How much of it is a story that you share with others? How does your story affect your character?

3. Consider your relationship to "looking up." Does personal identity depend on transcendence? Do you need to look up in order to form a stable and satisfying sense of self?

PART 2

———————

YOU ARE A SOCIAL BEING

6

Social Identity

"Persons come to know themselves in being known
by persons other than themselves."

DAVID JOPLING[1]

"Most people do not have infinite depths of individuality that
is theirs alone. What they believe to be their true inner self is
actually constituted by their relationships with other people."

FRANCIS FUKUYAMA[2]

HUMAN BABIES ARE about the most helpless and dependent creatures on earth. Whereas a human baby takes a good twelve months to walk unaided, a baby deer can stand within ten minutes of being born and can walk within seven hours. Even more stark is the contrast with reptiles, which typically leave their offspring to survive on their own as soon as they're born. Our babies, on the other hand, are utterly contingent beings. They start out life mirroring their parents, unconsciously imitating their facial expressions and gestures; it takes up to eight weeks even to recognize their own hands and to learn that they have bodies that can move. Needless to say, it's a lot of work looking after a newborn. Thankfully,

---

1   David A. Jopling, *Self-Knowledge and the Self* (New York: Routledge, 2000), 166.
2   Francis Fukuyama, *Identity: The Demand for Dignity and the Politics of Resentment* (London: Profile Books, 2019), 56.

it's a rewarding task; and it's a good thing baby toesies are so cute! All of this points to the fact that, developmentally, humans are formed in relation to other humans. We are profoundly and inescapably social beings.

The question then arises: Are our identities formed, even in adolescence and adulthood, in relation to others? Do you look around to find yourself? How important are other people for forming your identity? Sometimes an example with the volume turned up can be instructive. Consider the case of someone who shunned social contact for an extremely long time. His name is Christopher Knight. Back in 1990, at the age of twenty, Christopher parked his car on a remote trail in Maine and "walked away with only the most basic supplies. He had no plan. His chief motivation was to avoid contact with people."[3] He emerged from his solitude in 2017, twenty-seven years later, having been arrested for stealing from cabins in the wilderness where he was living.

As far as the rest of the world was concerned, when Christopher Knight formed a tribe of one, he ceased to exist. What is perhaps surprising is that, according to his own words, he himself also ceased to exist. In an interview about his decades-long solitary existence, he mused,

> "It's complicated. . . . Solitude bestows an increase in something valuable. I can't dismiss that idea. Solitude increased my perception. But here's the tricky thing: when I applied my increased perception to myself, *I lost my identity*. There was no audience, no one to perform for. There was no need to define myself. I became irrelevant."[4]

If there's no one to reflect back to you who you are, does a personal identity become superfluous? Is having one even possible? Surely, being known by others is essential for knowing yourself or even for having the need for a self.

---

3   Michael Finkel, "Into the woods: how one man survived alone in the wilderness for 27 years," *The Guardian*, March 15, 2017, https://www.theguardian.com/.

4   Finkel, "Into the woods."

In this chapter, we explore further the idea that in order to form your identity and to know yourself, you need to look around. We'll do this in two ways. First, by filling out the picture of human beings as social animals, with reference to a range of research from the social sciences. And second, with four personal stories, including my own, that illustrate the need to be known.

The Social Animal

When it comes to knowing yourself, social psychologists speak of the "looking-glass self," a term coined in 1902. It refers to our tendency to understand ourselves by perceiving what others make of us. In other words, the self is the result of learning to see ourselves as others see us.[5] The great Scottish poet Robert Burns is credited with saying: "Oh would some power the gift give us / To see ourselves as others see us."[6] Apparently, each of us has that power, for seeing ourselves as others see us is the experience of every human being.[7]

Human beings are social animals. A growing body of research—some parts surprising, some parts amusing—indicates the extent to which we are profoundly relational creatures and pushes against any notion that anyone is a self-made self. I will make five general points in connection with this fact, drawn from David Brooks's excellent work, each one striking at the heart of expressive individualism. The following five points are my own synthesis of the relevant studies:

1. You were largely formed by your parents.
2. Your thoughts are not entirely your own.

---

5 "Looking-glass self," Wikipedia, last modified June 2, 2021, https://en.wikipedia.org/wiki/Looking _glass_self.

6 Robert Burns, "To A Louse, On Seeing One On A Lady's Bonnet, At Church," in *Poems and Songs of Robert Burns*, Project Gutenberg (website), accessed October 28, 2021, https://www.gutenberg .org/; language modernized.

7 Of course, some people with significant cognitive impairment might be exceptions to seeing themselves as seen by others.

3. Your mind is not exclusively your own.
4. Your behavior is shaped by the company you keep.
5. You don't know yourself that well.

You were largely formed by your parents. Parents effectively pass on to their children an identity, which the child then accepts, revises, or rejects in adolescence. But even if you feel you have discarded the ready-made version of you, the influence of your parents and family of origin remains pervasive and powerful. To cite a bizarre example, consider your name, something you had no choice in. One study found that

> people named Dennis or Denise are disproportionately likely to become dentists. People named Laurence or Laurie are dispropor-tionately likely to become lawyers. People named Louis are dispro-portionately likely to move to Saint Louis, and people named George disproportionately move to Georgia. These are some of the most important decisions in people's live, and they are influenced, if only a bit, by the sound of the name they happen to be given at birth.[8]

Your thoughts are not entirely your own, as much as you like to believe that you think for yourself. And it's not just those presently around you that affect your thinking:

> The truth is, starting even before you were born, we inherit a great river of knowledge, a great flow of patterns coming from many ages and many sources. The information that comes from deep in the evolutionary past, we call genetics. The information revealed thou-sands of years ago, we call religion. The information passed along from hundreds of years ago, we call culture. The information passed along from decades ago, we call family, and the information offered

8   David Brooks, *The Social Animal: The Hidden Sources of Love, Character, and Achievement* (New York: Random House, 2012), 208.

years, months, days or hours ago, we call education and advice. But it's all information, and it all flows from the dead to us, and to the unborn. The brain is adapted to the river of knowledge and its many currents and tributaries, and it exists as a creature of that river the way a trout exists in a stream. *Our thoughts are profoundly moulded by this long historic flow, and none of us exists, self-made, in isolation from it.*[9]

Your mind is not exclusively your own. Human beings are able to function in a social world because of our network of minds created by our mammalian limbic systems, which resonate with the minds of others, enabling us to partially permeate each other's thought and behavioral worlds. As Brooks writes, "Human beings understand others in themselves, and they form themselves by re-enacting the internal processes they pick up from others."[10] As he points out, our "minds are intensely permeable. Loops exist between brains. The same thought and feeling can arise in different minds, with invisible networks filling the space between them."[11]

Your behavior is shaped by the company you keep. Once again, a somewhat humorous and mundane example makes the point:

At restaurants, people eat more depending on how many people they are dining with. People eating alone eat least. People eating with one other person eat 35 percent more than they do at home. People dining in a party of four eat 75 percent more, and people dining with seven or more eat 96 percent more.[12]

The impact of the behavior of others can have an effect on how you behave even when you don't notice it. Yawning, for example, is highly

9   Brooks, *The Social Animal*, 32; emphasis added.
10   Brooks, *The Social Animal*, 39.
11   Brooks, *The Social Animal*, 41.
12   Brooks, *The Social Animal*, 172.

contagious.[13] Indeed, imitation is a powerful human instinct, and it takes very little for it to kick in:

> Friends who are locked in conversation begin to replicate each other's breathing patterns. People who are told to observe a conversation begin to mimic the physiology of the people having the conversation, and the more closely they mimic the body language, the more perceptive they are about the relationship they are observing. At the deeper level of pheromones, women who are living together often share the same menstrual cycles.[14]

Most importantly for our purposes, *you don't know yourself that well,* which makes looking inward to find yourself problematic. What are you like in terms of your personality? "Numerous studies have shown that there is a low correlation between how people rate their own personality and how people around them rate it."[15] The same goes for how people regard themselves in terms of moral behavior and with respect to their achievements. One study found that half of college students said they would call out a sexist comment made in their presence. However, "when researchers arranged for it to actually happen, only 16 percent actually said anything."[16] Many studies show that people overestimate how much they know, and, if successful, how much of it was due to their talent and grit. One Harvard professor argues that "we have a psychological immune system that exaggerates information that confirms our good qualities and ignores information that casts doubt upon them."[17]

Many human beings are comically and infuriatingly overconfident. And apparently, self-confidence bears little relationship to actual competence:

---

13   Brooks, *The Social Animal*, 284.
14   Brooks, *The Social Animal*, 210.
15   Brooks, *The Social Animal*, 370.
16   Brooks, *The Social Animal*, 219.
17   Brooks, *The Social Animal*, 220.

A great body of research finds that incompetent people exaggerate their own abilities more grossly than their better-performing peers. One study found that those who scored in the bottom quartile on tests of logic, grammar, and humor were especially likely to overestimate their abilities. Many people are not only incompetent, they are in denial about how incompetent they are.[18]

Brooks's summary concerning human beings as social animals is blunt but accurate: "We don't know ourselves. Most of what we think and believe is unavailable to conscious review. We are our own deepest mystery."[19] As Michael Horton insists, "the 'self'— understood as an autonomous individual—does not exist."[20] The notion of a self-made self is naive at best; to recall and counter *The Greatest Showman*, no one marches to a beat that they alone drum. So much for "nobody can teach me who I am."[21] When it comes to your personal identity, you have been schooled by others from before you were born.

You are not just an individual. You are not your own creation. You did not invent yourself. You exist in a web of relationships. You are a social animal. Your identity is constituted in relation to other people and in being known by them. Indeed, the social and psychological sciences are increasingly defining personhood in relational terms. The self is no longer seen as an isolated and individual phenomenon but as something formed within a network of relationships and neural connections, a being-in-relation.

Most of the subtle influences that I have noted in this section operate at the level of the subconscious. You are not the product of your own conscious deliberations and choices. When it comes to forming your

18 Brooks, *The Social Animal*, 220.
19 Brooks, *The Social Animal*, 245–46.
20 Michael Horton, *The Christian Faith: A Systematic Theology for Pilgrims on the Way* (Grand Rapids, MI: Zondervan, 2011), 87.
21 Recall the advice in the book *Wisdom* mentioned in chapter 1.

identity, your subconscious does the bulk of the work. The research that Brooks cites shows that the unconscious mind is the realm "where character is formed and most of our most important life decisions are made—[it is] the natural habitat of the social animal."[22] You and I might like to think of ourselves as boldly expressing our individuality in order to find our true selves, but the truth is that rather than being a single, soaring eagle, eyeing our prey from a great height, we are more like a honking goose in a tight V-flight formation.

But don't misunderstand my goose analogy. It's not about repressive conformity but interdependence. Geese provide an excellent example of synergy. "As each goose flaps its wings, it creates 'uplift' for the birds that follow. By flying in a V formation, the whole flock adds 71 percent greater flying range than if each bird flew alone. When a goose falls out of the formation, it suddenly feels the drag and resistance of flying alone. It quickly moves back into formation to take advantage of the lifting power of the bird immediately in front of it."[23]

Like these geese in formation, we humans are also wired to be interdependent, secure in a network of relationships, with invisible connections and indissoluble ties. "If we have as much sense as a goose, we stay in formation with those heading where we want to go. We are willing to accept their help and give our help to others."[24] We fly best together, in harmony and unison, bearing our own burden and also sharing the burdens of others. And as any goose will tell you, it's the only way to fly!

In order to know yourself and be yourself, you need to be known intimately and personally by others. But it doesn't end there. You also need to be truly loved by them. Being known and loved are the key ingredients to every personal identity worth inhabiting.

22 Brooks, *The Social Animal*, back cover.
23 This illustration has been used frequently. See, e.g., Richard L. Daft, *The Leadership Experience*, 4th ed., Silo.Pub (website), 2010, https://silo.pub/the-leadership-experience-with-infotrac.html.
24 Daft, *The Leadership Experience*.

Personal Identity and Being Known

To explore further the nature of the link between personal identity and being known, I want us to consider four very different life experiences. We learn:

1. from sisters Lisa and Bea that being known is a reassuring and beautiful thing;
2. from my own experience that being known can replenish self-knowledge;
3. from bereaved husband Josh Vincent the irreplaceable value of being known; and
4. from an elderly Belsen concentration camp survivor that the need to be known lasts a lifetime.

A regular feature in my weekend newspaper is "The Two of Us," which looks at the friendship of two individuals. It's a typical human-interest story that focuses on how two people relate and what they mean to each other. Spouses, parents and children, friends, coworkers, and siblings are the standard fare. One article that stood out for me recently concerned the relationship between two sisters. When talking about her sister, Lisa, Bea commented, "Lisa sees the best in me. . . . There's something reassuring and beautiful about someone really knowing you."[25] It is true to say that we often feel "ourselves" when we are around those who know us best.

This has certainly been my experience. In January 2000, I returned to live in Australia after sixteen years living overseas. Reentry was a bit bumpy. I had less than two weeks to find somewhere to live, set up home, and settle three children into schools before starting a new job teaching at a high school, for which I had no formal training. In addition to these challenges, my sense of self had taken a battering. My

---

25 "The Two of Us," *Sun Herald*, November 22, 2013.

personal identity gauge was pointing toward empty, and the light was flashing. Slowly getting on top of things and making new friends kept the motor running, but refueling came from renewed contact with those who knew me best.

Two old friends, Frank and Martin, were especially helpful. I had known them most of my life and we had kept in contact while I was overseas for the previous sixteen years. Martin likes to tell the story of asking me to dice an onion on our first bushwalk as teenagers. My not knowing that you had to peel it first left a lasting impression, it seems. Frank was a flat mate in my early twenties and happily recalls my early attempts at cooking, which included serving up a relatively raw Chili con Carne. Back living in Sydney after so many years away, I went on regular overnight bushwalks with Martin, and Frank called me every Sunday night. If I was having trouble remembering who I was, then being known by Frank and Martin helped me to remember. There is indeed something reassuring and beautiful about someone really knowing you.

Josh Vincent, a thirty-eight-year-old father of three young boys, lost his wife to a seven-and-a-half-year battle with cancer. He wrote a moving blog post in response to the question he was asked frequently: "What is it like to lose your wife?" His answer, in short, was that he had lost the one who saw him. Here is some of what he shared from his journal:

> "What is it like to lose your wife?" A number of words come to mind. One is "invisible." I feel invisible in plain sight. Not physically invisible; I'm a big guy, so it's hard to miss me, and so many have blessed me and my boys with care and attention. So I'm not saying I don't feel cared for; I actually feel unworthy and humbled by people's kindness.
>
> I mean "invisible" almost in the sense of when a girl looks at a guy in a movie and says, "You see me." She means there is a person

in this world who gets her, who understands her with a depth of intimacy no one else does. Of course, in the movies, they usually say this after knowing each other for five minutes. But after 14 years with Cari, I felt like she *saw* me—all of me—and loved me anyway. The good. The bad. The ugly. She saw my imperfections and challenged me to grow.

And now the one person who saw me is gone. The only one who could read my every glance and anticipate my response is no longer available. There is no replacing 14 years of being seen by someone every day and night. You can't replace a soul who covenanted to stay with you no matter what. I miss the warmth and safety of that—the unrivalled beauty of it. So there is a real sense in which a crowded room makes me feel more invisible because she's not there—the one I always looked for in a crowd, the one who saw me and was for me no matter what.[26]

The experience of Josh Vincent is not unique. In his treatment of romantic love in *The Social Animal*, David Brooks makes the same connection between deep love and intimate knowing that Josh Vincent so painfully and beautifully describes. Note the way Brooks portrays the budding romance of the two main characters in the book:

Harold and Erica were never more alive than in the first weeks of their love for each other. One afternoon they were sitting on the couch at Harold's place, watching an old movie. "*I know you*," Erica said after a lull, apropos of nothing, peering into Harold's eyes. Then a few minutes later she fell asleep on Harold's chest. Harold went on watching the movie and shifted her head a bit so he could be comfortable. She made a soft nuzzling sound.[27]

26 Josh Vincent, "I Feel Invisible After My Wife's Death," The Gospel Coalition (website), January 28, 2019, https://www.thegospelcoalition.org/.
27 Brooks, *The Social Animal*, 212; emphasis added.

To be known intimately and personally is a big part of being truly loved. It is surely among the most valuable and cherished experiences on earth. Does anyone know you and love you in this way? Such deep and personal knowledge is not limited to erotic love but also appears in the best of friendships and family relationships.

Social researcher Hugh Mackay's book *What Makes Us Tick?* looks at the ten desires that drive human beings. They include the desire to connect, to be useful, to belong, for love, and so on. The chapters are deliberately not numbered so as not to give any suggestion of a hierarchy of desires. But according to Mackay, the most important desire is the desire to be taken seriously, which he explains as the desire to be noticed, to matter, to be appreciated, to be valued, to be remembered—that is, to be known. We all say, to quote him, "please recognize me and acknowledge me."[28]

In Mackay's view, however it's expressed, the desire to be known by others drives us for the entirety of our lives. He cites a heartrending example:

> Helen Bamber, the British campaigner for the care of torture victims, has described the experience of holding a dying woman in her arms after the liberation of the Belsen concentration camp at the end of World War II.
>
> As the woman rasped out the horrific account of her experiences in the camp, Bamber said to her: "I am going to tell your story." This seemed to calm the distressed woman. "I think she knew she was going to die," Bamber said. "She didn't want to die and [her story] not be told—that nobody would know." This was a woman anxious, even at her death, not to be ignored or forgotten. When all other desires have left us or become irrelevant, we are left with the desire to be acknowledged, identified, appreciated, and remembered.[29]

28 Hugh Mackay, *What Makes Us Tick: The Ten Desires that Drive Us* (Sydney: Hachette, 2010), 4.
29 Mackay, *What Makes Us Tick*, 4.

The Need to Be Known

In order to know yourself, rather than just looking only inward and following your heart, you need to look around to others in recognition that you are a social creature; we know ourselves in being known by others.

Ironically, in our day of finding and knowing yourself, of looking inward to define yourself, the desire to be known by others is as strong as ever. Quirky American author Mitch Albom points to the rise of celebrity culture in this connection played out in light of the impermanence of our lives:

> To think that you died and no one would remember you. I wondered if this was why we tried so hard to make our mark in America. To be *known*. Think of how important celebrity has become. We sing to get famous; expose our worst secrets to get famous; lose weight, eat bugs, even commit murder to get famous. Our young people post their deepest thoughts on public Web sites. They run cameras from their bedrooms. It's as if we are screaming, *Notice me! Remember me!* Yet the notoriety barely lasts. Names quickly blur and in time are forgotten.[30]

Albom's musings raise some key questions for the topic of personal identity: What does it take to satisfy our longing to be known? How does one make one's mark? Does death erase our identities? In addition, I wish to ask: Is being known by other human beings enough? What has your identity as a social being got to do with transcendence? What does the Bible do with the fact that we are social beings? Do you need to look up as well as around to find yourself?

Questions for Reflection and Discussion

1. This chapter argued that you are a social animal in that you were largely formed by your parents; your thoughts and mind are not entirely your

---

30 Mitch Albom, *For One More Day* (New York: Hyperion, 2006), 24.

own; your behavior is shaped by the company you keep; and you don't know yourself that well. Which of these resonate with you strongly? Which are harder to swallow?

2. Think about your own web of relationships. Who has had a formative impact on you? How does being known affect how you view and understand yourself?

3. What do you know of being loved? How has this shaped your identity or sense of self?

Known by God

"Wouldn't it feel wonderful to be completely known?"
MAGGIE WILKEN (CHARACTER IN *THREE WOMEN*, BY LISA TADDEO)[1]

"For now we see in a mirror dimly, but then face to
face. Now I know in part; then I shall know fully,
even as I have been fully known [by God]."
THE APOSTLE PAUL (1 COR. 13:12)

THERE IS SOMETHING precious and beautiful about someone really knowing you. That was certainly my experience when things went pear-shaped back in the 1990s. I had close friends who kept in touch with me, generously offered hospitality and practical assistance, and patiently engaged me in long and repeated conversations. One of the main benefits of such kindness was in connection with my shaken sense of identity. I was having trouble remembering who I was, given all the changes that had taken place in my life, and being known by my closest friends and having them pay attention to me was a great comfort and reassurance. As we saw in chapter 6, as social beings, we know ourselves in being known by other people.

---

1   Justine Toh, "The unbearable wonder of being completely known," ABC Australia, February 19, 2020, https://www.abc.net.au/.

Parents knowing their children is particularly important for a child's sense of identity. Parents not only reflect back to their children their identities but also play a big role in forming those identities. Children are named by their parents and receive their earliest experiences from them. Parents pass on their own tastes, values, and worldview to their children. Indeed, parents play a big part in the formation and maintenance of their children's identity, especially when they are young. At best, parents are those who know us well and hold a more complete memory of our lives than anyone else.

But as valuable as it is to look around in order to find yourself, being known by other people for self-knowledge has its limitations. All human relationships are imperfect, given that they can be clouded by our self-interest and selfishness. No one knows you perfectly, and not all of what they make of you is accurate. And human relationships end, whether through breakdown, when people move away, or when people die.

In this chapter, we will explore the idea that God's knowing us as his children offers the foundation for a stable and satisfying sense of self and can contribute to living a good life. Our lifelong need to be known is met most profoundly in being known completely and fully by God our Father, who gives us our identity as his beloved children. And that identity changes everything.

If we look around to be known by others, we look up to God for the same reason.

Known by God

Does God know you and me personally? And if so, how does that affect my identity?

The Bible affirms the critical role of being known both by other human beings and by God for personal identity. In the storyline of the Bible, this capacity for harmonious relationships, both with other human beings and with God, is interrupted by human disobedience.

If Adam and Eve forfeited the blessing of being known intimately and personally by God, faith in God is what restores that knowledge.

Significantly, the main characters in the Old Testament are explicitly said to be known by God, including Abraham, Moses, David, and the prophet Jeremiah.

> Abraham: "For I have known him . . ." (Gen. 18:19, my translation).
> Moses: "I know you by name" (Ex. 33:12).
> David: "You know your servant, O Lord God!" (2 Sam. 7:20).
> Jeremiah: "Before I formed you in the womb I knew you" (Jer. 1:5).

We must be careful here not to confuse two sorts of knowledge—namely, factual knowledge, the idea that God knows all about us, and relational knowledge, the notion that God knows someone personally. Some languages mark these two types of knowledge with different words. German, for example, uses *wissen* and *kennen* to refer to knowing *something* and knowing *someone*, respectively. The Hebrew, Greek, and English languages use the same verbs "to know" for both.

To say that God knows someone does not simply mean that God knows about them. "If, to use the language of 2 Corinthians 5:11, God's omniscience means that '*what we are* is known to God,' God's relational knowledge means that '*who we are* is known to God.' . . . If God's omniscience is an attribute of God that speaks of his transcendence and overlaps with his omnipresence,[2] his knowing us concerns his immanence and is related to his love."[3]

Note too that being known by God is directly connected to the question of personal identity. At one critical point in the biblical narrative, King David offers to build God a *house*, in the sense of a temple. Fond

---

2   Consider the juxtaposition of omniscience and omnipresence in Ps. 139:1–4 ("You know when . . ."), followed by 139:5–10 ("You hem me in . . .").

3   Brian S. Rosner, "'Known by God': The Meaning and Value of a Neglected Biblical Concept," *Tyndale Bulletin* 59, no. 2 (2008): 208–9.

of a good pun, God responds in the negative and tells David that he will build him a *house*, in the sense of a dynasty. David replies: "*Who am I, O Lord God, and what is my house, that you have brought me thus far?*" (2 Sam 7:18; 1 Chron. 17:16). Two verses later, David answers the question himself: "What more can David say to you? For *you know your servant, O Lord God!*" (2 Sam 7:20; see also 1 Chron 17:18). If David wonders who he is, the answer is that he is known by God.

And in both the Old and New Testaments, this is true of all believers. All of God's people are known by God.

> Israel: "You only have I known / of all the families of the earth"
> (Amos 3:2).
> The church: "Now that you have come to know God, or rather to
> be known by God" (Gal. 4:9)

But what is the nature of this intimate knowing? Believers in Christ are known by God in the same way that a father knows his child. This can be seen most clearly in Galatians 4, where Paul asserts that believers are "known by God." The prior verses (Gal. 3:26–4:7) expound the doctrine of God's adoption of believers in Christ. In the NIV, the section is accurately entitled, "Children of God," for these verses are indeed the longest exposition of adoption in the Bible. ("Son" in Galatians 3–4 is generic, inclusive of both men and women—Paul uses the language of sonship since it was sons who were the heirs in the ancient world.) On no less than four occasions, Paul tells the Galatian Christians that they are sons of God (3:26; 4:6; 4:7, twice in this last verse):

> *In Christ Jesus you are all sons of God, through faith.* . . . But when the fullness of time had come, God sent forth his Son, born of woman, born under the law, to redeem those who were under the law, *so that we might receive adoption as sons.* And because you are sons, God has sent the Spirit of his Son into our hearts, crying, "Abba! Father!" *So*

you are no longer a slave, but a son, and if a son, then an heir through
God. (Gal 3:26; 4:4–7)

When Paul describes the Galatian Christians in 4:8–9 as those who
are known by God, he has not left the theme of adoption behind. Paul's
preference for being known by God over knowing God in Galatians
4:8–9 as a description of them is thus understandable: it fits better with
their identity as children of God, which he has just spent so much time
expounding. Therefore, a fuller answer to the believer's question, Who
am I?, is that a believer is known by God as his child.

Names and Stories

In recent times, when acts of terrorism are perpetrated, the media typically does two things to remember and honor the victims: list their names
and tell their life stories in brief. Both are essential ways to communicate
their identities. The most basic thing about a person's identity is his or her
name, and what defines people are their stories. Being known intimately
and personally by God includes both these dimensions of our identities.

God knows his children by name. When Jesus compares himself to
a shepherd in John's Gospel, he makes the point that "he calls his own
sheep by name" (John 10:3). Not only does God know his people by
name; he sometimes changes their names as a sign of his thorough
involvement in their lives and an indication of his plans for them.
Examples include God changing Abram's name to Abraham, Sarai's to
Sarah, Jacob's to Israel, and, in the New Testament, Simon's to Cephas.

The theme of naming as knowing is also often reinforced in the Bible's
narratives, where often the characters who are named are the faithful
to whom God is unwaveringly committed. In Exodus 1, the pharaoh
is not named—he is just "the king of Egypt." But Shiphrah and Puah,
the lowly Hebrew midwives, are named (Ex. 1:15). Similarly, in Ruth 4,
Boaz is named, but the guardian-redeemer who refuses to buy the land
from Naomi for fear of endangering his own estate is not. Tim Keller

points to something comparable in the New Testament, in the parable of the rich man and Lazarus in Luke 16: "The rich man, unlike Lazarus, is never given a personal name. He is only called 'a Rich Man,' strongly hinting that since he had built his identity on his wealth rather than on God, once he lost his wealth he lost any sense of self."[4]

If your life is characterized by faith in and obedience to the Lord, like Shiphrah, Puah, Boaz, and Lazarus, then God knows you by name, and your identity is secure in him. Your name is written in the Lamb's book of life, a book written "from the foundation of the world" (Rev. 17:8).[5] So important are our names to God that he records them in what the Bible describes as "the book of life" (see Ps. 69:28; Rev. 13:8; 20:15; cf. Luke 10:20).

But there is also a book in God's metaphorical library that confirms that he knows the stories of our lives, not just in brief but in every detail. In Malachi 3:16, God is said to keep "a book of remembrance," an ongoing account of the words and deeds of each and every one of God's people. God knows and takes note of the lives of his children, not to condemn us, but to reassure us that he knows us intimately and personally. God's people are those to whom he is attentive—"a book of remembrance was written before him of those who feared the LORD and esteemed his name" (3:16). He treats us as his "treasured possession," and "will spare them as a man spares his son who serves him" (3:17). His loving attention applies to both the ups and downs of our lives. In Psalm 56:8, the psalmist asks God to "put my tears in your bottle. / Are they not in your book?"

Whereas the *knowledge of God* might sometimes seem ethereal and removed from our daily lives, the fact that we are *known by God*, even in our darkest days, is a great comfort. God knows us when our struggles with our own identity feel hidden from everyone else.

---

4   Timothy Keller, *The Reason for God: Belief in an Age of Skepticism* (London: Penguin, 2009), 78.

5   In Heb. 12:23, having your name "enrolled in heaven" is synonymous with being a member of "the church of the firstborn" (ESV margin note), suggesting once again a link between divine adoption and being known by God.

The Five Tests of the Good Life and Being Known by God

What difference does it make to receive your identity, not from looking inward, but from God, by looking up and hearing that you are his beloved child? A good way to ask this is to run it by the five tests we used earlier, to see how being known by God helps us deal with suffering and disappointments, pride and envy, the weak and lowly, enemies and injustice, happiness and pleasure.

In chapter 3, I argued that the self-made self did not fare well on the tests of the good life, with the utopia complex; outrage culture; the rise of narcissism, self-centered not-in-my-backyard thinking; and the happiness paradox being called as witnesses against it. Does being known by God intimately and personally supply any resources to help pass the tests of existence, ego, ethics, enemies, and enjoyment?

1. The Existential Test: Suffering and Disappointments

How does being known by God as his child help us to cope with suffering and disappointment?

Who are you if the things that define you—be they your relationships, employment, health, or whatever—are diminished or stripped away? A shaken self-perception is among the most painful side effects of adversity. As it turns out, the most common practical benefit of being known by God in the Bible is being comforted. According to the prophet Nahum, "The LORD is good, / a stronghold in the day of trouble; / *he knows those who take refuge in him*" (Nah. 1:7). J. I. Packer, author of the best-selling book *Knowing God*, claims that there is "unspeakable comfort" in being known by God.[6] Let's try and speak about it.

One of the things that people need when facing serious hardship is the encouragement that others know what you are going through. As Hugh Mackay puts it, "We place a high value on the people who are

6 J. I. Packer, *Knowing God* (Downers Grove, IL: InterVarsity Press, 1993), 37.

prepared to listen attentively and sympathetically to us. Being truly, seriously listened to feels like a welcome and precious gift."[7]

The comfort of being known by God when in distress ranges from his specific and active care, in which he meets the need in question, to a more general notion of consolation—that of being known, as a parent knows their child. Psychologist Maureen Minor likens God to the ideal parent who offers his children his loving attention and a secure attachment that provides "a safe haven and a secure base from which to engage the world."[8] It seems that being known by God can help provide a stable and secure identity, not unlike that which good-enough parents hope to give to their young children. Being known by God meets our deepest need to be acknowledged and valued when such things are most needed.

This can be the case irrespective of practical assistance. When a young child stubs a toe, she might need some medical attention. But she also needs the reassuring embrace of a caregiver. When confronted with uncertainty and hardship, being known by God offers this sort of comfort. In psychological terms, according to Loyola McLean, "The benefits of such consolation also extend psychologically to the affirmation of one's lovability, one's value and one's belonging to someone that can be internalized in a positive schema of self and potentially then accessed at times of challenge."[9] In times of distress, we often feel worthless and unloved, as if no one cares or even notices. Being known by God puts the lie to these destructive thoughts.

The three lowest points in the history of ancient Israel were slavery in Egypt, wandering in the wilderness, and exile in a foreign land.[10]

7   Hugh Mackay, *What Makes Us Tick: The Ten Desires that Drive us* (Sydney: Hachette, 2010), 29.

8   Maureen Miner, "Back to the Basics in Attachment to God: Revisiting Theory in Light of Theology," *Journal of Psychology and Theology* 35 no. 2 (2007): 112–22.

9   Loyola M. McLean and Brian S. Rosner, "Theology and Human Flourishing," in *Beyond Well-being*, ed. Maureen Miner, Martin Dowson, and Stuart Devenish (Charlotte, NC: Information Age, 2012), 77.

10 See also Brian Rosner, "Known by God," Ridley College (website), June 11, 2015, https://www.ridley.edu.au/resource/known-by-god-2/

In all three cases, God comforted his people by reassuring them that he knew them in their distress. When "the Israelites groaned in their slavery" and "cried out" to God for help, "God saw the people of Israel—and *God knew them*" (Ex. 2:23–24, my translation). With respect to Israel's wilderness wanderings, God comforts the Israelites with the reassurance that he knew them there in the wilderness too: "It was *I who knew you* in the wilderness, / in the land of drought" (Hos. 13:5). When in exile, the nation feared that God had forgotten them. In response, he insists that there is less chance of him forgetting them than of a mother forgetting her child:

> Can a woman forget her nursing child,
>   that she should have no compassion on the son of her womb?
> Even these may forget,
>   yet *I will not forget you*. (Isa. 49:15)

In each of these extreme situations, even if the alleviation of their suffering was some way off, knowing that God had taken notice of their anguish was the first step in its alleviation. It affirmed their identity as those who belonged to him. Their plight had not escaped his notice.

Those who are known by God, and know that they are known, have good resources to endure the hardship and disappointment that life inevitably throws at them and to maintain a healthy sense of self.

2. The Egotism Test: Pride and Envy

Does being known by God as his child help to manage pride and envy?

Pride is the inordinate desire to be seen as better in some respect than other people and to make a name for yourself. Intriguingly, both motives can be seen in the story of the Tower of Babel (Gen. 11), the archetypal story of human pride. In Genesis 11:4, the builders announce their intentions: "Come, let us build ourselves a city and a tower with its top in the heavens, and let us make a name for ourselves."

God's response to the building project in 11:5–7 is dripping with irony. If the tower was meant to reach to heaven, God has to "come down" from heaven even to see it! God regards even our most outrageous ambitions as puny. And instead of gaining notoriety, God said of their city and tower that "its name was [to be] called Babel" (11:9); in Hebrew "Babel" sounds like the word for "confused." The "name" they made for themselves (11:4) was one of derision.[11]

Speaking personally, pride is an occupational hazard for those of us who write books. Book sales and best-seller lists are means of measuring whether an author is building a reputation and standing out from other authors in the crowded book market. My motivation in writing this book, for example, can easily slip from wanting to help a range of people to wanting to be well-thought-of and admired. The next easily taken step is to view colleagues and peers as competitors and threats to my notoriety, and to treat them shabbily. It can also lead to bemoaning their success and secretly enjoying their setbacks. Pride, especially in league with envy, is the death of community. Whereas wanting to make the most of your talents and opportunities as well as taking some pleasure in your achievements is only natural, pride can easily lead to a consuming desire to stand out from the crowd and to a neglect of or indifference to the needs of others.

Being known by God can be part of the vaccination against human pride and the damage it causes in our relationships. It can help us deal with the insecurity that fuels our pride by reminding us that our identities are secure in God. We are less likely to reach for the sky and make a name for ourselves if our names are already known in heaven (Luke 10:20). And the recognition that God has marked you out means that you should feel less concerned about making your own mark.

11 See also Brian Rosner, "Making a Name for Yourself and Reaching the Sky," Ridley College (website), February 2, 2017, https://www.ridley.edu.au/principals-blog/making-name-reaching-sky/.

3. The Ethics Test: The Weak and Lowly

Do those who are known by God as his children have good warrant for responding in love to the weak and lowly?

Those who are known by God and adopted into his family are to imitate God their Father. It is at this point that we see the profoundly formative nature of the identity of being children of God, known by him, for behavior and character. To be known by God is to be a child of God, secure in his love, accepting this identity as a gift from him, consciously putting it on and behaving in ways that are in keeping with it.

To be known by God as his child is to reflect the family likeness. Take the call to love that flows from being children of God that we find in Ephesians, just one example from Paul's letters. Ephesians 5:1–2 makes the imitation of God the grounds for a life of love: "Therefore be imitators of God, as beloved children. And walk in love" (Eph. 5:1–2).

Note that the command to love is based not only on God's example but also on the status of his children as themselves "dearly loved" (5:1 NIV). Indeed, it is only when people feel loved and secure enough in their own identities that they can turn from self-interest and act in the interest of others in love. Love is the quintessential divine attribute, and even on its own, the call to "walk in the way of love" (5:2 NIV) is a call to walk in God's footsteps. The metaphor of walking also underscores the regular and everyday requirement of loving behavior. And that broad call to loving behavior is grounded in the identity of believers as God's children, as those known and loved by God.

In the Sermon on the Mount, Jesus encourages his disciples to give to the needy (Matt. 6:2) by reminding them that "your Father knows what you need before you ask him" (Matt. 6:8). Remembering that we are dearly loved children of God, who knows our every need, is a powerful motivation to respond in love to those less fortunate than ourselves.

4. The Enemy Test: Adversaries and Injustice

Do those who are known by God as his children have similarly solid grounds for being concerned about justice and not responding vengefully to enemies?

Certainly, the justice of God is just as prominent in the Bible as the love of God; "the Lord of hosts is exalted in justice" (Isa. 5:16). Likewise, in both testaments of the Bible, God's children are to reflect his character and seek to live justly. In Micah 6:8, to walk humbly with God is to "do justice, and to love kindness." And Amos calls believers to "let justice roll down like waters, / and righteousness like an everflowing stream" (Amos 5:24).

Those who are known by God as his children are to reflect the family likeness. Taking just one example, the injunction from Jesus to not retaliate against those who oppose you is firmly anchored in the identity of being a child of God. Jesus tells his disciples to love their enemies, "that you may be children of your Father who is in heaven" (Matt. 5:45, my translation).

5. The Enjoyment Test: Happiness and Pleasure

Does being known by God bring lasting joy and happiness?

The happiness movement is based on positive psychology, a discipline that seeks to discover not so much the cures to human mental health problems as to uncover what makes human beings flourish. One of the key findings is that people who are grateful feel happier:

> In positive psychology research, gratitude is strongly and consistently associated with greater happiness. Gratitude helps people feel more positive emotions, relish good experiences, improve their health, deal with adversity, and build strong relationships.[12]

12 "Giving thanks can make you happier," Harvard Health Publishing (website), August 14, 2021, https://www.health.harvard.edu/.

Two practices to promote thankfulness recommended by the Harvard Medical School are:

Keep a gratitude journal. Make it a habit to write down or share with a loved one thoughts about the gifts you've received each day.

    Count your blessings. Pick a time every week to sit down and write about your blessings—reflecting on what went right or what you are grateful for. Sometimes it helps to pick a number—such as three to five things—that you will identify each week. As you write, be specific and think about the sensations you felt when something good happened to you.[13]

Both are good ideas. But my point is that they are much more easily and consistently undertaken if you have someone to thank! Many things in life are not gifts directly from human beings. The person whose identity is based on God's personal knowledge of their situation and needs has much to be grateful for. As Jesus affirmed in the Sermon on the Mount, God knows how to give good gifts to his children (Matt. 7:11). It is easier to maintain a sense of gratitude in such circumstances than if your lot in life is due merely to blind chance and an indifferent universe. Perhaps surprisingly for a secular medical school, Harvard acknowledges the potential of faith in God in this regard. Another of their six tips for cultivating gratitude is to pray: "People who are religious can use prayer to cultivate gratitude."[14]

Having an all-seeing and all-loving heavenly Father can even prompt joy and gratitude for life's difficulties and hardship. James counsels that there can be joy even in suffering if you know that God knows what you are facing, and there might be some benefits in store:

Count it all joy, my brothers and sisters [ESV margin note], when you meet trials of various kinds, for you know that the testing of

13   "Giving thanks can make you happier."
14   "Giving thanks can make you happier."

your faith produces steadfastness. And let steadfastness have its full effect, that you may be perfect and complete, lacking in nothing. (James 1:2–4)

It is easier to give thanks under all circumstances if you believe that "all things work together for the good of those who love God . . . and are known by him" (Rom. 8:28, my translation).

At this point, I should offer a caveat. I am not arguing that all believers are more resilient, humble, loving, compassionate, and happy than all nonbelievers. Nor even that the self-made self necessarily leads to poor outcomes on my five tests. I'm not even sure how such measurements would be made. People's identity formation script is just one factor among many that will affect their behavior. My point is simply that, in my judgment, those who are known by God intimately and personally are well equipped to deal with the questions of existence, ego, ethics, enemies, and enjoyment and have deep resources from which to draw in responding in positive ways to life's challenges.

Known and Loved by God

Being known by God as his child has both individual and corporate implications. As with all families, it implies a family likeness and thus carries with it the expectations of certain behaviors. With respect to our five tests, being known by God can bring comfort in the face of adversity, meeting a deepfelt need for unconditional love and being known in the midst of distress. It can provoke a healthy humility, releasing us from the futile drive to establish our own significance and to assert our superiority over other people. With regard to the weak and lowly, it can help us to "be imitators of God, as beloved children. And walk in love" (Eph. 5:1–2). When dealing with enemies and anger, it can prompt us to imitate God as we "do justice, and . . . love kindness," (Mic. 6:8). And it can also support a life of gratitude, leading to lasting joy and happiness, even when life is tough.

Different people find the Christian faith attractive for a variety of reasons. Some are moved by the offer of forgiveness of their sins, by the hope of eternal life in a dark world, by the ideals and experience of a loving Christian community, by the teaching and example of Jesus, by the notion of God saving the world through a costly sacrifice, or by the paradox of God saving the world, not through a display of power or wisdom, but through the weakness and foolishness of a crucified messiah. In every case, there is a real and felt need that faith in God meets.

Does anyone become a Christian because of the experience of being known personally and intimately by God? Perhaps not many would put it in exactly those terms. But I know of at least one who comes close. Sarah Irving-Stonebraker is Senior Lecturer in Modern European History at Western Sydney University. She wrote an article explaining how she moved from atheism to Christian faith, in which she mentions the very thing I've been talking about in this chapter. Note the way in which Sarah's need to be known in order to ground her identity is met in being fully known and loved by God:

> I grew up in Australia, in a loving, secular home, and arrived at Sydney University as a critic of "religion." I didn't need faith to ground *my identity* or my values. I knew from the age of eight that I wanted to study history at Cambridge and become a historian. *My identity lay in academic achievement.* . . . One Sunday, shortly before my 28th birthday, I walked into a church for the first time as someone earnestly seeking God. Before long I found myself overwhelmed. *At last I was fully known and seen and, I realised, unconditionally loved.*[15]

So we have seen that looking around to others and up to God—that is, being known by both others and God—plays a strong role

---

15   Sarah Irving-Stonebraker, "How Oxford and Peter Singer drove me from atheism to Jesus," The Veritas Forum (website), May 22, 2017, http://www.veritas.org/.

in providing our sense of self and dealing with our identity angst. But taken alone, even these are not enough to truly help us form a coherent sense of self. We are not static, timeless creatures; our lives progress through time, and so our identities are shaped not just moment to moment, but by the overarching narratives we hold to and view ourselves within. It is this idea of humans as story-telling animals that we will investigate next.

Questions for Reflection and Discussion

1. Perhaps you have thought often about knowing God, but less about being known by God. What is different about viewing the relationship from this perspective?

2. Some people find the idea of being truly seen and known by God more disturbing than comforting. If that's you, what parts of Scripture discussed in this chapter bring a sense of comfort?

3. Consider again the five tests of the good life: the existential, egotism, ethics, enemy, and enjoyment tests. As you consider the possibility of being known by God, truly and intimately, what feels hard or constrained in these areas of life? What feels freeing and more possible?

PART 3

———————

YOU ARE YOUR STORY

8

Narrative Identity

"We tell ourselves stories in order to live."

JOAN DIDION[1]

"Our life stories are who we are. They are our identity."

JONATHAN GOTTSCHALL[2]

"Everyone lives and operates out of some narrative identity,
whether it is thought out and reflected upon or not."

TIMOTHY KELLER[3]

TELLING YOUR OWN story is at the heart of expressive individualism. We might even say that our day is characterized by "incessant autobiography," a term coined by C. S. Lewis in his little book *An Introduction to Paradise Lost.*[4] I hesitate to use the term, given that Lewis coined it to describe the self-absorbed narcissism of the character of Satan in Milton's masterpiece, *Paradise Lost!* But "incessant autobiography" is a fitting way of describing how everyone seems to be feverishly telling their life stories on the various platforms of social media. It is possible

1   Joan Didion, *The White Album* (London: Weidenfeld & Nicolson, 1979), 11.
2   Jonathan Gottschall, *The Storytelling Animal: How Stories Make Us Human* (Boston, MA: Mariner, 2013), 161.
3   Timothy Keller, *The Reason for God: Belief in an Age of Skepticism* (London: Penguin, 2009), 15.
4   C. S. Lewis, *An Introduction to Paradise Lost* (Oxford: Oxford University Press, 1961), 102.

today to document your life story in considerable detail and publish it widely on a daily basis. Where you are, what you're doing, whom you're with, how you're feeling, what you're eating, how it's all affecting you, and on it goes. Not everyone is obsessed with telling their stories in this way, but the possibilities for doing so seem to multiply, and the potential for constantly narrating our lives out loud underscores the role of our stories in each of our personal identities.

Along with looking around to others, we look backward and forward at our life stories in order to find ourselves.[5] We all know this. When we first meet someone, along with noticing their gender and race, guessing their age and learning their name, we might ask about their cultural background, occupation, significant relationships, and where they live. Going deeper, a more penetrating question is to ask them about their story: "What is your family background? What in your past has made you who you are today? Where are you heading in life? What defines you?" Human beings tell stories about themselves that matter.

Life Stories

The expressive-individualism approach to narrative identity is entirely predictable. Each of us chooses the stories that define us (or at least we think we do). And, in our stories, *we* take the starring role, as well as act as director, producer, script writer, illustrator, narrator, and marketing director.

What is your story? How would you answer the following questions?

What in your past has made you who you are today?
What events have defined you?
Where are you heading in life?

---

5   Richard Bauckham, *The Bible in the Contemporary World: Hermenuetical Virtues* (Grand Rapids, MI: Eerdmans, 2015), 138–39, observes that "the human self has no timeless existence outside of the temporal reality that we can only describe in narrative."

What are your aspirations, hopes, and dreams?

Have there been any times when you've lost the plot or gone off script?

Stories have "sculpting power."[6] And this is certainly the case with the stories we tell about ourselves. Alistair McGrath is right: "The story we believe we are in determines what we think about ourselves and consequently how we live."[7] There is no doubt that a key dimension of personal identity is the story you inhabit. According to Gottschall,

> Story teaches us facts about the world; influences our moral logic; and marks us with fears, hopes, and anxieties that alter our behaviour. . . . Research shows that story is constantly nibbling and kneading us, shaping our mind without our knowledge or consent. The more deeply we are cast under story's spell, the more potent its influence.[8]

One of my favorite radio programs is called "The Year that Made Me." It's an interview show with famous guests talking about themselves and their life stories, specifically the year that was most formative for them. Here's a sample of how five celebrities answered the question, What was the year that made you?

Footballer Chris Judd: 2004, his first Brownlow medal

Actress Lisa McCune: 2001, the birth of her first child

Novelist Tim Winton: 1978, a terrible car accident

Children's book author Alison Lester: 2006, pneumonia and a
    week-long coma

Comedian Akmal Saleh: 1978, the sudden death of his father[9]

---

6 Gottschall, *The Storytelling Animal*, 152.

7 Alister McGrath, *Deep Magic, Dragons and Talking Mice: How Reading C. S. Lewis Can Change Your Life* (London, Hodder & Stoughton, 2014), 47.

8 Gottschall, *The Storytelling Animal*, 148.

9 *The Year that Made Me*, ABC Sunday Extra with Julian Morrow, accessed October 26, 2021, https://www.abc.net.au/.

Now you might expect the defining moments of famous people to be something they achieved, some triumph for which they are famous. And, on that score, the sportsman Chris Judd doesn't disappoint; note that it wasn't just his Brownlow medal, but his first one, that made him—he won two![10] The actress Lisa McCune highlights a genuinely identity-changing event—namely, becoming a mother. But, intriguingly, the other three point to negative experiences as the defining events of their lives: Tim Winton, a car crash; Alison Lester, a coma; and Akmal Saleh, a death. And note that in the case of comedian Akmal Saleh, the event was not one that happened to him, at least directly—namely, the death of his father. Indeed, a defining event can be an achievement or a failure, something you do, or something done to or for you. It can also be something that happened before you were born, such as some national event or family experience.

Shared Stories

A person's story begins before that person was born. My father was born in Vienna, Austria, in a Jewish family. He was an only child, and as a young teenager, he and his parents fled Europe soon after Hitler took over Austria in 1938. They headed for Shanghai in China where there was an international settlement that accepted stateless refugees. They spent ten years there, in "the Waiting Room," as the settlement has since been called. All three became Christians soon after their arrival. In 1949, after the war was over, they immigrated to Australia. My father met my mother, an Australian, in Sydney, and they married in 1953. Seeing as I didn't come along until 1959, how can that be a part of my own life story?

It is in fact quite common for family histories to have an impact on a person's identity. In my case, my father's history affects a number of things about me, including my attitude to education (which my father

---

10 The Brownlow Medal is awarded to the "best and fairest" player in the Australian Football League during the home-and-away season.

missed out on), to refugees, to Jews and Judaism, to European history and culture, playing chess, food, music, and so on. Of course, my life has had many other influences. But my experience is not unusual. Such "second hand" memories, in which you are not present or the primary actor, are testimony to the formative power of larger narratives for personal identity, stories of which we find ourselves a part and which we share with others.

Another such shared story shaping personal identity is your national identity—in my case, an Australian nationality. National identity is all about past events that shape national character in the present. A nonindigenous Australian character, for example, cherishes the values of mateship, classlessness, and the "fair go." This is in part due to the convict origins of my country's first settlement in the eighteenth century. Other nation-defining events also contribute to the national character, such as the heroism of the failed Gallipoli campaign of 1915 in World War I, which is commemorated on Anzac Day each year on April 25. Such events had a levelling effect on society as the struggles of ordinary people became chiseled into the nation's memory. Why do I barrack for the "underdog" in most sporting events when my team is not involved? Why do I think it fair enough when "tall poppies," prominent people in society, get cut down to size? Because such sentiments are part of the Australian narrative identity.

Your story is fundamental to your personal identity, but it's not an individual story. Being social animals, we live in shared stories. It is a mistake to think that our life stories are simply our own making and played out in isolation from others. The metanarrative, or big story, in which each of us lives is a combination of defining moments and goals and expectations of life related to stories handed to us by our families and related to the stories of our nations, ethnicities, social classes, and religious faiths.

And this is true even in our day. One of the ironies of expressive individualism is the fact that in many cases it leads to conformity.

Trevin Wax observes, "A restless, individualistic pursuit of happiness evolves into a strange conformist impulse. We think we're blazing our own path, but the paths we take look strangely like everyone else's."[11] As we saw in chapter 6, we are inescapably social creatures.

In my view, there are two big stories to which the vast majority of people in the West subscribe today, and these are playing a big role in forming people's identities. They are the story of *secular materialism* and the story of *social justice*.[12] Both are fueled by the movement of expressive individualism. Like any good story, they each have a basic plot and setting, key turning points, central themes, stock characters, conflicts to be resolved, and an anticipated climax. While they are understandably attractive in various ways, both are seriously flawed. As life stories go, they are ultimately unsatisfying because both have a truncated view of human nature and a distorted view of reality.

I am not suggesting that the narrative identity of every person in the West follows one of just two scripts. In my view, secular materialism and social justice are simply the two dominant personal identity stories that find varied expression in a number of different settings and contexts. It's even possible to subscribe to a mishmash of both; human beings are notoriously inconsistent. These two big stories are like literary genres that house a number of subgenres—just as the genre of drama comes in crime, teen, horror, and legal versions; and comedy can be black, romantic, or slapstick. Under secular materialism, we will consider the subgenres of Enlightenment Progress, the Sexual Revolution, and Consumerism. And under social justice, we will treat the narratives of

---

11 Trevin Wax, "The Faithful Church in an Age of Expressive Individualism," *Kingdom People* (blog), The Gospel Coalition (website), October 22, 2018, https://www.thegospelcoalition.org/.

12 See McGrath, *Deep Magic, Dragons and Talking Mice*, 70, who lists the stories of progress and victimhood as the two big identity formation stories of our time: "Some live under the story of individual progress of the sort peddled on daytime talk shows, that the self is the most important thing there is and that more or better information will organically produce better selves. Still others subscribe to the victim metanarrative, that their personal choices have little impact on the world they live in."

the marginalized and those of their allies—those not affected themselves by discrimination but nonetheless committed to and defined by such issues and aware of their own privileges.

In order to understand and appraise the big stories of secular materialism and social justice, we will look at the fundamental *problems* they address, the significant *turning points* in the past that frame their stories, the nature of the *struggle in the present* in which they are engaged, and the *future hopes* they espouse. In other words, we will examine the main themes of the stories, as well as their beginnings, middles, and ends. Following an analysis of these four pillars of each of the big stories and their subgenres, we will consider their shortcomings and why I regard them as unhelpful and inadequate narrative identities.

Ending up in the wrong story for your narrative identity can have disastrous consequences. In connection with the increase in mental health issues for adolescents across Western countries, psychologist Michael Crossley argues that "depression frequently stems from an incoherent story, an inadequate narrative account of oneself, or a life-story gone awry."[13] Do you have an adequate narrative account of yourself? What is your narrative identity? What life story are you living?

Questions for Reflection and Discussion

1. How does the fact that you are your story affect your personal identity?

2. Are you in complete control of your story? Are you the sole author and narrator? How much of it is a story that you share with others?

3. How does your story affect your character?

---

13 Reported in Gottschall, *The Storytelling Animal*, 175.

9

The Story of Secular Materialism

*"The Enlightenment saw human reason as the pinnacle
of history and the implementation of science and
technology as hastening towards a better future."*

TREVIN WAX[1]

*"The myth of progress fails because it doesn't in fact work . . .
because it would never solve evil retrospectively; and because
it underestimates the nature and power of evil itself."*

N. T. WRIGHT[2]

THE BIBLE CONTAINS some strident condemnations of greed, perhaps the most famous of which is the judgment that "the love of money is a root of all kinds of evil" (1 Tim. 6:10). But it is also not naive about the challenges of poverty. In the only prayer in the book of Proverbs, the sage asks God to spare him from both riches and poverty, fearing that the former would lead him to forget God, and the latter to curse God (30:7–9). Indeed, the apostle Paul confirms that both conditions of life bring distinctive difficulties: "I know how to be brought low, and

1 Trevin Wax, *Eschatological Discipleship: Leading Christians to Understand Their Historical and Cultural Context* (Nashville, TN: B&H Academic, 2018), 101. My discussion of the three forms of secular materialism builds on Wax's insightful treatment.
2 N. T. Wright, *Surprised by Hope: Rethinking Heaven, the Resurrection, and the Mission of the Church* (New York: Harper One, 2008), 87.

I know how to abound. In any and every circumstance, I have learned the secret of facing plenty and hunger, abundance and need. I can do all things through him who strengthens me" (Phil. 4:12–13).

While riches can lead to a selfish outlook on life, there's nothing pleasant about genuine poverty. There's also something to be said for ambition. It is hard to argue with John Stuart Mill, who wrote that "it is better to be a dissatisfied Socrates than a satisfied pig."[3] Many people have material ambitions for their children and seek to provide better for their families. The Bible condemns ambition, but only of the selfish variety (Phil. 2:3).

But can goals of improving your lot be taken too far? In this chapter, I look at how materialistic ambitions can take over your life and put you in a story that ultimately fails to deliver on its promises.

The Story of Secular Materialism

What is secular materialism? By "secular," I simply mean the worldview that takes no notice of religious or spiritual matters; one that doesn't look up, if you like. Secular in this sense is often pitted against sacred. Technically, "materialism" is the related theory that nothing exists except matter. A more common meaning of the term refers to the belief that material possessions and comforts are the most important things in life. Given that I argued in chapter 5 that human beings are inevitably drawn to the spiritual, I am not suggesting that many people subscribe strictly and consistently to secular materialism in the fullest sense of these terms. Instead, I believe that many people, whether consciously or not, act as if matter is all that exists and that material things are all that matters.

We will consider three varieties of the story of secular materialism. The first is the overarching version that sets the scene for the other two—namely, Enlightenment progress. If Enlightenment progress con-

---

3   Quoted in Robert Wuthnow, ed., *Rethinking Materialism: Perspectives on the Spiritual Dimension of Economic Behavior* (Grand Rapids MI, Eerdmans, 1995), 179.

cerns a paradigm shift in thinking that has transformed whole societies in the West, the second and third versions of secular materialism, the sexual revolution and consumerism, are more focused on individuals and their behavior. In all three cases, the influence of expressive individualism is clearly evident in the narrative identities that they produce. Stories of secular materialism regard happiness as the highest goal of life, reject external authority, and believe unwaveringly in the value of individual freedom.

Enlightenment Progress

The Enlightenment tells a story of progress, upward and onward, from an unsatisfactory past toward an attractive vision of a better future.

The Problem	Constraints on personal freedom
Past Turning Points	The Renaissance and the Age of Reason
Present Struggle	Progress through the development of science, technology, and education
Future Hope	The triumph of reason and enlightenment

THE PROBLEM

The Enlightenment's key emphases on progress and freedom indicate that the problem it seeks to solve concerns the stagnation and subjection of the preceding periods of human history, and its lingering effects in the present world. Peter Gay defines the Enlightenment as seeking "freedom from arbitrary power, freedom of speech, freedom of trade, freedom to realize one's talents, freedom of aesthetic response, freedom, in a word, of moral man to make his own way in the world."[4] The word *enlightenment* itself gives a clue to the movement's self-characterization as emerging from darkness—in particular, from the Dark Ages (also known

---

4   Peter Gay, *The Enlightenment: An Interpretation—The Rise of Modern Paganism* (New York: Knopf, 1966), 3.

less pejoratively as the Middle Ages). Indeed, Enlightenment thinking predisposes one to view any period prior to the seventeenth century as benighted. Prior to the Enlightenment, "history was a register of crimes, a tale of cruelty and cunning, at best the record of unremitting conflict."[5]

PAST TURNING POINTS

In terms of major movements in history, the Enlightenment is often mentioned in the same breath as the Renaissance, which is usually dated as taking place just prior, during the fourteenth to seventeenth centuries. If the Enlightenment put reason and science to the fore, the Renaissance, with its catch cry of "back to the sources," is known for its reinvigoration of art, architecture, and literature.

Another key turning point for Enlightenment progress is the rise of reason and the supposed demise of religion. Enlightenment thinking pits reason against religion and predicts the triumph of the former over the latter. In this narrative, the age of reason in the seventeenth and eighteenth centuries is the turning point of history, freeing humanity from primitive religious superstitions and pointing to a brighter future. Such assumptions remain with us to this day.

PRESENT STRUGGLE

The Enlightenment story in the present is about progress through the development of science, technology, and education. It is humanity coming of age and casting off its immature and primitive past. Behaving rationally and maturely is the means of progress, and the potential benefits of such progress are thought to be unbounded.

FUTURE HOPE

The Enlightenment project must not be seen merely as an awakening to the potential of reason and science. It is deeply committed to a grand vi-

5   Gay, *The Enlightenment*, 32–33.

sion of human flourishing in the future. The notion of progress is at the heart of the Enlightenment project, powered by the engines of science and technology. But there is nothing modest about the expectations that accompany such progress. Immanuel Kant, a major Enlightenment thinker, wrote that the "proper destiny [of human nature] lies in such progress."[6] The language of "destiny" is telling.

CRITIQUE

The first statement to make is that the language of enlightenment has broad appeal, not least from a Christian point of view. Indeed, light and darkness are common motifs in the Bible, with the former depicting an unsatisfactory state of affairs, and the latter pointing to the solution. The prophet Isaiah wrote that "the people who walked in darkness / have seen a great light" (Isa. 9:2), and Jesus is called "the light of the world" (John 8:12).

Enlightenment progress has undoubtedly brought enormous benefits to individuals and society. Modern medicine, for one, has relieved untold suffering and prolonged life in ways that the first Enlightenment luminaries could not have imagined. The average life expectancy has gone from less than 40 years old in late Middle Ages England to over 70 for the whole world in 2017. In developed countries, the number of people living to 100 is doubling every 13 years and is predicted to go from 455,000 in 2009 to 4.1 million in 2050.[7] Similar chapters in the story of progress could be told for science and technology.

However, the story of Enlightenment progress includes some serious distortions, and it has failed to deliver on its promises in key respects. In short, it has an overly negative view of the past, a rosy view of the present, and a naive view of the future. Worst of all, it underestimates human evil.

---

6   Immanuel Kant, "What is Enlightenment?" in Peter Gay, *The Enlightenment: A Comprehensive Anthology* (New York: Simon & Schuster, 1973), 387, quoted in Wax, *Eschatological Discipleship*, 116.

7   "Life expectancy," Wikipedia, last modified September 22, 2021, https://en.wikipedia.org/.

With respect to history, Enlightenment progress suffers from what C. S. Lewis called "chronological snobbery," the thinking that earlier times were always inferior to the present.[8] Overconfidence in ourselves in the present inevitably undervalues the past. This can be seen when people speak of being on the wrong and right sides of history to promote a progressive position. But even in terms of science and technology, the past cannot be written off as primitive and unsophisticated. This fallacy is easily refuted. Take, for example, the aqueducts in ancient Rome, which were a feat of engineering to rival almost anything in our day; consider the roof of the Pantheon in Rome, the two-thousand-year-old Roman pagan temple, still standing today, which remains a puzzle of engineering in terms of mass and precision.

But more importantly, the Enlightenment conviction that reason will lead to an infinitely better world in moral terms has been proven wrong. The problem with human beings is not just our dull heads but also our hard hearts, which have not changed. Jesus warned that "out of the heart come evil thoughts, murder, adultery, sexual immorality, theft, false witness, slander" (Matt. 15:19). And the prophet Jeremiah lamented that "the heart is deceitful above all things, / and desperately sick" (Jer. 17:9). In the twentieth and early twenty-first centuries, we find glaring testimonies that humanity remains cruel and in conflict, with two world wars, chemical weapons, nuclear armament, several mass genocides, continued poverty, environmental degradation, and so on.

Finally, reason has not gutted religion and forced it into decline as predicted,[9] the reason being that, rightly understood, reason and religion are complementary forms of knowledge and not in competition. The assumption that faith is anti-intellectual is false. While there are unfortunate exceptions, historically, belief in God actually spurred the

8   C. S. Lewis, *Surprised by Joy* (1955; repr., San Diego, CA: Harcourt, Brace, Jovanovich, 1966), 207–8.
9   See chapter 4, "We Look Upward."

search for knowledge rather than obstructing it.[10] The origin of science is a case in point. It is commonly assumed that the roots of science can be traced back to the Greeks of the sixth century BC. But Aristotle's polytheistic worldview, with its many gods, none of whom created the eternal universe, could take things only so far. The worldview that really got science going was the older Hebrew notion that the universe was created and upheld by God. As John Lennox, Professor of Mathematics at the University of Oxford, puts it, "The foundation on which science stands, the base from which its trajectory has swept up to the edge of the universe, has a strong theistic dimension."[11]

The much-maligned doctrine of creation presumes order in the universe. With his polytheistic worldview, Aristotle was left to deduce from fixed principles how the universe ought to be, a methodology that did not permit the universe to speak directly. Belief in a Creator God has meant that for centuries, the goal of scientists has been to discover the rational order that has been imposed on the world by God. There's every reason to look for the laws of nature, if there is a Lawgiver. The history of ideas reveals that education in the Western world has prospered, not in spite of, but precisely because of its Judeo-Christian foundations.

Are you committed to the narrative identity associated with Enlightenment progress? Do you think science and technology will solve the world's problems? Or do you agree that the human heart is the ultimate spoiler and will always block humanity's path to its "proper destiny," to recall Kant's words? The next two versions of the story of secular materialism take things in a more personal direction.

The Sexual Revolution

The Sexual Revolution took place during the 1960s, '70s, and '80s. Sexual liberation was its aim.

---

10 Content in this paragraph and the next is adapted from Brian Rosner, "Does a Belief in God Hold Back Students?" Centre for Public Christianity (website), August 14, 2022, https://www.public christianity.org/.

11 John Lennox, *Can Science Explain Everything?* (London: Good Book, 2019), 61.

The Problem	Sexual repression and moral codes that constrain sexuality and sexual conduct
Past Turning Points	Sigmund Freud, the pain-and-pleasure paradigm, and the pill
Present Struggle	Removing social norms and sexual taboos, and fulfilment through the release of sexual desire
Future Hope	Sexual emancipation and the authentic expression of the true sexual self

THE PROBLEM

The problem that the sexual revolution confronted was the sexual repression of the moral codes that had constrained sexuality and sexual conduct in the West from the Dark Ages through the nineteenth-century puritanical Victorian period and, despite numerous challenges, remained in place through to the compliant 1950s. If the sexual revolution began in the 1960s, the 1950s are a cipher for everything that is wrong with society.

The resulting guilt and shame of such restrictive codes were seen as not only unnecessary but, more importantly, preventing people from following their hearts and being themselves. In seeing sexuality and sexual expression as integral to personal identity and happiness, the sexual revolution was an early manifestation of the expressive individualism that I am critiquing in this book.

PAST TURNING POINTS

Undoubtedly, there are many things that spurred the revolution, most of which are common themes of secular materialism. Three specific developments are noteworthy.

First, the highly influential Austrian psychiatrist Sigmund Freud (1856–1939) theorized that unconscious repression of sexual desire is fundamentally unhealthy and causes numerous problems. The 1936 book *The Sexual Revolution*, by one of Freud's students, Wilhelm Reich, was clearly ahead of its time on this score. Reich insisted that what was needed in society was "a radical change in the conditions of sexual life to counter the disgraceful medieval sexual legislation that inflicts harm on humanity."[12]

A second turning point that continues to drive the Sexual Revolution concerns a change in the dominant worldview in the West today. Anthropologists sometimes characterize human cultures according to the major drivers of behavior and values. Ruth Benedict proposed three such frameworks. In the broadest terms, she theorized that Western cultures are driven by guilt and innocence, Arab and Asian cultures by honor and shame, and animistic cultures by fear and power. Guilt and innocence cultures make decisions around whether something is right or wrong; honor and shame cultures around what brings honor to your family or community, or what might bring shame; and animistic cultures around how to influence the spirit world that controls day-to-day life. Intriguingly, when Adam and Eve fall in Genesis 3, they are guilty, ashamed, and afraid.[13]

However, missiologist David Williams has suggested that the West has undergone a profound paradigm shift with regard to the fundamental axis of its decision-making. In place of the guilt-and-innocence worldview, he believes we now increasingly subscribe to a pain-and-pleasure framework for living. Williams elaborates, and connects the trend to Freud:

Of course, the language of pain and pleasure is nothing new. The pleasure principle is a cornerstone of Freudian psychoanalysis. Freud argued that human beings have always been driven by an instinctive desire to seek pleasure and avoid pain. . . . In a pain–pleasure worldview, you make decisions based on what feels good to you and

12 Wilhelm Reich, *The Sexual Revolution: Toward a Self-Regulating Character Structure*, trans. Therese Pol (New York: Farrar, Straus and Giroux, 1974), preface to the 3rd ed. (1945), xvii, quoted in Wax, *Eschatological Discipleship*, 138.

13 I am indebted to an unpublished lecture by David Williams, Church Missionary Society Director of Training and Development, for this analysis and the following discussions.

what makes you happy. Your identity is as a pleasure seeker and a pain avoider.[14]

In light of Western societies putting the highest value on the avoidance of pain and the pursuit of pleasure, it is hardly surprising that the sexual revolution has largely won the day.

Third, what really kickstarted the sexual revolution was the birth control pill, or "the pill," as it came to be known. It was first approved for mass use in the United States in 1960. And it made casual sex less risky, breaking the nexus between sex and pregnancy. It is no accident that the sexual revolution got moving in the decade following its release. The pill was no less significant for breaking sexual taboos than the machine gun for ending the cavalry in modern warfare or the lightbulb ending candlelight.

PRESENT STRUGGLE

In line with expressive individualism, the sexual revolution asserts that the real me has desires that need to be expressed to be true to myself. The task of removing social norms and sexual taboos is an ongoing obligation. And individuals are encouraged to find fulfillment by discovering their true self and essence, and expressing it to its full potential. As Roger Scruton observes, the thinking is that "to deny [sexual desires'] release is to *repress* them, and repression of the sexual urge is also oppression of the individual."[15]

However, it is important to note that many people who subscribe to the belief in fulfilment through the release of sexual desires are in monogamous, long-lasting relationships and regard sexual activity outside of those relationships as "cheating." Some of the old sexual boundaries have not gone away. But there is a sense in which the sexual revolution

14 Williams, unpublished lecture.
15 Roger Scruton, "Is Sex Necessary? On the Poverty of Progressivism's Fixation on Sexual Liberation," *First Things* (December 2014): 35.

has redefined marriage in transactional terms; marriage is the means to self-fulfillment and, in such circumstances, entails a commitment that in reality is conditional on successfully serving that end.

Consistent with the major tenets of expressive individualism, the sexual revolution sees its struggle against four impositions: from anything outside the individual concerned, from society, from previous generations, and from religion and politics that might seek to limit sexual expression.

FUTURE HOPE

The goal of the sexual revolution is sexual emancipation—everyone doing what feels right in his or her own eyes. The hope is to produce a society where no one falls short of his or her potential and where each of us can authentically express our true selves in all matters sexual.

CRITIQUE

The first thing to say is that the Bible agrees that humans are sexual beings. Genesis 2 is unique among ancient Near Eastern accounts of creation, with its focus on the creation of woman. Genesis 2:20–25 makes clear not only Adam's need for a mate but also the differentiation and complementarity of males and females, the incompleteness of one without the other, and the norm of sexual intimacy: "Then the man said, 'This at last is bone of my bones / and flesh of my flesh; / she shall be called Woman, / because she was taken out of Man'" (2:23). A similar point is made more concisely in Genesis 1:27, where it is said that in creating humankind, God created "male and female." Ken Mathews notes that the "Hebrew terms for 'male' and 'female,' as opposed to man and woman, express human sexuality."[16]

However, as narrative identities go, defining your existence in terms of your sexuality is limited, and making sexual release the purpose

---

16 Kenneth A. Mathews, *Genesis 1–11:26*, New American Commentary 1A (Nashville, TN: Holman Reference, 1996), 173.

of your life is tiring, to say the least. It can also be an excuse for self-centered behavior. Scruton explains the attraction of the sexual revolution as well as its unintended outcome:

> My pleasures are mine, and if you are forbidding me them you are also oppressing me. . . . Self-gratification acquires the glamor and moral kudos of a heroic struggle. For the "me" generation, no way of acquiring a moral cause can be more gratifying. You become totally virtuous by being totally selfish.[17]

Furthermore, making sex all about personal pleasure ignores its other key dimensions—namely, procreation and partnership. Sex has more than one purpose; it has both societal and social implications. It is even questionable whether the view that sex is purely for self-expression and pleasure is good for all of those concerned, especially women. Russell Moore asks,

> Is it really an advance for women that the average adolescent male has seen a kaleidoscope of images of women sexually exploited and humiliated in pornography? . . . [Or] the adolescent girl facing the pressure to perform sex acts on her boyfriend, or else lose him?[18]

The disturbing prevalence of violence in pornography and the phenomenon of "sex before kissing" as the common experience among young girls are among the dire consequences of expressive individualism's approach to sex.

Single people and those not able to have sex for a range of reasons also become "roadkill" when the meaning of life is couched in terms of sexual performance. Such people are left to feel that they are diminished

17 Scruton, "Is Sex Necessary?," 36.
18 Russell Moore, *Onward: Engaging the Culture without Losing the Gospel* (Nashville, TN: B&H, 2015), 171–72.

beings, falling short of the glory of self-fulfillment. Taking for granted the Bible's positive take on marital sex, Richard Hays rightly notes,

> Scripture (along with many subsequent generations of faithful Christians) bears witness that lives of freedom, joy, and service are possible without sexual relations. . . . Never within the canonical perspective does sexuality become the basis for defining a person's identity or finding meaning and fulfilment in life.[19]

Consumerism

What is consumerism and how does it play out as a narrative identity? Consumerism defines human beings in terms of our purchases and what we contribute to society as paid workers. As an extension of Enlightenment progress, consumerism holds out the promise of the freedom to choose the lifestyle you want. As a form of secular humanism, it places the highest priority on material things and their accumulation. That consumerism concerns more than just possessing things can be seen from advertisements that connect possessions to personal identity. An advertisement for a luxury condominium or apartment complex reads, "Define Yourself." And the Seiko corporation would have us believe: "It's not your hair. It's not your car. It's not your perfume. It's your watch that tells most about who you are."[20]

Susan White explains how consumerism tells a story with a beginning, a middle, and an end:

> If there is any overarching metanarrative that purports to explain reality in the 20th century, it is surely the narrative of the free-market economy. In the beginning of this narrative is the self-made, self-sufficient human being. At the end of this narrative is the big house,

19 Richard Hays, *The Moral Vision on the New Testament* (New York: HarperCollins, 1996), 390–91.
20 Seiko advertisement cited in "So busy checking watches, there's no time for anything else," *The Sydney Morning Herald*, January 10, 2004, https://www.smh.com.au/.

the big car, and the expensive clothes. In the middle is the struggle for success, the greed, the getting-and-spending in a world in which there is no such thing as a free lunch. Most of us have made this so thoroughly "our story" that we are hardly aware of its influence.[21]

The Problem	Falling short of material prosperity
Past Turning Points	The rise of capitalism and the achievement of material goals
Present Struggle	The accumulation of possessions, financial security, and enjoying one's life to the full
Future Hope	Material comfort and happiness

THE PROBLEM

The problem that consumerism seeks to solve is different for different people. If financial security and independence is the goal, the starting point might be the proverbial growing up on the wrong side of the tracks, the struggles of an immigrant family, or just the weight of expectation that every new generation will exceed the material prosperity of their parents. Aspiration, for all sorts of reasons and with mixed motives, defines the consumerist narrative identity.

PAST TURNING POINTS

In general terms, the turning points of the story of consumerism coincide with the Industrial Revolution and the rise of capitalism. Looking further back, the change from limited goods agrarian economies in the ancient and medieval worlds to unlimited goods economies made it possible to become wealthy without necessarily impoverishing your neighbors. In the former, to increase the size of your farm, for example, required decreasing the size of someone else's. In unlimited goods economies, at least in principle, wealth creation does not bear such a

21   Susan White, "A New Story to Live By?" *Bible in TransMission* (Spring 1998), 4.

cost. More recently, the saturation of societies in advertising at every turn, pitching every new product as essential for a fulfilling life—be it somewhere to live, something to drive, something to eat, something to wear, or somewhere to play—marks a significant development. The 1980s are sometimes said to be the high point of naked avarice, with the famous line from Michael Douglas's character in the 1987 movie *Wall Street* summing things up: "Greed is good." But greed has never gone away.

PRESENT STRUGGLE

The goal of the story of consumerism is the accumulation of possessions in the hope of financial security and enjoying one's life to the full. Of course, many people's motives for aspiring to acquire material goals are not entirely selfish. More money can mean a better education for your children, more leisure time with your spouse or friends, or better health. But we ought not to underestimate the power of consumerism on our everyday lives.

With reference to the North American context, Wax explains how consumerism has taken hold of the calendar and, true to the values of secular humanism, has succeeded in replacing religion as structuring time:

> Today the calendar is structured around consumerism. Thanksgiving is the precursor to Black Friday and Cyber Monday sales, carrying us through the shopping season of Christmas, . . . to Valentine's Day, Mother's Day, Father's Day, Memorial Day, and Labor Day. . . . These are the seasons, the rhythms that give shape to contemporary society. Note how most of these "holidays" are not "holy days" in the old sense but "shopping days." When the purpose of life is consumption, then time is refigured to help people consume more and better.[22]

22 Wax, *Eschatological Discipleship*, 167–68.

Envy of those just above you on the ladder of success and the inability ever to be content in any area of life drives both daily activities and long-term dreams. In fact, those who "make it" are said to be living the dream.

FUTURE HOPE

The future hope of consumerism is the story of going from being a "have-not" to having it all. If the highest goal in life is happiness, and you subscribe to secular materialism, then a vision of material comfort is hard to resist.

CRITIQUE[23]

In recent years, a number of academics and social commentators have questioned the rampant materialism of the Western world. They argue that if people are trying to get rich in order to be happy, it isn't working. Elizabeth Farrelly wrote that over several decades, "Western happiness has declined precisely in tandem with the rise of affluence."[24] Similarly, Ross Gittins claims that there is actually "evidence that those who strive most for wealth tend to live with lower wellbeing."[25] Amusingly, in response to the lure of personal success, Jim Carrey states, "I think everybody should get rich and famous and do everything they ever dreamed of so they can see that it's not the answer."[26]

Material possessions seem to have a built-in obsolescence, not just in terms of their use-by dates, but with respect to the pleasure they bring. The joy of a shiny new car or comfy sofa or whizbang computer diminishes over time. Psychologists call it habituation; they offer de-

---

23 Content in this section is adapted from Brian Rosner, "Greed as a False Religion," *Ethics in Brief* 12, no. 5 (2008): 1–4. See also Rosner, *Greed as Idolatry: The Origin and Meaning of a Pauline Metaphor* (Grand Rapids, MI: Eerdmans, 2007).

24 Elizabeth Farrelly, "In search of a cure for paradise syndrome," *The Sydney Morning Herald*, October 28, 2006.

25 Ross Gittins, "How to be happy," *The Sydney Morning Herald*, January 2, 2006.

26 Jim Carrey, "Quotes," Goodreads, accessed October 29, 2021, https://www.goodreads.com/.

creased stimulation as we become use to, or habituated to, them. They go from your new car, new sofa, or new computer to just being your car, your sofa, or your computer.

Some critics of greed have compared it to a religion. One newspaper article carried the title, "In greed we trust" (instead of "in God we trust").[27] When high profile stockbroker Rene Rivkin died, one published obituary spoke of his "once-loyal entourage of supporters who worshipped their high priest at the altar of wealth."[28]

As it turns out, the comparison of greed with a religion is hardly original. The New Testament warns not infrequently of the religious power of money. Jesus charged that people either serve God or Mammon— that is, possessions (Matt. 6:24; Luke 16:13). The apostle Paul believed that some people's god is their belly (Rom. 16:18; Phil. 3:19), and he condemned greed as a form of idol worship (Col. 3:5; Eph. 5:5). What are we to make of the comparison of greed with religion? Are the New Testament denunciations of greed in terms of idolatry just arresting hyperbole? Can such extreme rhetoric help us in the fight against greed today?

The first thing to notice is that Jesus's and Paul's comparisons of greed with religion were more innovative in form or expression than in content. The Old Testament paves the way for them with its strong association between wealth and apostasy. In the Old Testament, it's not that the rich inevitably abandon God; rather, becoming wealthy raises the possibility. With riches comes the temptation to trust in oneself rather than God. The rich sometimes feel that they have no need of God; they have made other arrangements.

Material things as a threat to devotion to God is underscored in both Old and New Testaments. Take, for example, Deuteronomy 8:12–14, which warns those entering the promised land not to allow

27 "In greed we trust," *The Economist*, October 30, 1997, https://www.economist.com/.

28 Rene Rivkin, quoted in "Pity the poor man," *The Sydney Morning Herald*, May 3, 2005, https://www.smh.com.au/.

their prosperity to lead them to abandon the Lord. In Luke's Gospel, with reference to the teaching of Jesus, the dangers that riches pose to entering the kingdom of God are evident in the parable of the rich fool (12:13–21), the encounter with the rich ruler (18:18–30), and in the calls to renounce possessions and give to the poor in order to enter the kingdom of God (14:33; 18:22).

The concept of greed as a religion has deep roots in the Bible. What are we to make of Paul's explicit comparisons of greed with idol worship in Colossians 3:5 and Ephesians 5:5? In what ways are greed and idolatry alike? Over the centuries, three answers to this question have been suggested. Whereas most twentieth-century interpreters see *love* as the point of similarity, the Reformer Martin Luther identified *trust*, and the early church father Chrysostom *service*. Do the greedy person and the idolater love, trust, and serve their money and their idols, respectively? All three are in fact correct.

The Bible underscores love, trust, and service as three core responses of the believer in relation to God, and faults both the idolater and the greedy person for foolishly misdirecting these same three. Both idolaters and the greedy set their hearts on inappropriate objects. Both rely on, trust in, and look to their treasures for protection and blessing. Both serve and submit to things that demean rather than ennoble the worshiper. The mammon saying in Matthew and Luke confirms this troubling teaching. Jesus warns about excessive love of wealth and a forbidden service of wealth: "No one can serve two masters, for either he will hate the one and love the other, or he will be devoted to the one and despise the other. You cannot serve God and money" (Matt. 6:24).

Greed is idolatry in that, like the literal worship of idols, it represents an attack on God's exclusive rights to human love, trust, and service. Material things can replace God in the human heart and set us on a course that is opposed to him, even arousing his jealousy.

Is greed a religion today? It does seem that for many people, material possessions hold a place in their lives that was once occupied by belief in God. The economy has achieved what might be described as a sacred status. Like God, the economy, is capable of supplying our needs without limit. Also, like God, the economy is mysterious, dangerous, and intransigent, despite the best managerial efforts of its associated clergy. If once our most vivid experiences were religious, today they involve money rituals. The modern-day equivalent of the city cathedral is the shopping complex.[29]

As we already noted, what Christianity claims that God expects of believers—namely, love, trust, and service—may well characterize our relationship with money. A glance at the palpable glee on the faces of game show contestants confirms our love of money. You can literally buy "securities" and "futures." Most disturbingly, as the French ethicist Jacques Ellul put it, "We can use money, but it is really money that uses us and makes us servants by bringing us under its law and subordinating us to its aims."[30]

The ultimate solution to the insatiable grasping for, and obsessive hoarding of, material goods that marks our age is not simply to say no to something of limited value, but to say yes to something better. Jesus's concluding exhortation on the subject of greed in the Sermon on the Mount amounts to such a redirection of desire: "the Gentiles seek after all these things. . . . But seek first the kingdom of God and his righteousness" (Matt. 6:32–33). Like all idols, money fails to deliver on its promises. If the root cause of materialism is misdirected religious impulses, then the ultimate solution is still faith in the true and living God who alone gives the security and satisfaction that each of us craves.

The Bible's critique of idolatry is not just that it offends the God who is described as jealous, but the fact that idols are gods that fail. Idol worship leads only to the disappointment and embarrassment of those who trust in them. Thus, we may surmise, one problem with deifying your work or wealth is that ultimately they fail to deliver on

29 See also Brian Rosner, *Beyond Greed* (Kingsford: Matthias Media, 2004), 50.
30 Jacques Ellul, *Money and Power*, trans. LaVonne Neff (Downers Grove, IL: InterVarsity Press, 1984; repr., Eugene, OR: Wipf & Stock, 2009), 47.

their promise to supply the lasting sense of significance, security, and satisfaction that each of us craves.

An Unsatisfying Trilogy

In this chapter, we have examined three different versions of the story of secular materialism: Enlightenment thinking, the sexual revolution, and consumerism. I've named them as narratives that are going nowhere—stories that fail to deliver on their promises by misjudging the effect of ever-increasing personal freedom and underestimating the depths of human depravity. In the end, those living the stories of secular materialism fall prey to idols that fail to bring the security, significance, and satisfaction that each of us craves; idols are gods that fail, be they human progress in general, sexual fulfilment, or material possessions. Next, we will examine the second big story that many people are inhabiting in the West today—namely, the story of social justice.

Questions for Reflection and Discussion

1. How much has the story of Enlightenment progress been your own story? How does it align or misalign with your understanding of human history?

2. In your opinion, what is good and right about the narrative of sexual freedom? Where does it miss the mark?

3. Material comfort and happiness have a lot going for them, and poverty is genuinely troubling. How do you navigate the story of capitalism and consumerism for yourself?

The Story of Social Justice

*"Render true judgments, show kindness and
mercy to one another, do not oppress the widow,
the fatherless, the sojourner, or the poor."*

ZECHARIAH 7:9–10

"There are those who turn justice into bitterness."

AMOS 5:7 (NIV)

WHEN I WAS GROWING UP, social justice was a big part of my family's values. As I mentioned in chapter 8, my father and his parents had
experienced the cruel injustice of persecution, having fled Nazi terror
in Austria in 1938 and finding asylum as refugees in Shanghai. They
emigrated to Australia in 1949, again fleeing an emerging authoritarian
regime. My father then met and married my mother. My grandparents
lived in the back rooms of our house through to my early teenage years.
Antisemitism irreversibly changed the course of their lives. Dad's father
was a bank manager with a doctorate, and his grandfather a medical
doctor. Unlike the two Dr. Rosners before him, Dad missed a formal
education, spending his teenage years in the privations of his life in
China. In Australia, he worked as a clerk for an oil company. In addition, the family's considerable wealth had been left behind in Austria,
ruthlessly confiscated by the new regime. In this light, without any

144 PART 3: YOU ARE YOUR STORY

sense of resentment—our family did not dwell on what might have been for my father and his parents—I grew up believing racism to be a terrible evil.

My father was anything but xenophobic. He loved migrants of all sorts, for some years teaching English to "new Australians," as they were called, in a community college. A family joke was that Dad learned more of their languages than they did English. The church we belonged to was near emergency accommodation for new arrivals in Australia, many of them refugees. Often, such people would turn up for the morning service. Guilty of xenophilia, the love of foreign people, Dad had no trouble learning their names—they were people from places like Vietnam, Eastern Europe, and the Middle East—while at the same time struggling to remember the names of the regulars at church. He also delighted in learning to greet them in their mother tongues. Compassion for the outsider runs deep in my veins.

But how does social justice work as a narrative identity? Like secular materialism, the social justice narrative identity is a breed of expressive individualism. If the former is based on the belief that the world will improve dramatically as the scope of individual freedom grows, the latter believes unwaveringly that certain aspects of a person's identity—such as their gender, ethnicity, or sexuality—are of paramount importance. Also, like the story of secular materialism, the story of social justice perceives problems that need to be solved and runs a compelling narrative of past turning points, present struggles, and future hopes.

The story of social justice views the world as a place of cruel injustice, whereby resources and opportunities are unevenly distributed, privilege is concentrated on a few, and action needs to be taken to create societies that promote diversity and equality. Before embarking on our evaluation of two versions of the social justice story, the narratives of the marginalized and those of their loyal allies, I want to point out up front that the Bible teaches that we should be committed to the protection and care of all people, especially the marginalized and disadvantaged. Indeed, unlike secular materialism, the story of social justice is attractive to many Christians, and for good reason.

Justice in the Bible

The concept of justice in the Bible covers more than simply the punishment of wrongdoing. The Bible regularly pairs justice with acting righteously and behaving with mercy, love, kindness, and compassion. For example, "Render true judgments, show kindness and mercy to one another, do not oppress the widow, the fatherless, the sojourner, or the poor" (Zech. 7:9–10). And God calls all people to seek justice for those most vulnerable to suffering injustice.

Justice in the Bible is rooted in God's character and creation:

"The Rock, his work is perfect,
    for all his ways are justice.
A God of faithfulness and without iniquity,
    just and upright is he." (Deut. 32:4)

If humans are called to do justice, "the Lord God, who made heaven and earth . . . executes justice for the oppressed" and "loves those who live justly" (Ps. 146:6–8, my translation). God's character includes a zeal for justice that leads him to love tenderly those who are socially powerless. "But the LORD of hosts is exalted in justice" (Isa. 5:16).

Throughout the Old Testament, God's people must "learn to do good" and "seek justice" (Isa. 1:17). When Job confronts his accusers, he insists,

"I put on righteousness, and it clothed me;
    my justice was like a robe and a turban.
I was eyes to the blind
    and feet to the lame.

I was a father to the needy,

and I searched out the cause of him whom I did not know."

(Job 29:14–16)

Similarly, the Prophets rail against injustice and insist that the right worship of God cannot exist without loving justice. Amos threatens judgment on "those who oppress the innocent and take bribes / and deprive the poor of justice in the courts" (Amos 5:12 NIV). Amos calls believers to "let justice roll down like waters, / and righteousness like an ever-flowing stream" (5:24). The prophet Micah sums things up well: "What does the Lord require of you / but to do justice, and to love kindness, / and to walk humbly with your God?" (6:8).

Jesus's teaching and ministry continues to underscore the central place of justice. Mary prophesies that Jesus will fill the poor but send the rich away empty (Luke 1:53). When John the Baptist's disciples ask Jesus if he is the Messiah, he points as evidence to his care for the downtrodden, including the blind, lame, deaf, those with leprosy, and the poor (Matt. 11:4–5). Echoing the Old Testament Prophets, Jesus accused the Pharisees of concentrating on religious observance while neglecting "justice and the love of God" (Luke 11:42). For Jesus, a lack of concern for the poor is not a minor oversight, but instead reveals that a person is at odds with God. In the parable of the sheep and the goats, the true sheep of Jesus are those who have a heart to help the hungry, the stranger, the poor, the sick, and the imprisoned (Matt. 25:35–36).

The Bible reveals the God of justice, who demands justice from his creatures. It also gives full voice to human cries against injustice. With this in mind, the story of social justice as a narrative identity is very attractive. How does it work? Is it an adequate story on which to base your personal identity? Is it the right way to see the world? How is it affecting individuals and societies as a whole?

Social Justice as a Narrative Identity

Human history is full of heartbreaking episodes of the horrendous ill-treatment of various groups of people. A visitor from another planet would soon need to learn the concepts of prejudice and discrimination to have any chance at understanding our world's past and present as well as its ruling inhabitants. In the story of social justice, far from rolling on like a river and a never-failing stream, justice is in permanent drought and righteousness barely a trickle.

Examples of social injustice abound and are too many to even sample. I'll cite just a couple to give a taste.

With respect to sexism, women's suffrage (the right of women to vote in elections) was not granted in Australia until 1902, in the United States 1920, and the United Kingdom 1928. In 1980s Australia, an unmarried woman would have trouble getting a mortgage approved.

As an example of racism, consider the experience of Australian indigenous soldiers who served in the Second World War. When Aboriginal men returned from the war, they were still not allowed to be citizens of the country they risked their lives defending, and, unlike the white men they fought alongside, they were not given a pension or a land grant. Few people today could fail to be moved to indignation by such injustices.

The story of social justice divides the world into three groups: the oppressors; the oppressed; and those on the side of the oppressed. The last two form two distinct social justice narrative identities, which I will treat under the headings of "The Marginalized" and "Their Loyal Allies," respectively.[1] The two have much in common, and I will offer my reflections of the social justice narrative identity by way of critique in a single concluding section.

---

1   I have intentionally avoided terms like *victims* and *the woke*, which are increasingly signals of a culture war in which I want no part.

The Problem	Injustice against various minority groups
Past Turning Points	Egregious examples of historical injustice and marks of genuine progress
Present Struggle	Against all forms of racism, sexism, homophobia, and transphobia, among other identity-based evils
Future Hope	The transformation of society and human nature itself.

The Marginalized

THE PROBLEM

The problem that social justice narratives seek to address is injustice, both past and present, against various minority groups. Such groups vary in size and in magnitude of discrimination, with race, gender, and sexuality being the most prominent.

PAST TURNING POINTS

The key turning points in the various narratives of the marginalized concern egregious examples of historical injustice and marks of progress in the long struggle toward equality—in other words, a series of low points and high points. With respect to racism against African Americans in the United States, for example, the key turning points are things like slavery, segregation, the assassination of Martin Luther King Jr., police brutality, and hate crimes, on the one hand, and the Civil Rights movement, interracial marriage, and a black president, on the other.

Similar defining moments appear in the narrative of overcoming sexism, with the denial of access to education and employment, unequal pay and having no right to vote among the low points, and the overturning of some of these being the high point, or at least progress. For gay and lesbian people, critical shared memories would include the prohibition and punishment of homosexuality and the legalization of same-sex marriage. For transsexual people, a similar story is told, with societal stigma, harassment and violence, and a long history of persecution, to the recognition of their full humanity, preferred labels, and access to medical treatment and healthcare.

PRESENT STRUGGLE

In short, the story of social justice is the struggle to overcome all forms of racism, sexism, homophobia, and transphobia, among other evils, exposing the numerous historical injustices and opposing present-day wrongs.

One of the strategies is what is sometimes called identity politics, where groups of people form alliances based on skin color, race, gender, or sexuality and press for action on their relevant concerns and grievances.

FUTURE HOPE

While it is difficult to generalize, the story of social justice is often driven by a grand vision of a transformed society in which the world is put to right. In the most extreme form of identity politics, the movement is "an ideological worldview that promises to sort out every inequity, not just in their own lives but every inequity on earth."[2]

The Loyal Allies

The allies of the oppressed in society are those who are not themselves victims of injustice, but rather people who side with the marginalized and are no less determined to right the wrongs of the past and present. These people are alert—or awake, if you like—to the pervasive presence of identity-based injustice in society.

THE PROBLEM

Many of those who identify with underprivileged groups see the fight for equality as requiring the exposing and opposing of all forms of

---

2   Douglas Murray, "Crowds running us over a cliff," *The Australian*, September 14, 2019, https://www.theaustralian.com.au/.

racism and bigotry, which they regard as far more prevalent than most people realize. They see themselves as defending the marginalized by speaking out on open and hidden prejudice and the resultant inequality.

PAST TURNING POINTS

Along with being shaped by the same historical examples of atrocities against various identity groups in society that the victims of such injustice find significant, the loyal allies of the marginalized credit their own awakening to education. Their eyes have been opened to the deep problems that continue to dog Western countries, and they are determined to expose them. Developments in tertiary education lead the way to becoming sensitive to social justice issues, especially studies dealing with race and gender.

PRESENT STRUGGLE

Those on the side of the oppressed tend to regard those not with them as being against them. The activist playbook glossary includes terms such as:

White privilege—the societal benefits that white people enjoy over non-white people

White fragility—the defensiveness of white people when confronted by examples of racial inequality and injustice

Microaggression—commonplace negative prejudicial slights or insults suffered by culturally marginalized groups at the hands of the dominant group, whether intentional or not

Unconscious biases—social stereotypes about certain groups held by individuals that are outside their conscious awareness

Cultural appropriation—the adoption of elements of a disadvantaged minority culture by members of the dominant culture

De-platforming—the shutting down of controversial speakers whose views might offend a minority group

Cancelling—the removal of parties from public life or employment for expressing offensive opinions

What we learn from the first four items in this list is that if you are part of the dominant group in a society and you are not a loyal ally of the oppressed, then you are the problem. And, we might add that denial is futile, given that your participation in oppressing minority groups can be subconscious.

FUTURE HOPE

There is nothing modest about the hopes of allies committed to the cause of social justice. Many proponents are committed not just to the righting of wrongs but to the transformation of society and even human nature itself.

Critique

The story of social justice is powerful, tapping into genuine grievances and striving to address injustice. Its basic convictions are correct: there has been horrendous prejudice and discrimination in the past; such prejudice and discrimination still exist to some extent; and we should address ongoing injustice. But there are also serious problems with the movement.

Both the marginalized and loyal ally narratives are driven by a commitment to expressive individualism, finding yourself by looking inward and seeing the world in such terms. In doing so, as I pointed out in chapter 2, many people elevate and absolutize one aspect of their identity (e.g., their race, gender, sexuality, and so on), which connects them to a group that shares these features and brings with it the template of a life story. Such narratives are often driven by a legitimate desire to seek justice for the group. However, they can also lead to a distorted view of the world in which every situation is judged in simplistic ideological terms, and an ugly tribalism emerges. At worst, such groups can be united not by common objects of love but by their mutual hatred for other groups.

The story of social justice has a tendency to divide humanity into goodies and baddies. The idea that if only we could reform or remove the baddies then everything would be fine is naive, to say the least. The problem is that all human beings, and not just one group of people, are capable of both good and evil. Aleksandr Solzhenitsyn famously wrote,

> If only there were evil people somewhere insidiously committing evil deeds, and it were necessary only to separate them from the rest of us and destroy them. But the line dividing good and evil cuts through the heart of every human being.[3]

A major problem with the story of social justice is that those following its script often wear thick and distorting lenses through which to view the world and blinkers to screen out information that doesn't fit the narrative. The story of human rights in the twentieth century is actually one of progress and steady accumulation. But the current swell of social justice proponents acts as if things have never been worse. Doubtless, there is more to be done. But the rhetoric can be overblown. It is one thing to identify an inequity; it is quite another to propose a solution that will actually make a difference, let alone fix things, and not make things worse. Pretending there are easy and obvious answers to complex problems is unhelpful.

To keep to this narrative, some peoples' experiences and stories need to be bracketed out in order to maintain the rage. For example, many women experience discrimination in the workplace; one woman I know described her life experience in settings with men as one where she has consistently "deescalated, apologized, placated, downgraded my own

---

3   Aleksandr Solzhenitsyn, *The Gulag Archipelago: An Experiment in Literary Investigation,* vol. 1 (1973; repr., London: Vintage, 2002), 31.

skills/experience, gone silent."[4] This is her experience, and it is a griev-ous one. But some women also flourish under male leadership, and others find themselves silenced and disempowered under a female boss. Both men and women can be longwinded, insensitive, ignorant, and arrogant. Both men and women can be lousy leaders. Confirmation bias is a big problem for ideological narratives like social justice, where any new evidence is always interpreted as confirming existing beliefs.

Ironically, the victim status can become one of power and privilege, and there is evidence that some people attempt to take advantage of it. Take, for example, the rising numbers of people who claim Indigenous or First Nations heritage for themselves on dubious grounds. In the United States, they are known as "race-shifters," in Canada "Pretend-ians," and in Australia "box-tickers." To put it crudely, if being white is being devalued, then there is a temptation to adopt a more valuable color. Australian academic Victoria Grieve-Williams, a Warraimaay historian from the New South Wales mid-north coast, said, "In Aus-tralia the race shifting phenomenon is pervasive and well recognised by Aboriginal people. The race shifters hold the power, they stifle debate and resist scrutiny in various ways, including attacking Aboriginal people who ask who they are in our cultural terms."[5]

Who the bad guys are is also a changing landscape. There is a kind of ladder of marginalization, whereby if a man and a woman are in dispute, the woman must be right; if a white woman and a black woman are in dispute, the black woman is right; and so on. The absurdity of such reckonings should be self-evident if we remember that all human beings are capable of evil. In the end, we are all oppressors in one way or another.

Further, the idea that prejudice and discrimination are all that is wrong with the world and is confined to one group is absurd; the

4 Social media post.
5 Caroline Overington, "Harmful: warning issued to 'race shifters,'" *The Australian*, July 2, 2021, https://www.theaustralian.com.au/.

distribution of human evil is far deeper and wider. All three supposedly discrete groups—the oppressed, their allies, and the oppressors—have their distinctive failings: the oppressors may well be prone to prejudice, discrimination, bigotry, and nepotism; the oppressed can easily fall into a place of irresponsible laziness and entitlement, destructive envy, and bitterness; their allies can be guilty of self-righteousness, bullying, and group think. And all three groups should be wary of pride, greed, sexual exploitation, selfish ambition, corruption, violence, deception, ruthlessness, malice, and raw self-interest. Human evil is the original diverse and inclusive industry.

On many college campuses, questions of personal identity have moved from being peripheral to holding central place in the search for truth. For example, Standpoint Theory insists that our view of the world is always shaped by our class, race, and sex, and so the perspectives of marginalized groups are uniquely valid. While a previous generation of students were trained to avoid ad hominem arguments and strive for objectively valid views, today we are much more likely to inquire as to a speaker's intersectional credentials before considering what they have to say or deciding not to listen at all.[6]

Standpoint theory and intersectionality have their legitimate place. My white, middle-class maleness determines much of my behavior, along with shaping the expectations of those around me concerning how I dress and act, the opportunities I have enjoyed, and the roles that I play. But that is not the whole story, as is the case with so many of us. Part of my background is also my father's refugee experience and immigrant status, and my upbringing in a working-class suburb of a major city. To lump me into one group is hardly fair.

Growing up, I considered myself fortunate compared to the refugees who turned up at church on some Sundays. But in my first year at college, I was taken aback by fellow students who wanted to know

6 Thanks to my colleague Andrew Judd for his insight on these matters.

what school I went to and what sort of car I drove; I struck out on both counts. I went to a working-class public school and drove an old clunker. When I attended parties at the homes of more affluent friends, we dined later in the evening than I was used to and often ate food of which I'd never heard. Privilege is a relative matter and not easily defined in simple terms.

Journalist and academic Stan Grant points out the difficulty of assigning one identity marker with reference to filling out something as innocuous as a census form. Does he check the box for indigenous? If he does, isn't that a denial of his non-indigenous grandmother? He complains: "I will not be anything that does not include my grandmother. . . . I will not put a mark in a box that someone has decided contains me."[7] Understandably, he resists not only the victim status but also the label that you are only one side of your heritage.

Some people with an indigenous background likewise prefer not to be boxed into a category. Stan Grant introduced Kodie Bedford on his *One Plus One* interview program with the words, "She was a journalist, she's a writer, she's a storyteller—just don't call her an Aboriginal storyteller."[8] Identity is often more complicated than group labels, which frequently tell only part of a much bigger and richer story.

Grant has a balanced take on the story of social justice and identity politics as they relate to his own indigenous Australian heritage. Notice his insistence that social justice is a narrative identity, both with great explanatory power and with clear limitations:

This has become a powerful narrative for many indigenous Australians. It is a history I was raised on: the story of invasion and dispossession, racism and segregation, passed down through the

---

7   Quoted in Francis Fukuyama, *Identity: The Demand for Dignity and the Politics of Resentment* (London: Profile, 2019), 83.
8   "ABC News, One Plus One: Kodie Bedford," ABC Australia, January 18, 2021, https://www.abc.net.au/.

generations of my family. These stories are painful and vivid. They have marked me—at times, I have felt, indelibly. History is where we locate ourselves; it is the foundation of identity. It can help explain so much ongoing suffering and injustice. But it can become a crippling narrative. It has been my struggle—the struggle of all of us—to move beyond it. Not to ignore it or airbrush the worst aspects but to lift its weight from my shoulders. I have no desire to be bound to a history of misery—or, worse, to revel in it.[9]

Greg Lukianoff and Jonathan Haidt helpfully distinguish two sorts of identity politics: common-enemy and common-humanity. Whereas the latter humanizes its opponents and appeals to their humanity, the former demonizes its opponents, lays all the blame at their feet, and seeks to destroy them.[10] Clearly, both exist, but too often the story of social justice drifts into a common-enemy mindset.

A striking example of cultural appropriation and the response of loyal allies of the perceived oppressed occurred when Keziah Daum, a young Caucasian woman from Utah, wore a bright red silky cheongsam (a Chinese dress) to her prom and then posted a photo on Twitter. One offended Asian young man posted a response: "My culture is NOT your ******* prom dress." His post was then liked 200,000 times and retweeted 50,000 times. Such public shaming—flogging might not be too strong a term—is not uncommon. Indeed, in our globalized world, the threshold for being labelled racist or a bigot, homophobic or transphobic, is now quite low by standards of even a few years ago.

Keziah defended her decision to wear the dress: "To everyone causing so much negativity: I mean no disrespect to the Chinese culture. I'm simply showing my appreciation to their culture. I'm not deleting

9   Stan Grant, "Identity politics traps the indigenous mind in cycle of grievance," *The Australian*, April 28, 2018, https://www.theaustralian.com.au/.

10 Greg Lukianoff and Jonathan Haidt, *The Coddling of the American Mind: How Good Intentions and Bad Ideas Are Setting Up a Generation for Failure* (London: Penguin, 2018), chapter 3.

my post because I've done nothing but show my love for the culture."
Her post was liked over 100,000 times, with many defenders of Daum
being of Chinese background.[11] Apparently, one person's cultural appropriation is another person's cultural appreciation. A more divisive dress
has perhaps never been worn, which testifies both to the power of the
internet and also to a potential problem for the story of social justice.

Not all of the problems of women are the patriarchy. Not all of the
problems of people of color are racism. Not all of the problems of the
LGBTIQ+ communities are social stigma. And removing those problems will not produce the new world that we all long for. That, of course,
doesn't mean that we shouldn't address injustice. But a simplistic approach to social justice issues is unhelpful and can be counterproductive.

Then there are the inevitable losers in the desired new world order.
And not every complaint is simply white or male fragility. Can we
really blame all men when a woman is raped or murdered? The typical
response from some men awake to social justice issues is to call for a
change in the culture of toxic masculinity. Such issues should be addressed, and there is definitely work to be done. But other more personal contributing issues such as homelessness, violent pornography,
and drug addiction are often ignored because they don't fit the script
of prejudice and discrimination. The most successful anti-violence
programs in Australia, for example, target repeat offenders and focus
on substance abuse, mental health, unemployment, and parenting
advice.[12]

One feminist changed her views when she had a son: "The real
oppressor to women is not men in general, it is men who have been
misguided about what it means to be real men. In the defense of women
everywhere, I realized I now had to defend boys too—starting with my

11 Daniella Greenbaum, "Nonsensical critics are accusing an 18-year-old girl of cultural appropria-
    tion and racism—and they're missing something much bigger," *Business Insider Australia*, May 3,
    2018, https://www.businessinsider.com.au/.

12 Richard Guilliatt, "The reckoning: one city, four murders," *The Australian*, October 18, 2019,
    https://www.theaustralian.com.au/.

own."[13] And not every loser in identity politics is a white male. Some successful women or people of color rightly express their discomfort at policies of positive discrimination and quotas when they are left looking as though they did not actually deserve their success.

The biggest problem for the story of social justice is that in underestimating the breadth and depth of human evil, and restricting evil to a group of oppressors, we not only create new injustices but also engender naively optimistic future hope. The world will not be put right simply by opposing multiple forms of prejudice and discrimination, as unjust and ubiquitous as these might be. What we need is a truly radical transformation of the world and all of its inhabitants.

With that in mind, the Bible not only reveals the God of justice, who demands justice from his creatures and gives full voice to human cries against injustice, but also proclaims that God determines to restore justice to the whole earth.

The letter of James, the brother of Jesus, is a case in point. It confronts injustice, especially exploitation of the poor. James challenges God's people to make justice a mark of their lives and to take a stand on behalf of the oppressed in the fieriest terms: "Come now, you rich, weep and howl for the miseries that are coming upon you. Your riches have rotted and your garments are moth-eaten. Your gold and silver have corroded, and their corrosion will be evidence against you and will eat your flesh like fire" (5:1–3). James also recommends waiting patiently for the Judge to bring justice and reverse fortunes: "Be patient, therefore, bothers, until the coming of the Lord. . . . The Judge is standing at the door!" (5:7, 9). Bringing these two threads together, the letter directs people both to look up for God to bring justice to the earth on the last day and to allow the hoped-for justice of the kingdom of God to permeate their lives in the present by caring for those in need (1:27; 2:14–26).

---

13   Ashley Simpo, "This Is How Having A Son Changed Feminism For Me," ScaryMommy (website) April 19, 2017, updated October 29, 2020, https://www.scarymommy.com/.

Overall, I judge the story of social justice to be an inadequate basis for narrative identity. For all its good intentions, it has serious fault lines running through its foundation. It can lead to an unhealthy sense of entitlement, it is divisive, it offers an incomplete diagnosis of what is wrong with humanity, and although its transformative vision of the future is inspiring and worthy, it lacks the means to get there.

Narrative Identity Without Looking Up

If the story of secular materialism, by seeking fulfilment in gods that fail, turns out to be a tragedy, the story of social justice can so easily turn into a farce, seeking to set the world right in a way that falls far short and leads to ever more conflict and discord. The fatal weakness of both stories is that they seek to produce narrative identities without looking up.

Do you need transcendence to construct a stable and satisfying life story, one that addresses the injustice of our world with grace and truth? I believe you do, and I call as witnesses two recent movies (both of which I recommend):

In the 2017 Ritesh Batra film *The Sense of an Ending*, to paraphrase the marketing, a man (Tony Webster, played by Jim Broadbent) becomes troubled by his past and is presented with a mysterious legacy that leads him to reconsider his current station in life. The movie opens with the narrator wondering:

> How often do we tell our own life-story? Do we adjust, embellish, make sly cuts and create a new reality? And when everything is coming off the rails, how are we to know that our lives are entwined, forever?[14]

The movie is not as nihilistic as this makes it sound. But the plot does underscore the fact that telling your own life story is a tall order

---

14 *The Sense of an Ending*, directed by Ritesh Batra (London: BBC Films, 2017).

and prone to self-serving interpretations of key events. It's hard enough working out the genre and where everything fits, let alone arranging a satisfying ending.

In the 2016 Lone Scherfig film *Their Finest*, a secretary turned script-writer for propaganda films (Catrin Cole, played by Gemma Arterton) joins the cast and crew of a major production while the Blitz, the German bombing of Britain during 1940–1941, rages around them.

In one scene on a beach, Arterton's character discusses with her fellow scriptwriter (Tom Buckley, played by Sam Claflin) the tragic death of another character's grandson, who was hit by a tram while on shore leave from the war. Her colleague muses, "Why do you think people like films? It's because stories have structure, shape, purpose, and meaning. When things turn bad, it's still part of a plan. You know, there's a point to it. Unlike life."

Does your life story lack structure, shape, purpose, and meaning? That would certainly describe how I felt when my life derailed in Scotland in the mid-1990s. Not only were my hopes and plans for the future altered but many of my cherished memories were damaged, some even feeling like they belonged to someone else. According to literary critic Gary Saul Morson, "Closure and structure mark the difference between life as it is lived and as it is read about; and real people live without the benefit of an outside perspective on which both closure and structure depend."[15]

Viewed from "under the sun," to borrow the description of human life from the book of Ecclesiastes (1:9), the vast majority of people's lives do not seem to move toward a satisfying ending or any sense of resolution. Our lives appear to be driven in large part by random events, and they do not proceed in any predictable direction over the long course, as much as we try to manipulate them. Writing your own life story seems impossible.

---

15   Gary Saul Morson, *Narrative and Freedom: The Shadows of Time* (New Haven, CT: Yale University Press, 1994), 38.

The worldview that excludes the transcendent, looking up, has often led to pessimistic nihilism and the conclusion that human existence is utterly meaningless. Yet Christians believe that God provides the necessary "outside perspective" of which Morson speaks. In other words, looking up gives our lives both structure and closure, and can provide us with a more adequate narrative identity.

So how does it work? What does a narrative identity based on looking up to the God of the Bible look like? What difference does it make? And how do you live it? What is the problem that the story of God's people sets out to solve? What are the past turning points in that story? What is the present struggle? What is the future hope? And what sort of critique might be levelled against the people living the story of God's people? I will flesh out some answers to these questions in the next three chapters.

Questions for Reflection and Discussion

1. What about the story of social justice resonates strongly with you? If you're a Christian, how does it align with your understanding of God as a God of justice? Where does it diverge?

2. Perhaps you identify as marginalized in one or several ways, or maybe you align yourself with particular oppressed groups through allyship. How is it to consider this identity within the bigger narrative of secular materialism, as we have done in this chapter?

3. The main critique of social justice in this chapter is its polarizing tendencies. Solzhenitsyn writes that "the line dividing good and evil cuts through the heart of every human being." How might you approach the issues and causes you care about while holding onto a more nuanced understanding of human beings as neither "all good" nor "all bad"?

The Life Story of Jesus Christ

*You died, and your identity is now hidden with Christ
in God. When Christ, who is your life story, appears,
then you also will appear with him in glory.*

THE APOSTLE PAUL (COL. 3:3–4, MY TRANSLATION).

*"It is in fact more important for us to know what God
did to Israel and in God's Son Jesus Christ, than to
discover what God intends for us today. The fact that Jesus
Christ died is more important than the fact that I will die.
I find salvation not in my life-story,
but only in the story of Jesus Christ."*

DIETRICH BONHOEFFER[1]

YOU ARE YOUR STORY. To find yourself, you need to look backward and forward. Defining moments from the past and your future hopes and destiny define you. But as much as we might like to think of ourselves as the narrator and main protagonist, and as writing our own script, each of us participates in shared stories.

Most people in the West are part of two big shared narrative identities, living their lives as part of the story of secular materialism or the

---

1   Dietrich Bonhoeffer, *Life Together* (1954; repr., Minneapolis, MN: Fortress, 1996), 62.

story of social justice, or some combination of the two. In this chapter, we consider a third shared story, the narrative identity commended in the Bible—namely, the story of the people of God. We begin by briefly examining this story in general terms under the same headings that I used in chapters 9 and 10: the problem the story addresses, past turning points, present struggle, and future hope.[2] The most surprising aspect about the story of God's people is that it is based on the template of the life story of Jesus Christ.

The Story of God's People

As different versions of expressive individualism, the two big shared stories of secular materialism and social justice have one thing in common: both are essentially self-help stories, committed to a high view of human freedom to improve the lives of those in the story substantially and the world dramatically, without looking up. In that respect, the story of God's people could not be more different; to use my favorite Scottish preposition, it is a rescue from "outwith" ourselves.

The story of God's people is the ultimate indictment of the heart of the expressive individualism message. It asserts that you don't have it within you to define yourself or to live the good life. You need an intervention from outside of yourself. You need a rescue. As N. T. Wright puts it, "The problems of this world are solved not by a straightforward upward movement into the light but by the Creator God going down into the dark to rescue humankind and the world from its plight."[3]

There are other key differences between the narrative identities produced by expressive individualism and the story of God's people. The first two stories underestimate the problem that afflicts individuals and society, and are overly optimistic about how to fix it. The third story, on

---

2   The four headings correspond to traditional categories of systematic theology: the fall of Adam and Eve, redemption, sanctification, and eschatology.
3   N. T. Wright, *Surprised by Hope: Rethinking Heaven, the Resurrection, and the Mission of the Church* (New York: HarperOne, 2008), 87.

the other hand, is both the bleakest and the brightest. When it comes to genuine and lasting change, we human beings left to ourselves are without hope; we are as good as dead. Thousands of years of human history confirm this. But the good news is that a dramatic intervention has taken place and a date has been set for our final and complete transformation. Unlike other stories, the story of God's people claims to have both structure and closure. But, it's important to note, we are not the stars of the show.

The Problem	Pervasive evil—the flesh, the world, and the devil
Past Turning Points	The death and resurrection of Jesus Christ, our substitute and representative
Present Struggle	Enduring wilderness and exile, opposing evil, and putting on Christ
Future Hope	The resurrection of the body, the new heaven and new earth

The Problem

The story of God's people agrees with the other two stories that human ignorance, mortality, prejudice, and discrimination are serious and abiding problems that dog the human race. However, its diagnosis goes deeper and is more radical. It acknowledges not just the extraordinary acts of generosity and kindness that humans can accomplish but also the fact that we are all capable of unspeakable acts of malice and cruelty. The tendency to act in pure self-interest is a universal blight on the human race, covering every age group, race, and culture. And it is the root cause of injustice and untold misery; it includes all of us.

Jesus is often depicted as the champion of love, and for good reason. But he was anything but naive regarding human nature. In the Sermon on the Mount, he not only expected people to love their enemies (Matt. 5:44) but also described his own hand-picked disciples, along with the crowds, as "evil" (Matt. 7:11). And far from recommending that we follow our hearts, he believed that "out of the heart come evil thoughts, murder, adultery, sexual immorality, theft, false witness, slander" (Matt. 15:19).

The human race is nothing if not complex. There are those who give humanity a good name and those whose inhumanity brings us shame. In a disaster zone, some search for survivors while others loot homes and businesses. The same human race that boasts Einstein and Mother Teresa, Shakespeare and Leonardo Da Vinci, Frank Lloyd Wright and Marie Curie, must own up to producing Hitler and Stalin, weapons of mass destruction, feats of genocide, and a litany of heinous atrocities. Humans are both the pièce de résistance of the world and "a piece of work," both peacemakers and peace breakers.

The problem of evil in the human heart is that it can grip and bind us and make us more and more insensitive to the selfishness of our own behavior and its harmful effects on others. The fact that we are social beings makes the ripple effects of human pride, lust, and greed go far and wide. Anyone who has known someone with an addiction will be aware of the power that drugs, alcohol, gambling, or pornography can exercise over a person and also the devastating impact they have on those connected with them. Unflatteringly, Jesus condemned all of us as addicts of selfish behavior when he stated, "Truly, truly, I say to you, everyone who practices sin is a slave to sin" (John 8:34).

But the Bible offers an even more disturbing account of evil. Not only is the human heart "deceitful above all things, / and desperately sick" (Jer. 17:9), but the world itself is a place in which evil thrives—and there is "the evil one," a leader of spiritual beings hell bent on multiplying evil.[4] The problem that the story of God's people seeks to solve, then, is the pervasive, seemingly intractable, and ensnaring power of evil. We need both deliverance from the power of evil and forgiveness

4　See Graham Cole, *Against the Darkness: The Doctrine of Angels, Satan, and Demons* (Wheaton, IL: Crossway, 2019).

for our own evil actions. We also need ourselves and the world to be put right in righteousness and justice.

Past Turning Points

In both the Old and New Testaments of the Bible, God's people are defined by the story of their redemption, by shared memories and a common defining destiny. In the case of Israel, it was release from slavery in Egypt and the prospect of entering the promised land. Michael Horton explains the significance of such shared memories for personal identity with reference to the Old Testament people of God:

> The present generation makes history their story. . . . History is not only rendered contemporary; it is internalized. One's people's history becomes one's personal history. One looks out from the self to find out who one is meant to be. One does not discover one's identity, and one certainly does not forge it oneself. . . . Instead, it is the consequence of what are presented as the acts of God. . . . Israel began to infer and to affirm her identity by telling a story.[5]

For followers of Jesus Christ, the turning points in our story are release from the reign of sin by the death of Christ and the hope of eternal life. In a passage like Colossians 3:3–4 (see the quotation at the beginning of this chapter), the life story of Christ is the Christian's narrative identity. Christ not only died in our place; there is a sense in which we also died with him. We share his death, and we will share his resurrection.

This is why Paul can say in Galatians 2:20, "I have been crucified with Christ. It is no longer I who live, but Christ who lives in me. And

---

5 Michael Horton, *The Christian Faith: A Systematic Theology for Pilgrims on the Way* (Grand Rapids, MI: Zondervan, 2011), 86–87. See also David DeSilva, *Sacramental Life: Spiritual Formation Through the Book of Common Prayer* (Downers Grove, IL: InterVarsity Press, 2008), 168: "The greatest danger for the Israelites on entering the Promised Land was forgetting the story of God's redemption and salvation and that they would then start living out another, distorted story."

the life I now live in the flesh I live by faith in the Son of God, who loved me and gave himself for me." Indeed, Paul's language of "putting on" Christ (or the new self) in several of his letters is a call to embrace this very story as one's own and live according to it.

Believers in Christ look back and internalize the death and resurrection of Jesus Christ, remembering it as something that changes who we are today and who we will be in the future. Christians see their life story fitting into and mirroring the life story of Jesus Christ. According to Alistair McGrath, "Christianity doesn't just make sense of things. It changes our stories. It invites us to enter into, and be part of, a new story."[6]

The cross is the answer to the postmodern objection that all metanarratives, including the Christian one, are by definition self-serving and oppressive. Rightly understood, the Christian story into which we are invited is one that champions the oppressed and calls for self-sacrifice.

While it is true that each of us has a unique story, all of our stories are part of some bigger story. In both the Old and New Testaments of the Bible, the people of God are defined by the story of their redemption, by shared memories and by a common defining destiny. In the case of Israel, it was release from slavery in Egypt and the prospect of entering the promised land; for followers of Jesus Christ, it is release from sin by the death of Christ and the hope of eternal life. Of course, how well Christians inhabit the story of Jesus Christ and are shaped by it makes all the difference.

Present Struggle[7]

The Bible provides a number of helpful ways in which to think about our struggle against moral evil in the present as we await our defining destiny at the return of Christ. One example is the way in which be-

---

6   Alister McGrath, *Deep Magic, Dragons and Talking Mice: How Reading C. S. Lewis Can Change Your Life* (London: Hodder & Stoughton, 2014), 47.

7   Content in this section is adapted from Brian Rosner, "The Coronavirus Crisis as a Wilderness Experience," The Gospel Coalition Australia (website), May 25, 2020, https://au.thegospel coalition.org/.

lievers are encouraged to compare themselves with the people of Israel in the wilderness journeying toward the promised land.

The theme of wilderness is widespread in the Bible. Adam and Eve were banished from the Garden; Cain was sent into the land of Nod; Abram wandered from his father's household; Moses fled to Midian; David was an outlaw on the run, living in caves; and John the Baptist was a voice of one calling in the wilderness. They all experienced times of dislocation, isolation, and deprivation. And the Bible recognizes the hardship of such experiences. The wilderness is "a land of deserts and pits, . . . / a land of drought and deep darkness" (Jer. 2:6), the habitation of demons (Matt. 12:43), and a place of alienation and wandering (Luke 8:29; 15:4).

The paradigmatic wilderness experience was the forty-year meandering of the people of Israel in that "great and terrifying wilderness" (Deut. 1:19) that delayed their arrival in the promised land after their miraculous escape from Egypt. In the New Testament, Jesus's temptations in the wilderness following his forty-day fast recapitulates Israel's experience. Wilderness is a big part of his life story. As it turns out, all of God's people effectively live in the wilderness, in between the times of our past redemption and our final rest. Indeed, 1 Corinthians and Hebrews address believers in Christ as wilderness Christians (1 Cor. 10:1–13; Heb. 3:16–19).

What, then, is God doing when we find ourselves in the wilderness? Addressing the Israelites about to emerge from "the waiting room," as it were, Deuteronomy 8:2–5, a text Jesus turns to in his own wilderness experience, answers this question:

> And you shall remember the whole way that the Lord your God has led you these forty years in the wilderness, that he might humble you, testing you to know what was in your heart, whether you would keep his commandments or not. And he humbled you and let you hunger and fed you with manna, which you did not know, nor did

your fathers know, that he might make you know that man does not live by bread alone, but man lives by every word that comes from the mouth of the Lord. Your clothing did not wear out on you and your foot did not swell these forty years. Know then in your heart that, as a man disciplines his son, the Lord your God disciplines you.

God does three things for those stuck in the wilderness—which, in one sense, is all of God's people in every age. First, he tests us. God uses the wilderness to determine what is in our hearts (8:2) and discover the limits of our obedience. Sadly, Israel failed the test and instead tested him ten times (Num. 14:22) in return, by grumbling (Exod. 14–17; Num. 11) and committing idolatry (Exod. 32; Num. 25; Deut. 9:7). It is certainly true that times of difficulty lay bare the condition of our hearts. And life is full of such times. Seeing our lives through the lens of wilderness, we do well to be vigilant against the sins of sloth, selfishness, and self-indulgence, along with grumbling and idolatry. This is the context in which our struggle against all kinds of evil is set.

Second, God also provides for us. The good news in Israel's wilderness sojourn was that God provided manna, quail, and water from the rock, and he continued to lead them, despite their disobedience. Their clothes did not wear out, and their feet did not swell. Troubling times can cause us to doubt the goodness of God. The key thing is to notice and celebrate the evidence of God's kindness and continued care, even amid hardship and adversity. In our wilderness lives, it is natural to lament what God has taken away; we are also to thank God for what he gives us.

And third, God forms us as his children. God used Israel's time in the wilderness to humble the nation, "as a man disciplines his son" (Deut. 8:5). God turned the various tribes of former Egyptian slaves into a nation. At the end of their wilderness experience, they had become one people, under one God, with one national goal: the conquest of Canaan. God can use the discomfort and privations of the wilderness for our good. His ultimate purpose is to conform us to the image of his Son. We can know that God uses whatever happens in our lives to test our hearts, to provide for us and reassure us of his goodness, and to form us as his children as we wait in confidence for our promised future with him.

As odd as it sounds, the narrative identity of believers in Christ is tied up with the life story of Jesus Christ, which itself echoes the experience of God's people in the Old Testament. With respect to the question of personal identity, if we wonder who we are, Jesus Christ is the one and only perfect human being. In one sense, there are only two basic identities in the world. In the book of Genesis, Adam, the first human being, is the prototype of us all, created in God's image but flawed and marred by sin. Jesus Christ is the second Adam, the one who gets it right, and the prototype and forerunner of all who put their trust in him.

With Jesus, we see what new humanity looks like. As Oliver O'Donovan puts it, "The new man Christ is the pattern to which we may conform ourselves."[8] But it's not just a matter of imitating him. In the Gospels, there is a call to follow Jesus literally. But the New Testament letters, written after Jesus rose from the dead and ascended to heaven, never talk about following Jesus. "Following" is inadequate language to describe Christ's impact on our identity. The apostles prefer to describe people as being "in Christ" rather than following him.

The language of being "in Christ" is among the most puzzling in the New Testament. While it can mean that we belong to Christ, on occasions it means something more. Paul can use the notion of being "in Christ" to indicate that we actually participate in Christ's very identity: "if anyone is in Christ, he is a new creation" (2 Cor. 5:17). And the goal of Paul's pastoral ministry is to "present everyone mature in Christ" (Col. 1:28).

---

8   Oliver O'Donovan, *Resurrection and Moral Order: An Outline for Evangelical Ethics* (Leicester, UK: Apollos, 1994), 143.

Andrew Cameron has explored the idea of finding your identity "in Christ":

> Whoever we think our selves to be, Jesus' humanity encompasses and "decodes" everyone's diversity, all journeys and every vocation. To be truly human involves knowing him and participating with him. Somehow, to participate "in Christ" is to begin a new voyage of discovery. We do not lose our past stories, yet we increasingly understand our selves in reference to Jesus Christ.[9]

The new self we are to put on is Jesus Christ, who represents God's new humanity. It is not that we thereby lose our individuality. But who we are is brought to completion in him.

The defining moment of the lives of those living the life story of Jesus Christ is his death on a cross. The direction of our lives is set by that defining moment. Living authentically, then, becomes the task of living in accordance with your new identity and regularly performing your signature move. According to Colossians 3, we died and rose to new life in union with Christ (3:1–4). That is our "moment of truth," the memory of which defines us forever. It changes everything for us. And we would not be who we are were it not for Christ's death and resurrection.

And the signature move that grows out of that identity is the act of love. Our conduct is to be compassionate, kind, humble, gentle, patient, and forgiving, all of which grow out of "love, which binds everything together in perfect harmony" (3:14). Just as our identity as children of God was forged through an act of amazing love, so too we are to live lives of costly, selfless, others-centered love.

It is not that other identity markers and what you do with your life are of no consequence for your personal identity if you are a believer in Christ. Your race, gender, family, occupation, marital status, and

9   Andrew Cameron, *Joined-up Life: A Christian Account of How Ethics Works* (Nottingham, UK: IVP, 2011), 114.

so on are important, but they are not all-important (see chapter 2). Obviously, life events and experiences can have a lasting impact on your identity and conduct. But at the most profound level, if you are a believer in Jesus Christ, what sets the course for your life and keeps it on track is your identification with Christ and imitation of him, and being known and loved by God as his child. Putting on that identity will determine the sort of man or woman, worker, friend, neighbor, father or mother, son or daughter that you will become.

Future Hope

The future hope for God's people is that on the final day, God will lay bare the injustice of our world, judge the world in righteousness, and have mercy on those who have put their trust in him.

At the heart of the Christian's hope is the resurrection from the dead. At its best, the church tells the story of a new world that began when Jesus rose from the dead and lives in the light of that world-changing event. The New Testament connects this destiny to that of Jesus Christ, who was raised from the dead: "We were buried therefore with him by baptism into death, in order that, just as Christ was raised from the dead by the glory of the Father, we too might walk in newness of life" (Rom. 6:4–5).

Who am I if death is my ultimate destiny? What would life look like then? In Isaiah 22:13, the prophet depicts the reaction of the inhabitants of Jerusalem when the city was under siege. With the ruthless Assyrians at the door, they are facing the grim prospect of annihilation. With such a destiny, they decide to party like there is no tomorrow: "Let us eat and drink, / for tomorrow we die." Paul quotes this text in 1 Corinthians 15:32 to point to the futility of life without the direction and motivation given by the resurrection of Jesus.

There are exceptions, of course; unbelievers can live lives that are not dissolute and self-indulgent. But it is not just Christians who think life without the hope of resurrection lacks purpose. Some philosophers agree. While existentialism stresses human individuality and freedom, it is also often deeply pessimistic. In lay terms, for many, in the face of death, life is pointless.

A. N. Wilson is an English author. Among his biographies are books about Tolstoy, C. S. Lewis, John Milton, and Sir Walter Scott. For much of his adult life, he was not a believer. In fact, in his biography of Jesus, Wilson tried to show that Jesus was no more than a failed messianic prophet. However, in recent years, he has changed his mind. At the heart of his new-found faith is the resurrection of Jesus from the dead, which he believes is "the ultimate key to who we are." At Easter 2009, Wilson wrote an article in which he contrasted the story of materialist atheism with the Christian story, and tells us something of why he finds the latter so compelling:

> Materialist atheism says we are just a collection of chemicals. It has no answer whatsoever to the question of how we should be capable of love or heroism or poetry if we are simply animated pieces of meat.
>
> The Resurrection, which proclaims that matter and spirit are mysteriously conjoined, is *the ultimate key to who we are*. It confronts us with an extraordinarily haunting story.
>
> J. S. Bach believed the story, and set it to music. Most of the greatest writers and thinkers of the past 1,500 years have believed it.
>
> But an even stronger argument is the way that Christian faith transforms individual lives—the lives of the men and women with whom you mingle on a daily basis, the man, woman or child next to you in church tomorrow morning.[10]

A story arc is the overall narrative in episodic storytelling media such as television or comic books. On a television program, for example, the

---

10   A. N. Wilson, "Religion of hatred: Why we should no longer be cowed by the chattering classes ruling Britain who sneer at Christianity," *Daily Mail* (website), April 11, 2009, https://www.daily mail.co.uk/; emphasis added.

story arc is the governing trajectory that unfolds over many episodes. All the episodes are moving toward a death, a wedding, a car crash, or some other climax that the scriptwriters have had in the mind from the beginning. And when you watch one episode, even if in one sense it can stand on its own, it forms part of a larger narrative that is told over the whole series. The events in individual episodes take on full significance only when you know the story arc to which they contribute. Being known by God and putting on the new self is about remembering your story arc.

The most unexpected twist in the story of Christian hope is the idea that the Christian's story arc is the same as that of the rest of creation. In Romans 8:19–21, Paul believes that not only are Christians looking forward to the final consummation but also "the creation waits with eager longing" (8:19a). What is it waiting for? Believe it or not, the creation is waiting for the same thing believers are waiting for: "for the revealing of the children of God" (8:19b, my translation).

Paul explains, as best he can,

> For the creation was subjected to frustration, not by its own choice, but by the will of the one who subjected it, in hope that the creation itself will be liberated from its bondage to decay and brought into the freedom and glory of the children of God. (8:21–22)

Things are not the way they're supposed to be. This is true of me, in all my well-intentioned, and sometimes ill-intentioned muddle of a life. It's true of the communities in which I live and work. It's true of you, too. It's true of whole countries. Even the world itself, Paul reckons, feels like it has been "subjected to frustration . . . [and wants to be] liberated from its bondage." Disobedience to God, sin, has brought death to us all. The good news is that God intends to reverse this tragedy. Raising Jesus from the dead was the first step in the process. The return of Jesus to put the world to right is the future hope of those seeking to live the life story of Jesus Christ.

Critique

In the rest of this chapter, we measure the narrative of the life story of Jesus Christ against the five tests of the good life. As you might expect, I regard the life of Christ to be a superior narrative identity template for living the good life to the main alternatives offered in our day, those based on expressive individualism—that is, secular materialism and social justice. However, before seeking to make that case, it is important to confess that Christians do not always live up to the life story of Jesus Christ, me included.

Indeed, the history of the church offers plenty of ammunition to its critics, including the violent crusades, torturous inquisitions, cruel witch hunts, the oppression of women, unspeakable child abuse, and reprehensible corruption among church leaders. Talk of following the pattern of Christ's selfless life story seems a million miles away from what many would say is the behavior of those who claim to follow Christ. Rather than putting self-interest to death, Christians can behave as selfishly as everyone else. Speaking personally, I find the appalling conduct of fellow believers to be the biggest discouragement from persevering in the Christian life. And I have close friends who no longer believe because of Christians behaving badly. Two things prevent me from losing heart and giving up.

First, as the major documentary *For the Love of God* puts it, "The church is better and worse than you ever imagined." Along with the inexcusable wickedness perpetrated at times in the name of Christ, we must recognize that "the origins of Western values like human rights, charity, humility, and non-violence [go] back to the influence of Jesus"[11] and the reversal of the world's values by the cross.[12] And there are many

---

11   "For the Love of God," Centre for Public Christianity (website), 2020, https://www.public christianity.org/.

12   On the profound positive influence of the Christian faith on Western civilization, without ignoring the failings, see Tom Holland, *Dominion: The Making of the Western Mind* (London: Little, Brown, 2019); and John Dickson, *Bullies and Saints: An Honest Look at the Good and Evil of Christian History* (Grand Rapids, MI: Zondervan, 2021).

inspiring examples of followers of Christ actually following his example of selfless love, both historically and in the present.

Second, in one sense, the bad behavior of God's people, along with the good, should not surprise us, since the Bible itself does not hide the fact that religious people can behave badly. Tim Keller points out that one scholar has documented "how [Karl] Marx's analysis of religion as an instrument of oppression was anticipated by the Hebrew prophets Isaiah, Jeremiah, Amos, and even the message of the New Testament gospels. . . . Marx was unoriginal in his critique of religion—the Bible beat him to it!"[13] When it comes to treating others badly, the problem lies not in the life story of Jesus Christ but in the failure of those who claim to follow the script to do so authentically and consistently.

I find it of great help and comfort that the Bible calls out the bad behavior of God's people and also provides the resources for their renewal, and mine too. Keller writes, "While the church has inexcusably been party to the oppression of people at times, it is important to realize that the Bible gives us tools for analysis and unflinching critique of religiously supported injustice from within the faith."[14] This capacity for self-critique sets the Christian narrative identity apart from others. It is worth remembering that every Sunday in church services around the world, the people of God begin by confessing their own sins, including not loving their neighbors as much as they love themselves.

At Anglican churches in Australia, we pray,

Merciful God,
our maker and our judge,
we have sinned against you in thought, word, and deed,
    and in what we have failed to do:

---

13 Timothy Keller, *The Reason for God: Belief in an Age of Skepticism* (London: Penguin, 2009), 58.
14 Keller, *The Reason for God*, 60.

we have not loved you with our whole heart;

we have not loved our neighbors as ourselves;

we repent, and are sorry for all our sins.

Father, forgive us.

Strengthen us to love and obey you in newness of life;

through Jesus Christ our Lord. Amen.[15]

The Five Tests of the Good Life and the Christ-Story Self

How does the narrative identity of the life story of Jesus Christ perform in practice, in terms of the questions of existence, ego, ethics, enemies, and enjoyment? As we have already seen with the signature move of sacrificial love that arises from the Christ story, the Christian narrative identity gives clear moral direction to those people whose identities are shaped by the death and resurrection of Christ.

1. The Existential Test: Suffering and Disappointments

Does living the life story of Jesus Christ help people to cope with the inevitable suffering and disappointment that life throws their way? Having your story defined by death on a cross is a constant reminder that life is full of injustice. As John Swinton puts it, "As Christians, we locate and interpret our suffering within the narrative of the life, death and resurrection of Jesus."[16]

Paul makes this very point in an odd verse in his second letter to the Corinthians, where he says that "we always carry around in our body the death of Jesus, so that the life of Jesus may also be revealed in our body. For we who live are always being given over to death for Jesus' sake, so that the life of Jesus also may be manifested in our mortal flesh" (2 Cor. 4:10–11 NIV). Paul understands his experience of being

---

15 The Anglican Church of Australia, *A Prayer Book for Australia* (Mulgrave, Victoria: Broughton, 1999), 126.

16 John Swinton, *Raging with Compassion: Pastoral Responses to the Problem of Evil* (Grand Rapids, MI, Eerdmans, 2007), 112.

"afflicted in every way, but not crushed; perplexed, but not driven to despair" (2 Cor. 4:8) as a sharing in Jesus's sufferings.[17] When we suffer, as the Phillips paraphrase of 2 Corinthians 4:10 says, "we experience something of the death of the Lord Jesus." And that identification with Jesus's death is necessary for "the life [story] of Jesus to be revealed in our body" (2 Cor 4:11, my translation).

To remember the death of Jesus when we suffer can assist us when our lives don't go according to plan. There are many layers to suffering, one of which is its seeming meaninglessness. It is common for Christian people who experience loneliness, pain, shame, exclusion, and any form of unjust suffering to find comfort and hope in the shame and pain of Jesus's unjust crucifixion.

Speaking personally, when I hit rock bottom some twenty-odd years ago in my own crisis of identity, it helped me greatly in dealing with feelings of rejection and abandonment to remember that on the cross, Jesus had been rejected and abandoned by God, no less. It would be easy to respond that my suffering should not be compared to the suffering of Jesus. But that is exactly what Paul recommends.

When we remember the suffering of Jesus in the midst of our own troubles, and carry around in our bodies the death of Jesus, some beneficial results ensue: "For as we share abundantly in Christ's sufferings, so through Christ we share abundantly in comfort too." (2 Cor. 1:5). As Paul states in Romans 5:3–4, rightly understood, our "suffering produces endurance, and endurance produces character, and character produces hope" (see also James 1:2–4). The shared memory of the death of Jesus gives meaning to our suffering and instills in us a measure of comfort and hope.

---

17 Several features of the passage underscore the connection between the sufferings of Paul and Christ. For example, the same verb to "be given over" is used for the "giving over" of Jesus to death (see Rom. 4:25; 8:32; 2:20; 1 Cor. 11:23). Paul says that he is "always being *given over to death* for Jesus's sake" just as Jesus was *"was given over for our trespasses and raised for our justification"* (Rom. 4:25, my translation). Also, the four uses of the simple name "Jesus" (in 2 Cor. 4:10–11) draws attention to the earthly life of Christ.

2. The Egotism Test: Pride and Envy

Does living the life story of Jesus Christ equip people to handle the temptations of arrogance and pride? Having your story defined by death on a cross spells the death of selfish ambition.

The story of which believers are a part actually has a remedy for pride at its very heart. The clearest call for humility—putting the interests of others ahead of our own—in the New Testament is in Philippians 2, and it explicitly calls believers to live a life shaped by the cross of Christ:

> Do nothing from selfish ambition or conceit, but in humility count others more significant than yourselves. Let each of you look not only to his own interests, but also to the interests of others. Have this mind among yourselves, which is yours in Christ Jesus, who, though he was in the form of God, did not count equality with God a thing to be grasped, but emptied himself, by taking the form of a servant, being born in the likeness of men. And being found in human form, he humbled himself by becoming obedient to the point of death, even death on a cross. (Phil. 2:3–8)

Believers are to be humble, valuing others above themselves, in imitation of Christ, who humbled himself to the point of death on a cross.

The early church was a complete anomaly in the social world of its day in terms of its composition. The wealthy and the poor, masters and slaves worshiped alongside each other, and the New Testament contains warnings against showing partiality in church meetings and offering the best seats to the well-off (James 2:3).

The virtue of humility was virtually unknown in the ancient world before the revolution of the cross of Christ. The humble were considered servile, and the notion of putting the interests of someone below your station in life ahead of your own would have been regarded as madness. But that is exactly what the life story of Jesus Christ represents.

3. The Ethics Test: The Weak and Lowly

Does living the life story of Jesus Christ enable people to respond well to the weak and lowly who populate the world and inevitably cross our paths? Having your life story defined by death on a cross challenges worldly values of human strength and brilliance.

The fact that God saved the world through a shameful execution rather than through some impressive display of human power or wisdom turns the values of the world upside down. And as Paul insists in 1 Corinthians 1, in keeping with the message of Christ crucified, the people of God are constituted in the main by the misfits and nobodies, not the well-born and well-to-do: "But God chose what is foolish in the world to shame the wise; God chose what is weak in the world to shame the strong" (1 Cor. 1:27). Those living the life story of Jesus Christ are to treat the weak and lowly as equals.

While there are troubling counterexamples, I have seen such values played out in subtle and quiet ways in a number of churches. The best churches have a diversity of membership, in terms of age, background, status, and so on, who are united on an equal basis in one body. To cite one example, Peter is a former senior politician, at home with world leaders, and yet on Sundays he would, as a matter of course, greet one mentally disabled member by name, sit and chat with her. Those living the life story of Jesus Christ have every reason to act in such ways.

4. The Enemy Test: Adversaries and Injustice

Does living the life story of Jesus Christ empower people to respond well to their enemies? The New Testament call to nonretaliation and forgiving your enemies is rooted in the story of Jesus Christ. Jesus himself called on his disciples to turn the other cheek and backed it up with his own extreme example. When faced with those who did him violence to the point of death, he prayed for their forgiveness. And in Paul's letters, the call to forgiveness recalls Jesus's work on the cross in securing our forgiveness: "forgive one another, as God in Christ forgave you" (Eph. 4:32).

Bill is a Christian friend who is wanting to demolish his aging house and rebuild on the block of land. His neighbor, living in a large two-story home, has repeatedly and strenuously opposed the modest rebuild on trivial grounds to the point where the plans have been held up in local government for two years and counting. At the same time, the neighbor's son, who is studying for a college science degree, regularly visits Bill for assistance with his school assignments. It does not even occur to Bill to do anything but to continue helping. His admirable response of nonretaliation and love, I believe, has to do with Bill's narrative identity. He is living the life story of Jesus Christ, and that is what defines him.

5. The Enjoyment Test: Happiness and Pleasure

Does living the life story of Jesus Christ bring lasting joy and happiness? Oddly, the cross is once again the answer. For the final say in Christ's life was not his hideous death, but rather his vindication and return to life: "for the joy that was set before him [he] endured the cross, despising the shame, and is seated at the right hand of the throne of God" (Heb. 12:2). The genre of Jesus's life story, which we are called to live, is U-shaped. No matter how steep the dip—and death on a cross is as low as it gets—lives that are conformed to the life story of Jesus Christ anticipate a rising from the depths to glory in the presence of God.

I know a number of Christian women younger than I who are living with serious cancer diagnoses. Along with the expected anxiety and sadness, their examples of remaining engaged in life, continuing to show concern for others, and maintaining a calmness in the midst of sometimes dire circumstances speak to the quiet contentment and even joy that living the life story of Jesus Christ brings. If dying with Christ defines us, no less significant is our defining destiny with Christ, the very prospect of which brings great joy in the present, even in midst of real hardship and suffering.

Living Christ's Story

We live the stories to which we subscribe. Narrative identity informs behavior and shapes who we are in the world. Alistair McIntyre said it well: "I can only answer the question 'What am I to do?' if I can answer the prior question 'Of what story or stories do I find myself a part.'"[18] The choice for all of us is between a starring role in our own short story, the genre of which could be a tragedy or a farce, or a bit part in the grand story of God and the redemption of the world.

As can be seen from the five tests, living Christ's story, as a child of God united to Christ, offers us a stable and satisfying sense of self. The shared memory of dying with Christ gives meaning to our suffering and instills in us a measure of comfort and hope. We have good grounds to be humble and consider others more important than ourselves, in imitation of Christ, who humbled himself to the point of death on a cross. Similarly, the weak and lowly we come across are to be respected and assisted, given that in the cross, God chose human weakness as the means of saving the world; in identifying with Christ in his death, we die to pure self-interest and are raised to live lives of sacrificial love. In contrast to outrage culture, the story of Jesus Christ calls on his disciples to turn the other cheek in imitation of his own extreme example. And, like Christ, we can endure hardship for the joy set before us in the future when we will be vindicated along with him when God puts the world to right.

But it's not just about believing the storyline. It's about inhabiting it. Stories have the power to inspire imagination and imitation. N. T. Wright notes the relevance of living Christ's story for our world today:

We live in a world where, increasingly, people are clutching at straws, unable to glimpse a story which would lead the way into true peace,

---

18 Alasdair MacIntyre, *After Virtue: A Study in Moral Theory* (Notre Dame, IN: University of Notre Dame Press, 1981), 216.

freedom and justice. The Christian gospel offers such a story. But to tell it truly, you have to be living it.[19]

In the final two chapters of this book, we unpack further how to live the story of God's people.

Questions for Reflection and Discussion

1. Consider the life story of Jesus Christ. How do this chapter's descriptions of its problem, past turning points, present struggles, and future hope align with your own understanding of the Christian narrative?

2. We examined the "five tests" in light of being known by God a few chapters back. Here, we bring in a different angle—that of being "in Christ." In what ways does this different angle shift your view of how a Christian worldview meets the challenges of these tests?

3. What is it like to consider yourself as a "bit part" in God's grand narrative, rather than the hero or heroine of your own tale? A disappointment? A relief?

19 N. T. Wright, *God in Public: How the Bible Speaks Truth to Power Today* (London: SPCK, 2016), 33.

PART 4

———————

THE NEW YOU

12

Losing Yourself

*"Whoever finds his life will lose it, and whoever
loses his life for my sake will find it."*
JESUS CHRIST (MATT. 10:39)

"You are not your own."
THE APOSTLE PAUL (1 COR. 6:19)

IN THIS FINAL PART of the book, I want to describe from two different angles the Christian alternative to the self-made self's flawed practice of looking only inward to find yourself. In this chapter, we ponder some striking differences between the two identity formation strategies in question. In this and the final chapter, I will suggest some practical ways in which to embrace the new self and make it your own.

Expressive individualism can be summed up in two assertions:

1. To be yourself, you have to find yourself.
2. You belong to yourself.

In our day, both statements seem self-evident and beyond dispute; they are hardly bold claims. The first is almost tautologous, needlessly saying the same thing in different words; how else are you going to be yourself other than by finding yourself? These days, to be yourself is to find yourself, and to find yourself is to be yourself.

The second could be a main point in a solemn declaration of human rights: What is the alternative to belonging to yourself? Being subject to some external authority is almost the definition of oppression.

Yet, as shocking as it might sound, the Bible is in fundamental disagreement with both of these cardinal principles of expressive individualism and recommends a different pathway to self-knowledge and a stable and satisfying sense of self. Two sayings, one from Jesus Christ and the other from the apostle Paul, make the point, both sounding as if they were deliberately provocative rebuttals of expressive individualism.

In direct opposition to the imperative advice to find yourself, Jesus said, "Whoever finds his life will lose it, and whoever loses his life for my sake will find it" (Matt. 10:39). And in a flat contradiction of the principle of personal autonomy, Paul stated bluntly, "You are not your own."

Let's take them one by one.

The Paradox of Personal Identity

Even though there is a growing consensus in our day that the way to find yourself is by looking inward, there are good reasons to think otherwise. Not least of these is the incoherence of the strategy of expressive individualism in general terms and the way it is playing out. Modern identity formation is riddled with embarrassing ironies, with yawning gulfs opening up between what is asserted or appears to be the case and what is an unfortunate reality. In many ways, expressive individualism is leading to outcomes that are the opposite of what we expect:

- We are told to look inward to find ourselves, but inevitably we still look to the approval of others to shore up our sense of self.
- We use social media to define ourselves, but the same tools leave us more exposed than ever to how others perceive us.
- We pursue our desires with a passion, but even when we get what we want, we are left feeling discontent and dissatisfied.

- We seek to rid the world of prejudice and discrimination, but to bring that about, we invent new forms of prejudice and discrimination.
- We regard religion as the imposition of an oppressive external authority, only to find ourselves looking up to things unworthy of our devotion that enslave and dehumanize us.
- We seek to live our unique stories, only to find ourselves plugging into big, shared stories.
- Worst of all, we place the highest premium on finding ourselves, only to find it harder than ever to do so.

But there is one irony in connection with the subject of identity formation that dates back two thousand years: Jesus's insistence that those who find themselves will lose themselves and those who lose themselves will find themselves. More accurately, it is a paradox, an assertion that is true even though on first glance it seems contradictory. A paradox is a profound irony.

Jesus's advice against trying to find yourself is puzzling, to say the least. John Nolland calls it "deliberately riddling and paradoxical."[1] As it turns out, it appears to have been one of his favorite sayings, turning up in all four Gospels and in three different versions:

"Whoever loves his life loses it, and whoever hates his life in this world will keep it for eternal life." (John 12:25)

"For whoever would save his life will lose it, but whoever loses his life for my sake will find it." (Matt 16:25; see also Mark 8:35; Luke 9:24)

"Whoever finds his life will lose it, and whoever loses his life for my sake will find it." (Matt. 10:39).

1 John Nolland, *The Gospel of Matthew*, The New International Greek Testament Commentary (Grand Rapids, MI: Eerdmans, 2005), 442–43.

190 PART 4: THE NEW YOU

All three sayings warn that certain actions will lead to losing your life: loving your life, seeking to save your life, and finding your life. And another entirely different action is recommended in order to keep or find your life—namely, hating your life and losing your life.

The first two appear in contexts in which there are hints that the physical lives of Jesus's disciples are under serious threat. The issue in these texts is whether a follower of Jesus is willing to die for Jesus. Jesus warns his followers that seeking to save their earthly lives by denying him would result in losing eternal life. And he reassures them that losing their physical lives for his sake will result in protecting their true lives.

However, the third one seems to be saying something different, something broader and more general. When it comes to losing your life by finding it, and vice versa, in Matthew 10:39 the "life" at stake is the same one on both sides of the saying. Unlike the other two sayings, it is not a contrast between earthly and eternal life. "Life," in Matthew 10:39, as in the other texts, translates the Greek word *psyche*, from which we derive the English words *psyche* and *psychology*. In this context, it comes close to what we mean by personal identity, the subject of this book. Leon Morris writes that "life here [in Matt. 10:39] means very much what we mean by 'self.'"[2] Hence, this is one way to translate the verse: "Whoever finds oneself will lose oneself, but whoever loses oneself for my sake will find oneself."

In the first part of Matthew 10:39, to find yourself is the equivalent of pursuing a self-made self. It is to find your own way, to seek your own personal happiness above all else, to focus on pursuing your life dreams, to follow relentlessly your own path, with little thought to those around you who might, in fact, get in your way. Jesus is not condemning ambition or achievement in itself. Rather, finding yourself in the first half of Jesus's saying is about focused self-creation, the essence of expressive individualism. According to Jesus, in the ultimate

2   Leon Morris, *The Gospel according to Matthew*, The Pillar New Testament Commentary (Grand Rapids, MI: Eerdmans, 1992), 268–69.

tragic irony, seeking to establish your own identity results in losing your identity.

But also, according to Jesus, in order to find yourself, your true and lasting identity, you need to relinquish the quest for self-assertion and look in another direction. Jesus opposes the notion that to know yourself, you need to find yourself. The paradox of personal identity is that those who gaze inwardly to find themselves will lose their identities, and those who look elsewhere, to the interests of others, will find their true identity. Or as Morris says, "To concentrate one's best energies on oneself is to destroy oneself, whereas to lose oneself in the service of Christ and others is to find oneself."[3]

But Jesus doesn't just warn those looking for themselves that their search will fail. Moving to the positive alternative to seeking to find your life and thereby losing it, the motivation he supplies for losing your life, not seeking to establish yourself, is that it is done "for my sake." C. S. Lewis put it this way:

> Give yourself up, and you will find your real self. Lose your life and you will save it. . . . Look for yourself and you will find in the long run only hatred, loneliness, despair, rage, ruin and decay. But look for Christ and you will find him, and with him everything else thrown in.[4]

Excessive self-focus is the root of pride, and pride produces a distorted view of the self. The Bible faults the proud on this very point: "For if anyone thinks he is something, when he is nothing, *he deceives himself*" (Gal. 6:3). In Jeremiah 49:16, the prophet writes that the pride of your heart has deceived you (see also Obad. 3). And in Isaiah 16:6, the problem with Moab's pride is that her boasts are empty. Even though the proud spend a lot of time thinking about themselves, they don't actually know who they are.

3   Morris, *The Gospel according to Matthew*, 268–69.
4   C. S. Lewis, *Mere Christianity* (1952; repr., London: Font, 1997), 187.

However, contrary to much popular thinking, humility is not about thinking poorly of yourself. Jason Meyer writes that "humility is fundamentally a form of self-forgetfulness as opposed to pride's self-fixation."[5] Tim Keller agrees: "The essence of gospel-humility is not thinking more of myself or less of myself, it is thinking of myself less."[6] When Paul warns against pride, he does not say to think little of yourself: "I say to everyone among you not to think of himself more highly than he ought to think, but to think with sober judgment" (Rom. 12:3).

The Bible nowhere recommends thinking about yourself in some exaggeratedly low way or ignoring your achievements. If pride involves self-promotion and elevation, humility is not about self-degradation and demotion. Rather than causing you to think less of yourself, humility leads you to thinking less about yourself. The humble, although thinking less about themselves, know themselves more accurately than do those who are proud. Or as Jesus put it, those who risk losing themselves know themselves better than those who seek to find themselves.

The model for this way of finding yourself is Jesus's own life story, as we saw in the previous chapter. Jesus is the paradigm of the paradox of personal identity. He lost himself in the service of others and found his true identity as Lord of all in the process. Jesus is the ultimate illustration of Matthew 10:39: "Whoever finds his life will lose it, and whoever loses his life for my sake will find it." And he sets the pattern for all of us who want to find a stable and satisfying sense of self. Tim Keller calls it the freedom of self-forgetfulness and the path to true joy.[7]

The Rejection of Personal Autonomy

A second statement from the Bible that collides head on with expressive individualism is Paul's words in 1 Corinthians 6:19: "you are not

---

5   Jason Meyer, "Pride," in *Killjoys: The Seven Deadly Sins*, ed. Marshall Segal (Minneapolis, MN: Desiring God, 2015), 12.

6   Timothy Keller, *The Freedom of Self-Forgetfulness: The Path to True Christian Joy* (Leyland: 10Publishing, 2012), 32.

7   The title of Keller, *The Freedom of Self-Forgetfulness: The Path to True Christian Joy.*

your own." In our day, we pride ourselves on our independence and freedom from all external authorities. The notion that no one can tell you who you are has almost credal status. And true freedom is thought to be found in defining yourself for yourself. Postmodernism has made a living out of suspecting anyone who seeks to impose their views on anyone else as doing so in order to subjugate others.

Yet even in our day of insisting on the priority and benefits of personal autonomy, there are some contexts in which belonging to someone else is still seen in a positive light. A young child lost in a shopping mall makes no complaint when his parent turns up and claims him as the parent's own. Likewise, while it is open to abuse, true romantic love has at its heart a mutual belonging. Countless love songs, starting with the Song of Solomon in the Bible, contain refrains along the lines of "my beloved is mine, and I am his" (2:16; see also 6:3). Indeed, the social animals that we are, nothing gives us more of a sense of value and worth than being loved to such an extent that we belong to another. Far from distressing or oppressive, such an embrace reassures and liberates us.

Indeed, love is the context of Paul's startling assertion that you are not your own. The words following Paul's rejection of personal autonomy in 1 Corinthians 6:19–20 explain why you belong to another: "you were bought with a price." You belong to another because you are loved beyond measure. That love was expressed in the high cost of your redemption: "you were ransomed from the futile ways . . . not with perishable things such as silver or gold, but with the precious blood of Christ" (1 Pet. 1:18–19); "God shows his love for us in that while we were still sinners, Christ died for us" (Rom. 5:8).

Just as the pattern of Christ's humiliation and exaltation shows us the way to find yourself, the same cross of Christ proclaims that God has claimed you as his very own; you belong to him. But surrendering of yourself in this way does not lead to the eradication of your self or an oppressive subjugation. On the contrary, in losing yourself and belonging to one who loves you with an everlasting love, you will find your true self.

Living the Life Story of Jesus

What does it actually look like to relinquish your personal autonomy and belong to God? And how do you go about it? There are six things you can do to inhabit the life story of Jesus Christ and make it your own. The practices I have in mind are common to almost all Christians. Many Christians would not realize their identity-forming and identity-confirming power; nonetheless, they are the means to losing yourself and finding yourself in Jesus Christ, whether or not those performing them know it. Living the life story of Jesus Christ combines looking back and forth to your story with looking up to the narrative that defines you most profoundly.

The practices are not designed to achieve or construct the new identity of being a child of God, but rather to live more in keeping with that identity, to exist more authentically within it. In our day, when an individual or corporation says or does something offensive, they often quickly apologize, hoping to defuse the explosion of outrage of the callout culture and so avoid being "cancelled." Such apologies usually end with the words, "that's not who I am," or "that's not who we are." They insist that the unacceptable remarks in question were out of character. It's certainly true that identities carry with them a set of behaviors that produce a settled character. Putting on the new self is all about remembering who you are and behaving in accordance with that character.

The language of taking off the old self and putting on the new self appears in Colossians 3:9–11, in the context of being conformed to the life story of Jesus Christ. Believers in Christ are those who died with Christ, have been raised with him and whose destiny is tied up with his glorious appearing (3:1–4). Significantly, in another passage (Rom. 13:14), when Paul tells believers to put something on, it is Jesus

Christ himself: "put on the Lord Jesus Christ." Clearly, the new self is modeled on the character and person of Jesus and in particular his sacrificial death on behalf of others. You find yourself not just by losing yourself but by being found in Christ.

The first thing that you must do to claim the story of Jesus Christ as your own life story is put your faith in Christ and get baptized. Galatians 3:26 makes this clear, where faith in Christ, becoming a child of God, being included in Christ's life story, being baptized, and being clothed with Christ are all linked together in one package: "So in Christ Jesus you are all children of God through faith, for all of you who were baptized into Christ have clothed yourselves with Christ." Faith is the open hands of receiving the undeserved gift of being a child of God, known and loved by him. And baptism is the rite of initiation into this identity. In direct contradiction of expressive individualism, in baptism, we affirm that we are "not closed, self-sufficient autonomous units"[8] but rather connected to others in a shared story. Baptism speaks of our shared memory and defining destiny that form our identity in Christ. We die with Christ to self-interest and self-assertion and we rise to new life now and most fully in the future.

Second, in order to live the life story of Jesus Christ as your own, you can remind yourself of the problem, past turning points, present struggles, and future hope of your life story by reading and hearing the Bible. The Bible tells the human story and the story of those united to Christ. From our creation as God's offspring in the garden, through our ruinous rebellion, to God's determination to set things right, the human story, "warts and all," is the main plot of the Bible's larger narrative. And the history of Israel as God's chosen people, from the covenant promises through Abraham, the conquest, kingship to the exile and return, all leading to the work of Christ on the cross, are the main turning points

---

8 James K. A. Smith, *Desiring the Kingdom: Worship, Worldview, and Cultural Formation*, Cultural Liturgies 1 (Grand Rapids, MI: Baker Academic, 2009), 186.

of every believer's narrative identity.[9] The Bible also speaks of our defining destiny of being revealed as God's children when Christ returns. In reading the Bible and hearing it preached, we learn not only about God but also about ourselves and our true identity.

Third, you can rehearse the defining moment and signature move of your life story by taking Communion. The Communion service is an identity-forming and -confirming emblem of the gospel. In eating and drinking the symbols of the broken body and shed blood of Christ, believers are prompted to look in all the right directions to find themselves. We look back to a shared memory, forward to our defining destiny, around at our brothers and sisters in the family of God, and up to God in faith, hope, and gratitude.

With regard to the function of liturgy and storytelling in general, James K. A. Smith claims that we are defined by what we desire or love, which is bound up with our view of human flourishing. Liturgy, then—and Smith argues that the world is full of competing liturgies—helps to shape and cultivate our desires. Being human takes practice, and liturgy is where we learn. Smith contends, for example, that in the Communion service, we are placed in the midst of the story of God's work: "It's as if the story we've been hearing and rehearsing now comes live with illustrations."[10] For Smith, sharing in the Lord's Supper is supremely transformative: "Just as a song makes words stick in our memory, so the sights, smells, and rhythms of the Eucharist seem to make the story both come alive and wriggle into our imaginations in a way that wouldn't otherwise."[11]

Fourth, you can express your allegiance to the life story of Jesus Christ, and not some other story, by saying the creed. Saying the creed,

---

9   Paul writes to the Christians in Corinth concerning "*our* fathers" (1 Cor. 10:1), referring to the history of the nation Israel. Matthew opens the New Testament with a genealogy that demonstrates the continuity of "Jesus Christ, the son of David, the son of Abraham" (1:1) with the story of Israel.

10   Smith, *Desiring the Kingdom*, 198.

11   Smith, *Desiring the Kingdom*, 199.

if done well, affirms the story to which we belong. When we say the Apostles' Creed, for example, we repudiate the creeds of alternative visions of what it means to be a human being in our day, including the narrative identities of secular materialism or social justice. In affirming that we are part of the story of God, Christians at the same time deny that they are part of another story. N. T. Wright argues that when we recite the creed, we affirm that "we are renewed as this people, the people who live within this great story, the people who are identified precisely as people-of-this-story, rather than as people of one of the many other stories that claim for attention all around."[12] Or as Smith puts it, "In reciting it [the Creed] each week, we rehearse the skeletal structure of the story in which we find our identity."[13]

Fifth, you can celebrate your narrative identity and imagine your destiny by singing, along with others seeking to live the same story. Singing corporately offers praise to God and reinforces the identity of God's people. Singing is also one means by which we inhabit our destiny as God's people. We confirm that we belong to a different world. In this sense, singing can be a deeply subversive activity, asserting that our ultimate allegiance lies outside of the dominant narrative and social identities of our day.

Sixth and finally, you can put dying to sin and rising to new life in Christ into practice daily by living in a manner worthy of the gospel of Jesus Christ (Phil. 1:27; see also Eph. 4:1). In the words of Jesus himself, those who wish to follow him must "take up his cross daily" (Luke 9:23). We are to live cruciform lives, putting self-interest to death and serving others in costly love.

To put on the narrative identity of the life story of Jesus Christ, put your trust in Christ and get baptized, read and hear the Bible, take

---

12 N. T. Wright, "Reading Paul, Thinking Scripture," in *Scripture's Doctrine and Theology's Bible: How the New Testament Shapes Christian Dogmatics*, ed. Marcus Bockmuehl and Alan J. Torrance (Grand Rapids, MI: Baker, 2008), 64.

13 Smith, *Desiring the Kingdom*, 192.

Communion, say the creed, sing the faith, and, most importantly, live the gospel. Jonathan Gottschall observes that "the more absorbed readers are in a story, the more the story changes them."[14] Following these six practices will plant God's grand story deep in your spirit and psyche, and transform your behavior. It is the ultimate rejection of personal autonomy, a giving up of yourself to find your true self in the life story of Jesus Christ.

Questions for Reflection and Discussion

1. "Whoever finds his life will lose it, and whoever loses his life for my sake will find it." (Matt. 10:39). How have you understood this paradoxical teaching in the past? How can it inform your search for identity in the future?

2. Humility is often associated with self-abasement. What does it do for you to think about it as self-forgetfulness, or "thinking of yourself less"?

3. Does relinquishing autonomy sound like a wise or foolish idea to you? What would it look like practically to surrender to God? Which of the six practices outlined in "Living the Life Story of Jesus Christ" are already a part of your own practices? Are any on the list calling for your fresh attention?

14   Jonathan Gottschall, *The Storytelling Animal: How Stories Make Us Human* (Boston, MA: Mariner, 2013), 151.

13

Finding Yourself

"We are grass, no doubt of it. But with a sense of history we can have a perspective that lifts us out of our very brief moment here. Certainly, this is one purpose of biblical narrative."

MARILYNNE ROBINSON[1]

"The Scriptures function as the script of the worshipping community, the story that narrates the identity of the people of God."

JAMES K. A. SMITH[2]

IN THE 1990S, I worked at the University of Aberdeen in Northeast Scotland. In those days, Aberdeen was a center for the booming oil industry in the North Sea, and I had some friends who worked offshore on the oil rigs in various capacities as engineers, helicopter pilots, and the like. Their working lives gave them an odd existence, with extended periods offshore, alternating with a few weeks back home. One friend worked as a submariner and would sit in a confined space at the base of the rig or on the floor of the ocean with just one workmate for two

---

1   Marilynne Robinson, *The Givenness of Things: Essays* (New York: Farrar, Straus and Giroux, 2015), 154.
2   James K. A. Smith, *Desiring the Kingdom: Worship, Worldview, and Cultural Formation*, Cultural Liturgies 1 (Grand Rapids, MI: Baker Academic, 2009), 195.

weeks at a time. I can't imagine a more unattractive work environment.
Still, it was an essential element of the whole enterprise. Sometimes
enduring uncomfortable conditions in order to examine something
significant that is hidden from sight is worth the effort, especially if it
uncovered a fault that threatened to bring down the whole enterprise.

As you have accompanied me through this book as we've examined
how we form our identities at the very bottom of the cultural iceberg,
I trust you haven't found it too claustrophobic! Taking a careful look
at expressive individualism has been a tad uncomfortable at times, I'm
sure. But, as I hope you agree, ultimately it is worth the effort.

We began this book in part 1 with a description and appraisal of expressive individualism, the view that the only place to look to find yourself is
inward. I judged the movement to be fatally flawed for three reasons: looking only inward to find yourself produces a fragile self, easily destabilized
and lacking in genuine and lasting self-knowledge (chapter 2); it is failing
to lead to the good life, too easily producing selves that are self-deceived,
self-absorbed, and self-centered (chapter 3); and it is faulty in its foundations (chapter 4), because in order to find yourself you also need to look
around, backward and forward, as well as upward to God (chapter 5).

A better identity formation strategy, one that acknowledges that we
are social beings and have narrative identities, is to form a self that is
known intimately and personally by God (part 2) and conforms to the
life story of Jesus Christ (part 3). In the previous chapter, I pointed out
that rather than finding yourself and belonging to yourself, Christian
faith insists that the path to secure and joyful self-knowledge involves
losing yourself, relinquishing your personal autonomy and belonging
to your Father in heaven.

In this final chapter, I will attempt to answer four questions with
positive and practical advice:

1. How can you embrace the identity of being known by God as
   his child?

2. What sort of conduct and character does this new identity produce?

3. What does the corporate life of the new identity look like?

4. Can a Christian approach to identity formation accommodate the concerns and use the language of expressive individualism?

Knowing Yourself as You Are Known by God

Having suggested six ways in which a person can put on the life story of Jesus Christ in the previous chapter, I now want to discuss practices that can enable a person to put on the identity of a child of God known and loved by him. I recommend three, which pertain to how we relate to God and the people of God: listening to God; speaking to God; and becoming a committed and vulnerable member of a local church faith community. Being known by God includes looking around to your relationships and upward to your most defining relationship.

The principal way in which we listen to God is by reading and hearing the Bible. In the Bible, we learn about not just God but also ourselves. The Bible tells you who you are and also who you aren't. From cover to cover, God tells his people who they are: you are a chosen people, a royal priesthood (1 Pet. 2:9); you are wonderfully made (Ps. 139:14), the apple of God's eye (Ps. 17:8); you are the light of the world, the salt of the earth, a city on a hill (Matt. 5:13–16); you are the temple of the Holy Spirit (1 Cor. 6:19) and belong to the body of Christ (1 Cor. 12:12–30); you are a new creation (2 Cor. 5:17); you are a child of God, known by him (1 John 3:1). Equally, God reminds his people that they are not among those who do not know God, who are darkened in their understanding, separated from the life of God, children of wrath, sons of disobedience (see Eph. 4:17–18). If with Adam we are banished as rebellious sons and therefore experience "death before death," in Christ we hear God say in Scripture, "You are my beloved son, in whom I am well pleased" (see Matt. 3:17). Almost every page of the Bible contributes to self-knowledge. It provides satisfying answers to three of life's most fundamental questions: What is a human being?

Who am I? Who are we? Reading the Bible is like looking in a mirror: it reminds you who you are (see James 1:23–24).

Speaking to God in prayer is a second vital practice if you wish to know yourself as you are known by God. Timothy Keller writes, "Prayer is the only entryway into genuine self-knowledge."[3] Or as Ed Clowney explains, "In prayer we rightly seek the joy which the presence of the Spirit brings, the knowledge of the Father and the Son. Yet the highest goal of prayer is not to claim the Lord as our inheritance, but to be claimed by him as his own."[4]

In order to pray effectively, we need God's help to overcome not only our weakness but also our ignorance: "we do not know what we ought to pray for" (Rom. 8:26 NIV). And God facilitates our prayers not only through helping us in our weakness but also by knowing our heart (8:27)—that is, our deepest emotions, thoughts, and desires. Jesus makes the same point just before giving the model prayer to his disciples in Matthew 6: "Your Father knows what you need before you ask him" (6:8). Being known by God makes prayer possible.

The third practical thing to do to know yourself as you are known by God is to establish and maintain deep connections with other people who belong to God. Jack O. Balswick, Pamela Ebstyne King, and Kevin Reimer stress the relational dimension of Christian worship, community, and identity:

> Progress toward becoming a mature reciprocating self is fostered best within a network of relationships characterised by uncon- ditional love, grace, empowering and intimacy. The goal of the maturation process is to become a person with the capacity and

---

3   Timothy Keller, *Prayer: Experiencing Awe and Intimacy with God* (London: Hodder & Stoughton, 2014), 18.

4   Edmund P. Clowney, "Prayer," in *New Dictionary of Biblical Theology* (Downers Grove, IL: IVP, 2000), 691; emphasis added.

inclination to reciprocate each of these characteristics: *to love and be loved, to forgive and be forgiven, to empower and be empowered,* and *to know and to be known.*[5]

This has certainly been my experience. I have been involved in churches for extended periods in five countries where I've lived. All of them had their problems. But in every case, in the midst of the messiness and challenges of what Christians call fellowship, I came to know and be known by people, many vastly different from me in key respects, whose lives and caring interactions with me and each other helped all of us to live more fully our identity as children of God. We can be known and loved not only by Jesus Christ but also by the body of Christ.

I am aware that this is not everyone's experience of church life. And for that I am deeply sorry. Churches and Christians who act in ways that hurt their members have lost the plot of the life story of Jesus Christ which they are meant to be living. As I noted in chapter 11, the New Testament itself anticipates such bad behavior and gives clear instructions for dealing with it.

The Conduct and Character of the New Identity

What sort of conduct and character should being known intimately and personally by God produce? While a full answer to this question is the subject of another book, a glimpse of authentic Christian living can be seen in the famous beatitudes in Jesus's Sermon on the Mount. David Brooks, self-described as a committed Jew and admirer of Jesus, something of a "border stalker" between the two closely connected ancient faiths of Judaism and Christianity, says this about the Beatitudes: "The beatitudes are the moral sublime, the source of awe, the moral purity that takes your breath away and toward which everything points.

5 Jack O. Balswick, Pamela Ebstyne King, and Kevin S. Reimer, *The Reciprocating Self: Human Development in Theological Perspective* (Downers Grove, IL: IVP Academic, 2016), 351.

204   PART 4: THE NEW YOU

In the beatitudes we see *the ultimate road map for our lives*."[6] Critical
for our purposes, Jonathan Pennington describes the Beatitudes as "the
true way of being that will result in happiness and human flourishing,"[7]
echoing the major goals of expressive individualism. But, as we will see,
the Beatitudes take a significantly different route to meet those goals:

> Blessed are the poor in spirit, for theirs is the kingdom of heaven.
>
> Blessed are those who mourn, for they shall be comforted.
>
> Blessed are the meek, for they shall inherit the earth.
>
> Blessed are those who hunger and thirst for righteousness, for
> they shall be satisfied.
>
> Blessed are the merciful, for they shall receive mercy.
>
> Blessed are the pure in heart, for they shall see God.
>
> Blessed are the peacemakers, for they shall be called sons of God.
>
> Blessed are those who are persecuted for righteousness' sake, for
> theirs is the kingdom of heaven.
>
> Blessed are you when others revile you and persecute you and utter
> all kinds of evil against you falsely on my account. Rejoice and be
> glad, for your reward is great in heaven, for so they persecuted the
> prophets who were before you. (Matt. 5:3–13)

If expressive individualism directs a person to build their own kingdom, Jesus enlists us in service of the kingdom of God. He replaces a
superficial search for happiness with a promise of comfort to those who
mourn the imperfect and unjust state of our world. In place of the bold
living of those who think "you only live once," he commends the meek
as those who will be rewarded in the life to come. He promises success to
those hungering for righteousness and justice by humble means. Instead

---

6   David Brooks, *The Second Mountain: The Quest for a Moral Life* (London: Allen Lane, 2019), 246;
    emphasis added.

7   Jonathan T. Pennington, *The Sermon on the Mount and Human Flourishing: A Theological Com-
    mentary* (Grand Rapids, MI: Baker, 2017), 54.

of mercilessly calling out, shaming, and punishing wrongdoers, he praises showing mercy. Rather than telling people to follow their hearts, Jesus assures the pure in heart that they will see the living God. To the peace-breakers intent on ridding the world of injustice by force, Jesus highlights peacemaking. In view of the inevitable persecution of those pursuing his vision, Jesus promises a place in his kingdom. Indeed, Jesus pronounces those living in these ways to be truly happy and blessed by God.

But the Beatitudes are not a self-help guide, a to-do list where you do your best and hope for the rest. Jesus himself is the model of the life he recommends to his followers in the Beatitudes. As Brooks notes, "Jesus is the one who shows us what giving yourself away looks like."[8] The Beatitudes are about the life story of Jesus and his invitation to his followers to live the same story. Jesus is his own example when it comes to expounding the conduct and character of his disciples as sons and children of God. Matthew's Gospel makes this clear. We see Jesus mourning (Matt. 26:38); he is described as meek (11:29) and is an example of righteousness as he fulfils all righteousness (3:15). He leads the way in showing mercy (9:27; 15:22; 17:15; 20:30–31). He comes to bring peace (12:15–21; 26:52). He is himself persecuted to the point of death (see esp. 26:67; 27:30). To live the Beatitudes, you need the help of Jesus Christ, who alone can enable you to live his life story.

The Corporate Life of the New Identity

What does the corporate life of the new identity look like? The New Testament answers this question on almost every page. Paul's closing instructions to a church in first-century Greece are one compelling example and still apply today:

We urge you, brothers, admonish the idle, encourage the fainthearted, help the weak, be patient with them all. See that no one repays

8   Brooks, *The Second Mountain*, 246.

anyone evil for evil, but always seek to do good to one another and to everyone. Rejoice always, pray without ceasing, give thanks in all circumstances; for this is the will of God in Christ Jesus for you. (1 Thess. 5:14–18)

This ancient manifesto, addressed to brothers and sisters in the family of God, those known and loved by their heavenly Father, is a radical alternative to the rife expressive individualism that is ruining our day. And, recalling the five tests of the good life, building a community on these lines goes a long way to helping those involved to cope with life's inevitable hardships and disappointments, deal with destructive pride, leave room for the weak and lowly, respond to injustice in practical ways, and lead lives of lasting joy and quiet contentment.

I can think of inspiring examples of each line of instruction, none of which are earth-shattering or newsworthy, at least not in terms of how the media functions in our day. But they are the kinds of things that are in tune with the new identity of the people of God. There's Bruce, a successful corporate executive who, without fail, for over a decade helped out with a soup kitchen every Friday night. And Barb, an elderly widow, who took into her home and provided accommodation to refugee Muslim young men. And Greg, a lawyer who used his considerable means to fund numerous charitable projects and served tirelessly on governance boards pro bono. And Adam, a single man who moved out of his apartment and back in with his parents in order to give two friends, a newly married couple, somewhere to live for six months. Or my mother, who gave anonymously to people in need throughout her life, even though it was often beyond her means. Across the world, there are innumerable cases of generous, hospitable, and kind behavior of believers in Jesus Christ, consistent with the vision of the self-giving sacrifice of a crucified Lord. Such people are quietly staying on script in bit parts in God's grand story of the kingdom of God.

The Values and Language of Expressive Individualism

This book offers a thorough critique of expressive individualism, the notion of looking only inward to find yourself. Along with pointing out the shortcomings of the movement, I have also sought to commend a positive alternative strategy of identity formation, looking in other directions, in addition to inward: around to your relationships, backward and forward to your story, and up to God for your most defining relationship and to become part of his story.

In chapter 2, I noted some of the benefits of expressive individualism: inclusion, self-reflection, and authenticity. Here I want to suggest briefly that the Bible's approach to identity, when properly undertaken, can also bring these benefits. The community that is living the life story of Jesus Christ should be inclusive in the best sense. Churches are to be groups of people who don't normally belong together, united on an equal basis in one body: "Here there is not Greek and Jew, circumcised and uncircumcised, barbarian, Scythian, slave, free; but Christ is all, and in all" (Col. 3:11). And Christian faith at its best brings a unity without obliterating cultural differences or making one culture dominate another. The basis for that unity is the mutual love for Jesus Christ, who loves us all and gave himself for us.

The value of self-reflection is actually anticipated in the Bible. Paul sees us as whole beings, determined from within; humans have an "inner being."[9] But the inner person is not there to be discovered, affirmed, and celebrated unconditionally, but rather strengthened and renewed: "[I pray] that according to the riches of his glory he may grant you to be strengthened with power through his Spirit in your inner being, so that Christ may dwell in your hearts through faith" (Eph. 3:16–17); "Though our outer self is wasting away, our inner self is being renewed day by day." (2 Cor. 4:16). Such renewal begins

---

9   The term is rendered differently in English versions as inner "man" (NKJV), "person" (NET, HCSB), "self" (ESV), "nature" (NRSV), "humanity" (REB), or as "human nature" (NJB).

by admitting that what we find within is not perfect or sufficient. As Paul counsels in Romans 12:3, we are to think about ourselves "with sober judgment."

As it turns out, the value of living authentic lives, true to ourselves, is the heart of the Bible's call to moral transformation. The Bible knows that knowing who you are leads to conduct in keeping with your identity. That is the point of much Christian doctrine: reminding believers who we are in Christ. In that light, it is imperative in our day that Christian teaching on identity be expressed in forms familiar to our current context.[10] Such a project is beyond the scope of this book. But it is a challenge that needs to be met, and there is ample scope. Should you be true to yourself? Be true to your new self! Should you do you? You should do the new you!

The Prayer of the Authentic Self

As a final summary and challenge, I want to focus our attention on a prayer that has been said by millions of Christians around the world for two thousand years—namely, the prayer in the Sermon on the Mount, recorded in Matthew 6:9–13, that Jesus taught his followers to say. Praying the Lord's Prayer is a powerful critique of and substitute for expressive individualism. This can be seen when put alongside a satirical "prayer" that I have written that sums up the key emphases of expressive individualism: The Prayer of the Authentic Self.

The heart of expressive individualism is looking inward to find your true essence and identity—that is, your authentic self. In the Prayer

---

10   Graham Stanton, *Wide-Awake in God's World: Bible Engagement for Teenage Spiritual Formation in a Culture of Expressive Individualism* (Eugene, OR: Wipf & Stock, 2020), 116, argues that "there is little value in arguing that authenticity ought not to be a central feature of our culture, not least because it is an argument that makes the false assumption that, even if won at the intellectual level, there would be any hope of dis-embedding this ubiquitous value from the modern social imaginary." Stanton's book is an example of contextualizing Christian identity formation for youth ministry.

of the Authentic Self, I have personified that inner essence, which in our day, to all intents and purposes, has attained a hallowed or sacred status. Other tenets of expressive individualism evident in the prayer are a commitment to personal happiness as the highest goal in life, the unchallengeable status of personal desire, the rejection of all forms of external authority, the lauding of individual freedom, and the narrative of triumphant personal achievement and experience. In the prayer, the self-made self looks around to others, but only to defeat its perceived enemies. And it looks backward and forward, but only to its own individual life story, from birth to "the kingdom of me." It looks forward to the goal of fulfillment, seventh heaven, not meant metaphysically, but rather as the state of intense happiness or bliss. Certainly, the prayer doesn't involve any looking upward.

The Lord's Prayer	The Prayer of the Authentic Self
Our Father in heaven,	My essence within,
hallowed be your name,	help me to find my authentic self,
your kingdom come,	my kingdom come,
your will be done,	my will be done,
on earth as in heaven.	from birth to seventh heaven.
Give us today our daily bread.	Give me today my daily spread.
Forgive us our sins	Forgive not my enemies
as we forgive those who sin against us.	as I suppress those who sin against me.
Lead us not into temptation	Lead me not into self-doubt
but deliver us from evil.	but deliver me from all external authorities.
For the kingdom, the power,	For the kingdom, the power,
and the glory are yours	and the glory are mine
now and for ever.*	now and for ever.
Amen.	Amen.

* The concluding lines to the Lord's Prayer ("For the kingdom, the power, and the glory are yours now and forever") were probably not originally part of Matthew's Gospel. They appear in later manuscripts. For that reason, English versions like the ESV and NIV include them only in the margin or as a footnote. I include them here as part of the most-commonly recited version of the prayer.

The Lord's Prayer, on the other hand, reminds us of and reinforces key elements of the primary relational and narrative identities of all believers in Jesus Christ, helping us to look around, backward and forward, as well as upward.

The opening address of the Lord's Prayer could not be more different from the project of expressive individualism. The plural pronoun "our" replaces the focus on you as an individual with the focus on you as part of a group. And the appeal to "our Father in heaven" is a look upward rather than inward. Having God as your Father also relates to our final destiny as God's fully fledged children.

To pray for God's kingdom to come means to pledge allegiance to the rule of the one true God and to locate your life in the narrative of God's unfolding plan. Likewise, to pray, "your will be done, on earth as in heaven," is to live now in the light of your defining destiny as part of that kingdom. It is also an implicit renunciation of both self-assertion and the desire to build your own kingdom.

To ask God to "give us today our daily bread" is an admission that our lives are in God's hands and that he knows how to give good gifts to his children. It is also a call to reject consumerism and materialism. The petition to "forgive us our sins, as we forgive those who sin against us" brings both comfort and a challenge, reminding us of our status as forgiven sinners and calling us to reject taking revenge on those who have wronged us. Finally, the request to "lead us not into temptation, but deliver us from the evil," expresses our inherent weakness and vulnerability, and the extent of our need to look up and be found by God.

The Lord's Prayer closes by turning our gaze unmistakably upward, confessing that the kingdom, power, and glory belong to God alone. Before its final manifestation, the person praying vows that they will not live for their own kingdom, in their own power, or for their own glory. In short, the Lord's Prayer reminds us that our identity is found in Jesus Christ and his coming kingdom. Praying the Lord's Prayer marks out the main lines of the story of which all believers are a part: it reminds us to whom we belong, to what we are committed, what we need, and where we are headed.

If you are not a believer in Christ, I wonder how you have responded to this book. Do you agree that, despite certain benefits, looking only inward to find yourself has serious problems? Do you discern that the self-made self is fragile, faulty, and failing? How about your social identity? Do you find being known and loved by God as his child an attractive way of finding a stable and satisfying sense of self? And what about your story? Do you see the limitations of the secular materialist and social justice narrative identities? Are you drawn to the life story of Jesus Christ? Do you sense a need to look up?

The Lord's Prayer is not just a prayer for those who already belong to Jesus Christ. Earlier in this chapter, I mentioned that the entry point into the life story of Jesus Christ involves putting your faith and trust in him. I know of no better way to start that journey than praying the Lord's Prayer from the heart.

Our Father in heaven,
hallowed be your name,
your kingdom come,
your will be done,
on earth as in heaven.
Give us today our daily bread.
Forgive us our sins
as we forgive those who sin against us.
Lead us not into temptation
but deliver us from evil.
For the kingdom, the power,
and the glory are yours
now and for ever.
Amen.

Questions for Reflection and Discussion

1. If you have an identity as one who is known by God, united to Christ, and part of a new body (the church), what helps you to make that identity your own? If you are new to this identity, what might help you own it more?

2. What could it look like for you to "do the new you"?

General Index

Scripture Index

GIULIANI

THE RISE AND TRAGIC FALL
OF AMERICA'S MAYOR

ANDREW KIRTZMAN

Simon & Schuster Paperbacks

NEW YORK   LONDON   TORONTO
SYDNEY   NEW DELHI

Simon & Schuster Paperbacks
An Imprint of Simon & Schuster, Inc.
1230 Avenue of the Americas
New York, NY 10020

First Simon & Schuster trade paperback edition September 2023

SIMON & SCHUSTER PAPERBACKS and colophon are
registered trademarks of Simon & Schuster, Inc.

For information about special discounts for bulk purchases,
please contact Simon & Schuster Special Sales at 1-866-506-1949
or business@simonandschuster.com.

The Simon & Schuster Speakers Bureau can bring authors to your
live event. For more information or to book an event, contact
the Simon & Schuster Speakers Bureau at 1-866-248-3049
or visit our website at www.simonspeakers.com.

Manufactured in the United States of America

1   3   5   7   9   10   8   6   4   2

Library of Congress Cataloging-in-Publication Data is available on file.

ISBN 978-1-9821-5329-8
ISBN 978-1-9821-5330-4 (pbk)
ISBN 978-1-9821-5331-1 (ebook)

For Kyle

Contents

Author's Note

The title of researcher only begins to describe the role David Holley played in this project. He worked on it daily for over two years, elevating the quality of this book incalculably. His extraordinary reporting and analytical skills are reflected in every page.

I thank him for his talent, dedication, and friendship. Can't wait to do it again.

—Andrew Kirtzman

Preface

I first met Rudy Giuliani over breakfast at a midtown Manhattan hotel in the summer of 1992. After serving as a newspaper reporter for more than a decade, I took the risk of my journalistic career and crossed the Rubicon into television, accepting a job as an on-air political reporter for NY1, Time Warner's twenty-four-hour news channel.

My arrival there coincided with the start of Giuliani's grudge match against the incumbent mayor, David Dinkins, who had beaten him by a slim margin in 1989. At breakfast Giuliani was polite and amiable, spending most of the time laying out his path to victory. The power dynamic was largely in my favor, as he was a losing candidate trying to impress upon me his viability. He was impatient for the rematch to begin.

The station assigned me to cover his campaign—I became its Giuliani reporter. I filed a story about him several nights a week for the next nine years.

Giuliani was enormously accessible at first, cultivating reporters just as he had in his United States attorney days, a strategy that helped make him one of the country's most celebrated crime fighters. He was candid and outspoken, and his campaign organization was still on the improvisational side, with a few close aides running the show, along with a larger-than-life campaign strategist, David Garth, a gruff bulldog of a man who had famously helped elect John

Lindsay and Ed Koch and was intent upon electing his third New York mayor.

Garth was working to soften the lawman's sometimes snarling persona from the 1989 race, filming campaign commercials of Giuliani on park benches talking nostalgically about his love of the New York Yankees as a kid growing up in Brooklyn.

As the campaign revved up, something changed. My phone started blowing up each night after my stories aired, a foul-mouthed Garth hollering at me for what he called biased coverage. The antagonism coming from the campaign grew so intense that it began withholding the candidate's daily schedule from the station, forcing our assignment desk to rely upon other news organizations to keep up with Giuliani's public events. Similar situations were playing out at other news organizations across the city; the campaign decided on a strategic level to keep the city's journalists on the defensive to blunt their perceived bias against a white Republican candidate running to unseat the city's first Black mayor.

I was getting hit by all sides. As I was being targeted by the campaign for being adversarial, I was being eyed by some within the station as being too sympathetic to the candidate. In fact I was growing fascinated by him. The city was in decline and Giuliani was increasingly tapping into the public's anxiety about disorder in the streets and ambivalence about David Dinkins, its often hapless mayor.

Giuliani was severe, brilliant, angry. He had grown as a candidate since his loss four years earlier, immersing himself in issues he had failed to study the first time around, and emerging with innovative proposals. His campaign's attacks on me were annoying on a personal level but intrigued me as a reporter. Dinkins was running a predictable campaign reflecting the career politician he was, with a union endorsement here, a politician's endorsement there. Giuliani was inventing something from scratch.

I was fascinated by his perpetually spinning moral compass.

The Catholic school graduate framed policies not as good or bad but rather as right or wrong. He had a dark, Machiavellian streak, yet managed to wrap his problematic acts in a cloak of righteousness. The Giuliani campaign motto was "One City, One Standard," a thinly veiled accusation that Dinkins was taking sides on the racial battlefield. He claimed the high ground in that war—what could be more fair than a single standard?—but was stirring up resentment among his base of blue-collar white voters, who were already suspicious that Dinkins was showing favoritism to Black communities.

Giuliani won the rematch, and for the next eight years I covered him with continuing astonishment. The new mayor shed his nice-guy act the moment he walked through the doors of City Hall. His daily press conferences were studies in combat, him hurling daily fusillades of insults at reporters, accusing them of asking stupid questions, distorting facts, or acting "jerky"—one of his favorite expressions. He was intent on blowing things up to effect change; every initiative became an over-the-top drama.

When I became a host of the station's nightly political show, *Inside City Hall*, his aides played games to keep us in check. When they approved of our coverage they'd offer up high-level officials as guests. When they perceived a slight—which was constantly—they denied us access to even the most low-level administration figures. Garth continued to call me nightly after every show, mixing insults with flattery. The manipulations were endless.

The mayor seemed to enjoy his parries with my colleagues and me at his daily press conferences, but otherwise kept most of us at arm's length. When I published a book about his mayoralty in 2000, he announced that he wouldn't read it.

The dynamic between us changed on September 11. I experienced that day with him, interviewing him in a sweat as we hurried north on Church Street, away from the destruction. He had narrowly escaped the implosion of the first tower; when the second tower collapsed we ran for our lives.

From that moment on I became part of his 9/11 story. He related his experiences with me in his 9/11 Commission testimony, in his *Time* "Person of the Year" interview, and in his book, *Leadership*. For years following that life-altering day he would break into a smile when we ran into each other, and bring up our experience.

For better or worse, I probably did more to inform the world about Giuliani's performance leading the city through the tragedy than any other person, save Giuliani himself. I wrote a new chapter about our experience for my book about him. I relayed the story of his actions in countless interviews for television, newspapers, radio, and documentaries.

Then I picked up the Giuliani story where it left off. He had flamed out as a presidential candidate, and his business ventures were raking in unimaginable amounts of cash, much of it earned from dubious clients. I wrote stories about it for magazines and newspapers, and spoke critically about his profiteering off of his achievements on 9/11. We returned to our original roles in each other's lives.

In the fall of 2019, I began writing this biography. Giuliani was working as Donald Trump's attorney, causing enormous trouble with his friend, and watching his own reputation go down in flames.

My colleague David Holley and I conducted hundreds of interviews with people who had been close to Giuliani at different points in his life, including his friends, aides, business associates, Trump White House officials, and others. We read through memos, documents, and public schedules from his mayoral archives, which were not available to the public at the time I wrote my first book. We recorded his daily radio shows and podcasts, and watched countless televised interviews going back to his prosecutor days.

Despite the implosion of his once godlike reputation—or, rather, because of it—I remained as fascinated by him as I'd ever been. Unlike Trump, whose character and values never changed in his path to power, Giuliani was leading the latest—perhaps the last—of his many lives. He has fascinated me from the moment I met him to this day.

In October 2019 I reached out to him for an interview. He was a central protagonist in the Ukraine scandal at the time, the catalyst for President Trump's first impeachment, and a growing figure of ridicule over a series of bizarre television interviews. Several days after my first text to him he responded that the timing was off, and that he needed to "work through privileges."

A week later I wrote him again to give him a heads-up about a forthcoming piece that I had written about him for the *Washington Post*. "It's focused on the moral aspect of your leadership, which has always fascinated me," I stated, positing that it had served him better at some times than at others. His response betrayed a deep frustration.

"My moral compass has always been clear to me," he wrote. "Sometimes I act in a politically correct way and I am lionized, and sometimes the same me comes to a different conclusion in good faith than the Democratic Regime of Thought and I am demonized.

"And sometimes you really threaten to uncover their underlying corruption and they try to destroy you."

He was clearly angered by the growing chorus of criticism aimed at him from all sides of the political spectrum. I wrote that I was eager to hear more.

"Maybe, let's see," he wrote me. "Always believe rational discussion can reveal the truth. Others disagree with me and say the major media is so anti-Trump they will say or do anything to take him down.

"I believe this will really hurt America irreparably and hope for some balance, but I see no evidence of it yet."

I followed up with him several times. I sent numerous notes in the ensuing months, as his role in one scandal gave way to another, and public ostracism intensified. I asked to have coffee with him, wished him Merry Christmas, and offered my best wishes when he was hospitalized with Covid. Occasionally he would call me by accident—I'd hear him speaking with people in the background. But he had chosen to halt our conversations.

I haven't heard from him since.

—Andrew Kirtzman

I don't care about my legacy. I'll be dead.
—RUDOLPH WILLIAM LOUIS GIULIANI

Introduction

The circus began moments after the Concorde hit the runway.

Rudy Giuliani and his entourage, so large that it filled the entire aircraft, stepped down a small staircase onto the tarmac at London's Heathrow Airport on the evening of February 12, 2002. The most celebrated leader to emerge from the September 11 attacks arrived for four days of almost incomprehensible hero worship, including his knighting by Queen Elizabeth.

The chairman of British Airways, Rod Eddington, greeted him like a head of state. Camera flashes lit up the scene as he presented the former mayor with a cap and bomber jacket inscribed with Giuliani's name.

"For me it is particularly significant to have this recognition from our good friends, the government of Great Britain," Giuliani told reporters.

The next day, he rode past crowds hanging over barricades, and through the majestic wrought-iron gates of Buckingham Palace. It was just four days since Princess Margaret had passed away, leaving her grief-stricken sister to carry out her duties in her famously stoic manner. Guests were instructed by the palace to wear black out of respect. Giuliani stepped out of his car dressed in a black morning suit with a silver striped tie, white handkerchief, and an American flag lapel pin.

His companion, Judith Nathan, was at his side, sporting a hat with a playful black bow to accent her somber attire. The accessory had triggered an angry blowup at the hotel hours earlier, as turmoil was plaguing the trip behind the scenes. But Nathan and Giuliani had their game faces on, and were clearly pleased to be at the center of the extraordinary pageantry.

Organ music filled the palace's Grand Ballroom as guests were presented to the queen. There were over one hundred people receiving honors, among them his former fire commissioner Tom Von Essen, and police commissioner Bernie Kerik. But only Giuliani would receive an honorary knighthood. An attendant announced the former mayor's arrival in a booming stentorian voice that would have impressed Oliver Cromwell.

"For services after the September 11 tragedy, the most excellent order of the British Empire, to be an honorary knight commander, civil division, the honorable Rudy Giuliani, lately Mayor of New York."

Because he was not a British citizen, Giuliani was not bestowed the knighthood on bended knee on the velvet investiture stool, nor did the queen tap a sword on his shoulder in benediction. But to listen to him afterward, she seemed as taken with him as he was with her. They spent an unusual amount of time chatting ("maybe two minutes," an NPR reporter said), and she smiled as they spoke.

"She congratulated me on my leadership during a very horrible time," Giuliani recalled, "and said it must have been horrid and awful. She said she had watched a lot of what happened and what I had done, and wanted to express her admiration.

"I said I was receiving it on behalf of not myself but all the police officers, firefighters, rescue workers and the heroic people of New York . . . Then she said when we concluded, 'I hope you're having less stress now,' and I told her I was."

The dreamlike quality of the visit continued after the knighting. Giuliani was feted at a banquet by the Lord Mayor of London and driven to 10 Downing Street for a joint press conference with Prime Minister Tony Blair, who lavished praise on him. That night, he was the star of the show at a rollicking benefit for 9/11 families held at Babylon, Sir Richard Branson's restaurant at the Kensington Roof Gardens in London. Giuliani had the crowd roaring with a shtick featuring an exaggerated Brooklyn accent.

Paul McCartney posed for a picture with his arm around Judith, who clutched Giuliani tightly on her other side, with Branson squeezed in. All had their palms out doing a "That's show business" pose. Andrew Lloyd Webber, Simon Cowell, and what seemed like a convention of British entertainment icons mingled around them.

All the adulation was magnified a thousandfold by international television coverage, which Giuliani's team encouraged by feeding live interviews with the former mayor like coal to a fire.

Everyone was game for the hero narrative. "What's important in all of this, of course," reported CNN's Walter Rodgers, "is that the Londoners are seeking information and counsel from Giuliani on how to bring down the city's horrific crime rate. Giuliani's obviously the man to do it."

The extraordinary thing about this heady experience was how unextraordinary it was for Giuliani. The knighthood was just another stop on the circuit for a man well on his way toward becoming one of the world's most celebrated figures.

Six weeks earlier, *Time* named him its "Person of the Year," portraying him on its cover with the headline "Tower of Strength." Three months earlier, he addressed the United Nations General Assembly, an honor usually reserved for heads of state. A week before that, Oprah Winfrey introduced him as "America's Mayor" to twenty thousand cheering fans at a Yankee Stadium 9/11 memorial service. Interspersed between the events were pilgrimages from world leaders, such as France's Jacques Chirac, who dubbed Giuliani "Rudy the Rock."

It was not until two years later that the national 9/11 Commission sorted out Giuliani's role in the disaster, and catalogued a list of catastrophic mistakes by his administration that left hundreds of police and firefighters vulnerable on that awful morning. There was an argument to be made that Giuliani had cost lives on September 11 rather than saved them.

But try telling that to a public that was desperate for someone to take charge on the day that Islamic terrorists hijacked American planes and flew them into skyscrapers and the Pentagon; when office workers trapped in the towers jumped to their deaths to escape the infernos; when two of the tallest buildings on earth imploded. On a day of terrifying anarchy, when civilization itself seemed to be threatened, Rudy Giuliani seemed to be the only person in charge. He was methodical, calm, and compassionate. He radiated competence. That made an indelible impression upon millions of frightened people, from Brooklyn bartenders to the Queen of England.

And he was determined to capitalize on it.

Giuliani had other things on his mind on this winter day beyond the royal costume ceremony. Two months earlier, he had registered a new company with New York's secretary of state named Giuliani Partners that formed the launchpad for his post-9/11 career, a venture that would gross over $100 million in the coming years. One of Hollywood's most powerful agents had negotiated a book deal that would fetch him another $3 million. Washington Speakers Bureau was booking engagements at up to $200,000 per speech.

Such was Giuliani's epic career that he was already a historic figure *before* 9/11. Fifteen years earlier, as United States attorney for the Southern District of Manhattan, he won unprecedented convictions of Mafia leaders and Wall Street traders that elevated him into the pantheon of the most celebrated prosecutors of the twentieth century. Less than a decade later, he was declared "the city's most important politician of his generation" on the front page of the *New*

York Times for spearheading New York's turnaround. He had been so famous so many times that his knighting by the Queen of England was little more than a sugar high.

Two decades later, seventy-six-year-old Rudy Giuliani could still draw a crowd. A battalion of camera crews and dozens of national political reporters encircled him in a parking lot in a dingy industrial section of northeast Philadelphia. It was November 7, 2020, four days after Election Day, and his client, the president of the United States, had lost his reelection bid. Instead of conceding, Donald Trump was gearing up to overturn the results, egged on by Giuliani more than anyone.

If this event had taken place in the 1980s, Giuliani's entrance into the battle over the presidency would have been an almost cinematic moment, with the most admired and feared prosecutor in America joining the side of an embattled president.

But the Rudy Giuliani stepping up to face the media on this dreary morning was a changed man. Far from the monkish ascetic from the U.S. attorney days, years of overindulgence had left him hunched and overweight, a square box of a man with a self-satisfied grin.

He was despised by millions who once celebrated him. He was Trump's enabler, a reckless force behind a scandal that led to one impeachment, and he was well on his way to sparking a second. He was error-prone, forgetful, sloppy, a drinker. His judgment failed him badly. In recent months he was duped by a Soviet agent, made a laughingstock in a major motion picture, and burned by his alignment with crooks and thieves who were now facing prison time. His gaffes on behalf of the president, his eruptions of anger on live television, made him fodder for late-night comedians. His enthusiastic journey into the shadowy recesses of corrupt foreign governments triggered a criminal investigation by the same U.S. Attorney's Office he once led.

Most of his loyal aides had fallen away by now, many of them embarrassed to be associated with their longtime mentor. His lone sidekick was Bernie Kerik, his former police commissioner, who'd served three years in jail for tax fraud and perjury. "I got about five friends left," Giuliani confided to an aide.

It was about to get worse.

Trump alerted the world with a tweet earlier in the day that Giuliani would be holding the press conference at the Four Seasons in Philadelphia. The president soon clarified himself: the location was actually Four Seasons Total Landscaping, a family business on a forlorn street in a near-deserted industrial district. When reporters arrived they were directed to its parking lot, down the street from a porno shop and a crematorium.

This was to be Giuliani's opening salvo as the new general in the war over the election. It turned into more of an exploding cigar.

He made one spurious accusation after another to argue the case that Trump was being robbed of the presidency. He accused Pennsylvania Democrats of stealing Trump's victory in the state. He disparaged the mail-in ballots that had won the election for Joe Biden.

"Those mail-in ballots could have been written the day before by the Democratic Party hacks that were all over the convention center," he said. "What I'm saying to you is, not a single one was inspected as the law required. . . .

"The same thing was done in Georgia, the same thing was done in Michigan, the same thing was done in North Carolina," he said. "It seems to me somebody from the Democratic National Committee sent out a little note that said 'Don't let the Republicans look at the mail-in ballots. At least not in the big Democratic hack cities that we control. . . .'

"Joe Frazier is still voting here," he alleged. "Will Smith's father has voted here twice since he died."

He asked a Republican poll watcher, Daryl Brooks, to step up to the mic and tell the press what he'd witnessed on election night.

"We don't know if people were voting twice or three times," Brooks said. "They did not allow us to see anything."

White House lawyers were appalled at the conspiracy mongering. Virtually everything Giuliani charged was false. Some law firms the White House signed up for the ballot challenge withdrew from the effort after viewing the press conference. Daryl Brooks turned out to be a convicted sex offender. "Giuliani wrecks Trump campaign's well-laid legal plans," *Politico* reported.

As always, the president's lawyer was resolute in his beliefs.

"This will be a very, very strong case," he told reporters. "And I know you won't accept it because of your hateful biases. But let's see if you can try thinking rationally."

That night, Kate McKinnon appeared on *SNL*'s "Weekend Update" segment dressed as Giuliani. She gave him wide, crazy eyes, a sinister voice, and spindly fingers splayed demonically across his chest.

GIULIANI: Did you see my press conference today? It was at the Four Seasons. Fancy!

ANCHOR: Sounds fancy, but it was at a landscaping company called Four Seasons. Was that a mistake?

GIULIANI: What? No.

The anchor, Colin Jost, asked Giuliani what his plans were for the future.

"I will be fine," he said. "I always land on my feet, upside down from the ceiling."

At that, someone threw a head of lettuce in his face.

* * *

What happened to Rudy Giuliani? So many people asked that question when America's Mayor reappeared in 2016 as a leading player in the Trump psychodrama, a tragic figure who'd lost his way.

Some argued that he had changed since the 9/11 days, while others insisted that he was always this way. It usually depended upon whether you admired him or hated him; not a lot of people fell in the middle.

As anyone who had been close to him can tell you, he was not always the sad, pernicious figure who stood in the parking lot of Four Seasons Total Landscaping. Yet his personality didn't change with the flip of a switch either.

His descent was the result of a series of moral compromises made over the years as the temptations of power and money grew. There were any number of opportunities to do the right thing when he did the opposite. By the time he reached an advanced age all those compromises left him an empty vessel, filled with a desire for power and little more. Alcohol, and a toxic marriage, were exacerbating factors, though not the cause.

This is not just a story of Giuliani's rise and fall, but of his many rises and falls. Few figures in American life have climbed so high and fallen so low so many times. The Giuliani story is an opera of triumphs and disasters, downfalls and comebacks. The lives of millions were affected along the way.

Ultimately the measure of a leader is not what he does or even why he does it, but rather how he affects the lives of the people he leads. That answer tracks Giuliani's trajectory. He had titanic accomplishments, far more numerous and consequential than those of most elected officials. He brought a new level of accountability to Wall Street; reversed the fortunes of a declining city; led a nation out of the depths of despair. But his willingness to do the wrong thing for his own benefit caused misery for those who stood in his way, from stockbrokers to Haitian refugees to young Black men on the streets of New York. This giant of American government capitalized on the country's divisions for his own benefit, and nearly brought down a president—twice—all the while wrapping himself in a flag of rectitude.

By the twilight of his career, a man once venerated for his integrity and incorruptibility had evolved into one of the most cynical figures in American life, a latter-day version of himself that would have appalled the young Rudy Giuliani.

In the end he was a captive of his insatiable self-interest. This is the story of the heroism and the havoc that it caused.

CHAPTER I

Morality

A blizzard of red, white, and blue confetti filled the sky above Manhattan's Lower Broadway on the morning of October 19, 1960, all but obscuring the sight of presidential candidate John F. Kennedy and his wife, Jackie, riding atop a slowly moving Chevy convertible inching its way past a million cheering supporters. It was the largest ticker-tape parade down Manhattan's Canyon of Heroes since General Douglas MacArthur was celebrated for his triumphs in the Pacific.

The crowd size was ballooning so quickly that police were growing nervous that things could spin out of control. Jackie worried that the sides of the car were starting to bend from the mobs pressing against it. At Wall Street, Jack rose from his seat to address the throng over a loudspeaker (*"In 1960 the people say yes to progress!"*), but the roar of the crowd, and the wailing of police sirens trying to contain it, drowned out the sound of his voice. The people of the city were giving the Democrat a tumultuous lift into the final stretch of his campaign for president against Vice President Richard Nixon.

Earlier in the morning, three miles away in a far more sedate Brooklyn neighborhood, a pudgy Catholic school senior named Rudy Giuliani decided to commit the almost unheard-of sin of cutting school to get a glimpse of his political hero. Bishop Loughlin Memorial High School was a serious place, where it was close to

11

unthinkable to run afoul of the Christian Brothers who ran it. But Kennedy fever had been sweeping the city's Catholic schools, and Giuliani was set on meeting him.

John Maceli, a classmate in Giuliani's homeroom, wasn't a particularly close friend of his—they had barely socialized—but he was game for the adventure. The two boarded the GG train, a traveling sardine can that transported hordes of men and women around Brooklyn and Queens each morning. Maceli was in it more for the kick of cutting school than for the politics, but Giuliani was jubilant at the prospect of seeing Kennedy in person.

The crush of parade-goers at the subway exit was even more oppressive than the squeeze inside their subway car. The teenagers squirmed their way forward until they reached a wooden police barricade along the route. When the senator's car appeared in the distance, the crowd exploded in cheers. Giuliani joined in the delirium, chanting *"Jack! Jack! Jack!"*

As Kennedy's car neared, Giuliani decided he wanted to meet him. It was a crazy idea—he'd have to leap over the barricade to get to him—and Maceli warned him against it. But Giuliani wasn't asking his permission. Leaving Maceli behind, he climbed over the barrier, jumped into the parade route, and sprinted toward Kennedy's car. Before anyone could stop him, he caught up to the convertible. JFK smiled at a beaming Rudy Giuliani and shook his hand.

Neither his idolizing of Kennedy nor the audacity it took to greet him were surprising to Giuliani's friends. Even in high school he was so focused on politics that they voted him Class Politician. A few years later he told a girlfriend he would be the first Italian Catholic president.

As an adult, he romanticized his upbringing as something close to perfect. He was born on May 28, 1944, in an era so distant that it seemed lifted from a black-and-white newsreel. FDR was president and D-Day was a week away. *Going My Way*, starring Bing Crosby as a young priest battling the old order, was the number one movie in America. Elvis Presley was just nine years old.

He spent his early childhood in East Flatbush, in an immigrant neighborhood once known as Pigtown, where modest cookie-cutter houses teemed with first- and second-generation Americans striving to climb past the bottom rung of the economic ladder. His parents, Harold and Helen, second-generation Italian Americans, lived in Helen's mother's two-family house on Hawthorne Avenue, a red-and-tan brick building a block away from Kings County Hospital, where the poor of Brooklyn gave birth to their children and grieved for their loved ones.

Not everyone went to church, but many banked their hopes for their children upon a good Catholic education. From the moment Giuliani entered kindergarten until the day he enrolled in law school, the majority of his teachers were nuns, priests, and Christian Brothers. Each class began with a prayer (*"Let us remember that we are in the holy presence of God"*).

Bishop Loughlin didn't appear special from the outside. It was a foreboding brown and brick building in a dicey part of Fort Greene; students were warned to remain within a two-block perimeter in order to avoid crossing paths with neighborhood youth gangs. "It always looked like a prison to me," said Maceli. But it was a jewel in the crown of the Brooklyn Diocese, a scholarship institution for the system's high-achieving male students, almost all of them lower-middle-class kids from first- or second-generation Italian and Irish families.

The boys at Loughlin wore jackets and ties, studied hard, and didn't talk back to the Christian Brothers, men in long black robes who took vows of poverty and chastity to devote themselves to their educational mission. "The brothers were real authority figures," said Joseph Centrella, a high school classmate. "If they said do it, we did it."

It's not hard to understand why Giuliani thrived at Loughlin. He was a serious student who enthusiastically embraced the dogmatism that sat at the Catholic institution's core. "If you didn't have his same beliefs, there was something wrong with you," said Edwin Betz, a classmate.

Pale and broad-shouldered, with deep, dark eyes and a jet black pompadour, Giuliani spoke with the gravity of an older man, his words filtered through a soft lisp. His yearbook photo depicts a grave-looking young man with an accusatory expression, an apostolic figure in a dark suit and bow tie. While his friends were dancing to Chubby Checker and the Shirelles, he preferred Puccini to pop stars, and founded the school's opera club. While they were sneaking cigarettes on side streets, he was sitting in half-empty classrooms studying the doctrines of the Catholic faith in the school's catechist club.

The hierarchical structure of the Church, its focus on respect for authority, and its emphasis on morality made an indelible impression upon him, and continued to influence his thinking as he grew older. He took enormous pride that his family members included a firefighter and four cops, the personification of authority.

"I'm going to tell you how I conduct myself," he told a radio audience a half century later. "I try to do what is right. I try to live up to what my father and mother told me: If it's right, you go straight ahead, you square it with God and you square it with the mirror every morning when you're shaving. And I do."

The paradox was that he viewed all of his actions through the lens of morality, even when they were morally questionable. His belief in conformity, and the responsibility of leaders to enforce a moral order, would have huge consequences later in life, as he vaulted from one position of enormous power to another, determined to stamp his view of right and wrong on every situation. The language of morality would govern his words, his politics, his personal life. His belief in the infallibility of his views rendered him impervious to criticism and self-doubt, which would prove to be his greatest asset and his eventual undoing.

It took Giuliani a good amount of moral jujitsu just to get through childhood. He was educated by teachers preaching godliness, while his family members were a motley crew that included police officers, loan sharks, and thugs.

"Three cousins killed within five years," wrote the investigative reporter Wayne Barrett, who uncovered the criminal past of Giuliani's family in 2000. "A mob uncle and cousin. A cop uncle protecting the mob uncle."

The most problematic of all for him was his father.

On April 2, 1934, a milkman named Harold Hall entered an apartment building on East 96th Street in East Harlem, a stop on his rounds to collect payments from tenants. It was the same neighborhood in which Harold Giuliani earned his livelihood as a burglar.

Harold Giuliani's dreams of becoming a professional boxer had long since died, done in by vision problems that had him squinting and blinking through thick eyeglasses. He'd been forced to wear them since the age of six, and was ridiculed mercilessly by his classmates, ripping at his self-esteem and saddling him with a permanent chip on his shoulder. The collapse of his boxing prospects left him with no career to speak of, and no outlet for his anger beyond the satisfactions of criminal activity.

The elder Giuliani and an accomplice were apparently aware of the milkman's schedule. They crouched in wait for Hall behind a dimly lit stairwell on the first floor, awaiting his arrival. He entered the building shortly after noon.

"As I started up the stairway I saw the gun stare me in the face," the milkman later testified. "The man with the gun said to me, 'Get behind the stairs.'" Giuliani's accomplice rifled through Hall's pockets and pulled out $128. "Pull down your pants," the accomplice ordered, and when Hall refused Harold yanked his pants down to his ankles, tied his hands and moved on to his feet. They were interrupted when police rushed into the building. Harold was arrested; his friend got away.

A psychiatrist for the city's Department of Hospitals who was appointed by the court to evaluate Harold found him to be a sad and troubled man—a highly aggressive "personality deviate" immune to other people's feelings. His report characterized Giuliani's aggression as "pathological in nature."

"He is egocentric to an extent where he has failed to consider the feelings and rights of others," the psychiatrist's report stated. "He has developed a sense of inferiority which, in recent years, has become accentuated on account of his prolonged idleness and dependence on his parents."

Harold spent a year and four months behind bars at Sing Sing Correctional Facility in upstate New York. Upon his release he cycled through jobs, spending time as a salesman, and later as a plumber's assistant at the Brooklyn Navy Yard when Rudy, his only child, was born. Hoping to earn more money with a family to support, Harold went to work at Vincent's Restaurant, owned by Rudy's uncle Leo D'Avanzo, serving as muscle for Leo's vast loansharking and gambling operation.

Harold brandished a baseball bat, cracking heads and breaking kneecaps when Leo's debtors ran late on their payments. "People in the neighborhood were terrified of him," a customer at Vincent's told Barrett.

The potential for damage that a violent, pathologically self-centered father can inflict upon a child is incalculable. Rudy Giuliani has steadfastly portrayed his father as a gentle, loving man who taught him his most valuable lessons, from treating people with respect to the importance of paying taxes. "He would say over and over, 'You can't take anything that's not yours. You can't steal. Never lie, never steal,'" he recalled in 2001.

The depiction of a benevolent father was a far cry from the damaged, menacing figure that Harold's psychiatrist diagnosed.

"I had a very healthy relationship with him," Giuliani reflected in a 1987 interview. "In measuring myself against him, I always felt a little inadequate because I couldn't give as freely and easily to people as he did. I felt more resentment about it."

But he also betrayed a glimpse of what life was like growing up with a man of mercurial moods. "He'd give away his last penny to somebody in need," he said. "But he was also crazy, had a crazy personality. He had very strong opinions. If you didn't know him, you could've thought he was very dictatorial.

"He had a terrific sense of humor, but not being perfect, he also had a very bad temper," he said. "He could get angry in a second, then three or four minutes later he'd feel terrible about it."

In contrast to Harold, who led an often directionless existence, alternating between thuggery and menial jobs, Rudy's mother Helen was controlled and focused, with firm ideas about how to raise her son.

She had her job cut out for her handling not only a child but a husband with a history of violence, as well as a hodgepodge of hoodlums in the family and at Harold's bar whom she couldn't get Rudy far enough away from.

She was a fiercely intelligent woman and a voracious reader who graduated high school at sixteen after skipping two grades, dreaming of becoming a teacher. Her father died shortly after, so she instead went to work as a secretary to support her six siblings.

She was a tough, protective woman, and, by all accounts, a strict but loving parent. Growing up, Rudy was deeply attached to her, but worried about disappointing her. "My mom pressured me to succeed," he reflected years later. "But the pressure was heavy."

Andrew Kirtzman

Her expectations were for academic excellence, whereas Rudy was an average student at a young age. When he did come home with A's, he could find her withholding, demanding A-pluses from him. It wasn't surprising that he would grow up to be a driven man.

"She was pretty domineering, pretty strong, and intelligent," said a Giuliani friend. "He wanted to please her very badly."

He was the center of her universe, for all the positives and negatives that can entail. "She was the one who gave him the support that he needed," said Joan D'Avanzo, who married one of Helen's many nephews. "She was the driving force behind Rudy."

For all his troubles, Harold cared enough about his son to extricate Helen and him from his world of loan sharks and broken bones when Rudy was seven years old. Helen's mother sold their East Flatbush home and the family hightailed it out of Brooklyn in 1951, trading bus fumes for the smell of fresh-cut grass in Garden City South, Long Island.

The suburb was a hub of middle-class white flight, an affordable refuge where parents needn't be concerned that their children would encounter people of different races on their way to school. The Giuliani family's street, Euston Road, was lined with maple trees and small, two-bedroom Cape Cods, modest homes for families climbing their way out of the lower-middle class.

Giuliani eventually won a prestigious scholarship to Bishop Loughlin back in Brooklyn. Each year the Brooklyn Diocese admitted just two students from each parish in Brooklyn, Queens, and Long Island to the school, tuition free. Giuliani was one of them, and spent hours each day commuting by train from the lush green fields of Long Island to the garbage-strewn streets of north Brooklyn.

Whatever was taking place inside the Giuliani home motivated Rudy to prove himself to the world with a vengeance. After school let out each day, kids on Euston Road would play stickball in the glow of the setting sun. They were always searching for older kids to play

18

with, but Rudy, looking stiff in the white dress shirt that was part of the Loughlin uniform, waved them off, preferring to sit on his stoop and read. "He pretty much kind of kept to himself," said John Connor, a neighbor.

While he didn't run for class president at Loughlin, he served as campaign manager for someone who did. George Schneider was one of three candidates in the race. The two others, Anthony Shanley and Joseph Centrella, were doing the usual—hanging up posters and banners, buttonholing students in the corridors, promising to push for better food in the lunchroom. Giuliani took it to another level, driving a campaign vehicle through the streets around the school, blaring Schneider's message to students as they emerged bleary-eyed from their subways in the morning.

When the day arrived for the three candidates to speak to the student body, Shanley rose before the audience in the school auditorium and made his case, asserting among other things that his opponents were too busy with other activities to hold office.

Giuliani sprang from his seat in the audience. Speaking in an accusatory tone that he would perfect as an adult, he all but called Shanley a hypocrite, ticking off a list of extracurricular activities that Shanley was involved in. "If you're saying these guys have too many activities, what about yourself?" asked the future prosecutor.

No one had anticipated such a harsh challenge. No one even had a campaign manager until Rudy Giuliani took over George Schneider's effort. Shanley offered a brief rebuttal to Giuliani's accusation and sat down.

Giuliani's tactic may have worked in a limited sense; Shanley lost. But Schneider did, too. Centrella, the third candidate, squeaked by them both.

Not everyone was impressed with Giuliani's aggressive style, but all that certitude made for an enormously self-confident teenager. In his senior year, he accompanied his class on a trip to Washington,

D.C. Late one night at their hotel, they plunged into an epic water fight, racing back and forth to their bathrooms to fill up pitchers and douse one another in the hallways. They started pouring water under bedroom doors.

Word reached the hotel manager. He stormed up to the floor and encountered a disaster scene. Halting the bedlam, he ordered the students to pack their bags and vacate the hotel within ten minutes.

Things got quiet fast. Soaked in water and stopped in their tracks, the students grew panicked that they'd face expulsion from Loughlin. No one could think of a way out of the crisis until Giuliani spoke up.

"He's bluffing," he said. "I'm going to sleep."

His classmates, terrified, followed his lead, went into their rooms, and slept the night. The manager never returned.

It made a big impression on his friends. "He doesn't let fear run his emotions as readily as others would," his friend Peter Powers said. "He has this uncanny knack to know when he's right and to believe in it."

As Giuliani thrived at school, his father was attempting to earn an honest living in the suburbs by turning in his baseball bat for a shovel, taking a $3,500 a year job in 1959 as a laborer at a school district in nearby Lynbrook. He moved the family to a new home, in North Bellmore, and kept the job for almost three years. It ended badly.

In the spring of 1961 he was arrested for allegedly loitering for "immoral purposes" in a public park, according to Jack O'Leary, Rudy's homeroom teacher at Bishop Loughlin and a family friend.

Harold claimed he was doing deep knee bends in the restroom to help with a constipation problem. The police apparently let him off without filing charges. But the trauma of the arrest, evoking a criminal past he had tried to forget, took its toll. According to O'Leary, Harold suffered a nervous breakdown.

Unemployed, he drifted back to Leo's bar in Brooklyn, picking up his bat again to support his family.

"Our glorious political history abounds with payoffs, bribes and bought state legislatures," railed a columnist for the *Quadrangle*, the student newspaper of Manhattan College, in 1964.

"Ars Politica"—the art of politics—was a platform for Rudy Giuliani to condemn the fools, hypocrites, and scoundrels who did not share his politics. "Barry Goldwater was an incompetend [*sic*], confused and sometimes idiotic man," he wrote. New York's mayor Robert Wagner was "selfish, self-centered, power hungry."

The author was young and liberal, but he wrote like an old scold.

"The Republicans will either nominate a 'winner' candidate or a loser," he wrote about the 1964 New York Senate race. "This means they will either pick a candidate they feel has the best chance of winning, or concede the election and put up a patsy who will walk, talk, eat and drink for four months, just to pass the time of day." (Kenneth Keating, the Republican incumbent, went on to lose to Robert F. Kennedy, a Giuliani hero.)

The columnist was happy to sit in judgment of others. There were no shades of gray to him, just black and white, right and wrong. The Kennedys were virtuous; Goldwater was a hack.

It was not surprising to his friends and family members that Giuliani considered becoming a priest after he graduated from Loughlin. He agonized over the prospect with teachers and friends, and visited seminaries to get a sense of what life in the Church would be like. Ultimately, he told the *Christian Science Monitor*, he decided against it due to his "budding interest in the opposite sex."

Instead, he enrolled at an all-male Catholic college.

In a city of sprawling universities with great national footprints, Manhattan College was a modest commuter school, tucked away on a hill overlooking Van Cortlandt Park on the northern edge of the metropolis. Despite its name, it was in the Bronx, and it shared little of its namesake borough's modernity, values, or ambivalence toward religion.

It was a rigorous, conservative institution, with a redbrick chapel whose cupola and crucifix towered above its small, bucolic campus. The neatly groomed young men who attended the college, all dressed in jackets and ties, were taught by Christian Brothers, as at Bishop Loughlin. Giuliani studied in a program that revolved around the Great Books movement, in which the traditional Western canon was used as the basis for teaching history, philosophy, and science. While students at NYU were reading Kurt Vonnegut and James Baldwin, Giuliani and his classmates were studying Plutarch and Thoreau.

There was a seriousness of purpose to the place; it was pure vanilla, but deeply intellectual. "We spent all our time reading," said Bernard McElhone, a classmate. "It produced people who thought they had a grip on how Western civilization developed and maintained itself."

Giuliani enrolled in the fall of 1961 as part of a troika. Peter Powers, Alan Placa, and he attended Bishop Loughlin together, and grew as close as brothers. Giuliani was the pugnacious leader of the pack, while Placa and Powers, soft-spoken and cerebral, were content to play supporting roles in his unending dramas. Powers, a born gentleman, tempered Giuliani's extreme impulses when he ran too hot, a role he would reprise again and again in the years to come. Placa, who would become a priest, was there for Giuliani, and vice versa, when trouble visited them both.

The decade's political and cultural upheavals were coming to a head. JFK had been sworn in as president eight months earlier, promising a new generation of leadership. The KKK was hurling firebombs at Freedom Riders in Alabama. Pope John XXIII declared it was time to "open the windows [of the Church] and let in some fresh air" in advance of Vatican II.

Manhattan College closed its ears to the sounds of change, but even within its conservative confines Giuliani was considered so rigid that people took notice. Some students were starting to chafe at the college's strict dress code, but he wasn't among them. "The whole world was taking off its tie," said McElhone. "Then there was Giuliani, showing up in a suit. He was sort of odd, and standing out in a strange, anachronistic way." The leading fraternity on campus rejected him. "He was too opinionated, too much of a straight arrow," a frat member told the New York *Daily News*.

He worked feverishly for Robert F. Kennedy's campaign for U.S. Senate, traveling to train stations near his Long Island home at 5:30 a.m. Powers was a conservative Republican, and the two of them went at it for hours over dinner at the Giuliani home in Long Island. One night, Powers and his date emerged from a Long Island movie theater to discover that Giuliani and Placa had plastered his car with Kennedy stickers.

Giuliani told anybody who'd listen about his political aspirations. "He told me he wanted to become the first Italian-Catholic President of the United States," Kathy Livermore, his girlfriend at the time, told the *Daily News*. "He liked to say, '*Rudolph William Louis Giuliani III, the first Italian-Catholic President of the United States.*'"

While other classmates partied at off-campus bars, Giuliani begged off. "Down at the bottom of the hill at Manhattan was the Pinewood," recalled Gene Hart, a classmate. "That was a shuffle-board hangout. A few dollars would pass hands when we had two-hour breaks between classes.

"You had to pass the library to get there," he said. "Some people would stop in the library, like Rudy. Some people would keep walking."

And so it went for the four years Rudy Giuliani spent in college, a Kennedy fan leading an Eisenhower lifestyle. On the day JFK was assassinated in November 1963, he was on campus, dressed in an ROTC uniform.

Believers in conformity were not hard to find at Manhattan College, but it struck far more of his contemporaries as odd when Giuliani and Peter Powers entered NYU Law School in 1965. They arrived in Greenwich Village like visitors from another era, two young men in suits and ties venturing outside of the Catholic education bubble for the first time in their lives. They had watched the beat generation come and go from the sidelines, and were just as happy to skip the burgeoning counterculture movement blossoming in the streets outside their classroom buildings.

"The first time I attended a class in which a prayer wasn't said at the beginning of class was my first day at NYU Law School," Giuliani recalled. "I was so confused I began by making the sign of the cross and then I looked around and realized people were staring at me."

He and his sidekick were hopelessly square—it never occurred to them to experiment with marijuana—but not immune to the boozy allure of the bars and clubs that lined Bleecker Street. "It was the greatest fucking place in the world," Powers recalled.

When the two entered as freshmen, security guards were still requiring male students to lift up their sweaters to prove they were wearing ties. But they had stumbled into a cultural revolution. In the span of a year the institution underwent a striking transformation. Gone were the shirts and ties, replaced by jeans and sandals. The place was pulsating with political activism.

A burgeoning number of law students, inspired by the civil rights movement, were taking up public interest law, traveling down South to represent Black citizens suffering under segregationist housing, employment, and election laws, and representing civil rights demonstrators tossed into jail cells after bloody confrontations with local sheriffs. Others were taking community-organizing jobs in underserved neighborhoods, funded by President Johnson's War on Poverty.

Law school student civil rights groups were popping up on campuses around the country, agitating for voting rights, women's rights, and gay rights; many held their annual conventions at NYU Law School.

"It was the most politically organized, sophisticated, activist class you've ever seen," said Sylvia Law, a member of Giuliani and Powers's class. "We had been at the Mississippi Freedom Summit. We had been arrested. . . . There was nothing like this class."

Inside the NYU dorms the music was getting louder, hair was growing longer, and drug use was skyrocketing.

"There was a change in the atmosphere from '65 to '68," said Norman Siegel, an NYU Law student who years later tangled with Giuliani as a civil rights attorney. "You had to be aware of that, and make a conscious choice of whether you were open to that kind of change in your thinking and outlook toward other people."

It was a lot to swallow for two straitlaced Bishop Loughlin boys raised to respect authority. Powers had to step around protesting students blocking his way to class. "I remember sometimes not being able to get down the hall because they'd want to lie down for a half hour or something and protest, which I thought violated my rights," he recalled.

Giuliani, a liberal Democrat, had more sympathy for the cause than his friend, but showed little interest in joining in. "Rudy was never into changing the law," said David Finkelstein, a classmate. "He was into upholding the law."

While his classmates were getting their noses broken by riot police at antiwar protests, his political activism consisted of doing grunt work for Long Island political clubs as a Democratic state committeeman.

The students in his social circle weren't public interest types; they were young men who were on track for jobs at white-shoe law firms, which paid first-year associates $15,000 a year to push paperwork for partners. "What he was known for was that he smoked big stogie cigars, and he played bridge," Law recalled. "He was like a good ol' boy.... By good old boy, I didn't mean to say he was overtly racist or sexist or anything like that. He was just not that interesting."

Giuliani conceded years later that he'd sat out the 1960s. "Just exactly how I missed it, I can't describe," he said. But if he was out of step with its culture, he was discovering his life's mission. A man taught to revere authority was increasingly drawn to the law, a profession whose very purpose was to respect the rules.

"I went in with the mental attitude that if I enjoy it, I'm going to stay," he told a reporter. "If I don't, I'm going to leave, get a master's degree in history or something."

Years later, he made discovering the law sound like he'd entered the priesthood.

"I began to view my love of debate as pointing toward a new calling—to the law, where I could indulge that enthusiasm to the full," he said.

He made the *Law Review* at the end of his freshman year, an appointment that came with on-campus housing. He packed up his things and moved out of his parents' house in Long Island, and immersed himself in his legal studies.

He graduated NYU Law School magna cum laude in 1968, the same year Martin Luther King Jr. and Bobby Kennedy were assassinated. Race riots were ravaging cities across the nation. The outcry against the Vietnam War was dividing parents from their children. Crime and disorder were running rampant in the streets of New York.

Armed with a law degree and a towering self-confidence, Giuliani set upon his mission to impose order on a world spinning out of control.

CHAPTER 2

Justice

The United States Courthouse in Foley Square is an imposing building in Lower Manhattan, with a six-hundred-foot tower that looms ominously over the judges, attorneys, and supporting players in the justice system who pass through its Corinthian pillars each day. It's where Julius and Ethel Rosenberg were sentenced to die, and where the government failed to stifle the publication of the Pentagon Papers.

It's also where generations of federal prosecutors at the U.S. Attorney's Office for New York's Southern District made their careers. And it's where, in the fall of 1974, a young prosecutor named Rudy Giuliani first blazed into the public eye with his quest to take down a corrupt United States congressman.

The politician and the prosecutor were outwardly calm and confident as they faced off in court the morning of October 1, but privately both men knew the enormous stakes at hand in what was one of the biggest corruption cases of the Watergate era.

On the stand was Bertram Podell, the powerful Brooklyn Democratic machine veteran who, at forty-eight, ran his political affairs with a self-certainty common among the untouchable. Opposite him was Giuliani, an assistant U.S. attorney on the rise. It was already an epic event—a congressman facing charges of conspiracy, bribery, and conflict of interest—when Giuliani rose just after 10 a.m. to cross-examine him.

The questioning quickly became a master class in breaking down a steely opponent with a thousand cuts. Giuliani laid out his case that Podell had accepted a total of $41,350 from Florida Atlantic Airlines in exchange for helping to secure a new route to the Bahamas—a U.S. congressman secretly operating as their representative. He grilled Podell about praising the airline in a meeting with the Bahamian minister of transport.

"Did you introduce yourself as Congressman Podell?" Giuliani asked.

Yes, Podell said.

"You told him it was a good, reliable company?" Giuliani continued. Yes again.

"Did you tell him that you were being paid to say that, being paid $1,000 to say that?"

"I don't think I was being paid to say that, Mr. Giuliani," Podell retorted. "That's a very unfair thing for you to say."

All the trademarks of Giuliani's pugnacious style were on display in court that day: the provocations, the relentlessness, the determination to get into the head and under the skin of his opponents—to own the adversary. But fueling his performance was a deeper conviction: a righteousness aimed at those he saw as frauds and liars, as unworthy pretenders to high government office, as enemies of the people who believed, as he did, that corruption and grifters had to be expunged from public service. That righteousness was Giuliani's North Star, a source of strength, and, ultimately, a fatal flaw.

Podell was by no means an easy mark, his conviction hardly a sure thing for the legions of New Yorkers who were following the case against the prominent politician. A Navy veteran who had volunteered for World War II before Giuliani was even born, he was so popular he had not lost an election in twenty years. And from his powerful perch, as soon as the criminal charges hit the newspapers, he launched a public damage control operation. He blasted the U.S. Attorney's Office as a puppet of President Nixon, claiming prosecutors were going after him to deflect from the mushrooming Watergate scandal. He declared it a "badge of honor to be known as public enemy number one of the most corrupt administration in the 200-year history of this nation."

Podell's lawyers called a parade of federal officials as character witnesses, including fellow congressman Ed Koch, who testified that his colleague's reputation for truthfulness and honesty was "excellent." Koch was then cross-examined by Giuliani: two future leaders of New York City, one grilling the other. Giuliani got Koch to admit under oath that this was not the first time he'd vouched for the integrity of a corrupt lawmaker.

Podell had long insisted he'd done nothing wrong, claiming he had never touched any dirty money. But in the third week of the corruption trial, as the cross-examination began, he met his match.

Giuliani was already a rising star in the U.S. Attorney's Office. He was promoted to lead the Official Corruption unit the very same month Podell was indicted. In his discount department store suits and awkwardly parted mop of dark hair, he cut a sharp contrast to the polished, smooth-talking congressman. But the young prosecutor was hungry; he'd been preparing for weeks using his colleague Michael Mukasey as a stand-in for Podell in practice sessions. Giuliani "kept telling himself how bad it was what this guy had done, to psych himself up," Peter Powers told the *Washington Post*. When he stood up in the courtroom to cross-examine Podell, he was ready.

The inquisition went on for hours, with Judge Robert Carter often interjecting to referee, telling the congressman to quit being evasive and ordering Giuliani to cool it when he went over the top. At one point, Giuliani slammed a book on a table, prompting exclamations of "Objection!" from Podell's attorneys.

"No dramatics, Mr. Giuliani," the judge admonished.

But Giuliani was withering, and the congressman's composure began to crack. Podell's cool dissolved completely when Giuliani claimed a $29,000 campaign contribution was actually a bribe from the airline to land that new route to the Bahamas.

"That's a lie!" Podell yelled.

"Who's telling the lie, Congressman?" Giuliani retorted.

"You are, sir," Podell said, incensed. "You are."

Giuliani then produced the $29,000 check from an executive at the airline. "Didn't he hand you a blank check and didn't you write in the name of the payee?" Giuliani asked.

"It looks like my handwriting," Podell admitted.

"It sure does," Giuliani said.

The *New York Times* described the young prosecutor as "a boxer closing in on a battered opponent." Sitting at the prosecution's table, Mukasey, Giuliani's co-counsel, said Podell was so shaken at one point that he pressed his thumb on the lens of his glasses hard enough to pop it out of the frame.

Shortly after 1 p.m., Judge Carter recessed the court for lunch, after which the cross-examination was scheduled to resume. It didn't happen. Podell's lawyers walked up to Giuliani as he was eating a sandwich. They wanted to discuss a plea, and three hours later, they had a deal.

When court went back in session, Podell withdrew his not guilty plea and copped to lesser conflict of interest charges. Gone was the swagger of earlier that morning. In a whisper, the congressman admitted to "knowingly and intentionally" representing the airline, though he said he didn't know he was breaking the law.

The congressman was fined and sentenced to six months in

prison. His political career was over. But Rudy Giuliani's ascent was just beginning.

In retrospect it made perfect sense that the two occupations Giuliani chose between as a young man were priest and prosecutor. Both held the allure of judging right from wrong, and enforcing codes of behavior. Strictly speaking, a priest enforces moral codes and a prosecutor legal ones, but in his case the lines blurred. "It gives you a chance to do only what's right," he said of a prosecutor's job. Yet much of what he did wasn't moral at all.

His version of his rise as a prosecutor is a cinematic tale of a once-in-a-generation talent driven to defeat the forces of criminality. It comes with its own dramatic soundtrack, a building drumbeat tracking his march, with a triumphant crescendo. The reality bears more than a passing resemblance: he was the real deal, an extraordinarily gifted lawyer and born leader who conducted a historic crusade to rid his city of the rot at its core. But the full story also includes elements of cruelty, self-aggrandizement, and hypocrisy. In his march to success, he revealed himself a damaged man.

In 1967, a strong record at New York University Law School landed the young Kennedy fan a $150 per week internship at Richard Nixon's law firm, Nixon, Mudge, Rose, Guthrie, Alexander & Mitchell. He was twenty-three and one of thirteen interns in the office. "He seemed not to know his way around," said Frederick Lowther, a fellow intern.

When Nixon, accompanied by his future attorney general, John Mitchell, sat down with the group—"What do you guys want to talk about?"—some peppered him with questions about Vietnam, and whether the U.S. should mine the major port of Haiphong Harbor. Giuliani held back, and didn't say much. "His interest in politics seemed to be local," Lowther said.

Peter King, another intern and a future congressman, found him "shy and too nice a guy" at first, but his opinion changed. In a lunchtime conversation, another intern praised New York's former Republican senator, Kenneth Keating. *"You're a fucking liar!"* Giuliani shouted. *"He's a drunk!"*

King watched uncomfortably as the barrage of attacks continued. Arguing politics with Giuliani "was as though I had attacked his religion. . . . Suddenly, he'd be yelling and his eyes were popping out."

When it came time to offer jobs to the interns, Nixon's law firm passed on him.

His fortunes would change the next year, thanks to a man who became his mentor, and a woman who became his wife.

The story of Rudy Giuliani and Regina Peruggi begins in the lazy summertime months of their teenage years in the tiny Long Island hamlet of Sound Beach, named for its proximity to the mighty Long Island Sound.

Evangelina Giuliani, Rudy's paternal grandmother, rented a bungalow each summer, bringing the tribes of the extended family together for weekend gatherings on the beach, where conversations mixed with the squealing of seagulls, and a salty mist breezed off the ocean.

Gina and Rudy were second cousins; Rudy's father, Harold, and Gina's father, Salvatore, were first cousins. Her family had a house close to Evangelina's, and were regulars at the weekend feasts Evangelina organized.

Gina could be quiet around new people, but to her friends and family she was funny, warm, and intelligent; she grew up to become a college president.

The two cousins hit it off at an early age—Rudy took her to his high school junior prom, with their fathers serving as chaperones.

When he entered Manhattan College, he'd swing by her house after class. "He worshipped her," recalled one of her closest friends, Pat Rufino, who spent weekends at the Sound Beach family get-togethers. "Here's this guy, almost three or four times a week, stopping by to hang out with a bunch of high school kids . . . he had a crush on her. Big time."

Rudy was pale and disciplined, an old soul in a young man's body whose idea of fun was listening to Verdi in his living room. But there was an intensity to him that many found compelling. "By the time I met him when I was in high school and he was in college he already had a circle of people following him around," said Rufino. "He was very, very smart, and very articulate. People were very drawn to him. He was always the leader.

"I remember thinking he was going to eventually be president when I was fifteen years old," she recalled. "There was something about him that made you think he was going to be a big deal."

His romance with Peruggi didn't truly blossom until his final year at NYU. She was coming off a broken engagement and turned to her cousin. "They were dating two minutes later," Rufino said. "It was kind of like he was standing there waiting."

The couple had an easy chemistry; they were smart and confident, and ran with a group of close friends. "We all drank like crazy in college and in our twenties," said Rufino. "I mean really it was insane."

They were married on October 26, 1968, at St. Philip Neri Church in the Bronx with more than a hundred friends and family as witnesses. Giuliani's old Bishop Loughlin pal Alan Placa was best man, and Rufino was Peruggi's maid of honor. After the vows, everyone drove to a beach club for the reception, and the newlyweds had their first dance to Frank Sinatra's "All the Way."

Soon after their Virgin Islands honeymoon, he passed the bar exam. It was November 5, 1968—Election Day. Richard Nixon won the White House and Rudy Giuliani became a lawyer.

The couple moved into a tiny walk-up apartment on East 58th Street in Manhattan, right off tony Sutton Place. Giuliani landed a clerkship, and Gina worked as a drug counselor at a state jail. One Saturday every month, friends came over and Giuliani played opera music for them.

Peruggi learned a lot more about her new husband's passions as his career took off.

He was clerking for Judge Lloyd MacMahon of the Federal District Court in Manhattan. A former mob-busting prosecutor, he had a fierce reputation; even his friends were terrified of arguing cases in his courtroom. "He was offended and upset when lawyers were not prepared," Giuliani recalled. "There was no fooling him."

MacMahon told his clerks that every hour in court required four hours of rehearsals and role-playing, a roadmap Giuliani would follow when preparing to eviscerate Bertram Podell on the stand.

Giuliani and Jon Sale, a fellow clerk, spent hours in court watching the lawyers of the U.S. Attorney's Office in action like rapt theatergoers, "seeing how cool it was and how interesting it was and what great lawyers most of them were," Sale recalled. Giuliani discovered his true calling as a prosecutor.

MacMahon, famously hard to impress, was taken with Giuliani. "He said from the beginning that Rudy was the best law clerk he ever had," Sale recalled. The judge set about opening doors for his young protégé in ways that would send Giuliani's career into orbit.

He also used his clout to keep one door shut, and may have saved his life. Giuliani won student deferments through college and law school, but became eligible for the Vietnam War draft when he graduated NYU. Eager to avoid serving, he applied for an occupational deferment, but was rejected because deferments were typically reserved for positions the government considered essential. Law clerk wasn't one of them.

He was fortunate enough to have found a powerful federal judge as his mentor, however, and when MacMahon made the case himself the draft board saw the light. Thanks to MacMahon's intervention, the government declared Giuliani too indispensable to serve, and spared him from fighting in a war that killed almost sixty thousand Americans.

The combat that interested Giuliani took place in courtrooms. Armed with a recommendation from MacMahon, he was hired as an assistant U.S. attorney in Manhattan's Southern District. Giuliani was just twenty-six years old, and a federal prosecutor.

In his first year as an assistant U.S. attorney, he started off small, working on one case involving a stabbing, and another involving an illegal still, but moved up to work on explosive police corruption cases. He spent endless hours pumping sources for information on dirty cops, and proved so adept at the job that a movie and a book—*Prince of the City*—portrayed his partnership with a police informant, Bob Leuci.

His free time with Gina evaporated. "He used to work really, really late," said Rufino. "But half of the time he was working late he was screwing around with people in his office."

Giuliani's wife found another woman's jewelry in the house. Women she didn't recognize rang their doorbell, looking for him.

"He cheated on her pretty much the whole time they were married," Rufino said. "Obvious stuff that was really tacky."

Her husband denied to her that he was cheating, telling her it was all in her head—"gaslighting her," said Rufino. "He was emotionally and mentally terribly destructive."

Leuci, Giuliani's star informant, has described the cheating as flagrant. "Rudy Giuliani preferred WASPy women, blondes," he said. "He hit on everybody, hit on them all, all the time. He bounced around the Village. He was pretty wild."

The couple separated, only to reunite a short time later when a new opportunity presented itself to the ascendent prosecutor.

After five successful years as an assistant U.S. attorney—fresh off his victory in the Podell trial—Giuliani was connected by Mac-Mahon to the incoming U.S. deputy attorney general, Harold "Ace" Tyler, who was joining Gerald Ford's administration as the second most powerful official in the Justice Department. He hired Giuliani as his aide.

Gina and he moved to D.C. She found them a gracious high-rise apartment, where they hosted parties packed with top Justice Department officials. It was a proud moment in Giuliani's life; he liked to show friends his office, located in the same building where Bobby Kennedy once presided. On the wall behind his desk was a framed newspaper article reporting Podell's guilty plea.

But between his workaholic tendencies and his philandering, the couple's relationship deteriorated beyond repair. When Jimmy Carter was elected president in 1976, two years into their time in D.C., Tyler moved to New York to become a partner in a private law firm and brought Giuliani with him. The marriage didn't survive.

Giuliani's patrons at the Justice Department had been Republicans, and he began a political migration from his liberal roots, first declaring himself an independent, then completing his evolution in 1980, when he changed his registration to Republican one month after Ronald Reagan won the presidency. The explanation he offered was that the Democratic Party had swung too far to the left.

Two months after Reagan's election, he was tapped for a big job: associate attorney general, the third most powerful position at the Justice Department. Just thirty-six years old, he became the youngest associate attorney general in American history.

Two days before Rudy's confirmation, Harold Giuliani died of prostate cancer. Deep in mourning, he drove around his old Brooklyn neighborhood with Judge MacMahon and a close friend from his days at the U.S. Attorney's Office, pointing out landmarks from his youth. He later said it was the most painful event of his life.

For the rest of his days as a public figure, Giuliani invoked his father's name frequently, always quoting his sage advice. "My father used to say, 'The first thing that's important—you respect me,'" he recalled. "'The rest you'll understand.'"

Raised by a violent ex-con and exposed to thugs and mobsters growing up, Rudy was working at the pinnacle of the government criminal justice system. If it pained him to keep the details of his strange childhood secret, he didn't let on. All his friends and associates saw was a relentlessly ambitious figure, driven by some inner radar that set him on a perpetual search-and-destroy mission against his obstacles and adversaries.

Peter Powers liked to say that his best friend lacked a fear gene. It was apparent when Giuliani jumped barricades to shake a president's hand; slept soundly after helping to wreck a hotel floor; or cheated on his wife.

Triumphing over fear was a guiding principle to him. "My father was one of my heroes because he had such a tremendous ability to control—overcome—fear," he once recalled.

A powerful man bereft of self-doubt can accomplish great things or cause tremendous damage. As he rose to prominence, Giuliani increasingly demonstrated his capacity for both, with far more people impacted than just a long-suffering wife.

In the autumn of 1981, sixty-seven Haitian refugees jammed into a thirty-foot boat, a vessel so ramshackle that its only waterproofing was a coat of mud. The conditions on their island were intolerable; Haiti was the poorest country in the Western Hemisphere, with an average income of $250.

For decades, the country had been ruled by a father-son team of tyrants: first François "Papa Doc" Duvalier and then his son, Jean-Claude, known as "Baby Doc." Both declared themselves presidents for life, using the brutal secret police known as the Tontons Macoutes to crush dissent and spread terror throughout the country. Free and fair elections were scrapped; journalists were detained and tortured. Tens of thousands were killed. The Haitians who sought refuge in America pleaded that they were running for their lives.

The passengers on the overcrowded vessel had a run of luck at first, fleeing without harm where others had been shot and killed by Haitian police firing from the mainland to prevent their escape. They had almost made it to shore when their boat encountered rough waters just a mile off of Miami. It capsized, throwing them overboard. Nineteen men and fourteen women, one of them pregnant, drowned.

Horrifying stories such as these were becoming increasingly common. In 1980 alone, 25,000 Haitian refugees arrived on the shores of South Florida, a small percentage of the 150,000 asylum seekers, most of them Cuban, arriving in the Mariel Boatlift. The Reagan administration looked favorably upon the Cuban refugees, largely granting them asylum to escape the regime of Fidel Castro, who was considered an enemy by the president and his Cuban American supporters.

The Haitians were another story: Duvalier had made friends with the administration, despite the widespread corruption and brutality of his regime. Granting him his wish, Reagan declared Haitians economic, not political, refugees and ordered them detained and returned to their home country, where they faced brutal consequences.

The man chosen to enforce his order was Rudy Giuliani.

In April 1982, he traveled to Haiti and met with Baby Doc Duvalier as well as the feared Tontons Macoutes. The prosecutor swallowed whole his assurance that there was no campaign of political persecution taking place. "There is not a problem, a major problem, a systematic problem of political repression in Haiti," Giuliani testified at a subsequent court hearing in Miami. "A situation of political repression does not exist, at least in general, in Haiti."

He callously dismissed the heart-wrenching images Americans were seeing of desperate refugees being held in American detention camps. Television news programs "would show these pathetic people sort of holding hands and kissing each other, and then say that this man and wife were separated by this cruel, vicious government," he said. "These people don't come over with marriage certificates. And they keep claiming that different people are their wives."

He injected alarming racial stereotypes into the debate. "If you let the men into the women's camps, they go around raping them," he insisted, making no such allegations against the Cubans whom the administration embraced.

Giuliani had once marveled that becoming a prosecutor allowed him to do "only what's right," but chose career success over protecting the lives of thousands of terrified refugees. It was a stance that earned him widespread scorn, but deep gratitude from the administration. His loyalty to the president was absolute. Ronald Reagan would not be the last to experience it.

By February 1982, Donna Hanover, an anchor at WCKT-TV in Miami, was realizing her ambitions in the television news business after years toiling in some decidedly unglamorous places. Compared to her previous gigs in Utica, Columbus, and Pittsburgh, Miami was paradise, just one career rung away from New York, the most prestigious media market of them all.

She was blond-haired and green-eyed, with the statuesque bearing and polite, frozen smile of a television hostess. A Justice Department colleague of Rudy Giuliani's who met her at a wedding in Tennessee set the two of them up on a blind date.

Giuliani's work enforcing the administration's immigration policies required him to travel to Miami frequently; he had his assistant give Hanover a call.

"His secretary called me up and said, 'I understand you want to interview Mr. Giuliani,'" Hanover recalled. "And I said, 'Well, yes. That's fine.'" She scolded him later on. "You should really get your personal relations and your press relations straightened out," she said.

The two had a long, romantic dinner—Giuliani said he fell in love with her "immediately"—and she interviewed him the next day.

It took just three weeks for Giuliani to tell Hanover he loved her. On the sixth week he proposed. They were at Disney World, of all places, at a conference for prosecutors. She said yes, quit her job, and moved to Washington.

Giuliani was still married to Peruggi, who had moved on with her life. The two divorced at the end of the year, but that would not be the end of their story. Hanover and her fiancé would have to wait as Giuliani tied up a loose end.

At the beginning of 1983, John Martin Jr., the U.S. attorney for the Southern District of New York, informed the Reagan Justice Department that he intended to resign. Giuliani quickly became the frontrunner to replace him.

As associate attorney general supervising all the U.S. attorneys across the country, becoming a U.S. attorney was technically a step down. But by doing so, Giuliani would be giving up a bureaucratic position to head the most prestigious prosecutor's office in the nation in the largest media market in the country. It was an opportunity to claim center stage.

He was also privy to cases brewing behind the scenes that had the potential to make a star of whoever took the job.

On October 14, 1982, President Reagan took the short trip from the White House to the Department of Justice's Great Hall to deliver a landmark speech on crime. Much of the press coverage focused on his war on drugs, but his remarks about organized crime represented a turning point in the generations-long battle between the feds and the Mafia.

"For many years, we have tolerated in America, not just in the illegal and highly dangerous drug traffic but in many other areas, a syndicate of organized criminals whose power is now reaching unparalleled heights," Reagan said, standing between enormous aluminum-clad statues of a woman in a toga and a half-naked man.

"It controls corrupt union locals; it runs burglary rings, fences for stolen goods, holds a virtual monopoly on the heroin trade; it thrives on illegal gambling, pornography, gun-running, car theft, arson and a host of other illegal activities. . . .

"The time has come to cripple the power of the mob in America."

The Mafia was deeply embedded into the fabric of urban America, terrorizing businesses and labor unions, driving up prices in the construction industry, selling narcotics to America's teenagers. Reagan's speech was a call to bear down on the mob with the full weight of U.S. law enforcement.

Hundreds of FBI agents and prosecutors were deployed to field offices across the nation to bolster Reagan's war. They were armed with powerful new laws loosening wiretapping restrictions and enabling prosecutors to pursue entire mob families rather than just individual members.

John Martin's Southern District had been building cases against the five Mafia families for years. They were bombshell cases that were almost baked, making whomever succeeded him a lucky man.

Giuliani accepted the Southern District position and was sworn in on June 3, 1983, by Judge MacMahon. Within two years, Martin's role in the Mafia cases would be all but forgotten. New York had a new sheriff, and he was eager to let people know it.

"I think we can end traditional organized crime," Giuliani predicted boldly to the *New York Times* a month after his arrival. He portrayed the fight against the mob as a personal one, an effort to avenge the honor of his fellow Italian Americans, who had long suffered from the stigma the Mafia had given them. The media ate it up.

While he was eager to personify the war on the mob, the cases against the Five Families had been largely constructed by the time he arrived—they weren't his. He solved that problem before he even walked through the doors of his new office.

As Giuliani tells the story, he experienced a eureka moment that changed crime-fighting history while still at the Justice Department. It happened, he said, while watching a *60 Minutes* interview with mob boss Joseph Bonanno, who had inexplicably decided to publish his memoirs.

In his book, Bonanno described the inner workings of "the Commission," a ruling council comprised of the bosses of all Five Families.

According to Giuliani, he realized that instead of going after the Five Families individually, it would be better to go after them as a single, corrupt organization, an audacious move that, if successful, could decapitate the mob with a single case.

"I dreamed up the tactic of using the Federal Racketeer Influenced and Corrupt Organizations Act (known to *Sopranos* fans by its acronym 'RICO') to prosecute the Mafia leadership for being itself a 'corrupt enterprise,'" Giuliani wrote in his book *Leadership*.

"I realized that Bonanno's description of how the families were organized provided a roadmap of precisely what the RICO statute was designed to combat. As soon as I became the U.S. Attorney I was able to hoist Bonanno by his literary petard."

There are strong arguments that Giuliani distorted the truth to make himself the hero of what came next. Ron Goldstock, director of the State Organized Crime Task Force, has described a meeting two months after the new U.S. attorney arrived in New York in which it was he who proposed using the RICO statutes against the Five Families to Giuliani, instead of the other way around.

Goldstock said he told Giuliani that law enforcement wiretaps were revealing that the families were gathering regularly, *Godfather*-style, to set ground rules and resolve disputes. He said Giuliani grew excited that he could take down organized crime in one fell swoop. Giuliani has denied Goldstock's version of events.

What is indisputable is that the new U.S. attorney attacked the case with a vengeance over the following months. There was no need to start a new investigation; the evidence had already been gathered for the existing cases. All that was necessary was to wade through hundreds of hours of wiretapped conversation to locate specific references to the Commission.

Energized, Giuliani traveled to Washington to brief William French Smith, the attorney general, about the Commission concept, and request jurisdiction over narcotics enforcement in the region, a slap in the face to the Southern District's rivals at the Eastern District offices in Brooklyn. The attorney general, who had worked closely with Giuliani in Washington, granted him jurisdiction, and threw in funding and personnel. By 1984, 350 FBI agents and one hundred police detectives were working on mob cases.

The decision to scramble the cases against the Five Families after years of preparation and shift the focus to the Commission wasn't universally embraced.

Walter Mack, the irascible chief of the Southern District's Organized Crime Unit, was a graduate of Harvard and Columbia Law School, and a former Marine in the Vietnam War. He once said that the closest adrenaline rush to combat was arguing a criminal trial as a prosecutor. "It causes you to focus," he said.

Mack had nurtured the five mob family cases over many years; the Commission case was threatening to destroy his work. "It completely stripped off from all of those family investigations the very best evidence at the very top," he said. "There was Rudy grandstanding himself as this great organized crime guy. . . . It was just really more of a selfish act that had risks to it."

Mack was infuriated that Giuliani was taking credit for work done under John Martin, and appalled by his insatiable need for attention. The grand indictment press conference was becoming a staple of the evening news. When prosecutors charged eight men with planning to sell weapons to Iran and the Irish Republican Army, he held a press conference and provided machine guns as props. When the feds busted heroin rings doing business in five cities, it was Giuliani who announced it.

Then there was "Federal Day" in September, an initiative that flooded a neighborhood with hundreds of FBI agents and produced mass arrests of low-level drug dealers. Their crimes were traditionally the province of local, not federal, prosecutors, and it wasn't clear what good a single day of activity by the feds each year would accomplish. But it made Giuliani seem like a champion of the people.

The high-profile antics were a marked contrast to Martin's low-profile style, and struck traditionalists as unseemly. But the media was enchanted.

"A Real-Life Perry Mason," ran a *Newsweek* headline. "Giuliani sees himself as a crime fighter, and he believes that he can do that best in New York," it reported. "That may be, but some of his associates say that the politically savvy Giuliani might also use his position at center stage to build up a base from which to run for office."

His hunger for press became something of a running joke among his Southern District subordinates. But Mack wasn't in a laughing mood; he took his concerns about the media offensive to the new boss. Not long afterward, a member of Giuliani's inner circle—derisively known around the office as the "YesRudis"—informed him that Giuliani was unhappy. "He thinks you're not on the team," he said.

After years spent working on the cases Giuliani was borrowing from, Mack was demoted. "It pissed the shit out of me," he said.

But there was also a sense of excitement in the office; Giuliani was spearheading groundbreaking cases, and drawing national—even international—attention to them. For all his showboating, many there considered him an inspiring leader.

"He was just always there, totally into the law," said Daniel Richman, a prosecutor under Giuliani. "At no time did you see any throwing of weight around or anything other than a clear analytic focus that had integrity at its core."

With the media focused on the Southern District as never before, Giuliani took a risk near the end of the year that could have blown up in his face: obtaining a secret annulment of his marriage to Peruggi. He wanted to marry Donna Hanover in a Catholic ceremony, but his divorce from Peruggi prohibited it. It fell upon his boyhood friend Alan Placa, a priest and a law school grad, to figure out how to solve the problem.

Placa learned from research that the Church required special dispensation for second cousins to marry; Rudy and Gina had never obtained it. In order to invalidate his marriage to Peruggi, Giuliani claimed that he and his wife thought they were *third* cousins. Family members on both sides have disputed that bitterly, contending that the couple knew all along how they were related. But the Church granted Giuliani's wish, ruled their marriage improper, and wiped it off the books.

Peruggi was shocked when she learned of his plans. "She basically felt like she had been betrayed," said Pat Rufino.

Giuliani cheated on Peruggi throughout their marriage, proposed to another woman before they were divorced, and moved to annul their union without her knowledge. It was a remarkable way to treat a wife. Rudy and Donna tied the knot on April 15, 1984.

* * *

In late February 1985, FBI agents fanned out across New York to arrest the leaders of New York's five organized crime families. They were indicted on fifteen counts of racketeering, an epic moment in the history of the government's war on organized crime. They were five aging Italian men at the top of the Genovese, Gambino, Lucchese, Colombo, and Bonanno crime families, men with names like "Fat Tony" Salerno, "Tony Ducks" Corallo, and "Big Paul" Castellano.

Three hundred other alleged organized figures had already been indicted over the previous two years, including twenty-four members of the Gambino crime family arrested in one fell swoop on homicide and racketeering charges, in a case spearheaded by Walter Mack. But that was all a prelude to the announcement that Giuliani made at a packed news conference, attended by over a hundred members of the media.

He entered a windowless room filled with television crews, photographers, and reporters. He was accompanied by a group of top law enforcement officials.

"This is a bad day, probably the worst ever, for the Mafia," he said. "This case charges more Mafia bosses in one indictment than ever before," he added, branding the defendants the mob's "ruling council." FBI director William Webster, who flew in for the event, called the indictments "historic."

It was a watershed moment for Giuliani, and the start of an extraordinary run. One twelve-day period the following year would capture the extraordinary sweep of his efforts to combat organized crime, malfeasance on Wall Street, and government corruption.

On November 19, 1986, a jury found four mob bosses and several of their associates in the Commission case guilty; many received one-hundred-year sentences. The fifth mob leader, Paul Castellano, leader of the Gambino crime family, was murdered before he got to trial; three men in trench coats working for his own organization riddled him with bullets as he stepped out of a limousine outside Sparks Steak House in midtown Manhattan.

Seven days later, Giuliani won the conviction of Stanley Friedman, the enormously powerful Bronx Democratic Party leader, climaxing a crusade to expose a vast municipal corruption scandal that had riveted the city. Giuliani tried the case himself, forfeiting the opportunity to try the Commission case because Friedman's was the more complex trial of the two—a high-stakes decision. But the risk paid off; the conviction positioned him for a potential mayoral run in 1989.

The same two-week period saw a turning point moment on Wall Street. Giuliani announced that Ivan Boesky, an icon of a delirious era in the financial sector, had agreed to plead guilty to a criminal charge and pay a $100 million fine for insider trading. Giuliani was the skunk at the party, ruining the fun with a relentless assault on corruption in the market. His successful pursuit of Boesky led to even bigger triumphs: the arrest and conviction of Michael Milken, the wildly successful king of junk bonds, and the subsequent collapse of Drexel Burnham Lambert, the investment powerhouse that epitomized the industry's free-for-all culture.

His remarkable successes—he seemed to present the public with the scalp of a new titan every week—cemented his image as a fearless crusader against the corruption and entitlement of New York's political, financial, and social elites.

"Every era has a law-enforcement figure or two who captures the public imagination, who turns the job of police officer or prosecutor into 'crime buster' and makes the fight against evil appear to be a personal vendetta," the *New York Times* proclaimed in June 1985.

The article described a starstruck woman gushing over him in an elevator ride (*"You're the one in the papers—with the mob!"*) and tabulated his media appearances (two television appearances that week, five the week before). It featured blistering criticism of his pursuit of media attention, and in particular his press conferences, derided as "unethical," "prejudicial," and "unbelievable" by the administrator of the New York State Commission on Judicial Conduct.

Giuliani contended that his public shaming of his prosecutorial targets served a purpose. "It's very hard to convince them that I do it because I feel a government office should be open, and I have an obligation to maximize public education and public knowledge," he said, though that didn't explain why he posed "playfully" in his bed with Donna for a magazine profile.

"He gets a bad rap for talking in length with the press, but he's like that with everybody," Hanover told the reporter. "He'll stay up talking for hours with friends; he's interested in everything. That's what I like about him. I like smart men. I've always found that very sexy."

Her husband's addiction to the media, and television in particular, helped to magnify his accomplishments. He was a master interview, crisp and disciplined, strategic in his comments, and cool under pressure.

The attorneys on the other side of the cases he was publicizing weren't amused. Giuliani's press conferences were models of character assassination, painting his targets as guilty long before trial. His opponents howled that he was tainting the jury pool.

A case in point was the prosecution of Bess Myerson, a front-page circus of a case that became known as the "Bess Mess." Giuliani was its ringmaster.

Myerson, who was raised in a lower-middle-class housing co-operative in the Bronx, was the first Jewish woman crowned Miss America in 1945, and remained a beloved icon to Jewish New Yorkers for much of her life. She was beautiful, elegant, and well-spoken, highly in demand by presidents and mayors seeking to associate with a woman of her stature. During the 1977 mayor's race she was a constant companion to Ed Koch, who was unmarried and suspected by some of being gay. His campaign manager, David Garth, believed Koch would have lost the race without her. Koch subsequently named her his cultural affairs commissioner.

In the summer of 1983, she gave a $19,000 per year special assistant's job to Sukhreet Gabel, the daughter of Hortense Gabel, a veteran State Supreme Court judge who was presiding over the divorce case of Myerson's boyfriend, Andy Capasso. Soon after Sukhreet was hired, Judge Gabel cut Capasso's alimony payments to his ex-wife by two thirds to $500 a week, and child support almost in half to $180. The press caught on, and prosecutors took notice.

Robert Morgenthau, the Manhattan district attorney, passed on the case, worried about its flaws. Giuliani had no such compunctions; he indicted Myerson, Capasso, and Judge Gabel in October 1987. Speaking to reporters, he called the $19,000 position "part of a bribe."

"When you are sitting on a case where the correspondent in a matrimonial matter employs your daughter, that is a matter that should cry out for investigation," he said.

The law required more than the appearance of a quid pro quo, though: prosecutors had to prove that there was an explicit agreement. Thus did Sukhreet Gabel, an eccentric thirty-nine-year-old who spoke openly about her history of depression and electroshock therapy treatments, secretly record her phone conversations with her mother and try to lure her into admitting she had made a deal with Myerson (she failed).

The spectacle spilled into farce, as Sukhreet, Giuliani's star witness, bathed in the media glow, singing at a cabaret and getting a televised facial makeover. She portrayed herself as a loving daughter, and brought roses to her mother at the defendant's table prior to testifying against her. Judge Gabel, half blind, was nurturing and supportive of her, offering an insight into why she had reached out to dozens of potential employers, Myerson included, to find a position for her troubled daughter.

Jay Goldberg, Capasso's lawyer, was incensed at both the prosecutorial overkill and Giuliani's use of the media to aid his case. "Giuliani tried to bury the people under the avalanche of prejudicial publicity," he said. "I mean you couldn't turn the page for a day without reading some sort of terrible story about Bess and Andy."

When members of the jury pool were interviewed by the judge, John Keenan, Goldberg said, "everybody said they believed the defendants were guilty. Everyone."

In the end, Myerson, Capasso, and Gabel were found not guilty, the determining factor being the sight of a troubled daughter testifying against her mother. It was an embarrassing loss for Giuliani at a sensitive moment, as he was considering a run for mayor. "This is a case that had to be tried," he maintained.

His final months as U.S. attorney were less a victory lap than a moment of reassessment by the public.

Criticism over his methods mounted in February 1987, when he had three Wall Street traders arrested, handcuffed, and marched across their trading room floor without so much as an indictment; Giuliani dropped the charges three months later. "I should have slowed it down and I should have found out how complex the case was," he conceded.

More high-profile cases ended in acquittals—most prominently his case against Imelda Marcos, the widow of former Philippines president Ferdinand Marcos—or were reversed on appeal. The backlash against Giuliani was crystallized in a March 1989 ruling from Federal District Court Judge John Sprizzo, who threw out the indictments of seven defendants in a major heroin trafficking case known as "Pizza Connection II."

"There is in your office—and I notice it not only in this case but in other cases—a kind of overkill, a kind of overzealousness, which is not even, from my viewpoint as a person who has been a prosecutor, rationally related to any legitimate prosecutive objectives," the judge said.

By then, Giuliani had already left the job to campaign for mayor. On his way out the door, the *Daily News* ran a photo of him with an automatic pistol with a silencer. "GOOD NEWS FOR BAD GUYS," read the headline, "Crimebuster Giuliani steps down." Similar stories popped up in newspapers from St. Louis, Missouri, to London, England.

"I hope the legacy we leave is the continued emphasis on the need to reform the way in which we do business and practice politics," he told reporters at his last press conference.

Giuliani evolved in significant ways in the years that followed, but the zeal he brought to the Southern District never faded. Nor did his propensity for overkill, or his addiction to media coverage. But his stages grew larger.

CHAPTER 3

Combat

On a cloudy mid-September morning in 1992, Rudy Giuliani and two young aides piled into a car outside his mayoral campaign headquarters on Lexington Avenue and headed downtown to City Hall. Phil Caruso, the flame-throwing president of the Patrolmen's Benevolent Association, was staging a protest rally, and invited him to speak. The candidate didn't need convincing.

In the aftermath of the Rodney King riots in Los Angeles, Mayor David Dinkins, the city's first African American mayor, had proposed the formation of an all-civilian board to review complaints of police misconduct. The union, no fan of Dinkins to begin with, was incensed.

When he arrived at the scene, Giuliani encountered a massive crowd of burly off-duty officers in street clothes clogging the streets and waving protest signs. Ten thousand of them had shown up, fuming over the mayor and bearing signs ranging from resentful to racist (*"Dump the Washroom Attendant"*). They were focused less on the proposal and more on the man pursuing it. Chants of *"Dinkins must go!"* boomed through the streets at football stadium volume.

To say it was a friendly crowd for the Republican mayoral frontrunner would be an understatement. Like many of them, Giuliani was an outer-borough Roman Catholic from a blue-collar background with a family full of cops. Like them, he was contemptuous of Dinkins. The crowds parted for him "like Moses," said his press secretary, Ken Frydman, and started to chant *"Rudy!"*

Things had started to go wrong by the time their car pulled up. The plan was for the crowd to march around City Hall with banners and picket signs, but thousands broke away from the route and toppled wooden barriers, jumped on top of parked cars, and stormed the plaza in front of the building as on-duty cops looked on like spectators. They packed the steps leading up to City Hall's front doors, effectively seizing control of the building. A few of them strung huge cloth banners between the building's grand columns, with scrawled lettering reading DINKINS MUST GO and DINKINS YOU SOLD OUT THE NYPD.

Beer flowed, and the crowd grew rowdy. Security officers inside City Hall placed bars across the doors in fear of protesters storming inside. Emergency calls went out to police headquarters to send in reinforcements. The rally was turning into a riot.

Caruso called Giuliani and asked him to head for the City Hall steps to urge the crowd to vacate the plaza. Someone handed the candidate a bullhorn, and he waded through the throng to the steps of the building. Whatever he said was drowned out, but some heeded his call and followed him out of the plaza.

He walked to the flatbed truck outside the perimeter of the building, where thousands were gathered, and hopped up to the makeshift stage. After a handful of other politicians delivered their speeches, Giuliani took the mic and the crowd roared.

Shedding his suit jacket and rolling up the sleeves of his white button shirt, he ripped into Dinkins.

"The mayor doesn't know why the morale of the New York City Police Department is so low," he said, jabbing his finger in the air. "He blames it on me, he blames it on you. The reason the morale of the Police Department of the City of New York is so low is one reason and one reason alone: *David Dinkins!*"

The crowd cheered, and broke into chants of *"Dinkins must go!"* Fired up, Giuliani laid into the administration's policies as *"bullshit!"* which led the crowd to start chanting *"bullshit!"* back.

Jimmy Breslin, the tabloid columnist, would paint a devastating portrait of the crowd's behavior the next day. Standing with a group of them, the cops taunted the writer for being roughed up in the Crown Heights race riots the previous year.

> The cops held up several of the most crude drawings of Dinkins, black, performing perverted sex acts. And then, here was one of them calling across the top of his beer can held to his mouth, "How did you like the n——s beating you up in Crown Heights?"
>
> Now others began screaming . . . "How do you like what the n——s did to you in Crown Heights? Now you got a n——r right inside City Hall. How do you like that? A n——r mayor."

Soon afterward, the protesters marched to the Brooklyn Bridge, jamming its roadways and blocking traffic.

Giuliani—who later claimed he didn't witness any racist behavior—drove back to the office exhilarated. It wasn't until he watched the television coverage of the riot that he realized he'd come off looking like the leader of a lynch mob.

From the moment Jimmy Walker was spied cavorting with a Ziegfeld Follies showgirl in the Roaring Twenties, New Yorkers have come to expect their mayors to be larger than life, capturing their imaginations while keeping things under control. The best of them have succeeded at both.

David Dinkins came into office in 1990 with the promise of upholding that tradition. While he lacked the pugnacity of Fiorello La Guardia and Ed Koch, and the charisma of John Lindsay, he carried enormous stature as a historic figure, the first Black mayor elected to run one of the world's great cities.

A liberal Democrat, he prevailed in 1989 in a bitter race against Giuliani, less than a year out of the U.S. Attorney's Office, who ran as the Republican and Liberal Party candidate. Dinkins's narrow victory sparked jubilation among African Americans across the nation, and instantly transformed him into a civil rights icon.

"November 7, 1989, is a date that will live in history," he proclaimed on the night of his triumph. "We passed another milestone on Freedom's Road, a victory not for African-Americans alone but for all New Yorkers and all Americans."

He had an elegant dignity to him, with an innate graciousness and a kind, grandfatherly manner. Drained from twelve years of Koch's effective, entertaining, and exhausting reign, the public embraced the lower-key figure.

But Dinkins's victory turned out to be the high point of his mayoralty; a cascade of crises overwhelmed him virtually from the moment he took office. The bottom was falling out from the city's economy; New York was hemorrhaging private-sector jobs—330,000 vanished by the end of his term. A million New Yorkers were on welfare, and unemployment was rising. The municipal payroll exploded by fifty thousand workers under Koch, helping to widen a budget deficit climbing into the billions. With Wall Street sputtering and the housing market cooling, tax revenues were plummeting.

Nothing in Dinkins's background prepared him to deal with a problem of this magnitude. A proud veteran of the Harlem Democratic political machine, he had served as a city clerk, performing marriages and rubber-stamping legislation, and then as Manhattan borough president, a position that gave him a vote on development proposals. He was short on executive experience, and indecisive, particularly when faced with decisions that could hurt the city's most vulnerable citizens.

Sidestepping hard choices whenever possible, he spent four years in an excruciating search for outside aid to stave off the threat of bankruptcy, a state takeover of the city's finances, or both. The federal government, the municipal unions, Wall Street bond raters—no one in a position to bail out the city had enough faith in his stewardship of the city's finances to give him the break he was looking for.

He lurched from one extreme to the next, granting generous raises to friendly unions, then laying off workers. He implemented the largest tax increase in city history, which did little to dissuade bond rating agencies from threatening a catastrophic downgrading of the city's bond rating. Inevitably he was forced to cut back on essential services, curtailing garbage collection and closing fire companies.

Much of the problem was not of his making, but solutions eluded him. His heart was set on lifting up the poor, not cutting back on the services they depended upon. "We must never, never abandon the compassion, the concern and the caring which are the hallmarks of our government," he said. "Bond ratings are important, but our bond with the people is every bit as important." The soaring oratory was of little solace to a public suffering filthy streets and other declining services.

Such was Dinkins's plight that the fiscal crisis was not even his biggest problem. The city seemed rudderless in the face of ballooning crime and a deterioration of public order.

Nine months into his first term, *Time* magazine encapsulated the problem in a cover story titled "The Rotting of the Big Apple." It portrayed a city beset by crime and disorder, with almost two thousand murders per year, and streets filled with vagrants.

"Even the basic rudiments of civil behavior seemed to evaporate along with the glitter of the boom times," it stated. "Every day 155,000 subway riders jump the turnstiles, denying the cash-strapped mass transit system at least $65 million annually. The streets have become public restrooms for both people and animals, even though failure to clean up after a pet dog carries fines of up to $100. What was once the bustle of a hyperkinetic city has become a demented frenzy.

"The city has spun out of control."

With tourists being assaulted, and in one notable instance murdered, and children in city housing projects being gunned down in the crossfire between street gangs, Dinkins launched a study to examine police staffing needs. Days turned into weeks. The *New York Post*, no friend of his, captured the mood of the city with a headline reading "*DAVE, DO SOMETHING!*" Ultimately, he pushed through the hiring of an additional six thousand officers. They would not come on line for another two years.

Distrustful of his own police force, and despised by the rank and file, Dinkins seemed helpless in the face of spiraling racial conflagrations, including an epic riot in Crown Heights, Brooklyn, in 1991 that was sparked by the killing of a Black child by a speeding vehicle that had fallen behind a motorcade carrying the grand rebbe of an Orthodox Jewish sect. Rioters and looters created a state of siege in the Orthodox Jewish community for three days until police commanders finally got the situation under control.

The conditions provided a perfect opening for a lawman to enter the picture and promise to clean up the town.

Giuliani had had four years to hone his thinking on the issues after the 1989 loss, and emerged in 1993 with a coherent vision that dramatically contrasted with that of his opponent.

He argued that the liberal establishment was driving the city into the ground in the name of compassion. Restraining the police out of concern for civil liberties was allowing violent crime to paralyze minority communities. Concern for the rights of the homeless was creating havoc in the streets. A welfare system designed to protect the poor was entrapping a million New Yorkers in a cycle of dependence. His list went on and on.

His proposals to crack down on crime included a focus on quality of life, a term encompassing the daily indignities New Yorkers dealt with on the way to work, from people sleeping on subway seats to homeless people urinating against buildings. He had become a student of George Kelling and James Q. Wilson's Broken Windows theory, which held that small crimes, left unchecked, lead to bigger crimes, much as one rock thrown through a window leads to others. The cops had to stop looking the other way on the rampant disorder plaguing the streets. Dinkins scoffed at the notion, but it resonated deeply with New Yorkers.

"We have a city to save," Giuliani told a crowd of voters with messianic fervor.

A demoralized public that would have once shunned his ideas proved willing to listen. With his political guru David Garth softening Giuliani's image with gauzy commercials featuring him rhapsodizing about his love of the Yankees, the candidate's behavior at the police rally started to fade into memory.

The racial undertones of the Giuliani-Dinkins rematch were never far from the surface; Giuliani was a white prosecutor running against a Black mayor in a city shaken by a race riot. Each side vowed disingenuously to refrain from playing the race card. Giuliani's campaign slogan, "One City, One Standard," played to white voters resentful of Dinkins's perceived favoritism toward the Black community. President Bill Clinton, meanwhile, starred at a Dinkins fundraiser and all but accused white voters of turning on the mayor because he was Black. "Too many of us are still too unwilling to vote for people who are different than we are," he proclaimed.

Governor Mario Cuomo, the Democrats' liberal champion, may have played the most decisive role in the race, signing off on a bill soon after Dinkins's 1989 victory that placed a referendum on the 1993 ballot in Staten Island, the city's most conservative borough, calling for its secession from the city. It was a popular measure on the island, even though the decision was up to the legislature, not them. On election night, the Staten Island vote swelled by twenty thousand compared with 1989, and helped push Giuliani over the top. His margin of victory, around 2 percent, mirrored Dinkins's margin over him four years earlier.

The victory was met by an explosion of joy at Giuliani's election night event at the Hilton. "My administration will be universal in its concern, sensitive to our diversity and evenhanded in every way possible," he said in his victory speech. "Nobody, no ethnic, religious or racial group will escape my care, my concern and my attention."

It was a promise he would break many times over.

On a humid March evening in 1994, police officer Sean McDonald stood watch outside of a condemned apartment house on Shakespeare Avenue in the Bronx, a seedy commercial strip in one of the city's most dangerous neighborhoods. He was serving out a dreary assignment, guarding an empty building in the wake of an electrical fire. The Buildings Department had asked the Police Department to prevent people from entering the structure, and the job fell to the twenty-six-year-old cop, barely two years out of the academy.

At approximately 7:30 p.m., two people approached him and pointed to a commotion taking place at a nearby tailor shop. McDonald crossed a thoroughfare and entered the Filo Fashion Tailor Shop, a mousehole of a store. Two men were emptying the cash register. The owners were tied up in the back room.

McDonald drew his gun and yelled at the men to freeze. He frisked Javier Miranda, and attempted to do the same with Rodolfo Rodriguez. A scuffle ensued, and Rodriguez pulled a Smith & Wesson .38 out of his pocket and unleashed a fusillade of bullets. The robbers flew out of the store, as McDonald staggered outside, collapsing in a puddle of water. He died soon afterward.

Twelve hours later and six miles south, hundreds of members of the city's political and business elite streamed into the grand Metropolitan Ballroom of the Sheraton Times Square hotel for a breakfast forum on urban crime featuring Giuliani and his mayoral counterparts in Washington, D.C., Boston, and Miami. A red, white, and yellow banner with the logo of the *New York Post*, the event's sponsor, stretched across a giant mirror at the front of the room.

As audience members settled in, grabbing a last Danish from the buffet table, Rupert Murdoch, the paper's owner, welcomed the audience from a podium bearing a poster with an image of a revolver. "As last night's terrible murder of Sean McDonald confirms, crime dwarfs every other issue confronting urban America," the media mogul said.

Giuliani, dressed in a gray suit and gray tie, was the first to speak. A sense of gravity fell over the room when he brought up McDonald's death.

Last night's murder is an attack on what holds us together as New Yorkers and Americans. We're held together by law. And we're held together by respect for the law. That's what America's all about. That's how America started, and that's the principle that keeps us all together.

Not a common ethnic background, not a common religion, but our respect for each other, exemplified in our respect for the law. Police officers carry that respect into every community, into every part of our city.

Officer McDonald last night was responding to try to help other people. When he responded, he didn't ask what religion they were, what race they were, what ethnic background they were. He didn't ask if they were poor or rich. He responded to try to help, and now he's dead.

... Remember that [police] are carrying for us respect for the law. We have to respect them, and support them, and we have to understand that we, together, can come through this. Realizing that mutual respect for each other, and for the law, is going to save us.

He uttered the word "respect" seven times in the first three minutes. While the other leaders at the dais spoke in talking points, preening a bit, loudly punctuating their most dramatic lines with outrage, Giuliani—thin, monkish, severe—spoke without notes in a low, solemn voice. Eschewing standard platitudes about crime, he used the tragedy to deliver a sermon straight from the halls of Bishop Loughlin.

We look upon authority too often and focus over and over again, for 30 or 40 or 50 years, as if there is something wrong with authority. We see only the oppressive side of authority. Maybe it comes out of our history and our background.

What we don't see is that freedom is not a concept in which people can do anything they want, be anything they can be. Freedom is about authority. Freedom is about the willingness of every single human being to cede to lawful authority a great deal of discretion about what you do.

They were the words of an autocrat. Some in the audience were shocked by the comment, but it should have been clear to them by then, three months into his term, that it was not an aberration, but rather the guiding principle of his mayoralty. Nothing in his campaign, or even his tenure as a prosecutor, prepared the public for his dictatorial impulses.

A week after his inauguration, police received an emergency call with a report of an armed robbery at a Nation of Islam mosque in Harlem. When police entered the ramshackle building and raced up its stairs, they were attacked by members of the Black nationalist organization, livid at the intrusion.

Eight officers were injured, including one who was pushed down a flight of stairs and another whose nose was broken. One of the assailants captured an officer's gun.

With the members of the group barricaded, Giuliani saw his moment to make a statement to the world that the era of weakness was over.

He dialed up the commanders on the scene. "I want arrests!" he demanded. William Bratton, his new police commissioner, was stepping off a plane at LaGuardia Airport to begin his new job when the mayor called him with the same demand. Bratton persuaded Giuliani after a good deal of pushback to give his commanders time to defuse the situation. Eventually the occupants filed out of the building. It turned out that the robbery call that led the police to the building was bogus.

Four days later, Reverend Al Sharpton entered the picture. A gifted preacher and a canny strategist, he specialized in parachuting into racial donnybrooks and twisting the city into knots. Whether he was a racial arsonist or a civil rights hero depended upon whom you asked, but mayors had learned the hard way that it was a lot easier to work with him than against him. In the words of Deputy Mayor Bill Lynch, Dinkins's political guru, "it was better to have Sharpton pissing in your tent than pissing on it."

Giuliani was having none of it. To him, acquiescence to Sharpton was just one more accommodation that had helped run the city into the ground. He saw an opportunity to send a message that the era of racial blackmail was over, and pressured Bratton to cancel a meeting he had scheduled with mosque leaders that Sharpton intended to join. The group was turned away when they arrived at One Police Plaza.

Sharpton fumed—"We're not going to go back to being disregarded and disrespected!"—but Giuliani was resolute. "We have spent way more time on Reverend Sharpton than it's really worth," he told reporters, slamming the door of City Hall shut on one of the most feared power brokers in New York. It would take years for Sharpton to exact his revenge.

A week later, as the mayor emerged from a Martin Luther King Jr. Day celebration in Harlem, reporters pressed him for a response to criticism from Black elected officials that he had neglected to seek their input during the controversy. He replied with a complaint about *them*, noting with irritation that he had an amicable private talk about the matter with Charles Rangel, the dean of the city's congressional delegation, only to watch the congressman turn around and criticize him to reporters.

"I want to reach out to all of the communities in the city," Giuliani said. "It has to be a two-way street. And they're going to have to learn how to discipline themselves in the way in which they speak."

The condescension did not go over well. "It's outrageous," said Harlem councilman Adam Clayton Powell IV. "He's speaking to us like we are his children."

It was quite a feat to offend the entire Black leadership of the city after just eighteen days in office. But Giuliani was offering no apologies. He was making comments like that every day. Each subject of his wrath earned a lecture on moral behavior. When the mother of a robbery suspect condemned the police for killing her son, he blamed it on her. "Maybe you should ask yourself some questions about the way he was brought up and the things that happened to him," Giuliani lectured her on the radio.

The mayor was giving New York a lesson in authority. When the city's Legal Aid attorneys went on strike, stranding thousands of defendants without legal representation, he was furious. He canceled their contract with the city and gave them twenty-four hours to return to work or be replaced. The strike was over by nightfall.

Mayors had tried and failed for years to persuade the leaders of the Metropolitan Transportation Authority, an independent body, to cede control over the transit police to allow for a cost-saving merger with the New York City Police Department, which the mayor controlled. Facing resistance, Giuliani went straight for the nuclear option, freezing the city's $300 million contribution to the authority. Faced with fiscal starvation, its leaders surrendered the force to him.

The ultimate vehicle for asserting control was the city's almost $32 billion budget, larger than that of some countries. In February, one month into his mayoralty, he unveiled his plans to restructure, pare down, and sell off city services.

He spent weeks preparing for it. The MBAs and CPAs on his financial team who helped him craft the plan were struck by how quick a study he was. "He would recall every number on that page to a decimal point," recalled Joe Lhota, his finance commissioner at the time, and a future deputy mayor. "It was absolutely scary."

Walking into a room packed with elected officials, Giuliani warned on live television of a "fiscal emergency" if major structural changes weren't made to the way government operated. It was quite a show: he worked without notes, and displayed a mastery of complex details, flicking through slides showing one calamitous trend after another. It was a stark departure from Dinkins's budget briefings, at which he ceded much of his time to his budget officials. At Giuliani's presentation, his budget director, Abe Lackman, sat behind him quietly.

He called for a $1 billion cut to city agencies, $300 million in union givebacks, and a reduction of fifteen thousand workers from the payroll. But there were no layoffs or cutbacks; instead he unveiled a slew of innovations and audacious proposals.

He cut a deal with the unions to offer buyouts in exchange for changes to antiquated hiring rules. Instead of cutting services he streamlined the bureaucracy, and proposed merging city agencies and privatizing some public hospitals. He imposed finger imaging for welfare recipients to weed out fraud, kicking off a massive effort to reduce the rolls. A city of eight million people could not afford to have a million of them on public assistance, he argued.

The proposals triggered an avalanche of protest, but in the end the City Council gave Giuliani most of what he wanted. It was a first step toward stabilizing the city's careening finances, and proving to a weary public that New York was actually governable.

Long before Donald Trump mesmerized the American public with his antics, Giuliani perfected the art of government as high theater. His mayoralty was a sequence of shocking episodes, some alarming, some comic, many a combination of the two. The cast of characters in his opera changed from week to week but for the diva at the center of it all. He lived to shock, sometimes doing so intentionally, other times when he couldn't help himself.

The most striking episode of his first year in office revolved around the 1994 governor's race. Mario Cuomo, perhaps the Democratic Party's most revered liberal icon at the time, was running for a historic fourth term, a major lift for any incumbent, and facing his first tough challenge in years from Republican candidate George Pataki, a little-known state senator and former mayor of the small upstate city of Peekskill.

Cuomo's opponent was as bland as they came, with a standard-issue Republican platform and prepackaged talking points. He was a veritable creation of New York senator Al D'Amato, a wily and enormously powerful Republican, who was a bitter nemesis of the mayor's going back to his prosecutor days. The national GOP eyed Pataki as a giant-killer.

It was clear from the start that Giuliani's heart belonged to Cuomo, who helped boost Republican turnout for his 1993 campaign with the Staten Island secession referendum, and who commissioned a devastating election-year report on the Crown Heights riots that portrayed Dinkins and his team as incompetent. Like Giuliani, Cuomo was an Italian American, authentic, and devoted to the struggling city.

Pataki courted Giuliani's endorsement, which should have been a given for a fellow Republican. But the mayor was proving elusive, at one point making the candidate wait two hours on a bench at City Hall while Giuliani visited a crime scene. Pataki gave up and left.

Pataki's advisors urged Giuliani's political aides to persuade their boss to at least stay neutral in the race, and most—though not all—of them urged the mayor to do just that. Giuliani held his cards close to the vest, however, and built up so much suspense that when his staff scheduled his announcement press conference television stations cut into their programming and carried it live. Oprah was pre-empted for Giuliani.

Walking to the Blue Room podium, sweating profusely and carrying written comments—a rarity—he announced his verdict.

"The election this year presents a fundamental dilemma causing many of us probably to do the same thing, agonizing over a decision we have to make, the choice we have to make for governor," he said.

"From my point of view, as the mayor of New York City, the question that I have to ask is, 'Who has the best chance in the next four years of successfully fighting for our interests? Who understands them, and who will make the best case for it?' Our future, our destiny is not a matter of chance. It's a matter of choice.

"My choice is Mario Cuomo."

As heads turned in newsrooms across the city, he ripped into his fellow Republican. "Senator Pataki has almost uniformly voted against the interests of the city and often the metropolitan region.... Mario Cuomo is his own man. I prefer dealing with someone who is his own man.

"The sense that I've gotten from George Pataki is that it is very much a campaign out of a political consultant's playbook. There are clichés, there are slogans, there's the right soundbite, there's the right position. You become specific only for as long as you have to, and then you become general again."

For all the conservative policies the mayor adopted on the way to City Hall, he was at heart a moderate, and showed no reservations about supporting a proud Democrat. The astonishing heresy of his endorsement of Cuomo, the seemingly suicidal betrayal of his own party, was pure Giuliani. He stubbornly trusted his instincts, even when he risked disaster.

Pataki's numbers crashed in the immediate aftermath, nosediving from a 7-point lead to a 13-point deficit. Arthur Finkelstein, D'Amato's Republican strategist, sensed an opening, however. He launched a campaign to foment a backlash in the conservative upstate strongholds, stoking long-standing resentment of the city by claiming the endorsement was part of a secret deal in which Giuliani backed Cuomo in exchange for massive amounts of state aid.

Intoxicated by his dramatic effect on the race, Giuliani persuaded the Cuomo camp to send him on an upstate endorsement tour. It proved catastrophic, as crowds of jeering Pataki supporters organized by the campaign greeted him in cities from Rochester to Utica with signs reading "Traitor!" and "Let's Make a Deal!" Fistfights broke out in Syracuse. The television coverage was disastrous. Giuliani had made the Cuomo campaign all about him, and brought it crashing down, along with Giuliani's political fortunes. Cuomo lost to Pataki by 3 points.

Giuliani was scarred—Pataki refused to speak to him for weeks. It was a riveting drama, but just one of many.

William Bratton, the new police commissioner, was a picture of cool, a tough, poker-faced cop with a ruddy complexion and an air of smooth self-confidence. He had served a widely acclaimed tour as New York's transit police chief before becoming police commissioner in Boston, where he was born and raised. But his swagger was pure New York.

"We will fight for every house in the city," he proclaimed with Churchillian flair upon his appointment. "We will fight for every street. We will fight for every borough. And we will win."

Giuliani and he made for a formidable pair, a famed prosecutor and a celebrated police commissioner vowing to clean up the town. "Get off the drugs, get off the booze, get off your ass, and get a job," Bratton warned the homeless. It was almost heresy to talk that way in the liberal metropolis. But not in Rudy Giuliani's New York.

Bratton's first act was to clean house of the upper ranks of the department. He was an innovator, and the team he assembled reflected it. His most important hire was Deputy Commissioner Jack Maple, a barrel-chested spark plug of a man with a bowler hat, bow tie, and spectator shoes. He was a crime-fighting visionary; one night over drinks with Bratton, he started spitballing strategies and jotting down his thoughts on a napkin. The result was the groundbreaking CompStat system, a high-tech, data-driven apparatus that allowed the high command to chart crime patterns block by block in real time.

The CompStat room at police headquarters became mission control for the department, with maps projected on big screens indicating where crimes were being reported at any given moment.

"Basically, where you saw the dots, that's where you wanted to put the cops," Maple said in 1999.

Giuliani's message to the cops was that they were free to do their jobs—the restraints of the Dinkins era were off. Bratton told them they were expected not only to respond to crime but to prevent it. It entailed confiscating a lot of guns.

Officers swooped into the streets of Bedford-Stuyvesant, Harlem, and other minority communities, stopping and frisking young men they suspected of carrying weapons. To be a Black man in the Giuliani era was to be treated as a potential criminal; the mayor's one Black deputy mayor, Rudy Washington, was stopped and frisked so frequently that the mayor's office issued him a police identification badge.

The mayor's quality-of-life offensive was equally aggressive. Laws against fare beating, urinating in public, and pot smoking were enforced under Giuliani's Broken Windows initiative. The homeless were rousted from the streets and forced to move along. Summonses for minor crimes ballooned from 175,000 to 500,000. The number of arrestees cycling through the Rikers Island jail system swelled by over 15,000. Misdemeanor arrests more than doubled.

Giuliani had crime statistics delivered to his door each morning, and regularly dialed up his police commissioner to press for even more aggressive action. The constant pressure on the department to boost arrests was a huge threat to the civil liberties of people of color; complaints of police abuse rose 50 percent. But the protests of politicians and civil liberties groups were largely ignored by the public, as conditions in the streets improved, and crime fell across the board.

Aside from Maple, who looked like a 1920s dandy, Bratton's crew included John Miller, the dashing public information chief, who traded in his perch as a television crime reporter for the adrenaline rush of crime fighting; and John Timoney, a gruff deputy commissioner and the department's highest-ranking uniformed officer. Bratton's squad was a cocky bunch, fighting bad guys and taking on the old guard by day, and regaling one another with war stories at night at Elaine's, the Upper East Side celebrity watering hole. The tabloids loved their Untouchables act, though the suits down at City Hall were less amused.

Bratton's rise coincided with that of Cristyne Lategano, the mayor's enormously controversial young press secretary (she later married and changed her last name to Nicholas). Her remarkable trajectory was one of the most consequential story lines of Giuliani's mayoralty, and it intersected—disastrously—with the commissioner's.

She was a relative newcomer to Giuliani World, hired midway through the 1993 race as a late-inning replacement for Ken Frydman, the campaign's voluble press secretary. She was just twenty-eight years old, but had worked for several campaigns and came recommended by previous bosses as a tireless worker.

When Giuliani won he named her his City Hall press secretary, with the expectation that a more seasoned pro would be hired as communications director to look over her shoulder. But that appointment never materialized after the leading candidate turned down the job, leaving Lategano, a relatively inexperienced staffer, to put together City Hall's vast communications operation herself.

The members of Giuliani's inner circle—mostly white, male lawyers—had long histories with him, starting with Peter Powers, who'd grown up with him. They paid little mind to the young newcomer. She was a hard worker, constantly in motion, always a little too stressed to smile.

Phil McConkey, the ex-Giants receiver who employed her during his New Jersey congressional run, said Lategano "would throw herself in front of a truck to protect her boss." Giuliani discovered her loyal streak while tooling around the city with her on his way to his press events. Most press secretaries try to serve two masters—their bosses, and the reporters demanding information about them—but she felt no divided loyalties. Eschewing efforts to charm City Hall's reporters, she took to berating them for biased coverage, and regularly went over their heads to complain to their editors. It was pure antagonism from day one.

The mayor had long since concluded that a white prosecutor who'd beaten the city's first Black mayor would never get a fair shake from most reporters, and he relegated them to his enemies list. The sound of Lategano giving them hell was music to his ears.

The two developed a routine; Giuliani would start his mornings with her, his chauffeur picking her up in his white Chevy Suburban at her apartment as early as 6 a.m. Together they would go over news coverage in the car on their way to his morning events.

His aides started to take note of the burgeoning relationship; how she would squeeze next to him during crowded rides, sit at his table at luncheons, layer mustard on his hot dogs at outdoor events. When the two were in City Hall she'd eat lunch with him in his office.

Word of her influence spread throughout the government. "Commissioners would line up like planes on a runway outside her office to get permission" for their plans, an aide said. "They were petrified of her."

The young press secretary learned early that the way to remain indispensable to Giuliani was to play to his suspicions. She divided the world into two camps; those who were loyal to him, and those who were pursuing their own agendas. Black politicians, most of whom supported Dinkins, were relegated to the latter category. Her influence had grave implications for the city, as Giuliani's failure to show even basic respect to leaders of color came back to haunt him.

"She brought out the worst in Rudy," said a longtime aide, echoing the views of virtually every aide. "When bad things were happening, instead of having reasonable people around him, saying

'Rudy, we should think this out,' Cristyne would be the one saying 'Bullshit!'"

Powers and other senior aides woke up one day to realize that she had become Giuliani's most influential advisor. "Nine people would agree on something in a meeting," recalled an advisor. "Ten minutes later, [Giuliani] would call and say he'd changed his mind. You'd go back to his office and say 'What happened?' And she'd be sitting with him." Eventually, Powers, the mayor's closest friend and wisest advisor, left city government, frustrated over her overwhelming influence.

Lategano was Giuliani's kindred spirit, in perfect sync with him on most issues, and sharing his mistrust of others. His obsessions became hers; she was so focused on controlling the actions of the agencies and officials around him that the Department of Environmental Protection was ordered to run the daily reservoir levels by the City Hall press office before releasing them to the *New York Times* weather page.

Her biggest target of all was Bratton.

There was no one in city government as crucial to Giuliani's success as the police commissioner. The crime rate, which had already started to fall in the last years of the Dinkins administration, plummeted when the quality-of-life and stop-and-frisk campaigns commenced and CompStat realigned police deployment. Arrests shot up 25 percent in the first two years of the administration, and murders plummeted by almost 40 percent, a far greater reduction than most other cities were experiencing with the end of the crack epidemic. The streets grew safer: the number of gunshot victims in the city plunged by 35 percent.

Giuliani watched with a wary eye as the media credited his commissioner for the remarkable turnaround. The mayor worked virtually around the clock; he turned up at every major fire, every major crime scene, every water main break, any hint of an emergency. He was constantly on the 11 p.m. news holding impromptu press conferences in the street to describe the night's emergency. New Yorkers saw a relentless, indefatigable leader.

Yet Bratton continued to poll better than him, got better press than him, and probably had more fun, as he increasingly popped up at A-list events on the Manhattan social circuit.

The more threatened Giuliani became, the more he moved to rein Bratton in. "The mayor really wanted to be the police commissioner," Bratton later recalled. "Denny Young [the mayor's counsel] and Peter Powers reinforced that he was the police commissioner, and I was the first deputy."

City Hall started insisting on approving his appointments and promotions, vetting his appearances, and controlling the information he shared with other elected officials. "Anybody on whatever enemies list they had, everything had to be cleared through them," he said.

When President Bill Clinton visited a Brooklyn precinct house in 1994, Bratton was stunned when the mayor's deputies told him to stay away. "They were snubbing the president of the United States over some pissing match."

The mayor banned his staff, Lategano included, from Elaine's. While close to John Miller in the early days of the administration, she became increasingly confrontational, berating him late at night for media coverage of his boss. She ordered the NYPD press department to forward all interview requests to her.

Bratton felt Lategano's growing hostility to his team correlated with the amount of grief the mayor was giving her. "She'd be the one that would bear the brunt of his ranting and his raving," he said. "What she began to do was exactly what an abused child does. They try to displace the anger.

"She was universally despised," he said.

Bratton's gang laughed to one another about the dressing-downs they were receiving in the downstairs conference room at Gracie Mansion. "We used to joke that they'd throw the windows open so that it'd be ice cold in there, and when they attached the electrodes they'd throw cold water on you so when they threw the electricity on it'd hurt even worse," Maple recalled in 1999. "You had to basically engage in dark humor because they were in many respects a sadistic group of people."

In February 1995, Giuliani lowered the boom on Bratton's press operation, ordering John Miller to fire his staff. The department, Giuliani said, was "out of control." Miller resigned in protest.

It was arguably the mayor who was most out of control, however, as his friends and staff believed he was having an affair with his press secretary. The two were keeping late hours on weekdays and weekends, and staff started receiving strange orders from the top; they were forbidden from sending First Lady Donna Hanover his weekend schedule. "He'd be down in the office watching *The Godfather* with Cristyne," recalled one.

Friends and advisors—including Powers, and Giuliani's political guru, Ray Harding—tried to bring up the subject of the alleged affair with him and warn about its powder keg potential. "I'm not talking about it," the mayor snapped.

In September 1995, the relationship exploded into public view. "THE WOMAN BEHIND THE MAYOR," blared the cover of *New York* magazine. "WHY DOES EVERYONE HATE THIS WOMAN?" read the inside headline. An anonymous mayoral aide was quoted extensively.

> Her staff hates her because she treats them like shit. City Hall people hate her because she's young and arrogant and treats them like shit. The pressure to handle the Bratton problem is growing, and everybody has identified her as the press problem.

She's got the threat of death hanging over her. But every once in a while she has these quiet, tender moments with the mayor. He never defends her at meetings, in public, but sometimes when they're alone he tells her, "I think you're doing a great job and don't think I don't appreciate your work."

Giuliani's marriage to Donna Hanover was thrown into turmoil by the reports, but Lategano—who denied they were having an affair—wasn't going anywhere. The same couldn't be said for Bratton. On January 15, 1996, with the city experiencing the biggest two-year crime drop in its history, *Time* magazine put the commissioner on its cover, wearing a trench coat with his collar turned up in front of a squad car with flashing lights. The headline was "FINALLY WE'RE WINNING THE WAR ON CRIME."

Two months later, he was gone.

Lategano (who declined to be interviewed) made no apologies at the time for how Bratton was treated. Though she denied that she was advising the mayor to stay away from Black leaders, it was just that concern that fueled her initial doubts about the commissioner.

"Here we are, seven days into the new administration, and the police commissioner is meeting with Al Sharpton—it made no sense whatsoever," she said, referring to the Harlem mosque conflict. "It was a wake-up call that maybe Bratton wasn't the right choice."

She played coy about her influence over the mayor. "You're only as powerful as people allow you to be, or as much as they think you are," she said. "But I was really just the director of communications. I was the press gal."

If Giuliani's treatment of Bratton was shoddy, the ordeal he put schools chancellor Ramon Cortines through bordered on sadistic. Unlike the police commissioner, Cortines did not work for him—he was appointed by an autonomous Board of Education. The fact that he could not exercise control over Cortines drove him crazy.

The chancellor was a nationally respected education leader who had run numerous school districts. He'd already put in his retirement papers at the San Francisco school system when he was recruited to become an assistant education secretary in the Clinton administration. New York came calling as he was waiting for Congress to confirm him, and he was hired by the board two months prior to Giuliani's election.

He was soft-spoken and courteous, with a receding hairline and the demeanor of a patient schoolteacher. It wasn't clear why Giuliani chose to bully him; his appointment was championed by Giuliani's allies on the Board of Education, and he shared the mayor's opposition to universal condom distribution, and other lightning-rod programs favored by progressives. His primary offense seemed to be that he didn't have to take the mayor's orders.

New York's was the nation's largest school district, with a million students in its aging school buildings. Half of its students couldn't read at grade level. Many schools were plagued by violence, and the bureaucracy was famously byzantine; for years, its leaders struggled to figure out how many employees worked there. Giuliani wasn't looking for incremental improvements—he wanted to "blow up" the system, in his words. Waging an unsuccessful effort to persuade the state legislature to hand him control, he set out to get the new chancellor to do his bidding.

Cortines was given the Bratton treatment soon after the mayor took office. Mayoral aides summoned him to Gracie Mansion's basement conference room in February 1994, and made him wait two hours for Giuliani. When he arrived, he requested that Cortines lay off 2,500 employees as a first step toward reducing the bureaucracy. Cortines maintained that he was noncommittal, but Giuliani thought they'd come to a deal.

At the end of March, the chancellor released a plan to shed fewer than half that number, sending the mayor into a rage. "Don't tell me there are only six or seven hundred useless bureaucrats at 110 Livingston Street," he fumed to reporters, referring to the Board of Education headquarters building in Brooklyn. "Part of the problem could be that coming from out of town maybe he doesn't realize he's been captured by the bureaucracy." The personal attacks were starting.

That night, he summoned Cortines back. This time there was no request, just a threat: fire 2,500 people—including his press secretary and budget director, who had questioned Giuliani's demands in the press—or he would appoint a "monitor" to oversee the board. The experienced prosecutor was using bare-knuckled intimidation tactics. But Ray Cortines wasn't a criminal—he was a mild-mannered educator.

Cortines believed Giuliani was more interested in skimming the savings from the layoffs to help him balance his own budget. But he was cornered, and he caved on the 2,500 figure, with an agreement to spread the layoffs out over fifteen months. The Giuliani team gave him twelve hours to fire his two aides. When the meeting ended, Giuliani had his press office issue a release—after midnight—announcing that Cortines had agreed to the cuts.

The next morning the chancellor refused to fire his aides. "My integrity is not for sale," he announced. Giuliani delivered on his threat to name a monitor to evaluate his work. Cortines had to be talked out of resigning by the governor.

The antagonism only grew over the following months. The chancellor was working long days to improve the system, and math and English scores started inching up. But Giuliani dismissed the results as meaningless. The two continued to tangle in the media, sometimes daily. In December, Giuliani called on Cortines to resign, reprising the refrain that he had been "captured by the bureaucracy."

Cortines was flummoxed. "He's made it very clear that no matter what I do or say, unless I acquiesce to all his wishes that I am not a good manager and I am not showing leadership," he stated. "If the Board of Education doesn't think I'm doing a good job they should get rid of me. I don't work for the mayor."

The board responded by giving him a new two-year contract.

As the back-and-forth escalated Giuliani's attacks grew increasingly personal. "He shouldn't be so sensitive about it," he said, ridiculing the chancellor's attitude as "precious."

"The chancellor should stop it," Giuliani said. "He should grow up, and what he should do is understand that he has got to embrace change and stop whining about it, and stop playing the little victim."

Cortines was gay, and from a generation of schoolteachers who had learned the hard way to refrain from discussing their sexual orientation publicly. Knowing that Cortines would not call out Giuliani on his homophobic remarks made the spectacle that much more painful to watch.

Realizing that the torture was never going to end, Cortines walked into the board president's office in June 1995 and handed in a note of resignation. He signed it *"No regrets! Ray Cortines."*

Decades later, he reflected on the experience, saying that overall it was a positive one because of the progress he was able to make in the city's classrooms. "I don't have any hard feelings," he said. "I left New York on my terms."

He sounded less philosophical when recalling a last story about his time as chancellor. Soon after resigning, Cortines said, he had a conversation about Giuliani with his incoming successor, Rudy Crew.

"He said, 'Well I won't have any problems, I know how to deal with him,'" Cortines recalled. "And to myself, I said 'Bullshit.'"

CHAPTER 4

Trouble

New York's Inner Circle Dinner is an annual rite for the city's political class, a boozy black-tie charity event filling the Hilton Hotel's grand ballroom with hundreds of politicians, reporters, lobbyists, and assorted government hacks and bottom-feeders. It's a celebratory affair, with fat-bellied reporters and government spokespeople warbling off-key in ribald skits skewering politicians.

The highlight is the rebuttal performance by the mayor, which can be memorable and sometimes wildly inappropriate, as when Mayor Ed Koch sang and danced in an afro wig in 1980, sparking a walkout by Harlem's congressman Charles Rangel. Happy to push boundaries to their extreme, Rudy Giuliani in his fourth year in office appeared onstage in full drag with the cast of the musical *Victor/Victoria*, a jaw-dropping moment that fed his bottomless appetite for shocking people. His performance as "Rudy/Rudia" amused the city but triggered head-scratching in Middle America. That did not dissuade him from donning a gray wig and a floral dress to play an Italian grandmother almost nine months later on *Saturday Night Live.*

The event is usually an edgier, if more parochial, version of the White House Correspondents' Dinner, brasher and looser than its Washington counterpart, but lacking its celebrity wattage. But to attend it on the night of March 11, 2000, was to be at the center of the political universe. Organizers sold one thousand tickets, and the midlevel editors who usually populated the sea of candle-lit tables were replaced by their publishers, craning their necks like tourists to view the entrance of the most famous woman in America.

It had been sixteen months since New York senator Daniel Patrick Moynihan announced that he would not run for reelection, setting off a frenzy of maneuvering by potential candidates for the office, chief among them the city's mayor. When the news leaked that First Lady Hillary Clinton was interested in the seat, the buzz exploded into something closer to a frenzy.

Giuliani was well into his second term in office, having dispatched his Democratic rival, Manhattan borough president Ruth Messinger, by 16 points in 1997, albeit with the lowest voter turnout in decades. So complete was his dominance over the city that he even beat her on her home turf, Manhattan's famously liberal Upper West Side, where voters sheepishly pulled the lever for the Republican authoritarian because their streets were safer, cleaner, and saner.

Though a poor fit for a senator's job—working with others to build consensus wasn't exactly his forte—the prospect of a prize fight against a Clinton was too intoxicating for Giuliani to resist. He entered the race as the runaway favorite for the Republican nomination.

The media went into hyperventilating mode over the prospect of a titanic battle between Clinton and the city's larger-than-life mayor. Swept up in the fight-of-the-century euphoria, he crisscrossed the country with the goal of raising $20 million for the battle.

The candidates had yet to cross paths until this evening, however, and the atmosphere inside the grand ballroom was electric. Giuliani was chatting with guests at his table when a cloud of Secret Service agents, campaign aides, and reporters entered the ballroom, followed by camera crews bathing their blinding lights on the woman at the center. The first lady was "looking like Cleopatra in full regalia," the writer Gail Sheehy recalled, "gowned to the floor in a pyramidal coatdress of black satin. Her neck girdled in a collar of jewels. Her golden hair, swept high, shimmers."

The army of handlers and photographers moved slowly through the crowd as Clinton widened her eyes and flashed a joyous smile with every handshake and kiss on the cheek for her new friends in New York politics. Escorted by New York *Daily News* publisher Mort Zuckerman, a billionaire developer and political ally of the Clintons, she worked her way through the throngs of well-wishers to Giuliani's table and tapped him on the shoulder. "Good evening, Mr. Mayor," she said. Startled, he sprang up from his seat, flashed his Cheshire cat smile, and shook hands with her under a shower of flashing strobe lights.

The crowd was filled with senators, members of Congress, and chairs of *Fortune* 500 companies, but they were relegated to the role of spectators and supplicants, standing in line for the opportunity to meet Clinton. It was thirteen months since her husband had been impeached in the aftermath of the Monica Lewinsky scandal, which loomed over her candidacy even after his acquittal in February.

When the curtain rose on the reporters' show, the jokes at her expense were merciless. They ridiculed her as a clueless out-of-towner. "I can't wait to get to Shea Stadium, where I can watch my favorite team, the Yankees," a television reporter playing Clinton announced. Informed that the Yankees played at Yankee Stadium, she shrugged. "We live in Chappaqua now, you know," she explained. "That's Indian for 'The Land of Separate Bedrooms.'"

Then a reporter playing Bill Clinton broke into song.

> Yes, it's true, I've been a guy who sometimes strayed
> Made you feel so foolish that you just got played
> Now I need to know, I need to know
> Does your Bubba Bill get to stay or go?

With a thousand eyes trained on Clinton for signs of embarrassment or anger, she donned her famous glassy-eyed gaze, with an occasional laugh or a gentle wince to prove that she was enjoying herself. It couldn't have been easy, but she survived the ordeal intact.

Escorted backstage, she encountered Giuliani again as he prepared to go on stage for his rebuttal performance. Her presence jarred him.

"Well, I hear you're the real star," she said.

"We're gonna see, we're gonna see," he replied. "I like doing it."

"I can't wait to see it," she said, as reporters recorded their chess match.

The mayor was watching his adversary upstage him at his own shindig. With Clinton returning to her seat, he finally got off a good line for reporters. "I'm very, very encouraged at the fact we're drawing lots of out-of-towners to this performance of mine," he told them. Then he set about reclaiming the spotlight.

The curtain rose on Tony Carbonetti, dressed as a hospital orderly, wheeling Giuliani into his psychiatrist's office, where the mayor's pal Elliot Cuker sat with a notebook.

"My main problem is with anger," the mayor said. "I'm just so angry."

"Anything in particular?"

"Yes, the goddamned press!"

For nearly thirty minutes, he proceeded to take the audience on a revealing tour of his psyche. Intended as self-parody, it had the uncomfortable ring of truth.

"I'm not paranoid," Giuliani said to Cuker. "I just don't trust anybody."

The lights went down. Two mammoth movie screens lit up with a film starring Giuliani, Cuker, and a bevy of celebrities. The mayor was on a Manhattan street, angrily berating a cab driver played by

Danny Aiello. "That guy is nuts!" the actor turned to the camera and exclaimed. After a series of Giuliani tirades, the video faded to the mayor dressed as the Beast from *Beauty and the Beast*, storming through the venerable restaurant Le Cirque, disrupting people's meals, picking at Henry Kissinger's lunch. "What is wrong with that guy?" asked the famed restaurateur Sirio Maccioni.

And so it went, one celebrity after another wondering why the man was filled with so much rage.

Back on his psychiatrist's couch, Giuliani struggled to understand the root of his temper. Cuker urged him to get in touch with his feminine side.

The house lights dimmed again and the film resumed. Giuliani was shopping for perfume at a department store—dressed, yet again, in full drag. Reprising the role of Rudy/Rudia, swathed in a pink gown and a big blond wig, he browsed the aisles, only to bump into Donald Trump.

"You know, you're really beautiful," Trump said, lasciviously. "A woman who looks like that has to have her own special scent."

"Oh thank you," Giuliani replied in a high-pitched shrill. Spraying perfume on his neck, he asked Trump for his opinion of the scent. The developer leaned in for a sniff. "I like that," he said.

"This may be the best of all," Giuliani said, giving himself a spritz to his bosom. Trump, turned on, buried his face in the mayor's breasts, earning a slap in the face. "Oh you dirty boy!" the mayor vamped. "Donald, I thought you were a gentleman." Trump shrugged to the camera. "You can't say I didn't try."

The two seemed to be having the time of their lives acting out this misogynistic fantasy together. It was right out of Milton Berle, a childish display of machismo by two aging alpha males. The mayor's performance ended, improbably, with him back onstage clad in a white polyester suit, disco dancing with the cast of the Broadway musical *Saturday Night Fever*.

The night made for a strange but riveting tableau, the feminist hero forced to endure ridicule for her husband's infidelity and then watch her rival splaying his issues with women and anger across the stage. One had to wonder what was going through Clinton's mind as she watched Giuliani baring his id with abandon, putting the world on notice that he could do anything he pleased in his city, including wearing a dress.

But few in the audience picked up on the full depth of Giuliani's audacity this evening. Sitting quietly at his table in place of Donna Hanover, hiding in plain sight in a room packed with hundreds of reporters, was the woman with whom he was having an affair.

Late one night in May 1999—a year prior to the Inner Circle event—the mayor decided to spend a night chomping on a cigar at Club Macanudo on Manhattan's Upper East Side.

It was the start of the Memorial Day weekend, and residents of the area were clearing out of town for their beach and country houses, casting a blanket of quiet over the streets.

The neighborhood is Manhattan's wealthiest, where doormen stand guard outside rows of canopied co-op buildings housing members of the city's capitalist elite. The mixture of affluence and privacy creates an allure of exclusivity that appeals enormously to a certain type of person.

The air inside Club Mac, as regulars know it, is similarly rarefied. A plush throwback of a restaurant, it's the kind of place where prosperous old lions grind their cigars into plates of half-eaten steak and mashed potatoes, and retire for whiskey nightcaps to swap stories with their business and social equals.

Some have likened its interiors to a James Bond set, with its dress code, dark lounges, mahogany furniture, and extensive cigar collection. In truth, the place was just three years old, created by an upscale cigar maker to look like it had been around forever. Giuliani, a decidedly unmodern man, felt right at home there.

It was a respite at a tumultuous moment. Things were going wrong for him, as he was paying the price for a lot of bad decisions.

The streets outside City Hall had lately been filled with demonstrators. Hundreds of sidewalk vendors marched down Broadway in Lower Manhattan to protest his move to rid them from the city's busiest sidewalks. Housing activists filled the streets when his welfare reform measures grew increasingly punitive; he had ordered that the city's homeless earn their right to sleep in city shelters by performing menial work, cleaning trash off of park benches alongside of welfare recipients forced into labor in exchange for benefits. A court had to order him to permit the poor to apply for food stamps at the city's welfare centers.

He was at war with his friends and his enemies, to the point at which it was hard to tell who was who. Governor Pataki and he were barely on speaking terms. After hounding his first schools chancellor out of office, his *second* schools chancellor, Rudy Crew, was threatening to resign over the mayor's push to allow parents to spend their share of government education funding on private schools.

He grew increasingly vengeful. When the City Council overrode his veto of a bill dictating homeless policy, he announced his administration was placing homeless shelters in the districts of the councilmembers who voted against him. When the Campaign Finance Board defied his plan for funding special elections he threatened to cut off its funding.

"This is a chief executive who is out of control," railed Councilmember Stephen DiBrienza, a target of the mayor's wrath.

Going into 1999, his job approval rating was at 60 percent, and New Yorkers approved of the way things were going in the city by nearly a three-to-one margin.

The city was safer; the sense of menace in the streets was lifting, and the sound of gunshots in the city's most dangerous neigh-borhoods was fading. Residents of the city's poorest neighborhoods were able to walk down their streets at night without fearing for their safety. Businesses in those communities were sprouting up. Giuliani was the hero of the turnaround, with the costs of his crime-fighting success hidden from much of the public.

That changed in the early morning hours of February 4.

Amadou Diallo was a slight, soft-spoken West African immi-grant, barely into his twenties, who spent his days scratching out a living by hawking tube socks and videotapes as an employee of a discount store on 14th Street in Manhattan. He lived in a tiny apart-ment on Wheeler Avenue in the Soundview section of the Bronx, a gritty tenement neighborhood plagued with one of the highest crime rates in the city.

As usual, he put in a twelve-hour day peddling his wares to bar-gain hunters in front of the store, stepping inside five times to kneel down on a rug in a cramped storeroom to pray. When night fell, he took the long subway ride home.

At around midnight, after saying good night to his roommates, Diallo decided to go out and get a meal. At the same time, four white young plainclothes police officers from the New York City Police De-partment's Street Crime Unit were cruising the area, scanning the sidewalks for trouble.

The unit had been around for years at the Police Department, but had grown in prominence under Giuliani. Its officers were charged with operating on the streets of the city's most dangerous neighbor-hoods, and were skilled at confiscating illegal guns from individuals, a mission not meant for the faint of heart. They traveled in unmarked cars, wearing bulletproof vests under street clothes. Their slogan was "We Own the Night," and members distributed T-shirts in 1996 with a quotation from Hemingway: *"Certainly there is no hunting like the hunting of man, and those who have hunted armed men long enough and liked it, never really care for anything else thereafter."*

Their ferocity had a natural appeal to the mayor and his police commissioners, who marveled at the unit's success: it was a comparatively tiny unit—less than 2 percent of the force—but it accounted for 40 percent of the illegal guns the NYPD was confiscating. Ignoring warnings from the leaders of the unit that he was moving too fast, Police Commissioner Howard Safir, appointed by Giuliani to replace Bratton, almost tripled its size from 138 to 380.

The department's tactic of choice was stop-and-frisk: anyone deemed suspicious—usually young Black men—was thrown against a building and patted down for weapons. In 1998, the unit frisked more than 27,000 people and made 4,647 arrests, meaning that 22,000 mostly Black men were unnecessarily accosted by members of the unit. Department-wide, 175,000 New Yorkers were frisked during the fourteen-month period beginning January 1998. Half of them were Black.

One of the officers in the car, Sean Carroll, noticed Diallo standing outside his building.

"He was standing on the stoop," the officer later testified. "It appeared he was looking up and down the block. . . . He steps back into the vestibule, like he doesn't want to be seen."

"I got something on the right," Carroll told the others. "We gotta check it out."

They exited their car and started moving in on Diallo. He grew nervous, and moved back toward the building's vestibule, digging his hands into his pants pocket.

"His right side is digging," Carroll said. "He's frantically opening, trying to get through that door. He's looking at us, looking at us. I'm saying, 'Police, show me your hands, show me your hands!'"

Instead, Diallo pulled an object out of his pocket. Carroll

screamed *"Gun!"* and began shooting. Bullets ricocheted off the building, making it seem that Diallo was firing back at them. When another officer, Edward McMellon, fell backward while firing at Diallo, his partners assumed he'd been shot. They unleashed a hailstorm of gunfire, forty-one shots in all, spraying Diallo's small frame with bullets to his heart, lungs, liver, kidneys, spinal cord, and spleen.

When the gunfire ended, silence fell upon the scene. Carroll moved in on Diallo to seize the weapon from his hand. All he found was a wallet. *"Where's the fucking gun?"* he screamed in panic.

The reality of what he and his partners had done set in. "I rubbed his face," Carroll testified. "I said, 'Please, don't die!'"

It was a catastrophe that New Yorkers learned about within hours of the shooting. Word made its way to the West African community, and then to the media. It did not take long for furious demonstrations to spring up in the Bronx. "OH GOD! COPS KEEP KILLING 'R' BABIES" read a sign held aloft at the site.

As fury grew, Giuliani sensed the threat that the uproar posed to the perception of his crime-fighting achievements, the beating heart of his mayoralty. Standing at his lectern facing a crowd of reporters and photographers in City Hall's Blue Room, he said the shooting was "one of great concern," and cautioned against a rush to judgment. He showed far more passion in defense of his department.

"It would be very unfair to jump from this incident to accuse an entire police department and to take away from them credit they deserve for being just about the most restrained police department in the country," he said.

But that was exactly what was happening. Police killings had fallen since the Dinkins years, but Dinkins's police were not ritually humiliating minorities on the streets of their communities. Giuliani argued that it was precisely those neighborhoods that were benefiting from the aggressive crime fighting taking place in their streets, and some residents concurred. Many others saw it as a police occupation directed by a racist.

The furor proved a boon to the adversaries Giuliani had long since banished to political Siberia, Sharpton and Dinkins most prominently. Perhaps the only New Yorker more divisive than Giuliani, Sharpton created a masterpiece of political theater. He organized daily acts of civil disobedience outside of One Police Plaza, with a growing number of politicians and celebrities offering themselves up for arrest in support of the cause. Over one thousand people in the course of a month were arrested for sitting down outside the department's doors and refusing to budge, producing jarring daily images of elected officials, many of them Black, being taken away in handcuffs.

Sharpton was elevating police brutality to the forefront of the city's agenda, and embarrassing the mayor. His protests were nonviolent, and embraced by the elite who once disdained him. He grew in stature by the day. "Giuliani is on the run," he proclaimed.

The public learned to its astonishment that Giuliani had been refusing to meet with New York's Black leadership for *years*. Egged on by Cristyne Lategano, he divided the world between friends and enemies, and these were Dinkins people. The revelation led to a series of awkward, hastily arranged meetings between Giuliani and state comptroller Carl McCall, the state's highest-ranking Black official, and C. Virginia Fields, Manhattan's Black borough president, which were covered by the media as if they were historic events.

Fields, mild-mannered and conciliatory, held her tongue, and graciously agreed to meet with the man who had treated her so shabbily. It wasn't until years later that she revealed her feelings. "I don't like to define people this way, typically," she said. "But he was just an absolute, out-of-control racist."

Safir, the stone-faced police commissioner, made things worse at every turn. His answer to the outcry was to print up tens of thousands of palm cards for police officers reminding them to be *polite*. On the eve of a City Council hearing on the Diallo crisis, he was caught on-camera in a tuxedo at the Academy Awards.

As the anger in the streets grew, so did Giuliani's. "This is a great publicity stunt," he complained to reporters. "Can't you figure it out? It's a publicity stunt, and you are, as usual, sucked into it." But his advisors were starting to panic. He allowed his pollster, Frank Luntz, to convene a midtown focus group on the situation. As the participants discussed Giuliani's lack of empathy with minorities, he lost patience. "This is a waste of time!" he shouted at Luntz. "I've learned nothing from this. I am not going to turn against the police. I am not going to give into the mob mentality.

"I would rather not be mayor than do something unprincipled," he said.

True to form, he never displayed the slightest bit of doubt in his position during the greatest crisis of his mayoralty. There was always a principle involved in his unending dramas, a moral cause to defend. In this case, as in others, the principle dovetailed with his political interests; it would come off as a capitulation to start apologizing at this late date.

The public, unlike the mayor, was having plenty of second thoughts. His supporters were turning on him; his approval ratings plunged over 30 points to the lowest showing of his mayoralty. His veneer of invincibility was shattered. *New York* magazine portrayed him as a battered Superman being pelted with eggs. "THE FALL OF SUPERMAYOR" was the headline. And Hillary Clinton was preparing to capitalize on it all.

The people he normally could count on to give him strength were either gone or keeping their distance. Peter Powers, his best friend, was back in private practice. Cristyne Lategano, his devoted alter ego, was fading from the scene as Giuliani and Donna Hanover tried reconciling; the media took notice when he and Hanover shared a dance at Gracie Mansion on the night of Safir's son's wedding. Two nights later, Lategano walked into a Giuliani fundraiser and essentially told reporters that she was leaving town. "I already have the footprint on my back," she said. "I know you all want me to leave."

Three days after Lategano said her goodbyes, Rudy Giuliani decided to have a smoke at Club Mac.

Love can find you anywhere, as can trouble. Both visited Giuliani when Judith Nathan walked through Club Mac's doors that night.

A sales manager for Bristol Myers Squibb, the pharmaceutical giant, Nathan was twice divorced and living with her boyfriend in Manhattan when she met the mayor. She was there with an employee to cement an agreement between the company and Dr. Burt Meyers, an infectious disease expert at Mount Sinai Hospital. It happened that Meyers was treating Giuliani's mother, Helen, for a diabetes-related problem.

Accounts differ about who pursued whom; Nathan says that Giuliani insisted that she join him at his table, where he was sitting with Denny Young, his counsel and right-hand man, and that she refused. Only when she passed by his table did they chat, she claims. Wearing a Yankees jacket over a white collared shirt and black tuxedo tie, he began to flirt with her.

It was "one of those moments you remember forever," she recalled. "He said 'Are you not happy with the job I'm doing?'"

"Honestly, I have no clue," she said she replied.

Both were smitten. "It was the thunderbolt," Giuliani recalled years later, borrowing a line from *The Godfather*. "Our attraction was instantaneous. There was almost something mystical about the feeling."

A few days later, he sat at his desk at City Hall shooting the breeze with Tony Carbonetti, his soon-to-be chief of staff, and Matt Mahoney, Carbonetti's deputy. He fiddled with Nathan's business card, deliberating like a teenager whether to call her. His wife and two children were uptown at Gracie Mansion.

Carbonetti was appalled. "I have a bad feeling," he said. "Don't fucking do this."

"It will be fun," Giuliani insisted. "She's a great girl."

His flirtation with disaster horrified his close aide. But this was the same man who endorsed Mario Cuomo for governor; who threatened to fire every Legal Aid attorney in the city; who wore a dress at the Inner Circle. He was never as excited as when he took risks, the more perilous, the better.

He and Nathan began seeing each other almost every night. Nathan says he told her he loved her on their third date.

When she left for a business trip to Bermuda, the mayor called her every night. "Rudy doesn't sleep," she told her confidante.

She started popping up more frequently at the mayor's side. Elliot Cuker frequently hosted the two at his midtown cigar bar, Cooper Classic Cars and Cigars, giving the couple a discreet place to rendezvous.

The assistants who served as gatekeepers at City Hall were learning about her as well. "It was just like one day she was kind of on the scene," said one.

"One day she would call and she'd say 'This is Judith for the mayor.' I was like, 'Uh, he's busy.' And everybody was like 'No no no! Put her through, put her through!'"

As the press speculated about whether Rudy and Donna were reconciling, the mayor's staff was sneaking Judith into City Hall to see him, using the pretense that she was a friend of Kate Anson, the mayor's scheduler.

"Security would call Kate and say, 'Oh your friend Judith is here,'" recalled the assistant. "If there was anybody around it was never her coming to see the mayor. It was just her coming to see Kate."

Giuliani brought Nathan into his world with barely a heads-up. It was a club she hadn't asked to join, and which eyed her warily.

To call his world insular would be an understatement; his aides and sidekicks barely left his side from early morning until late at night. When the workday ended they reconvened at steakhouses and Italian restaurants. All of their favorite spots seemed to have a connection to somebody. "There was always a reason they could trust being there, and they knew it would never get out," said a Giuliani confidante.

To Nathan, his cast of characters seemed like transplants from the 1950s, their dinner tables filled with steaks, pasta, tumblers of scotch, cigars, and overflowing ashtrays. Giuliani's crew included Ray Harding, the rotund, Camel-smoking leader of the Liberal Party, speaking in a slow, conspiratorial cadence that led a journalist to liken him to a one-man smoke-filled room; Cuker, the dapper, bow-tied cigar bar owner; Howard Koeppel, the jolly, pistol-packing, gay millionaire car dealer; and perhaps a dozen staffers and deputy mayors who rarely left his side.

To Nathan they were a strange bunch. Giuliani explained to her that politics attracted odd characters.

The mayor relished his role as paterfamilias. He was garrulous, indefatigable—he drew his energy from people. His crew luxuriated in his company and competed for his approval. He never seemed ready to call it a night. He didn't just like being around people; he needed it. His new girlfriend came to realize that Giuliani hated being alone.

Central to Nathan's justification for her affair with Giuliani was her contention that his marriage to Donna was effectively over by the time the two started dating. After a month together, she claimed that he showed her a written separation agreement, signed by Rudy and Donna, that outlined the facts of their estrangement, a legal prelude to a divorce filing. It allegedly stated that Donna would remain in Gracie Mansion while Giuliani served out his term.

Nathan has not produced a copy of the alleged document, however, and some people close to Giuliani dispute that it existed at the time.

Nathan was a complex figure. Born Judi Ann Stish in Hazleton, Pennsylvania, a former coal mining town, she alternately presented herself as an affluent and powerful executive and a small-town girl, fond of pulling out her TJ Maxx card to demonstrate her humble values: "I'm a Maxximizer," she often said.

She was smart, engaging, and hyperkinetic, with boundless energy, like her new boyfriend, and a natural ability to turn a stranger into a confidante in the span of a conversation. She had a nurturing side—she was trained as a nurse—and a deep loyalty to those she cared for. She looked at Giuliani with adoring eyes.

He was a familiar figure to her; her father, Donald Stish, whom she worshipped, was an old-school Italian, like Giuliani. Both were towering figures in her eyes.

Others in her life were less enchanted with her than the mayor was. Her ex-husband Bruce Nathan portrayed her in his divorce papers as shallow, materialistic, and cruel.

"Unlike my wife, I was not a social climber," he stated, adding that her "'main goal' in life was: being involved with whatever was 'the in thing' at the moment. Whether it was: belonging to the 'right church' by converting from Catholicism to Presbyterian; playing bridge with the 'right people' . . . enrolling [their daughter] Whitney at the 'right schools' in order to further my wife's social aspirations; wearing designer clothes and jewelry; and vacationing at the fashionable Hamptons."

She could be vicious, he alleged; when she lost her temper, he said she would call him a "kike" and a "Jewboy."

Judith accused Bruce of spousal abuse, and alleged he assaulted her.

But it was Bruce's description that rang true to Giuliani's aides, who came to regard her as deeply manipulative and obsessed with status and money. Their main concern in the spring of 1999, however, was that the mayor was cheating on the first lady. And the person most concerned was Tony Carbonetti.

Baby-faced and genial, Carbonetti's devotion to his boss ran deep. Their family connections reached back more than half a century: Louis Carbonetti, his grandfather, was Harold Giuliani's best friend, and Lou Jr., Tony's father, was a friend of Rudy's growing up. True to his preference for keeping things in the family, the mayor named Lou Jr. to head the city's Community Assistance Unit, and twenty-five-year-old Tony as his appointments director, dispensing patronage jobs to political supporters.

It was a measure of Giuliani's loyalty that he promoted Tony to chief of staff even after his father was forced to resign for lying on his financial disclosure forms about his debts, among other scandals. Nine years after that, he would plead guilty to three counts of perjury for lying about a conflict of interest while running a Brooklyn nonprofit. But Giuliani's bond with Tony only deepened, as the mayor increasingly came to rely upon his aide's political acumen.

Nathan and Carbonetti immediately sensed a threat in the other. She told people that she tried to win him over, presenting him with gifts, such as a leather computer case, which she claimed she later found in a City Hall garbage can. "I knew he was going to be an adversary," Nathan said. (Carbonetti claims his girlfriend at the time threw it away because he wasn't using it.)

Her efforts to woo him came to a dead end at a diner in upstate New York, when Giuliani was making the rounds for his potential Senate run. Nathan invited Carbonetti to dinner.

She reminded him of the acrimonious relationship the staff had with Lategano, and asked him how they could avoid the same sorry outcome. "What can I do to make you not hate me?" she asked.

"Stay the fuck out of his life," Carbonetti responded.

She was stunned. "I can't stay out of his life. We love each other. You can't tell two people not to love each other."

"Well, you're just going to complicate things. You're going to be a distraction, and it's going to be ugly. You're going to take us off message."

Nathan had never heard the term "off message" before. The phrase stuck in her craw.

Out of loyalty to the boss, Giuliani's core staff worked hard to conceal the affair. They frequently staffed his dates with Nathan to give him cover in case reporters or photographers spotted the couple together. They half-jokingly called themselves his "Alibi Squad."

But the mayor's entourage would never accept Nathan into their circle. "It didn't matter who I was or what I did or what I could bring to the table," she told a confidante. "I was a threat to their power, because they perceived that I wanted power. They did the same thing to Cristyne."

Carbonetti saw it differently. "She's a horrible human being," he said.

Far from staying away, no one would play a larger role in Rudy Giuliani's life in the years to come than Judith Nathan. Her priorities became his priorities, shaping the decisions he made, and changing the course of his career. Within a few years almost every member of Giuliani's entourage was gone.

CHAPTER 5

Pals

"Tonight: Donald Trump! Need we say more?"

Larry King, CNN's craggy prime-time interviewer, sat face-to-face with New York's dashing celebrity developer on the evening of October 7, 1999. Trump was there to announce that he was forming an exploratory committee to run for president. It was a publicity stunt—it would be sixteen years before he got serious about running—but the ratings were always good for him, and King treated it as if it were a historic event.

"Most people who form exploratory committees, that's that major step toward going," King said, egging him on.

Trump played coy. "Well, it's a step."

"Can you say it is a major step?"

"I don't think I can say it's a major step. . . ."

"And the decision by sometime in January?"

"Sometime January or February, early part of February."

"Two, three months in there, right?"

"I would say about that, yes, Larry."

It was a mindless conversation. Only when the subject veered off topic did the developer say anything revealing.

"What do you make of the Hillary-Giuliani—I know you're a big fan of Giuliani," King asked.

"I am, and I like her very much, but I think Rudy—and as I said before, he's been the greatest mayor in the history of the city of New York. . . . [He] really helped the city, and he's been a great mayor. Maybe some people don't like him and some people love him totally.

"I happen to be in love," he said.

He caught himself and tried to backtrack on the comment, but it was a telling moment. Trump rarely gushed about anyone besides himself, but there was something about Rudy Giuliani that made him swoon.

The mayor and he were rarely seen together, but their behind-the-scenes dealings were far more frequent than most people knew. It was a relationship based on a symbiotic mix of friendship, respect, and self-interest, a dynamic that would last a lifetime.

Trump had endless needs of city government. He was a developer whose business thrived on subsidies and tax breaks, and depended upon agencies for variances, permits, and other approvals. It was in his interest to cultivate the mayor and his aides. Giuliani, for his part, gained from his campaign contributions, advocacy, and assorted benefits of being on Donald Trump's good side, including sky-high praise on national prime-time television interviews.

But the relationship wasn't purely transactional; each saw much to admire in the other. They were old-school, outer-borough brawlers who took pleasure in bludgeoning their opponents. Both valued loyalty above competence, with the sky the limit for those who passed the test. They were forever striving to prove their loyalty to each other.

The bond was on display in October 1998, when Trump broke ground on Trump World Tower, a development slated to rise across from the United Nations building on Manhattan's East Side—"the tallest and most luxurious residential tower in the world," he boasted.

The plans were comically out of scale with the neighborhood, a $360 million, 750,000-square-foot bronze-colored glass edifice rising seventy-two stories (he exaggerated and claimed it was ninety stories). It was three hundred feet higher than the U.N. building, then the tallest building in the area.

Trump quietly purchased air rights from the owners of surrounding buildings, which sidestepped the need for height variances, and allowed him to avoid onerous zoning hurdles. He simply applied for a building permit, which the city's Buildings Department summarily granted.

Community members, blindsided, went ballistic. For half a century, developers had honored the city's 1947 agreement with the U.N. restricting the size of new developments in the vicinity. Trump claimed "most people" believed the agreement was never consummated.

As he began selling apartments for more than a million dollars each with barely a beam planted in the ground, protests flooded City Hall from well-to-do neighbors, many of whose views of the East River stood to be ruined by his trophy building. No less than Walter Cronkite wrote a complaining letter to Giuliani on May 25, 1999, on behalf of the Beekman Hill Association, a community group. He urgently requested a meeting to discuss what he called the "peculiar" Buildings Department decision. A week later, the mayor received a similar letter from Citicorp's legendary CEO, Walter Wriston.

A few weeks went by seemingly without a response from the mayor. Cronkite, angered, fired off another letter to him, complaining about his lack of responsiveness to their complaints about Trump's "monstrous building."

"I am disappointed to learn that you apparently have turned a deaf ear to the rather distinguished hundreds of citizens (and the even more numerous citizens of no public distinction) who are protesting the 90-story Trump residential Tower he is rushing to build at 47th and First," wrote the most trusted man in America.

U.N. secretary-general Kofi Annan weighed in with his own letter, insisting that the mayor revisit the Building Department's decision.

It wasn't just irate neighbors who were disturbed by the city's green light. The chairman of the City Planning Commission, Joe Rose, sent an internal memo to Deputy Mayor Randy Levine stating that he was "not comfortable" with some of the Building Department's conclusions that led to the approval. Lacking the power to cancel the permit, Rose moved to overhaul the zoning code's height regulations so that no one could pull a Trump-style maneuver again.

Giuliani ignored the objections. Cornered at an event by a community leader, he demurred, calling the matter "a very complicated legal question."

Many of the project's opponents were more respected, accomplished, and powerful than Donald Trump, giants of New York who weren't accustomed to the kind of shoddy treatment they were receiving from the mayor. But he seemed happy to treat them with disrespect. His treatment of Trump was another story.

Eight days after Cronkite sent his irate second letter, the mayor walked through the grand, solid-bronze doors of the venerable Marble Collegiate Church on Fifth Avenue for the funeral of Fred Trump, Donald's father. He marched up the center aisle's red carpet, past dozens of pews filled with hundreds of members of the city's corporate and political elite, stepped up to the dais, and turned to the audience. Fred's casket, covered in white roses, was a few feet away.

"Fred Trump was a very big man, a giant," Giuliani told the crowd. "Fred Trump not only helped to build our city, but helped define it."

Donald, who told a biographer that he considered it a sign of weakness for a man to cry, listened quietly as the mayor praised the family patriarch, describing Fred, once more feared and loathed than his son, as a hero who contributed incalculably to the city's greatness.

Such acts of kindness and respect flew back and forth between the mayor and Trump. The developer maintained a back channel to the administration through Deputy Mayor Randy Levine, a skilled troubleshooter for the mayor and a die-hard Republican. Trump provided him with a steady stream of Senate campaign intelligence, keeping him abreast of which members of the establishment were raising money for Clinton. Most were intimate affairs charging invitees as much as $25,000 a pop, such as developer Larry Silverstein's fundraising dinner aboard his yacht ("Rubber soled shoes please"). Trump typically scrawled a note on the invitations, and directed them to "Randy L."

He also kept an eye on Giuliani's adversaries. When Ed Koch held a party for his book attacking the mayor, *Giuliani: Nasty Man*, Trump forwarded the invite to Levine, with a note reading "Randy L Not nice!" The information was of minor value, but it was Trump's signal of fidelity to the mayor.

Interspersed with the gestures of his support were notes about the U.N. project. When an executive at Rose Associates, a real estate conglomerate, wrote a letter to shareholders of a nearby building urging them to oppose the tower, Trump forwarded it to Levine, questioning Joe Rose's impartiality as city planning commissioner. "Randy—this is Joe Rose's family company—what do you think—?"

When a friend sent Trump a letter claiming that most people he'd spoken with supported the tower, Trump mailed it to Levine. "Randy—Most People are Strongly in Favor," he scrawled in black marker. When the billionaire David Koch, who opposed the project, ran into local opposition for attempting to expand his Palm Beach mansion, Trump sent Levine a *Palm Beach Daily News* story about it, ridiculing Koch's hypocrisy.

Trump's adversaries were apoplectic over Giuliani's refusal to speak with them. Former Diners Club chairman Seymour Flug was reduced to ambushing Giuliani on a street corner as he was exiting his SUV and handing the mayor a letter of opposition to the tower.

Trump was too smart to work Giuliani overtly, but he reached out when something was guaranteed to please him. When *New York Observer* columnist Joe Conason speculated that Trump was surreptitiously working to land Giuliani the Independence Party's support for his Senate race, Trump sent the column to Giuliani ("It is always a pleasure to hear from you," the mayor replied).

His correspondences—half intended to help Giuliani, half intended to help himself—continued unabated through the duration of the fight over the tower. As Cronkite and company waited for a phone call from the mayor that never came, Trump was nuzzling his face into Giuliani's breasts in their Inner Circle video.

On August 7, 2000, Trump's mother, Mary, died. Giuliani attended the wake and once again spoke at the funeral of a Trump parent.

"I will never forget your friendship!" Trump wrote to Giuliani afterward. "You are a very special person and I will always be with you no matter what course you follow!"

Three months later, Trump's opponents exhausted their legal efforts to stop the tower, and he proceeded to build the tallest residential building in the world, as promised. Flug reacted with disgust. "Every time a New Yorker, or anyone else, for that matter, passes by this monstrosity," he told a reporter, "they should think of Mayor Giuliani and Mr. Trump."

In August 1999, the cover of the Sunday *New York Times Magazine* featured a relaxed Rudy Giuliani flashing a wide smile, his leg crossed casually over his knee, under a headline reading "Introducing Mr. Nice Guy."

The story, by James Traub, set the stage for Giuliani's epic ("Miltonic") race for the Senate against Clinton, and described a candidate at peace with himself.

The Mayor's aides insist that in the last few months they have seen a New Rudy emerge. He's playing golf with his son, Andrew—on a weekday! He's wearing goofy sunglasses! He's smiling, really! The chilly Mayor was even seen wrapping a fatherly arm around a City Hall employee. And it has been weeks since he has lashed out at his critics, or fumed at the hypocrites who beset him. "He ain't cranky anymore," says one of his top aides, who would rather not have his name associated with the sentiment that the Mayor was formerly cranky.

The story prompted eye rolls at City Hall, as the anonymous aide was hiding the real reason for Giuliani's new disposition: he had been hit by a thunderbolt.

He and Judith were inseparable. At dinner with his aides, they were playful and affectionate, sharing stories and nibbling at each other's food. Sometimes he would rhapsodize her with a song. They were together so frequently that it started to seem normal to his aides.

On weekends he traveled with Nathan to her small condo in the Hamptons, often driven by members of his security detail, and accompanied by Giuliani's young body man, Manny Papir. As aides were feeding cover stories to reporters that he was on golf trips with Andrew, he was lighting up cigars on Nathan's patio and relaxing in the soft glow of the setting sun. Sometimes they would dine at local restaurants. The *East Hampton Star* took note of it in two cryptic sentences buried near the end of a story titled "October Fish Takes Tournament."

"Speaking of marlin, Mayor Rudolph W. Giuliani and a friend seemed to be enjoying dinner at the Johnny Marlin restaurant down on the Montauk docks Sunday night," it stated. "He was seated under the giant blue marlin mount." Then the story moved on to an item about a local fisherman hooking a thirty-eight-pound striped bass.

Nathan wasn't the only reason the mayor was in a buoyant mood.

The administration was regaining its footing. The Amadou Diallo protests were all but over, and Hillary Clinton was floundering.

The first lady, who had never run for office before, was making an alarming number of mistakes. When her husband granted clemency to members of the FALN Puerto Rican terrorist group, a war broke out between Hispanic leaders and police unions. Stuck in a vise of her husband's making, she exhausted every rhetorical escape route until finally picking her poison and calling for her husband to reverse his decision.

A few months later, she traveled to the Mideast, ostensibly on White House business but mainly to demonstrate her mastery of foreign affairs to the New York electorate. She scheduled appearances in Israel and in the West Bank, in a Clintonian effort to appeal to every audience and offend no one. It didn't work out that way. Appearing at a joint press conference with Suha Arafat, the wife of PLO leader Yasser Arafat, Clinton sat passively as Arafat delivered a blistering speech falsely accusing the Israeli military of firing poison gas at Palestinians. In the face of scorching criticism for remaining silent during the diatribe, Clinton pinned the blame on her interpreter.

Her supporters cringed at her inability to untangle herself when controversies arose. But the mayor was elated, and used every weapon in his arsenal to rattle her. He yanked permission for Tina Brown to hold a star-studded debut party for *Talk Magazine* at the Brooklyn Navy Yard after the celebrity editor placed Clinton on the cover of her first issue. The next month, he ordered his aides to raise the Arkansas flag above City Hall. The moves were over the top, and guaranteed to drive Democrats crazy.

Like the president he would serve decades later, Giuliani had an instinctive ability to press the outrage button at whim. In his first term he fomented public uproars to shatter the complacency that allowed city services to decline, crime to rise, and budget deficits to soar. But as his political aspirations grew, he increasingly created these spectacles to serve his own needs.

Exhibit A was the holy war against the Brooklyn Museum in the fall of 1999.

The once staid institution intentionally courted controversy by importing a British exhibit titled "Sensation," set to open in October. The exhibit's catalogue featured, among other things, mannequins of naked children mimicking sex; a cow sliced into twelve pieces; a man hanging from a cross-shaped tree with his penis severed; and a portrait of a child killer made from the handprints of children. The piece most guaranteed to offend, say, an old-school Catholic mayor, was a portrait of the Virgin Mary, flanked by images of vaginas and anuses, and baring a clump of elephant dung on her left breast.

Giuliani, genuinely offended, lashed into the exhibit at a press conference. "The idea of, in the name of art, having a city-subsidized building having so-called works of art in which people are throwing elephant dung at a picture of the Virgin Mary is sick," he said.

He moved to cut off $7 million in public funding for the museum, appalling the art world, editorial boards, and civil libertarians. Polls showed New Yorkers opposed his move two to one.

He wasn't playing to the city, though; his audiences were conservative upstate voters and national Republican donors. The man who once ridiculed Barry Goldwater as confused and idiotic hired Goldwater's former aide Richard Viguerie, a right-wing direct mail specialist and a founder of the Moral Majority, to produce a fundraising letter highlighting his campaign against the museum.

"The left-wing elite opposes me," wrote the mayor who had endorsed Democrat Mario Cuomo five years earlier, "because I have shown that a Republican can win elections by wide margins even in a Democratic stronghold like New York City with a bold unapologetic Ronald Reagan–style conservative agenda."

The letter went on to advocate for school prayer and posting the Ten Commandments in the nation's classrooms.

To hammer home the message, he took his show on the road, delivering a full-throated endorsement of Republican values and excoriating the museum exhibit at the Ronald Reagan Library in Simi Valley, California, and then bragged about his actions on Fox News. His rhetoric grew more incendiary by the day. "I don't want any money coming out of my pocket to pay for this kind of sick demonstration of clear psychological problems," he told reporters. "This should happen in a psychiatric hospital, not in a museum."

It was vintage Giuliani, unleashing his moral fury while cheating on his wife and selling out his political principles. Ultimately the courts ruled against him and forced the city to continue funding the museum.

Giuliani's espousal of liberal causes had ceased in 1994, after Newt Gingrich led the Republican takeover of Congress, and Republican George Pataki seized the governorship from Cuomo. Giuliani's welfare policies, advocacy of school vouchers, and other positions were part of his conservative turn. But this was the first time that he embraced right-wing social causes. It was making a lot of New Yorkers cringe, but Fox News and the Republican Party ate it up. His dalliance with the political right was just beginning.

On April 26, 2000, Donald Trump grabbed a black marker and scrawled a note to the mayor. Friends of Giuliani, the campaign organization, had sent Trump a press release hailing the candidate's 14-point lead among upstate voters, conducted by John Zogby, the preferred pollster of the GOP.

"RUDY—This is great!" Trump wrote in large letters on the bottom of the page. "Keep fighting."

Trump was doubtless aware that there was nothing to celebrate that week. Giuliani's upstate lead was a small part of a far gloomier story; the past six weeks had seen a neck-and-neck race turn into a statewide 10-point lead by Clinton. And things were getting worse.

New Yorkers were accustomed to having an over-the-top mayor. But what transpired over eight weeks in the spring of 2000 was closer to lunacy.

The sequence of events that turned the world upside down for Rudy Giuliani began six weeks earlier, not long after Giuliani shook hands with Hillary Clinton before one thousand guests at the Inner Circle Dinner at the Hilton. Nineteen blocks away from the midtown hotel, in a seedier part of town, three plainclothes narcotics detectives were cruising through the rain, hunting for drug dealers.

In the wake of the Diallo fiasco, NYPD brass reined in the Street Crime Unit, and watched, predictably, as gun seizures plummeted and the murder rate rose. Under pressure from City Hall to squelch the trend, Police Commissioner Safir launched "Operation Condor," a $24 million effort to flood the city's high-crime neighborhoods with narcotics officers. Instead of searching for illegal guns, the police this time were dispatched by the hundreds to rid the streets of drug dealers. Like the Street Crime Unit's stop-and-frisk onslaught, it was brutally effective; narcotics officers made over twenty thousand drug busts in just two months.

City Council members, irritated over the program's price tag, hauled Safir in for a hearing on March 13, at which he defended the program. Murders were up, he said, and drug dealing was a major reason.

"As we eliminate drug gangs and drug criminals, there will be fewer people shooting each other," he testified.

Three days later, Operation Condor reached its disastrous culmination.

The Distinguished Wakamba Cocktail Lounge was a hole in the wall a few blocks south of the city's wretched Port Authority Bus

Terminal, off Times Square. The area was a no-man's-land of dive bars, prostitutes, and drug dealers, a tempting target for cops looking to put points on the scoreboard. As it was, Detectives Anderson Moran, Julio Cruz, and Anthony Vasquez had already made eight marijuana busts that day before spotting Patrick Dorismond standing outside of the Wakamba.

Their precinct commander, suspecting that the Bloods gang was selling crack in the area, dispatched the three to perform buy-and-bust stings. Moran played the customer, while his two partners worked as backup "ghosts." All three wore street clothes.

Dorismond came from a prominent family in Haiti—his father and brother were famous musicians. Patrick's occupation was less glamorous; he worked as a private security guard near Macy's, supporting his two children.

With his partners watching from a discreet distance, Moran approached Dorismond and his friend outside the bar, pretending to be a buyer. "Have any krills?" he asked, using street language for crack.

Things unraveled in seconds. Dorismond took offense, flew into a rage, and threw a punch. Detectives Cruz and Vasquez came running, and Vasquez pulled out his firearm. One of Dorismond's friends yelled *"Gun!"*

A melee ensued, and Dorismond grabbed Vasquez's hand holding the gun, twisting it until at one point it neared Vasquez's head. It was a life-and-death struggle, with the two men virtually chest to chest. The gun went off—no one could tell who pulled the trigger—sending bullets ripping through Dorismond's aorta and killing him almost instantly.

He was the fourth unarmed Black man killed by police in thirteen months, and when word spread activists and elected officials were incensed. Three weeks earlier, the four officers involved in the Diallo case had been acquitted by a jury that concluded his death was an accident. Lingering anger over the acquittal inflamed the atmosphere around Dorismond's killing.

The usual players in New York's race wars took their places. Al Sharpton, surprisingly low-key, called for calm, and urged New Yorkers to withhold judgment until the facts came in. Giuliani did so as well, appearing at a press conference with Safir at his side. He spoke in a low, solemn voice.

"I would urge everyone not to jump to conclusions, and to allow the facts to be analyzed and investigated without people trying to let their biases, their prejudices, their emotions, their stereotypes dictate the results," he told reporters, expressing no condolences to the Dorismond family.

It was a matter of principle to Giuliani that he stand in the way of those calling for the heads of the three detectives. As in the Diallo case, he felt it would be immoral to play to the crowd and sell out his officers.

But morality didn't get in the way of what he did next.

On the same morning that he cautioned against a rush to judgment, he authorized the NYPD to release Dorismond's criminal and court records—including, inexplicably, his sealed juvenile record, an unheard-of move of questionable legality. The records showed that Dorismond had been arrested three times over nine years: once for hitting someone; a second time for criminal possession of a weapon, where no weapon was found; and a third for robbery and assault when he was thirteen (contained in the sealed record). He was never convicted of a crime; he pleaded guilty to two disorderly conduct violations.

Giuliani launched a blistering campaign to discredit a man who had been shot dead by police after minding his own business. With demonstrators marching in midtown chanting *NYPD murderers!* he escalated his attacks on Dorismond's character.

"People do act in conformity very often with their prior behavior," he said on *Fox News Sunday* from a VFW hall on an upstate campaign swing. The media "would not want a picture presented of an altar boy, when in fact maybe it isn't an altar boy, it's some other situation that may justify, more closely, what the police officer did."

Dorismond actually had been an altar boy, and a student at Bishop Loughlin, no less. But no apologies were forthcoming. As in the Diallo conflict, Giuliani pointed out that police shootings under his watch were at a record low. But the statistics didn't resonate with the public nearly as much as his lack of compassion. His moral absolutism was creating havoc; he refused to visit Dorismond's family, saying to do so would send the wrong message about who was to blame.

Not to be dissuaded—his aides gave up trying—he then went after Dorismond's *girlfriend*, who had the temerity to praise her dead companion on television. He authorized the release of more police records indicating that police had been called when Dorismond allegedly assaulted her. "That Mr. Dorismond spent a good deal of his adult life punching people was a fact," Giuliani said.

With the temperature hitting a boiling point, Dorismond's funeral in Brooklyn descended into a riot. Five thousand people escorted the body to a church as protesters screamed anti-Giuliani chants and clashed with police. Twenty-three cops were injured, and twenty-seven people were arrested.

Giuliani's statewide lead over Clinton evaporated, and the floor collapsed on his approval ratings, which sank to the lowest point of his mayoralty. Clinton was beating him three to one in his own city and would soon tie him upstate. His support among Black city residents was so minuscule that the *New York Times* poll couldn't even measure it.

As tempers in the streets rose, so did Giuliani's. There was no distinction to him between an attack on the cops and an attack on him, and politically that was probably true. No mayor in history had ever bound himself to the city's police as he had. It was his army.

In the end, a grand jury concluded that Detective Vasquez did not intend to kill Dorismond, and declined to indict him. Giuliani cited that decision, like the acquittal of the officers who shot Amadou Diallo, as vindication of his refusal to cave to mob rule. History would remember it as the moment he smeared an innocent dead man.

The mayor was under even greater pressure than people realized. Amid the tumult of the Dorismond conflict, he was struggling with a spiraling health crisis.

Three weeks after the killing, he received a phone call from his doctor as he and Judith were riding to a campaign fundraiser at the Binghamton Country Club in upstate New York. A routine checkup the previous day showed his PSA levels were high, a warning sign for prostate cancer.

At the same time he was struggling to salvage his Senate campaign, he was undergoing a sequence of medical tests, and waking up in the middle of the night with anxieties about his health. Each successive test produced worrisome results. On April 25—the day Donald Trump dashed off his congratulatory note to him—Giuliani was at Mount Sinai Medical Center, undergoing a biopsy that would confirm he had prostate cancer.

On April 27, he walked into the Blue Room in City Hall, which was filled to capacity with reporters. What seemed like his entire staff was gathered in a corner. Dressed in a navy blue suit, white shirt, and red tie, he waited patiently for people to take their seats. Television stations were broadcasting live.

"I was diagnosed yesterday with a—prostate cancer," he began. "It's a treatable form of prostate cancer that was diagnosed at an early stage."

He delivered the news calmly, factually, and candidly, as was his way in crises. He answered questions patiently, and was unusually game to answer questions about his feelings. Reminded by a reporter that his father died of the same disease almost two decades earlier, he said the diagnosis "[brought] up very painful memories."

"I miss my father every day of my life," he said. "He's a very, very important reason for why I'm standing here as the mayor of New York City."

"Will you be a nicer guy now?" asked Rafael Martinez Alequin, a press gadfly.

"No way," he answered to laughter.

Over the next few days his news commanded the front pages, good wishes poured in from every which way, and the political world engaged in will-he-or-won't-he speculation over the fate of his Senate campaign. Hillary Clinton called him to express her support.

The outpouring of sympathy continued for five days. On the sixth it came to a screeching halt.

The tabloids had gotten wind of a story and held on to it out of respect for his medical condition. The gates flew open in the pages of the New York *Daily News.*

"*Rudy & Friend Dine & Dine,*" ran the headline of Mitchell Fink's gossip column.

"Rudy Giuliani hasn't let the diagnosis of prostate cancer slow him down," the columnist wrote. "A day after he stunned the city with news of his condition, there he was at 11 p.m. Friday dining on mussels in marinara sauce—but no linguini—with a friend at Cronies on Second Avenue.

"Then, Sunday night, he and the same friend reappeared at the restaurant, this time sitting in a more open section of the eatery....

"One restaurant staffer opined that the mayor was with his wife, but shown a picture of Donna Hanover, he said it wasn't her. Giuliani's office had no comment."

The rival *New York Post* had been working on the story as well but had held its fire. The next day the editors' patience came to an end. "Here's the first look at the mystery woman who's been spotted dining quietly with Mayor Giuliani," it reported, revealing Judith Nathan's name near three blurry photos of the two.

The mayor had tempted fate for over a year. The only surprise was that it took the press this long to catch on.

That afternoon reporters bombarded him with questions about the "mystery woman."

"She's a good friend, a very good friend," he said. "Beyond that, you can ask me questions, and that's exactly what I'm going to say."

The pandemonium that followed was both opera and soap opera, a mammoth scandal exploding under the glare of a nation already transfixed by his race against the first lady. But it wasn't Hillary Clinton who was the star of this production.

In short order the secrets the couple kept over the previous year tumbled out into the headlines—their dinners with Giuliani's team, trips to the Hamptons, quality time at Elliot Cuker's cigar bar, attendance at official Gracie Mansion events. It was a mesmerizing train wreck. Mayor, Senate candidate, cancer patient, adulterer—Giuliani was in a tabloid league of his own.

He was a master at waging wars in public, but this went beyond the usual Giuliani epic; never in his career had he come off as such a villain. In a matter of a few weeks he had divided the city over race, sparked a riot, and gotten caught cheating on his wife. All his speeches about values, the lectures about civility, the piety about the Ten Commandments in classrooms, were laid to waste. The hypocrisy was breathtaking.

Not until Donald Trump transfixed the nation years later by bragging about groping women would a public figure find himself in so much trouble in the middle of a nationally viewed election.

Joe Bruno, the powerful Republican State Senate majority leader, was a gray-haired, old-school rural conservative from upstate Rensselaer County, where his pastime was horseback riding at his thirteen-acre ranch. He was not the kind of man to find amusement in the fun and games taking place at New York City Hall, where there didn't seem to be an adult in sight. Watching his party's prospects of winning a U.S. Senate seat collapsing with Rudy Giuliani's marriage, he telegraphed his anger in a radio interview.

"I'm hoping they can reconcile their differences and do whatever it is they think is in their best interest and their families' because it certainly isn't conversations that we want to keep having publicly," he said.

Giuliani got the message. That morning he scheduled a press conference on the outdoor terrace of the elegant Bryant Park Grill in midtown. He took a question about Bruno's comments, but instead of addressing them, launched into a rambling account of his marital troubles.

"This is very, very painful," he began, looking stressed. "For quite some time it's probably been apparent that Donna and I lead in many ways independent and separate lives.

"It's been a very painful road and I'm hopeful that we'll be able to formalize that in an agreement that protects our children, gives them all the security and all the protection they deserve, and protects Donna."

After announcing his intention to divorce the first lady, he then turned to the subject of Judith. "I rely on her, and she helps me a great deal. And I'm going to need her more now than maybe I did before. These are decisions that I have to make, you know, at a very difficult time...

"I don't really care about politics right now," he said. "I'm thinking about my family, the people that I love and what can be done that's honest and truthful and that protects them the best," he said.

It was hard at the moment not to sympathize with him. He

seemed deeply distraught; his eyes were red. "My emotional state is, I'm very sad," he said. "And I feel terrible."

It seemed like the conclusion of the saga of Giuliani's troubled marriage to Donna Hanover, who had kept a low profile since he acknowledged his affair with Nathan. But hours after her husband's press conference ended, her press office sent out a media alert for her own press conference at Gracie Mansion. Television satellite trucks descended upon the mayor's residence.

Hanover stepped out of the mansion with her hands clasped, and walked up to a mass of reporters stationed in the driveway. It turned out that she had been blindsided by her husband's announcement.

"Today's turn of events brings me great sadness," she said, her voice quivering. "I had hoped to keep this marriage together. For several years, it was difficult to participate in Rudy's public life because of his relationship with one staff member.

"Beginning last May, I made a major effort to bring us back together. Rudy and I re-established some of our personal intimacy through the fall. At that point, he chose another path. Rudy and I will now discuss the possibility of a legal separation."

The television news veteran was a professional at this game, and picked a moment to inflict maximum damage, alleging on live television that Giuliani had cheated on her not once but twice, the first time with Cristyne Lategano.

Far from getting his house in order, as Joe Bruno demanded, Giuliani had brought the conflict to a higher level. Bruno, Pataki, and virtually every Republican witnessing the circus were aghast. The Senate race, the mayoralty—all were lost in the unreality of the mayor and his wife turning on each another.

One surreal development begat another. Two days after the dueling press conferences, the mayor and Nathan took his press secretary Sunny Mindel out for her birthday to Tony's Di Napoli, an Upper

East Side Italian restaurant, and then went for a romantic ten-block stroll up Second Avenue after dinner. The couple was accompanied by a swarm of photographers. "WALKING MY BABY BACK HOME," the front page of the *Daily News* read the next day.

Giuliani no longer seemed sad. He was proud to walk with his girlfriend, and wanted the world to know it. There was never a moment of remorse for what he had inflicted on his wife, children, party, or the public. He passed his own moral litmus test with flying colors.

The takeaway that would haunt him for the rest of his career was that he announced to the public that he was divorcing his wife before he informed her, the act of a twisted mind. It did not come out of the blue, however; the two had discussed divorcing numerous times.

"They tried to reconcile for a period of time after Cristyne left," said an aide. "We were all very hopeful. Everyone wanted him to have a happy home life. Everyone wanted him to make up with Donna. Peter [Powers] and Tony [Carbonetti] and everybody else tried to help, but it fell apart very quickly. Then Judith popped into the picture."

With the cat out of the bag, and cancer hovering over him like a dark cloud, Giuliani spent the next week agonizing over the Senate run. His closest advisors made pilgrimages to Gracie Mansion to argue their cases. Powers, languishing in self-imposed exile after losing his power struggle with Lategano, returned to his best friend's side, as he had so many times over the years. "Rudy, there are a lot of sharks in the water," he told him. "The smart thing to do is, let's fight another day."

Adam Goodman, his media advisor, made an impassioned presentation to the contrary, arguing that the mayor's only chance of rescuing his career would be to fight his way back and capture the seat. Withdrawing would confirm to his Republican critics, still smarting from the Cuomo endorsement, that he didn't care about the party.

Those critics would not have been wrong. As state Republicans were printing "RUDY" posters for the upcoming nominating convention, the candidate's mind was elsewhere. On the night of May 18, he appeared at a televised town hall at Manhattan's 92nd Street Y hosted by Andrea Mitchell of MSNBC. Sensing a rare moment of vulnerability, she pressed him for his reflections.

The cancer diagnosis, he said, "involves thinking about your life, mortality, the quality of your life."

Astonishingly, he confessed to regretting his shoddy treatment of Patrick Dorismond's family. "I made a mistake," he said. "I should have conveyed the human feeling that I had of compassion and loss for the mother. I think if I could do it over again, I would try to balance it more."

With the clock ticking down to the state convention and Republicans at their wits' end, his agonizing ceased after a poor night's sleep on May 19. When the sun rose he called some friends, hosted his weekly radio show, and then instructed his aides to call an afternoon press conference. By noon, television satellite trucks encircled City Hall, and local and national news crews inside the building waited in a line that snaked down long corridors leading to the old Board of Estimate chamber, a stately hall with fifteen-foot white marble columns and wooden church pews.

At 3:30 p.m., Giuliani, dressed in a dark suit, white shirt, and crimson tie, swept into the room with virtually every member of his staff. Hundreds of his supporters jumped to their feet, and gave him a standing ovation.

He quieted the crowd. "I'm a very fortunate man, and this is one demonstration of why I'm a very fortunate man," he began. "God has given me a lot, and whatever obstacles that are placed in your way, I think the way to deal with it is to try to figure out how to make it make you a better person.

"The reason I'm such a fortunate man is that I have people that love me and I love them, and they care for me and I care for them, and that's the greatest support that you can have in life. And I think I'm fortunate because I probably have a few more people like that."

He was at his plainspoken best, speaking from the heart with simple eloquence. He confessed that he'd had trouble making this big decision—"which has never really happened to me," he said. "I've always been able to make decisions.

"But something very beautiful happens," he continued. "It makes you figure out what you're really all about and what's really important to you. . . . And I guess because I've been in public life so long, in politics, I used to think the core of me was in politics, probably. It isn't.

"I've decided that what I should do is to put my health first," he said grimly. "This is not the right time for me to run for office."

A reporter asked him if this signaled the end of his political career.

"I don't think I'm thinking about politics," he said. "I don't know, I'm thinking about—I'm thinking about deeper, deeper things than that."

Then, as he had done on election night in 1997 and other moments of high emotion, he promised to reach out to Black New Yorkers whom he'd estranged during his mayoralty. "I want to extend my mayoralty and try to overcome some of the barriers that are there," he said.

Giuliani had left a path of destruction a mile long over the previous two months, laying waste to his marriage, his party, and the city's racial fabric, only to announce in a soul-searching speech that he'd realized that there was more to life than politics.

It was hard to keep up with the self-serving tap dance, but there was a genius to it. He came off as hugely sympathetic, Lou Gehrig announcing his retirement to a grieving public, calling himself the luckiest man in the world.

Somewhere, perhaps, Donald Trump was watching this master of political theater taking control of a crisis by providing the public with a mesmerizing show, with himself cast as the hero.

The speech ended in a hail of applause. Television photographers turned off their lights, and Giuliani made his way to the exit with his entourage, a hurricane blowing out to sea.

CHAPTER 6

Mistakes

On January 8, 2001, Giuliani and his security detail circled the upper level of City Hall's soaring white marble rotunda, past the landing where Abraham Lincoln's body lay in state in 1865, and entered the City Council chambers. It was a grand old room, dating back to 1897, with mahogany panels, high muraled ceilings, and giant portraits of Revolutionary War heroes. George Washington, dressed in his general's garb, his palm resting on his horse, loomed over the crowd below.

A roar of applause greeted the mayor as he marched to the front of the room to deliver his final State of the City speech. Aides propped a giant image of the city skyline behind him, obscuring the dais; he had no need of a podium, as he never read from a script. A huge photo of the twin towers of the World Trade Center loomed over his right shoulder.

The man who'd ignored, terrorized, and exhausted so many of the officials in this room was applauded magnanimously. Perhaps it was the knowledge that he was recovering from cancer, his face glistening under the klieg lights. But it was also a recognition that this was the beginning of his farewell tour. He was term limited, and his mission was coming to an end.

The warmth ran both ways. He paced back and forth, daytime-show-host style, as relaxed as he'd ever been in public. His talk—it didn't feel like a speech—was expansive, generous, wistful. "It's a State of the City speech that I wasn't sure last year at this time that I was going to give," he said, referring to his illness. The year had turned out to be "a gift."

His usual ominous tone was replaced with optimism; he sounded like a man who'd been given a new lease on life. "It's got to be one of the most rewarding, one of the most fulfilling, and one of the most wonderful jobs in the world," he said of the mayoralty, "mostly because of all of the people of the City of New York who work together so well." There were plenty of moments in the past when the line would have been delivered for a laugh, but not this morning.

He thanked his adversaries by name and tossed out buckets of crowd-pleasing new projects and programs, a convention center here, a new park there. He unveiled a massive, billion-dollar affordable housing program, which housing activists had been pleading for without success since the dawn of his mayoralty.

"We should do something else for the Bronx, because we haven't done enough for the Bronx," he said of the city's poorest borough, 80 percent Black and Hispanic and all but ignored by him over seven years. He tossed them a new military academy.

"I feel like Giuseppe Verdi did when he sat down and wrote 'Falstaff,'" he said. "He put in it thousands of themes, like all these things that he had in his head that he didn't get to develop in other operas. He stuck it all in 'Falstaff.'"

New York was a far different city on this day than it was when he assumed the mayoralty from David Dinkins seven years earlier. You could read it in the numbers and feel it in the streets.

Crime was down nearly 60 percent. The murder rate was even lower; 1,250 fewer New Yorkers were killed in 2000 than in 1993. Car thieves stole more than 111,000 vehicles the year before Giuliani took office. The count was down to less than a third of that.

City streets were not just safer; they were cleaner. Seventy-five percent of streets were rated clean when he was elected; the figure was now over 85 percent.

The city's tax burden was the lowest in thirty years. Eleven million more tourists per year were jamming the city's hotels. The local economy had finally joined the national upswing, buoyed by the booming tech industry. New skyscrapers and apartment towers were springing up across the city.

The improvements sparked a seismic change in how Americans saw New York, and how New Yorkers felt about their city. In the 1970s, as services deteriorated and crime skyrocketed, 800,000 New Yorkers, fed up with dangerous, filthy streets, fled the five boroughs. The run for the exits reversed dramatically in the 1990s (which began with Dinkins in City Hall); the population ballooned to its highest point in history, more than compensating for the exodus.

The administration's crackdown on crime and disorder seemed to many like the work of a totalitarian regime, his police force mercilessly rousting the homeless from the streets and perpetually stopping and frisking Black men for guns and other weapons. "This is America in the 21st century, not Chile in the 1970's [sic]—you can't just stop everyone," said Mark Green, the city's public advocate.

But the results were indisputable. The restoration of order gave the most dangerous neighborhoods an almost post-wartime feel, and was sparking an economic rejuvenation in once-blighted commercial districts. The ability to take a train at night without fear of getting mugged was almost a shocking experience for New Yorkers.

The absence of mentally ill homeless men and women loitering in playgrounds or urinating against apartment buildings returned the streets to normalcy. Many city parks that had long been surrendered to hoodlums and drug dealers were reclaimed by families.

To be a New Yorker in January 2001 was to feel Giuliani's presence wherever you went. You thought of him when you noticed less graffiti on your walk to work, and felt safer on your subway ride. You cursed him when you were stopped and frisked, hassled for smoking pot, or ticketed for drinking in the street. He loomed large when police shut down your favorite nightclub, or closed a neighborhood sex shop. Your relatives from out of town were raving about their visit to the city and the mayor who'd made it safe for them.

Every New Yorker had an opinion about Rudy Giuliani. But to love him or hate him was to acknowledge that someone was in charge.

"New Yorkers don't talk about crime the way they used to, or about welfare or quality of life issues or perhaps even the budget," wrote James Traub in the *New York Times* a few weeks after Giuliani's speech. "New Yorkers don't give credit for good intentions the way they used to: New Yorkers now expect a mayor to do something about problems, not pontificate about them. This is Giuliani's New York."

It was for this reason that his popularity rebounded after each of his dramas. It would become accepted wisdom in the years that followed that his polarizing reign left him politically spent in his last year. But the facts showed otherwise. In mid-August, 55 percent of New Yorkers approved of the job he was doing, a robust showing for any politician. The public was more optimistic about the city's future than at any time in almost a quarter century, and a good percentage credited the mayor.

Giuliani ended his talk on an optimistic note.

"It's going to be a very aggressive year, and a very active one, because I just have one more year to contribute whatever unique thing I can contribute to the city in my administration," he told his audience. "And we're going to try to have as good a year as possible."

The mayor earned the right to take a bow. But by the time his farewell tour commenced, he and his team had fumbled or ignored some critical challenges so badly that it likely cost people their lives eight months later.

Luke Healy was in mortal danger. The thirty-six-year-old firefighter was trapped in the burning basement of a two-story Queens home, desperately calling for help over his state-of-the-art Motorola radio. No one was responding.

He tried again. "MAYDAY, MAYDAY, MAYDAY!" There was no response. He tried a third time, a fourth—seven calls for help, and none of the members of Engine Company 305 heard him. They were just outside the house.

Healy, thick-jawed and muscular, wasn't even supposed to be there. His shift was ending when the alarm for the basement fire came in at 5 p.m. on March 19. Instead of heading home to his family, he hopped on the engine and sped with his team to Forest Avenue.

The fire was intensely hot, and thick smoke obliterated visibility. Worse, his oxygen supply was close to empty. As he tried to exit, following the fire hose back out the way he came in, he discovered an object blocking the path. He tried to go around it, but in the darkness lost the hose and his pathway out.

He was at risk of suffocating, and it seemed no one could hear his pleas for help. He decided to run through the darkness, hoping he wouldn't slam against a wall or fall onto something far worse.

A lieutenant was staring into the abyss of the basement when he saw the two yellow lines on the sleeve of Healy's jacket. He grabbed Healy and pulled him to the stairs. Healy gasped for relief.

For the department, the incident triggered bad memories.

In 1993, Islamic extremists set off a truck bomb at the World Trade Center that killed six people and injured more than a thousand. As they fought the blaze, firefighters discovered that their radios—Motorola Saber I's—were useless inside the towers. Signals got jammed, radio channels were overloaded, and voices didn't reach the highest floors. Firefighters were unable to communicate with the police; the two departments' radios literally operated on different wavelengths.

It took another eight years of bureaucratic delays to replace the Saber I with a new product—the Motorola XTS 3500. When the department finally distributed the high-tech replacements, Luke Healy almost lost his life.

The firefighter's brush with death set off a storm of bad press for the Giuliani administration.

"FDNY recalls new models after firefighter's close call," a *Newsday* headline read. Healy's Mayday calls had actually been received, but by another engine company more than ten blocks away. His own company, standing just outside the basement, couldn't hear a thing.

The new radios were promoted as offering a few new and critical features that the Saber I's lacked—in particular, an ability to connect firefighters with police officers on the same radio frequency. If successful, the new units would be a game changer, with the potential for saving lives.

The department had deployed close to four thousand of the new units five days prior to the Healy incident. Almost immediately, reports streamed in to the FDNY about the same problems he faced, including dead spots and messages that failed to deliver.

The fire union was outraged that the new devices, which cost the department millions of dollars, and had taken years to select, had failed. In response to the criticism, Giuliani could have revved up pressure on his agencies to fix the problem, but that wasn't how he operated when he was attacked.

"This isn't about reality, this is because the union is bitter over the fact that the commissioner had to discipline a few people and they're being petulant," he said angrily, referring to the recent firing of two fire officials.

He was wrong. An investigation by City Comptroller Alan Hevesi detailed years of bungled decisions and questionable practices in the administration's selection of the new radios. "Sending firefighters into burning buildings with radios that have not been properly field-tested is irresponsible and dangerous," he said at a news conference. He cut off further payments to Motorola.

Again, the mayor reacted angrily. Hevesi was running to succeed him; Giuliani accused him of pandering to the union. "There are better ways to get their endorsement than to kind of roll over for them," he told reporters.

Hevesi's report, while damning, overlooked the role of a key player in the radio fiasco, an administration technology department employee named Deborah Spandorf. Her story would end tragically.

She was a midlevel employee at the Department of Information Technology and Telecommunications, with a talent for working the bureaucracy to scare up gizmos on short notice, whether it was a deputy mayor's cell phone or a new dispatch console for the Sanitation Department. She pushed the Fire Department to purchase the Motorola XTS 3500s and other Motorola products with such zeal that competitors filed complaints that they had been squeezed out of the purchasing process.

Little known at City Hall was that her sister, Marian Barell, was a lobbyist for Motorola. (Barell denied knowing her sister worked for the city on Motorola projects, saying the two weren't close.)

In April, the administration vowed to fix the new radios and get them back into service, but nothing happened. The Fire Department redistributed the old Saber I's—the same ones that malfunctioned at the Trade Center in the 1993 bombing, and which didn't permit the uniformed services to communicate with one another. The consequences were catastrophic.

*   *   *

By the time of Healy's brush with death, the city's Office of Emergency Management had been up and running for seven months. The facility, located on the 23rd floor of 7 World Trade Center, was a glitzy hive of activity, fifty thousand square feet of television monitors, aerial photos, computers, bulletproof walls, generators, and a six-thousand-gallon fuel tank.

Giuliani endured months of ridicule for allocating $15 million to a "bunker," with its hotline to the president, and a sofa bed "where he can nap between bouts of saving the city from scourges such as blackouts, hurricanes and killer germs," scoffed the *Washington Post.* The concept became a symbol of his paranoia. "If Giuliani wants to build a bunker only for the people he trusts, all he needs is a phone booth," quipped the City Council speaker, Peter Vallone.

But it was an idea ahead of its time, a model of disaster management that would be replicated in cities across the nation. It unfortunately had a fatal flaw.

OEM was an outgrowth of Giuliani's frustrations with getting timely information out of his police department during emergencies. NYPD ran disaster response out of its own emergency center, and guarded its information jealously. The last straw for him came when he only learned about a major water main break by watching the evening news.

The man he turned to for help was Jerry Hauer, a nationally recognized disaster response expert who had once worked at the city's Emergency Medical Service. He was an innovative thinker in a blood-and-guts profession, with a long list of degrees and a world of experience in the science of disaster. He had the air of a spy, with a low, sotto voce voice and a bone-dry sense of humor. But he also had a taste for the kind of news media stardom that only a capital like New York could provide. Giuliani persuaded him to quit his job running Indiana's emergency response system and come back to the city to create a cutting-edge operation outside the purview of the Police and Fire Departments.

There were only eight people working at the NYPD center, and Giuliani hated going there; his presence sent a signal that the Fire Department was not part of disaster planning, he felt. Plus, the press room was too small. He wanted a far larger operation on neutral ground, with a chief who reported directly to him.

He and his new hire grew close; they smoked cigars at night and on weekends at Club Mac and on Gracie Mansion's porch. When Giuliani discovered to his horror that small beetles had bored their way into his cigar collection, it was Hauer he called in a panic (he packaged them into Tupperware containers and froze them).

Hauer went scouting for facilities to house the new OEM, from underground locations to a courthouse to a ferry. The option he preferred was a space at MetroTech, a modern office complex in downtown Brooklyn, right across the river from City Hall. "The building is secure and not as visible a target as buildings in Lower Manhattan," he wrote in an internal memo.

The idea was a nonstarter—Giuliani wanted the center to be within walking distance of City Hall. Hauer was nervous that Lower Manhattan was a terrorist target, especially in light of the 1993 bombing at the Trade Center. But the next best choice was at 7 World Trade Center.

In many ways it was an ideal space. The building housed several federal agencies, and was outfitted with all sorts of security measures designed to thwart attacks. Hauer went along with it, but the Police Department was adamantly opposed. An NYPD memo obtained by the *New York Times* outlined a host of dangers, including the Trade Center's history as a terrorist target. "This group's finding is that the security of the proposed O.E.M. Command Center cannot be reasonably guaranteed," wrote Daniel Oates, the commander of the intelligence division.

Giuliani stood his ground, and ordered the facility built at the Trade Center site. "We knew that the area was still a target," Hauer said. "That was always in the back of your mind."

Once it opened, OEM proved enormously beneficial to the city's emergency response efforts. It was a different story when a cataclysm struck in September.

While the clock was ticking down on Giuliani's mayoralty, there was always time for another psychodrama in his life. In the spring, the public witnessed the extremes of his capacity to nurture and to destroy, to love and to hate.

He had been sorting out people as either heroes or villains since his days at Bishop Loughlin, but as he grew older his radar for enemies widened. In the months following his State of the City speech, he found the most unlikely target of them all in his wife.

Other mayors might have found it challenging to conduct extramarital affairs while still living in the official residence with their wife and children. But Giuliani wasn't an ordinary mayor.

Following his withdrawal from the Senate race the previous year, he underwent radiation treatments almost every day for five weeks to kill the cancer cells in his prostate—a brutal regimen that had him in so much pain that he could barely stand at times. Driving in a van toward a campaign event for a Bronx state senator one afternoon, he told his driver to pull over. He jumped out of the car and threw up.

It was a miserable, terrifying experience that he endured while running city government. "When I did actually sit down and unburden myself about the fear and the worry, I turned to Judith," he later wrote. "She was the one who took care of me the most."

Nathan, trained as a nurse, introduced him to specialists she knew through her pharmaceutical company job, peppered them with questions, and made sure the patient followed their instructions. It was she, rather than Giuliani's wife, who got him through the ordeal. "I don't know how I would have done it without her," he wrote.

The experience only worsened his relationship with Donna Hanover, whom he had sued for divorce but continued to live with at Gracie Mansion. Banished to a downstairs guest room, he complained to friends that she was deliberately awakening him at sunrise each morning by exercising on a treadmill above his ceiling in the creaky old house. "They really disliked each other and they were really mean to each other," said an advisor.

As his health improved he didn't so much nudge Hanover out of her public role as throw her overboard. He took Nathan to George W. Bush's inauguration and Bernie Kerik's swearing-in as police commissioner. They waved to the crowds together at parades, and donned bathrobes for a pajama-party fundraiser. He assigned her a security detail, at a cost of $100,000 in taxpayer money per year. And she began attending events at Gracie Mansion. The press dubbed Nathan the "First Companion."

On May 7, a fuming Hanover filed for a restraining order to bar her from Gracie Mansion, sending the media into orbit over their disastrous marriage once again.

To the mayor, an enemy was an enemy, whether it was Bill Bratton, Ray Cortines, or his wife. Instead of trying to make the mess go away as quietly as possible, as most politicians might do, he hired the famed divorce attorney Raoul Felder, a tabloid celebrity with an insatiable appetite for publicity. He landed at the doorstep of the city's newspapers like an Easter miracle.

Felder quickly set about trying to destroy Hanover's reputation. At a May 11 courtroom hearing, he portrayed her as an opportunist "trying to cling to a marriage that has been dead for years," in order to "get her name in the newspapers, make more movies, advance her career."

"She will stay in Gracie Mansion until they take her screaming, scratching and kicking out of that place," he told Acting Manhattan Supreme Court Justice Judith Gische. "I suppose we're going to have to pry her off the chandelier to get her out of there."

Most New Yorkers knew Hanover as a dignified figure. Felder was out to change that. "She's howling like a stuck pig," he said.

The media soaked up the revolting spectacle, but Judge Gische wasn't impressed. She ruled in Hanover's favor, banning Nathan from the mansion and ordering her to stay away from Giuliani's two children, Andrew and Caroline.

The mayor was not pleased.

Hanover took pride in her role as first lady, championing charities she held dear, and throwing events for them at the mansion. The day after Gische's ruling, Tony Carbonetti dashed off a private memo to her.

"In light of the quite public parting of the ways between Donna Hanover and the Mayor, it is obviously disingenuous and inappropriate for Donna Hanover to continue to act as First Lady or in any way as a representative of the Mayor," he wrote.

"With regard to events and programs outside of Gracie Mansion in any way connected to the City of New York, Donna Hanover will no longer serve as First Lady and my office will designate spokespersons, as appropriate, to act on behalf of the Mayor of the City of New York."

He was not done humiliating her. He contacted the Susan G. Komen Breast Cancer Foundation, of which Hanover was honorary chair, and notified them that she was being yanked as hostess of an upcoming event she was scheduled to host for the group. Hanover learned about it from charity officials.

The battle had the air of a Jerry Springer episode, facilitated by a mayor who would do anything to win, even at the expense of a woman he had loved and fathered children with. That his constituents were witnessing this car crash was of little matter to him, as he knew they cared far more about how he had improved their neighborhoods than how he treated his wife.

It felt somehow fitting that the next character to walk onstage would be Donald Trump. The developer, a tabloid fixture himself, was devouring every moment of the story like everyone else, and wanted in. Five days after Judge Gische issued her ruling, he penned an open letter to Giuliani in *New York* magazine.

"I think the best thing for you to do would be to sit down with each other in a room, without your lawyers, and see if you can settle it," he wrote. "Raoul Felder is a nice man, but I think he loves the press. The one who's having the best time in this case is Raoul."

Ultimately it was the mayor who moved out of Gracie Mansion. Howard Koeppel, Giuliani's car dealer buddy, had visited him there with his future husband, Mark Hsiao, and got a personal tour of his miserable existence, from his downstairs bedroom to Donna's treadmill above it that was waking him up in the mornings. "I don't know how much longer I can stay here," Giuliani told them.

"Why don't you come stay with us?" Koeppel offered offhandedly. Giuliani was noncommittal, but days later showed up at their three-thousand-square-foot Upper East Side apartment with an overnight bag. "I didn't know he was going to stay six months," Koeppel recalled.

The press had a field day with their sitcom existence, a macho, old-school Italian mayor living with a gay couple in an apartment decorated with a statue of David and Tiffany lamps. But it was a warm and loving environment for a man who'd spent months contending with a serious illness and a crumbling marriage. On Sunday nights, Judith would join them for dinner at Bill Hong's Chinese restaurant nearby, and the group would come back to watch *The So-*

pranos. In the mornings, Mark made Giuliani breakfast and Howard helped pick out his ties. When he left for work he'd give them both a kiss on the cheek.

It was from their building that he emerged to greet the morning on September 11.

CHAPTER 7

Catastrophe

Alarm bells clanged inside the Duane Street firehouse at 8:33 a.m. on September 11, 2001. There was a report of a gas leak on the corner of Lispenard and Church Streets, a dingy stretch of run-down restaurants and storefronts seven blocks away.

Battalion Chief Joe Pfeifer, the leader at the cavernous old building, had already worked fifteen hours of his twenty-four-hour shift. The twenty-year veteran of the department stood out as the adult of his rambunctious crew; he was soft-spoken and analytical, with the bearing of an accountant, or a doctor, always calm and strategic when hell broke loose. The department had put him in charge of three other firehouses in Lower Manhattan.

His crew's fire trucks pulled up outside of Seaworld Seafood, a dive where you could grab a deep-fried cod sandwich and a stack of fries for $4.50. He plucked a handheld gas meter from the truck and waved it over a sewer grate. The firefighters checked the surrounding buildings and found no odor. A boring run.

Above them, a panicked flight attendant inside a Boeing 767 was on the phone with an American Airlines flight services manager, reporting that her plane had been hijacked. A group of al-Qaeda terrorists had seized control of the cockpit after slitting a passenger's throat with a box cutter and overpowering the captain and first officer. Mohamed Atta, who had gone to flight school for this moment, was sitting in the pilot's seat.

The attendant, Madeline Sweeney, described what she was seeing outside her window.

> I see water. I see buildings. I see buildings. . . . We are flying low. We are flying very, very low. We are flying way too low. Oh my God we are flying way too low. Oh my God!

The plane, flying at such a low altitude that Pfeifer could read the American Airlines logo on its fuselage, sped through the air at 443 miles per hour and sailed like a projectile into the North Tower of the World Trade Center, piercing the building's steel columns and exploding into a fireball that mushroomed into the morning sky. Hundreds of office workers between the 93rd and 99th floors were killed instantly.

The crowds watching the destruction fourteen blocks away froze in disbelief. Pfeifer jumped into his car and radioed just twelve seconds later. "We just had a plane crash into upper floors of the World Trade Center," he said in a steady voice. "Transmit a second alarm and start relocating companies into the area." Seconds later he called in again. "We have a number of floors on fire. It looked like the plane was aiming toward the building. Transmit a third alarm."

His driver sped downtown as Pfeifer delivered orders from the passenger seat, craning his neck to get a better view of the inferno. By the time he arrived at the enormous white marble lobby of the North Tower, he had called for 150 firefighters; the number would grow to close to one thousand over the next hour. Steel and glass were raining down from the giant crater nearly a quarter mile above the lobby. Thick, black smoke was billowing out of the building. There were crashing sounds coming from outside the entrance.

Pfeifer barely had time to position himself in the lobby's fire command station when, at 9:03 a.m., a second plane commandeered by terrorists barreled nose-first into the South Tower next door. Nine thousand gallons of jet fuel poured out of the plane, sending a massive fireball exploding from the middle of the building. All fifty-six passengers were killed, along with those working between the 77th and 85th floors. Whatever doubts anyone had about whether the nation was under attack vanished.

The evacuation of thousands of workers inside the North Tower alone would have been an immense undertaking. Now the task was doubled.

A fire chief's job is to bring order to chaos, but insurmountable problems started to snowball from the moment Pfeifer arrived. Most if not all of the building's ninety-nine elevators were knocked out of service, meaning the only way for firefighters to reach the trapped and the injured was to climb the stairs of the 110-story building. Pfeifer and a growing number of other chiefs streaming into the lobby were ordering hundreds of firefighters, each of them lugging seventy pounds of equipment, to climb the tower in search of people to rescue. One of them was Lieutenant Kevin Pfeifer, Chief Pfeifer's brother. The two locked eyes for a moment before Kevin made his way upstairs. It was the last time they would see one another.

The periodic crashing sounds coming from outside escalated. Firefighters walked closer to the building's doors, and realized it was the sound of falling bodies smashing on top of the plexiglass canopy over the entrance. Desperate men and women were jumping out their office windows to escape the 2,000-degree heat from the burning fuel. The sounds continued throughout the morning, one every minute or so, providing a sickening soundtrack as the commanders tried to make decisions.

Eight years of efforts to improve communications in the towers since the 1993 terrorist bombing were being put to the test. The mayor had built the Office of Emergency Management Command

Center to coordinate fire, police, and other agencies' responses to emergencies. The Port Authority, which ran the complex, installed repeaters at 5 World Trade Center to boost radio signals. The city lobbied the feds successfully for a UHF channel to expand the number of radio channels, one of them designed to allow the Fire and Police Departments to communicate with each other. And a mayoral department specializing in communications technology had distributed a few dozen special 800-megahertz radios to fire and police commanders to permit them to share information with one another.

But one by one the systems failed. The plane crash into the North Tower wiped out the building's public address system, robbing building security and Fire Department commanders of a means to communicate with the tens of thousands of office workers in the building. Pfeifer and others couldn't get the repeaters to work, and assumed they were broken. The protocols for using the special 800-megahertz radios had never been agreed upon by the Police and Fire Departments, so most commanders didn't bother to carry them.

The Fire Department's new XTS 3500 radios were gathering dust since being pulled out of service earlier in the year after Luke Healy's near-fatal experience in a Queens basement. Eight years after the old Saber I radios failed them in the 1993 bombing, firefighters were back in the same buildings, relying upon the same failed radios, and experiencing the same problems.

The sheer number of firefighters using the radios was a huge challenge. So many transmissions going on simultaneously created a cacophony of chatter that made it hard to hear anyone clearly.

The story was vastly different for the Police Department. The majority of police officers were communicating on radios using the new UHF channel, and experiencing few major problems, whereas the Fire Department's Saber I's did not operate on UHF. Their information-gathering machinery was far more advanced than that of the Fire Department; there were police outside and inside the towers; there were police helicopters in the air, police boats in the Hudson River, and a sophisticated police dispatch system coordinating the efforts.

But the Police Department, like the FDNY, was an island unto itself. There were no high-ranking police officials in the building telling Fire Department officials what they knew, just as there were no Fire Department officials sharing information with the police. The communications gap was a recipe for disaster.

Managing the movements of so many firefighters at once in the twin towers represented an unprecedented logistical challenge, but their chiefs had decades of experience that prepared them for this task. Yet they couldn't direct their crews if they couldn't communicate with them. Unlike their police counterparts, most of the firefighters circulating through the towers could only communicate with one another from short distances. The men risking their lives to save thousands of people in the burning buildings were falling further out of communication with each stairway they climbed.

The situation grew exponentially worse over the next hour.

Richie Sheirer, the city's Office of Emergency Management chief, began the morning at an 8 a.m. meeting at City Hall, five blocks north of the Trade Center. The topic was the upcoming unveiling of a new memorial planned to honor Brooklyn Dodger legends Jackie Robinson and Pee Wee Reese. "I was in heaven, sitting between Ralph Branca and Joe Black," he recalled.

The players were heroes of Sheirer's growing up in the Brooklyn projects, where his parents worried he'd wind up in jail, or dead, from hanging out on the streets. Instead, he found refuge in a local Boys and Girls Club of America, and when he grew older he began a career as a dispatcher for the New York City Fire Department.

He was the president of the dispatcher's union when he met

Giuliani in the 1993 campaign, and helped the candidate land the union's endorsement over David Dinkins. The two hit it off, and Sheirer worked as a driver for the candidate, schmoozing it up with him as he shuttled him to campaign events. When Giuliani won, Sheirer's career in the department took off. He rose through the ranks to become a top aide to Fire Commissioner Howard Safir; when Giuliani picked Safir to succeed Bill Bratton as police commissioner, Safir brought Sheirer along.

He was a squat, bespectacled curmudgeon, with a big heart and a deep loyalty to the man who shepherded his rise. The feeling was mutual. When Jerry Hauer, OEM's founding commissioner, announced his intention to leave in 1999, rumors flew that Sheirer was up for the job. Senior staffers were alarmed, viewing him as a Giuliani crony, a career dispatcher light on emergency management experience.

"Don't worry, Rudy isn't that crazy," Hauer assured them. He was stunned when Sheirer got the job.

The Police Department had close to forty thousand officers, larger than the armies of many countries. The Fire Department, the nation's largest, employed almost nine thousand firefighters and another four thousand emergency medical workers. They were mammoth, century-old fiefdoms with deeply ingrained cultures and a historic distrust of each other, a problem that had bedeviled generations of mayors.

In July 2001, just two months prior to the attacks, Giuliani attempted to settle endless feuding between the two departments by signing an executive order creating an incident command rubric outlining which side of the two-headed monster was supposed to take the lead in various types of disasters. But it was widely ignored by the two departments.

Hauer feared that if Giuliani expected the OEM director to knock heads and force the Police and Fire Departments to work together in emergencies it was never going to happen under Sheirer. "He didn't have the respect of the departments," he recalled.

Sheirer's meeting with the Dodger legends was interrupted by a loud "pop" sound; he thought a transformer somewhere had exploded. Then his phone rang; an OEM Watch Command staffer told him that a plane had crashed into the Trade Center. He stepped outside onto the portico and saw a plume of black smoke rise from the tower. He knew it wasn't caused by a wayward pilot. There were going to be terrible losses, he thought.

For reasons that remain unclear, Sheirer chose not to head to the OEM Command Center at 7 World Trade Center to coordinate the response by the Police and Fire Departments, and other emergency services, which were sending hundreds of vehicles with screaming sirens to the site. Instead, he and some aides headed straight for the North Tower.

Sheirer, who died in 2012, told *New York* magazine a month after the attacks that he used the three cell phones clipped to his belt to ask the Pentagon to freeze the airspace; to tell the Coast Guard to seal the harbor; and to request backup search-and-rescue teams from the state.

He did not, by anyone's account, use his time on the ground to attempt to unify the police and fire commands, which were stationed three blocks apart. Nor did he try, short of that, to get the departments to send high-ranking members to the other's posts to share information. Perhaps things were happening too quickly for him to react. Or perhaps he realized, as Hauer feared, that the departments wouldn't take orders from him.

Inside the towers, terrified office workers were dialing 911, pleading with emergency operators for someone to rescue them. The operators were at a loss as to what to tell them—no one was informing them that evacuation orders had been issued; that heading upstairs to the buildings' roofs was fruitless because the doors were locked;

that there was a single passable stairway in the North Tower that a handful of people above the flames had discovered.

Absent this information, the operators fell back on the standard advice for high-rise fires, urging people to stay in place and await help. It was contrary to what Pfeifer was trying desperately to communicate to them: Head to the stairwells. Flee the towers.

OEM might have helped avoid the miscommunications by feeding the 911 call center information from the Police and Fire Departments. But Sheirer and his aides weren't at OEM in the first hour. When a false rumor started to circulate that a third plane was headed toward the Trade Center complex, OEM was evacuated and shut down. The building it was in collapsed later in the day.

Robbed of OEM's capacity to coordinate the rescue efforts, the fire chiefs in the lobbies of the North and South Towers lost yet another way out of their communications nightmare. Their radios were failing, the police weren't talking to them, and the public address system was down. Their last pipeline to the outside world collapsed with the closure of OEM. Chief Pfeifer and his colleagues at the North Tower command post didn't even have a television; people watching the catastrophe from their homes had a better idea of what was going on in the tower than they did.

There was only one person who could have made a difference.

Rudy Giuliani was wrapping up a breakfast with Bill Simon, an old Southern District colleague, and Denny Young at the Peninsula hotel on Fifth Avenue and 55th Street when his bodyguard got an urgent call from Deputy Mayor Joe Lhota down at City Hall. The loud "pop" sound that Sheirer was hearing a floor above shook Lhota's windows. When Lhota ran outside to the City Hall steps, he saw black smoke rising from the Trade Center.

He called Patti Varrone, a member of Giuliani's police detail.

"How near are you to the mayor?" Lhota asked. "Five feet away," she said. A plane, he told her, perhaps a twin-engine Cessna, had hit the Trade Center. She relayed the information to Young, who informed the mayor in his whisper-quiet voice.

Giuliani, Young, and two members of his detail barreled downtown in an SUV, across 42nd Street and down Seventh Avenue, where they saw doctors and nurses at St. Vincent's Hospital prepping outdoor triage centers for mass casualties. As they approached Canal Street they saw a "big flash of fire," as Giuliani recalled—the second plane careening into the South Tower.

Police Commissioner Bernie Kerik was taking a shower in his private bathroom at his office on the 14th floor of police headquarters when his chief of staff, John Picciano, knocked on his door and gave him the news. He threw his clothes on and jumped into his black Chrysler Concorde with two aides and two bodyguards. He called Giuliani; they agreed to meet at the towers.

When they arrived on the scene the air was filled with the acrid smell of burning jet fuel, and shattered glass was raining down from the buildings. Screaming fire trucks and ambulances arrived every other minute, their massive tires splashing through small rivers of blood, glass, and body parts. Terrified office workers were pouring out of the buildings. Giuliani looked skyward; his eyes followed a man who jumped out of a window a hundred stories high, and plummeted down into the roof of a nearby building. Other people were diving out their windows two at a time, some holding hands.

The mayor and his police commissioner walked to West Street, where the top brass of the Fire Department had set up an outdoor command post with a clear view of both towers. Pete Ganci, the fifty-four-year-old chief of department, was with First Deputy Commissioner Bill Feehan. They were the lions of the FDNY; it was lore that Feehan, seventy-one years old, knew the location of every fire hydrant in the city. Giuliani, who loved cops and firefighters, venerated them.

"Can we get helicopters up to the roof and help any of those people?" he asked Ganci.

"My guys can save everybody below the fire," he said. He didn't need to spell out the rest.

Giuliani asked him what he should tell people. "To get out of the building," Ganci said. "We have enough men there to help them." He wasn't aware that 911 operators were urging them to do the exact opposite.

As for those who could escape the buildings, "tell people to go north, get 'em out of here," he told the mayor.

According to Giuliani, his only suggestion to Ganci was that he move their command post to a safer location, as objects from the deteriorating towers were plummeting down around them. "They planned to relocate further north," the mayor recalled.

At that, Giuliani and Kerik said goodbye to them. He caught sight of Father Mychal Judge, the Fire Department chaplain. Judge was a jovial character, but he looked stricken. Giuliani stretched out his hand to the priest. "Father, pray for us," he said. "I always do," he responded.

With OEM out of commission and City Hall evacuated, Giuliani's goal was to set up a space for his aides and him. The police identified a Merrill Lynch office at 75 Barclay Street, not far away, and were already setting up landlines inside.

He had previously ordered an aide to find Fire Commissioner Tom Von Essen, who was with Joe Pfeifer and the other chiefs inside the North Tower. "It's really important that we all be together at the command post so that we can make decisions," he told an aide. "Get him and bring him to us."

Giuliani had been through enough disasters to know how crucial it was to bring the heads of the responding departments together to coordinate their efforts—he'd done it at countless emergency scenes in the past. In calling for Von Essen, the fire commissioner, to join

Kerik and him at the Merrill Lynch office—along with Sheirer and others—the mayor thought he was doing just that.

But it was the Fire Department commanders on the ground—Ganci and Feehan outside the towers, Joe Pfeifer and other chiefs inside—who needed to work together with the police. Instead, the cops and firefighters were at separate command posts, blocks apart, operating in their own silos.

Von Essen, the fire commissioner, wasn't even in the Fire Department's uniformed chain of command; when he traveled to the North Tower he was told to leave. "You're not supposed to be here," Deputy Chief Peter Hayden told him. "It's too dangerous."

Giuliani was the only person who had the authority to order the two departments at the scene to merge their commands, or at least to send high-ranking officers to the other's to share information. But by his own account he didn't do so. Even when Ganci told him he planned to move the Fire Department post north, the mayor didn't suggest, much less order, the two departments to join forces.

Years later, Von Essen was candid about what went wrong. "There should be a representative from the Police Department there," he said. "There should be a high-level chief from the Fire Department there. They should be controlling the operation from that command post. That day the police did not hook up with the Fire Department. I don't know why."

Giuliani would argue the opposite—that the two departments had different missions that required different locations. To agree with Von Essen would be to admit making a mistake at the most important moment of his career.

More likely, the mayor wasn't thinking strategically in the overwhelming chaos of the moment, with bodies falling around him and blood running through the streets. He was focused on his own mission, which was to get his trusted aides together with him.

The results of his inaction became clear soon after he departed.

Over at 7 World Trade Center, where OEM had just been shuttered, an Emergency Medical Services division chief named John Peruggia was standing in the lobby when he was introduced to an engineer for the city's Buildings Department. The engineer warned him that the structural damage to the towers was so extreme that they were in danger of collapse.

Alarmed, Peruggia pulled over an emergency medical technician, Richard Zarillo, and told him to run to the Fire Department command post and tell them to evacuate the towers—Peruggia couldn't reach them by radio. "You see Chief Ganci and Chief Ganci only," he told Zarillo.

The EMT raced through the madhouse scene on the streets until he spotted Ganci aide Steven Mosiello and told him that the buildings were in imminent danger. Mosiello walked Zarillo over to Ganci.

"Chief, these buildings are in imminent danger of collapse," Mosiello said.

"Who the fuck would tell you something like that?" Ganci asked.

"Richie, come over here and tell the chief what you just told me."

Zarillo relayed the engineer's information to the chief.

It was too late. Thirty seconds into their conversation a deafening roar emanated from the South Tower directly in front of them and the tower started to buckle. *What the fuck is that?* Ganci yelled. They went running for their lives.

Inside the North Tower the ground started to shake as if an earthquake had struck. The marble walls cracked, and glass fixtures fell from the ceiling. It made a "monster locomotive sound," Pfeifer said, like standing under a train trestle, its noise growing louder and scarier. The ceiling started to give out. People thrown off their feet scurried on their hands and knees in a panic to escape crashing objects.

In the darkness, Pfeifer ordered an evacuation of the building on his radio. Some firefighters heard the command, many did not.

As the deafening noise slowly abated, Pfeifer felt his way through pitch-black corridors, stepping over debris, gagging on smoke and dust.

He felt something at his feet. Grabbing a flashlight from an aide, he knelt down and spotted a priest's white collar. It was Father Judge, the Fire Department chaplain. Pfeifer felt for a pulse and found none. The priest, who had entered the lobby only a few minutes earlier, was killed by falling debris. Firefighters lifted up his limp body, caked in dust, and carried it out of the building and into a nearby church.

Pfeifer opened an exit door into the daytime sun. He and the others were under the impression that the floors above them had collapsed—they had no way of knowing that the tower next door had been destroyed.

It was in the following twenty-nine minutes that the loss of OEM, the failure of the radios, and a lack of a unified command—all the result of Giuliani administration mistakes or inaction—had the deadliest consequences.

The mayor would suffer endless ridicule in years to come for siting his emergency command center at 7 World Trade Center, a proven terrorist target. But its closure and ultimate destruction was no laughing matter. The result was catastrophic.

Soon after the South Tower collapsed, police helicopters encircling the burning North Tower radioed in a harrowing message. "About 15 floors down from the top, it looks like it's glowing red," one pilot reported. "It's inevitable."

"I don't think this has too much longer to go," radioed another. "I would evacuate all people within the area of that second building."

The police on the ground received the message and relayed it to their officers in the North Tower, who reacted with so much urgency that some slid down the stairwell banisters.

But no one told the Fire Department. The two departments' radios weren't compatible, and there were no commanders physically near each other's command posts to share the helicopter pilots' information. OEM was designed to keep all the departments in the loop in situations like this. But OEM was deserted.

The North Tower was filled with firefighters intent upon rescuing civilians. Some who heard the evacuation orders chose not to comply. Others took their time, unaware that the South Tower had collapsed, and that helicopter pilots were issuing dire warnings. A few overheard the news from the radios that police in the stairwells were carrying, and raced frantically to alert their fellow firefighters of the imminent collapse. Many didn't believe them.

"Had I known the full picture, my message to evacuate would have been preceded with the words 'Mayday, Mayday, Mayday'—signaling the urgency to get out of the building," Pfeifer recalled. "I could only imagine how that warning would have been a game changer for all of us in the North Tower, including my brother."

Giuliani and his team had entered the Merrill Lynch office on Barclay Street at 9:50 a.m., about an hour after the first plane hit the tower. By then his crew had swelled to about twenty-five commissioners and aides.

He and his deputies started working the phones. The mayor, sitting in a cubicle near the back of the office, was connected to Chris Henick, deputy assistant to President Bush, who informed him that the Pentagon had been attacked. Giuliani asked to speak with the president, but the White House had been evacuated; Henick said Vice President Dick Cheney would call him back. Cheney's assistant called him soon afterward and asked him to hold. The line went dead.

The building started to shake. A titanic earthquake sound erupted outside of the building. *"It's coming down, everybody down!"* yelled

Joe Esposito, NYPD's chief of department. People dived under their desks. "What the hell is happening?" Tony Carbonetti yelled.

Giuliani, still sitting at his desk awaiting Cheney's callback, thought Esposito was referring to a radio tower toppling off one of the towers. But the reality that the South Tower was imploding became clear soon enough. Chunks of concrete and steel started smashing through the office windows. Smoke and debris filled the air outside the building until it turned dark as night.

Detective John Huvane grabbed Giuliani's arm. "Boss, we've gotta get out of here," he said. The crew went scrambling for a way out.

The group wandered through the basement, a maze of hallways mostly leading to dead ends. They encountered one locked door after another, until two maintenance men appeared out of nowhere and led them to a working exit, much to their relief. When the doors opened into the sunlight of Church Street they entered a new world. The streets were covered in white dust, and there was a stillness in the air. The usual throngs of pedestrians were replaced with survivors covered in soot, walking in a daze.

A half hour earlier, I'd been awakened in bed by a ringing phone—my mother, frantically urging me to turn on the television. Half-asleep, I switched on NY1, my station, and saw two burning towers spewing horrible clouds of black smoke into a clear blue sky.

I called the station's assignment desk, which was in a state of commotion, and asked how I could help. I could hear Steve Paulus, the station manager, yell "Tell him to find Giuliani."

I flew out of my apartment with a press pass around my neck, flagged a taxi, and somehow persuaded the frightened driver to turn his car around and head downtown toward the towers. I was heading to 7 World Trade Center, hoping the mayor would be at OEM overseeing the response.

My driver had the radio on, and the urgency was escalating by the minute, "a situation that you thought couldn't get any worse getting progressively worse," as an anchor on WINS radio put it. We were speeding downtown, perhaps ten blocks north of our destination, when the crackle and boom from the destruction of the South Tower jolted us. I watched it collapse into itself from my window, sending massive plumes of black smoke and bright sparks shooting into the sky.

A few minutes later my driver lost patience, slammed on his brakes, and ordered me out of his car. A frantic woman got in as I got out, puzzled at why I would give up a precious ride away from the mayhem.

The white ash on the ground and the eerie quiet in the air evoked the aftermath of a nuclear attack. No one was on the street except two nurses walking hurriedly together; one of them stopped, and mercifully reached into her purse and pulled out a face mask for me.

I tried to call my station but service was down throughout Lower Manhattan. A policeman spotted me and yelled at me to get off the street—"It's going to blow!" I waved my press pass at him as if it could protect me, and protested that I had to find the mayor. He looked at me quizzically. "He's right over there," he said.

Amazingly, Giuliani was ten feet away with Sheirer, Kerik, Von Essen, and a clutch of deputy mayors and aides. His pants were covered in dust from the collapse of the walls inside the office from which they'd just escaped. Our eyes locked and he waved me over. "Come with us!" he said.

We went north together, the remaining North Tower belching clouds of black, tarry smoke behind us. It was a desperate moment; there was no longer a city government to speak of—its leaders were standing in front of me looking like war survivors. There was no OEM, City Hall was evacuated, phone service was down at police headquarters, and now the temporary post inside the Barclay Street offices was lost. Giuliani's team didn't even have a car.

We walked as the mayor's group discussed next steps, weighing and discarding location options to set up yet another temporary command center. Giuliani turned to me every few minutes to urge me to inform viewers to evacuate downtown Manhattan. I barely had a working cell phone.

A volcanic noise erupted behind us. We turned around and saw the North Tower buckle and collapse, each floor pancaking onto the one below it. It produced a crackling thunder sound, and flashes of brilliant light shot up into the sky as a tower that once pierced through clouds disintegrated. The collapse produced an epic plume of smoke and ash that grew higher and wider as the tower collapsed into itself. The billowing smoke was so massive that satellites picked up the image from outer space.

A hurricane of debris rushed toward us. John Huvane, protecting the mayor even with his own life in danger, threw his arm around his neck and bolted north. The rest of us followed suit, racing until it was clear we had outrun the storm. We slowed down as it faded into the background. I was covered in sweat.

Giuliani soon resumed the conversation about where to relocate city government. He was as controlled as I'd ever seen him, speaking in conversational tones, never raising his voice. Peter Powers may have overstated things when he said his friend was missing the fear gene, but if the mayor was terrified he was hiding it well.

Our motley crew walked another half mile in search of a landing. We trekked into the Tribeca Grand, one of Manhattan's trendiest hotels, earning stares from its fashionable clientele—it felt vaguely ridiculous. The mayor, Kerik, and Von Essen stared at the glass atrium with concern, then turned around and headed outside to resume the march.

The crowds off to the sides were growing larger, and started to cheer the mayor on, which annoyed him—he put his finger to his lips and shushed them. Somewhere in our odyssey Giuliani the bully vanished, replaced by a calm and fatherly figure. At one point along our walk he encountered a Black police officer who smiled nervously at him; he touched her cheek gently, as if to assure her she'd be okay. This was the man who once said Black New Yorkers should be grateful to him that they were alive.

People across the country were watching the destruction of the towers and the attack on the Pentagon with anxiety, their sense of safety fading with each image of survivors caked in dust, running for their lives.

There was no frame of reference for what they were witnessing. Americans who had been checking their BlackBerries and browsing through their morning emails moments before the planes struck could barely comprehend this attack on their soil. Even those old enough to remember Pearl Harbor might never have envisioned a broad-daylight attack on Manhattan.

It didn't help that President George W. Bush was a virtual nonpresence. He recorded a two-minute videotaped statement after learning about the attacks while reading to children in a second-grade classroom in Sarasota, Florida. Then he disappeared for much of the day, secluded at an Air Force base in Nebraska. In a moment of consuming terror, pillars of the nation seemed to be collapsing with barely anyone in charge.

Eventually we arrived at a small firehouse—Engine Company 24—in SoHo. No one was home—the firefighters were at the Trade Center. It was a measure of the anarchy of the moment that the people charged with getting the city under control were standing around a locked door, trying to figure out how to break in.

Huvane grabbed a fire extinguisher and started banging it against the door handle without success. A detective tried to break the door down with his body, slamming himself against it until it proved futile. An officer pulled out his gun, and aimed it at the lock, alarming the mayor's entourage and sparking cries of *"No!"* Time ticked by without a solution. Finally a police emergency vehicle pulled up outside the firehouse. Someone got a crowbar and jimmied open the firehouse door.

The office that Giuliani and his team squeezed into seemed no bigger than a walk-in closet. But it had a television and a landline, which was all they needed. Shortly before 11 a.m., he dialed NY1 and went on the air live with anchors Pat Kiernan and Sharon Dizenhuz.

"The first thing I'd like to do is to take this opportunity to tell everyone to remain calm and to the extent that they can, to evacuate Lower Manhattan," he told them. "We've been in contact with the White House and asked them to secure the space around the city."

"Can you give us any sense—there are so many people watching now who must have loved ones down in that area and are concerned," Dizenhuz said.

"My heart goes out to them," Giuliani said. "I've never seen anything like this. I was there from shortly after it happened and saw people jumping out of the World Trade Center. It's a horrible, horrible situation and all that I can tell them is that every resource that we have is attempting to rescue as many people as possible."

There was no sugarcoating. "The end result is going to be some horrendous number of lives lost," he said. "I don't think we know yet, but right now we have to just focus on saving as many people as possible."

Police cars and other emergency vehicles pulled up outside the firehouse. Staff from City Hall filed in. The mayor signed off on a location for yet another makeshift emergency command center—a police academy facility on the East Side—after first checking with Von Essen, "knowing the rivalry between the FDNY and NYPD," he later recalled. The entourage filed out of the firehouse and into police vehicles.

They arrived to find a small army of police with machine guns guarding the building. Once inside they gathered in a conference room. Giuliani started asking questions: How many people were killed? What was the condition of the remaining structures at the Trade Center site? How much personnel would be needed for the rescue operation? Calls were made to the president's team, and the heads of federal agencies. Governor Pataki arrived.

They went through the details of the massive search-and-rescue operation required; they needed floodlights, bulldozers, respirators, masks, a million pairs of gloves.

Tragic news kept streaming in. Estimates of Fire Department casualties kept rising, first one hundred, then two hundred, then over three hundred—the worst mass casualty in the department's history. Father Judge was dead. Ganci and Feehan were missing and would be found dead. The mayor's personal assistant, Beth Petrone, learned that her husband, Terry Hatton, leader of an elite Fire Department rescue unit, was gone.

At 2:35 p.m., Giuliani stepped in front of cameras with Pataki, Von Essen, Kerik, and others. There was no time for his staff to stage-manage the event, no mayoral podium or appropriate backdrop; they stood on a tiny platform with a metal art deco clock behind them. He had no notes.

"Today is obviously one of the most difficult days in the history of the city and country," he said. "The tragedy that we're all undergoing right now is something that we've had nightmares about—probably thought wouldn't happen. My heart goes out to all of the innocent victims of this horrible and vicious act of terrorism. . . .

"We will strive now very hard to save as many people as possible. And to send a message that the city of New York and the United States of America is much stronger than any group of barbaric terrorists. That our democracy, that our rule of law, that our strength and our willingness to defend ourselves will ultimately prevail.

"I'd ask the people of New York City to do everything that they can to cooperate, not to be frightened, to go about their lives as normal. Everything is safe right now in the city."

Reporters pressed him for numbers. The towers' capacity was 35,000; how many had perished?

Giuliani had resolved not to answer that question until he was given reliable figures. "The number of casualties will be more than any of us can bear ultimately," he said.

The soft-spoken tone he was using was familiar to his aides, but it was a revelation to much of the outside world. He knew what the public needed to hear: Don't be frightened. Everything is safe.

Giuliani hadn't rescued anyone from a burning building; the true heroes were the firefighters and others who trudged up the stairwells of the towers as panicked office workers stormed down them. His biggest contribution lay in his words.

"The city is going to survive," he said at an evening press conference. "We're going to get through it. It's going to be a very difficult time. I don't think we yet know the pain we're going to feel when we find out who we lost. But the thing we have to focus on now is getting the city through this and surviving and being stronger for it."

He traveled back and forth to the Trade Center several times that day, surveying the hellish moonscape of rubble, and fires that wouldn't stop burning for days. Well past midnight, Bernie Kerik and he agreed to call it a night. Kerik, who lived in New Jersey, started heading to police headquarters to sleep on his office couch, but halfway there had a change of heart and decided to see the destruction one more time.

The aide who was driving him swerved the car around and drove down to Church Street, where the long march had begun the previous morning. Kerik got out of the car and walked toward the smoking ruins. The site was awash in klieg lighting, as hundreds of workers dug furiously for survivors amid the beeping sounds of bulldozers.

The police commissioner saw a small group walking his way—the mayor and a tiny entourage. They spotted each other and smiled. Giuliani came up to Kerik and kissed his cheek. "I just had to see it one more time," he said.

Giuliani's courage in the face of near death, his absence of fear when all was falling apart, and his candor with the public was a study in leadership. Over the coming weeks and months, he attended over two hundred firefighter funerals, a demonstration of extraordinary compassion from a leader who had struck so many as heartless. His eloquence grew by the day.

Five days after the attacks, he traveled to St. Killian's, an old red-brick church in Farmingdale, Long Island, to eulogize Chief Pete Ganci, who died while trying to rescue his men from the collapse of the South Tower.

Giuliani walked to the altar, where Ganci's white chief's helmet rested on his casket. He spoke in a soft voice.

I can't make sense of this incident. I can't imagine anyone will for some time. But there is one thought that occurred to me earlier as I was sitting here listening to [Fire Department Chaplain] Father Delendick. Maybe, just maybe, the purpose of this horrible and terrible attack, if it has a purpose at all, maybe it's to test us. Maybe it's to find out if Americans today are as strong as Americans were in the beginning, when we forced our independence.

Maybe it's to test us to find out if we were as strong as we were when we had to fight to keep ourselves together as a Union and end slavery. Maybe it's to test us to see if we were as strong as our fathers and grandfathers were in ridding the world of Nazism and communism. Democracy doesn't come at an easy price, and we've all heard that said, but I don't know if we ever experienced it. We experienced it on Tuesday.

At the end of his eulogy he asked the crowd to stand and applaud for Ganci, to show his family what he meant to them, and to leave the children in his family with a memory of his being cheered as a hero.

The mayor was growing in stature as the world watched him closely. Heads of state trekked to visit Ground Zero, and to pay homage to the heroic leader of New York City. Giuliani gave tours to Vladimir Putin, Tony Blair, and Jacques Chirac. He received standing ovations on the street, in restaurants, on television. "Rudolph Giuliani is the personification of courage," proclaimed David Letterman, fighting back tears.

His legion of critics, shaken by the apocalyptic events, saw him in a new light. "He moves about the stricken city like a god," wrote *New York Times* columnist Bob Herbert, previously one of the mayor's harshest critics. "People want to be in his presence. They want to touch him. They want to praise him. The governor defers to him. The president seems somehow inadequate beside him.

"On Central Park West, a woman searching for just the right superlative for the man who is guiding New York through the greatest disaster ever to hit an American city finally said he's not like a god, 'He is God.'"

Giuliani's Fire and Police Departments evacuated approximately fifteen thousand people from the towers and the streets around them on September 11, possibly the largest rescue effort in American history. His work getting the city up and running after the devastation— much of it executed by Sheirer—was masterful.

But his administration's ineptitude also may have cost people their lives that day. At least 121 firefighters died in the North Tower in the twenty-one minutes after police helicopter pilots concluded that it was about to collapse, a message that was never shared with the Fire Department.

Countless firefighters never heard their commanders' evacuation orders on the grievously inadequate radios they were equipped with. The National Institute of Standards and Technology, in a $23 million study, stated "a preponderance of the evidence indicate[d] that emergency responder lives were likely lost at the WTC resulting from the lack of timely information-sharing and inadequate communications capabilities."

The tragedy of the radios was hammered home on October 1, when Deborah Spandorf, the city information technology official who pushed to replace the ineffective Saber I radios with the failed Motorola XTS 3500 devices, was found dead in her apartment, floating facedown in her bathtub. Two weeks earlier she had traveled to the city's makeshift emergency center on Manhattan's Pier 92, and passed out from what she saw. One of the apartments in her East 86th Street building belonged to Rudy Giuliani and Donna Hanover.

Years after the Trade Center attacks, the national 9/11 Commission concluded in its report that Giuliani's incident command system "did not function." It stated that the failure of the radios was a "contributing factor" to the fatalities, but not the primary one.

His performance on September 11 was a tapestry of inspired leadership and fatal mistakes. The public saw only part of the picture that terrible day; the rest was shrouded in adulation for years. He became a living legend, America's Mayor.

The options available to Giuliani were limitless. It was inconceivable that the legend could have an expiration date.

CHAPTER 8

Experts

Fresh out of graduate school in June 1993, an admirer of Rudy Giuliani's named Manny Papir stepped into the candidate's Madison Avenue headquarters and volunteered for his mayoral campaign. Earnest and friendly, with wire-rimmed glasses and a smile that could light up a room, he had high hopes of kickstarting his career by working for the prosecutor who was vowing to save the city.

The son of Cuban immigrants, he became one of the few Spanish speakers on staff, and he made himself useful by translating campaign coverage in the city's Spanish-language newspapers. When he came across what seemed like pro-Dinkins bias, he'd flag it for the campaign chiefs, who were often incredulous at what he'd found.

"Why didn't anyone else say anything about this?" Peter Powers would ask him.

Papir spent much of his childhood working in his parents' bodega in Atlanta, where his father taught him the value of hard work. "I learned early on that bosses like people who work, who produce," he said. When he wasn't laboring inside campaign headquarters, he was out on the streets working as a "barker," beseeching pedestrians to come meet the candidate.

The eager-beaver attitude paid off. When Giuliani beat Dinkins in November, he was rewarded with an assistant press secretary's job at City Hall.

His work ethic gained him points there as well. When Papir's colleagues balked at working weekends, he volunteered. Within a few months he was working as a body man for Giuliani, riding with the boss in the Ice Cream Truck, the nickname for the white SUV that ferried him around the city. It was a heady experience to get so much face time with the mayor; Papir was there for his every need, from fetching him lunch to fixing his collar.

The more his boss's trust in him grew, the more sensitive his assignments became. When Giuliani started seeing Judith Nathan, his job was to pick her up at her apartment building on Friday afternoons, and whisk them to her condo in the Hamptons for under-the-radar weekend interludes. Papir would check into a nearby inn with the security detail, always at the boss's beck and call.

Like Cristyne Lategano before him, he discovered that there was opportunity in Giuliani's fear of being alone, and his need to travel with a confidant at all times. Papir's proximity made him a valuable conduit for politicians and others seeking access to the mayor; his phone rang throughout the day with calls from people seeking a few minutes of Giuliani's time.

It was a role he cherished. Staffers far higher up in the pecking order sought him out for intel on the boss. "Every one of his uber loyalists would come up to me after denying things in the press, and say 'That didn't happen, did it?'" he laughed.

Papir wasn't as talented or as ambitious as Lategano; he was happy just to be Rudy's body man, and live in the reflected glare of his larger-than-life boss. "No one spent more time with him," he boasted. "No one."

All that access made him a natural threat to Nathan, who, like her boyfriend, was prone to seeing enemies all around her. "He was extremely powerful," she recalled. "Manny was the body man, and nobody got to Rudy without Manny. Nobody."

The closer the mayor's aides got to the mayor, the louder the alarm bells rang for Nathan. Papir was up there with Tony Carbonetti on her enemies list.

"Manny hated anyone close to Rudy—anybody," she said. "It took me a couple of months to realize he was trying to come between us."

The saga of Judith and Manny, and their war over Rudy Giuliani's affections, was a symbol of the sad and sometimes comic path that Giuliani chose to follow after September 11. Far from building upon the extraordinary stature he earned from lifting up the country in its darkest hour, he took it for a wild spin, cashing in on his fame, and gambling with his reputation.

The stars of his next act were opioid manufacturers, a Texas good ol' boy, an accused pedophile priest, and clients with oceans of money. When the inevitable explosion ensued between Giuliani's girlfriend and his gatekeeper, it was just another day at the office.

In the weeks that followed the attacks on the Trade Center, Giuliani's preference was not to leave the mayoralty at all. It wasn't hard to fathom why, in light of the continuing accolades from world leaders, the standing ovation in Congress, and the showering of affection from twenty thousand people at Yankee Stadium. New Yorkers were literally cheering him in the streets.

His actions on September 11 brought him into the orbit of the world's most important leaders, chief among them President George W. Bush. Riding with Giuliani and his aides during a September 14 visit to Ground Zero, Bush remarked to Tom Von Essen that he looked exhausted, and asked if he'd gotten any sleep. "Well, my wife came home last night, and I got lucky, so I'm feeling better today," the fire commissioner quipped, as Giuliani and Bernie Kerik shook their heads. "You're the only guy in this car who got lucky last night," Bush replied with a grin.

It was political nirvana for a mayor who up until then had always cared far more about power than money. In the weeks after the attacks, he wrote that he wanted to retire to Staten Island, the capital of blue-collar, white-ethnic New York.

With the rescheduled city primaries looming—the original date was September 11—he and his team launched a brazen behind-the-scenes campaign to twist the rules to allow him to remain in office past the required end of his term. Arguing that he was indispensable to the recovery, he tried and failed to convince City Council leaders to overturn the term limits law and free him to run for a third term. When that fell flat, he tried to persuade Governor George Pataki to cancel the election altogether, according to the former governor. After thinking it over, Pataki shot the idea down. (Giuliani called Pataki's story "bullshit.")

Then he went public with a wild proposal to extend his term by three months, justifying it as necessary for continuity, and to "maintain the unity that exist[ed] in the city." Such was his celestial stature that even the leading Democrat to succeed him, Mark Green, agreed to the idea, as did Mike Bloomberg, the billionaire mogul who was running for mayor as a Republican. The proposal died in the state legislature, but not before triggering bad memories of Giuliani's authoritarian ways.

Foiled, the next best goal was to anoint his successor. Green, the Democratic nominee, was a proud adversary of the mayor's as the city's public advocate, a kind of official government gadfly. Giuliani did everything in his power to thwart him.

Jerry Hauer, Giuliani's cigar buddy and OEM's creator, had left City Hall in 2000, but in the wake of the attacks was asked to establish a center for victims' families—Judith Nathan was also given a prime role—and to advise Giuliani pro bono on preparations for future attacks. Hauer gladly agreed, but it soon fell apart when he chose to endorse Green. Giuliani called him from his car upon learning the news. "If you do that, you're done," he told Hauer. When Hauer stood his ground, the mayor yanked his credentials to the family center.

The mayor picked his moment to endorse Bloomberg, the underdog in the race, at the end of October, just in time to air an endorsement commercial during the World Series. His seal of approval turned the election on its head and landed Bloomberg the mayoralty.

Facing life as a civilian, Giuliani's job prospects were limitless. There were any number of ways to cultivate his new role as an American statesman. Elected officials across the political divide were urging him to take charge of the city's $20 billion rebuilding effort. Speculation grew that he would join Bush's cabinet. Every conceivable door was open to him; he could run a foundation, a corporation, a law school. All would have preserved his Olympian stature.

But long before September 11 he and his closest aides had settled on a plan to open a consulting firm catering to corporate and government clients. The premise was that, having cracked the code for turning around the country's premier city, demand for their expertise would be strong. Mostly, it was a way of keeping the gang together until Giuliani ran for another office. "The idea of going our separate ways was really kind of traumatic," recalled Janna Mancini, a City Hall staffer. "At that point, whatever somebody asked us to do, if we could stay together we would have agreed to it."

But the deification of Giuliani on 9/11 changed the equation. He was now one of the most admired people in the world. Everyone wanted a piece of him. There was serious money to be made.

A handful of aides were dispatched to put together the financing for the new venture, but most of the company's future partners were still working at City Hall, and didn't have the bandwidth to think through its mission or structure. Time flew by without the firm having so much as a name.

On New Year's Eve, Giuliani's final day in office, he took a last sentimental swing through the city, swearing in a new class of firefighters, cutting a ribbon on a new police station, announcing funding for a new Staten Island elementary school, and ringing the closing bell at the New York Stock Exchange. At his valedictory press conference in City Hall's Blue Room, he was as jovial and self-deprecating as he'd ever been, thanking reporters and bringing City Hall's longest-serving janitor to the podium for a special mention.

When a reporter asked him if he planned to marry Judith Nathan, he smiled.

"I'm going to do the best I can to keep my personal life as personal as possible—not that I've succeeded at that very well in the last eight years," he deadpanned. The room broke into laughter.

His final announcement was that he and a handful of his closest aides were going into business as Giuliani Partners LLC. He said they had formed a strategic alliance with the accounting giant Ernst & Young; company officials stood by as he vaguely described his new firm's mission of "find[ing] companies and operations we can expand and assist."

Two years earlier, he had handed Ernst & Young an eyebrow-raising $20 million in tax breaks as an incentive to move its headquarters to 5 Times Square, sparking head-scratching among budget watchdogs, since the developer of the land had already received $236 million in breaks as part of the Times Square redevelopment effort. Now the company and he were going into business together.

That night, hundreds of thousands of boozy celebrants jammed Times Square in the frigid cold to welcome in the new year. Sharpshooters were stationed on rooftops throughout the area, a sign of a changed world. Giuliani was the star of the night, standing on a raised platform in winter garb with Judith, dressed elegantly in a black coat and red kerchief. At midnight, the iconic crystal-paneled ball descended down the spire of One Times Square, and the crowd exploded into a roar under three thousand pounds of red, white, and blue confetti. The moment felt like a national catharsis, an explosion of joy that America was still standing after the attacks.

As "Auld Lang Syne" boomed and confetti filled the night sky, the cameras zoomed in on America's Mayor and Nathan, and a national television audience watched them kiss. It felt like the final scene of an epic movie.

The next day, the party continued downtown at the ornate Tweed Courthouse for Bloomberg's inauguration gala.

Well into the early morning, Matt Mahoney, one of the few mayoral aides still sober, accompanied Giuliani and Nathan out of the party and onto Chambers Street, where the air still reeked of smoke from Ground Zero three and a half months after the attacks. The two men had a poignant conversation, filled with thank-yous, and talked about their futures at Giuliani Partners. Then Giuliani and Nathan stepped into a car. "I'm going to play some golf in Florida," he told Mahoney. "I'll see you at the office when I get back."

"Great," said the aide, waving farewell to the couple.

As the car drove away, Mahoney realized that no one knew where the office was.

The alliance of Giuliani and Ernst & Young made perfect sense on paper. Giuliani's fledgling consulting firm, with fifteen staffers, won instant credibility by partnering with a revered global brand, which employed tens of thousands of people. And E&Y had a vast and lucrative platform of clients that Giuliani's firm could access. For the accounting firm, Giuliani brought prestige, a record of success governing the nation's financial capital, expertise in law enforcement, and deep Washington connections.

E&Y had built a solid reputation, hour by billable hour, over almost a century and a half. The deal offered the accounting firm the ability to upsell their clients on additional consultative services that Giuliani Partners could provide, piling on more billable hours. The partners at Giuliani's firm had a sexier model in mind, however, which was basically to leverage the boss's star power for stratospheric fees.

But it wasn't clear what Giuliani Partners actually *was*, even to its founders. It was billed as a management consulting firm, but none of them had management consulting experience; the top brass were lawyers, cops, firemen, and political types. The boss's name was synonymous with crime fighting, so the company could credibly seek out security contracts. But the team's ambitions ran far beyond helping companies figure out how to spy on their employees.

Joe Lhota was the one member of Giuliani's inner circle at City Hall with extensive business and financial expertise. The former deputy mayor for operations was a Harvard MBA, who had worked in the private sector for decades. But he declined to join the firm. "I didn't understand what they were going to do," he recalled. "I still don't understand what they were going to do."

The firm may not have had a coherent business plan, but it did have a founder who was one of the most beloved men on the planet. And that was worth a lot. Management consulting was only the beginning. Giuliani's fame and reputation for integrity could be squeezed like a washcloth for all types of moneymaking ventures: investment banking, real estate—the possibilities were endless. Slapping the Giuliani logo on virtually any kind of business could send its prestige into orbit.

"There was a sense that for him and all the partners, this was their moment to cash in," said Mancini. "That sort of became the end goal."

E&Y furnished the firm with a sparkling new office suite on the 24th floor of the new tower at 5 Times Square, doubtlessly grateful for Giuliani's tax abatements. He took the corner office, which he decorated with a seat from the old Yankee Stadium, a humidor for his cigars, framed photos of Judith Nathan, and a sign on his desk reading "I'M RESPONSIBLE." Judith took an office next door to his, and had exercise equipment installed.

The hallways teemed with mayoral alumni. All the founding partners except one hailed from the administration. Spokespeople, advisors, schedulers, bodyguards, drivers, advance people—all took the trip uptown with him from City Hall. Bernie Kerik and Tom Von Essen, his police and fire commissioners, were made senior officers of the firm, though their status was so ill-defined that when Kerik showed up he was surprised to see his name on a door.

"Is this really happening?" he asked Mahoney, who himself hadn't been given a title. "I didn't know we were doing this. It probably would have been good if somebody told me."

There were two outsiders, each of them suspect in the eyes of the team.

Roy Bailey, a Texas insurance executive, was made a partner. He was an impeccably groomed, backslapping businessman, straight out of the boardroom, with a soft spot for conservative politicians—Rick Perry among them—and a talent for raising rivers of campaign cash. He was smooth as silk, and his ability to charm a stranger was legendary in Texas circles. "He could sell used cars easily—any used car," Republican congressman Pete Sessions told a reporter.

Growing up in Waco, Bailey's grandfather made him stand at the door of the First Baptist Church on Sundays, and greet every visitor. "Sometimes my grandfather would poke me and say: 'Look them in the eye, boy. That's how you get to know them,'" he recalled.

Bailey and Giuliani met during the mayor's short-lived race against Hillary Clinton. The hot-tempered New Yorker and the buttery-smooth Texan immediately hit it off. Giuliani made frequent trips to the state for fundraisers that Bailey helped to organize, as there was no shortage of Texans eager to torpedo the ambitions of a

Clinton. When he pulled out of the race, it was Bailey who helped hatch the plans to take the Giuliani show to the private sector.

Giuliani saw in Bailey a man with unlimited connections, access to a mountain of capital, and a Texas-sized vision of Giuliani's commercial potential. Bailey saw Giuliani as his ticket out of town. "I've always wanted to play in the big leagues," he said. "This is the biggest league."

The Texan presumably could have played the role of experienced businessman in the group, having run a large insurance firm, but client work wasn't in his portfolio. He was a salesman, a connector. And he soon became a Giuliani sidekick. "They had great chemistry," a partner recalled. "When he'd come up from Texas we'd tell Rudy, 'Roy's in town,' and he'd say 'Let's go out with him.'"

The crew from City Hall was somewhat amused, and somewhat appalled. "He was the nicest bullshit artist I've ever met," said one senior executive.

Giuliani would benefit enormously from his presence as time went on. To others, bringing a slick Texas salesman into the inner sanctum only reinforced the soulless mission of the firm.

Alan Placa was Bailey's temperamental opposite. He was soft-spoken, modest, and cerebral. He was also a priest accused of being a pedophile.

Like Peter Powers, Placa was like a brother to Giuliani; the three attended Bishop Loughlin and Manhattan College together before Placa decided to enter the priesthood. It was Placa to whom Giuliani had turned to obtain his annulment with Gina Peruggi. Placa rose to become a high-ranking advisor at the Diocese of Rockville Centre on Long Island, placed in charge of, among other things, investigating charges of sexual assault by priests.

In April 2002, his career was coming to a crashing halt. The

Suffolk County district attorney opened a grand jury investigation into allegations against the Long Island diocese, including accusations that Placa abused boys in the 1970s and used his position to develop policies to protect other priests. The diocese suspended him in June and forbade him from celebrating mass or wearing his priest's clothing.

Two months later, he was given an office at Giuliani Partners and hired as a senior vice president at a salary of over $300,000. Aside from vetting an occasional speech for the boss, a partner said, "He did nothing." Giuliani, intensely loyal to his friend, kept him on even after a grand jury the next year accused Placa of being "cautious but relentless in pursuing his victims," allegedly touching boys through their clothes. It also accused him of heading up a conspiracy to protect accused pedophile priests by shuffling them from parish to parish.

Placa denied the allegations and decried the destruction of his reputation. "I'm not even a human being," he complained to the *New York Times*. "I'm a monster." The statute of limitations saved him from prosecution, and a Vatican court cleared him of the charges six years later.

If Giuliani was concerned about his team's lack of qualifications to solve the problems of America's corporations, he didn't show it. They were family, forged over a lifetime and bonded forever on September 11. Like Donald Trump, loyalty was far more important to him than a good résumé. Besides, he believed they knew all they needed to know. They would teach governments to implement the principles of CompStat and Broken Windows; help them reinvent themselves as he had reinvented city government; manage as boldly as he'd managed the city. It was a conceit, barely fleshed out beyond a handful of long conversations over Italian dinners.

As it turned out there was little need for worry. Many of his clients were primarily focused on buying the imprimatur of America's

Mayor. There were any number of former elected officials available for hire, but godlike figures were hard to come by.

No company was more brazen about its intentions than Purdue Pharma, the maker of OxyContin, the painkiller whose widespread abuse was spawning a generation of young opioid addicts across rural America. Hundreds had already died from overdoses by the time the company came knocking in 2002. Purdue was facing almost three hundred lawsuits, and the Drug Enforcement Administration was investigating the firm's misleading claims and aggressive marketing tactics.

Purdue's chief attorney was blunt about his reasons for hiring the firm. "We believe that government officials are more comfortable knowing that Giuliani is advising Purdue Pharma," he said, according to the pharma company's literature. "It is clear to us, and we hope it is clear to the government, that Giuliani would not take an assignment with a company that he felt was acting in an improper way."

Giuliani was happy to join the cause. In hiring America's Mayor, they received the services of a man with nonpareil clout with the Bush administration. It wasn't just that he could get a meeting with anyone; it took courage for a government official to say no to a national hero.

Despite insisting that he wasn't in the lobbying business, Giuliani met with DEA chief Asa Hutchinson twice in early 2002—once at Giuliani Partners—to try to persuade him to rein in his investigators and give Purdue more time to get its house in order. Bernie Kerik had been dispatched to Purdue's New Jersey manufacturing plant to help tighten security, he pointed out. They argued that investigators should give Purdue time to fix its issues. Hutchinson asked his investigators to keep him briefed.

The pharmaceutical company agreed to pay a $2 million fine— investigators recommended ten times that amount—over their record keeping. Purdue admitted no wrongdoing, which allowed it to continue along its destructive path. Giuliani went on to help protect the company from even deeper trouble in the years that followed.

Just months after leading America through a historic crisis, Giuliani was earning millions by protecting a company whose actions were contributing to the overdose deaths of America's young people. A man who could find a moral justification for any decision invoked his cancer history to make his choice sound principled. "I understand the pain and distress that accompanies illness," he said in 2002. "I know that proper medications are necessary for people to treat their sickness and improve their quality of life."

There were innumerable organizations waiting in line behind Purdue to secure the Giuliani stamp of approval. In 2002, the integrity of the betting system used by the National Thoroughbred Racing Association was called into question amid the so-called Breeders' Cup Pick Six scandal, in which three former fraternity brothers managed to rig the system for a $3 million payout from a single race (they didn't get the money). Around the same time, the state comptroller and attorney general considered inquiries into the association's practices. With the organization's reputation teetering, it turned to Giuliani Partners to give its good name a thorough rinse.

It announced that Giuliani would investigate the betting system, and bring "independence and credibility" to it. The former mayor all but bestowed his blessing on the association from the outset. "The NTRA should be applauded for its immediate response," he said.

Industry observers were appalled. "It's not clear what anyone will be getting for his money other than the current credibility of the Giuliani name . . . given the firm's lack of expertise in either technology or racing," wrote Steven Crist, the publisher of the *Daily Racing Form*.

Nine months later, Giuliani Partners released a report finding no evidence of systemic fraud. Instead, it recommended upgrades to NTRA's system—and that the industry continue to monitor itself.

The income from the firm and his other activities was making Giuliani a rich man. In his final year as mayor, he had earned a salary of $195,000, and claimed through his divorce lawyer that he had just $7,000 on hand. A year later, Donna Hanover claimed he was making $1 million per month.

His outside income was even more eye-popping. He signed a $2.7 million advance on a book deal with Harvey and Bob Weinstein's Miramax Books, and delivered over a hundred speeches in his first year, crisscrossing the country for $100,000 or more per appearance. For all his ambitions for his firm, he was barely at the office.

There was no modern precedent for this level of cash-in for a New York City mayor. David Dinkins, his predecessor, was spending his post-mayoralty earning a living as a professor at Columbia University. Ed Koch was making good money authoring books and serving as a rainmaker for a prominent law firm. But Giuliani was in an altogether different orbit. He'd leveraged his mayoralty to make himself spectacularly wealthy.

For thirty years, he'd chased the narcotic high of power, rarely displaying an interest in material possessions. As prosecutor and mayor, he purchased suits at a Bancroft store for $299. He eschewed trendy restaurants in favor of neighborhood mom-and-pop joints. But when the cash spigot opened after September 11 he put up scant resistance to the seductions of wealth. He began to dress better, eat at better restaurants, socialize with wealthier people.

Ten months after vowing to retire in Staten Island, he paid $4.77 million for a 3,100-square-foot, nine-room co-op on 66th Street and Madison Avenue, one of the most coveted addresses on Manhattan's Upper East Side. Two years later he purchased a $3.2 million house in the Hamptons with nine bedrooms, seven bathrooms, a swimming pool, screening room, gym, wine cellar, and steam room (which Judith converted into a walk-in humidor to keep his cigars moist). That same year, he bought a Palm Beach apartment for Judith's parents for $410,000.

Members of his inner circle noticed a growing fondness for creature comforts. The man who spent eight years as mayor riding through the city streets in a Chevy Suburban SUV was now insisting on traveling by private jet. His Washington Speakers Bureau standard contract required transportation with a Gulfstream IV or larger, a minimum two-bedroom hotel suite with a king-sized bed on an upper floor, and four additional rooms for aides and security.

"People started treating him like a king, and I think he liked it," said a longtime aide. On a nighttime flight to Europe on a Gulfstream jet, Giuliani grew upset that the plane didn't stock cashmere blankets. "It was stunning," the aide recalled. "He would never have done that three or four years before that. Not possible."

Fairly or not, his friends and aides laid the blame on Judith and her social aspirations. He accompanied her daughter and her to debutante balls, an unfathomable concept to his entourage. "He wouldn't spit on these people once," recalled a former aide.

But he showed few signs of unease with his budding nouveau riche lifestyle. He played golf in the Hamptons and Palm Beach, and made rounds on the charity circuit, ditching his dark business suits for powder blue sport jackets, bright pocket squares, and chinos— the uniform of old-school WASP society. In the years that followed he accumulated memberships at eleven country clubs and purchased two more homes.

His creeping materialism was fueling an insatiable appetite for cash. To fund his new lifestyle—as well as an enormous $6.8 million divorce settlement with Hanover—he pushed for increasingly extreme fees.

In 2002, Tommy Mottola, the legendary chairman and CEO of

Sony Music Entertainment, invited Giuliani's team to his office at
Sony Tower, the Philip Johnson postmodernist masterpiece on Madison Avenue. He outlined a dire situation to the Giuliani team: the
rise of the internet, led by the file-sharing site Napster, was creating
a piracy crisis that was posing an existential threat to the industry.
The five biggest music companies had joined forces to combat the
problem, and needed help.

"It's going to require a legal mind, it's going to require a political
mind, and it's going to require someone who understands how to
manage," Mottola said. "We need to figure out a way to get either
legislation, or enforcement, or regulation, and we need someone to
work with different industries."

Giuliani barely touched the sushi that he was offered ("He
wasn't exactly a sushi guy," said a colleague), but was excited by
the challenge. It was the perfect assignment for the firm, one that
wasn't based solely around Giuliani's fame. Mottola was looking to
him for his government connections, legal expertise, and gravitas
to make all the players fall into line. "We were made for it," said a
partner.

Giuliani crafted a proposal for Mottola with a staggering price
tag of over $10 million, causing internal concern that he was pushing
the envelope, to say the least. But Giuliani figured that each of the
five music companies could kick in $2 million.

He was wrong; the companies were flabbergasted by the ask, and
rejected the proposal immediately. The opportunity evaporated in a
haze of greed.

Perhaps the most telling illustration of Giuliani's new life as a
mercenary lay in the paid speeches he was grinding out like confetti.

In the weeks following the 9/11 attacks his oratory soared. His
eloquence was inspired by grief, compassion, and a sense of history,
as when he delivered his farewell address as mayor to a rapt audience
at St. Paul's Chapel across from Ground Zero.

Our enemies insanely commit suicide to serve some irrational purpose. And they think that we are afraid—they used to think that we are afraid to die for what we believe in. And the reality is that we don't want to die. And we don't believe that it's our right to make that choice for ourselves. We think God only has that right.

But the reality is that we're just a few blocks from a site in which hundreds and hundreds of men and women freely by choice gave up their life. First, to protect the lives of other people. And secondly, to preserve the dignity and honor of the United States of America while under attack.

This war will go on for some time: to find the terrorists, to eliminate terrorism, to eliminate terrorists. I don't know how long it will go on. It will go on probably for a longer time than we would like. But I hope you realize that we have already won it. We have already won the war. It's just a matter now of finishing it. And that isn't easy. And it's going to mean more sacrifices and more lives lost. It could even mean more attacks. I don't know. But I know we won.

The man you could book to speak to your colleagues or classmates for $100,000 and a ride on a Gulfstream jet was a wholly different figure. He was Rudy Giuliani the motivational speaker, extolling six banal principles of leadership, punctuated by endless allusions to 9/11, and peppered with mobster impersonations. It was a marketing tie-in to *Leadership*, his book.

"The first principle of leadership, I believe, is understanding who you are, what you are and what you stand for and being willing to stand for something," he told eight thousand students at the University of Buffalo. "It comes down to what happened on Sept. 11."

His words were those of a self-help author, with his tales of 9/11 the standout feature.

"To be a leader, and an effective one and a good one, you have to be an optimist," he said. "Nobody follows a pessimist.

"When I say leadership, I don't just mean running a large organization or small organization. I also mean running your life because you need leadership to get through life."

His speaking-fee haul in 2002 was estimated at $8 million.

Tumult was a constant companion to Giuliani; it accompanied him at every step of his career, and plagued his every relationship. Most politicians spent their lives trying to avoid it; he fed off of it. It was quintessential Giuliani that his trip to Europe to be knighted by the Queen of England turned into a public triumph and a personal disaster.

The debacles never ended when it came to his personal relationships, and because there was virtually no line separating his private and public lives, havoc in one area caused havoc in the other. And that is where the story of Manny Papir and Judith Nathan comes in.

The Europe trip took place six weeks after he'd left the mayoralty, as the firm was taking shape and the office at 5 Times Square was under construction. Giuliani pulled out all the stops for the glamour event; he filled the Concorde with a large party of friends, family, and colleagues.

The cast went beyond the usual gang of aides and security. There was Jim Turley, the CEO of Ernst & Young; Giuliani's uncle Rudy, a retired police officer; Randy Levine, the president of the New York Yankees and a former deputy mayor, and his wife, Mindy; Bernie Kerik; Tom Von Essen; and Giuliani's assistant Beth Petrone.

A Giuliani trip anywhere was always a zoo; his aides were noisy, sleep-deprived, and self-important, attributes acquired from years with a New York City mayor. Those qualities more or less blended in back in Manhattan, but were less endearing to, say, guests and managers of a quaint 145-year-old London hotel.

The St. James's Hotel and Club was the epitome of a proper British establishment. The staff spoke in whispers; the rooms were elegant and understated. Giuliani's aides entered its lobby yelling into their cell phones, shouting to colleagues, and making requests for special treatment. "It was the quintessential ugly Americans, carrying around that little map of the world where New York City is the size of the universe, and London is a pin-dot," said a member of the entourage. "I don't know how many times they'd ask us to quiet down. You'd think no one else was getting knighted."

No one was more demanding than Judith Nathan. And no one got the brunt of her demands more than Manny Papir.

In the months leading up to September 11, Nathan began to win the grudging respect of some of Giuliani's friends, who appreciated her dedication to him during his prostate cancer crisis. In the weeks following the attacks, many saw her as his rock of stability, helping him cope with the crushing pressure of mourning the dead and trying to bring a devastated city back to life. It was hard to watch her gaze at him and not be struck by her adoration.

But when Giuliani was transformed overnight into an international hero, it wasn't just his life that changed in an instant. As his fame exploded, and the money started pouring in, Nathan developed clear ideas about who they were, and how they deserved to be treated.

Tension was mounting between Nathan and Papir long before the Concorde took off from New York for England. According to Nathan, she worked hard to win him over when the two first met, inviting him to dinner at her 96th Street apartment. "Manny used to love it when I would play piano," she said. "He would sing."

But things went south quickly. Frustrated that she couldn't call Giuliani directly—all her calls had to go through Papir—she bought

Giuliani a second phone. "From that moment forth, Manny hated me," she said.

In her eyes, three of Giuliani's closest handlers—Kate Anson, his scheduler; Sunny Mindel, his press secretary; and Papir—were doing their best to poison her relationship with Giuliani. "Manny Papir had total control—and Kate Anson and Sunny Mindel had total control—over him," Nathan said.

Her complaints had a whiff of paranoia. The mayor's circle of friends and staff came to see her as dangerously manipulative. Giuliani and she fought constantly, and she could be vicious.

"Rudy would tell me 'Who do you think you are?'—'I know who I am,'" Nathan said. "'*Who the fuck are you, your father was in Sing Sing.*' That's what I would say—literally that's what I would say to him."

Giuliani's handlers were both appalled and threatened by her. "It was a power struggle from day one," said a friend of Giuliani's. "All these guys wanted control of him—they'd hitched their wagons to Rudy years ago. Everybody saw the White House in their futures. Judith was derailing that train.

"The more Judith started to interfere, the more the Rudy people clamped down, and it became a war of wills that permeated every aspect of his life, down to what tie he was going to wear."

Like Cristyne Lategano before her, Nathan played to his suspicions, raising questions about the motives of the people closest to him. And just as with Lategano, he allowed her to drive away the people closest to him. His two children, Andrew and Caroline, loathed Nathan so deeply they stopped speaking to him for years. According to a friend of Nathan's at the time, she bragged that she removed their contact information—and Tony Carbonetti's—from Giuliani's phone (Nathan denied it).

Carbonetti, Giuliani's longtime political advisor, was too powerful to push around. But Manny Papir, the young body man, was another story. "She treated him like an indentured servant," said one aide; "a vassal," said another.

Papir was smoldering when they arrived in London. Colleagues tried to persuade him to brush off her abuse, but his resentment seeped out in not-so-subtle ways.

"He was getting a little too reckless, being snippy with her, and with good reason," said a member of the entourage. "But this was the boss's wife he was rolling his eyes in front of, and she was able to sell that to Rudy that he was being disrespectful to her. I felt so sorry for him. He was really buckling under the weight of Judith's demands and waiting for Rudy to come and save him."

But Giuliani, so quick to anger in public, was oddly passive when it came to dealing with personal conflict. He rarely fired people himself, leaving the unpleasantness to his deputies, and was reluctant to intervene in staff disputes. The entourage member felt he was worried that to confront Nathan would be to risk her causing a scene, or demanding to get on a plane back home. "She was always on the edge of leaving."

Giuliani and Nathan arose early on the morning after their arrival at the St. James. They had a packed day ahead of them, starting with a 7:15 a.m. breakfast event with hundreds of corporate executives at the Park Lane Hotel, followed by the 10:15 a.m. knighting ceremony at Buckingham Palace. Things went wrong virtually from the moment they got out of bed.

The queen's request that attendees wear black in honor of Princess Margaret's passing forced the guests to scramble for new outfits. Judith dispatched Papir, who arrived in the country a day before the rest of the party, to find her a hat for the occasion. He went shopping at Harrods hours before their plane touched down, bitter at having to fetch clothes for the boss's wife.

He and Nathan disagree about what happened next. According to Nathan, Papir waited until the last minute, then presented her with a hideous creation designed to humiliate her. "It had, like, red feathers meant to look like horns.

"I think he did it on purpose," she said. "His goal was to keep me from going to the knighting." She said Giuliani was furious. "Rudy went nuts on Manny," she said, and ordered him to go back to Harrods to bring back additional choices.

Papir, who dismissed her accusations as ludicrous, said a salesperson at Harrods selected a half dozen hats for her consideration, and delivered them to the St. James for her inspection. Nathan disparaged them all, he said, and complained to Giuliani, who gave Papir more of an eye roll than a tongue-lashing.

The one thing Papir and Nathan agree upon is that the incident poisoned their relationship for good. "I remember from that moment forth, when Manny dropped off those hats, he wanted to kill me," she said.

According to Papir, the hat incident was "the spark that lit the flame."

The burlesque reached its climax a few days later, when the Giuliani road show moved to Baden-Baden, Germany, a picturesque spa town, where he was scheduled to accept an award.

Nathan was exhausted. She had developed a cold, and injured her ankle going down a flight of steps. At event after event, Giuliani was being mobbed by media and greeted like a conquering hero. "He wanted me at everything," she said.

At the same time, Papir was buckling under the challenges created by Judith's whims. She prevailed upon Giuliani to extend their stay an extra night, which had Papir frantically rebooking hotel rooms and car transportation, and trying to persuade an irritable pilot to keep his plane stationed in the town for an additional day.

At the hotel, Nathan overheard Papir disparage her to a colleague. "Where's the princess?" he asked.

She grabbed a member of the security detail, who heard it as well, and headed upstairs to tell Giuliani. Not long afterwards, Tony Carbonetti and Bruce Teitelbaum fired Papir. There were no farewells.

"I was kicked out with zero severance, zero help, and no one from the mayor on down thought to call or help," Papir said years later. "I was forgotten.

"It was all her, and ultimately his character, that doomed me," he said. "I take no joy in knowing that the warning signs that we all saw regarding Judith were so clear to us, and he ignored them."

Papir recalled the conversations he would have in the car with Giuliani about his disastrous experiences with women. "It's actually something I tried to convince Rudy of: Dude, you suck at relationships. Stop having them."

The problems with Nathan, and the disintegration of Giuliani's most important relationships, were both a cause and an effect of his wayward turn after September 11. His friends were puzzled that this famously ascetic man was increasingly focused on money and material things, and had chosen in his mate a woman who was passionate about both.

But his creeping decadence was an outgrowth of a painful reality, which was that his power had drained away. When he left the mayoralty, he lost his grip on the zealous mission that had driven him his entire career, which was to wield power and impose his view of right and wrong on others.

As mayor, he had an army of forty thousand police officers and a $40 billion budget at his disposal. As a prosecutor he had enormous say over people's freedom. Now all he could do was talk about what he'd once achieved, bask in the applause, make money off of it, and find increasingly meaningless ways to spend it. This brilliant man, with his peerless record of accomplishment, chose a shallow existence to fill the void.

Eventually he would start to miss the power he'd lost, and seek to recapture it in ways that grew increasingly desperate.

CHAPTER 9

Rambo

On a balmy summer morning in 2001, Mayor Rudy Giuliani placed a call to his police commissioner. Bernie Kerik picked up the phone, but a howling noise in the background made it hard to hear him.

"Where are you?" the mayor asked. "It sounds like a wind tunnel."

The wind was in fact blowing furiously behind Kerik. He was scaling like Batman up a tubular suspension cable swerving to the top of the Brooklyn Bridge, taking baby steps to avoid falling onto speeding traffic below.

"How did you get up there?" Giuliani asked him, raising his voice so Kerik could hear him.

"I walked on the fucking pole," he replied.

The mayor paused for a moment. "Why would you do that?"

An aide had basically dared Kerik to make the climb, pointing out that members of the department's Emergency Service Unit had to do it all the time in practice drills. No other police commissioner, Kerik recalled, "ever had the balls to do it."

But why would they? Why was the city's police commissioner risking his life while much of the city was still in bed?

It was the kind of question that he must have gotten many times over the course of his improbable career. If there was risk involved, Bernie Kerik was your man.

He looked like a drill sergeant, with a compact body built like a tank, a bushy mustache, and a shaved head. His eyes moved discreetly around a room, always casing for signs of trouble. He was perfectly cast for the tough-guy jobs he'd held: chief investigator for a hospital that catered to Saudi Arabia's royal family; prison warden at the Passaic County Jail in New Jersey; undercover narcotics detective in Harlem; New York City correction chief; New York City police commissioner.

He was a rogue with a compelling life story. His mother, a prostitute, abandoned him at the age of two, and was likely murdered by a pimp when he was nine years old. Growing up in a rough neighborhood in New Jersey, he dropped out of high school, earned a black belt in karate, and found his calling in the military and law enforcement. He'd engaged in so many gun battles as a cop that his nickname was "Rambo." Every other word out of his mouth was a profanity. Giuliani loved him.

"I wasn't a politician," Kerik said. "I wasn't one of these fucking bean counters."

The two met in the run-up to Giuliani's first campaign against David Dinkins in 1989. At the time Kerik's hair ran down to the middle of his back, he wore six diamond earrings, and sported a big goatee. "I looked like fucking Charles Manson," he recalled.

The candidate had been the subject of death threats since his prosecutor days, and was most comfortable when surrounded by plainclothes cops with mics in their sleeves and guns under their jackets. He got a kick out of Kerik, but also saw him as a protector, a pit bull who'd growl at anyone who came too close. When Giuliani made a second run against Dinkins in 1993, his new friend became a driver and advance man, tooling around with him from one campaign event to the next. He called Giuliani "Boss."

Kerik's career blossomed with Giuliani's election in 1993. The new mayor placed him in a middle-management position at the city's Department of Correction, which ran the massive Rikers Island prison complex, a notorious haven for violence.

In 1995, he was summoned to Gracie Mansion, where the mayor informed him over a bottle of wine that he was promoting him to deputy correction commissioner. Kerik hesitated, pointing out that he had only managed a single prison as warden of the Passaic County Jail prior to joining the NYPD, but Giuliani wasn't concerned. He led him to a room downstairs, where Deputy Mayor Peter Powers was waiting with a group of other aides. Each stepped forward and gave Kerik a kiss on the cheek.

"I wonder if he noticed how much becoming part of his team resembled becoming part of a Mafia family," Kerik recalled. "I was being made."

He proved wildly successful. He was a relentless taskmaster at Rikers, paying 2 a.m. visits to the complex, firing incompetents, arresting prisoners who committed violent acts in jail. Serious crimes plummeted by over 90 percent, from over ninety stabbings and slashings a month to seven. The mayor promoted him to the top job in 1998.

Two years later, Giuliani once again tapped him for a job far above his experience level, naming him police commissioner even though he'd never made it to the rank of sergeant, and hadn't graduated high school. Several advisors opposed the appointment because of his lack of experience, but Giuliani had an intuitive trust in Kerik. He waved their concerns away as so much bedwetting.

"I believe that the skill I developed better than any other was surrounding myself with great people," he wrote in *Leadership*.

That sense of infallibility got Giuliani into huge trouble down the line, as his judgment of people was often terrible. Though his love for Kerik was genuine, he placed a premium on how loyal people were to him, how much attention they paid him, and how much they could help him. For those who passed that test he was willing to overlook a lot.

Kerik was the temperamental opposite of his rigid, joyless predecessor, Howard Safir; he was colorful, street-smart, and foul-mouthed, all pluses in a city that preferred its leaders larger-than-life. He brought his tornado style to the department, making five arrests *himself,* collaring, among others, a convicted murderer wanted on carjacking charges. Rank-and-file morale, which sank after the Diallo uproar, rebounded, and relations with the city's Black community improved due to his aggressive outreach to neighborhood leaders. Crime, which had already fallen by around 57 percent when he arrived, fell another 11 percent by the time his term ended.

Kerik worshipped the mayor, describing him as "the most single-minded brilliant person" he'd ever met. Giuliani referred to him as "the brother I never had," and became godfather to both of Kerik's daughters.

When the World Trade Center was decimated by terrorists, Kerik was by Giuliani's side, and became perhaps the second most recognizable national figure from the tragedy. He wrote a best-selling autobiography, and signed a deal with Miramax for a movie based on his life.

There were odd moments in his stint as commissioner that raised questions about his ethical compass. Newspapers reported that he or his staff sent homicide detectives to question and fingerprint Fox News employees when Judith Regan, his book publisher and girlfriend, lost her cell phone and necklace at a taping there. The city's Conflicts of Interest Board fined him $2,500 for using police officers to conduct research for his book. Giuliani looked the other way.

The mayor was far from alone in his fondness for his Runyon-esque commissioner. In his travels with Kerik through the ash and steel graveyard of Ground Zero, President George W. Bush developed a deep admiration for him. Like Giuliani, the president disdained stuffed shirts, and found Kerik's hardscrabble life story inspiring. Only later would he and Giuliani question whether they'd placed too much faith in someone so attracted to danger that he considered scaling the top of the Brooklyn Bridge just another Saturday morning.

Bush was already a weakened leader by the time he took office in January 2001. Many Democratic voters considered his victory over Al Gore illegitimate from the bitterly contested election results in Florida and the Supreme Court ruling that halted the recount there with Bush ahead by just 537 votes out of almost six million. The disputed victory deprived him of a mandate, though his campaign had offered few revolutionary proposals to begin with. The agenda in his first eight months in office meandered from cutting taxes to creating a massive new Medicare entitlement, leaving members of his own party lukewarm. If there was a through line to his presidency it was hard to recognize it.

The September 11 attacks changed everything. In the span of a morning, Bush's administration was transformed into a war presidency. In an address to a special joint session of Congress on September 20, he declared war on terrorist groups and the countries granting them harbor.

"Our grief has turned to anger, and anger to resolution," he told the nation. "Whether we bring our enemies to justice, or bring justice to our enemies, justice will be done."

He peered up at the guests seated in the House Gallery.

"Tonight, we welcome two leaders who embody the extraordinary spirit of all New Yorkers," he said. "Governor George Pataki and Mayor Rudolph Giuliani." The chamber erupted in cheers.

Pataki lacked Giuliani's passion, and talent for capturing the spotlight, and never became a national figure. It was Giuliani who was forever bonded with President Bush and the wars he waged that night.

It was quite an alliance. Both men's fortunes turned around on that fateful morning. Giuliani woke up on September 11 a lame-duck mayor with an uncertain future, and went to bed an international celebrity with stratospheric wealth in his future. Bush was transformed from a modestly admired president to a wildly popular one; his polling skyrocketed 35 points in the span of a week, and hit 90 percent after he addressed Congress. At the end of the year Gallup released its list of most admired men. Bush ranked first, and Giuliani was third, right above the pope.

The two were in political lockstep; Giuliani made that clear in a speech of his own eleven days after Bush's address to Congress. Local officials don't usually get invited to address the United Nations General Assembly, except perhaps to welcome foreign dignitaries to their city. But Giuliani was speaking less as a mayor when he stepped into the Assembly Hall on October 1, and more as the conscience of a wounded country.

"Look at that destruction, that massive, senseless, cruel loss of human life, and then, I ask you to look in your hearts and recognize that there is no room for neutrality on the issue of terrorism," he said. "You're either with civilization or with terrorists. On one side is democracy, the rule of law and respect for human life. On the other, it's tyranny, arbitrary executions and mass murder. We're right and they're wrong. It's as simple as that."

Giuliani's view of the world was doubtlessly impacted by watching people jump to their deaths from the burning towers, hugging sobbing children at firefighter funerals, and mourning the deaths of his own friends. It wasn't hard to imagine why he asked Bush if he could be the one to execute Osama bin Laden.

But by marrying himself to Bush politically, and adopting his and Vice President Dick Cheney's hawkish views, he was aligning his ideology to his self-interest. He reinvented himself as a foreign policy hawk, opening up a candy store of political and financial benefits with the administration.

The two weren't friends; it was more a marriage of convenience. Bush had the beloved hero of America's worst terror attack validating his war policies. Giuliani was granted a national stage, entrée to the highest echelons of the Republican Party, and a wide-open door to the White House and government agencies for his clients. It was worth millions to him.

His stump speech was an ode to Bush and the war on terror, with his September 11 parables playing on a never-ending loop. When the White House began its drumbeat for war against Iraq, he marched at the front of that parade, comparing Saddam Hussein to Hitler and warning against Neville Chamberlain–style acquiescence in the face of evil.

"We sometimes repeat our mistakes," he told a country club audience on Long Island. "In the future, as we look at what's necessary, we cannot let down our guard.

"I have a very strong view that it's imperative that we remove Saddam Hussein and do away with his regime," he said. "You have to take pre-emptive action. As time goes by, Saddam Hussein will become more and more dangerous."

It was a refrain he echoed repeatedly. When the White House suggested that Saddam was harboring weapons of mass destruction he sang that song as well. "I see Iraq as part of the overall effort to remove the capacity for biological, chemical warfare and the possibility of using weapons of mass destruction," he told Wolf Blitzer in a CNN interview.

When he wasn't joining Bush at fundraisers or hosting him in the city for 9/11-related events, he was at the White House for meetings or "purely social visit[s]," as he told reporters in July 2002. Inevitably, his appearances with the president led to speculation that he would join the administration, either as secretary of homeland security, or as Bush's 2004 running mate, requiring Bush to bump Cheney off the ticket. The buzz took on a life of its own, forcing administration officials to deny the baseless reports.

As it turned out, it wasn't Giuliani that Bush wanted. It was his protégé.

"Welcome to a free Iraq," Ambassador L. Paul (Jerry) Bremer said to Bernie Kerik, leaning in for a handshake inside Saddam Hussein's old office inside the Republican Guard Palace in Baghdad. It was May 19, 2003, less than two months since the American invasion of Iraq, and Kerik's first day as interior minister of the Iraqi Coalition Provisional Authority, a job for which the White House plucked him out of Giuliani Partners with barely any notice.

Eighteen days after George W. Bush stood on the deck of the USS *Abraham Lincoln* under a banner reading "Mission Accomplished," the euphoria over the U.S. military's stunningly efficient defeat of Saddam's forces was fading. From the moment the smoke from the invasion cleared it became obvious that the administration's assumptions about post-liberation conditions were astonishingly wrong. The Iraqi people were not greeting the U.S. as liberators. The Iraqi army, police force, and government bureaucracy all but collapsed, surprising officials who expected to find the foundations of Iraqi society still intact. The country's vital infrastructure—power stations and water supplies—was crippled. The streets were in a state of anarchy, with looters ransacking businesses and government offices. The sound of gunfire filled the air.

Jay Garner, the retired lieutenant general sent by the White House to serve as the first American administrator in Baghdad, focused on reestablishing Iraqi self-governance to allow the Americans to exit the country fairly quickly. But after just one month on the job the president replaced him with Bremer, a longtime friend of Vice President Dick Cheney's chief of staff, Scooter Libby.

Chief among Bremer's priorities was ridding the government of Saddam loyalists, who belonged to the Ba'ath Party, a hugely controversial strategy within the administration. But the utter chaos of the situation gave Bremer something close to a free hand, and he received permission from the president to dissolve the Iraqi army and cleanse Ba'ath Party members from the top ranks of the Iraqi government.

The decision proved catastrophic; 500,000 Iraqi soldiers and other military officers were released into the streets and left to fend for themselves, embittered, and susceptible to the appeals of insurrectionists. The move fueled a civil war that fractured the country and kept the American military engaged in Iraq for much of the next decade.

Bremer did not dissolve the police, but its ranks plummeted in the course of the invasion, and the dismissal of all its top officials under the de-Ba'athification policy crippled its command structure. The streets were plagued with lawlessness, and Bremer needed someone to rebuild the force virtually from scratch.

Bush's rationale for appointing Kerik wasn't hard to understand: Who better to rebuild a police force than the former leader of the nation's largest police force, a 9/11 hero, and a former Mideast security expert? Plus, he was on Team Bush, and could be counted on to parrot the White House party line.

Kerik inherited a shambles. Tens of thousands of police personnel had fled in the war, leaving the streets in chaos. It was just four weeks since the cessation of combat, and the infrastructure of the department ceased to exist. Saddam had destroyed all the personnel records, so even if officers wanted to return, Kerik had no way of distinguishing between the good guys and the bad guys. "There was no vetting process," he said. It was impossible to recruit without rebuilding the entire system.

A plan was devised to create a police training site in Hungary, but that government pulled out at the last minute. Kerik said he met with the King of Jordan and persuaded him to host the facility, but the process dragged on for months.

It wasn't the painstaking task of rebuilding a bureaucracy that inspired him. Kerik was at heart a crime fighter, and the rampant disorder in the streets was what got his adrenaline going.

"I was fucking excited," he wrote in his memoirs. "My entire career had been one of living on the edge, being in the heart of the action, dealing with life-and-death situations. This would be no different. . . .

"I'm not sure exactly why I'm like this, or where it comes from," he wrote. "Like many little boys, I loved to play cops and robbers, games of combat, fantasizing about being the hero, the good guy who saves the day."

It was an honest description of what motivated him, and not all that different from how a lot of cops might describe themselves. But it wasn't clear that what Iraq needed was an action junkie.

Kerik threw himself into policing, working eighteen hours a day "in a hundred degrees in the shade," he recalled. Appalled by the methods the police employed under Saddam—"ripping out toenails and fingernails, pounding nails through a person's palm"—he submitted a restructuring plan to Bremer recommending the imposition of minimum standards, training, and accountability. "They were more like savages than police," he recalled.

The insurrection was growing by the day, the mayhem exacerbated by Saddam's release of 38,000 prison inmates, many of them rapists and murderers, prior to the American invasion. Kerik and his team ran dangerous nighttime raids, busting kidnapping gangs, car theft rings, and other criminal outfits.

Conducting high-risk operations in a war zone played to his strengths, but Army officials were infuriated that he was infringing on their turf. "They'd get tips and they'd go and actually raid a whorehouse," Lieutenant General Ricardo Sanchez, the commander of U.S. forces at the time, recalled in 2008. "I went to see Kerik and asked him to knock it off. . . .

"He is a very energetic guy," Sanchez said. "He is very confident—overconfident to an extent—and he is very superficial in his understanding of the requirements of his job. His whole contribution was a waste of time and effort."

Kerik—who denied raiding houses of prostitution—felt that Sanchez lacked respect for the Iraqi police. But Sanchez was just one of several American officials who turned sour on him. Robert Gifford, the senior advisor to the Iraqi Interior Ministry, said Kerik assured him upon his arrival that he wouldn't be getting in his way. "I'm here to bring more media attention to the good work on police because the situation is probably not as bad as people think it is," Gifford said Kerik told him. "I'm not here to get into your shit."

September 11 made Kerik a celebrity, and soldiers sought his autograph, and posed with him for photos. Reporters seemed more interested in speaking with him than Bremer, according to the war correspondent Rajiv Chandrasekaran. Gifford told him that when he sat down to brief Kerik, "he didn't listen to anything. He hadn't read anything except his emails. I don't think he read a single one of our proposals."

Kerik called Gifford's account "completely ludicrous" and said Gifford had a grudge against him based on personnel issues.

But there was no question that Kerik was soaking up attention from the media. He conducted a series of print and television interviews after his arrival, marveling at the Bush administration's success. He told *Time* that he saw "a 100 percent change" for the better in just his first week on the job: "People are starting to feel more confident," he said. "They're coming back out. Markets and shops that I saw closed one week ago have opened." The story was more about the celebrity crime fighter than the crime situation itself, with a headline reading "Can a New York Cop Tame Baghdad?"

A study of the Iraq war by the RAND Corporation in 2009 did not look kindly on his tenure.

"Kerik has been roundly criticized by senior and junior CPA officials for being a terrible manager and planner, and costing the CPA significant time in building police capacity," the report stated, referring to the Coalition Provisional Authority, the temporary governing body.

"We didn't realize until late in the game that Kerik didn't have any interest in administrative details," it quoted Clayton McManaway, Bremer's deputy, as saying. "He was running around on operations, and he didn't like to do planning and budgeting. We lost months with the police under Kerik. Equipment hadn't been ordered and contracts hadn't been put in place."

Kerik ran a "shoestring" effort to retrain officers, according to the study. The Army decided to work around him and train members on its own.

Some who worked for him felt differently, admiring the same qualities that made him popular among the rank and file in New York.

"When he came into the office he didn't sit down with me, he sat down with the officers," recalled General Ahmad Albayati, his right-hand man. "He listened to them."

Slowly, he said, police started trickling back to work once Kerik was able to persuade them that the American-led force wasn't the enemy. But the situation was dire. "We didn't have enough equipment to do our job," said Albayati. "We didn't have enough guns to protect ourselves."

Kerik left Iraq after just four months. The police force had 32,000 members by then, less than half of what he said was required. The American media celebrated him as the "Baghdad Terminator." But not everyone was sad to see him go.

"After four months, Kerik left Baghdad, to the relief of many," the RAND study found. Fred Smith, a CPA official interviewed by RAND, described Kerik's departure with contempt. "He paraded around the palace with a full entourage of photographers as he bid Jerry Bremer and others farewell," he said. "He was headed back to the States and a Rose Garden event with the President."

It was, in fact, the South Lawn where President Bush welcomed him home.

"Because of his leadership, his knowledge, and his experience, he was able to stand up a police force in Baghdad in a very quick period of time," Bush told reporters. "Bernie went there and made a big difference."

When it was his turn to speak, Kerik addressed the skeptics.

"I listen to the press, and I listen to some of the public, some of the criticism," he said. "And they talk about, it's taking too long. Well, try to stand up 35 police stations in New York City. It would take you about 11 years, depending on who is in the City Council."

"Bernie, you're a good man," Bush said.

His confidence in Kerik confounded the officials who worked with him in Iraq. They would be even more surprised a year later, when the president showed just how much he believed in him.

On a rainy morning in May 2004, Rudy Giuliani and a large entourage pulled up behind a village of television satellite trucks parked in front of the New School in Greenwich Village. A crowd gathered outside of the building, unable to squeeze into the Tishman Auditorium inside, which was packed to capacity. Someone hung a large banner on a nearby building reading "NEVER FORGET."

When Rudy, Judith, and his aides walked into the auditorium they were greeted with a storm of flashing cameras and blinding klieg lights. Members of the National Commission on Terrorist Attacks Upon the United States—the 9/11 Commission—sat at the front of the room, and a large audience of firefighters and family members of people who perished in the attacks sat at the other end. Giuliani walked to the center of the room, and seated himself at the witness table. His entourage filled up the entire row behind him.

In the two and a half years since planes exploded into the twin towers, killing almost three thousand people, accounts of the former mayor's mishandling of the crisis had mounted. The public was learning about the Fire Department's faulty radios, and other administration mishaps. A growing number of rescue workers at Ground Zero were developing cancer and respiratory ailments from inhaling air filled with pulverized concrete, jet fuel, asbestos, and other toxic particles, and accusations were flying that Giuliani's administration had downplayed the dangers and failed to protect them. And firefighters were livid that he curtailed search-and-rescue operations prior to recovering the remains of more than two hundred fallen colleagues.

This was Giuliani's moment of reckoning.

The controversy over his handling of the disaster triggered an explosion the previous day when Bernie Kerik, Tom Von Essen, and Richie Sheirer appeared before the panel. Commission member John Lehman, a former Navy secretary, characterized the mishandling of the radios, and the city's haphazard response system, as "a scandal ... not worthy of the Boy Scouts." Accusations flew, and Von Essen told reporters after the event that if he'd had the opportunity, "I probably would have choked him."

Commission members were greeted in the morning by tabloids in full outrage mode. "INSULT" read the cover of the *New York Post*, with a photo of a firefighter kneeling at Ground Zero and an editorial reading "Memo to 9/11 Commission: This man is a New York hero. Not a Boy Scout." The *Daily News* advised Lehman to "get down on his hands and knees and beg forgiveness of the public servants he insulted if he wants to preserve a scrap of his reputation."

The stage was set for a brawl with Giuliani. As television stations threw to live coverage, Thomas Kean, the commission chair and former New Jersey governor, called the hearing to order and swore him in. Giuliani, dressed in a dark striped blue suit with an American flag on his lapel, commenced his testimony.

"Mr. Chairman, members of the commission, we're all hurt, we're all damaged, we're all very, very angry, and we're all feeling the loss of heroes that we loved," he said.

". . . there are many in this country that have been personally touched, sometimes manyfold, by the losses on September 11, 2001. But we have to channel our anger toward doing all that we can to prevent and ameliorate any future attack, because by all predictions further attacks are going to come."

His therapist's tone threw everyone off their game. He was America's Mayor, there to heal, not divide.

"Our enemy is not each other, but the terrorists who attacked us, murdered loved ones, and continue to offer a threat to our security, safety, and survival."

The commission was searching for answers to the mounting questions about his handling of the radios and recovery operation. But he had other ideas.

"Maybe it would be helpful if I just outlined quickly what I did in the first hour or two that morning," he said.

He proceeded to tell The Story, a minute-by-minute account of his heroics on September 11. For twenty-four minutes he described his breakfast with Bill Simon at the Peninsula hotel, the race down to the Trade Center, his encounter with Pete Ganci, Bill Feehan, and Father Judge, his escape from 75 Barclay Street, the trek up Church Street, the arrival at the firehouse, and his journey to the police academy.

> I saw a man hurling himself out of the 102nd, 103rd, 104th floor. And I stopped, probably for two seconds, but it seems like a minute or two. And I was in shock. . . .
>
> All of a sudden I could see outside a tremendous amount of debris and it looked—it first felt like an earthquake and then it looked like a nuclear, a nuclear cloud. . . .
>
> We heard another tremendous noise, realized that the second building had now come down and saw the cloud from the second building come up the streets. . . .
>
> At that point, I was able to reach the White House and the Defense Department again.

It was a story the country had heard countless times since that apocalyptic morning; his words were lifted virtually word for word from his book, *Leadership*, and numerous interviews. But it was mesmerizing. The room was rapt as he recounted an almost biblical tale of a journey out of hell and march toward the light.

It was a head fake, as the commissioners had come for answers about failures in his administration, not a self-serving war story. But when he concluded it was too risky to challenge him.

"Your leadership of that day and in the days following gave the rest of the nation, and indeed the world, an unvarnished view of the indomitable spirit and the humanity of this great city," said commission member Richard Ben-Veniste, "and for that I salute you."

Lehman, public enemy number one in the morning tabloids, gushed further. "There was no question to the world that the captain was on the bridge," he said.

Kean described Giuliani as a "great, great leader."

The questions they proceeded to ask were velvety soft. Giuliani brushed aside the radio problems, suggesting that firefighters perished in the North Tower not because they didn't hear the evacuation orders, but because they didn't want to evacuate. That led the victims' family members in the audience to lose patience. "Talk about the radios!" one yelled. Another shouted "Stop kissing ass!" at the commissioners.

Years later, Kean and Vice Chair Lee Hamilton called the Giuliani hearing "a low point" in the commission's history, and all but conceded that he had intimidated them.

"We did not ask tough questions, nor did we get all of the information we needed to put on the public record," they wrote. "We were affected by the controversy over John Lehman's comments, and by the excellent quality of the mayor's presentation."

Giuliani used his September 11 story like a Get Out of Jail Free card; it was sacrilege to second-guess him. He would never again be held to account for his mistakes.

On May 24, 2003, Giuliani married Judith Nathan, against the advice of virtually everyone close to him. Tony Carbonetti said he urged his boss not to marry her "every day for about two years," and in fact had Fox News chief Roger Ailes join Giuliani and him for dinner one night to try at least to convince him to sign a prenup (he refused). Most of Giuliani's friends characterized his feelings for Nathan as a mixture of love and fear.

The wedding reflected the couple's plunge into high society. Donald Trump, Henry Kissinger, Beverly Sills, and Barbara Walters joined four hundred guests at a glittering affair held under a tent on the lawn of Gracie Mansion, where Mayor Michael Bloomberg performed the ceremony. Giuliani wore a custom-tailored Brioni suit, and Judith wore a satin Vera Wang wedding dress embedded with Swarovski crystals. The most talked-about fashion statement, though, was the diamond and pearl tiara sitting atop her head, which gave the event the feel of a coronation of some sort. "All that was lacking was the horse-drawn coach," wrote *New York Times* fashion writer Ruth La Ferla.

The extravagance struck Giuliani's friends as a middle finger to Donna Hanover, who'd battled tooth and nail to keep Nathan out of the building when she was first lady. "It was sad that it was at Gracie Mansion, where Donna raised their children," said Mindy Levine, one of Judith's bridesmaids.

The media concurred. "Wearing that sparkling tiara was a former-mistress-now-wife's equivalent of doing an elaborate touchdown jig," wrote Robin Givhan in the *Washington Post*. "It was perfectly understandable that Nathan would want to be queen for the day, but she did not have to be as callous as Marie Antoinette."

But the bride and groom were clearly smitten. Toward the end of the evening, they made their way to the press area. "I would like to introduce my wife, Mrs. Giuliani, and you can see how fortunate I am," Giuliani told reporters proudly. He gave his wife a kiss on the lips for the cameras.

Theirs was an unorthodox relationship, but it was their marriage, no one else's. Judith considered the three years that followed as the happiest of their lives together. When they weren't jetting around the world for Rudy's speaking engagements, they were socializing with the society set, attending fundraisers in Manhattan, the Hamptons, and Palm Beach.

He had odd quirks; Judith said he kept a baseball bat under his bed in case of burglaries. "Wherever we lived we had to have a baseball bat under the bed if it was one of our houses," she said. "Wherever we were—in Palm Beach, in the Hamptons, in the city—he would say that that was his preferred method of defense." She felt it was a way of connecting with his father, Harold, who kept a baseball bat under the bar at Uncle Leo's restaurant.

His other habits were more gentle, though just as old school. When he left for work in the mornings, he penned loving notes.

"Honey, notice how nice I leave house [sic] everyday. For a man—not bad, and it's because I respect and admire how nicely and neatly you keep everything. You're a very good 'homemaker'!"

He wrote "I love you" and drew a heart around the words.

The logo on the note was torn from a memo pad reading "Bracewell & Giuliani," a new law partnership he'd entered into.

Giuliani was leveraging his fame into a wildly successful amalgam of business and politics that had money gushing in and politicians lined up at his door. There was a fine line separating his financial and political lives that grew increasingly faint over the years, until there was no line at all.

The memo pads bearing his imprimatur were piling up. In addition to Bracewell & Giuliani and Giuliani Partners, there was Giuliani-Kerik, a security consultancy (later named Giuliani Security & Safety); Giuliani-Von Essen, which had a fire and safety focus; Giuliani Security & Safety-Asia, an arm of the security business focused on Japan; Giuliani Capital Advisors, a lucrative investment banking firm that recorded almost $84.7 million in revenue in its 2004 fiscal year; and numerous other projects. Giuliani bragged that the employees on the payroll of his companies and law firm numbered in the hundreds.

The explosion in business dovetailed—not so coincidentally—with the rise of his political clout. The good times reached their zenith in the fall of 2004.

President George H. W. Bush's war to liberate Kuwait from Iraq in 1991 took just six weeks to complete and ended victoriously. By comparison, his son's war was almost a year and a half old by the start of the Republican convention in August 2004, and was spinning out of control. The military's position in Fallujah was deteriorating, and the revelations of the atrocities at the Abu Ghraib prison, at which CIA and Army officials tortured, raped, and sodomized prisoners, were still reverberating. The very premise of the war—that Iraq possessed weapons of mass destruction—had collapsed.

With John Kerry, the Democratic candidate, hammering away at the White House's mismanagement of the war, the Bush team moved to refocus the race away from Iraq and back to terrorism, and turn the contest into a referendum on which candidate could keep Americans safe. They chose New York's Madison Square Garden as the convention site to highlight the attacks on the Trade Center, and turned to America's Mayor to make the case.

The 9/11 attack wasn't the subtext of the convention's first night—it was the entire focus of it. Bernie Kerik kicked off the proceedings with a short speech praising the leadership of Giuliani, Governor Pataki, "and most importantly, our commander in chief, President Bush." Firefighters praised Bush in a videotaped tribute. Later, the house lights dropped, bathing the arena in blue, and the words "September 11, 2001" flashed on a screen. Three widows of 9/11 victims told their stories, with cameras cutting to close-ups of weeping delegates. A singer, a former police officer, delivered a touching rendition of "Amazing Grace."

With emotions stoked, convention staff distributed posters to delegates reading "A Nation of Courage," and the MC introduced the next speaker, *"the man who embodies the courage, strength and heart of New York City, Rudy Giuliani!"*

The crowd rose to its feet and cheered, as some broke into chants of "RUDY!" The backdrop changed to a photo of the Empire State Building and the city skyline at dusk.

Walking to center stage, Giuliani looked buoyant. He blew kisses to the audience and waited with a broad smile as the cheers died down.

"I've never seen so many Republicans in New York City," he joked. "I finally feel at home!" The quip had a ring of truth.

He validated Bush's leadership against terrorism right off the bat. "It was here in 2001 in Lower Manhattan that President George W. Bush stood amid the fallen towers of the World Trade Center and said to the barbaric terrorists who attacked us, 'They will hear from us.'

"They have heard from us!" Giuliani said, triggering an ovation.

With the audience in his grip there was no reason to raise his voice. He was calm, logical, and magnanimous.

"Neither party has a monopoly on virtue," he said. "We don't have all the right ideas, they don't have all the wrong ideas. But I do believe there are times in history when our ideas are more necessary, and more important, and critical when we are facing war and danger."

Inevitably, he launched into The Story, describing the moment he watched a man jump out of the tower, seeing "the flames of Hell," escaping 75 Barclay Street, and watching the massive cloud from the collapse of the North Tower rush toward him on Church Street.

There was a gamble to putting Giuliani out there to tell his heroic story, since he was famous only because Bush was missing in action on September 11. But any doubts were allayed when he bestowed the ultimate benediction upon the president.

Shortly after escaping the collapsing Barclay Street building, Giuliani said in a quiet voice, "without really thinking, based on just emotion, spontaneous, I grabbed the arm of then–Police Commissioner Bernard Kerik, and I said to him, 'Bernie, thank God George Bush is our president.'"

It was a curious claim—he hadn't mentioned it in any of his big speeches before—but the only person who could contradict it was the police commissioner, who was seated next to former president George H. W. Bush, nodding in agreement.

The crowd exploded into chants of *"Four more years!"*

The moment was the high point of the love affair between Rudy Giuliani, Bernie Kerik, and the president of the United States. In three months the bubble would burst.

Bush won his race against Kerry in November, beating him by a healthy margin in the Electoral College and by a little more than 2 points in the popular vote. He set about reshuffling his cabinet almost immediately, bidding farewell to Tom Ridge, his homeland security secretary, who was widely seen as an ineffective leader of the sprawling new department.

Bernie Kerik was sitting in his office at Giuliani Partners when he received an email from Dina Powell, at the time the director of the White House Presidential Personnel Office. "Give me a call," she wrote.

In a brief conversation, she asked Kerik to fill out a short form with his Social Security number, date of birth, and other basic information. She didn't say why.

Powell got back to him shortly after he sent it in. "The president is looking for a replacement for Tom Ridge," she said. "This is extremely confidential. I know you're close to Giuliani, but I'd ask for the time being, don't have this conversation with anybody."

Kerik was thrilled. For the next week he spoke repeatedly with the White House, as staffers dug for any problems in his background. At one point he almost lost interest when they suggested he would need to take a multimillion-dollar loss on his stock in Taser International, a stun-gun manufacturer. Soon after going to work at Giuliani Partners, he had joined the company's board and set about pitching the product to police departments across the country. He was wildly successful—sales increased tenfold—and the value of his stock options ballooned to $6 million. The problem was that Taser was seeking business from the Department of Homeland Security—a clear conflict of interest. Only after some reassurance from Powell that they could work around the problem did he agree to be considered for the secretary's position.

About a week after his initial call with Powell, Tony Carbonetti popped into his office and told him that Giuliani was aware that he was up for the job—he'd spoken with the president. Carbonetti and Kerik drove down to Washington for a meeting in the Oval Office.

"Good morning, Bern, sit down," Bush greeted him. "I'm looking for a secretary of Homeland Security. You want it?"

Kerik was stunned—he thought he was there for a job interview. "Yes sir," he replied.

"It's yours," Bush said. "I know what you've done for Rudy and the NYPD. I've seen you myself, I've seen you in action. What I need is somebody that can go and break some china to get the job done."

Kerik was once again being promoted way beyond his level of experience. He had spent little time in Washington, had never run a federal agency, and had only recently earned a high school diploma through a correspondence course. No one knew his vision for Homeland Security, or if he had one, because nobody asked. Bush's appointees in Iraq felt he performed incompetently while there, but their reports either didn't reach the president or didn't concern him. (General Ricardo Sanchez, the U.S. military leader in Iraq, said he was "flabbergasted" at Kerik's nomination.)

Carbonetti said that on the trip back home to New York he asked Kerik if there was anything in his background that might cause problems for the nomination. "He said no," Carbonetti recalled.

The prospect of Kerik's joining the cabinet excited both of his patrons. After two years of Tom Ridge, a stolid institutionalist, Bush wanted a leader who could tear through the bureaucracy and get things done. As for Giuliani, installing his sidekick at such a high level meant more government access, a potential windfall of new clients, and higher fees. His influence in the Republican Party, and fundraising potential, would grow even deeper.

On December 3, 2004, the president announced Kerik's nomination, calling him a "dedicated, innovative reformer who insists on getting results."

The media went to work. The *Washington Post* revealed on December 8 that Kerik was fired as chief of investigations for the Saudi hospital and deported from the country for surveilling its employees. Tabloids had already reported on Kerik's $6 million windfall from selling some of his Taser International stock in the days leading up to the nomination, but on December 9, the Associated Press reported that Taser had sold stun guns to the agency he was about to lead—and wanted to sell more. That day, the *Post* examined why multiple homicide detectives had been assigned to find Judith Regan's cell phone.

The White House learned far worse. The New York *Daily News* was preparing a report that Kerik had ties to an alleged mob-connected company through a close friend, Larry Ray, from whom he allegedly accepted tens of thousands of dollars in cash and gifts shortly before Ray was indicted for an alleged Mafia-run stock scam. Ray was the best man at Kerik's wedding.

Another landmine exploded behind the scenes. Staff members at Giuliani Partners preparing Kerik's records for his background check informed him that his nanny was an illegal immigrant. He had already assured the White House that she was a citizen, but it turned out the Social Security card she produced belonged to someone else.

It was a mess. Just seven days after Bush announced Kerik's selection, the nominee walked into Giuliani's office and closed the door. His boss and he walked through the details and came to the conclusion that he had to withdraw as nominee. Giuliani gave Kerik a tearful hug.

Rudolph Giuliani in the 1961 Bishop Loughlin Memorial High School yearbook. While other students were sneaking cigarettes, he was studying the doctrines of the Catholic faith in the school's catechist club. BISHOP LOUGHLIN 1961 YEARBOOK

Giuliani with his first wife, Regina Peruggi, and Ken Feinberg. The two men were assistant U.S. attorneys together in the early 1970s. Peruggi was shocked when Giuliani filed for an annulment claiming he discovered they were second—not third—cousins. COURTESY DEDE FEINBERG

FBI director William Webster and Giuliani announce indictments in "the Commission" case in February 1985 at Federal Plaza in Manhattan. Webster called the indictments "historic." ALAN RAIAI/NEWSDAY RM VIA GETTY IMAGES

Giuliani celebrates his victory over Mayor David Dinkins with Donna Hanover and supporters on November 2, 1993. HAI DO/ AFP VIA GETTY IMAGES

Police Commissioner William Bratton at City Hall with Mayor Giuliani in February 1995. Bratton polled better, got better press, and was popping up at A-list events, prompting the mayor to turn on him. GERALD HERBERT/NY DAILY NEWS ARCHIVE VIA GETTY IMAGES

Cristyne Lategano with Giuliani in 2000. The two were keeping late hours on weekdays and weekends, and staff started receiving strange orders forbidding them from sending First Lady Donna Hanover his weekend schedule. PAT CARROLL/NY DAILY NEWS ARCHIVE VIA GETTY IMAGES

"Rudia" and Trump in a video shown at the 2000 Inner Circle dinner in Manhattan. "You know, you're really beautiful," Trump said, lasciviously. "A woman who looks like that has to have her own special scent."

NYC Police Commissioner Bernie Kerik scales the Brooklyn Bridge in the summer of 2001. No other police commissioner "ever had the balls to do it," he boasted. RALPH E. SMITH

September 11: Richard Sheirer, Giuliani, John Huvane, and the author on Church Street after the attacks. The group went running when the North Tower collapsed behind them and a hurricane of debris headed their way.

Giuliani, President George W. Bush, Senator Charles Schumer, and Fire Commissioner Tom Von Essen at the World Trade Center site three days after the September 11 attacks. STAN HONDA/AFP VIA GETTY IMAGES

Giuliani and Judith Nathan celebrate New Year's Eve in Times Square on the last day of his mayoralty, December 31, 2001. "I'm going to do the best I can to keep my personal life as personal as possible—not that I've succeeded at that very well in the last eight years," he deadpanned. PAUL J. RICHARDS/ AFP VIA GETTY IMAGES

Judith and Rudy at his knighting ceremony at Buckingham Palace in February 2002, a sign of his international celebrity. The selection of her hat led to an aide's firing. NILS JORGENSEN/ SHUTTERSTOCK

Giuliani at the GOP presidential debate at the Ronald Reagan Presidential Library in May 2007. Asked for a yes-or-no answer to the question: "Would the day that Roe v. Wade is repealed be a good day for America?" Giuliani replied, "It would be okay." JAMIE RECTOR/GETTY IMAGES

Giuliani introduces Donald Trump at a campaign event in August 2016 in Wilmington, North Carolina. Many of Giuliani's advisors were appalled that he backed the candidate. "We begged him not to do it," said one. SARA D. DAVIS/ GETTY IMAGES

Rudy Giuliani at the James J. Fox cigar bar in London with Lev Parnas (left), Igor Fruman (on his cellphone), and an unidentified man. FROM GIULIANI EMAIL WITH PHOTO OBTAINED BY PRO PUBLICA

Fruman, Giuliani, and Parnas. "They were perfect," Giuliani told the *New York Times*. "They did everything I wanted, and they never got involved in asking questions."

Caught in a compromising position in *Borat Subsequent Moviefilm,* thirteen days before the 2020 election.

Giuliani in the parking lot of Four Seasons Total Landscaping on November 7, 2020, upon being told the networks had called the election for Joe Biden.

Giuliani charges election fraud at a November 19, 2020, press conference. "I've seen all of you taking pictures right now, and I can anticipate what your headlines are going to be," fellow lawyer Jenna Ellis said angrily. DREW AN-GERER/GETTY IMAGES

The president called Kerik offering to fight on for the nomination, but his nominee declined. He prepared his letter of withdrawal to the president.

That triggered a call from Andy Card, Bush's chief of staff.

"Listen," Card told him. "I know you've been around, but take my word for it, when we release that letter and people realize that you're down, every cockroach you've ever had a problem with, they're going to crawl out from under their rocks."

The withdrawal was a huge embarrassment for the White House and for Giuliani. Both cited the nanny problem as the reason, never acknowledging the cascade of far more serious problems.

The bombshells about his past kept falling long after the nomination was pulled. On December 10, *Newsweek* revealed that in 1998 a warrant was issued for his arrest when he didn't respond to a subpoena related to a condo he owned in New Jersey. He settled the issue, making the warrant go away, but hadn't disclosed it during his vetting, the magazine reported.

Three days later, the *Daily News* broke the worst story of them all. Its story was headlined, "BERNARD KERIK'S DOUBLE AFFAIR LAID BARE."

Former NYPD Commissioner Bernard Kerik conducted two extramarital affairs simultaneously, using a secret Battery Park City apartment for the passionate liaisons, the Daily News has learned.

The first relationship, spanning nearly a decade, was with city Correction Officer Jeanette Pinero; the second, and more startling, was with famed publishing titan Judith Regan.

His affair with Regan, the stunningly attractive head of her own book publishing company, lasted for almost a year.

Dramatically, each woman learned of the existence of the other after Pinero discovered a love note left by Regan in the apartment.

Subsequent reports revealed that the Battery Park apartment was designated for use by exhausted rescue workers at Ground Zero.

Why would a high official—a police commissioner—act so recklessly? Why was Giuliani so blind to all this, if in fact he was? Why did he give Bernie Kerik all that power in the first place? Why did he recommend him to the president of the United States?

That night, Giuliani and Judith traveled to Washington for a holiday dinner party at the White House. They also attended a taping of the annual Christmas concert with the president and first lady. Riding with them in a limousine, Giuliani apologized to Bush for the Kerik disaster. Aides later said Bush felt it wasn't necessary.

Sitting together in that limousine, shaking their heads over the debacle they had unleashed, the two might have asked each other why it never occurred to them that Kerik's love of risk-taking could extend to his personal life. Or why they had romanticized him and his Rambo story so much that they overlooked the warning signs that flashed bright red all around him. "The two of them had an infatuation with him," said Carbonetti.

With the fallout from the scandals continuing, Kerik resigned from Giuliani Partners on December 22.

The most extraordinary aspect of the Bernie Kerik story was that it did not end there. It would take years, but his value to Rudy Giuliani rose again. And George W. Bush would not be the last president to develop a crush on him.

CHAPTER 10

Frontrunner

There's a famous story in Rudy Giuliani's circle about the night that he became mayor in 1993. It was a nail-biter; David Dinkins had beaten him by fewer than fifty thousand votes in their first match-up four years earlier, and the margin of victory in their rematch was expected to be just as slim.

Over one thousand supporters jammed the ballroom of the New York Hilton, nursing their drinks in little plastic cups as they watched returns stream in on giant screens above the stage. The first votes trickled in from more liberal parts of the city, driving up Dinkins's numbers, while the results from Staten Island, the most conservative borough, lagged behind. When the borough finally reported in, Giuliani took the lead and the mayoralty.

The room exploded. It was a seismic event for the city, as a Republican prosecutor promising sweeping change defeated an incumbent mayor and the city's Democratic establishment despite a five-to-one party enrollment disadvantage.

Squeezed into his suite with him upstairs with the politicians, power brokers, and hangers-on was Giuliani's eighty-four-year-old mother, Helen, a head shorter than the people surrounding her. She was as discerning and shrewd as her son, and seemed to be taking it all in. As his friends tell it, the mayor-elect sought her out to give her the news that he'd won the mayoralty. She wasn't surprised. "I thought you'd be president by now," she said.

By the time he shook John F. Kennedy's hand at a ticker-tape parade in 1960, Giuliani was already passionate about politics, and it wasn't long afterward that he started talking about his dreams of becoming the first Italian American president. It was an ambition stoked by Helen's sky-high expectations for her only son, and her lack of tolerance for failure. When he stood atop the steps of City Hall to be sworn in at his second inauguration in 1998, she once again made it clear that the mayoralty was just a stepping-stone. "Someday, I will see him sworn in as president," she told reporters.

The idea was being taken more seriously inside the building than she may have known that morning. Giuliani started taking steps toward a 2000 White House run as soon as his second term began.

He convened a meeting of his closest aides at the Grand Havana Room, the Fifth Avenue cigar bar that served as a clubhouse for the boss and his crew. Adam Goodman and Rick Wilson, two Florida-based political advertising men, were brought in to lead a discussion about his potential path to the presidency.

The two passed around copies of a plan they had spent weeks developing, and proceeded to walk through the strategy, which began with an acknowledgment that the idea of a New York City mayor running for president was a stretch. Giuliani's profile in the heartland wasn't very high, and Middle America wasn't crazy about New York to begin with.

Goodman didn't get much further than that. Members of the inner circle started challenging their assumptions. The mayor was greeted enthusiastically when he traveled to Iowa and New Hampshire to test the waters. He had turned New York around. He was a rock star.

"[They felt] that he just had to put his name up and remind people about the things he did in New York and suddenly he would win every dairy farmer, every soybean farmer, and every Chamber of Commerce small business person in the state," Goodman said. "There's something called confidence and there's another thing called the delusion of confidence."

The fact that no New York City mayor had ever jumped straight to the White House, and that his positions on abortion and other social issues were out of step with the Republican mainstream, barely dented their enthusiasm. Nor did the fact that Giuliani lived his life in a maelstrom of personal chaos. But much as they downplayed them, those realities would catch up with him before he could fulfill his mother's hopes.

Giuliani may well have run for president while still mayor in 2000 if Daniel Patrick Moynihan's Senate seat had not opened up. Having passed on a White House run, he knew when he left City Hall at the end of 2001 that the next realistic opportunity would not come for another seven years, since George W. Bush was still in his first term.

So he bided his time. He passed on the opportunity to run for governor against George Pataki in 2002, and against Eliot Spitzer in 2006.

Giuliani Partners was where he wanted to be until 2008. When Bush was pilloried for his administration's bungling of Hurricane Katrina, which destroyed much of New Orleans in 2005, he called Giuliani personally and asked him to take over as the rebuilding "czar," which could arguably have given the president a chance for a reboot in the quagmire. Giuliani traveled to New Orleans and held some meetings there, but turned down the offer.

In Giuliani Partners, he had cleverly constructed a machine capable of exploiting his blizzard of opportunities, financial and political. It swept up cash, pushed open doors, and ran on a fuel of politics and money. His partners and senior staff were both corporate consultants and political operatives, able to switch hats at a moment's notice.

Roy Bailey was a prime example. As a rainmaker, he was equally capable of reeling in a business client as a campaign donor. In 2005 he struck the mother lode.

Bailey was one of Texas's top Republican fundraisers, and he hung out with like-minded types—country club conservatives who ran companies, sat on hospital boards, and wrote checks to grateful politicians.

Pat Oxford was one such man. He was the managing partner at Bracewell & Patterson, a venerable four-hundred-person Houston law firm, whose blue-chip clients ranged from Bank of America to the Republic of Kazakhstan, where the firm had an office. It was midway down the food chain of Texas's mighty law firms, eclipsed by powerhouses like Baker Botts, the legendary firm named for the family of former secretary of state James Baker. Oxford was a giant in Texas Republican politics, a connected fundraiser and donor, and an advisor to the Republican elite. President Bush called him "Oxy."

Bailey first introduced him to Giuliani at the Republican convention in 2004. While Giuliani was electrifying delegates with his September 11 stories, the Texans discussed their mutual interests. Oxford was eager to lift Bracewell & Patterson into a higher orbit of prestige, and seeking a partner to establish a beachhead in New York City. Bailey knew a deal when he saw one.

On March 31, 2005, Giuliani and Oxford walked into a room filled with reporters at the Waldorf-Astoria hotel on Park Avenue, and announced the birth of Bracewell & Giuliani. The former mayor and U.S. attorney bestowed his famous name on the firm and agreed to serve as a rainmaker and help recruit lawyers to the New York office.

Oxford said he was looking forward to Giuliani showing his firm "how it is to play in the bigs." Giuliani portrayed it as a kind of homecoming. "People who know me are not surprised. They know how much I enjoy practicing law and how much I have missed it."

It was an enormously lucrative deal for Giuliani. Bracewell agreed to pay Giuliani Partners $10 million, and an annual salary to him of at least $1 million, plus a slice of the profits. The financial windfall was just the beginning; the venture opened the door to a vast universe of Texas power brokers, campaign donors, and clients.

It was a timely marriage for someone planning a run for the White House. By 2006 he and his team, led by Tony Carbonetti, were deep into conversations about the race, and he was increasingly being asked about the possibility by reporters.

Calculating his chances of winning in 2008 was difficult because of his singular role in American life. He was more popular than the pope, and revered for his leadership. The presidency seemed like a natural progression. "He felt that voters should have the opportunity to give him the job," said an advisor.

But if his status in American politics was unique, so was the challenge he was facing. No Republican with a pro-choice, pro-gay, and pro–gun control record had ever won the Republican presidential nomination. He'd also be asking social conservatives to overlook his exhaustively documented history as an adulterer. While his name recognition was sky-high, the chattering class believed that he'd fizzle like a busted balloon once voters learned about his record.

The political terrain was also problematic. His two major competitors would also be courting the moderate Republican vote, and had advantages he didn't. John McCain, the beloved war hero and maverick Arizona senator, won New Hampshire by 18 points in 2000, and Governor Mitt Romney of neighboring Massachusetts had a semi-home-field advantage.

But Giuliani and his team had been convinced of his destiny going back to their meeting at the Grand Havana Room in 1998. Now he had the September 11 halo, and in the five years since the Trade Center attacks his popularity had allowed him to plow through every obstacle in his way. He was the exception to every rule. Why should the presidency be any different?

For years, he relied upon a tiny crew of loyalists—all from New York—to advise him. But no one in his circle had ever run something as sprawling and complex as a presidential campaign. As uncomfortable as it felt to invite outsiders into their tight circle, there was no choice.

On November 10, Giuliani filed papers to form an exploratory committee, which enabled him to raise and spend money. A month later, he hired Mike DuHaime, the political director of the Republican National Committee, to lead the committee and then transition to campaign manager.

DuHaime was only thirty-two, but had made a prodigious rise to the top echelons of the party. He was already a practiced hand in national politics, having overseen races in eleven Northeastern states for the Bush campaign, and seventy-five congressional races for the RNC. A boyish New Jersey native, he considered the mayor a heroic figure, having watched from across the river as he led New York's turnaround, and revived its spirits after 9/11. DuHaime dined with both McCain and Romney to discuss the race, but he was so enamored of Giuliani that he reached out to him proactively and offered his services.

Karl Rove, Bush's political guru, cautioned DuHaime on the move, warning him that it would be difficult for a pro-choice New York moderate to win in conservative states like Iowa and South Carolina. But the strategist wasn't dissuaded. "You watch," he told him.

Oxford, appointed campaign chairman, set about working his magic in Texas. He and Roy Bailey lured T. Boone Pickens, the famed oilman and corporate raider, and Tom Hicks, the owner of the Texas Rangers baseball team, into joining the Giuliani campaign committee, and introduced the future candidate to dozens of the state's top Republican fundraisers.

When Oxford was asked whether Giuliani was too liberal for the party, he sidestepped the question by pointing to his enormous popularity. After dining with him at a downtown Houston restaurant, he told a reporter, Giuliani got a standing ovation when he stood up to leave.

DuHaime recognized that entire swaths of the electoral map would have to be completely written off because of Giuliani's moderate views. He was leading the pack in national primary polls, sometimes by double digits, but his strength was with voters in large states like New York and California, whose primaries were not until Super Tuesday, February 5. Giuliani would need to survive the eight January primaries and caucuses in more conservative states that came before it. And he was behind in most of them.

Ed Goeas, his pollster, conducted three sets of focus groups in Iowa, the first contest of the cycle, and declared it hopeless. Success hinged on New Hampshire, the second of the early contests, and Florida, the seventh. There were large numbers of moderate Republicans in both states who'd be open to his message. If he didn't at least come close in both states it would be difficult if not impossible to remain in the race, much less win it.

In retrospect, Goeas believed that the best day of Giuliani's presidential campaign was the day he announced his candidacy. "It was downhill from there," he said. But that was too generous. Things started to go wrong even before he entered the race.

The unofficial start of the contest was November 8, 2006, the day after the midterm elections. They were a disaster for the Republicans and the Bush administration; Democrats won control of both houses of Congress and six governors' seats, the strongest Democratic wave in two decades. The country was eager to be done with Bush and the war he waged.

The atmosphere around Giuliani's candidacy was electric. He was mobbed during his nationwide campaign appearances on behalf of Republican candidates, as Americans flocked to get a glimpse of America's Mayor. He was leading all the Republican presidential candidates in national polls. In November 2006, he was ranked the most popular politician in the nation.

Many, if not most, of his fans outside of New York knew him primarily from watching him on television on September 11. They were about to get a much closer glimpse. It took just two days into the new year for them to learn that chaos was part of the package.

On January 2, 2007, a photo of his smiling face filled the front page of the New York *Daily News*, beside a headline reading "RUDY LOSES PREZ PLANS." A two-page spread inside the tabloid detailed the contents of a confidential, 140-page planning document prepared by an unnamed Giuliani campaign official that was leaked to the paper. It contained handwritten notes about his political challenges, fundraising information, and travel schedules.

The notes ticked off his vulnerabilities—"Business," "Kerik," "Judith," and "Social Issues"—and questioned whether they would prove to be insurmountable.

"Are there any other big items of worry?" the writer of the document asked. In the left margin were the words "False comfort with #'s"—apparently referring to the candidate's sky-high polling.

The story was written by Ben Smith, a thirty-year-old reporter working out of a dingy basement press room at New York City Hall. A source "sympathetic to one of Giuliani's rivals for the White House" slipped him the binder in a furtive handoff on a street corner in Greenwich Village. Smith wrote that his tipster found it at a campaign stop in one of Giuliani's multicity blitzes for Republican candidates.

The misplacement of such a sensitive document, and its capture by a reporter, was a huge embarrassment to Giuliani, and raised questions about the competence of his campaign before it officially began. But more troubling was his staff's concern that his personal baggage could kill his candidacy. Their cocky self-assurance when he first considered a run back in his mayoral days now came with a whiff of anxiety. "All will come out—in worst light," it read. "Does any of it cause RWG to lose his luster? Confidence? Donors to drop off? Drop out of race."

The campaign went on the attack. Giuliani's press secretary, Sunny Mindel, a committed loyalist, called Smith and berated him for publishing the document without sharing it with her. According-ing to Smith, she ended her tirade at him with some parting words: "Bow to Mecca, shithead."

The memo's focus on social issues reflected the campaign's deep concern about his record on abortion, gay rights, and gun control. The goal of selling him to conservatives was near futile; the only way to do it was to change his views altogether. Candidates altered their core principles all the time—Romney did a complete flip on all three issues in preparation for the race. But Giuliani had been lecturing the public about his principles his entire career. How could he aban-don his beliefs with the eyes of the nation on him? The dilemma bedeviled him throughout the campaign, and in many ways came to define it.

The obvious play was to steer the conversation to his selling point: his leadership on September 11 and his hawkish views on fighting terrorism. Polling showed that Republicans trusted him to deal with that life-and-death issue far more than any of his compet-itors. It was the subject he most wanted to talk about, and the one his fans most wanted to hear. But with 9/11 almost six years in the past, the issue had plummeted as a priority with Republicans; when New Hampshire voters were asked by pollsters what they wanted the candidates to talk about, terrorism ranked fifth.

But 9/11 was the strongest hand he had to play, and he played it relentlessly. On his first trip to New Hampshire, he traveled with Judith to Bretton Woods, in the state's North Country, to speak at the Littleton Chamber of Commerce's annual supper. When he arrived at the Mount Washington Hotel, he was met with a massive press contingent. It was minus 9 degrees outside.

The place was packed. As he waded through the crowd, people brought up 9/11 before he could. A little girl came up to him and said she'd lost a cousin that day. The local fire chief's wife asked him to sign a book about the people who died in the tragedy.

When he reached the front of the room to speak he didn't disappoint. He warned the crowd that even small towns like theirs were in danger of terrorist attacks, pointing to Shanksville, Pennsylvania, where United Airlines Flight 93 crash-landed on the way to Washington, D.C. He said he had recently spoken to a high school graduating class there. "But for the grace of God and the bravery of the people who brought that plane down those kids wouldn't be with us," he said, gravely.

He also covered another favorite talking point, about the leadership he exhibited that dark day. He had virtually branded the word since 9/11; *Leadership* was the name of his book, the title of his speeches, and now the leitmotif of his campaign. "The single most important part of leadership . . . is to figure out what you believe, figure out what's important, have convictions, stand for something," he said.

September 11 was a subject he could sound tough on. Questions about social issues were another matter. When he couldn't avoid them, he dissembled, usually badly. A few weeks after traveling to

Bretton Woods, he appeared on Larry King's show to make his candidacy official. After giving the host his scoop ("Yes, I'm running"), Giuliani was pressed to explain his positions on social issues. His answers were contorted into knots.

KING: Let's move to some things domestic. You've had some quotes lately that—that seem contradictory. I know you're pro-choice, you've always been pro-choice.

GIULIANI: I am.

KING: Yet you'll say you'll appoint judges who are strict constructionists. If that's the case, they're going to vote to overturn "Roe v. Wade," which you don't want.

GIULIANI: I don't know that. You don't know that.

KING: Are you pretty sure that no matter who you appointed, "Roe v. Wade" will remain?

GIULIANI: I don't—nobody knows that.

KING: Would it hurt you if they overturned it and you appointed judges that overturned it?

GIULIANI: I don't think it would hurt me or help me or—it would be a matter of states making decisions or . . .

KING: You'd be indifferent to it?

GIULIANI: I wouldn't be—I wouldn't be indifferent to it. It wouldn't be the litmus test on which I would appoint somebody.

It was a plate of ideological mush, designed to somehow placate the right without caving on his long-held beliefs. His comments about gay marriage were even more confusing.

KING: Would you favor a constitutional amendment saying marriage is a man and a woman?

GIULIANI: Not if it remains the way it is now. Unless all of a sudden lots of states do what Massachusetts does, and kind of come at it from the other side, and decide that the Constitution says that—that you cannot have marriage between a man and a woman. If it stays the way it is, you don't need one.

A leader famous for standing up for his principles without apology was muddling his views in search of support. His moral beliefs seemed to melt into a puddle of banalities. In search of safe topics, he preached the importance of unity, and optimism, a message that he'd somehow forgotten to mention in his first thirty years in public life.

The platitudes and the obfuscations were on display in the first televised debate of the season, which was held at the Ronald Reagan Presidential Library in California. Lined up toward the far end of a stage with nine other Republican candidates in front of a video of a waving American flag, he mentioned "optimism" three times in his first answer alone. Then Chris Matthews, the moderator, asked for a yes-or-no answer to a question: "Would the day that Roe v. Wade is repealed be a good day for America?"

Mitt Romney replied, "Absolutely." Mike Huckabee said, "Most certainly." McCain answered, "Repeal." Then it was Giuliani's time.

"It would be okay."

What did that mean? "Okay to repeal?" Matthews asked.

"It would be okay to repeal. Or it would be okay also if a strict constructionist judge viewed it as precedent, and I think a judge has to make that decision."

The answer halted the flow of the debate, as Matthews kept trying to understand what he was saying. "Would it be okay if they didn't repeal it?"

"I think the court has to make that decision, and then the country can deal with it," Giuliani said. "We're a federalist system of government, and states can make their own decisions."

And so it went for the duration of the campaign, Giuliani splitting hairs on controversial subjects as the campaign chased conservative voters it would never attract.

"We all panicked and said how do we get him to check all the boxes?" said Tony Carbonetti, Giuliani's closest advisor and campaign leader. "You start bringing the Republican experts in—'This is how you need to answer gun control, you've got to intertwine this into your answer'—and we fucked with his head.

"We tortured the poor guy into being something he wasn't," Carbonetti said. "You ended up with a flawed candidate."

It wasn't just his beliefs he was watering down. His rhetoric was less fiery. His smoldering anger was missing. Gone was the mayor who threatened to fire every public defender in the city; who called a fiscal monitor "crazy," an animal rights advocate "deranged," and reporters "jerky." Where was the leader whose favorite slogan for New York was "We can kick your city's ass"?

A decade later Donald Trump would trounce his competition in New Hampshire with relentless bombast. Giuliani, who set the mold for that style, chose the opposite route. One morning, he grew upset reading a *New York Times* story that focused on his legendary temper. He told an aide he didn't want to be known for that anymore.

"That righteous anger wasn't coming out when [he] needed it," said Matt Mahoney, Carbonetti's deputy.

Campaign officials watched with concern as the boss acted increasingly entitled. He was a workaholic, feverishly sprinting across the country to fundraise. And he threw himself into the issues, constantly peppering his aides for statistics. But they were surprised by the lack of passion. "He was running almost not because he wanted it, but because he felt like he would be good at the job if he got it," said DuHaime.

Republicans in New Hampshire were perplexed by his lack of

interest in speaking with voters; on his April visit he held only two events, both invitation-only.

The famed control freak was delegating more, trusting decisions to consultants he barely knew. "He wasn't that plugged in," said a longtime advisor. "There wasn't a total commitment."

He seemed a spectator to his circumstances. One night in Iowa, traveling four hours in a car down endless stretches of pitch-black highways, he mused at what he'd gotten himself into. "Running for president, you have to be kind of crazy," he told his companions. "There was this fatalistic ambivalence to it," said one of them.

That quality became increasingly apparent during the cascading disasters involving his wife.

In March, Pat Oxford placed a call to one of New York's highest-profile communications strategists. Mike McKeon had a black belt in political combat. Blond-haired and green-eyed, with an Irishman's dark humor, he was the communications chief for Governor George Pataki back in the days when he and Giuliani were mortal enemies, thanks to the former mayor's endorsement of Mario Cuomo. It was a testament to McKeon's reputation that the Giuliani camp reached out to him.

Oxford told him that the campaign needed an aggressive New York communications pro to deal with reporters digging into Giuliani's record at City Hall; it required someone who knew the backstory to his controversies, and could play hardball with reporters. McKeon took the gig.

At their first meeting a few days later at Giuliani's campaign headquarters at the South Street Seaport in Lower Manhattan, McKeon learned a lot more about the assignment. It had little to do with Giuliani's mayoral record, and a lot to do with his wife.

The "Judi problem" was campaign shorthand for the aggravation, time consumption, and public relations nightmares that Giuliani's wife brought to the campaign. McKeon was the latest in a line of campaign aides tasked with keeping her under control.

"We want you to get Judith to call him less," Oxford said.

"What does that mean?" McKeon asked. "Call him on the phone less?"

"Yes," Oxford said. "If you get her down to a dozen calls a day that would be a victory." He said she was calling her husband many times that number (she claimed her husband called her just as frequently, an assertion no one in the campaign backed).

McKeon had been around long enough to know when someone was dumping a mess in his lap. But the crisis manager in him was intrigued.

People like Oxford and DuHaime were accustomed to working with political wives who'd been in the game for a while, and had an awareness of their responsibilities in a presidential campaign, no matter how dreary. Judith had never been a candidate's wife; her debut performance was on the biggest stage of them all.

The reviews weren't kind. The Washington crew, like their New York counterparts, were appalled at her knack for winding up her husband for her own purposes. On the night of a big debate, as his handlers were prepping the candidate backstage, she complained to Giuliani about the seat she'd been assigned. Giuliani grew worried, and staffers scurried to fix the problem. "It's really not where you want his mindset to be during a debate," sighed a strategist.

Judith called her husband when she heard that reporters were writing about her, or when she thought photographers were following her. Always worried that she would lose her temper, he would send staff scrambling down rabbit holes to chase down her reports. Some felt her perpetual calls were a means of control. "She would purposely do it to get him off his game," said an advisor close to both of them. "Key days you needed him to be in the game, she'd be in his ear, she'd be calling, she'd be complaining about something. She was a total distraction."

But she wasn't always imagining things. The idea that the next first lady could be the woman once labeled "The Mistress" on the cover of *People* magazine was an irresistible media storyline. Reporters were digging furiously for dirt.

Judith had mixed feelings about her husband running. A close confidante said she only found out about his intentions over dinner one night with Roy Bailey and him at a midtown steakhouse restaurant. "You're going to make the most beautiful First Lady since Jackie Onassis," Bailey allegedly told her, prompting Rudy to kick him under the table. According to the confidante, Judith walked out of the restaurant, sick.

As the campaign took shape and campaign staffers grew increasingly resentful of her, the hostility grew mutual. She told her husband that his campaign aides were amateurs who were bleeding the campaign dry, Tony Carbonetti above all. "They were so ridiculously incapable," she told a confidante. "The most dangerous people are people who don't know what they don't know."

Tasked with containing the mess, McKeon reached out to Judith's aides—she had at least one PR advisor of her own—and met with her at an Upper East Side coffee shop.

They went through her schedule. Stung by bad press, she had agreed to speak with New York *Daily News* reporter Heidi Evans for a profile. Evans was an investigative reporter, not a feature writer, which should have set off alarms. Judith's other commitment was to a major national television interview with her husband and Barbara Walters, an even higher-stakes effort to improve her image.

McKeon sat in on her interview with the *Daily News*. Evans, ever friendly while going in for the kill, revealed she had discovered a 1974 wedding certificate that suggested Judith had misled the press about the number of times she had been married. Rudy was her third husband, not her second. Between them, Rudy and Judith had been married six times.

McKeon, alarmed, called the candidate. "I'm aware of it," Rudy told him. "Well nobody else is," McKeon replied. "There's going to be a big story that she has this husband that no one's disclosed."

Giuliani had that fatalistic sound in his voice. "It is what it is," he said.

On March 23, 2007, the *Daily News* ran a front-page photomontage with Judith on the left and Rudy on the right, with the headline "*I did, I did, I DO!*" running down the middle. The story reported that in 1974, soon after graduating nursing school, Judith married Jeffrey Ross, a medical supplies salesperson, at a Las Vegas marriage chapel named Chapel of the Bells. When they divorced in 1979, Judith married her next husband just five days later.

"We appreciate the value of marriage," she quipped to Evans about Rudy and herself. Ross, she said, was "a terrific guy."

The story was picked up nationally, and thrust the worst possible subject for her husband onto the front pages. Reporters went hunting for reaction from conservative Republican voters. Stories about tensions between Giuliani staffers and Judith bubbled to the surface, filled with complaints from staff that she was interfering with scheduling and event planning, and using campaign personnel for her own purposes.

McKeon defended her publicly. "She is a positive force for Rudy, a very strong supporter for Rudy, and nothing but an asset to him and the campaign," he told a reporter. He meant none of it.

The fracas over her first marriage was nothing compared to what came next. In preparation for the Barbara Walters interview, the campaign scheduled a media training session for Judith, at which she was prepped with talking points about the first marriage and the affair she'd had with the mayor behind Donna Hanover's back. There was no such preparation for Rudy, thought to be a master at the craft.

Walters was a friend of Judith's, and lobbed softballs during the interview before asking whether it bothered her that she had dated a married man. Looking composed in a casual lime green sweater, Judith replied with flawless pabulum.

"It was a rocky road, absolutely," she said. "But when you have a partnership that is based on mutual respect and communication, the two of you know what's going on."

It was only when Rudy joined the interview that things went off the rails. "Hi, sweetheart," she said to her husband as he sat down. "Hi, baby, how are you?" he responded.

Walters asked a battery of questions about their unorthodox marriage, and the dysfunctions in his family.

WALTERS: There are also the questions, you know, we talk about morality and family values. I guess what I'm getting at, does it disturb you that your wife, whom you love very much, may be being blamed for the estrangement with your children?

GIULIANI: Well, this is my responsibility, not hers. She's done everything she can. She loves all the children.

Walters knew her subjects well, and seemed aware of his penchant for boasting about Judith's medical knowledge.

WALTERS (to Judith): Will you sit in on policy meetings?

JUDITH GIULIANI: Again, if he asks me to, yes, and certainly, in the areas of healthcare.

WALTERS (to Rudy): If and when you were president, would Mrs. Giuliani sit in on cabinet meetings?

RUDY GIULIANI: If she wanted to, if they were relevant to something that, that she was interested in, that would be something that I'd be very, very comfortable with.

The next day, the candidate's interest in his wife attending cabinet meetings was splashed across every newspaper. The *Daily News* branded her the "Secretary of Love." The campaign tried to clean up the mess, releasing a statement from Giuliani stating that she "obviously" would not be a cabinet member or attend most cabinet meetings, "if any." Her role would be to "educate Americans on preventing illness and promoting overall health."

The tumult wasn't over. Three days after the Walters interview, the *New York Post* ran a disturbing piece about Judith's job duties as a salesperson for a medical supply outfit that manufactured surgical staplers. The company conducted sales meetings demonstrating the stapling procedure on dogs, most of whom died afterward or were put to death. The headline was "JUDI'S JOB WITH PUP-KILLER FIRM."

As McKeon tried without success to explain the story away, an angry candidate stepped forward to tell the press to lay off. "Attack me all you want," Giuliani said. "There's plenty to attack me about. Please do it. But maybe, you know, show a little decency."

Not long afterward, the entire high command of the campaign was summoned by Judith to a meeting at the Palm, a venerable steakhouse in midtown Manhattan. Awaiting them at a large table inside a private room decorated with caricatures of celebrities were Rudy, Judith, and her personal representatives. As Pat Oxford, Mike DuHaime, Mike McKeon, and others filed in, Judith had her aides distribute nondisclosure agreements binding them to confidentiality under threat of legal action.

The campaign chiefs were taken aback. DuHaime refused to sign. "If you don't want me in the meeting, I won't come to the meeting," he told her.

With tension rising, Rudy walked up to the aide, asked for a copy of the NDA, and signed it. "If I'm ever elected I'm going to make you the head of the CIA," he told her, trying to lighten the mood. All except DuHaime relented (he was permitted to stay).

The topic was Judith's role in the campaign. While there was certainly reason to discuss damage control strategy, the scope went far beyond that. She and her advisors wanted her to have a larger role in the campaign, and solicited ideas for issues she could champion.

Ed Goeas, the campaign's Virginia-based pollster, had already been advised prior to the meeting to offer to hold focus groups on the subject as a peace offering to her. But Judith and her advisors wanted specific goals and strategies hammered out. Rudy and she were a team, like Bill and Hillary, and she wanted a plan to promote that. (Judith denies she compared them to the Clintons.)

Goeas was a longtime Washington hand, with traditional views on these things, but he also knew that Judith Giuliani was no Hillary Clinton. "If he is elected, the first lady picks a charity that she makes her focus," he said. But the campaign needed to be about her husband.

That didn't go over well. "You just want her to be like out of *Father Knows Best*, from the 1950s," one of her advisors charged.

"They're not voting for her, they're voting for him," Goeas said. "She doesn't get an issue to promote."

"What role should I play?" Judith asked.

"You're his third wife," he shot back. "What you should be is humble."

The room fell silent. A tableful of men were disparaging the ambitions of the candidate's wife. It was a good time for Giuliani to step in, but he stayed quiet. "He didn't want to fight with her, but he didn't want to shut her down either," Goeas said. "He left that for us."

The meeting only hardened the antagonism on both sides. She had a long-running feud with Carbonetti and other members of the old City Hall crew, but Goeas and others were national consultants, and they were fed up with her as well.

"In all my years of politics, and I worked my first campaign at twelve in 1964 when my dad was in Vietnam, I've never been put in a position like that of putting a wife in her place," Goeas said. "All I know was that I wanted to go back to Virginia."

In July 2007, Rudy and Judith played host to a special guest at their seven-thousand-square-foot home in the Hamptons. The couple had entertained dozens of political celebrities at their sprawling, nine-bedroom, two-story complex, which was situated on a lush, hedged-off compound overlooking a horse farm and acres of open land. But no guest was as special as Charlie Crist.

The silver-haired, preternaturally tanned governor of Florida had inordinate make-or-break power in the Republican primary. Giuliani was leagues ahead of the competition in national polls—18 points ahead in mid-July—but running far behind in the early states. Without a victory in Florida, his campaign could sink before Super Tuesday.

Crist had a deep relationship with John McCain, but the senator's campaign was imploding; he'd burned through his bank account, and dozens of employees were being let go. Crist's endorsement was up for grabs.

The governor was a political chameleon, so wily at the art of survival that he would run for office as a Republican or Democrat depending upon the situation. He was looking to play kingmaker in the presidential race.

His hosts went all out for their guest. Judith brought in a chef to cater their meals, and Rudy took him to the Hamptons' most exclusive golf clubs. The governor was given the run of the house—its gymnasium, steam room, swimming pool, and private screening room.

On Saturday night, they went out to dinner at a local restaurant with advisors to the two politicians. According to DuHaime, Crist uttered the magic words. "He promised the endorsement," DuHaime said. When they got back to the house, the group sat outside under a starry night sky smoking cigars late into the night. The next morning Crist and the Giulianis had a huge brunch on the back porch overlooking the garden. "He sat there and said he would endorse Rudy," Judith said.

The Crist endorsement became the secret amulet of the Giuliani campaign; knowing they had it allowed campaign officials to sleep at night. Giuliani planned to break the news to the world in early winter, when he would run ads in snowy New Hampshire. Then Giuliani could meet Crist in Florida for the endorsement. It would give the campaign an adrenaline jolt before voters went to the polls there.

Giuliani was polling a close second to Romney in New Hampshire. The Massachusetts governor was running ads attacking him for his positions on gun control and immigration, portraying the former mayor as liberal on the issues even though Romney was to Giuliani's left on them prior to the 2008 race. The governor's attack spooked Giuliani's campaign, which responded by airing television ads portraying Giuliani as a gun rights supporter, a backflip of his own.

Smudging his abortion rights stance had failed to make an impression in conservative circles; religious right leaders were so hostile to Giuliani over his pro-choice position that they were threatening to support a third-party candidate if Republicans nominated him.

The circus enveloping his private life didn't help. Andrew and Caroline, Giuliani's son and daughter, refused to campaign with him. They were children during their parents' war at Gracie Mansion, and grew up loathing Judith. "There's obviously a little problem that exists between me and his wife," Andrew told a reporter.

The feud prompted an unexpected defense of Andrew by Donald Trump, always game to join a media circus. "I play golf with Andrew, and Andrew is a very, very good golfer, by the way," he said on CNN. "And he loves his father. I don't think it's estranged at all. He totally loves his father and respects his father. And he loves his mother."

Giuliani shifted to gun rights as his entreaty to the right. The man who as mayor once attacked the NRA as "extremists," fought for an assault weapons ban, and sued gun manufacturers suddenly found his calling as a defender of the right to bear arms. The World Trade Center attacks had triggered a change of heart, he explained. "September 11 casts somewhat of a different light on Second Amendment rights; it maybe highlights the necessity for them more," he said in a speech to conservatives.

His biggest opportunity to explain his positions came on September 21, when all the candidates trekked to the NRA annual convention at the Capital Hilton in Washington, D.C., which was being televised on cable news. Speaking before a vast audience, Giuliani tossed out a succession of crowd-pleasers. "People have the right to protect themselves in their home," he said to applause. "The Second Amendment is a freedom that's every bit as important as other freedoms in the first 10 amendments. . . .

"Just think of the language of it," he said, reading the Fourth Amendment by mistake. "The language is, 'The people shall be secure'. . . ."

At that, a musical jingle emanated from his right pocket. He dug his hand into his pants and pulled out a cell phone. "Let's see now, this is my wife calling, I think." It was Judith.

"Hello, dear, I'm talking to the members of the NRA right now. Would you like to say hello? [awkward laughter]. I love you and I'll give you a call as soon as I'm finished, okay?"

He paused as she spoke to him. *"Okay, have a safe trip, bye-bye. Talk to you later, dear. I love you."*

He hung up to a smattering of applause. "It's a lot better that way," he said sheepishly.

His staff, shaking their heads in disbelief, had seen this movie before. His defining moment on gun control was ruined by another instance of marital dysfunction.

The sideshows dogging Giuliani snowballed. On November 9, Bernie Kerik was indicted on fourteen counts of tax fraud and other federal charges. A few weeks later, the *Village Voice* unloaded an exposé of Giuliani Partners' work for the government of Qatar, whose royal family had sheltered the mastermind of the September 11 attacks, Khalid Sheikh Mohammed.

Then came the most damaging story of all. Ben Smith reported that City Hall had found obscure pockets of the city budget in which to bury expense reimbursements for Judith's transportation to the Hamptons for secret weekend trips with the mayor. (The *New York Times* later concluded it was "not likely" that Giuliani's office intentionally buried the payments.) Subsequent reports revealed that Giuliani's police department was providing her with protection while he was still living with Donna. The pieces triggered coverage of the affair at the worst possible moment.

Then, on December 28, the *Times* reminded the public of what Giuliani was willing to do for a paycheck.

In 2006, Purdue Pharma, the maker of the addictive painkiller OxyContin, hired a legal defense team of "all-stars"—including Giuliani and another former U.S. attorney from New York, Mary Jo White—to fight off potential felony charges. A small U.S. Attorney's Office in Virginia was aggressively pursuing leads that the company and its executives were misleading the public about its painkillers.

Their efforts paid off. In May 2007, Purdue agreed to have its holding company plead guilty to a misdemeanor charge, rather than a felony, and paid a fine of more than $600 million. Because the holding company took the misdemeanor, Purdue was able to continue to sell its addictive drug, with deadly results. The executives charged in the case all escaped jail time.

In an earlier era, when Giuliani was considered a savior by millions of Americans, he might have floated above the disarray in his campaign. But by the end of 2007 the magic of September 11 was fading for America's Mayor. Repeating The Story could no longer shield him from the realities of his circumstances. Alarming his audiences with warnings of future 9/11's wasn't resonating in the quaint small towns of New England. His politics were out of step with his party, and his ideological contortions weren't working. His constant invocations of the Trade Center attacks were starting to attract ridicule. "There's only three things he mentions in a sentence," Senator Joe Biden quipped in a Democratic debate. "A noun, and a verb and 9/11." The audience exploded in laughter.

John McCain was now the story of the Republican primary. Battered and broke, he clawed his way back into contention by downsizing his campaign, shedding his poll-tested talking points, and speaking his mind on the Iraq War. He traveled on a shoestring with a band of fellow veterans, and dubbed it the No Surrender Tour. As his crowds grew larger, the media took notice. The comeback narrative was irresistible.

Giuliani reached for the amulet. The endorsement from Charlie Crist could conceivably save the day for him in New Hampshire, or at least help him lose respectably. But the Florida governor was suddenly nowhere to be found. Giuliani's calls were going unreturned.

On December 19, after almost a solid year as the Republican frontrunner, Giuliani lost his lead in the national polls. The candidate decided New Hampshire was a lost cause. The campaign ended its efforts there weeks ahead of the primary and moved its resources to Florida, writing off every state in between, leaving a path open for McCain to catch up with Romney. It was a stunning decision.

The outcomes for him in Iowa and New Hampshire were disastrous. Giuliani finished sixth in the Iowa caucuses on January 3, and five days later a surging John McCain won New Hampshire in a spectacular comeback victory. Giuliani came in fourth, behind Romney and Arkansas governor Mike Huckabee.

The night of the New Hampshire primary, Mike DuHaime

walked into a room where Giuliani was chatting with Tony Carbonetti, and offered to resign. The campaign told the press that their strategy all along was to skip all the early states, and a surprising number of reporters bought into it. But it was just spin.

"Mr. Mayor, this is not what we all thought about," DuHaime said. "It's not working out. Maybe what you need is a public break. You can go out and say the strategy didn't work, we're moving forward, and we're doing something different."

Giuliani looked at him quizzically. "Are you fucking kidding me?"

"I feel like this could be a breath of fresh air for the campaign if I resign," DuHaime said.

"Don't ever say that again," the candidate said. "That would never happen. We're going to figure this out together or we'll lose together."

The next morning, Giuliani and company packed their bags and hightailed it to Florida, where they remained for the following three weeks until primary day. By then fundraising had run dry. While the campaign raised more money than any other in the Republican primary, it burned through cash at an alarming rate. Anne Dunsmore, the chief fundraiser, left the campaign in late September out of frustration; money was going out of the door too fast, and the demands from above for more cash were overwhelming.

"They were just spending money hand over fist," she said. "They had a full-fledged presidential campaign the likes of which I've never seen in a nonincumbent race. It was being run by a bunch of former Bush campaign people who thought you should have four floors of a presidential campaign in downtown New York at a king's ransom."

With money in short supply, Ed Goeas had been unable to poll Florida for several weeks. He was worried the campaign was running a get-out-the-vote drive for people who were no longer supporting Giuliani.

By the time the race reached Florida, Giuliani was in free fall. Crist threw his support to McCain, who won the state, and ultimately the nomination. Giuliani came in third, with 15 percent of the vote. He dropped out of the race with just one delegate to show for his efforts.

He delivered his concession speech inside an Orlando hotel ballroom, broadcast live by the cable networks. He stepped up to a podium with a giant red-and-blue banner behind it reading "RUDY" and gazed out on a large and disappointed crowd. A dozen local Florida politicians took their place behind him. Judith stood to his right.

Mopping his forehead in the sweltering room, he opened with a Teddy Roosevelt quote extolling the virtue of a moral battle. "Aggressive fighting for the right is the noblest sport the world affords," he said.

With his lifelong dream crashing down in humiliation, he spoke in that purposeful way of his, talking about right and wrong, just as he'd done a thousand times since the day he rose from the audience at Bishop Loughlin to prosecute a candidate for class president.

"I don't back down from a principled fight," he said, "but there must always be a larger purpose—justice for an individual, hope for a city, a better future for our country.

"Elections are about fighting for a cause larger than ourselves," he said.

As he started to tick off the high points of his campaign, a woman in the audience with an unmistakable New York accent shouted out her support.

"They'll be sorry!" she yelled.

He blew her a kiss. "You sound like my mother," he said.

CHAPTER 11

Relevance

In 2013, insomniacs flipping through cable channels late at night were treated to a series of infomercials for LifeLock, an identity theft protection service. One showed a married couple standing outside their idyllic suburban home, examining a handful of bills with worried looks on their faces.

The pitchman for the product, seated in a distinguished wood-paneled room, was Rudy Giuliani, wearing his banker blue suit and American flag lapel pin.

"Looking forward to your tax refund? So are identity thieves."

With the same ominous tone he once used to warn Americans about terrorists, he urged viewers to arm themselves against internet hackers.

"Identity thieves steal from everyone—you have to protect yourselves," he said. "I protect myself with LifeLock."

He was followed by an announcer offering a sixty-day trial, plus a document shredder ("a $29 value—free!").

Giuliani had turned mercenary years before, but Americans had never seen that side of him, and there was something sad about watching an American legend joining the ranks of has-beens and forgotten television stars. They would be even sadder if they knew that the company he was pitching had paid a $12 million fine to the

Federal Trade Commission for misrepresenting its services and failing to keep its customers' information safe, and would be fined another $100 million a few years later for perpetuating the deception.

Giuliani was still a prosperous man, and legions of Americans remained enamored of his actions on September 11. But the epic failure of his presidential campaign was a crippling blow to his prestige. T. Boone Pickens, the Texas billionaire recruited by Roy Bailey, went public with his disgust in a written letter of apology to donors he recruited to the campaign. Giuliani "rode up to the grandstand and fell off his horse," he wrote. The humiliating campaign fiasco brought the former mayor's skyrocketing trajectory to a dead halt.

His slide down to infomercial pitchman began soon after he dropped out of the race in January 2008. The day after the Florida primary, he flew to the Reagan Library in Simi Valley, where the next GOP debate was scheduled for that afternoon. Giuliani and John McCain held a rushed endorsement press conference, warm words were exchanged, and McCain excused himself after taking just one question. "I think we've got to get ready for the debate," he said, walking offstage. With that, the race for president pulled out of the station and left Giuliani behind.

After stumping with McCain the first week of February, he and Judith fell off the radar for the rest of the month and part of March, and lost touch with many of his friends and close aides.

The staff at Giuliani Partners saw little sign of him in that period, and Pat Oxford announced at a Bracewell & Giuliani partners meeting in Texas that Giuliani would be taking time off to "decompress." While he popped up here and there at some McCain events, his public schedule was limited.

What precisely happened to Giuliani in the period following his crushing loss was known solely to Judith and him. The story that she tells is alarming. She describes his suffering a collapse marked by severe depression and alcohol abuse.

The failure of Giuliani's presidential bid tarnished more than his political career; it impacted his livelihood as well. Business at Giuliani Partners plunged 50 percent during the campaign, and the company was forced to let people go. The campaign had burned through more than $60 million and ended up $4 million in debt.

But what gnawed at him most was a creeping fear of irrelevancy. The flameout forced him to lower his sights from how to amass power to how to hold on to what he had left. When he offered a reporter a rare postmortem on the race in 2009 he betrayed his concern. "I think I should've fought Iowa harder," he told *New York* magazine. "That was the beginning of becoming irrelevant."

Relevance—the need to be at the center of the action—is basic sustenance for politicians, as critical for their egos as food for their bodies. Judith felt that her husband's Achilles' heel was his bottomless need for validation. It would lead him to make a lot of bad decisions.

The 9/11 icon had far less reason to worry about falling into obscurity than the average losing politician, but he had a lot further to fall. He'd spent his entire adult life famous, feared, or beloved. He was facing a long trip down.

He'd dreamed of becoming president from a young age, and blew his big moment when it arrived. He may or may not have won the Republican nomination with a smarter campaign strategy and without the perpetual distractions of his personal dramas, but emerging with just a single delegate was a catastrophic ending to a lifelong ambition. The outcome devastated him, according to Judith. "I couldn't get him out of bed," she said.

Eager to escape the dreary cold of February in New York, the two packed their bags and decamped to her parents' two-bedroom condo in Palm Beach, which Giuliani had bought for them. The couple lived in Palm Beach Towers, an upscale high-rise apartment complex, with views of the crystalline blue Intracoastal Waterway, a swimming pool, landscaped gardens, and nearby golf courses—a natural place to relax after a brutal campaign.

But Giuliani rarely left the apartment, spending his time sitting listlessly on his in-laws' living room couch, sleeping late in the bedroom, or smoking cigars in his bathrobe on the terrace facing a parking lot. Judith said he refused to socialize or sit for meals, even as her mother, Joan, tried to entice him with some of his favorite dishes: braciole, lasagna, pastitsio.

"It started to really worry me because he was waking up only if I would wake him," she said.

He became melancholy and self-pitying ("You should leave me"), she said. Her response—"You still have kids that love you, you have me, you have your health"—failed to assuage his sense of failure. "He just could not get over it," she said.

"He was in what, I knew as a nurse, was a clinical depression," she said.

She said he started to drink more heavily. While Giuliani was always fond of drinking scotch with his cigars while holding court at the Grand Havana or Club Mac, his friends never considered him a problem drinker. Judith felt he was drinking to dull the pain.

The situation was concerning enough to send the couple searching for a more discreet locale for his recuperation, as the press caught on to their stay at Palm Beach Towers, and photographers started popping up. In search of a friend to turn to, they found one in Donald Trump.

Long before the New York developer brought his unique brand of vulgarian chic to Palm Beach, Florida, Marjorie Merriweather Post, the heiress to the Post food fortune and at one point the wealthiest woman in America, constructed a vast palacio on twenty spectacular acres of Florida land stretching between the Atlantic Ocean and Lake Worth. She named it Mar-a-Lago, Spanish for "sea-to-lake."

The mansion she constructed on the property was as majestic as Versailles, or at least designed to look that way, with so much gold leaf in its living room ceiling that for a while the country ran out of the material. She imported Italian stone for its exterior walls and arches, Cuban marble for its dining room floor, and sculptures of parrots and monkeys commissioned in Vienna.

Running beneath the property's fifty-eight bedrooms, thirty-three bathrooms, tennis and croquet courts, swimming pools, and manicured lawns was a network of bomb shelters and tunnels that she had built during the Korean War. Even after Trump purchased the property in 1985 and converted it into a private club, the labyrinthian underground remained a secret to most people outside of Palm Beach. But it was that feature that proved most helpful when Rudy and Judith made their escape to the property in the early winter of 2008.

"We moved into Mar-a-Lago and Donald kept our secret," she said.

According to Nathan, Trump provided them with a hideaway that was secluded from the press and passersby, a safe space for an ailing friend who was a magnet for photographers. He had a perfect spot for them—a bungalow across the street from Mar-a-Lago that became part of Trump's private beach club. A small tunnel ran underneath South Ocean Boulevard, a narrow two-lane highway, allowing the Giulianis to walk to dinner beyond the glare of the press.

"No one would see us, so we could sleep here, go under the tunnel and go here and have dinner," she said, describing the walk from the bungalow to the larger house.

Though they didn't walk the grounds much, the Mar-a-Lago area was a tranquil environment in which to recover. It was also close enough to Judith's parents' home that she could run errands back and forth.

"During the period of time that we did that it was constant counseling for Rudy," she said. "I had various therapists speaking to him on the phone. He was in a chronic depression. He thought he was finished.

"And that was when Rudy, in my opinion, really went downhill and never came back. Rudy spent his whole life wanting to be president."

His drinking accelerated, she said, the beginning of a series of episodes in which he fell and hurt himself. "He was always falling shitfaced somewhere," she said.

Judith was known to exaggerate, and the depth of his depression is something that only she and Giuliani knew for certain, as they were largely isolated at the time. Their friends in New York said the two were out of touch with them.

Joe Lhota, the former deputy mayor, said his vague recollection was that Giuliani "kind of went into a cave—he kind of lost himself.

"No one heard from him for a while," Lhota said. He recalled that Tony Carbonetti told him at the time that Giuliani was "in a dark place."

Carbonetti now says that only Judith and Rudy know for sure how bad things were for his old boss. "There was a period where it was just the two of them for two or three months," he said. "She was the only person really spending significant time with him."

According to Judith, they avoided the social whirl at Mar-a-Lago during their stay, but spent a fair amount of time with Donald, "sometimes Melania," she said. "But more often than not it was just Rudy and I because Rudy was in a depression."

The two couples had never been a tight foursome. Judith, preternaturally social, found Melania guarded and reserved. Donald adored Rudy but was put off by Judith's braggadocio.

Over the years the couples attended each other's weddings, and got together occasionally, usually in larger groups, but sometimes it was just the four of them, as when they bumped into one another at Peter Luger's steakhouse in Brooklyn one night and decided to dine together. In the winter the Giulianis played golf at the Trump International Golf Club in West Palm Beach, and brunched with the Trumps and other New York snowbirds. Donald was always gracious when Judith needed help with a charity event, donating the use of one of his golf courses, or posing for photos and signing caps for her auctions.

It was the husbands who had a compelling kinship. The former mayor and the famous developer were two New York colossuses, dinosaurs from another time and place—or perhaps it was just a state of mind—in which powerful men flaunted their money and influence to prove their dominance over other powerful men, and wives were first and foremost arm candy, the more beautiful and diamond-bedecked the better.

"He would always come home and bring these beautiful gifts," Judith said of Rudy. "He wanted it to be ostentatious, he wanted me to walk down Madison Avenue with a big pearl necklace or a big diamond ring. He loved that it was emblematic for him of his not being, as he used to say, just a Brooklyn boy. He needed that validation."

But she clearly loved the lifestyle as much as he did, proudly posing in a cranberry bejeweled Carolina Herrera gown and Jimmy Choo shoes for the cover of *Avenue* magazine, a glossy society publication.

Both Trumps kept a protective eye on Judith and him, she said. According to a confidante of Judith's, she and Melania were practicing yoga on the beach one day when Melania spotted a Mar-a-Lago employee shooting photos of them. Melania called Donald, who marched to the scene and confronted the employee. After some back-and-forth, the man grudgingly handed Trump his camera.

When Trump saw the photos his employee had taken of his wife and Judith he fired him on the spot.

During their stay, Judith said she and Rudy decided to see a movie at a West Palm Beach shopping center one afternoon. It ended soon after it began. She said he stumbled out of the car, fell down, and gashed his forehead so badly he needed stitches.

Several weeks later, he made his first public appearance since arriving at Mar-a-Lago, traveling to New York to appear on *SNL*. He sat on the set of "Weekend Update" making self-deprecating jokes about the failure of his campaign. His makeup barely hid a large scar above his right eyebrow.

Giuliani's only mention of that period was to tell the *New York Times* in 2018 that he "spent a month at Mar-a-Lago, relaxing." But Judith contends that, eight years before Washington began talking about Rudy Giuliani and Donald Trump in the same breath, the future president took the failed candidate under his protective wing at a vulnerable moment. What's clear is that the two men's friendship survived when a hundred other Trump relationships died away like so many marriages of convenience. Giuliani would never turn his back on Trump, much to his detriment.

Loss can be debilitating, but it can also be liberating. Prior to the crash-and-burn of his candidacy there were lines Giuliani couldn't cross—ethical, moral, political. The pervasive glare of media scrutiny wouldn't permit it. But if the spotlight on Giuliani Partners wasn't completely extinguished after the race it was certainly dimmed. With less at stake to his reputation and fewer people watching, the restraints came off.

Coming home after a bruising loss, he encountered a changed landscape. Giuliani Partners was long past its heyday. Many of his closest confidants were gone or headed out the door. Bernie Kerik was facing jail time. The company was laying off employees; it would clear out of the Ernst & Young building within two years.

He was at a turning point, but his options were circumscribed by his extravagant lifestyle. At one point, he was supporting six homes and eleven country club memberships. In one six-month period alone he spent $12,000 on cigars and $7,000 on fountain pens.

Setting out to sate his materialistic needs, he went looking for money in all the wrong places.

On May 7, 2008, he held a press conference at NASDAQ headquarters in Times Square to endorse a mayoral candidate. Standing beside him, a foot taller, was Vitali Klitschko, a professional boxer nicknamed "Dr. Ironfist." He was a towering, chiseled figure resembling Ivan Drago, the Russian boxer in a *Rocky* movie, an Eastern European punching machine stretching six feet, seven inches tall.

Klitschko was running for mayor of Kyiv, the capital of Ukraine, and Giuliani, for some reason, was promoting his candidacy. "They need a leader like you, who can deal with corruption, who can deal with reform of government, which is so necessary," he told Klitschko in front of reporters.

As it happened, Klitschko was a client who was supposedly relying on Giuliani's advice on fighting corruption and crime. Advising him was a curious decision on Giuliani's part, only months after withdrawing his candidacy for president. It was also curious that Klitschko would fly halfway across the world for advice about criminal justice policy, especially for a campaign he hadn't yet won (he went on to lose). More likely, a photo op with America's Mayor carried credibility with the voters back home.

But Giuliani wasn't in it just for the potential consulting fee. Eastern Europeans were still big fans, presidential election or not, and business leaders and politicians were eager to tie their names to his brand. His entry point was Ukraine, and he was making new friends who could show him around.

He first visited the country in 2003, when he came to Kyiv to dedicate a September 11 memorial at the behest of a Ukrainian oligarch. His connection to the country deepened thanks to Vitaly Pruss, a New Yorker originally from Belarus, who did business in Eastern Europe through his company TriGlobal Strategic Ventures. Pruss caught on to Giuliani's appeal early, and invited him to make a paid visit to one of Russia's largest steel companies, which took place the next year. He became a prolific matchmaker for the former mayor in Ukraine, as well as Moscow; it was he who introduced Giuliani to Vitali Klitschko, among others.

The week after his Times Square press conference with Klitschko, Giuliani flew to Kyiv for a ceremony unveiling a monument to a Ukrainian helicopter designer, an odd event at which to find a former New York City mayor. Klitschko sponsored the event, and TriGlobal Strategic Ventures participated.

Deals started to happen. Seeking to leverage his fame in yet another field, Giuliani plunged into the real estate investment business with Jeffrey Berman, a Maryland investor and managing partner at TriGlobal, Pruss's company. "When we decided to put the fund together in my family, the money we wanted to go for was overseas money, and Rudy has a lot of traction overseas," Berman said. The goal was to raise as much as $750 million, and America's Mayor was an investor magnet.

Giuliani's headfirst plunge into Ukrainian affairs would lead to utter disaster in the years that followed, not just for him but for both the U.S. and Ukraine. If he had any compunctions about what he was getting into he never let on. The failure of his campaign freed him to chase money down dark avenues, and he did so without apology. The photos of him with his new Ukrainian friends showed a smiling man.

*　　*　　*

Incredibly, at the same time that he was continuing to swim in these murky waters, Giuliani was stoking speculation that John McCain might choose him as his running mate.

On July 20, the same day the press reported his real estate deal with Berman, Rudy and Judith flipped on their New York Yankees caps and took McCain to a ballgame. The three spent the day at Yankee Stadium in a box seat near the dugout, watching the home team play the Oakland A's. It was a loose, freewheeling afternoon, with the two men eating hot dogs with their sleeves rolled up under a baking sun. Fans cheered them both.

McCain and Giuliani were genuinely fond of each other, and spent much of the week chumming it up in limousines and hopping to fundraisers together. The friendship had survived their rivalry in the presidential race; Giuliani refused to attack McCain during the campaign despite the senator's broadsides on him, much to the frustration of his advisors.

Their public bromance heightened media speculation that McCain might put Giuliani on the ticket, something Giuliani didn't discourage. "I wonder if Rudy Giuliani might get a call to get vetted for VP?" Sean Hannity mused to the former mayor on Fox News. "Well, I don't seek anything. I really don't," Giuliani replied.

When it came time for McCain to make his choice, Giuliani didn't make the first cut; the campaign didn't even bother to poll on him. "In any meeting I was in, I don't recall Rudy ever being seriously mentioned," said McCain's pollster Bill McInturff.

Mike DuHaime, who moved over to the McCain camp from Giuliani's, said his old boss's pro-choice politics was an instant disqualifier. But Senator Joe Lieberman, who was a pro-choice former Democrat, almost made it onto the ticket; McCain was talked out of it at the last minute by aides who argued for Sarah Palin, much to his regret.

Giuliani was hurt by McCain's treatment of him. But McCain

chose him to deliver the keynote address at the upcoming Republican convention, which was part of the discussion between the two camps when Giuliani was preparing to drop out of the race and endorse him. It was as valuable a consolation prize as they came. With his business success tied to his political relevance, and his self-esteem dependent upon both, it was a priceless opportunity.

He was leading a dual existence, mixing it up with shady characters and making business deals in Eastern Europe while playing to the crowds as America's Mayor. Less than two weeks before McCain announced the keynote selection, Bracewell & Giuliani helped broker a deal to create Ukraine's largest cable provider.

On the night of Giuliani's convention speech in St. Paul, Minnesota, the crowd jumped to its feet and roared when he walked onstage, and barely allowed him to begin. Standing in front of a huge silhouette of the New York skyline, wearing his blue suit and red striped tie, he was buoyant.

"This already has been the longest presidential campaign in history, and sometimes to me it felt even longer," he quipped.

He ran through McCain's remarkable bio as a fighter pilot, prisoner of war, and maverick senator. But it was clear that his role was less to praise McCain than to take down Barack Obama.

"Everyone acknowledges that John McCain is a true American hero," he said. "On the other hand, you have a résumé from a gifted man with an Ivy League education. He worked as a community organizer."

He paused for effect and snickered, as the crowd laughed. "What? "I said, 'Okay, okay, maybe this is the first problem on the résumé.'"

He continued to belittle the qualifications of the first Black person nominated by a major party.

"Then he ran for the state legislature and he got elected. And nearly 130 times, he couldn't make a decision. He couldn't figure out whether to vote 'yes' or 'no.' It was too tough.

"He voted 'present.' I didn't know about this vote 'present' when I was mayor of New York City."

The audience roared with contempt.

Then, inevitably, he got around to his signature cause.

"They rarely mentioned the attacks of September 11, 2001," he said of the Democrats who had spoken at their convention a week earlier. "They are in a state of denial about the biggest threat that faces this country. And if you deny it and you don't deal with it, you can't face it."

And so it went for twenty-seven minutes in prime time, Giuliani praising McCain and ripping into Obama to roars from the audience for almost twice his allotted speaking time, costing the networks millions in lost advertising revenue.

A traumatic loss in the primaries liberated him to shed his bland candidate's veneer and revert back to who he was. He was lacerating, prosecutorial, sanctimonious, and cruel. But he was also clever, methodical, and riveting. For one last night, with the eyes of the nation upon him, he was Rudy Giuliani again.

In June 2012, the orchestra on the *Evening with Ivan Ivanovic* show in Belgrade struck up a brassy rendition of "New York, New York" as a studio audience cheered the entrance of America's Mayor, bounding down the steps of an illuminated glass staircase, flashing his toothy smile.

The host shook his hand, escorted him to his seat, and sat down behind a desk. It was a standard-issue, Johnny Carson–era interview set, right down to the nighttime skyline in the background and the coffee mug on Ivanovic's desk.

The show could have passed for a low-budget *Tonight Show* knock-off in an American city, but for the host's Slavic name and the fact that the skyline showed Belgrade, the capital of Serbia. Ivanovic, young and starstruck, told his guest that no American had ever appeared on his program.

"It's a big honor for me to have you here on my show," he said.

After some banter—he asked Giuliani for help getting him on the David Letterman show, prompting Giuliani to brag that he'd appeared on it over a dozen times—Ivanovic inquired what he was doing in Belgrade.

"We're here to give advice to Mr. Vucic, who is running for mayor, about economic development," Giuliani replied.

His client, Aleksandar Vucic, was running for office on a ticket with Tomislav Nikolic, a far-right presidential candidate known as "The Undertaker" for having once overseen cemeteries. Both men were alumni of Slobodan Milosevic's murderous regime, which prosecuted wars in the Balkans that saw 125,000 killed, including prompting NATO to launch air strikes that devastated much of Serbia. Milosevic was on trial for genocide by an international tribunal when he died in prison two years prior to Giuliani's appearance.

"How do you feel about [the bombings] now, after all this time has passed, after thirteen years?" Ivanovic asked Giuliani.

"I think the mayor should forget about it and move on to the future," his guest said, dismissively.

His gig for Vucic prompted the U.S. embassy in Belgrade to clarify that it wasn't taking sides in the election; then–Secretary of State Hillary Clinton fumed in a memo that his work for Vucic was "outrageous."

But for Giuliani it was just another day on the road. He had clients across the globe, a continuing benefit from the international fan club he had developed after his performance on September 11. The services he offered clients came with a unique benefit that a McKinsey or Bain couldn't begin to compete with: public support from a global hero.

New Yorkers who remembered Giuliani's probity as United States attorney would be astonished to read his client list, which read like a collection of villains from James Bond films.

Keiko Fujimori was a right-wing Peruvian presidential candidate whose father, former president Alberto Fujimori, was sentenced to twenty-five years in prison for murder and kidnapping. In 2011, she ran for his old position in the face of criticism that he was directing her campaign from his prison cell. Giuliani traveled to Peru, and maintained to the media, as he did for his client in Serbia, that his work was not political.

As in Serbia, he bestowed a tarnished client the validation of a legendary crime and corruption fighter. "I'm not here to get involved in the politics of Peru, but if she gets elected, I'd be very happy to help her," he told a television interviewer. Keiko Fujimori lost the election, and would later face money-laundering charges.

At the same time he was consulting the avenging scion of a homicidal dictator in Peru, and an acolyte of the leader behind ethnic cleansing in Bosnia, Giuliani was proselytizing for a group on the State Department's list of foreign terrorist organizations.

Mujahedin-e Khalq (roughly translated by U.S. officials to "People's Holy Warriors of Iran"), also known as MEK, was an Iranian militia group accused of slaughtering Kurds on behalf of Saddam Hussein after the 1991 Gulf War. In the years since, it proved remarkably adept at American public relations, rebranding itself as a pro-U.S. freedom-fighting group, and launching an expensive campaign to sign up reputable American public officials to deliver speeches on their behalf.

Giuliani was a particularly willing participant, penning op-eds and speaking forcefully at pro-MEK rallies, a major assist from a hardliner on terrorism. MEK's campaign succeeded: Secretary Clinton removed the group from the terrorism watch list in 2012. The State Department official who recommended the decision later excoriated Giuliani.

"'America's Mayor' has presented himself as a centurion in the fight against 'radical Islamic terrorism,'" wrote Ambassador Daniel Benjamin. "Yet he appears to feel that gorging at the table of Islamo-Marxist terrorists who have murdered Americans is in no way unseemly."

The prosecutor once revered for his rectitude was operating on a different moral plane a quarter century later. Now he was proselytizing for a pharmaceutical company that was hooking teens on painkillers; authoritarians running for office cloaked as moderates; terrorists rebranding themselves as freedom fighters; and an identity theft company that was deceiving its customers. Characteristically, he portrayed his actions on their behalf as based on principle. "You are the heroes," he told an MEK gathering. "You will be the freedom fighters and you will be honored in Iran's history."

Giuliani wasn't changing his stripes as much as surrendering to his worst instincts. The prosecutor who wrecked lives in search of fame; the mayor who destroyed reputations in pursuit of power; the husband who cheated on his wife—these men lived side by side with the leader who comforted grieving widows, and raced to help his friends in hard times.

At an advancing age, out of power, his lifelong dream unrealized, he grew decadent. He gained weight and continued to drink. He focused on superficial things—the acquisition of homes, appearances on the social circuit, a feverish pursuit of money. None of it added up to his meaningful roles as mayor or prosecutor.

He flirted publicly with running for governor against Andrew Cuomo and for U.S. Senate against Kirsten Gillibrand in 2009, and then president against Mitt Romney and others in 2012, only to back off each time in the face of formidable odds. He would never run for office again after 2008. Mayor of New York City was the only elective office he would hold.

With doors closing around him, his need to stay relevant became more desperate. Locked out of office and deprived of a platform—

he wasn't invited to speak at Romney's 2012 GOP convention—he started yelling louder to attract attention.

Giuliani had a history of adjusting his politics to suit his needs, dating back to 1980, when he became a Republican to land a job in the Reagan administration. He was a leading hawk during the war presidency of George W. Bush; when Barack Obama captured the White House in 2008 amid a tidal wave of enthusiasm, he became a member of the loyal opposition, critiquing the popular president but rarely condemning him. Obama's second term was another story.

By 2013, the country's politics was in a far different place than in 2008. The passage of Obamacare in 2010 triggered a nationwide outcry among right-wing conservatives, and invigorated the Tea Party. Their anger led to the rise of flame-throwers like Michele Bachmann and Ted Cruz.

The movement embraced figures who'd previously existed on the margins of the party. Donald Trump gained an unlikely national following for promoting a conspiracy theory that Obama was secretly a foreign-born Muslim. The racist charge caught on in pockets of the American right.

Giuliani, so politically milquetoast in the 2008 race that few could figure out whether he supported or opposed abortion rights and gun control, sensed the zeitgeist shifting. Conservative mainstreamers like House Speaker John Boehner were becoming an endangered species. The Republicans viewers wanted to watch on Fox News were alarmists, not institutionalists.

The burgeoning market in resentment politics was a perfect fit for a man who had perfected the craft at City Hall. Few American politicians were as practiced in the art of political outrage as Giuliani.

He got an opportunity to throw a bomb into the public conversation on November 23, 2014. It was three months after a white police officer named Darren Wilson shot and killed an unarmed Black man named Michael Brown Jr. on a street in Ferguson, Missouri. Protests over the shooting exploded into riots. For several nights, police battled protesters, stores went up in flames, and Molotov cocktails flew through the air. Missouri governor Jay Nixon declared a state of emergency.

The nation was on tenterhooks as a grand jury deliberated whether to press charges against the officer. On the day before it reached its decision, Giuliani traveled to NBC's Rockefeller Center studios to discuss the case on *Meet the Press*.

It was confounding that the show's producers chose to interview a politician despised by the Black community for his handling of police killings of Black men; perhaps the gauze of September 11 caused them to forget. But Giuliani had everyone remembering once the cameras blinked on.

He was joined by Anthony Gray, Michael Brown's attorney, and Michael Eric Dyson, a Georgetown University professor and frequent television commentator.

Dyson was incensed by the shooting, and criticized the governor's tactics to quell the rioting. "The police force is not to be an occupying force, they are to be there to protect and serve," he said.

Chuck Todd, the host, showed Giuliani statistics indicating the disproportionate percentages of white police officers patrolling the nation's minority communities, and asked for his reaction. The guest took the conversation in another direction.

"The fact is, I find it very disappointing that you're not discussing the fact that 93 percent of blacks in America are killed by other blacks. We're talking about the exception here," he said.

The temperature rose instantly. Dyson and Giuliani flew into an angry exchange, speaking over one another as Todd tried unsuccessfully to intervene.

DYSON: Black people who kill Black people go to jail. White people who are policemen who kill Black people do not go to jail. If a jury can indict a ham sandwich, why is it taking so long?

GIULIANI: It's hardly insignificant.

DYSON: I didn't say it was insignificant. . . .

GIULIANI: It is the reason for the heavy police presence in the Black community.

DYSON: Not at all. The police presence cannot make a distinction between those who are criminals and those who call the police to stop the criminals.

GIULIANI: What about the poor Black child that is killed by another Black child? Why aren't you protesting that?

DYSON: Those people go to jail. I do protest it. I'm a minister. They go to jail. Why don't you talk about the way in which white policemen have undercut the abilities of Americans to live?

GIULIANI: So why not cut it down so many white police officers don't have to be in Black areas? . . .

DYSON: They don't have to be. It's a matter of the effect of the state occupying those forces, sir.

GIULIANI: How about 70 percent to 75 percent of the crime in my city. . . .

DYSON: How about your attitude reinforces problematic perspectives that prevail in a culture, sir.

GIULIANI: Well, how about you reduce crime?

DYSON: Absolutely, when I become mayor, I will do that.

GIULIANI: White police officers won't be there if you weren't killing each other 70 to 75 percent of the time!

DYSON: Look at this! This is the defensive mechanism of white supremacy in your mind, sir.

Giuliani was unloading years of resentment from the Amadou Diallo and Patrick Dorismond controversies. His language reeked of sheer paternalism toward Black Americans. *"White police officers won't be there if you weren't killing each other...."*

The next day, the Missouri grand jury declined to indict Wilson, triggering the worst night of rioting since the shooting. "Burn this bitch down!" Michael Brown's stepfather Louis Head yelled to protesters outside of police headquarters. Rioters set fire to a dozen buildings and a pair of police cars as gunfire raged through the night.

Giuliani went on CNN the next morning, eager to push the racial button again. "The amount of crime in the Black community is excessive, 70 to 75 percent of the murders in New York City are committed by blacks," he said. ...

"When the president was talking last night about training the police, of course, the police should be trained," he said. "He also should have spent 15 minutes on training the community to stop killing each other."

The disparaging language—Black people needed to be trained not to murder—seemed designed to incite. But with the country convulsed by the violence in Ferguson, his comments just triggered some head-scratching.

Seemingly determined to shock his way back onto the nation's radar, he pumped up the incendiary language. Two months after his *Meet the Press* appearance, he attended a dinner for Wisconsin governor Scott Walker, a likely 2016 Republican presidential candidate, at the 21 Club in midtown Manhattan.

Filing into the windowless former speakeasy under low ceilings covered with antique toys and sports memorabilia, about sixty conservative businessmen and media figures settled into red leather seats to hear from one of the most talked-about contenders in the race. But it was New York's former mayor who stole the show.

"I do not believe, and I know this is a horrible thing to say, but I do not believe that the president loves America," Giuliani told the group about Barack Obama. "He doesn't love you. And he doesn't love me. He wasn't brought up the way you were brought up and I was brought up through love of this country."

The event was billed as a private dinner, but the remarks were picked up and reported by *Politico*. This time people took notice.

"America has been treated to a spectacle that New Yorkers grew accustomed to—and sick of—a long time ago," wrote columnist Errol Louis on the CNN website, "an outburst from ex-mayor Rudy Giuliani that is equal parts ugly, thoughtless and divisive."

"Do you think Rudy Giuliani has lost it?" ABC News's White House reporter Jonathan Karl asked at the White House daily press briefing.

"I think really the only thing that I feel is that I feel sorry for Rudy Giuliani today," Josh Earnest, the White House press secretary, said.

At another time in American politics, a comment such as Giuliani's might have been met with universal condemnation. In the new environment of heightened division, it just triggered more interview requests. On Fox News, Sean Hannity wondered if Giuliani actually had a point. Bill O'Reilly called Giuliani the *victim* in the matter, "because he experienced so much pain" on September 11, causing him to question those who didn't take terrorism seriously enough.

He worked hard to keep the controversy alive for the better part of a week. "Some people thought it was racist," he told the *New York Times* about his comments. "I thought that was a joke, since he [Obama] was brought up by a white mother, a white grandfather, went to white schools, and most of this he learned from white people. This isn't racism. This is socialism or possibly anti-colonialism."

Lest the coverage fade, he penned an op-ed about it for the *Wall Street Journal*. "Over my years as mayor of New York City and as a federal prosecutor, I earned a certain reputation for being blunt," he bragged.

While Giuliani was acting like a loose cannon, his inflammatory rhetoric wasn't random. Like Donald Trump, he was ginning up racial divisions to undermine the legitimacy of the country's first Black president. Questioning Obama's allegiance to America complemented Trump's questioning whether he was an American at all. The goal of both men was to portray America's first Black president as alien from the country he served. It was a point picked up in a prescient essay by Jeffrey Toobin in the *New Yorker*.

"Since Giuliani's disastrous run for the Republican Presidential nomination, in 2008, he has become a national embarrassment of a distinctive type," he wrote, quoting historian Richard Hofstadter's famous description of "the paranoid style in American politics," characterized by "heated exaggeration, suspiciousness, and conspiratorial fantasy. . . .

"The motivation behind the epithets from Giuliani and his allies will endure," Toobin warned, "and the resentments will find a new target, sooner rather than later."

Giuliani kept tossing grenades over the following months. "There's something wrong with the guy," he told the *Times* about Obama.

Much of the political world was laughing at his apparent kamikaze mission to destroy his own reputation. But on June 24, 2015, his efforts paid off. Walking into his apartment late one night after an appearance on the *Sean Hannity Show*, his phone rang. It was Donald Trump.

CHAPTER 12

Guardrails

In the summer of 2016, a dying Peter Powers was admitted to Calvary Hospital, a large hospice in the Bronx. Rudy Giuliani's best friend waged a quiet battle with lung cancer for several years until finally choosing to end his terrible ordeal by halting his dialysis treatments.

He carried different titles in a career largely devoted to his friend, all reflecting the second-banana role life had assigned him: member of Giuliani's high school opera club; manager of Giuliani's mayoral campaign; first deputy mayor in the Giuliani administration; advisor to the Giuliani presidential campaign. But the roles only half explained their relationship; they considered themselves brothers, their dynamic based not so much on loyalty as love. They were godfathers to each other's children. Their families spent holidays together.

Powers was a kind, measured tax attorney, a Goldwater Republican with simple rules for life and business. As deputy mayor for operations, in charge of day-to-day management over a sprawling government, he ran a remarkably tight ship, employing corny 1950s-era maxims. "You get what you inspect, not what you expect," he told city commissioners. Employees intimidated by the mayor came to him for advice in dealing with their mercurial boss.

While Giuliani was pale and severe-looking, barely capable of forcing a smile, Powers was ruddy-faced and folksy. He was sensible where Giuliani was impulsive, always the one to talk him out of crazy ideas, and mop up his messes. He counseled him through political crises, divorces, and bad marriages. David Garth, Giuliani's campaign strategist in 1993, likened Powers to Karl Malden in *On the Waterfront*, in the role of Father Barry, the levelheaded priest forever trying to calm the quick-tempered.

In his friend's final weeks Giuliani arrived at the hospital before anyone else each morning, and remained after everyone else left at night. "He took ushering my father out of this world as seriously as any other job," recalled Powers's daughter Heather Powers McBride. "He wasn't not going to sacrifice for sleep or food or anything else."

Bereft, he rarely left his friend's bedside, except to fetch a doctor to explain matters to the family, or to talk through the details of the wake and funeral. With her father near comatose, Heather and her sister tried in vain to communicate with him by calling his name. "Rudy would say *'Hey Peter!'* in a loud voice and my dad would wake right up until the very end," she said. "That was the voice that could rouse him.

"They were brought together for whatever reason in life. Until the very end the two of them had a very special connection."

When Giuliani lost Powers on July 7, his friends were taken aback by the depth of his grief. "He took the Peter Powers death harder than anything I'd ever seen," said one. "He was in bad shape," said another.

The death of Giuliani's best friend occurred during the most aimless period of his life. He was professionally and politically adrift, casting about for his place in the world, and grasping desperately for attention in ways that were doing grave damage to his reputation. His marriage to Judith, far from providing him with stability, was a growing source of tumult. The endless fighting, the constant advice from his friends to leave her (Powers among them), were wearing him down. As he processed Powers's death he careened from wistfulness to sadness to anger.

On the night before the wake, he placed a call to Bernie Kerik. It was his first call to his former police commissioner in a decade, when the indictments had started rolling in. Giuliani had all but washed his hands of him, going as far as to tell reporters "Bernie Kerik is history" in 2009. He had plenty of reasons to be angry, and legal and political reasons to stay away. But Kerik was crestfallen by his boss's abandonment, which was so total that Giuliani returned a horse statuette that Kerik's six-year-old daughter had sent him as a Christmas present in 2006.

Kerik was bitterly disappointed that Giuliani neglected to check on his daughters—Giuliani's godchildren—in the three years that he was in prison. "He was like family to me, someone I could never have abandoned," Kerik recounted. "But you live and learn."

After his release in 2013, he and Giuliani ran into one another in the Green Room of Fox News studios in midtown Manhattan, and shared a warm embrace. Nothing came of it until Powers died.

In his call to Kerik the evening before the wake, Giuliani asked him not just to come to the funeral home the next day but the day after as well. It was not an offer he could turn down—"He was torn up," Kerik said—but the prospect made him anxious. It wasn't just Giuliani he would be seeing, but all of Giuliani World, which had followed the boss's lead in shunning him.

Then there were the dozens, if not hundreds, of politicians and dignitaries who would be paying their respects, people Kerik once mixed with easily but who would be looking down on him as an ex-con. Before Giuliani called with his request, Kerik's plan was to "go in, pay my respects and get the fuck out of there." Since his release from prison, people had been looking at him differently—"like I committed homicide."

Filled with anxiety, he traveled the next morning to the Frank

E. Campbell funeral home on Fifth Avenue, which was surrounded by black SUVs and plainclothes security officers. "Everybody in city government was there," he said. "Every governor. If they didn't come for Peter they came for Giuliani."

"Nobody had seen me for years," he said. "I'd disappeared. And then suddenly I'm there."

Giuliani spotted him walking through the crowd and came over to him, flashing a smile and wrapping his arms around him. He planted a kiss on Kerik's cheek. Then he proceeded to walk him through the crowd, literally by the hand, as his old commissioner came face-to-face with members of the club who had long since discarded him. Giuliani barely left his side that morning.

At a separate event for his old City Hall crew a few weeks later at a midtown steakhouse, he made matters even clearer.

"You know I make it a practice not to speak about individuals because we're a team," he announced to the loyalists gathered in a private dining room. "But my prodigal son is back, and everyone needs to know that." At that, Bernie Kerik's old colleagues stood from their chairs and gave him a standing ovation.

Years later, Kerik lost his composure describing his old boss's act of love. Powers's death may have put Giuliani in a sentimental frame of mind. Or perhaps it sent him searching for a friend to fill the void.

But if his friend's death had Giuliani wearing his heart on his sleeve, it also caused him to act erratically. On the day of the funeral, hundreds turned out at St. Patrick's Cathedral, as close to a state funeral as New York City provides.

Giuliani's eulogy inside the vast Gothic chapel should have been the emotional high point of the service, but it was less personal than people expected; he bragged about the accomplishments of his administration at great length, describing how it brought an end to decades of liberal rule, and conquered a mindset that dragged the city into near bankruptcy. He gave Powers a good deal of credit for it, but to some in the audience much of the speech sounded like a paean to himself.

Toward the end he addressed Powers's two daughters, Heather and Krista.

"Your father had a dying wish," he said. "He told me he wants you to take care of Sylvia."

"Sylvia" was Powers's second wife, Sylvia Ng, who had been a factor in Powers's divorce from their mother. "We kind of pinched each other in the leg, and kept a half smile," Heather said. "I just waited for the moment to pass."

It was a curious performance on a major stage that left Giuliani's large, influential audience scratching their heads. It was just a warm-up to a speech to a far larger crowd that he was due to deliver just seven days later, when much of the nation would wonder what had gone wrong with him.

Donald Trump was in an ornery mood when he phoned Giuliani at his apartment on the night of June 24, 2015. Eight days earlier, he'd taken an escalator ride down to the lobby of Trump Tower and announced his improbable candidacy for the White House. Tonight he watched Giuliani on Hannity, one of his favorite shows, as he ticked off his preferences in the race.

HANNITY: Who's on Rudy Giuliani's radar in terms of . . .

GIULIANI: Jeb for sure.

HANNITY: Yes.

GIULIANI: Marco Rubio. You know, I like Senator [Lindsey] Graham.

HANNITY: That's the only mistake.

(LAUGHTER)

GIULIANI: Well, I like him very much. I love George Pataki, and I wish he could get traction. I love George . . .

HANNITY: He's not going to win! I know he's not going to win.

GIULIANI: Scott Walker I'd like to know more about.

HANNITY: Yes.

GIULIANI: Rick Perry I have a great fondness for.

Trump didn't make the cut.

"How long have they been friends of yours?" Trump asked Giuliani on the phone.

"Well, you know, Jeb, 10 years . . ."

"How long have we been friends?"

"Eighteen, 20 years."

"Are you mad at me?"

"No, I'm not mad at you."

"I'm running for president! You don't even mention me?"

Giuliani searched for words.

"I know you've got to take a little while to do an endorsement," Trump said, calming down. "You'll endorse me, though. I know you'll endorse me."

When the conversation ended, Giuliani dialed up Tony Carbonetti.

"Tony, he's serious," Giuliani said.

"Bullshit," he responded.

Much as he liked Trump, Giuliani shared the establishment's belief that he was little more than a novelty candidate in search of publicity for his company. In a race with no fewer than seventeen candidates, including Republican stars such as Ted Cruz, Rand Paul, Chris Christie, and John Kasich, all seemed more plausible than the *Apprentice* star. Giuliani, according to a former colleague, considered Trump a "carnival barker."

The conventional wisdom that he wasn't a serious candidate was reinforced by Trump's incendiary announcement speech. Mexico, he said, was "sending people that have lots of problems, and they're bringing those problems with us. They're bringing drugs. They're bringing crime. They're rapists."

But the Republican electorate took him plenty seriously. Three weeks after their phone call, Trump took the lead in the polls, and held on to it for the rest of the year.

So much was going wrong for Giuliani at the time that Trump's courting of him might have felt like sorely needed affirmation. Bracewell & Giuliani had been his prime cash cow since the 2008 race. As Giuliani Partners, his consulting firm, was wilting on the vine, the law firm bloomed. The consulting firm was doing about half the business in 2009 as it was before the presidential race, while revenues at Bracewell were up an equal percentage; between 2006 and 2008, the law firm's revenues shot up from $200 million to $300 million, thanks in no small part to Giuliani's rainmaking.

"He was a good partner for a while," a former Bracewell partner said. "He was worth his weight for some time, because he was able to get us access to pretty much anybody we were interested in representing. For clients we already had, he was America's Mayor. At dinners and stuff they were ga-ga over Rudy."

Bracewell employees were also ga-ga at first. "I remember him walking into the room and the energy of this person," said one. "He really had that charisma. Everybody felt it."

"He was perfectly personable, and as a law partner he was willing to do pretty much anything," said the former partner. "If you wanted him to do a dinner with a client he would do it. . . . Someone would be sitting next to him at a firm dinner and would ask him to speak at their teen's eighth grade graduation. He'd say sure."

He recruited talented lawyers to the firm, and though he did scant legal work, "his instincts on litigation were pretty damned good," said the partner. But after the debacle of the 2008 campaign, employees picked up a scent of desperation. He name-dropped more, and gave the impression that he cared about being seen as important. Concern at the Houston headquarters started to grow over news accounts of his incendiary political commentary. Lawyers were coming back from New York with stories about his boozy dinners at the Grand Havana Room. "There's trouble at home, too," a partner was told.

The last straw was his widely publicized remarks about Obama not loving America. Clients were threatening to walk. Partners were complaining to the top brass (managing partner Mark Evans took over leadership for Pat Oxford in 2008). "You've got to do something about this guy, he's gone totally off the reservation," said the former partner. "He said 'Yeah, I've started getting emails, we know.'"

On January 19, 2016, Giuliani announced that he was leaving his own company to go to work for the giant law firm Greenberg Traurig. Notably, he told Bloomberg Law that Greenberg's global reach was the deciding factor, citing its forty offices "in parts of the world where I spend a lot of time."

The collapse of his partnership with Bracewell was another destabilizing event in a tumultuous period. But he was about to find his new calling. Three weeks after he left Bracewell & Giuliani, Donald Trump won the New Hampshire primary.

In retrospect, his decision to align with Trump seemed obvious, but it took months before he warmed to the idea. He doubted Trump could beat Hillary Clinton in the fall. And he had little faith in Trump's campaign; the candidate was undisciplined, impulsive, and uninformed, and his motley organization seemed held together with chewing gum and Scotch tape. The whole endeavor seemed improvised. The candidate's extreme nativism was also way out of sync with Giuliani's more moderate politics.

But Trump was offering him a way back to center stage. The candidate had virtually no experience in electoral politics, scant knowledge of the issues, and virtually no mainstream Republican support. The void Giuliani could fill was vast—Trump badly needed help on both the politics and policy sides, and was in need of a confidant, someone of equal stature, someone he respected.

It was hardly the first time in Giuliani's life that fate placed a temptation before him and forced him to choose. But no decision in his career was as pivotal as the one he faced in the spring of 2016, when he was offered the opportunity to enter into an embrace with perhaps the least moral presidential nominee in modern times.

Part of the equation, perhaps the one that hurt the most, was that working for Trump would reverse their decades-long power dynamic, in which Giuliani as mayor was king and Trump a supplicant. Trump's fame was almost equal to Giuliani's, but not his stature, and not his influence. One was a reality show star, the other a former leader of millions, and a hero to hundreds of millions more. But it was Trump's ring that had to be kissed now. Giuliani had all but run out of juice; his last chance at relevance was to become a courtier to the host of *The Apprentice*.

Many of Giuliani's advisors were appalled at the idea. "We begged him not to do it," said one. But for a man who judged his worth in cable news appearances and speaking invitations, he didn't have much of a choice. There were not many presidential candidates calling him late at night and asking him to endorse them, and the one candidate who was doing so was hurtling toward the nomination like a comet.

On April 19, 2016, the morning of the New York primary, Giuliani took his place on an oversized white chair on the set of CNN's *New Day*, and told Chris Cuomo that he intended to vote for Donald Trump.

"It doesn't make sense to me that you are going to vote for Trump but that you won't endorse him," Cuomo said.

"Okay, so I'll endorse him," Giuliani said with a shrug. "But I'm not part of the campaign."

"But what's the difference?" Cuomo asked. "That's what I don't understand. Why don't you say, 'I'm Rudy Giuliani, I mean a lot in New York politics, I endorse Donald Trump?'"

"Okay, I'm Rudy Giuliani, I mean a lot in New York politics, I endorse Donald Trump," he responded. "But I'm not part of the campaign."

The strange dance reflected his unease. When Trump claimed speciously at the end of 2015 that Muslim Americans in New Jersey celebrated on the day of the September 11 attacks, Giuliani publicly expressed skepticism, pointing to the lack of video evidence. "If it doesn't show up, it's going to make him look really bad," he told CNN. His enthusiasm seemed to wax and wane even past the Cuomo interview. He told the *Jerusalem Post* in June 2016 that voters were ready to elect Trump "if he doesn't blow it."

But the chemistry between the two men was terrific, and over time he grew more enthusiastic. They were two old lions who enjoyed schmoozing together on the campaign plane, and Trump loved how energetically Giuliani fired up crowds before his speeches. He spoke to Giuliani with a deference that virtually no other aide received, a dynamic tracing back to the 1990s. Giuliani was a role model for him back then; his raw exercise of power, his use of bombast as a weapon, his relentless attacks on his critics and the media, all made a huge impression on Trump. His style set the template for Trump's view of the presidency "more so probably than any other political figure," said Jason Miller, Trump's communications strategist in 2016 and a Giuliani campaign aide in 2008.

Trump was far more forgiving of Giuliani's flaws than was his staff, some of whom viewed him as something of a crazy uncle. Stories about his excessive drinking were rampant. Mostly, they resented his close relationship with the boss.

Giuliani may not have agreed with Trump on fundamental issues, but temperamentally and stylistically it was a good match. His enthusiasm for throwing racial grenades into the public conversation could have gotten him thrown off other Republican campaigns, but it barely registered with Trump, who was already branding Mexicans criminals and Muslims terrorists. The cultural fit allowed Rudy to be Rudy; for the rest of the spring he continued to lecture the Black community about raising children to respect the police, and labeling the Black Lives Matter movement a domestic terrorist group.

The final guardrails on his behavior fell off the day Peter Powers died, costing Giuliani his last moderating influence. The trauma of losing his boyhood friend drove him even further into the arms of the developer.

"He got into it full-bore because his life was empty at that point," said a confidant. "Peter wasn't around, and he was just broken. It was something to do."

Trump rewarded him with a prime-time speaking slot on the first night of the Republican convention in Cleveland, a huge opportunity for a fading politician. There was light competition for the slot, as Republicans were avoiding the event, fearful of being associated with a divisive candidate with a 33 percent favorability rating. Dozens of senators and governors skipped it, as did four of the five living Republican nominees (Bob Dole attended). Corporate sponsors from Motorola to Walgreens bailed. The party could barely find a celebrity willing to speak; the best-known was Scott Baio—"Chachi" from *Happy Days*, a show that went off the air thirty-two years earlier.

The campaign filled speaking slots with Trump family members; relatives of citizens killed by illegal immigrants and soldiers who'd died at Benghazi (which the GOP blamed on Hillary Clinton); and right-wing extremist personalities like David Clarke, the Milwaukee sheriff who likened Black Lives Matter to ISIS. Giuliani was one of Trump's few prestigious validators.

On July 18, Giuliani traveled to the Quicken Loans Arena in Cleveland, bypassing protesters from Black Lives Matter and other groups, and entered the drab, shopping-mall-style structure along with thousands of delegates, supporters, and members of the international media.

He was already agitated over the killing of three law enforcement officers in Baton Rouge, Louisiana, the previous day by a Black man enraged at the police shooting of another Black man. And as he sat in the Green Room, he grew angry watching a speaker, Patricia Smith, holding back tears as she blamed Hillary Clinton for the death of her son, Sean, a foreign service officer killed in the attack on the American diplomatic compound at Benghazi.

At 10 p.m., America's Mayor walked onto a massive metallic stage set lined with green neon as cheering delegates waved signs reading "Make America Safe Again." He hadn't spoken at a convention since his speech eight years earlier in St. Paul, Minnesota, at which he methodically laid out his case for John McCain. He looked markedly older at seventy-two; his hair had thinned substantially, and his cheeks were more sunken. He seemed from the outset to be in an impatient mood, growing visibly frustrated trying to hush the cheering delegates.

"I am here to speak to you about a very serious subject: how to make America safe," he began. "The vast majority of Americans today do not feel safe. They fear for their children. They fear for themselves."

His face abruptly contorted into anger. "They fear for our police officers, who are being targeted with a target on their back," he said, making a clawing gesture with his right hand.

He brought up the killings of the three officers in Baton Rouge, and he thanked police everywhere for their dedication. His face grew red as he diverted from his prepared speech. *"When they come to save your life, they don't ask if you're Black or white—they just come to save you!"* he shouted.

The crowd jumped to its feet. His fury was growing.

"We also reach out our arms with understanding and compassion to those who have lost loved ones because of police shootings, some justified, some unjustified. Those that are unjustified must be punished. Those that are justified, we must apologize to.

"It's time to make America safe again. It's time to make America one again. ONE AMERICA!"

He was in a rage. He veered even further off-script.

"WHAT HAPPENED TO, 'THERE'S NO BLACK AMERICA, THERE'S NO WHITE AMERICA, THERE IS JUST AMERICA!' WHAT HAPPENED TO IT? WHERE DID IT GO? HOW HAS IT FLOWN AWAY?"

The crowd jumped to its feet and exploded in cheers. He was unhinged, arms flying, fists clenched, and mouth wide open, revealing a bank of tobacco-stained teeth, adding to the frightening tableau.

He looked like a dictator from some banana republic, waving his arms in anger, yelling at the top of his lungs, spouting the rhetoric of persecution and revenge. His voice rose and fell, a scream, a sentence, a scream.

"I am sick and tired of the defamation of Donald Trump by the media and the Clinton campaign. I am sick and tired of it!! THIS IS A GOOD MAN!!"

It was, among other things, a full-blown sellout, in which Giuliani forfeited what remained of his stature for the approval of his patron. It was as if he were channeling Trump himself, all rage and resentment, hitting decibel levels far exceeding Trump's. According to the author Michael Wolff, Trump called Fox News CEO Roger Ailes and asked, "Is he okay?"

Giuliani moved on to foreign policy, decrying Obama's reticence to use the words "Islamic extremist terrorism."

"In the last seven months, there have been five major Islamic extremist terrorist attacks on us and our allies," he said. "We must not be afraid to define our enemy. . . .

"For the purposes of the media, I did not say all of Islam. I did not say most of Islam. I said Islamic extremist terrorism. YOU KNOW WHO YOU ARE. AND WE'RE COMING TO GET YOU!"

His bellicosity, his paranoia, were turning an audience of aging suit-and-tie Republicans into an angry mob, cheering each hot-tempered explosion.

"THERE IS NO NEXT ELECTION! THIS IS IT. THERE IS NO MORE TIME FOR US LEFT TO REVIVE OUR GREAT COUNTRY!"

He clenched his right hand into a fist, and looked furious enough to punch someone. A single word passed through his lips: "GREATNESS!"

It was less a speech than a primal scream. But he could read a room. A more traditional speech would have fallen flat before a crowd conditioned by Trump to cheer conspiratorial rants and personal attacks. Giuliani's wasn't even the most extreme of the night. Lieutenant General Michael Flynn, a conspiracist forced into retirement by the Obama administration, whipped the crowd into a frenzy over Hillary Clinton and led thousands of delegates in a rabid chant of "LOCK HER UP."

Giuliani's friends were mystified that he was willing to toss out his 9/11 halo like a piece of cheap jewelry. The speech raised eyebrows in the media and political worlds about his stability ("Is Rudy Giuliani Losing His Mind?" *Politico* asked), but his fury dovetailed perfectly with the moment. In the age of Trump, outrage became a narcotic; nothing was too extreme.

On August 21, he appeared on Fox News and spread a fabricated rumor that Hillary Clinton was seriously ill. "Go online and put down 'Hillary Clinton illness,'" he told Fox News's Shannon Bream. "Take a look at the videos for yourself."

The assertion, based on nothing but misleading internet videos by Trump supporters, received major pickup in the mainstream media. Not long after questioning Giuliani's sanity, *Politico* gave him a platform to spread his newest bit of character assassination. "Giuliani: Press Ignores Signs of Clinton's Illness," ran its headline.

It was hardly alone. "Giuliani Fuels Clinton Health Rumors Again . . . and Again," stated NBC News. "Rudy Giuliani Stokes Rumors About Clinton's Health," reported Bloomberg Television, which reran his Fox interview, played a clip of a viral video questioning her health, and convened a talk segment about it. *USA Today*, with millions of daily readers, gave space to Giuliani for an op-ed.

"Recently, Fox News' Sean Hannity and the Drudge Report have openly discussed Secretary Clinton's series of falls, concussions and blood clots," he wrote. "Other news reports have noted Clinton's trouble walking upstairs, and Clinton was even filmed many times coughing excessively at routine campaign events.

"I did not come to a conclusion on this matter; I simply asked people to draw their own conclusions."

Instead of worrying his candidate, Giuliani was delighting him— Trump was fueling rumors about Clinton's health himself. Giuliani became a regular on Trump's campaign plane, and a golfing buddy, feeding the candidate opinions, rumors, and conspiracy theories. He became a minister without portfolio in the campaign, accountable to no one but the boss.

Trump pulled him in on all sorts of discussions, from foreign policy meetings to debate preparation. Giuliani had no foreign policy experience; his qualifications were based solely on his travels around the world working with foreign clients. But Trump didn't know many policy experts, and Giuliani was always around and happy to offer an opinion.

In the fall, the campaign asked Representative Michael McCaul, the Republican chairman of the House Homeland Security Committee, to participate in prep sessions with Trump in advance of his third debate with Clinton.

McCaul knew Giuliani well. They had worked together earlier in the year to persuade Trump to drop his call for a Muslim ban in favor of proposing restrictions on immigration from certain Muslim nations. It was a successful effort; Giuliani played a moderating influence on Trump, who ceased using the phrase "Muslim Ban," despite his fondness for the term.

Now, several months later, McCaul joined Giuliani at a debate prep session attended by Michael Flynn and a handful of others McCaul had never met.

The congressman came with an urgent request of Trump. As chairman of the Homeland Security Committee, he was getting briefed on the mounting evidence that the Russian government was interfering in the election, to the benefit of Trump. "We could tell that this was one of the biggest national security train wrecks coming down the tracks," said a senior House staffer.

McCaul outlined to Trump the magnitude of the threat to national security, and urged him to condemn the Russian efforts. Without a clear signal from you the interference could intensify, he warned.

Trump waved him off. "It's all just intelligence community bullshit," he said. Giuliani and Flynn concurred. Just intelligence community B.S. from deep staters, they agreed. The conversation ended there.

McCaul was stunned, lamenting to aides that the situation was crazier than he could have imagined. The people advising the man who might be the president were in total denial about Russian interference, McCaul said.

He was also alarmed at the foreign policy advice Giuliani and Flynn were giving Trump. "It was clear that Giuliani was unqualified to be advising Trump on foreign policy, national security, and especially cyber security issues," the staffer said. "His knowledge was so outdated that it wasn't relevant."

Giuliani was the global chair of cyber security and crisis management for his new employer, Greenberg Traurig. Having founded a security firm, and counseled clients across the globe about security, there was a logic to the title. But it was debatable how expert he was on the topic.

Soon after joining Greenberg, Giuliani served as a speaker at an offsite Greenberg gathering, held at an event space at the West Side Piers in Manhattan, perched on the Hudson River.

Greenberg, a Goliath in the legal world, was one of the last remaining firms to embrace suit-and-tie culture, and Giuliani, who never took off his jacket and tie, fit right in. There was a fair degree of skepticism among the ranks about his hiring—was it just his celebrity the firm was buying?—but he was politely received.

After dropping a lot of names—Israeli prime minister Benjamin Netanyahu's name kept coming up—the former LifeLock pitchman emphasized the importance of cyber security to corporate America, and the potential for expanding Greenberg's work in the burgeoning field. The idea of exploiting a growing opportunity for new business piqued people's interest.

An attorney raised his hand. "It's fine to emphasize the importance of protecting a company's digital information from outside intruders," he said, "but businesses are increasingly relying on cloud services. What advice do you have for clients about that?"

Giuliani was famously fast on his feet, but the question caught him off guard. "He gave an answer that was so vague and bullshitty that he wasn't even quite clear that he knew, what a cloud service was," said a shareholder.

The mood of the room, the shareholder said, changed palpably, from "'maybe this guy could be useful' to 'Are you fucking kidding me?'"

But Giuliani barely got a chance to prove himself. On October 6, he agreed to take a temporary leave of absence from the firm. His time was being taken up by the Trump campaign, and his public rampages were giving the firm's executives headaches, just as happened at Bracewell & Giuliani. Greenberg maintained a large lobbying presence in Washington, and his bombast in support of Trump, who was running far behind Hillary Clinton in the polls, was causing them grief.

Giuliani would need the time he was gaining back from the firm, though, as a video of Donald Trump emerged the next day that threatened to blow up the campaign.

"Rudy has always been a loyal soldier," Jason Miller, the Trump communications aide, recalled, "who would ride to the sound of the gun and dive in and volunteer when other folks might be running for the hills."

Trump discovered the depth of his loyalty on October 7, 2016, one month before Election Day. David Fahrenthold of the *Washington Post* obtained raw footage from an *Access Hollywood* shoot of Donald Trump riding a bus in 2005 with show host Billy Bush, headed to the set of *Days of Our Lives* for a Trump cameo.

Their banter was about Trump's prowess with women, and his language was so obscene that some news organizations aired warning notices before showing it. The two men began with a discussion about an unidentified woman.

TRUMP: I moved on her, actually. You know, she was down on Palm Beach. I moved on her, and I failed. I'll admit it.

UNKNOWN: Whoa.

TRUMP: I did try and fuck her. She was married.

UNKNOWN: That's huge news.

TRUMP: No, no, Nancy. No, this was [unintelligible]—and I moved on her very heavily. In fact, I took her out furniture shopping. She wanted to get some furniture. I said, "I'll show you where they have some nice furniture." I took her out furniture— I moved on her like a bitch. But I couldn't get there. And she was married. Then all of a sudden I see her, she's now got the big phony tits and everything. She's totally changed her look.

As the bus pulled in, they spotted the actress Arianne Zucker waiting to greet them.

TRUMP: Yeah, that's her. With the gold. I better use some Tic Tacs just in case I start kissing her. You know, I'm automatically attracted to beautiful— I just start kissing them. It's like a magnet. Just kiss. I don't even wait. And when you're a star, they let you do it. You can do anything.

BUSH: Whatever you want.

TRUMP: Grab 'em by the pussy. You can do anything.

The story dropped like a bomb on the race, with Republicans high and low denouncing Trump and withdrawing their endorsements. Many urged him to drop out. The Republican National Committee halted its financial support. Senate Majority Leader Mitch McConnell called the comments "repugnant," and urged Trump to apologize. The candidate did just that, releasing a video in which he chalked up the bus conversation to "locker room banter" and adding for good measure that Bill Clinton had done worse.

The second debate was two days away, and friends were suddenly hard to find. Trump loyalists scheduled to spin on his behalf on the network Sunday shows begged out, including his campaign aide Kellyanne Conway, RNC chief Reince Priebus, and former New Jersey governor Chris Christie.

For Giuliani it was a no-brainer to volunteer to step in; his future was tied to Trump's. And the saturation television exposure, no matter how unpleasant the topic, was golden for a politician on a downward slide. The campaign gave him the green light, sending a famous adulterer to explain Trump's behavior to America.

On Sunday morning his car barreled through the deserted canyons of midtown Manhattan, bouncing from one news headquarter to another for appearances on CBS, NBC, ABC, CNN, and Fox News. Each interview was difficult, as it was hard to defend the indefensible, but he gave it his best shot, condemning Trump's comments on one hand and minimizing them on the other. Some appearances were rougher than others. Jake Tapper on CNN was appalled.

TAPPER: This tape, which was recorded in 2005, on it, we hear Donald Trump behaving in, I think it's fair to say, a vile and disgusting way. It's not just the word he uses. He's essentially voicing a casual attitude toward sexual assault. What was your response when you first heard it?

GIULIANI: Well, I think it was the response of everyone else. They're horrible remarks. They're remarks you certainly don't want to hear from anyone, much less a presidential candidate. Then, when you reflect on it, he apologized for them. . . .

TAPPER: He's talking about actions that are sexual assault. And he was 59 or 60 years old when he said it. This wasn't something that he said when he was 18 years old. He is talking about a feeling of entitlement because he's a star. He can go up to women and grab them by the vagina, and it's OK, he won't get in trouble for it. It's really offensive on just a basic human level.

GIULIANI: Yes, it is . . . and gosh almighty, you know, he who hasn't sinned throw the first stone here. . . .

TAPPER: I will gladly tell you—Mr. Mayor, I have never said that. I have never done that. I'm happy to throw a stone. . . . I have been in locker rooms. I have been a member of a fraternity. I have never heard any man ever brag about being able to maul women because they get away with it, never.

GIULIANI: . . . the fact is that men at times talk like that, not all men, but men do.

TAPPER: You have talked like that?

GIULIANI: He was wrong for doing it. I am not justifying it. I believe it's wrong. I know he believes it's wrong.

When the dizzying round of appearances was over with he headed to LaGuardia Airport, where Trump and forty staffers were sitting on a tarmac waiting for him in a private Boeing 757-200. Staffers slapped him high-fives in the aisle for his yeoman efforts in defense of the candidate. Triumphantly, he sat down in a seat across from Trump.

"Man, Rudy, you sucked," the candidate said. "You were weak. Low-energy."

Giuliani sat in silence, humiliated.

He was not finished inserting himself into the action, however. On an October 25 appearance on *Fox & Friends*, he made a curious prediction.

"We got a couple of surprises left," he said, sitting with his three hosts on a beige couch. "Maybe in a little bit of a different way and you'll see and I think it will be enormously effective. And I do think that all of these revelations about Hillary Clinton finally are beginning to have an impact."

The next day he was back on the channel. "We've got a bunch of things up our sleeves that should turn this around," he said with a mischievous smile. His hostess looked puzzled.

Two days later, FBI chief James Comey stunned the nation with an announcement that the FBI was reopening its investigation into Hillary Clinton's private email server, an inquiry that had consumed her campaign until he closed it with fanfare in July. In a letter to Congress, he revealed that the agency had discovered tens of thousands of emails on a laptop belonging to former Congressman Anthony Weiner, whose wife, Huma Abedin, was Clinton's closest aide.

Comey's decision to go public with the probe eleven days before Election Day was highly unusual, and defied long-standing Justice Department guidelines prohibiting interference in elections. Several agency officials believed he released the information out of fear that the news was going to leak out. Comey was particularly concerned about the behavior of Rudy Giuliani.

Giuliani was having fun teasing it out. After playing cute on national television about his big secret, he went on a conservative radio program, hosted by Lars Larson, and bragged about his sources inside the FBI.

"The other rumor that I get is that there's a kind of revolution going on inside the F.B.I. about the original conclusion being completely unjustified, and almost a slap in the face of the F.B.I.'s integrity," he said about the Clinton investigation. "I know that from former agents. I know that even from a few active agents who obviously don't want to identify themselves."

Comey was so concerned that he ordered an internal investigation into whether Giuliani learned about the probe from his sources at the FBI's New York field office.

Comey denied that Giuliani's remarks forced his hand into revealing the reopened investigation, which blew up the election. As for Giuliani, he gave wildly different accounts of when and from whom he learned about the probe.

Two days before Election Day, Comey announced that nothing valuable was found on the laptop; the whole exercise had been for naught. Ordinarily it would have been good news for a candidate, but in this case it brought a Clinton scandal to the forefront of the race.

On Election Day, Trump pulled a historic upset over Clinton. He declared victory at the New York Hilton, in the same room in which Rudy Giuliani celebrated his win over David Dinkins twenty-three years earlier. In his speech, Trump singled out his friend. "I want to give a special thanks to our former mayor, Rudy Giuliani," he said to cheers. "Rudy never changes."

That night, Giuliani, buoyant from his role in the victory, stayed up celebrating with Trump and his family until nearly daybreak. Rudy and Judith were the only people to join the Trump family back at the apartment.

The day after the election he and Tony Carbonetti went for a smoke at the Grand Havana Room and had a good laugh over the improbable turn of events.

"What do you have to say now?" Giuliani asked his political advisor, who'd been skeptical of Trump's chances of winning.

"I got nothing to say," Carbonetti replied.

"You've got nothing to say? You've been giving me shit about this for months."

"I've planned for this day for the last six months," Carbonetti said. "I was going to sit here and tell you, 'All right, we've got to fix your image, rebuild it, but we can do it.' But this? I was not prepared for. I have absolutely nothing to say."

Giuliani deserved credit for his long journey back to relevance; it was a testament to his exquisite survival skills, his uncanny instinct for capturing people's attention, and his willingness to compromise his values. The downside to his comeback was that it was completely tied to a single, mercurial man, who was about to be sworn in as president of the United States. His efforts to prove himself to Trump were just beginning.

CHAPTER 13

Washington

On election night in 2016, John Bolton, the owlish former United Nations ambassador, walked into Rupert Murdoch's News Corp building on Sixth Avenue in midtown Manhattan. A Fox News contributor, he made his way to the Green Room of its brand-new, 3,700-square-foot, $30 million studio, and was assaulted by a visual cacophony of swirling lights, digital information boards, jumbo television screens, and high-intensity klieg lights. The place was glowing red, white, and blue.

Dozens of monitors, and a massive, flying-saucer-like "digital chandelier" were flashing election returns, which were expected to culminate in a win for Hillary Clinton.

Bolton was scheduled to sit on set at approximately 10 p.m.—pundits were certain she'd be declared the winner by then—to discuss the foreign affairs challenges she would inherit from Barack Obama. Instead, hours came and went as the contest grew unexpectedly close. Bolton killed time schmoozing with anchors and analysts, and kept himself caffeinated as the country awaited returns from pivotal states.

Deep into the morning hours, Karl Rove, the Republican strategist, was on set reminiscing about George W. Bush's victory in 2000 when a wild cheer erupted from the street outside the studio, causing him to lose his train of thought. Things grew quiet for a moment as Brett Baier, the anchor, held a brief conversation with someone speaking into his ear.

"We are going to make this decision now," he said. "The Fox News decision desk has called Pennsylvania for Donald Trump. This means that Donald Trump will be the 45th president of the United States, winning the most unreal, surreal election we have ever seen."

The station played a drumroll. The news ticker on the digital chandelier, glowing silver and red, flashed "DONALD TRUMP WINS PRESIDENCY."

"I just can't believe it," said Chris Wallace, the veteran anchor. "It just is stunning to me that he has won the presidency."

The coverage swung to Trump's victory speech, a surprisingly low-key affair filled with thank-yous, and then, finally, to John Bolton in the studio, answering questions about foreign policy at 3 a.m.

"I think reality is going to intrude very quickly," he predicted in his professorial monotone, skipping straight to the gloom, predicting that Trump could face crises from China to Russia in his first three months.

Before he'd gone on set, Bolton bumped into Wallace, who shook his hand. "Congratulations, Mr. Secretary," he said.

The ambassador was appreciative that Wallace thought he'd landed the secretary of state position, but, ever the realist, he didn't allow himself a moment to savor the possibility. There had been advance speculation about who the frontrunners would be if Trump pulled off an upset, "starting with Newt Gingrich, proceeding to Rudy Giuliani, then Mitt Romney, and then back to Rudy," he recalled.

Bolton could run rings around Giuliani when it came to foreign policy—his experience in the field stretched back decades, where Giuliani had none at all—but he knew that Trump owed Giuliani for his unswerving loyalty during a brutal campaign, and Giuliani was making no secret of his interest in the job.

The dynamic between the two reminded Bolton of an old Lyndon Johnson story. "I want loyalty," the former president said of a prospective hire. "I want him to kiss my ass in Macy's window at high noon and tell me it smells like roses."

"Who knew Trump read so much history?" Bolton thought.

Giuliani was on the airwaves as well that night. While Bolton was lingering in the Fox Green Room, he was being berated by Chris Matthews on MSNBC.

"Why did your candidate, and you yourself, refer to Hillary Clinton as sick and almost dying most of the campaign, and that she ought to be in prison?" Matthews asked indignantly. "You can't claim to run a clean campaign if you call your opponent on death's door and belonging behind bars."

"That's a perfectly legitimate conclusion," Giuliani replied, citing FBI statements about her email server, and alleging that she looked like she was slurring her words on the campaign trail.

With the election all but over, the host seemed to be venting months of pent-up anger.

"You're a smart guy," Matthews said. "You're a smart politician. I've known you forever. I didn't think there was anything wrong with you until this campaign."

Giuliani was taken aback. "I am proud of the way I conducted myself," he said.

All the conversation about Giuliani's stability—on television, on the campaign plane, in whispers from just about every corner of his universe—was giving Donald Trump pause about awarding him the most prestigious cabinet position. Like so many others, he worried that Giuliani had lost a step.

Certain assurances had already been made, however. Giuliani maintained privately that the president had promised him the secretary of state job numerous times during the campaign, and Tony Carbonetti, his political advisor, heard the same from Trump's team.

"People who were on the plane said to me, not once, not twice, but five times, that Trump told him 'If I win you can be secretary of state,'" he said.

But that was campaign talk, and now that things had gotten real Trump wasn't so sure anymore. In addition to his growing doubts about Giuliani's acuity, a campaign vetting team found so many client conflicts that it took twenty-five pages to list them. The media was detailing his work for the government of Qatar, MEK, Purdue Pharma, and a slew of sketchy foreign leaders. Senator Rand Paul was warning that he was concerned about Giuliani's "worrisome" ties to foreign governments.

Trump sounded him out about other positions: attorney general, homeland security secretary, even director of National Intelligence. But Giuliani wanted the moon.

The competition had their own drawbacks. Bolton was as right-wing on international affairs as they came—he called for bombing Iran—and Trump had trouble picturing him in the role. He was on the short side, with the look of a craggy intellectual, with wire-frame glasses and a bright, white, bushy mustache that the president-elect despised. Those things mattered to the president-elect.

Mitt Romney, the former Republican presidential candidate, was tall, handsome, and more corporate than either Giuliani or Bolton—right out of "central casting," Trump said—but was a blistering critic during the campaign, savaging Trump as a "phony" and a "fraud." That should have been a deal-breaker, but Trump remained intrigued.

And so it became a free-for-all.

Like everything in Trump's universe, the competition for cabinet jobs was staged for maximum entertainment value. Contestants were paraded before cameras, brought in for auditions, and pitted against one another. It was a strange vetting process, designed partly to test how the candidates played in public, and partly to feed the sadistic whims of the boss.

For the next two months, the lobby of Trump Tower became a carnival, with a steady stream of political celebrities entering through the front door and running the gauntlet of reporters and photographers camped out in the lobby like paparazzi at a red-carpet event. The walk from the Fifth Avenue entrance to the golden elevator bank was part business, part performance art. Reporters took notes of comings and goings—Rick Perry saying hello, Mike Huckabee waving goodbye—while others started showing up just for kicks, from Michael Moore to Kanye West to the Times Square Naked Cowboy.

Giuliani was named a vice chairman of the transition team, which gave him almost unlimited run of the place; unlike the more buttoned-up Republicans, he was happy to stop for interviews.

The contest for State picked up steam over the Thanksgiving holiday. Forever casting about for one more opinion, Trump polled his guests at Mar-a-Lago for their preferences among Giuliani, Bolton, and Romney. The former New York mayor was the favorite.

Over the weekend Giuliani made a dicey public play for the job in the pages of the *Wall Street Journal*. "I probably have traveled in the last 13 years as much as Hillary did in the years she was secretary of state," he told the paper. "My knowledge of foreign policy is as good, or better, than anybody they're talking to."

Without any government foreign policy experience to cite, he bragged about the number of countries he'd visited on business since leaving the mayoralty (eighty) and total foreign trips (150). "I've been to England eight times, Japan six times, France five times, China three times—once with Bill Clinton, by the way," he told the paper. "You can't say I don't know the world."

The campaigning backfired; Trump was angered by his public pressure. He had his aides reach out to Romney.

On November 29, the president-elect, Romney, and Reince Priebus, Trump's incoming chief of staff, met for dinner at Jean-Georges, the three-Michelin-star restaurant at the Trump International Hotel off Columbus Circle. Photographers snapped photos of the three dining on frogs' legs and scallops. It was a vintage Trump production, the enemy supplicating himself on his turf. "He loves it when the losers have to come and beg," said Jason Miller.

Soon afterward, he gathered his closest advisors together in his office overlooking Central Park on the 26th floor of Trump Tower. Virtually every member of his senior team was present: his daughter Ivanka Trump and her husband, Jared Kushner, Priebus, Kellyanne Conway, Steve Bannon, Hope Hicks, Dan Scavino. He asked for their votes on the secretary of state position, boiling the choices down to Romney and Giuliani. "Let's go around the room," he said. "Go."

They chimed in one by one.

"Rudy . . ."

"Rudy . . ."

"Rudy . . ."

And so it went. The majority voted for Giuliani.

"Wow, you guys are hard-core on Rudy," Trump said.

He thanked the team without rendering a verdict. And in fact he remained ambivalent. He had aides bring in Bolton.

The ambassador arrived at his Trump Tower office suite on December 2, just in time to see Robert Gates, the former defense secretary, exiting Trump's office, where the president-elect was sitting with Priebus and Bannon. Though curious, Bolton focused on the state of the world in the meeting, detailing challenges country by country. According to Bolton, Trump's two advisors told him afterward that the meeting had gone well, and that Trump "had never heard anything like that before."

Only later did he learn what Gates spoke to Trump about. Sensing that the president-elect was unsatisfied with his choices for State, Gates threw out the name of a wild-card candidate. ExxonMobil chief executive Rex Tillerson was a friend of his, and served on the board of the Boy Scouts of America, which Gates ran. He was silver-haired and distinguished, the epitome of an American corporate titan, and had extensive dealings with Vladimir Putin as part of his company's work in Russia.

Trump was intrigued. He interviewed Tillerson on December 6, and the candidacies of Bolton, Giuliani, and Romney died within a week.

Bolton suffered the indignity of learning in the *Washington Post* a year later why his candidacy sank. "Donald was not going to like that mustache," a Trump advisor told the paper.

Giuliani's consolation prize was an appointment as cyber security advisor to the president, mirroring his title at Greenberg Traurig. It might have been a stretch for a man who had trouble operating his cell phone, but it gave him a formal role in the administration, which was hugely helpful as he returned to the lucrative business of consulting for foreign governments and companies.

In March, he learned that Carbonetti was in Washington on business, and offered to let him tag along to a meeting with the president. Carbonetti knew Trump from the mayoral days, and was happy to accept.

When they entered the Oval Office, the president recognized Carbonetti right away, and immediately grew defensive. "You know it's not my fault, right?" he told him, bringing up the search process unprompted. "I offered him three different jobs!"

Giuliani's comeback wasn't yet fully realized, but Trump's victory was a turning point for him, as pivotal to his life as 9/11. Once again, he benefited from an upheaval not of his making, and leveraged it for enormous political and financial gain. The difference was that when he returned to the limelight, no one would confuse him for a saint.

Of all the international miscreants that Giuliani took on as clients—and there were many—none was as intriguing as Reza Zarrab, a Turkish-Iranian gold trader arrested by U.S. authorities in 2016 on money-laundering charges.

Young, clever, and cocky—he was married to a Turkish pop superstar—he built an improbable empire exchanging gold for oil and natural gas from Iran, helping to prop up the Iranian rial, its currency, when U.S. sanctions were strangling its economy. Exchanging Iran's products for gold instead of cash was a way of getting around the sanctions. At his business's height he boasted he was shipping a metric ton of gold each day, worth billions of dollars.

The epic scale of the enterprise made Zarrab staggeringly rich; he owned seven yachts, twenty houses, and a private plane. He was also lining the pockets of Turkish government and banking officials; he testified that he paid the Turkish minister of the economy more than $50 million, and the CEO of Turkey's Halkbank was found to have shoeboxes in his home stuffed with over $4 million in cash.

Such was Zarrab's fortune that upon his arrest in Miami—he claimed he was there to visit Disney World—he hired no fewer than sixteen attorneys from six different American law firms to get him out of trouble. They included Paul Clement, a former U.S. solicitor general, Benjamin Brafman, one of New York's most famous defense attorneys, and multiple former prosecutors.

The dream team turned out to be a bust, failing to get his case thrown out, or even change his bail arrangement. In March 2017, he changed course, bringing in an attorney to move his case from the courtroom to the White House.

It would be hard to imagine a more inspired decision than to hire Rudy Giuliani, or so it seemed. To call him a power lawyer at the time would be an understatement. At best, Washington's most connected attorneys could get their calls returned by a senior member of the Justice Department, or, perhaps, on a lucky day, a White House official. But Giuliani had an open invitation to the Oval Office.

Zarrab's arrest proved enormously troublesome to Turkey's autocratic president, Recep Tayyip Erdoğan, who had reason to worry that the gold trader would spill information about him to prosecutors to avoid prison.

Giuliani teamed with another high-powered Washington hand, Michael Mukasey, a former U.S. attorney general, and a close friend and colleague of his from his Justice Department days. Soon after their hiring by Zarrab in early 2017, the two jetted off to Turkey to meet with Erdoğan. In an affidavit Mukasey said they were pursuing a "state-to-state resolution in this case."

Barack Obama was president at the time of Zarrab's arrest, and Erdoğan was considered a thug by the administration. By the time Giuliani was brought on board America had a new president with a soft spot for despots.

In the fall, Secretary of State Rex Tillerson was called to join Trump for a meeting in the Oval Office. When he entered the room, he was surprised to see Giuliani and Mukasey sitting with the president.

"Guys, give Rex your pitch," Trump said.

At that, the two lawyers laid out a potential prisoner swap with Turkey, suggesting Zarrab be exchanged for an American pastor named Andrew Brunson, who was being held in a Turkish prison. Erdoğan had himself suggested other similar prison swap deals involving Brunson. Mukasey argued that as secretary of state, Tillerson had the power to spring Zarrab from prison and have him sent back to Turkey.

Tillerson was shocked. Trump didn't seem to understand, or care, that lawyers for an alleged money launderer were in the Oval Office urging the president of the United States to intervene in a criminal matter. Tillerson called the proposition highly inappropriate.

Instead of shutting down the matter, Trump sent the three men away with orders to iron out their differences. But Tillerson refused to meet with Giuliani about it again. Justice Department officials also closed the door on him, uneasy that he was urging officials from the president on down to take action to benefit a foreign leader without registering as a lobbyist.

Unable to win his release in court or in Washington, Zarrab pleaded guilty, turned state's witness in a case against a Turkish bank official, and testified that Erdoğan approved of the entire scheme.

Giuliani was characteristically defiant in defending his role in the case. "It happened to be a good trade," he told the *New York Times*, referring to the prisoner swap. "I expected to be a hero, like in a Tom Hanks movie."

Zarrab was just one of Giuliani's curious far-flung clients. His globetrotting took him back to Ukraine multiple times; in addition to delivering speeches, he signed on as a consultant to the city of Kharkiv, lending expertise to its leaders' crime-fighting efforts, and making new contacts with dark figures who would cause America untold grief in the following years.

Even at seventy-three, he was almost constitutionally unable to stay home for any length of time. The same drive that sent him racing to fires and homicides as mayor had him hopping frenetically from one foreign capital to another two decades later.

His need for constant stimulation wasn't limited to his professional life. On those weekends he was home in 2017 he and Judith were in perpetual motion in the Hamptons. There were political fundraisers to attend, dinner parties to throw, and charity fundraisers to be seen at; in less than forty-eight hours on one July weekend they attended the Rita Hayworth Alzheimer's Gala, the Watermill Center's Summer Benefit & Auction, and the annual Super Saturday event at Nova's Ark Project in Water Mill.

Every event gave him an opportunity to mix with New York's upper class, often with a glass of red wine or a tumbler of scotch in his hand. Rumors of his drinking were spreading from the Hamptons to the White House.

On August 15, he was rushed to a hospital for emergency surgery after taking a fall at a dinner party he and Judith hosted for friends at their Water Mill home. "I was a catcher from a very young age, and I have suffered with 'catcher's knee' for years," he told *New York Post* gossip columnist Emily Smith. "Then my knee gave way when I was walking on Sunday.

"I tried to get up but Judith ordered me not to move," he said. "If it hadn't been for her, the injury would have been a lot worse. I now call her 'Nurse Nancy.'"

Judith also sounded upbeat. "Of course, he's already working from his hospital bed, he's got the computers going, two phones, a couple of iPads and a Kindle," she told the paper. "He's not by any means down for the count."

Their united front kept speculation to a murmur. But Judith says the story was a ruse. "He was shitfaced," she said. "He had a cigar in one hand and a scotch in the other. He went down. It was hard to watch."

His fall was caused by a combination of alcohol that compromised his balance and a knee whose muscles were dissolved by constant cortisone shots, she said. Rushed to the hospital by his security detail, he underwent surgery and stayed bedridden for a long stretch.

"He agreed that this would be the ideal time to try to get clean," she said. "So we detoxed him at the same time he got medical care."

The experience sent him into another "massive depression," she said, another in a never-ending cycle of lapses and rebounds—his sixth, by her count.

"There's only so much anybody could do," she said. "I did everything I could do. I detoxed him, I rehabbed him. I did so much, and then they would just go and give it to him again."

"They" were his circle of friends and aides, whom she believed competed for her husband's time by tempting him with nights out at the Grand Havana Room, where his drinking would start up all over again. "It was really hard watching such a great man do this, and watching the people around him for their own agendas allowing him to do it," she said. "They should go to hell for that."

One of the guests who attended the party at which Giuliani fell said that while he drank that night, Judith appeared to be drinking even more heavily. The guest said Judith stormed over to Giuliani, irate that he had fallen on a wet surface.

Giuliani has denied that he had a drinking problem. Bernie Kerik called the notion "bullshit." Tony Carbonetti, Giuliani's closest confidant, declined on one hand to discuss Giuliani's drinking habits, but on the other laid the blame for it on Nathan, whom he detested. "If you spent an extensive amount of time with that woman you'd drink a lot," he said.

Trump himself expressed concern numerous times, particularly when Giuliani appeared to nod off at meetings. "He asked me if I thought Rudy was drinking too much," said a mutual friend.

MSNBC host Joe Scarborough, whom Trump took into his confidence for a short while after his victory, later told a similar story. "Donald Trump said during the transition that Rudy Giuliani was losing it, that he was a couple of steps behind, that he was falling asleep five minutes into meetings," he said. "Everybody around Donald Trump said [Giuliani] was drinking too much."

Giuliani's convalescence from his fall caused him to call off an August trip to Ukraine. Swearing to his wife that he would rein in his drinking, his physical and mental health slowly improved. "We became really close again then," Nathan said. In search of a way to keep his mind sharp, she reached out to the local Water Mill Bridge Club, and hired an instructor to come to their house for regular card lessons.

"They were very passionate, and very loving together," said Laura O'Reilly, the instructor. "They were all 'Yes honey, no dear.'"

Gradually, Giuliani graduated from crutches and walkers to a cane and then to normalcy. He left the Hamptons soon afterward, and resumed his travels where, according to his wife, he also resumed his drinking, calling from one business trip slurring his words so badly it was hard for her to understand him.

Things fell apart in the spring of 2018. He started to see a married New Hampshire hospital executive named Maria Ryan, denying it to the press despite mounting evidence to the contrary. Judith told her confidante that she started seeing someone as well.

On April 4, 2018, she filed for divorce in Manhattan Supreme Court, making this Rudy Giuliani's third marriage to collapse.

He gave the news to the *Post*. "In these divorce situations, you cannot place blame, it is 50/50, there are problems on both sides," he told the paper.

Giuliani's friends, who to a person saw Judith as a poisonous figure who destroyed his friendships and damaged his presidential campaign, could not have been more relieved. But he loved Judith deeply, and suffered with the dissolution of their nineteen-year relationship. "When the marriage fell apart, he drank heavily," said a former aide.

Judith reflected on the breakup several years later. "I wouldn't say that alcohol ruined the marriage," she said. "I would say that he cared more about politics than about anything else in his life. . . . All he cares about, and cared about then, was just keeping it together enough to appear publicly.

"I was the victim of his ambition, and you can quote me on that," she said. "All I wanted to be was a wife."

A few weeks after the divorce filing, Donald Trump invited Giuliani to dinner at Mar-a-Lago. The president, who never cared much for Judith, had a proposition for Giuliani that would take his mind off his problems. He made him an offer that would alter the course of his presidency.

Only fifteen months in office, Trump was drowning in scandal. Special Counsel Robert Mueller was investigating alleged collusion between his campaign and the Russians in the 2016 race. The U.S. attorney in Manhattan was probing hush money payments made by his lawyer to a porn star Trump had slept with.

His attorneys, John Dowd and Ty Cobb, persuaded him to hand over his records and fully cooperate with Mueller in order to get the probe over with as quickly as possible. One year and 1.4 million records later, with no end in sight and the president increasingly ignoring their advice, they resigned.

Trump was tired of the kid-gloves approach to the investigation. "Where's my Roy Cohn?" he famously lamented to his aides, referring to the late, infamously cold-blooded attorney and former mentor.

Trump was an impossible client, despised within much of the legal establishment, and notorious for not paying his bills. None of Washington's top Republican lawyers wanted the job. Giuliani happily accepted it.

The decision to bring him on was hotly debated within the president's circle. Jay Goldberg, Trump's attorney of twenty-two years, told him it was a terrible idea. "He's going to get you into trouble," he advised him. "He doesn't know when to stop."

Giuliani's hiring was exactly what General John Kelly, his chief of staff, had feared for months. The leader of the "Axis of Adults," the elders who tried to restrain Trump's worst impulses, Kelly had spent a year trying to keep the hotheads from Trump's campaign at bay. "There would be frequent conversations at the end of the day at Kelly's office," said a senior White House official. "It would be, 'Ugh, he wants Corey Lewandowski back, he wants to call Rudy.'"

It wasn't the first time Trump tried to bring Giuliani back into the fold. Early on, he raised the idea of creating a commission on radical Islamic terrorism and placing Giuliani in charge of it. It triggered furious internal opposition from staff who feared Giuliani would turn it into an ad hoc foreign policy power center, outside of the national security apparatus. Kelly let the idea die on the vine.

But a year and a half into his presidency, Trump was getting his sea legs, and chafing under the disapproving gaze of his establishment gatekeepers. He set about dismantling the Axis of Adults one by one, and replacing them with cronies and ideologues. Tillerson was ousted and replaced by CIA director Mike Pompeo, a Tea Party conservative; Lieutenant General H. R. McMaster, his national security advisor, was forced out and replaced by Bolton. Kelly would be out by the end of the year, replaced by an acting chief of staff, Mick Mulvaney, and then Mark Meadows, a founding member of the right-wing House Freedom Caucus.

On the face of it, Giuliani was a terrible choice to serve as Trump's attorney. At seventy-three, he was far past his prime as a lawyer, having barely stepped foot in a courtroom for nearly thirty years. He was disorganized, hot-tempered, and at times befuddled. His personal life was in shambles. And he had a drinking problem.

But in the alternate universe of Trump's White House, where bombast was the guiding principle, he was the most logical choice—perhaps the only logical choice. He was unconstrained by the mannered conventions that presidential lawyers were expected to practice. He was gleefully ferocious, an attack machine perpetually set to kill. He would say anything, do anything to win. He was, in short, just like Trump.

He debuted as the newest cast member in the Trump Show April 19, walking onstage into the most blinding spotlight of his career since 9/11. It was the perfect role for him, the famed prosecutor coming to defend the beleaguered president in his most desperate hour.

With typical bravado, he suggested to reporters that he could bring closure to Mueller's probe without breaking a sweat.

"I don't know yet what's outstanding, but I don't think it's going to take more than a week or two to get a resolution," he told the *New York Post*. "They're almost there."

"I've had a long relationship with Bob Mueller," he added. "I have great respect for him. He's done a good job. . . . I'm going to ask 'What do you need to wrap it up?'"

Following his story line, the *New York Times* quoted a source as saying that he was hired to "quickly resolve" the Mueller investigation. "Mr. Giuliani . . . is coming on board as a short-timer not only to appear on television but also to see if he can use his decades-long ties with Mr. Mueller to re-establish a working relationship with the special counsel's team," the paper reported.

The stories were way off. Giuliani wasn't going away anytime soon. And he wasn't coming to patch things up with Mueller.

Aware of the Justice Department's written policy that a sitting president could not be charged with a federal crime, Giuliani decided at the outset that the threat to the president was impeachment, not imprisonment. Impeachments could be influenced by public opinion. And the public watched a lot of television. Mueller, a famously straitlaced former FBI chief, was refusing to discuss the case. Whatever Trump and Giuliani said would go unchallenged.

With Trump's blessing, his new attorney embarked upon a media blitz to shape public opinion about both the Russia investigation and the hush money case. It was a tall order, requiring strategic messaging and disciplined execution. It quickly became evident that Giuliani was neither strategic nor disciplined.

He started the tour on friendly ground, appearing as Sean Hannity's guest on Fox News on May 2.

He seemed transformed from the man the public had last seen years earlier. In his heyday, his dark, penetrating eyes and steely demeaner betrayed a serious mind, forever processing his surroundings for threats or fools. The man sitting across from Hannity this evening was physically bloated, his face large and jowly, his portly frame squeezed uncomfortably into his suit jacket. His famed purposeful look, captured for eternity in photographs of him shouting orders on the smoke-filled streets near the World Trade Center, gave way to the pompous, self-satisfied grin of an overfed businessman.

He did his thinking out loud, improvising answers to each question. Asked by Hannity about reports that Trump's daughter Ivanka might be in Mueller's crosshairs, he responded with a flippant threat. "I would get on my charger and go right into their offices with a lance," he said. Asked the same question about Jared Kushner, her husband, he replied, "I guess Jared is a fine man, you know that. But men are, you know, disposable."

He was also extraordinarily mean. While smiling and comfortable around Hannity, who rhapsodized about their long friendship and dinners together, his personal attacks on Trump's adversaries were absurdly over the top. He criticized former FBI chief James Comey, fired by Trump for opening the Russia investigation, as a "disgrace," a "pathological liar," and a "perverted man." Hillary Clinton was a "criminal." The Mueller case, he said, had become a "witch hunt," using Trump's favorite phrase.

It was the opening salvo of a campaign to discredit the investigation through character assassination. Yet the scorched-earth strategy hit a wall when the subject changed to the hush money scandal.

Four months earlier, the *Wall Street Journal* revealed that Michael Cohen, Trump's trusted fixer, had paid $130,000 to the porn star Stephanie Clifford, whose stage name was Stormy Daniels, to keep quiet about a sexual encounter she had with Trump. The payment was made in October 2016, just a month prior to the election. Trump denied knowing anything about the payment, and Cohen echoed his denial.

When Hannity brought the matter up, Giuliani dropped a bombshell. "They funneled through a law firm, and the president repaid it," he said, casually.

Hannity was confused. "But do you know the president didn't know about this? I believe that's what Michael said."

"He didn't know about the specifics of it as far as I know," Giuliani said. "But he did know about the general arrangement that Michael would take care of things like this. Like, I take care of things like this for my clients. I don't burden them with every single thing that comes along. These are busy people."

After a commercial break, Hannity gave Giuliani one last chance to walk back his remarks.

"I think we were talking about two different things there," Hannity said. "I want to make sure . . ."

"Sure," Giuliani said. "I was talking about the $130,000 payment."

"Right. . . ."

". . . That was money that was paid by his lawyer, the way I would do out of his law firm funds or whatever funds, it doesn't matter. The president reimbursed that over a period of several months."

It wasn't clear that Giuliani understood what he had just done, which was to expose his boss's repeated denials as lies; turn the controversy into screaming, front-page headlines; and expose Trump and Cohen to criminal liability.

To make matters worse, Giuliani gave an interview to *Buzz-Feed News* later that night and contradicted his own suggestion that Trump didn't know the specifics of what he was reimbursing Cohen for. He recounted that Cohen explicitly complained to Trump after the election that he had not been reimbursed for the hush money he laid out. "We'll cover your expenses out of personal funds," Giuliani quoted the president as saying.

Blindsided White House staffers scrambled frantically to put out clarifying statements, and Trump and Giuliani tried haplessly over the following days to spin the unspinnable. The president ultimately confessed to funding the hush money payments, and landed on a talking point that most people agreed upon: "He's learning the subject matter," he said of his new lawyer. "He'll get his facts straight."

"Learn before you speak," Trump said. "It's a lot easier."

But Giuliani's blunders continued to pile up like a freeway crash. His appearance with George Stephanopoulos two days later was memorable.

STEPHANOPOULOS: The other day you . . . told BuzzFeed . . . that at some point after the 2016 election, Michael Cohen had complained to some people that he hadn't been paid by Donald Trump. And so then you said Cohen met with Trump and told him . . . that we'll cover your expenses, they work out this $35,000 a month retainer after that. So the president did know about this after the campaign?

GIULIANI: Can't say that. I mean, at some point, yes but it could have been recently, it could have been a while back. Those are the facts that we're still working on. . . .

STEPHANOPOULOS: But that's what you said. You said that to BuzzFeed.

GIULIANI: But here's the—but here's the—well, yes, I mean that—that's one of the possibilities and one of the rumors. The reality is . . .

STEPHANOPOULOS: You stated it as fact.

GIULIANI: Well, maybe I did. But I—right now, I'm at the point where I'm learning, and I can only—I can't prove that. I can just say it's rumor. I can prove it's rumor, but I can't prove it's fact. . . .

To make matters worse, he acknowledged that Cohen could have paid off *other* women on Trump's behalf.

STEPHANOPOULOS: You've said this was a regular arrangement [Trump] had with Michael Cohen. So did Michael Cohen make payments to other women for the president?

GIULIANI: I have no knowledge of that, but I would think if it was necessary, yes. . . .

Then he got himself in more trouble.

STEPHANOPOULOS: Are you confident the president will not take the Fifth in this case?

GIULIANI: How can I ever be confident of that?

Just one week into his media blitz, a story line formed that the president's new lawyer had lost his marbles. "Giuliani's conduct since joining the Trump legal team has been the subject of several private conversations in recent weeks among current and former Trump advisors and attorneys involved in the Russia investigation, who have been asking one another about the lawyer's drinking and other erratic behavior," *Politico* reported.

The story cited reports of his comings and goings to D.C. cigar bars and other hangouts, and suggested that he was drinking at the Grand Havana Room prior to his interview with Sean Hannity. "It's extremely insulting," Giuliani responded. "There's no proof of any kind that I take too much alcohol." But he didn't deny it.

Four days after the Stephanopoulos interview, his relationship with Greenberg Traurig came to an abrupt end. Giuliani, a $6 million per year shareholder, claimed it was his idea to leave. But the firm's leaders made it clear they were irked by his claim that attorneys commonly made the kind of payments that Michael Cohen made to Stormy Daniels.

Giuliani said he was glad the shackles from the law firm had come off. "The last year and a half, I haven't been on television," he told the *Times*. "Frankly, I've missed it."

That was clear in every appearance he made, even as the interviews turned increasingly hostile. He may have written his epitaph on *Meet the Press* in mid-August, when he argued to Chuck Todd that Mueller was seeking to interview Trump to lure him into a "perjury trap."

> GIULIANI: And when you tell me that, "You know, he should testify because he's going to tell the truth and he shouldn't worry," well, that's silly because it's somebody's version of the truth. Not the truth. . . .
>
> TODD: Truth is truth.
>
> GIULIANI: No, it isn't truth. Truth isn't truth! . . .
>
> TODD: Truth isn't truth? Mr. Mayor, do you realize what—this is going to become a bad meme.

The drumbeat of unforced errors irritated the president, who vented to staff about Giuliani's bumbling. But such was his respect for him that no one moved to rein him in; the speculation that his days were numbered never came to pass.

Besides, there was something distinctly Trumpian about his style; off-the-cuff, error-prone, dishonest, vicious. The more Giuliani got into the swing of things the more he adopted his boss's voice. His Twitter feed was filled with baseless charges and personal attacks aimed at Mueller's team.

"Headline: MUELLER OFFICIAL DELETES 19,000 TEXTS OF TRUMP HATING AGENTS as part of DOJ's evidence destruction program," he tweeted in December. "Where's the media outrage at destroying relevant evidence."

The accusation referred to former FBI employees Peter Strzok and Lisa Page, who had been removed by Mueller for sending each other anti-Trump messages, turning them into cannon fodder for the right. Two Department of Justice Inspector General reports discredited Giuliani's charge, finding that no one had destroyed the texts, only that DOJ staff had to recover them after a software glitch.

Giuliani tried anything that would stick. He charged, falsely, that Mueller's appointment was illegal; that he was trying to "frame" the president; that his staff was comprised of "sneaky, unethical leakers" and "rabid Democrats." He called on Attorney General Jeff Sessions to appoint an independent counsel to investigate the special counsel (and proposed he name one of Giuliani's closest friends to the job).

Trump and Giuliani waged their smear campaign virtually around the clock, with Fox News hosts amplifying their charges in prime time. Mueller refused to utter a single word in response.

In February 2019, Mueller's approval, down 4 points from October, stood at 43 percent. Only 21 percent of Republicans approved of the job he was doing, which was reason enough to celebrate in a White House focused almost solely on the Republican base. Trump, with an assist from Giuliani, succeeded in positioning the inquiry as just another partisan food fight.

When Mueller released his report in April, he found systematic Russian efforts to influence the election to Trump's advantage, but couldn't establish that Trump conspired with the efforts. He remained neutral about obstruction of justice allegations.

Trump's presidency was saved. But for Giuliani, the episode was devastating to his image. A leader once admired more than the pope, with an approval rating of 77 percent in 2006, was now a figure of derision, down to a dismal 32 percent. Almost half of Americans had an unfavorable opinion of him. All the damage was self-inflicted.

Asked by Jeffrey Toobin of the *New Yorker* in September if he was worried that his work on Trump's behalf would affect his legacy, he reacted with indifference.

"I don't care about my legacy," he said. "I'll be dead."

All that seemed to matter to him was the approval of a president who operated without a moral compass. Left to his own devices, Giuliani came close to destroying Trump's presidency.

CHAPTER 14

Joyride

"I hesitate to tell this story because people think I dreamed the whole thing," Rudy Giuliani recalled in 2002, "but it is literally true that I was nearly lynched."

As he tells it, his father dressed him in a New York Yankees uniform on the streets of Brooklyn when he was a child, putting him in harm's way in a neighborhood where love of the Brooklyn Dodgers was almost a religion.

"I was five years old and playing in that field when four or five kids grabbed me, stood me up by a tree, and put a noose around my neck," he wrote in *Leadership*. "My grandmother saw it all from her window and started yelling until the kids ran away. And it was all because I was wearing my Yankee uniform."

He told the story many times over the years, as much a testament to his moral convictions as proof of his devotion to the team. "I'm a real sports fan, whose lifelong loyalties don't evaporate when expedient," he wrote.

His loyalty to the Yankees was part of his identity. He was at the stadium when Roger Maris hit his sixty-first home run; when Reggie Jackson sent three consecutive homers sailing in Game Six of the 1977 World Series; when the team won its first championship in

302

eighteen years in 1996. He wore Yankees jerseys, decorated his office with Yankees memorabilia, and wore World Series rings.

It was only fitting that he celebrated his seventy-fifth birthday at the stadium. The catered event on May 28, 2019, was held at the George Steinbrenner suite, the largest and most prestigious luxury box in the stadium. No politicians were invited—it was strictly friends, family members, and a sprinkling of celebrity pals, such as Jeanine Pirro from Fox News and Cindy Adams from the *New York Post*.

The food was simple—Italian dishes from Arthur Avenue in the Bronx, milkshakes with cookies and sprinkles—and the vibe was casual. Each guest was given a red wine bottle with Giuliani's smiling face on it, with an inscription reading *"Rudy Giuliani—devoted father, loyal friend, and passionate leader who united a city during its darkest hours."*

With Judith out of the picture, his two children, Caroline and Andrew, came to celebrate his milestone after long stretches of estrangement. People delivered sentimental toasts. "It was beautiful," said Mindy Levine, an old friend who organized the event, and whose husband, Randy Levine, was the Yankees president and a former deputy mayor. "It was emotional for those of us who had been on a long journey with Rudy. There was some hope in the air."

Giuliani gave a short, heartfelt speech, pointing with emotion to the presence of his children, who seemed close to tears, and expressing his gratitude to be surrounded by so many relatives and friends.

The crowd was filled with people who had given much of their lives to him, only to find themselves left in the wake of his unseemly journey into Donald Trump's embrace. In truth, many of them were bitter at him for ruining his brand, and thus theirs. Those who made their careers off of their association with him were now being forced to apologize for it.

He was a vilified figure in his city; fans at the stadium were now booing him. "We were desperate at the time, watching a man seemingly self-destruct," Mindy Levine said. For one night, the father figure they respected seemed to reemerge. "This was a sign of the Rudy we missed," she said. "This was a sign of life."

As the party was getting started a security officer informed her that two men had arrived insisting they'd been invited. She looked over to the entrance and saw two squat, older men looking noticeably out of their element. The officer said their names were Lev Parnas and Igor Fruman.

She approached the two and asked them who they knew at the party. "Rudy Giuliani," Parnas said.

She made her way to the guest of honor. "There are these two people here—I don't know who they are," she told Giuliani. He peered over toward the door. "Oh no, no, they should be here."

Waved in, the two meandered through the crowd like tourists, snapping pictures, and pointing out Yankees artifacts to each other. Both spoke with thick Eastern European accents; Levine asked if they were from Israel, thinking that perhaps they were associates of Prime Minister Benjamin Netanyahu, a Giuliani friend. When they shook their heads, she pressed them on where they came from. "I didn't get a straight answer," she said.

Some in the crowd snickered that they looked like Russian mobsters. Fruman seemed particularly suspicious, with dark glasses and Coke-bottle lenses; some referred to him as "Lurch," the butler from the Addams Family. He was the shyer of the two, constricted by his halting English, and overshadowed by his gregarious business partner.

"Where are they from?" Levine asked Giuliani. "I'll tell you later," he said. "You're going to love them."

But while Parnas and Fruman stuck out conspicuously, the reality was that they were the true insiders at the event. In a room supposedly made up of Giuliani's closest friends, they were the only people in the room who knew what he was up to, and how haywire things had gone.

Giuliani always craved road buddies, stretching back to the City Hall days when Cristyne Lategano and Manny Papir squeezed into the mayoral SUV with him each morning. But by 2019 almost all his acolytes had fallen away, voluntarily or banished by Judith. Only Bernie Kerik and a few members of his old City Hall security detail remained at his side. Loath to be alone, he adopted Parnas and Fruman as his new sidekicks.

The two were at once his clients, business partners, cronies. They tagged along with him like appendages, clinging to his coattails wherever he traveled, be it to the White House or the Grand Havana Room. When President George H. W. Bush died in November 2018, he brought them, uninvited, to his state funeral at the National Cathedral, mixing with a crowd that included four presidents, heads of state, and Prince Charles.

Giuliani became honorary godfather to Parnas's son, and cradled him in his arms at his bris in a Boca Raton reception hall. Parnas referred to Giuliani as "my brother" in his text messages to him. "I loved his family, and probably him," Giuliani reflected. "And his partner, Igor Fruman, I also love and care about."

The relationship among the three was forged less by love than mutual interest, though. They were on an exhilarating, globe-hopping joyride, leveraging one another's access, clout, and connections for their financial and political gain. Above all, they shared a common interest in pleasing Donald Trump.

Parnas and Fruman were misguided groupies, eagerly following their righteous leader on a fanatical, and ultimately disastrous, mission. The two would end up convicted felons, while their mentor,

America's Mayor, fed the paranoia of a president, and coaxed him into actions so reckless that they consumed the nation and threw the country's foreign affairs into chaos.

But it was fun for a while.

The story of Giuliani and the White House Ukraine scandal had its roots, like so many Giuliani debacles, in the collapse of his run for president in 2008. With Giuliani Partners in decline, and money growing tight, he embarked on a feverish hunt for clients in the Eastern European capitals of the old Soviet Union, where his 9/11 heroics still had currency. Parnas and Fruman approached him in the summer of 2018 with a business deal. By then, the two were way ahead of him in discovering the profit potential in exploiting Ukrainian political and business interests to serve Donald Trump's political needs.

The business partners were U.S. citizens living in Florida, but had deep roots in Ukraine (Parnas was born there and raised in Brooklyn; Fruman was born in Belarus, and raised in Ukraine). Parnas was a born salesman, with a taste for Ferraris and diamond jewelry, and a history of business failures and court judgments. Fruman ran an import-export business, and was in charge of a real estate group that controlled a boutique hotel in Odessa, a Ukrainian city notorious for its mob activity, and a nightclub called Mafia Rave. More recently, they were looking for capital to finance a handful of projects, including an energy business and a financial services company.

They were hard-core MAGA, attending numerous Trump rallies in 2016, and networking feverishly with members of Trump's team, hoping to be accepted into his inner sanctum. Without any background in politics or government, their tickets to enter the gates of Trump World had to be purchased.

Skilled at leveraging other people's money for their benefit, they found a deep-pocketed Russian tycoon, Andrey Muraviev, who, according to a later grand jury indictment, was seeking to win retail marijuana licenses for a fledgling cannabis company, and was happy to shower American politicians with campaign donations to make it happen. He committed over $1 million for contributions to various candidates, which were made through Parnas and Fruman.

As the duo's political contributions grew, so did their access to American elected officials, which impressed their backer into funneling yet more money to them.

"Everything is great!!" Fruman wrote in a WhatsApp message to a go-between with the investor in October 2018. "We are taking over the country!!!!" Parnas proved the point by sending a photo of himself standing between Jared Kushner and Ivanka Trump. The same month, Fruman sent them a photo of himself with Florida governor Ron DeSantis with a message "Today Florida become ours forever!!!!"

The two hit paydirt on April 30, 2018, after they committed to a $1 million contribution to a pro-Trump super PAC, landing them a group dinner with the president himself. It was a risky investment—investigators later alleged Fruman took a loan against an apartment he owned to pay for it, and then donated $325,000 in the name of his and Parnas's energy business, which had no income. But the access they purchased was priceless.

The dinner was held in a small, elegant dining room at the Trump International Hotel in D.C. It couldn't have been more intimate; there was just one long wood table, decked out in fine china and small vases with freshly cut roses. There were fewer than a dozen guests; they included Donald Trump Jr., Jack Nicklaus III, the grandson of the famed golfer, and Roy Bailey, Giuliani's Texas buddy and business partner. When Trump entered the room, they stood and applauded.

His guests laughed each time he told a joke, and applauded when he boasted about his defeat of Hillary Clinton, his plans to build a wall at the Mexican border, and the cable television ratings that he said were skyrocketing because of him. Parnas waited patiently before making his asks.

At one point, he asked Trump to loosen banking regulations for cannabis companies. A bipartisan committee "would give you such a boost in the midterm with a lot of the millennials," he argued, unpersuasively. But Trump wasn't following the argument, thinking that Parnas was talking about legalizing marijuana. "In Colorado they have more accidents," he said. "It does cause an IQ problem."

Parnas had a second, more curious, ask, which involved Ukraine.

"A lot of the European countries, they're backstabbing us basically, and dealing with Russia," he said. "That's why you're having such difficulty. I think if you take a look, the biggest problem there, I think where you need to start is, we've got to get rid of the ambassador. She's still left over from the Clinton administration."

Trump was confused. "Where? The ambassador where? Ukraine?"

"Yeah," Parnas said. "She's basically walking around telling everybody, 'Wait, he's going to get impeached. Just wait.'"

"Really?" Trump replied.

"It's incredible. . . ."

"Get rid of her," Trump said. "Get her out tomorrow. I don't care, get her out tomorrow."

The president turned to an aide. "Take her out, okay? Do it."

And with that, Parnas poisoned the president's mind against U.S. ambassador to Ukraine Marie Yovanovitch, a woman Trump had never met, nor heard of.

Trump's ascension to power brought Giuliani and the two Ukrainians together at various functions, particularly at the Trump Hotel. Like most businesspeople who first encountered Giuliani, they were both starstruck, and intrigued by his potential to turbocharge their commercial interests. His credibility, which was for sale, had enormous value to two nobodies looking to attract investors.

The three hit it off immediately. They had multiple common interests; they traveled in Republican circles, did extensive business in Ukraine, and adored Donald Trump. The value proposition was clear: Giuliani was a cash magnet for foreign capital, and had enormous political influence. Fruman and Parnas had wealthy backers who could write him a big paycheck.

One of the business projects the pair was struggling to get off the ground was an insurance product designed to protect customers from identity theft and other cyber crimes. "If this seems a bit complicated, think of the company 'LifeLock,'" a September 12, 2018, investor letter stated. "Our model is almost identical."

The venture had gone nowhere for years, until LifeLock's most famous pitchman walked into their lives.

It didn't take long for a deal to come together. Parnas and Fruman raised $500,000 from a pro-Trump Republican donor to pay Giuliani to help market their new business, unfortunately named Fraud Guarantee, including a potential share in the company. "Rudy Giuliani is willing to put his name and reputation on the line, personally helping to bring future clients to the table," the investor letter stated.

It was striking how deep Giuliani's appetite for trouble was. He was in the public eye every day, castigating the Mueller investigation on television, hurling malicious accusations against Trump's critics on Twitter, enduring ridicule on late-night television for his public behavior, and contending with an endless stream of stories questioning his stability. He was signing deals with shady Ukrainians, defending a designated terrorist group at conferences, and fighting his wife in divorce court. The pressure from any one of those challenges might have triggered serious anxiety for someone else, but Giuliani seemed to revel in the maelstrom. His only fear seemed to be that it would stop.

It was in this environment that he took a call in November 2018 from an old Justice Department colleague who connected him with a source with a startling story to tell: the Ukrainian government had interfered in the 2016 election, with Joe Biden playing a material role.

At the time of the call, Robert Mueller was investigating Russia's meddling in the election, sparked in part by intelligence findings that Moscow had hacked into the Clinton campaign's email servers, and published confidential correspondences to undermine public support for the Democrat. Russia had also waged a disinformation campaign on social media to stir up discord in the race.

According to Giuliani, the source disputed Moscow's role, and suggested instead that the real scandal was a Ukrainian effort, secretly backed by the Democrats, to frame Russia, help Clinton, and damage Trump. The assertion was provably false; intelligence agencies and an endless number of investigative journalists determined that it was Russia that set in motion the effort to sabotage the election.

For Giuliani, the Ukrainian conspiracy theory, far-fetched as it was, represented a golden opportunity to discredit Mueller's investigation, save the Trump presidency, and cripple the candidacy of a 2020 Democratic presidential frontrunner in one fell swoop. The public would need to be persuaded that the national security apparatus of the American government was lying, and that Biden was a criminal sitting on millions of dollars in bribes.

Giuliani had a new purpose—to expose the truth as he saw it—and two Ukrainian sidekicks raring to help. "They were perfect," he told a reporter several months later. "They did everything I wanted, and they never got involved in asking questions."

On December 6, 2018, he accompanied Parnas, Fruman, and Parnas's son, Aaron, to the White House Hanukkah Party. The group's black Escalades bypassed hundreds of guests waiting in line, and pulled up in front of a private entrance, where a White House aide brought Giuliani to meet the president in the Oval Office and a second directed the Parnas entourage to the party.

Parnas and his son waited for about thirty minutes. When Giuliani ended his meeting with the president, he walked in all smiles. He told Parnas and Fruman they'd had a great meeting.

They were escorted to the Red Room, a parlor room not far from where the president delivered his holiday greeting to the crowd. When he was done, Trump waded through a throng of guests and walked down the hall to visit them. *"Where's my Rudy?"* he bellowed in a big, booming voice.

Spotting his attorney with his two associates, Trump walked up to the group and shook Parnas's and Fruman's hands. "Thank you for everything you're doing," he told them. Giuliani gave his companions a big smile.

The experience only deepened the bond between Giuliani and his two acolytes, particularly Parnas. "My brother I want to thank you soooo much for the most incredible experience I was able to have my son at the White House [sic]," he wrote Giuliani the next day. "You are the best and I truly mean it from my heart."

Over the following months Giuliani kept up a running conversation with Parnas over text while the two jetted around the globe on their cloak-and-dagger mission. At times it was more like a rant.

"On tarmac for almost one hour," Giuliani texted Parnas on the evening of December 18. "I think Mueller knew I was on this plane and is delaying it so he gets me to say whatever he wants me to say. But I'm just incapable of lying to save my own skin.

"He wants me to say that 35 years ago DT didn't pay two parking tickets," he texted. "You say so what's so important? Well they may have been right in front of then [sic] Soviet embassy. I WILL NOT BE BROKEN."

"Lol," Parnas responded. "Stand strong."

"I'm no rat," Giuliani replied.

The Cold War never quite ended for Ukraine. Europe's second-largest country, which shares a border with Russia, won its independence in the collapse of the Soviet Union in 1991, only for Russia to launch an insurgency in 2014 and then a full-scale invasion to reclaim the country in 2022.

It's an ancient country, dotted with gold-domed churches dating back to the Middle Ages, and the poorest country in Europe. But losing it in 1991 was an affront to Russia's national pride—Kyiv, its capital, was known as "the mother of Russian cities" to many Russians.

After the USSR collapsed, the country became a virtual playground for American and Russian geopolitical games. Its leaders were notoriously corrupt, their allegiances for sale to the highest bidder, and an atmosphere of intrigue permeated the government.

It was a perfect environment for an American conspiracist on a secret mission in 2018. It was hard to know whom to trust, but Giuliani set about granting audiences to anyone claiming to have dirt on Donald Trump's enemies, real or imagined. There were plenty of takers.

Parnas and Fruman connected him to elected officials and law enforcement figures who were happy to meet America's Mayor and gain favor with his client. The most valuable new friends were the former and current prosecutors general.

The equivalent of the U.S. attorney general, the holder of the position was expected to be the country's chief corruption fighter, targeting the rampant criminality that enabled Russia to manipulate the country's economy.

But even the corruption fighters were corrupt in Ukraine; the Obama administration and its European allies believed that Viktor Shokin, the prosecutor general from 2015 to 2016, was turning a blind eye to government malfeasance. In December 2015, then–Vice President Biden paid a trip to the country and threatened to block $1 billion in loan guarantees if Shokin wasn't fired. Left with no choice, Ukraine's president acceded to his wishes.

Parnas and Fruman set up an introductory call in December 2018 and then a longer Skype call between Shokin and Giuliani on January 23, 2019.

Shokin related a harrowing tale of American corruption. Biden hadn't forced him out because he was looking the other way on criminal activity, he alleged. To the contrary, the vice president had him removed because Biden was protecting his family's interests.

The principal protagonist in his story was Biden's son Hunter. In 2014, he was named to the board of the Ukrainian energy giant Burisma Holdings, a sinecure arranged by a business partner after Hunter was discharged from the Navy Reserve for testing positive for cocaine.

Burisma was under investigation for money laundering when Hunter joined its board, and the company likely brought him on with a host of other high-profile members, including a former Polish president, to whitewash its reputation. Hunter's life was in turmoil, and he turned a blind eye to Burisma's problems, which would haunt his father for years.

Shokin alleged that Burisma showered Hunter with millions, and that his father was protecting Hunter's interests by working to keep the prosecutor general's office from cracking down on corruption at the company. He said that Joe Biden had him fired before he could crack the case.

It was all music to Giuliani's ears, as Shokin undoubtedly knew it would be, but it was a lie. The Burisma investigation was dormant when Shokin was prosecutor general, one of the reasons he was fired. Biden was just one of many world leaders calling for his head; the International Monetary Fund, the European Union, and other European governments were pressuring Ukraine to fire him as well. And it was unclear how much Hunter was paid.

From Giuliani's standpoint, the allegations were a gift; where there were discrepancies he would fill in the blanks with speculation.

Things were picking up steam. A few days after the Skype call, Fruman arranged for Shokin's successor as prosecutor general, Yuriy Lutsenko, to fly to New York to meet with Giuliani. There was little need for arm-twisting; Lutsenko was as eager to meet with Giuliani as his host was to see him.

Lutsenko was a complicated figure, charismatic and so popular at points that he was considered a presidential contender. He'd gone to jail for helping to lead the pro-West Orange Revolution in 2004, and emerged a hero for it. But questions about his integrity were mounting. Marie Yovanovitch, the no-nonsense American ambassador to Ukraine, harbored doubts about his intention to curb corruption.

He was eager to gain favor with the Trump administration to ensure his political survival, hoping to persuade officials to fire Yovanovitch, as no one had followed through on the president's order to remove her after speaking with Parnas. Schmoozing up Giuliani was a major first step in his mission. And so he came to New York bearing gifts.

Over three days in late January, Lutsenko, Giuliani, Parnas, Fruman, and three others met around a table in a glass conference room decorated with New York Yankees memorabilia, snacking on bagels as they attempted to put together a case to smear Biden and Ambassador Yovanovitch.

Giuliani sat at the head of the table, while Lutsenko behaved "like a subordinate, trying to get a job," one of the Ukrainian participants recalled. The president's lawyer came off as a "smug, arrogant man," the visitor said. "A tank."

Giuliani had come to the meeting eager to prove that Burisma bribed the vice president through extravagant payoffs to his son in exchange for his help forcing out Shokin. Lutsenko was eager to please him, but his evidence was specious at best. He produced Latvian bank records that, he claimed, showed that a company owned by Hunter Biden and his business partner was paid $1 million by Burisma to lobby the vice president. The material was inconclusive, however.

Giuliani showed Lutsenko a video of Joe Biden bragging at the

Council on Foreign Relations that he'd forced Ukraine to fire Shokin in a matter of hours during his trip.

"Can you initiate proceedings against him on these grounds?" Giuliani asked the prosecutor.

Doubtful, he said.

Have you heard about the ambassador saying anything bad about Trump? he asked. Has she said that he'll be impeached?

Lutsenko and Yovanovitch were not on speaking terms, so he couldn't help on that front. But he claimed that he had evidence that the U.S. embassy was collaborating with another Ukrainian investigative agency, a bitter rival of his, and together they were operating the embassy as a Hillary Clinton "campaign headquarters." It was transparently manipulative to link the rival agency to Clinton, but Giuliani swallowed it.

"Can this be a reason for an investigation?" he asked.

Unfortunately, there was nothing illegal about it, Lutsenko said. "There is no such [law] as 'interference in the American elections,'" he told him.

And so it went for three days, Giuliani fishing for a pretext for Ukraine to announce an investigation that could end the Mueller inquiry and take down Biden.

Lutsenko's advice was to get the American government to open up an investigation of its own, and conduct it jointly with his office. It was a huge lift; William Barr, the incoming attorney general, would have to make that explosive decision if he were so inclined.

As it happened, a meeting with the U.S. attorney general was exactly what Lutsenko wanted. He was seeking U.S. cooperation on another investigation he had in mind, pursuing an American financial firm for allegedly laundering $7 billion in Ukrainian assets. There was also the matter of firing the ambassador who was making his life miserable. "We'll try to organize your meeting with the next attorney general, and you'll discuss all these topics," he said Giuliani promised him.

With the two dangling prizes in front of the other—a Ukrainian investigation for Giuliani, a meeting with Barr for Lutsenko—they agreed to continue to work together going forward. He and Lutsenko would reconvene in a Warsaw cigar bar just a few weeks later.

It left Giuliani deeply frustrated. On March 12, six weeks after their meeting in New York, he confided to Parnas that he was at a loss to prove his conspiracy theory.

"I've got nothing," he texted him. "The anti-corruption prosecutor made some very weak comments that are equivocal at best. And not consistent with the facts. Story would get blown up. Don't want to lead with my weakest hand.

"I need Poroshenko and the AG on the record about the ambassador and Biden," he wrote, referring to the former Ukrainian president, Petro Poroshenko, and Lutsenko. "Can u make that happen? Just starting to get cooperation from former AG Shokin. So we are moving in good direction."

There was a deep self-interest to his efforts—Lutsenko came close to hiring Giuliani as his attorney for a six-figure fee. Contracts were drawn up, only for Giuliani to back out at the last minute. "Originally, I thought I would do it," he later told the *New York Times*. "And then when I thought it over, I thought it would look bad."

It was an understatement. He had always lived dangerously, but this time he was playing with fire. People working to influence the American government on behalf of foreign countries were required by law to register as foreign agents. Giuliani claimed that he was acting as the president's attorney, not as a lobbyist. But it was arguable that he was breaking the law. Paul Manafort, Trump's 2016 campaign manager, was sitting in a Pennsylvania prison for, among other convictions, representing a Ukrainian president without registering as a foreign lobbyist.

Giuliani, Parnas, and Fruman spent much of their spring months playing spy games, traveling to far-flung countries for furtive meetings with a list of dubious characters; there seemed to be an unlimited travel and expense budget that someone was bankrolling. They were working outside of the purview of the United States government, landing meetings with foreign leaders and pressing them for action without the slightest input from the State Department.

There was no adult supervision to their adventures. Giuliani was using his position as the president's attorney to open doors in foreign capitals, meet with high-ranking government officials, conduct his detective work, and sometimes tend to client business. The sharp instincts for strategy that made him the most celebrated prosecutor of the 1980s had decayed into a rabid impulsiveness. He had turned the effort to destroy Biden into a moral crusade.

With Giuliani's cooperation, John Solomon, a friendly journalist at *The Hill*, wrote a series of conspiracy-filled articles about Yovanovitch and the Bidens in the spring, and even taped an interview with Lutsenko. The coverage came and went.

Lutsenko was crestfallen. "I thought that, after this interview, they would immediately open the Burisma case and I would receive the possibility, the opportunity, to see Attorney General Barr, and then to start with my seven-billion-dollar case," he told the *New Yorker*. Giuliani was similarly disappointed. "I figured the best way to do this now was to let them pick up on it, instead of my trying to force it on anybody," he said.

Trump was growing antsy. When he wasn't summoning Giuliani to the Oval Office he was calling his cell phone throughout the day. Giuliani had gotten his hopes up about Burisma and the 2016 election interference, and the president was obsessed with reports from the right-wing fringes that Clinton's email server was hidden away someplace in Ukraine. Giuliani was stoking his expectations.

Word was spreading in the West Wing that Giuliani had run

amok. John Bolton, Trump's national security advisor, sat in Oval Office meetings listening to Giuliani outline the Biden scandals, and was confounded by his "fantasies."

"They always seemed intermingled and confused," he recalled. "Even after they became public, I could barely separate the strands of the multiple conspiracy theories at work.... This whole thing was like a big bowl of spaghetti."

His opinion was widely shared by aides and cabinet members, but Trump was obsessed with Giuliani's theories. On a March 21 call with Bolton, the president complained that Ambassador Yovanovitch was "bad-mouthing us like crazy," and "saying some crazy shit about me and about you." Giuliani was egging him on, one conspiracist to another. In a call a few days later, Trump brought up Lev Parnas's allegation that she was predicting his impeachment. He once again ordered the diplomat fired, an order that aides continued to ignore.

There were no volunteers among the president's advisors to try to talk him out of relying on Giuliani's advice. "We almost certainly would have failed, and perhaps have also created one or more vacancies among Trump's senior advisors," Bolton said.

That left them to commiserate with one another. Bolton told Fiona Hill, a National Security Council official, that Giuliani was a "human hand grenade who is going to blow everybody up."

For all the noise he was creating, Giuliani was barely getting anywhere in his efforts. The Ukrainian government was resisting his pressure to announce an investigation into Biden, and his strongest ally, Lutsenko, was now giving him little more than lip service. And on April 21, the prosecutor general's career prospects collapsed, when Petro Poroshenko lost the presidency in an upset to Volodymyr Zelensky, a popular politician, former comedian, and no fan of Lutsenko's.

Trump called Zelensky that day to congratulate him, and the new president invited him to the inauguration, which would grant his regime enormous prestige. Trump said he would "look at the date."

Two days later, Trump summoned Bolton and acting chief of staff Mick Mulvaney to the Oval Office and demanded—yet again—that Yovanovitch be fired. Giuliani was on speakerphone, feeding him "third or fourth-degree hearsay," according to Bolton.

"He fired her again," Giuliani texted Parnas afterward.

"I pray that it happens this time," Parnas replied.

The boom fell on Yovanovitch the next day; she was ordered to relinquish the post on May 20, the day of Zelensky's inauguration.

Giuliani took a victory lap in a May 3 text to Parnas: "Boy I'm so powerful I can intimidate the entire Ukrainian government," he wrote. "Please don't tell anyone I can't get the crooked ambassador fired or I did three times and she's still there." But she was on her way out the door.

He felt no remorse. "I believed that I needed Yovanovitch out of the way," he later told the *New Yorker*. "She was going to make the investigations difficult for everybody."

With a Ukrainian investigation into Biden eluding Trump and him, Giuliani decided to take his case to the *New York Times*. He revealed in a May 9 interview that he would be traveling to Ukraine the following week to personally urge the incoming Ukrainian president to investigate his allegations. Never particularly on message in his interviews, he delivered some memorably off-kilter lines that didn't help the cause.

"We're not meddling in an election, we're meddling in an investigation, which we have a right to do," he told the paper.

The next day, he sent an extraordinary private letter to Zelensky requesting a meeting. It was a surprise to everyone in the White House except, perhaps, the president of the United States.

Dear President-Elect Zelensky: I am private counsel to President Donald J. Trump. Just to be precise, I represent him as a private citizen, not as President of the United States. This is quite common under American law because the duties and privileges of a President and a private citizen are not the same. Separate representation is not the same. . . .

In my capacity as personal counsel to President Trump and with his knowledge and consent, I request a meeting with you on this upcoming Monday May 13th or Tuesday May 14th. I will need no more than a half-hour of your time.

It was head-spinning. If Giuliani was representing Trump as a private citizen, why was he requesting an official act?

Giuliani never got his meeting. A public uproar followed the *Times* story, and his comments to the paper went over poorly at the White House. He was forced to cancel his plans, another setback to the cause. His frustrations growing, he went on Fox News that night and sent a veiled message to Zelensky that there was trouble ahead, charging that there were "enemies of the president" in Zelensky's orbit.

Unbeknownst to the public, he sent Parnas and Fruman to talk to a Zelensky aide instead.

They met secretly with the aide on May 12 at an outdoor café in Kyiv, in a scene worthy of a Bond film. The two henchmen attempted to strong-arm the incoming government official with an ultimatum. "I was told to give it to him in a very harsh way, not in a pleasant way," Parnas said of Giuliani's instructions.

Unless Zelensky agreed to investigate Biden and Burisma, Parnas threatened, U.S. military aid to Ukraine would be in jeopardy, and Vice President Mike Pence would cancel his trip to Zelensky's upcoming inauguration.

But the new government refused to cave—the official who met with Parnas blocked him on WhatsApp after the meeting. Parnas relayed the news to Giuliani in a call later that evening. "Okay," the boss replied. "They'll see."

The next day, Pence called off his plans to attend the inauguration.

For all the bullying tactics, the bottom was dropping out of Giuliani's efforts. Miffed that Giuliani never delivered on the meeting with Barr, and facing likely unemployment, Lutsenko dropped his American friend like a used cigar. "Hunter Biden did not violate any Ukrainian laws," Lutsenko told *Bloomberg News* on May 16. "At least as of now, we do not see any wrongdoing. A company can pay however much it wants to its board."

Blindsided, a fuming Giuliani called him in the middle of the night.

"Have you ever read your goddamn bribery statute? This takes a mental midget to do one plus two equals crime. You don't need to be a lawyer, Yuriy, you just need to be an honest man."

His argument, that Joe Biden's forcing Viktor Shokin out of office constituted bribery, made little sense. But he continued to repeat those words—*"Bribery! Bribery!"*—over and over, according to Lutsenko.

Giuliani told the *New Yorker* his investigation was "going along fine" until Lutsenko reversed course on Biden. "It undermined everything," he said.

Four days later, Zelensky raised the gold and bejeweled presidential scepter to cheers at his swearing-in ceremony inside Parliament. Instead of Pence, Trump sent a small delegation led by Energy Secretary Rick Perry.

The group reported back to the president in the Oval Office on May 23, delivering an upbeat report about the dynamic new president, and advising Trump to grant him an Oval Office visit. They misread their audience.

"I don't want to have any fucking thing to do with Ukraine!" Trump said. *"They fucking attacked me. I can't understand why. . . . They tried to fuck me. They're corrupt. I'm not fucking with them."*

Each time Perry interjected with a point he cut him off. *"I don't give a shit. . . . I want the fucking DNC server!"*

Perry, worried about the implications, argued that the U.S. couldn't allow Ukraine, a precarious ally in the struggle with Russia, to weaken.

"Talk to Rudy and Joe," Trump said. (Joseph diGenova, and his wife, Victoria Toensing, were Republican lawyers supporting Giuliani's efforts.)

Outraged, the president on July 25 took matters into his own hands, and called Zelensky himself.

The House Intelligence Committee operates in an office suite three floors underneath the marble floors of the United States Capitol. To enter, you need to punch in a code before passing through two sets of heavy doors wired for alarms, and surrender your cell phone, tablet, laptop, and headphones. The further back you walk, the higher your security clearance needs to be. The complex is known as The Bunker.

It was there that the overlapping scandals of the Trump administration converged in May 2019. Just around the time that Giuliani was celebrating his seventy-fifth birthday at Yankee Stadium, Diana Pilipenko, an expert on corruption and financial crimes for the Center for American Progress, reached out to her contacts at the committee. With a master's degree from Harvard in regional studies focused on Russia, Eastern Europe, and Central Asia, she scoured the Ukrainian newspapers regularly, and was intrigued by coverage of Rudy Giuliani and his corruption investigation.

The staff at the committee was immersed in the Mueller probe and Trump's financial dealings at the time. But Giuliani's activities raised enough eyebrows to prompt Daniel Goldman, its director of investigations, to reach out to a second source. The source sat down with Adam Schiff, the chairman of the committee, and Goldman, and painted a fuller picture of Giuliani's odd mission. No one had a clear fix on his role, though; was he on assignment from the administration?

On July 25, with media clamor growing, the staff was alerted to an official readout of a phone call that day between Trump and Zelensky.

"Donald Trump is convinced that the new Ukrainian government will be able to quickly improve image [*sic*] of Ukraine, complete investigation of corruption cases, which inhibited the interaction between Ukraine and the USA," the readout stated.

The summary wasn't from the White House, though—it was from the Ukrainian president's office. The White House version made no mention of Trump's desire to "complete" an investigation. The discrepancy tipped the scales in favor of a congressional inquiry.

Goldman had been on staff for only seven months; he and Schiff, both former prosecutors, had met at the MSNBC Green Room the previous year, and talked about Goldman doing some work for the intel committee. When the Democrats took control of the House in November 2018, he got the call to come aboard.

As they prepared their inquiry over the August recess, the committee received a call in confidence from an administration official who was deeply upset by what was taking place inside the White House, and by Trump's call with Zelensky in particular. He was advised to file a whistleblower's complaint.

The press got wind of it, media interest ballooned, and a battle of nerves ensued between the White House and the committee, which demanded to see the document. Subpoenas started flying and ultimatums were issued. On September 25, the White House took Washington by surprise and caved. It released not only the whistleblower complaint, but shortly afterward a reconstructed transcript of the call as well.

Schiff, Goldman, and the team gathered inside Schiff's office in the Bunker and pored over them. "We were sitting there reading through it, and at various points you would hear things like 'Holy shit' and 'Oh my God!'" Goldman recalled.

"In the course of my official duties, I have received information from multiple U.S. Government officials that the President of the United States is using the power of his office to solicit interference from a foreign country in the 2020 U.S. election," the whistleblower letter began. "This interference includes, among other things, pressuring a foreign country to investigate one of the President's main domestic political rivals.

"The President's personal lawyer, Mr. Rudolph Giuliani, is a central figure in this effort. Attorney General Barr appears to be involved as well."

The letter outlined a concerted effort by the president and his attorney to coerce the Ukrainian government into lying about the country's involvement on behalf of Democrats in the 2016 elections, and to smear the former vice president of the United States.

Exhibit A was the White House reconstruction of the president's call with Zelensky. At least a week prior to the July 25 conversation, Trump had ordered $400 million in aid to Ukraine frozen. In their conversation, he made clear what Zelensky needed to do to receive it.

ZELENSKY: ... We are ready to continue to cooperate for the next steps, specifically we are almost ready to buy more Javelins from the United States for defense purposes.

TRUMP: I would like you to do us a favor though, because our country has been through a lot and Ukraine knows a lot about it. I would like you to find out what happened with this whole situation with Ukraine ... the server, they say Ukraine has it. ...

ZELENSKY: ... I will personally tell you that one of my assistants spoke with Mr. Giuliani just recently and we are hoping very much that Mr. Giuliani will be able to travel to Ukraine and we will meet once he comes to Ukraine. I just wanted to assure you once again that you have nobody but friends around us....

TRUMP: ... Mr. Giuliani is a highly respected man. He was the mayor of New York City, a great mayor, and I would like him to call you. I will ask him to call you along with the Attorney General....

The other thing, there's a lot of talk about Biden's son, that Biden stopped the prosecution, and a lot of people want to find out about that so whatever you can do with the Attorney General would be great.

The documents provided the foundation for an impeachment inquiry.

"The best way I could describe the Trump Hotel is as a cesspool of Trump officials," Aaron Parnas, Lev's son, recalled. "It was just a little hub completely disconnected with the rest of Washington, D.C."

On any given evening, a visitor to BLT Prime, the hotel's restaurant, could share bar space with cabinet secretaries, senators, lobbyists, or perhaps one of the president's sons. But the Republican with the most celebrity wattage in 2019 was Giuliani, who held court at a regular table with a clear view of the lobby, and the Republican stars and wannabes as they came and went.

Fans were forever approaching him and asking to have their photos taken with him, and he happily obliged. Elected officials, Fox News anchors, and friendly politicians would come by to pay homage to him. Someone created a nameplate reading *"Rudolph W. Giuliani—Private Office"* that the hotel placed on his table each time he arrived.

On the afternoon of October 9, he had lunch with Parnas and Fruman before they left for a flight to Vienna; Giuliani planned to travel there the next day.

That evening, Aaron Parnas received an alarming call; his father and Fruman had been arrested at Dulles Airport as they prepared to board a Lufthansa Airlines flight to Frankfurt. Both were carrying one-way, first-class tickets.

Panicked, he knew who to call. "I just had to go to Rudy," he said. Giuliani and his father "were like long-lost brothers."

Over the next forty-eight hours, the two worked out of Giuliani's hotel suite, waging a frantic effort to get to the bottom of what happened. Giuliani's cell phone was buzzing all day with calls from Trump, and reporters were besieging him with interview requests. Giuliani was flummoxed. "What could he possibly have been arrested for?" he asked Aaron, with a straight face.

The source of Parnas and Fruman's downfall was the very thing that elevated them from nobodies to somebodies in the first place: the campaign contributions they'd showered upon Trump and others. They used shell corporations and other illegal sleights of hand to obscure that the money came from a Russian investor.

It was the end of the line for Parnas and Fruman, two determined opportunists who'd taken the joyride of their lives together. The exotic trips, White House parties, state funerals, and global cloak-and-dagger games came to a halt with the click of handcuffs. Giuliani fell conspicuously silent. Trump cut them loose altogether. "I don't know those gentlemen," he told reporters.

It was probably inevitable that the two would ultimately be chewed up and spat out by their powerful benefactors, but they seemed the last ones to realize it. "I felt like my family left me," Lev Parnas reflected. "They all clammed up."

Giuliani had reason to be distracted; the United States Attorney for the Southern District opened up an investigation into whether he broke U.S. lobbying laws in his Ukrainian pursuits on behalf of Trump. The man who rose to fame as the incorruptible leader of the district was now being examined by its prosecutors as a potential criminal target.

The biggest victims of the Ukraine scandal may not have been those who got caught up playing Trump and Giuliani's games, like Parnas and Fruman, or even those, like Marie Yovanovitch, who became innocent victims of them. Trump's withholding of military aid to Ukraine for his political benefit sent a signal that America's support for the country was tenuous at best. Among those watching was Russian president Vladimir Putin, who may have seen it as his opportunity to fulfill his expansionist dreams. His invasion of Ukraine in 2022 destroyed much of the country and resulted in tens of thousands of military and civilian deaths.

Giuliani never displayed any contrition for his part in the Ukraine scandal. Nor did he tone down his activities in wake of the criminal investigation into him. He emerged from the episode less an attorney than a fanatic, a dangerous man.

CHAPTER 15

Smeared

On December 3, 2019, the House Intelligence Committee released a report laying out the case for Donald Trump's impeachment. It was the culmination of weeks of nationally televised hearings, at which a parade of government officials, defying orders from the White House, testified about an elaborate scheme by the president and his attorney to destroy the reputations of Joe Biden and Marie Yovanovitch.

The document's portrait of Giuliani was of a malevolent and cynical operative waging a search-and-destroy mission on behalf of an immoral boss. One chapter after another focused on his complicity.

"Rudy Giuliani, on behalf of President Trump, led a smear campaign to oust Ambassador Yovanovitch. . . . Giuliani and his associates promoted false conspiracy theories about Ukraine colluding with Democrats to interfere in the 2016 US election. . . . Mr. Giuliani also made discredited public allegations about former Vice President Joe Biden and his son, Hunter, in an apparent effort to hurt President Trump's political rival in the 2020 presidential election."

There were any number of reasons for Giuliani to be devastated. His image as an American hero was in tatters. He had helped to bring about his patron's impeachment. A criminal investigation into his actions threatened to ruin him. Anyone with a modicum of self-awareness would be hiding in bed.

Instead, on the day before the report was released, he stepped off a plane in Budapest, Hungary, with a small entourage, and headed to meet a group of Ukrainians offering more dirt on the Bidens.

The trip was underwritten by One America News Network, the fringe right-wing cable channel that served as an extremist alternative to Fox News. The reporter on the trip, Chanel Rion, was OAN's White House reporter, and a promoter of QAnon conspiracy theories. The title of the series she was working on was "Ukrainian Witnesses Destroy Schiff's Case—Exclusive with Rudy Giuliani."

As heads turned at the sight of America's Mayor outside Budapest's airport, his party was escorted to a row of dark vehicles. The caravan took a forty-five-minute drive through the snowy back roads of the Hungarian countryside, headed toward what Giuliani called a safe house. It was spooky enough to prompt Christianné Allen, his twenty-year-old communications director, to take out her cell phone and text her whereabouts to her boyfriend "so somebody knew where I was."

They arrived at an isolated, twelve-room hunting lodge, emptied of guests and patrolled by security guards. Over the next two days, Giuliani played investigative reporter as cameras rolled; he sat with Rion at the corner of a large wooden table with a succession of Ukrainian ex-prosecutors, politicians, and political fixers, firing questions at them about Biden family corruption. Even Yuriy Lutsenko made a cameo ("I have no other way to protect my reputation," he told the *New Yorker*. "Why not?").

Giuliani was so pleased with the interviews that he burst into a joyous rendition of "God Bless America," singing along to a song on his iPad, in a morning ride to the airport on the way to his next shoot.

The group landed in Kyiv, Ukraine's capital, and headed to the outskirts of the city, driving through ramshackle villages on dirt roads toward their destination, a lush, mountainous resort named the Equides Club, with horse stables, a golf course, and upscale eateries.

Restaurant Chalet Equides was a few steps past the hotel's chocolate marbled foyer. Its menu featured delicacies like Siberian black caviar, red deer, and mouflon (wild sheep). The waiters there mostly recalled Giuliani's fondness for Glenmorangie, a single-malt Scotch whiskey.

He and Rion resumed their interviews inside a private room. Viktor Shokin, the rubber-faced former prosecutor general accused of corruption by U.S. officials, focused on his firing at the behest of Joe Biden—familiar territory. He presented Giuliani with a report, allegedly written by a Latvian prosecutor's office, that stated Burisma made payments to several members of its board—Hunter Biden among them—with money that was allegedly laundered through a complex series of bank transfers conducted by Burisma. There was no evidence that Hunter Biden participated in the transactions, or even knew about them. And there was no suggestion in the documents that Joe Biden was involved in any way. Giuliani filled in the blanks.

The more interesting interview was with Andriy Derkach, a portly Ukrainian Parliament member who was making the Burisma affair as much of a personal crusade as was Giuliani. He provided the crew with "leaked" documents and materials he said he obtained through a website he ran, tying the Bidens to a conspiracy against Shokin.

"I wish I'd met you earlier," Giuliani told him.

When the interviews concluded, Giuliani and his colleagues retired to the bar, where they smoked cigars, drank whiskey, and snacked on horsemeat sausages. Rion reported that the party had to make a hasty, middle-of-the-night dash to the airport when they received reports that one thousand Ukrainian soldiers had been dispatched to find them. She also reported that when they arrived at the

Kyiv airport George Soros was waiting for them there with "human Dobermans in little black Mercedes." Neither was true; she walked back both stories later on.

When Giuliani arrived in New York, Trump called him before he could exit the plane. "What did you get?" the president asked. "More than you can imagine," his attorney responded. He promised to produce a report with his findings.

Trump heralded the coming revelations to reporters. "He's going to make a report, I think to the attorney general and to Congress," he said. "He says he has a lot of good information."

But the president withheld a key fact from the public: his national security advisor, Robert O'Brien, had informed him in an Oval Office meeting that Giuliani was a victim of a Russian disinformation campaign created to influence the 2020 election. The U.S. government considered Derkach an active Russian agent. The information Giuliani was trumpeting was suspect.

Trump just shrugged. "That's Rudy," he told O'Brien.

There was no evidence that Giuliani knew about Derkach's identity, or that Trump informed him about it. On the contrary, it appeared that the president allowed his lawyer to go on making dubious accusations about Biden and Yovanovitch, calculating that having a dupe for Russia making spurious allegations on his behalf benefited him more than halting an effort to undermine another presidential election.

Giuliani's blockbuster report never materialized; all that resulted from the trip was an avalanche of tweets and YouTube videos. As for Rion, the story she aired about her trip with Giuliani portrayed his findings as "a devastating pile of smoking guns" that proved the impeachment effort was a "hoax that amounts to a coup."

"Some will call it treason," she said.

*　　*　　*

Two days after he returned to New York, Giuliani got a call from Judith. Their divorce battle was headed to court, and had become so acrimonious that they were lashing out at each other in the press.

"I feel betrayed by a man that I supported in every way for more than 20 years," she told the *New York Times*. "I'm sad to know that the hero of 9/11 has become a liar."

"Judith is vindictive," he told the *New York Post*. "She's doing all she can to string this out and shake me down for millions. She's on a campaign of hate, but she still loves using my last name to get a leg up in society . . . she's a social climber."

But with the trial a month away, Judith suggested that they meet privately to try to settle the matter to avoid a public spectacle. He agreed, and at eleven o'clock the next morning they met at the Metropolitan Club on the Upper East Side, an institution founded by J. P. Morgan and other wealthy New Yorkers in 1891.

Entering the stately, white palazzo through a grand marble entrance hall, with a ceiling covered in gold leaf and a mural of winged cherubs, the two Giulianis greeted each other with a warm, sentimental hug. "We both cried," Judith recalled.

She was struck by how much he had changed. "He looked so old and so fat, and so unhealthy," she said. "His teeth needed to be replaced—he was missing a laminate. His glasses were dirty. And he was limping from the torn muscle."

When they sat down for breakfast they talked about their lives without one another—he and Maria Ryan were growing inseparable—and he confessed to being worried about the criminal investigation into him, she said. "I'm doing pretty shitty," she said he told her. "They're lying about what I did."

When they got down to the business of dividing up the estate things fell into place relatively easily: the Manhattan apartment for him, the Hamptons house and guest house for her; one Palm Beach condo for him, her parents' Palm Beach condo for her. Cash was a different story. The two burned through it with abandon during their marriage—"$250,000 a month on sheer fun," she recalled—and he said he was hurting for funds to pay his mounting legal bills for the criminal and divorce cases. She agreed to forgo some upfront cash in exchange for a percentage of his future income.

The two jotted the agreement down and formalized it later that day. The marriage was over. Thanks to him, Judith had lived in luxury for seventeen years, and traveled to so many countries she'd lost count. She socialized with presidents, dined with foreign heads of state, met the Queen of England, and became a doyenne of New York society.

She had been torn to shreds in the media, and portrayed as a villain by Rudy's aides, friends, and, in the end, Rudy himself. The rough treatment prompted Ken Kurson, a longtime advisor to Giuliani, to write a guilt-ridden letter to her apologizing for failing to protect her from the "duplicitous, hurtful, and just plain odd behavior" of advisors during the presidential campaign. This, despite her having nursed him through his cancer crisis and being a loving wife, "the person with whom Rudy could relax, and whose hand Rudy held every time a plane took off.

"I never understood why your very existence caused so much resentment and even hostility from those who honestly do love Rudy," he wrote. "My only theory is that many of the people who surround Rudy want and expect him to be married not just to his work but to the people with whom he works."

With the wars over with, Judith claimed in retrospect that she felt only relief. But the wounds ran deep.

"I don't hate Rudy," she reflected. "I pity him at this point."

On December 18, the House impeached Trump on abuse of power and obstruction of Congress charges. It was only the third time in the history of the republic it had voted to file charges.

"SUCH ATROCIOUS LIES BY THE RADICAL LEFT, DO NOTHING DEMOCRATS," the president tweeted. "THIS IS AN ASSAULT ON AMERICA, AND AN ASSAULT ON THE REPUBLICAN PARTY!!!!"

White House aides were infuriated with Giuliani over the debacle. Many who raised their hands to support him for secretary of state in Trump's office three years earlier washed their hands of him. "I don't know if you could have found anyone who could have been a real Rudy ally or loyalist inside the White House after that," said a Trump aide.

The exception was Trump, who never blamed him for the debacle, publicly or privately. The day after the vote, the president welcomed him warmly at a fundraiser at Mar-a-Lago. "He was happy to see the mayor," Giuliani's aide Christianné Allen recalled.

Somehow, for all the insanity of Giuliani's efforts in Ukraine, their conspiratorial adventure brought them closer together. Just as they worked to take down Biden, so did they collaborate to discredit the investigation into their efforts. "They just kind of made the whole thing a big swirl," Jason Miller said. Anthony Scaramucci, Trump's onetime communications director, called Giuliani the "Secretary of Deflection."

The impeachment yielded some major dividends for the president. The House vote fell along partisan lines, inflaming Trump's supporters and creating a boon to his campaign. In the final three months of 2019, the reelection effort took in $46 million in contributions, a third of its entire take that year. His approval ratings never sank.

John Bolton felt that Giuliani had so much dirt on the president that Trump was too scared to cut him loose. It was a popular theory that was bolstered when Giuliani joked to the *Guardian* that he had "very, very good insurance" in case Trump threw him under the bus.

But their friendship was real. Trump knew that Giuliani always had his back, that he had been there for all his great crises, dating back to the *Access Hollywood* furor. "Rudy was there when a lot of you guys weren't," the president would snap at staff members.

But it was a twisted kind of loyalty. Heading into the 2020 election year, Trump was willing to let his attorney destroy his own reputation, place himself in legal jeopardy, and make a fool of himself in service to him. Giuliani, intoxicated by his importance to the president, and reliant upon the relationship to maintain his value to clients, seemed game for it.

It was a tragic dynamic to watch in real time, painful to those who cared for Giuliani, satisfying to those who hated him or his boss. "The thing about Rudy that he doesn't understand now is that Trump has hung him out to dry already," Rick Wilson, a Trump antagonist and former campaign aide to Giuliani, told an interviewer at the time. "He's already been killed. He just doesn't know he's dead yet."

Convinced of the righteousness of his path, and too blinded by zeal and self-interest to realize how his story would end, he barreled into the new year like a rottweiler let off his leash.

The election of 2020 had an epochal feel. Blue America viewed it as democracy's last stand against an unstable authoritarian, a man who lied so often that the *Washington Post*'s count total was over sixteen thousand by the start of 2020. Red America saw Trump as a defender of a vanishing way of life, and as a champion against the smugness of the urban elites. After three years of Trump, the country wasn't so much divided as at war with itself.

Giuliani's only major takeaway from the Ukraine fiasco seemed to be that he needed a better megaphone. Television interviewers were increasingly attacking him over his conspiracy theories. He watched Trump dictate his message to his base completely unfiltered each day through his social media channels and wanted in. He hired someone to bring him into the digital age.

In the fall of 2015, when Christianné Allen was a junior at Cloverfield High School in the suburbs of Richmond, Virginia, she decided to attend a school football game one evening. It turned out to be a humiliating experience.

She was a bright, ambitious student, model-beautiful (she had in fact once worked as a model), and a proud Christian conservative. She spent her free time working as an intern for Donald Trump's presidential campaign, which made her something of a lightning rod at school. When she walked into the stadium to watch the Cavaliers play, a crowd of students in the stands erupted in boos, then started to chant, *"Fuck Trump!"*

It was hardly an isolated incident. She was taunted in the hallways, and ridiculed by her classmates online. After months of harassment, and eager to start her career in conservative politics, she dropped out and enrolled in an online school run by Jerry Falwell's Liberty University.

"The need to begin defending our God-given freedoms in America has never been greater!" she wrote on her Facebook page.

In 2019, a friend at the conservative *Daily Caller* brought her together with Giuliani. Allen was working in political communications at the time, and was hoping to sign him up to speak at a conference. He gave her a job instead.

He was lucky to have her; she was young and idealistic while he was in the twilight of his career and increasingly isolated. He had spent the year wreaking havoc on the nation. It was nothing compared to the damage he was about to cause.

When she entered his life in September 2019, he had 300,000 Twitter followers, no Facebook or Instagram accounts, and had never hosted a podcast. Allen set about building out those platforms. She had a podcast set built in the den of his apartment, with cameras and warm lighting that gave the wood bookcases behind him a soft glow. In a run of luck, John Catsimatidis, a billionaire New York supermarket magnate and conservative donor, purchased WABC Radio and handed Giuliani a show.

For much of 2020, he communicated with the public on his own media channels. He was on camera or on the radio every day except Saturday, and tweeted as compulsively as the president.

His podcast, *Rudy Giuliani's Common Sense*, premiered on January 24, 2020, eleven days before the end of Trump's Senate trial. The opening animation was a swirl of patriotic music and images of Revolutionary War heroes, interspersed with photos of Giuliani as prosecutor, mayor, and 9/11 hero. Like the Thomas Paine classic, he said the show would "bring to bear the principles of common sense, and rational discussion."

"The Democrats would call it impeachment and the Republicans would call it a coup," he began, launching into a discourse that was part history lesson, part partisan screed. "What the Democrats have done is make Alexander Hamilton's nightmare a reality."

The focus of his first shows was the Ukraine conspiracy, a cause he refused to drop when many in his party were desperate to move on from it. The anger toward him for his role in the scandal only hardened his resolve to expose the truth. There was no one to shake him off his pedestal.

"I am under constant attack for representing the president of the United States," he complained, sitting at a desk, staring into the camera with his hands folded. "Lawyers who represent terrorists, lawyers who represent murderers, lawyers who represent very unpopular issues are considered heroes because our profession says everyone is entitled to a defense, except for opponents of Donald Trump."

He was defensive, pedantic, and boring. He spent his second

episode laying out the Biden case detail by detail, with characters with hard-to-pronounce Ukrainian names, descriptions of complex banking transactions, and fact after numbing fact about money transfers, phone conversations, black ledgers, accounting audits, alleged bribes, and on and on. The prosecutor whose withering questioning of Bertram Podell led the congressman to confess his guilt was making a case so confusing it was impossible to comprehend.

And then he cut to a commercial.

"I have very definite opinions on the best cigars for the right time and the right place . . . subscribe to Cigar Aficionado through the link on our website. You're going to really enjoy it. It's a great read!"

It was a cringey reminder of his mercenary side, and perhaps his cash crunch. But embarrassment wasn't in his emotional lexicon. And so his viewers sat at their computers week after week and watched him rail about Burisma and the Bidens, interspersed with ads of him smoking cigars and peddling magazine subscriptions.

He kept the Ukraine train chugging even after the Senate voted to acquit the president on February 5. "Acquitted for life!" Giuliani tweeted—and soon afterward announced he would go on a nationwide tour to educate Americans about Burisma and the Bidens.

His war was interrupted by good news on February 18. Bernie Kerik, who had rejoined Giuliani's entourage after his rescue from purgatory, received a call from Trump on his cell phone. Like George W. Bush before him, the president had grown fond of the roguish ex-cop, who had became a staunch supporter.

"Right now, as we're speaking, I'm signing your presidential pardon," Trump told him. "Your record will be expunged. Go on with your life."

After a rocket ship of a career that soared to epic heights and then exploded in flames, Kerik was back where he started, at Giuliani's side protecting him, fighting his fights, and keeping him company. He would stick by his boss until he was his last defender.

*   *   *

Giuliani and Allen had an early morning routine when they spent time in New York. She would leave the Park Lane Hotel, where he put her up, and arrive at his Upper East Side apartment with coffee and a breakfast sandwich.

He famously slept just four hours a night—"and not even in order," she said—and was at work at his dining table by the time she arrived, "folders up to his nose," rummaging through his legal work as daylight streamed in through his shades. "That's when he was at his happiest," she said. "He had the biggest smile on his face."

Her days with him were long and ran "a thousand miles an hour," between fielding nonstop press inquiries and producing his podcast and radio shows. "I almost had to make appointments to leave," she said.

Like many who worked for him, she saw his best side: paternal, playful, and generous. "He takes care of people who are his good friends," she said.

The chasm between his private and public sides was always vast, but perhaps never so much as in 2020. When he wasn't caring for his friends and loyalists, he was spewing venom.

Joe Biden spent January and much of February locked in a tight primary race with a group of far nimbler candidates, including Senators Bernie Sanders, Elizabeth Warren, Kamala Harris, and Amy Klobuchar, and South Bend, Indiana, mayor Pete Buttigieg. Biden was seventy-seven, and showing every year of it in his slow-footed debate performances. But in late February he shook off his slumberous start and won a decisive victory in South Carolina after landing a crucial endorsement from Congressman Jim Clyburn. The win cleared much of the field.

For years, Giuliani was forced to wear Biden's famous quip about him—the one about a noun, a verb, and 9/11—like a scarlet letter.

With the former vice president now the Democratic frontrunner, the comeuppance Giuliani sought wasn't so much his defeat as his destruction. As if branding Biden a criminal over the past year weren't enough, he launched a campaign to portray him as senile. His tweets the first week of March were savage.

"Biden can't complete a sentence. Imagine if you could cross examine him about the millions and millions the Biden Family Enterprise made selling his office?"

"Do we have to diagnose what is wrong with him? It's obvious."

"The Democrat party must think we, the American people, are idiots. In a year this man may not know his own name."

His invective wasn't confined to Twitter. He brought doctors on his podcast to diagnose Biden's cognitive state. He told an interviewer on *Fox & Friends* that the candidate had dementia.

There was nothing spontaneous about it; Trump and he coordinated the character assassination effort just as they portrayed Hillary Clinton as sick in 2016. "WOW! Sleepy Joe doesn't know where he is, or what he's doing," Trump tweeted March 3. "Honestly, I don't think he even knows what office he's running for!"

Thanks to Allen's efforts, Giuliani's Twitter following tripled to over one million in a matter of months; his podcast swung dramatically in viewership from day to day, but sometimes drew hundreds of thousands, and hit #3 on a ratings chart at one point. His radio show had an even wider audience. He appeared frequently on Fox News's prime-time shows, which drew millions.

The 2020 campaign was turned on its head by two convulsions in the spring. The Covid pandemic emptied America's streets, shuttering businesses and closing schools. Trump struggled haplessly to wish it away, blaming the media for overstating the problem, and predicting it would be short-lived. The administration's lack of preparation created shortages of everything from ventilators to toilet paper.

The police killing of George Floyd in Minneapolis on May 25 triggered a second upheaval. Americans were sickened by a video of Derek Chauvin, a forty-four-year-old white police officer, kneeling on the neck of the forty-six-year-old African American as he struggled to breathe, killing him for the sin of using an alleged counterfeit $20 bill. The murder triggered demonstrations across the country, some of them violent, and sparked a reckoning for the country over its treatment of Black citizens.

Unlike the pandemic, the Black Lives Matter movement presented an upside to a president whose success was based on stoking racial resentment among economically insecure white voters. And no one was as well positioned to exploit the opportunity for him as New York's legendary crime-fighting mayor.

"Now with 7 days of Mob rule of cities with mostly DEMOCRAT MAYORS, it is obvious that these Mayors are incapable of protecting their citizens," Giuliani tweeted on June 1.

On WABC the following afternoon, he demanded mass arrests in New York, where huge demonstrations were giving rise to looting. "Put 1,000 people in prison, you won't have a riot the next day," he said, sounding like a southern sheriff.

Corporate America embraced the Black Lives Matter movement as a catalyst for change, but to Giuliani it was a threat to society. It was certainly an opportunity to foment fear among the base. His Twitter feed became an endless ticker of apocalyptic warnings.

"WAKE UP! Black Lives Matter wants to destroy law enforcement, end bail, empty the prisons (including drug dealers as well as users), provide themselves with reparations, AND a full-time government income without the necessity of work."

"To support BLM is to support: Violence, Anarchy, Obliteration of history, Destruction of much of our Constitution, Common ownership of property, Destruction of Israel, the elimination of our American way of life. People are being fooled by Black Lives Matter."

In June, a transatlantic television audience got a heavy dose of his bleak prophesy on *Good Morning Britain*, which for some reason he agreed to appear on despite its 1 a.m. New York start time. Piers Morgan was on set in London, while Giuliani sat at his podcast desk in his New York apartment, dressed in a light blue sport jacket and giant tortoiseshell glasses, heavily pancaked with an orange tint.

For ten long minutes, the two fought over a single question, which was why Trump had recently tweeted out an infamous old quote from a bigoted Miami police chief—"when the looting starts, the shooting starts"—as he threatened to send the military to quell the violence on the streets of Minneapolis.

"That is an accurate statement, an accurate warning—that if you continue to loot, you will bring about violence," Giuliani argued.

"Why would any president say that?" Morgan asked.

The two went around and around on the question until Giuliani lost his temper.

MORGAN: It's one of the most infamous quotes in America.

GIULIANI: It is not, I've never even heard it before. I've been in law enforcement for 20 years Piers. I wouldn't have known where that came from.

MORGAN: Where did he get it from?

GIULIANI: What a bunch of garbage! . . .

MORGAN: Right, so you've just to clarify . . .

GIULIANI: Because you're a bunch of phonies! That's why!

The longer the two went at it the more personal the argument became.

MORGAN: Rudy, what happened to you?

GIULIANI: You are professionally unethical!

MORGAN: What happened to you, Rudy?

GIULIANI: Nothing happened to me. Nothing happened to me at all except . . .

MORGAN: You used to be one of the most revered people in America.

GIULIANI: . . . except watching how much you people lie and distort. You're disgraceful.

MORGAN: Let me just tell you something.

GIULIANI: You are disgraceful. YOU'RE DISGRACEFUL!

MORGAN: You know what Rudy, you used to be one of the most respected and revered people in America, if not the world. You were someone we looked up to. Someone who stood up for fairness . . .

GIULIANI: Oh, who wants to listen to you Piers. Really, I am. You can say anything you want because I have no respect for you, for the way you're covering this. . . .

MORGAN: Why has President Trump . . .

GIULIANI: What happened to me is the same thing that always happens to me: I happen to be in favor of truth and justice, and you people are in favor of a phony political narrative. You're a disgrace and the interview is over as far as I'm concerned.

MORGAN: You know what, Rudy, you sound completely barking mad.

Screaming interviews became something of a Giuliani hallmark. The previous fall, he and Chris Cuomo of CNN went down the Burisma rabbit hole in a sparring match so convoluted that Giuliani contradicted himself in the span of thirty seconds.

CUOMO: So, you did ask Ukraine to look into Joe Biden?

GIULIANI: Of course I did.

CUOMO: You just said you didn't.

GIULIANI: No, I asked them to look into the allegations which related to my client which tangentially involved Joe Biden in a massive bribery scheme.

It ended with Giuliani calling Cuomo "a total sell-out."

As 2020 progressed, he yelled, *"Shut up, moron!"* to a guest on Laura Ingraham's show, called a Bloomberg TV interviewer a "phony," accused a Fox Business anchor of "defamation," and tangled with MSNBC's Jonathan Capehart until the host asked, inevitably, "What happened to you?"

The question of what had gone wrong with America's Mayor, so prevalent that interviewers were pressing him for the answer on television, launched a guessing game in the media: it was alcohol; it was old age; it was Judith; it was senility, desperation, greed.

The most devastating contribution to the genre was a *New York* magazine story by Olivia Nuzzi, who interviewed him the day after he returned from Ukraine. She described an early afternoon car ride with him to the restaurant at The Mark, a five-star Upper East Side hotel. Sitting in the backseat with her, his fly unzipped, saliva dripping down his chin, he sang her an aria from *Rigoletto*, fumbled with three cell phones, and tossed around conspiracy theories linking George Soros to the media and Marie Yovanovitch. "Soros is hardly a Jew," he said of the Jewish philanthropist. "I'm more of a Jew than Soros is."

He attacked the Southern District prosecutors investigating him as "absolutely assholes" who were jealous that he was more successful running the office than they were. He scoffed when asked if he was an alcoholic. "The alcohol comes from the fact that I did occasionally drink," he said. "I love Scotch. I can't help it. All of the malts. And part of it is cigars—I love to have them with cigars. I'm a partyer."

When they arrived at the restaurant, he "fell over to his right and hit a wall" on the way in, Nuzzi wrote, and then ordered two Bloody Marys with his lunch. "I know you love them," the waiter replied.

His friends, Giuliani complained, were whispering that he was behaving strangely, then turning around and urging him not to damage his legacy. "My attitude about my legacy," he said, "is 'fuck it.'"

Going into the first general election debate on September 29, Trump was polling almost 10 points behind Biden. With more than 150 million voters expected to tune in, the pressure on him to perform was enormous.

The president loathed mock debates, and had already walked out on a few. "I'm the president, I already know how to do this," he told aides at an aborted session in July at his golf club in Bedminster, New Jersey.

But on the weekend preceding the big event, he agreed to participate in a series of practice sessions in the Map Room on the Ground Floor of the White House. In the same room in which FDR and Churchill plotted the direction of World War II, a group of presidential advisors were arrayed around a long conference table, while Donald Trump sat by himself with an ice bucket, three Diet Cokes, and a bottle of hand sanitizer.

Chris Christie was the leader of the debate prep effort, and played Joe Biden in the sessions, while Kellyanne Conway played the moderator. A few other aides sat in and offered strategic advice, including chief of staff Mark Meadows. To Christie's relief the first session, on Saturday, went well, as Trump was focused, and sparred enthusiastically.

The next day, September 27, the group reconvened. Only this time, Rudy Giuliani unexpectedly walked in. As the group ran Trump through likely questions, he repeatedly interrupted. *"Go to Hunter . . . go to Ukraine . . . go to the Biden family grift."*

The group had already discussed the possibility of Trump's raising the corruption issue at some point in the debate, preferably at a high level, so people could follow the details. Giuliani vehemently disagreed with the strategy. He gave them a taste of what his radio and podcast audiences were hearing each day.

"He's scrolling through his iPad, saying 'Ukraine this,' 'Hunter that,'" one aide recalled. "He had an amazing recall about everything Ukraine. He was like Rain Man when it came to Ukraine."

With the exception of Trump, who was "politely kind of dismissive" of the idea, everyone else in the room was adamantly opposed to turning the debate into a Hunter Biden inquisition. Christie, who never bought into the conspiracy to begin with, felt the scandal, if there was one, was impossible to explain in simple terms, and paled in comparison to Americans' larger concerns about Covid and the economy.

The session proceeded in fits and starts. Whenever an opportunity to interject presented itself, Giuliani went back to Burisma. "It was a distracting shiny object that he kept trying to put in front of the president," a participant recalled. "It was just a complete distraction."

Attempting to illustrate his points, Giuliani rummaged hopelessly through his notes, and tried unsuccessfully to play video clips on his iPad. "He was just kind of a big bumbling mess," said a participant.

Eventually Christie lost his patience. "We've got to stay focused here!" he admonished Giuliani.

No one was more frustrated than Meadows. According to Christie, he made it a point to block Giuliani from attending future sessions. Some aides deliberately gave him the wrong start time to the next day's practice session; he arrived just as it was ending.

Ultimately Trump blew the debate, not because of Hunter Biden but because of a disastrous decision to interrupt Biden's every answer and talk over Chris Wallace's efforts to rein him in. It triggered a free-for-all that reduced the event to a giant headache—"a hot mess inside a dumpster fire inside a trainwreck," in the words of CNN's anchor Jake Tapper; a "shitshow" in the words of his colleague Dana Bash. Trump's interruptions—over seventy by some counts—allowed Biden to produce the night's only memorable line in a spontaneous burst of frustration: "Would you shut up, man?"

Three days later the president's fortunes slid further when he tested positive for Covid, and spent three days in the hospital in a circuslike atmosphere. With the campaign in turmoil, Giuliani scrambled to find a bombshell to shake up the race. It made its way to the front page of the New York Post eight days later.

"BIDEN SECRET EMAILS," the paper screamed on October 14, over a photo of a smiling Joe and Hunter Biden. "Smoking-gun email reveals how Hunter Biden introduced Ukrainian businessman to VP dad."

The story quoted a purported memo to Hunter on April 17, 2015, from Vadym Pozharskyi, an advisor to the board of Burisma, thanking him for "giving an opportunity to meet your father and spent [sic] some time together." The story also quoted from an earlier email purportedly from him, in May 2014, asking Hunter for "advice on how you could use your influence."

The paper connected the dots between the alleged meeting and Joe Biden's threat to withhold aid to Ukraine eight months later, which was quite a leap. Both Bidens denied the meeting ever took place.

The provenance of the emails was more intriguing. According to the *Post*, they came from the hard drive of a water-damaged Mac-Book Pro that a man named Hunter dropped off in April 2019 at a small repair store in Delaware. Other reports revealed the owner of the Mac Shop in Wilmington, John Paul Mac Isaac, was legally blind, and could not say whether the customer was Hunter Biden.

Isaac said the owner of the laptop never returned. After scrutinizing the contents and growing alarmed, he said, he turned it over to the FBI, keeping a copy of the hard drive for himself. A Trump supporter, he grew frustrated over time with the agency's failure to act, and shared a copy with Giuliani's attorney, Robert Costello. The *Post* said Giuliani gave them the contents of the hard drive after the paper was first tipped off to its existence by Steve Bannon, who had been bragging about having it.

Giuliani expected the story to blow up the race, and in another election, and at another time in his life, it might have. But it instead became a bellwether of his collapsing credibility. The previous month, the Treasury Department outed Andriy Derkach, whom Giuliani interviewed in Ukraine, as an active Russian agent. Fearing that Giuliani was doing Russia's bidding, wittingly or not, mainstream media organizations treated the laptop as if it were radioactive and refused to go near the story. Twitter locked the *Post*'s account.

Giuliani's erstwhile allies deserted him. Secretary of State Mike Pompeo warned about the dangers of a "foreign element" "propagating information." Over fifty former national security officials, many of whom served in Republican administrations, signed a letter stating they were "deeply suspicious that the Russian government played a significant role in this case."

The *Post* reporter who wrote the story refused to put his byline on it. Fox News, a sister news organization, refused to run with the information that Giuliani offered them, and news-side anchors disparaged it on air. "It is completely unverified and frankly, Rudy Giuliani is not the most reliable source anymore," said Chris Wallace. "I hate to say that, but it's just true."

"Let's say, just not sugarcoat it," said Brett Baier. "The whole thing is sketchy."

Giuliani was furious. "The Pentagon Papers were stolen, but the press had no problem printing it," he complained on his radio show. "But it hurt *Republicans*."

A year later, *Politico* reporter Ben Schreckinger reported in a book that he authenticated two emails from the laptop, including Pozharskyi's April 17 note to Hunter thanking him for introducing him to his father. The *New York Times* concurred months later. Biden's advisors, who in 2020 denied the meeting took place, conceded that the two men actually did meet that night, but only in passing. The revelation did not mean that everything in the laptop was authentic, but if Giuliani weren't held in such universal low regard at the time, Biden might have spent part of the crucial final weeks of the 2020 race on the defensive.

The real October surprise for Giuliani took place a week after the *Post* published the laptop story. Unlike the Hunter Biden story, it captured the nation's attention.

In the spring of 2020, Giuliani traveled to The Mark hotel with a security aide to film an on-camera interview for a documentary about his career. Christianné Allen, his communications aide, dealt with the producers over the phone, ironing out logistics and technical issues.

The producers had an impressive website, with a list of well-known films to their credit, and knew their stuff when it came to the mechanics of a two-person shoot. "They checked every box," Allen said. Only later did she realize that their email addresses had one too many dots in them.

Allen routinely attended Giuliani's television interviews, but on the day of the shoot Giuliani asked her to fly to Washington to take care of other business; he traveled to The Mark with just the security aide.

The aide checked the hotel suite before Giuliani walked in, and then sat in a chair outside of the room during the interview so no one could get in or out without his okay.

The result debuted on October 23, thirteen days before the election. Giuliani provided the climactic scene of *Borat Subsequent Moviefilm: Delivery of Prodigious Bribe to American Regime for Make Benefit Once Glorious Nation of Kazakhstan*, starring Sacha Baron Cohen, the comedian and prankster in character as Borat.

Cohen deliberately timed the film to debut a few weeks before Election Day to inflict maximum damage on Trump's reelection effort. Giuliani, a man seen by so many as a loathsome icon of the Trump era, was the perfect target.

He was greeted at the hotel room by the twenty-four-year-old actress Maria Bakalova. In the movie, she played Borat's fifteen-year-old daughter Tutar; seeking to marry Giuliani, she showed up in the hotel room pretending to be a television reporter, sporting a tight aqua blue dress and bright red lipstick. Facing Giuliani in a chair so close to him that they were almost knee-to-knee, she blushed when she introduced herself.

"You are one of my greatest heroes," she said, in a thick Eastern European accent. "I will try my best, but because I'm super excited and nervous . . ."

"You relax," he said, chuckling. "I'll relax you. Want me to ask you questions?"

She giggled nervously.

"I'll relax you, okay?"

"I feel like I'm living in a fairy tale," she said.

"Here," he said leaning into her. He took both her hands in his and squeezed them. "You're going to do great, okay?"

She asked Giuliani two softball questions about Covid, pretending to read them nervously from her notes.

"China manufactured the virus and let it out," he explained to her, "and they deliberately spread it all around the world. I don't think anybody was eating bats. Did you ever have a bat?"

"Oh no," she said, "I don't think I will ever eat a bat."

He squinted his eyes and laughed out loud. Things grew increasingly flirty.

"If you eat a bat with me?" she asked him in broken English.

"Okay, I'll eat a bat with you," he said, laughing.

She leaned into him and put her left hand on his knee and kept it there for a second. The two had a drink of what looked like whiskey and clinked glasses.

"Never been in front of the camera, always been behind of the camera," she said.

"Oh I think you're going to look pretty good," he said, with a wide grin. "Yeah, you're going to look pretty good."

After a brief interruption from a sound technician—Giuliani didn't recognize that it was Cohen, dressed in a fake wig, mustache, and beard—Bakalova leaned over, placed her hand on Giuliani's knee again, and apologized to him.

"Apology accepted," he said. The setup was going according to plan.

"Shall we have a drink in the bedroom?" she proposed. They walked in together, drinks in hand.

Inside the bedroom, he asked for her phone number and address, and she leaned over him, dug into his shirt to remove his mic wire, as he tapped her on her hip.

After she pulled out the wiring he lay down on the bed, face up, and dug far into his pants to tuck his shirt back in. He was lying stretched on the bed, seemingly staring at the young woman, when Cohen barged into the room in underwear, a red nylon onesie, and a big V-shaped red bra. "She fifteen, she too old for you!" he yelled.

Giuliani jumped to his feet. "Why are you wearing this?" he asked.

"She's my daughter, please take me instead!"

Giuliani, stunned, darted out of the hotel room and took off with his security aide. "I was in prison many years!" Cohen yelled to him. *"I have techniques with my mouth!"*

Giuliani filed a police report on Cohen (who had hidden in a closet during the security sweep). He tried to blunt the impact of the prank by leaking his own version of the story to the *New York Post*, and charged that the movie was "a complete fabrication." But when it premiered October 23, the humiliation he endured was almost as cringeworthy as the scene itself.

Kate McKinnon pantomimed him masturbating on *SNL*. The next day, anti-Trump protesters in Manhattan pelted his car with eggs. Late-night hosts dined out on the story for days. "I take off a mic every night," gibed Stephen Colbert, "never once have I reclined on a king-size bed and launched a fact-finding mission into my own groin." Joe Rogan, the hugely popular contrarian podcaster who said he has a "love-hate relationship with conspiracies," called Giuliani "gross."

For all the damage Cohen intended, he couldn't have imagined how exquisite the timing of its release would turn out to be. A month after intelligence experts were accusing Giuliani of being a dupe for a Russian agent, the movie showed him vulnerable to such manipulation.

"'Borat Subsequent Moviefilm' captured Giuliani in a private, un-vetted, scotch-filled meeting at a critical moment in our country's history," the entertainment journalist Chris O'Falt wrote. "And remarkably, 11 days before the election, we have evidence of his inability to read the room, to suss out credible sources, and his capacity to be compromised by foreign entities."

Giuliani finished out the campaign lost in a sad, private echo chamber. With no apparent ability to feel shame, the epic humiliations of his year—the impeachment he triggered; his association with a Russian agent; the televised meltdowns; the movie that had the nation laughing at him—got processed as simply more injustice to be fought. Looking for someone to blame, he focused all his rage on Joe Biden.

On his November 1 radio show, he suggested that Trump appoint him to expose corruption in the Biden family.

"You little slimeball, and miserable father, hard for me to not spit in your face, the way you treat your kid, Joe," he said, referring to Hunter and his addiction problems. Later in the broadcast he called Biden a pervert.

On Election Day, for some reason, he spent thirty minutes doing a remote interview with RT, the Russian state-controlled network that broadcast propaganda for Vladimir Putin internationally. It was a curious decision, considering that he was already under fire for disseminating disinformation for Russia.

Instead of making a closing argument for Trump's reelection, Giuliani spent thirty minutes spewing conspiracies about the Bidens.

"There's only one reason [Hunter] has that drug problem—it's Joe Biden," he said, sitting at a desk wearing a gray wool fleece over his shirt and tie. "When this man was a young man, having a severe drug problem, instead of letting him live a life that was simple, [Joe] started to use him as a bag man to collect bribes for him."

He was making reckless charges, each with its own confusing set of facts. He pulled out his cell phone and held it up to the camera to show photos allegedly of Hunter smoking crack—taken, he claimed, from Hunter's laptop. The glass on the back of Giuliani's phone was shattered. All the audience could see was a blurry object in his hand.

He conducted an even more telling interview that afternoon with Steve Bannon, Trump's former political strategist, on his podcast, *Bannon's War Room*. Giuliani offered the president some advice about how to react to the election returns that evening.

"We should assume if he has a credible lead—a point or more— we'll call the state and we should put it in his column and we start off from there and then he should claim victory," he told Bannon. "I mean as early as possible to get the suspense over for the American people."

He had the opportunity to offer the idea to Trump a few hours later.

The East Room of the White House that night had an electric feel, packed with hundreds of staffers and celebrants under its crystal chandeliers. The president had a platform with a podium placed at the head of the room for what he expected would be a victory speech.

Giuliani spent his evening at a desk in the Red Room with his son, Andrew, scrutinizing the returns on a laptop in the same space that Abe Lincoln read his morning newspapers during the Civil War. Portraits of Dolley Madison, Woodrow Wilson, and JFK loomed above as the two followed the returns from swing states.

The father and son were not part of, or even communicating with, the Trump campaign high command, which was sequestered in a room one floor below. Their Red Room desk was an island unto itself, just as Giuliani was an unmoored figure in the building, invested with huge power but without a salary, an office, or the support, or even the respect, of the staff.

Covid had America's voters—particularly Democratic voters— fearful of gathering in crowded polling precincts. Trump had so downplayed the risk of Covid that experts were expecting a "Red Mirage" on Election Night—a big lead for Trump from voters who voted by machine, followed by a tsunami of Democratic absentee votes that would take days to count.

Trump and Giuliani spent months disparaging absentee ballots as a fraudulent system designed to steal the election from him, which was both false and wildly self-destructive because it discouraged Republicans from voting by absentee ballot. The stakes were enormous, as over 40 percent of voters cast their ballots by mail in 2016. Far more were expected in 2020.

Giuliani had it in his mind all day that Trump needed to declare victory early in the night, before the Red Wave started to recede. As the hours ticked by and the race tightened, he became more adamant that the president needed to kill the coming Democratic momentum in the crib. He pushed to speak with Trump, who was watching the returns on TV in his private residence.

Word reached the operatives downstairs, where campaign manager Bill Stepien set up a makeshift war room inside the Map Room. The team sent for Giuliani.

A small group, including chief of staff Mark Meadows, was waiting for him when he came downstairs. It was evident to some in the room that Rudy, who had been drinking, was intoxicated.

The Trump aides had little time, as developments in the race were breaking by the minute. "There were a lot more important things to do than talk to Rudy," said one. But they realized he needed to be placated, if only to keep him from going straight to the boss with his ideas.

"We just have to start saying we won," Giuliani implored them.

They were puzzled. "Won where?" asked one. "Just say we won," he insisted.

"Where are your numbers?"

He took out his iPad and started scrolling through his screen, hunting for data. It was a repeat of the scene back in September, when he disrupted Trump's debate prep in the same room, in front of the same disapproving crowd. "He's trying to hit refresh," a participant recalled. "He's got these big fingers pounding on the screen. Nothing was happening."

"Just pick a state and say we won!" he insisted. "Say we won Michigan."

Meadows grew frustrated. "It's irresponsible," he said. "We can't just be saying that." (Biden won Michigan the next day.)

"It just kind of got ridiculous," said an aide. "We were trying to keep Rudy, who was distracting and maybe drunk, away from Trump. What was supposed to be a five-minute kind of courtesy was just going on and on without any obvious ending."

They fell away and went back to work.

Upstairs, the mood was souring as the race grew tighter. At 11:20 p.m., Fox News all but blew up the evening, calling Arizona for Biden with 73 percent of the vote in. It was a crucial battleground state, and a Biden win represented a critical blow for Trump. As his aides made frantic calls to Rupert Murdoch and Fox executives to roll back the call, Biden went on television and said he was "on track" to win the race.

Giuliani's advice suddenly found a taker after he finally made his way to the private residence.

At 2:30 a.m., with partiers weary and plates of half-eaten sliders and French fries growing cold, Trump had his staff play "Hail to the Chief," and he walked up to the podium to speak to the nation. "This is a fraud on the American public," Trump said. "This is an embarrassment to our country. We were getting ready to win this election. Frankly, we did win this election."

It was another victory for Giuliani over his West Wing adversaries. The nation was in for another calamitous journey, with Donald Trump and his alter ego leading the way.

CHAPTER 16

Conspiracy

On January 10, 2021, ten weeks after Election Day, Maria Ryan, Rudy Giuliani's girlfriend, decided to send a letter to the president of the United States. Like Judith Giuliani before her, Ryan was more than just a romantic partner to her famous companion; he had made her a partner in his public life. She was half the team of *Uncovering the Truth with Rudy Giuliani & Dr. Maria Ryan*, his Sunday radio show, and president of Giuliani Communications, the company that operated his media channels. She was his closest confidante; wherever he went, so did she.

Like Judith and Cristyne Lategano, Maria met Giuliani while he was married to someone else. Ryan was CEO of Cottage Hospital, a small, thirty-five-bed facility in New Hampshire. When they were first spotted together at a resort hotel two hours from her home in the spring of 2018, he went to great lengths to deny they were dating—she was also married. But the public had long stopped caring about his marital dramas by then, and eventually the pretense faded.

Also like Giuliani's prior companions, Ryan was intensely protective of him, and of her primacy in his life. So it must have seemed only natural to her that she should write Donald Trump with a list of demands on his behalf.

Giuliani was working pro bono for the president, but as money grew tight for him, he and Ryan had pressed the campaign for compensation. Shortly after the election, she emailed Trump's campaign managers requesting $20,000 per day in legal fees for him, an enormous ask that would have made him one of the highest-paid attorneys in the country. The effort quickly backfired when word reached the media, antagonizing the president and making compensation even less likely. That did not dissuade her from bringing up the issue again in her January letter—this time with some additional requests.

"Dear Mr. President," she wrote on January 10, "I tried to call you yesterday to talk about business. The honorable Rudy Giuliani has worked 24/7 on the voter fraud issues. He has led a team of lawyers, data analysts and investigators."

She followed with three numbered items:

1) He needs to be paid for his services. I gave an invoice to Mark Meadows via Katherine Friess. As you know, he lost his job and income and more defending you during the Russia hoax investigation and then the impeachment pro bono.

2) The Medal of Freedom. Mr. Giuliani rarely asks for anything for himself. He is praying you present him with this on Friday, January 15 or Monday the 19 [*sic*].

3) General Pardon

At the bottom of the letter, she also hinted that he would like Trump to name him "an election prosecutor."

"Please call me if you'd like to discuss any of these items," she wrote at the end.

The invoice she referred to, sent to chief of staff Mark Meadows, was for $2.5 million plus expenses for Giuliani's legal fees. She sent an additional letter to Meadows requesting $45,000 for *her* services—"working in the campaign pursuing truth and justice for the president."

Ryan gave the letter to Friess, an attorney working with Giuliani, to send to Trump. Alarmed, she shared it with Bernie Kerik.

He was appalled by the audacity of her casual request for a pardon, $2.5 million, and a Medal of Freedom—and her giving Trump dates to choose from. As for the pardon, Giuliani had not been accused by the government of committing a crime at the time, but the investigation by the Southern District fueled speculation that Trump would grant him a pardon to shut down the probe. Giuliani denied he was seeking a pardon even as his girlfriend was writing letters lobbying for it.

Frightened by the potential for it ending in embarrassment for Giuliani, Kerik buried the letter in a drawer, hoping Ryan did not send them a different way.

Giuliani would insist he never sought a pardon, which was disputed by at least one White House aide.

The episode was a perfect distillation of the farcical, sometimes delusional, quality to his efforts in the final months of the Trump presidency. As in the Ukraine scandal, he committed reckless acts that were so damaging they had historic repercussions, and without a second's thought. In a lifetime of crusades, this was his grand finale, and it ended in a crescendo.

When the sun rose the morning after the November 3 election, there was no declared winner. Trump and Biden were running neck and neck in a handful of battleground states, where election officials were still wading through the monsoon of mail-in votes.

Trump's campaign to delegitimize the mail-ins revved into high gear. He dispatched Giuliani, his son and daughter-in-law Eric and Lara Trump, Corey Lewandowski, and election lawyer and former

Florida attorney general Pam Bondi to Pennsylvania, a critical bat-tleground state, where he was leading Biden by 700,000 votes, with 1.4 million mail-in ballots still to be counted. The president had rea-son to be worried, as Biden was winning almost 80 percent of the mail-ins so far.

Giuliani's group convened a press conference on a Philadelphia street, which was covered live by the cable networks. Their accu-sations flew like pinwheel sparks, shooting off in a hundred direc-tions. Eric Trump charged that volunteers for Biden hung posters and passed out flyers at polling locations, hardly the stuff of a stolen election, even if true. "Guys, this is fraud," he said.

Giuliani, with decades more practice at this sort of thing, railed against the "Democrat crooked machine of Philadelphia."

"They're not going to steal this election," he warned. "This is be-yond anything I've ever seen before."

He didn't come armed with specific allegations of fraudulent vote counting, just a bitter complaint that the campaign's poll watchers were kept so far away from the workers processing mail-in ballots at the Philadelphia Convention Center that they couldn't tell either way. "Joe Biden could have voted 50 times, as far as we know, or 5,000 times," he said. "Do you think we're stupid?"

An Election Day judge had already ruled that the Board of Elec-tion had followed the law, but Giuliani wasn't impressed. "Obviously a political hack," he said.

As for how far their poll watchers were being kept back, the num-bers varied depending on who had the mic. "Twenty or thirty feet away," said Giuliani. "Forty, fifty yards away," said Eric Trump. "At least thirty feet," said Bondi. A poll watcher named Jeremy Mercer whom Giuliani brought to the microphone said it was "hundreds, at least a hundred feet away."

Giuliani turned to Mercer to question him. "Could you tell us how many ballots approximately went through that process that you had no chance to observe?" he asked. "Based on the counts that we've heard, it's about 125,000, maybe more," Mercer replied. "Well, so that should be deducted from the count," Giuliani said, as though throwing away such a massive number of votes were nothing special.

Election Day corruption, Giuliani charged, wasn't limited to Philadelphia—it was prevalent in all the Democratic-controlled cities in swing states. "Quite possibly, we'll do a national lawsuit and really expose the corruption of the Democratic Party."

"We're going to win this election," he said. "We've actually won it—it's just a matter of counting the votes fairly."

The cast of characters, with their hyperventilating language and sloppy arguments, screamed B-Team—"something out of a Coen brothers film," quipped Jake Tapper on CNN.

The contempt was shared inside the Trump campaign.

Back in July, with Biden's lead over the president rising into double digits, Trump fired his campaign manager, Brad Parscale, and brought in a new team led by Bill Stepien, an operative close to Chris Christie, and election attorneys Justin Clark and Matt Morgan. The three were data-focused, with an aversion to publicity. Members of the crew were among those who tangled with Giuliani at Trump's debate prep in September, and on election night. To say that they were wary of him would be an understatement.

After the Philadelphia press conference, Bernie Kerik drove home to New Jersey. As he was settling in for the evening, Giuliani called him. "I talked to the president," he said, "and he's going to need help with the legal part. I need you to come back."

Like the military man he was, Kerik didn't question or complain—he packed his bag and drove back to Washington. In the morning, he visited his boss at his hotel suite and was told they had a meeting scheduled with the campaign's legal team at Trump headquarters in Arlington, Virginia. At 10 a.m., Kerik walked into a large, faux-modern industrial office, with exposed air-conditioning ducts and sweeping glass windows overlooking the Potomac. The place was littered with empty pizza boxes and other reminders of election night two days earlier.

He was joined in a large glass conference room by Giuliani, Maria Ryan, Christianné Allen, and Victoria Toensing and Joseph diGenova, the husband-wife legal team that assisted Giuliani in his Ukraine exploits. There was just one person he didn't know, sitting at the far end of the table, scribbling notes.

When the conversation in the room hit a lull, Kerik couldn't resist turning to the stranger in the corner of the room. "Excuse me, who are you?" he asked. He introduced himself as Matt Morgan, the campaign's general counsel. "What are you doing here?" Kerik asked. "Where is everybody?"

"It's just me—I'm going to help the mayor with what he needs," Morgan said.

"Really, dude?" Kerik thought. "One person? Where was the fucking team?"

The legal effort was not as robust as it should have been, but that was not the reason the meeting wasn't better staffed with Trump officials. "People didn't want to be associated with him," a senior campaign aide said of Giuliani. "Everyone just kind of avoided him." Morgan had drawn the short straw; someone from the campaign was assigned to babysit Giuliani's group every few hours.

But Stepien, Clark, and Morgan knew it was Giuliani who had the president's ear. While Clark and his legal team gamed out court challenges in swing states, the president's attorney was working outside the chain of command, feeding Trump sweeping conspiracy theories and pushing for far more dramatic steps. Trump soaked it up.

"STOP THE COUNT!" Trump tweeted the morning after Election Day.

"ANY VOTE THAT CAME IN AFTER ELECTION DAY WILL NOT BE COUNTED!" he tweeted the next day.

Giuliani's entourage started to swell after Election Day. His new compatriots were a crew of right-wing attorneys: Sidney Powell, who gained acclaim in MAGA circles for her representation of Michael Flynn; Boris Epshteyn, a Trump enthusiast known for his work as a commentator for the conservative Sinclair Broadcast Group; Jenna Ellis, a Christian conservative activist who authored a book arguing that the Constitution should be interpreted through a biblical perspective, and that gay marriage encouraged pedophilia; and, as the work ran into December, John Eastman, a conservative academic who once clerked for Clarence Thomas.

Stepien and his colleagues were mainstream Republican consultants, men who had steadily climbed the political ladder to the White House. Giuliani's new friends were a more colorful crew, hailing from the fringes of the party, only to be plucked from the shadows and thrust into the limelight by Trump. They were the kind of lawyers Southern District Rudy Giuliani would have disparaged as cranks. But as he set out to relive his days as the most feared prosecutor in America, his squad was no longer the Justice Department's best and brightest, but rather a motley crew of conspiracists and a homophobe.

The Giuliani and Trump campaign teams operated in separate orbits, sharing only a mutual contempt. Ellis referred to their group as Trump's "Elite Strikeforce." Stepien and his colleagues called themselves "Team Normal."

Their meetings were disastrous. Team Normal found Giuliani's crew—and Giuliani in particular—unprepared, disorganized, and ignorant of election laws. The Giuliani group spoke in the Trump lexicon: deep state, fake news, stolen election.

"They had no plan," a campaign official said. "They'd just be talking, nobody doing anything. It was bizarre."

One by one, Clark, Stepien, Morgan, and the others would quietly slip out of meetings with them and return to their desks. "People would just be like, 'Fuck this, I'm out,'" one said.

Keeping Giuliani from doing too much damage was a constant conversation among the high command.

"He was impossible to control," a senior campaign official said. "We were trying to run the campaign and provide sound advice to the president and it was a sideshow and a distraction all along the way.

"In the middle of all we were doing, we had to have a daily—multiple times daily, at times—conversation about what do we do about Giuliani. Do we keep him in headquarters? That was a real difficulty because he was a complete distraction, bossing twenty-three-year-old staffers around, who were getting him coffee, and getting him legal pads, and taking over the conference room.

"Or do we get him out on the road so we can actually get stuff done at headquarters and keep him away from the president because he's a bad influence on the president? Well, that was a problem too."

That became crystal clear on Saturday, November 7. With the mail-in vote overwhelmingly favoring Biden, the presidency was slipping from Trump's grasp. Giuliani and Kerik headed back to Pennsylvania.

"Lawyers Press Conference Four Seasons, Philadelphia. 11:00 a.m.," Trump tweeted at 9:35 a.m. He deleted it eight minutes later, then tweeted, "Four Season's Landscaping!" before deleting that a minute later. A minute after that, he tweeted, "Big press conference today in Philadelphia at Four Seasons Total Landscaping—11:30am!" Five minutes later, he tweeted again. "Lawyer's Press Conference at Four Season's Landscaping, Philadelphia. Enjoy!"

He wasn't the only person confused by the location. Marie Siravo, the owner of Four Seasons Total Landscaping in Northeast Philadelphia, located in an industrial neighborhood just off I-95, received a call at home about the same time from the manager of the Four Seasons Hotel in Philadelphia. "Are they coming to you or are they coming to me?" he asked.

For reasons neither she, a battalion of reporters, nor the president of the United States could figure out, the campaign asked to hold a press conference in her company's parking lot, a backdrop too forlorn for a school board candidate, much less America's Mayor. But Siravo's son called her from the office and told her to rush over. "Rudy Giuliani's at your desk, and I think he's talking to the Big Guy," he said. She and her husband did the hour-and-fifteen-minute drive in forty-eight minutes, in such a hurry they drove the wrong way down a one-way street.

She was beaten to it by a local political gadfly named Daryl Brooks, a poll watcher at the convention center claiming to have been prevented from observing the vote count. He arrived in time to see Giuliani and Bernie Kerik emerge from a black car. "This is the guy from 9/11," he thought. "Oh shit."

He found himself sitting with Giuliani in a conference room at the landscaping office when Trump called. Giuliani and Corey Lewandowski took the call in a nearby room and put him on speaker. "He was telling them not to be afraid, and to set the record straight," he recalled. "He was angry."

Giuliani's team wasn't aware that Brooks had served over three years in prison for allegedly exposing himself to two young girls. Their vetting process, if there was one, allowed these mishaps to occur again and again (Brooks claimed he was wrongfully convicted). But that slipup paled next to the derision Giuliani received for the location of the press conference, representing the president at a dreary parking lot in the middle of nowhere instead of, say, an upscale hotel bearing the same name.

Shortly before the event began a woman barged into the room where Giuliani was preparing and announced that CNN had called the election for Biden. Giuliani was furious. "How can they call an election?" he asked, his arms waving. "The press can't call an election!"

He emerged from the building into the asphalt lot, Trump posters taped to the wall behind him, and commenced the press conference as if nothing had happened, hammering away about the poll watching outrage, and tossing in new charges that dead people's names were showing up in some write-in ballots; others were backdated, he said. There was a "very strong circumstantial case" that 600,000 write-in ballots were tampered with, he charged.

He had no evidence. "It's not my job to determine if the ballots are right or not, it's their job," he said of the city's election officials.

Back in Washington, Team Normal was gathered at headquarters for a sobering moment with White House officials and family members, including Jared Kushner, Hope Hicks, Dan Scavino, Eric Trump, as well as White House lawyer Eric Herschmann and David Bossie, who headed the legal team until coming down with Covid two days later. They were taking a last look at the numbers, trying to decide as a group what to tell the president about a race that was ending badly.

"It's not looking good," Stepien told them, according to a person who was present. "We need to provide counsel to him about what his chances are, and how to close this out in the best way possible for him."

Giuliani and his press conference wasn't on their minds. "Honestly, we were just happy to have him out of the office," a campaign official said.

The bottom fell out soon enough. One news organization after another started calling Pennsylvania for Biden, and declared him the winner of the presidential race. The election was over.

Word started to travel through the press corps at Giuliani's event that the race had been called. By whom? Giuliani asked a reporter. "All the networks," a reporter said.

"Oh my goodness!" he cried out theatrically. "All the networks! Wow!" He raised his arms to the sky, as if praying to the gods. "All the networks! We have to forget about the law! Judges don't count!"

And at that, with the race called, reporters started packing up their notebooks and tape recorders and filing out mid-event. The press conference was a bust.

The Four Seasons mishap became such a national joke that the owners of the landscaping company sold over a million dollars of parody T-shirts in less than a month. It was a measure of how farcical things were becoming that the event would not even be Giuliani's worst laughingstock moment of the campaign.

Later in the day, Stepien, Clark, Miller, Bossie, and Herschmann traveled to the White House to deliver difficult news to the president in the Yellow Oval Room in his private residence. He was fresh off the golf course and wearing a white "Make America Great Again" cap. Stepien and Clark ran through the odds with him; the campaign needed to win a challenge in Wisconsin, another in Pennsylvania, and hope for the remaining uncounted votes to tip the scales in his favor in Arizona and Georgia. But the chances of turning the situation around were low, perhaps 5 or 10 percent. The subtext was that it was over.

Trump seemed to listen. Giuliani, however, had been telling him the opposite: that he had won the election, and needed to fight the malevolent forces intent upon stealing it from him. Stepien and the others waited while the president changed out of his golf gear, showered, and got dressed for dinner with Melania. While he was gone, they game-planned: he needed to understand the slim chances of winning. They repeated it when Trump came back. But he had no intention of giving up.

*　　*　　*

"This was a dishonest election," Giuliani said on his radio show with Maria Ryan the next day. "This is all about Marxism, communism, socialism," she added. "Fake news all the time, 24/7."

Their guest, Steve Bannon, declared flatly that Trump had won the race. "Seventy-one million people will never accept Biden's stealing of the election," he said.

Giuliani detailed the alleged voting scam with no proof. "Thousands upon thousands upon thousands" of dead people had voted in Pennsylvania, he said. "Very distinguished mathematicians" believed it was statistically impossible for Biden to have made up the 700,000-vote deficit with the mail-in vote. Observers were "locked out of polling places." Witnesses would attest to it.

A year after conjuring up a nonexistent scandal in Ukraine that led to the impeachment of a president, he was doing it all over again. The campaign's legal team had law firms across the country filing suits where there was a case to make, but his approach was of a wholly different nature. It wasn't a technical issue here or there he was talking about, but a national conspiracy.

"He had zero regard for whether something was factual or not," said a frustrated senior aide to the president. "It didn't matter. He just wanted the president to be happy. It was pretty remarkable. . . .

"I get why the president was listening to him," the aide said of Giuliani. "But I don't get why Rudy would tell him that."

It wasn't so much that Giuliani was telling Trump something he knew wasn't true; rather his own survival rested on it *being* true. Giuliani was seventy-six years old; his political and financial future, even his escape from prosecution, was dependent upon Trump's remaining in power. No one was as prepared to fight as hard to overturn the election results as he was.

He excelled at winding up the president on the alleged conspiracy as his aides were trying to calm him down. In an Oval Office meeting with Giuliani's team and White House lawyers on November 10, Trump vented his frustration that Attorney General Bill Barr was not investigating the stolen election charges. "Why isn't he looking into all the stuff that we're finding?" he asked Giuliani. "Isn't that what he is supposed to do?"

"Yes," Giuliani said, "if there's evidence of criminality, of intimidation, or of voter fraud, they have a criminal and a civil division and would both look at that."

Trump looked at Pat Cipollone, the White House counsel, standing next to Giuliani. "You were supposed to talk to the attorney general," he said.

"We have," he said. Eric Herschmann, the White House lawyer, had done so.

"Is he going to investigate? Is he going to look at this stuff?"

"I hope so." Cipollone shrugged.

"That's your answer? You hope so?"

Angered, Trump looked at Giuliani, who was sitting next to Bernie Kerik. "See? That's what I have to deal with," he said. "You have him," he said, pointing to Kerik. "I have that," he complained, alluding to Cipollone.

It wasn't fair to Cipollone, a frequent target of Trump's, since Barr was adamantly refusing to play ball. The DOJ had not found anything close to the level of irregularities that Giuliani was alleging. At his own Oval Office meeting with Trump a few weeks later, Barr called Giuliani's allegations "bullshit," and referred to his team as a "clown show."

Trump refused to concede, creating a nerve-wracking, split-screen situation for the nation, in which Biden was making transition announcements while Trump was claiming he'd won. Only a few Republicans dared acknowledge Biden's victory, and Senate Majority Leader Mitch McConnell, worried that angering Trump

would jeopardize two Senate contests in Georgia that were yet to be decided, declared the president "100 percent within his rights" to look into irregularities.

With the situation careening toward a constitutional crisis, tensions between the Giuliani camp and the campaign legal team exploded in a series of White House confrontations.

Clark, Stepien, and Jason Miller were waiting in the Cabinet Room for a meeting when Clark, the leader of the campaign legal team, was called into the Oval Office, where the president and others were discussing their litigation efforts in Georgia. Giuliani was on speakerphone, criticizing Clark's work and agitating for the campaign to file a federal lawsuit. "They're letting you down," he told the president.

Clark repeatedly explained that it was premature to sue, that the courts only entertained recount demands after races were certified.

"They're lying to you," Giuliani told Trump repeatedly.

Clark lost his temper. "You're a fucking asshole, Rudy!"

Trump didn't show his hand as their argument escalated. But his next move should have been obvious to anyone in the room.

Giuliani was staying at the Mandarin Oriental Hotel in New York, where Christianné Allen had turned a fifth-floor room into a media space for his radio show and media interviews. He went live on WABC at 3 p.m. His main target was the Dominion and Smartmatic voting machines that were employed by localities across the country on Election Day.

"It's actually mind-boggling when you look at it," he said. "Dominion software is a Canadian company. Why we are using a Canadian company to count our ballots is strange to start with.

"Its software really is Venezuelan," he said. "It's called Smartmatic. It was invented for Hugo Chávez to steal elections.

". . . One of the top people in Dominion is a very big vocal supporter of Antifa," he said. "The CEO of Smartmatic until a few weeks ago was a close associate of George Soros."

All of his statements were wrong. Dominion was founded in Canada but had moved its headquarters to the U.S. Smartmatic wasn't a Venezuelan company (two of its founders were Venezuelan, but it was founded in Florida). Smartmatic was a competitor of Dominion's, not its software supplier. The alleged ties to Chávez, Antifa, and Soros were fictitious.

In the midst of his disinformation spree one of his three cell phones rang; the caller ID read "White House." He cut to a commercial break and took one of his headphone earmuffs off to speak with the caller. The conversation ran twice as long as the break, so Allen had to call the control room in New York to tell them to fill the time with additional ads.

Before he went back on the air, Giuliani let Allen know that the president had just named him the new head of his legal team.

The United States Courthouse in Williamsport, Pennsylvania, sits nearly two hundred miles west and a world away from the imperious Foley Square tower in which Rudy Giuliani rose to fame as a young prosecutor. It is a four-story, utilitarian glass-and-brick building, so drab it could be a police station. Far from the pulsating energy of downtown Manhattan, Williamsport's population could barely fill half the seats at Yankee Stadium. Its claim to fame is being the birthplace of Little League Baseball and the location of Little League's annual World Series.

It was an unlikely setting for a hearing that could determine the winner of a presidential race. But that was Giuliani's intent on the morning of November 17, 2020, when he pulled up to the courthouse to argue the case himself. He was far heavier than he was back in his prosecutorial heyday, and walked so unsteadily that a security aide had to hold his arm when he walked up and down the building's steps.

When he entered Chief Judge Matthew Brann's courtroom and

walked to the plaintiff's table, wearing a navy suit and striped tie, it felt like a comeback attempt by an aging star.

His aim was to persuade the judge to block the certification of Pennsylvania's election results, and throw out nearly 700,000 mail-in votes. It was a wildly unrealistic goal, bordering on delusional. The campaign was losing far more modest cases in virtually every state in which it brought legal action, and law firms hired by the campaign were bailing out.

He had worked through the night preparing the suit earlier in the week, arguing in it that the election had been stolen from Trump by a coordinated, nationwide campaign of fraud perpetuated by the Democrats. But Clark's team had edited it heavily, and removed his wildest allegations, leaving him to argue a narrow complaint about two voters who claimed their ballots were improperly voided. That matter didn't interest Giuliani, so he argued the larger point anyway—how big-city Democratic bosses were rigging votes for Biden, and how Republican observers were being denied the right to observe vote counting.

He spoke with the clarity and force that had won him so many cases in his prime. But it was a radio show monologue he was delivering, not a courtroom argument over the narrow matter at hand.

"The best description of the situation is widespread nationwide voter fraud . . . and that is part of the reason I am here," he said. "Because this is not an isolated case—it is a case that is repeated in at least 10 other jurisdictions."

The Democrats had "made fools of" Republican poll watchers on Election Day by keeping them far away from the counting, he said, producing a handful of affidavits. But he had no evidence of fraud, and under questioning admitted his was not even a fraud case. To make things worse, an opposing attorney announced that another Pennsylvania court had just ruled against the Trump campaign on the poll watcher issue.

The judge was incredulous. "You're alleging that the two individual plaintiffs were denied the right to vote, but at bottom you're
asking this court to invalidate more than 6.8 million votes, thereby
disenfranchising every single voter in the commonwealth," he said.
"Can you tell me how this result can possibly be justified?"

Only 680,000 votes, Giuliani corrected him.

Lloyd MacMahon, Giuliani's mentor, would have been appalled
to see his former law clerk fumble through the hearing. When
Judge Brann asked him what standard of review applied to the case,
Giuliani seemed thrown. "I think the normal one," he said. Another
time, he told the judge, "Maybe I don't understand what you mean
by strict scrutiny."

But his biggest mistake was arguing the case at all. Brann's ruling a week later was scathing, and personal. "One might expect that
when seeking such a startling outcome, a plaintiff would come for-
midably armed with compelling legal arguments and factual proof of
rampant corruption," he wrote. "That has not happened."

Instead, Giuliani presented "strained legal arguments without
merit and speculative accusations . . . unsupported by evidence."

Giuliani's suit, he said, was a "Frankenstein's Monster."

It was a reality check from a responsible adult in a small Pennsylvania town intruding upon Trump and Giuliani's alternate universe.
It was short-lived.

Twelve days after the Four Seasons fiasco, Giuliani and his compatriots convened a press conference for dozens of journalists and a
live television audience in a lobby area inside Republican National
Committee headquarters in Washington. It was a small, claustrophobic space with low ceilings and more people than chairs; Bernie Kerik
had to watch it from the back of the room, over the shoulders of cameramen with their tripods. Christianné Allen watched from the side.

Giuliani opened with his usual speech about a centralized conspiracy by the Democrats to rig the election and keep Trump's poll

watchers from observing the count. To illustrate, he did an impression from *My Cousin Vinny*—"How many fingahs do I got up?"—cross-examining an elderly woman with bad eyesight in court.

He told the story of a worker who saw "thousands and thousands" of votes delivered by food trucks to a Detroit voting location in the dead of night. The ballots, he said, "were in garbage cans, they were in paper bags, they were in cardboard boxes, and they were taken into the center. . . ."

"I know crimes," he said. "I can smell them." He failed to note that a Michigan judge had already thrown out the worker's allegation as not credible.

The room was stifling hot, and Giuliani was sweating profusely. Rivulets of liquefied hair dye began streaming down his sideburns. Unaware, he mopped sweat from his cheeks and forehead, but not the sides of his face where the dye was trickling toward his jaw. The unfortunate spectacle was playing out on national television.

Allen was alarmed, and tried to get his attention from the side of the room. Giuliani saw her gesticulating but didn't understand what she was trying to tell him. She stood frozen, unsure whether walking up to him on live television and telling him to wipe the dye off his face would do more harm than good. "There were just thousands of clicks happening, and I knew that was going to be everywhere afterwards," she said.

Kerik, trapped behind the crowd of cameramen, was unable to get to the front of the room, and stood helplessly. He was a public figure himself, and had no misconceptions about how this would play out. "Nobody's going to pay attention to the fucking fraud," he thought.

The sight of Giuliani continuing to argue his case, oblivious to his predicament, was riveting television. Kerik wasn't altogether correct that the visuals of the event would be the only headline, though. Sidney Powell, towering over Giuliani and Jenna Ellis in a leopard-print cardigan, spoke next, and in a syrupy North Carolina drawl brought the absurdity of the crusade to new heights.

"What we are really dealing with here and uncovering more by the day, is the massive influence of communist money through Venezuela, Cuba, and likely China in the interference with our elections here in the United States," she began.

"The Dominion voting systems, the Smartmatic technology software and the software that goes in other computerized voting systems here as well—not just Dominion—were created in Venezuela at the direction of Hugo Chávez to make sure he never lost an election after one constitutional referendum came out the way he did not want it to come out."

The software was programmed to flip votes from Trump to Biden, she alleged. The flood tide of Trump votes "broke the algorithm," she added in a head-scratcher.

Her rant came without anything approaching evidence, a problem that Jenna Ellis, the next speaker, tried and failed to spin away. "This is basically an opening statement," she argued. "Putting on evidence takes time."

Ellis and Jason Miller, who was working for the campaign, pushed Giuliani to prevent Powell from speaking prior to the event. "We'll own her and all of her craziness," Miller said he warned him, arguing that Giuliani himself had at times expressed reservations about her conspiracy mongering. But he pushed back, saying Powell had "some really good points and ideas," and added, "star power." In fact, the gulf between Powell's arguments and Giuliani's was narrowing by the day; he'd been on the radio arguing much of what she alleged.

As the streaks of hair dye on his face turned into streams, Ellis seemed to grasp that the point of the press conference was lost. "I've seen all of you taking pictures right now, and I can anticipate what your headlines are going to be," she said angrily. Giuliani looked on quizzically.

The event set off alarm bells at the White House and campaign headquarters. Trump was said to be unsettled. Bill Barr, already distancing himself from Trump's crusade, found it "a grotesque embarrassment."

The campaign team in Arlington was appalled—"a complete embarrassment," said one official. Chris Christie called the conduct of the legal team "a national embarrassment." Christopher Krebs, who oversaw election security under Trump until he was fired for defending the election results, tweeted that it was "the most dangerous one hour and 45 minutes of television in American history—and possibly the craziest."

For his part, Giuliani never exhibited any embarrassment. "He didn't focus on it for more than thirty seconds," Allen claimed.

"When he was at City Hall, he would've been bugging out," Kerik said. "He was basically beyond that. The left-wing media was going to slaughter him anyway."

His streak of laughingstock episodes resumed on December 2 in a Michigan state government hearing room in Lansing. Sitting at the witness table with Jenna Ellis before the House Oversight Committee, he urged the state to toss out the election results that had already been certified, a mammoth ask.

"Look, the people who certified your election . . . what are they worth?" he asked.

His star witness was a freelance IT contractor for Dominion, Mellissa Carone, who claimed she watched polling officials run the same ballots through counting machines "at least 30,000" times at Detroit's convention center. She was the source of Giuliani's discredited claim that cartons of Biden votes were secretly delivered by food trucks in the dead of night.

Sitting next to Giuliani, his arms folded and his nose scrunched, she slurred her words, made nonsensical remarks, and appeared to be drunk.

Ballots, she said, had been found "in rivers," and "under rocks."

A puzzled state representative couldn't square her estimate with the poll book, which showed the number of absentee ballots cast. "We're not seeing the poll book off by 30,000 votes," he pointed out.

"What'd you guys do, take it and do something crazy to it?" she replied.

Carone later denied that she was drunk. Reporters discovered that she had just ended a year's probation for lying to police about sending lewd videos of her fiancé and her to his former wife.

Eight days later, Giuliani traveled to Georgia and charged to legislators that a video showed two low-level election workers, Shaye Moss and her mother, Ruby Freeman, rigging the election outcome, exchanging USB memory sticks "as if they're vials of cocaine." The fabricated charge sparked so many death threats against the women that one had to leave her home for two months.

The depth of Giuliani's cynicism was exposed at a meeting in Arizona with House Speaker Rusty Bowers, where he argued without proof that hundreds of thousands of undocumented immigrants and thousands of dead people in the state had voted for Biden.

"We've got lots of theories, we just don't have the evidence," Giuliani told an astonished Bowers.

It was Ukraine all over again—the president's lawyer, armed with a conspiracy he couldn't prove, using intimidation tactics to try to coerce people to validate it.

The month ended with a tragicomic twist. Giuliani for months had parroted the president in disparaging mask wearing to curb the spread of Covid, and waded proudly through crowds at his various stops unprotected. On December 7, Trump announced that his attorney had contracted the virus.

Giuliani was admitted to Georgetown University Medical Center and received Regeneron, a monoclonal antibody treatment unavailable to most Americans, thanks to Trump's arranging special treatment. "The White House physician helped a lot, the president helped a lot," Giuliani said. "They got me better in two days."

Washington Post columnist Dana Milbank wrote about the episode on December 14. His first line read "Rudy Giuliani is a horrible human being."

By mid-December the outlook for overturning the election results was bleak. The Electoral College affirmed Biden's victory, and the Supreme Court rebuffed efforts to throw out the votes in Texas and Pennsylvania. The campaign filed over sixty lawsuits across the country, and lost or withdrew almost every one of them. The story should have been over.

Trump remained stubbornly convinced the election was stolen from him, however, and rejected appeals by staff and friends to bow out gracefully. Some gave up trying. Barr resigned on December 14. Jared Kushner, Trump's most trusted advisor, checked out of the situation soon after Election Day rather than tangle with Giuliani over his conspiracy theories. The president's son-in-law jetted off to the Mideast to negotiate a rapprochement between Qatar and Saudi Arabia. (Not long afterward he landed a $2 billion Saudi investment into his private equity firm, sparking a Congressional inquiry.)

Kushner's decision to flee the White House removed Giuliani's only significant counterweight at a pivotal moment in history. The president was left with Giuliani, Powell, and the rest of the "Elite Strikeforce" team conspiracists to save his presidency. Meanwhile Biden was announcing cabinet appointments daily.

Trump began tossing out increasingly irresponsible ideas. The conversation turned to how the White House could order the seizure of thousands of machines. Trump was all for it.

The idea was not new. A Texas bar owner and retired Army colonel named Phil Waldron, a self-described information warfare specialist, had developed a proposal for a government takeover of the

machines after concluding that the election results had been manip-
ulated in Biden's favor by Chinese communists, big banks, and other
forces. Michael Flynn, once Trump's national security advisor, was
floating the specter of martial law. Instead of rejecting them as fanat-
ics, Giuliani traveled with Waldron to speak with state legislators,
and Trump invited Flynn to the White House.

Nineteen years after his failed effort to extend his term in office
after 9/11, Giuliani placed an astonishing phone call.

With Trump's encouragement, he called a contact at the Department of Homeland Security, Ken Cuccinelli, the acting deputy
secretary. He asked him whether DHS could impound the voting
machines. Cuccinelli took some time to study the matter. He ultimately informed Giuliani there was no legal way to do so.

Giuliani was out to dinner on December 18 when he was summoned to the White House. When he entered the Oval Office he
stepped into a war that had been raging for hours between Sidney
Powell, Michael Flynn, and White House lawyers. Powell and Flynn
had drafted executive orders for Trump, one to call in the military
to confiscate the nation's voting machines, the other to order Homeland Security to do so. Powell was also requesting that Trump appoint her special counsel to investigate election fraud.

Giuliani and Powell were already butting heads; as far out as he'd
gone in the crusade, he still saw himself as the same protector of the
law that he'd always been. Flynn and Powell's proposal to call in the
military was a nonstarter, he told Trump, unless there was evidence
of foreign interference in the election. Powell produced a handful of
affidavits that Giuliani dismissed as flimsy.

Giuliani had finally discovered a line he wouldn't cross when
confronted by someone who had no sense of boundaries at all. It's
possible that someone in the chain of command would have found
a way to halt a Trump executive order to confiscate the machines if
he had signed it, or that the courts would have stepped in to halt it.

But Giuliani stopped Trump before it was set in motion, and helped prevent a historic disaster.

The draft executive orders fell by the wayside, as did Powell's bid to be named special counsel. When the meeting ended, Trump told Giuliani he didn't want to see her back in the White House.

"We are in the eve of a day that will live in history," Giuliani announced to his radio audience on the afternoon of January 5. "Tomorrow January 6, 2021, will be written about in our history books, as long as we still have history—forever."

He didn't say which aspect of the following day's events had him most excited, as he had spent weeks working on different ways to reverse, delay, or nullify Joe Biden's election. Congress was required by law to count the electoral votes, a formality that Trump and Giuliani saw as an opportunity.

Working out of a makeshift war room at Washington's Willard Hotel, Giuliani oversaw a clandestine effort to pressure swing state officials to reject elector slates that favored Biden, and replace them with "alternate" slates favoring Trump. Those slates were hurriedly thrown together by pro-Trump forces, who sent fake certifications to Congress hoping to delay the January 6 count.

They were also lobbying Washington lawmakers to put the vote on hold to allow state legislatures time to change their elector slates. Trump was putting pressure on Vice President Mike Pence to delay the count of electoral votes unilaterally.

With the nation on edge in anticipation of the joint session, Trump's team was whipping the base into a frenzy by framing Congress's vote on the electors, and Pence's subsequent actions, as the moment to reclaim the nation from Biden.

"What they're saying is not just a cover-up, it's a cover-up of a massive crime, and God willing it's gonna come out before this country really starts heading in the wrong direction," Giuliani warned his listeners.

He neglected to highlight the biggest spectacle planned for the next day, an enormous "Save America" rally on the White House Ellipse, at which Trump and his allies, Giuliani included, would be speaking. Intended as a table-setter, it would become the main event.

On the morning of January 6, Giuliani left the Willard for the rally at around 10 a.m. He piled into a row of vehicles with Kerik, Maria Ryan, Andrew Giuliani, John Eastman, and Boris Epshteyn, and took a drive that turned into a crawl. Tens of thousands of rally participants jammed the streets around the Ellipse. Drivers dropped Giuliani's team off on a street corner, and they trudged through grass on the National Mall to get to the Ellipse.

The visual at the Ellipse was stunning; there was a giant scaffolding, swathed in sheer purple curtains, that framed the White House perfectly behind the speaker podium. American flags swayed in the breeze, and giant banners read "Save America March."

The crowd was filled with diehard MAGA fans and members of more than a dozen ultranationalist groups and militias, with names like Oath Keepers and Proud Boys. Some of the organizations had spent weeks planning acts of violence.

Giuliani took the stage to chants of *"Rudy!"*

Standing on the Ellipse stage, winding up the throng of restive protesters, he seemed an older, more desperate version of the Rudy Giuliani who stood with a bullhorn at the police rally outside City Hall twenty-eight years earlier. As in 1992, he was bathing in a mob's adoration, feeding off its anger, sharing its resentment. He had changed dramatically since that day, but not completely.

Facing the likely end of the Trump presidency, and with it his political influence, relevance to the media, and ability to attract clients, he made one last call to stop the train.

Wearing a black suit and red tie, he offered no opening quip, no thank-yous, no flattery to the crowd. He went straight to the point.

"Every single thing that has been outlined as the plan for today is perfectly legal," he began. Pence, he said, "can decide on the validity of these crooked ballots, or he can send it back to the legislators, give them five to 10 days to finally finish the work. . . .

"Over the next 10 days, we get to see the machines that are crooked, the ballots that are fraudulent, and if we're wrong, we will be made fools of. But if we're right, a lot of them will go to jail!"

He thumped the podium with his right hand. "So let's have trial by combat!" he said to cheers. "I'm willing to stake my reputation, the President is willing to stake his reputation, on the fact that we're going to find criminality there."

To anyone listening to him closely over the previous two years it wasn't surprising that he would invoke violence; it was an almost natural progression. He'd piled one conspiracy atop another over the months—the Mueller witch hunt, the missing Hillary Clinton email server, Biden and Burisma, the communist takeover, the Black Lives Matter threat, the secret laptop, the stolen election. An armed rebellion seemed almost like a logical response to the government criminality he had been depicting.

When his speech ended he and Kerik hung out backstage, but by the time Trump spoke at noon they were freezing, as neither had overcoats. Kerik prevailed upon the boss to head back to the Willard with him twenty minutes into the president's speech.

According to Kerik, they left without hearing Trump exhort the crowd to march to the Capitol and "fight like hell." Prompted by his exhortation, almost ten thousand protesters started marching. When they arrived, members of the frenzied crowd stormed through barricades and raced up the Capitol steps.

At 2:13 p.m. the first protesters breached the building, smashed windows, stormed through the corridors, and ransacked offices.

The televised joint session of Congress was adjourned, and Pence, Speaker Nancy Pelosi, and others were whisked away to secure locations. The violence left multiple people dead and hundreds injured, including more than 140 officers.

Giuliani's radio show began at 3 p.m.

"I'm not there at Capitol Hill, but I'm watching it right across the street from me here in this room, on television, and it looks crowded, flags going back and forth," he said. "But it looks extraordinarily peaceful, almost quiet."

The media, he said, was "going to find some kid who stole something they shouldn't have stole and they're going to blame it on Trump not telling them to stay the heck away from Washington. . . .

"This looks almost like an inaugural," he said. "There's nothing disruptive about it."

He knew more than he let on. Four days earlier, he predicted to Cassidy Hutchinson, an aide to Trump's chief of staff Mark Meadows, that January 6 would be a "great day," she recounted to a House committee investigating the riots.

"We are going to the Capitol," Giuliani said. "It's going to be great. The president is going to be there. He's going to look powerful."

When Hutchinson asked Meadows about it, she said he replied, "There is a lot going on, Cass, but I don't know—things may get real, real bad on January 6."

Deny reality as Giuliani tried, his efforts to usurp the Electoral College vote fell apart in Congress at an evening session filled with fury at Trump. Both chambers and Pence approved the Electoral College vote and certified Biden as president.

It was Trump, not Giuliani, who bore the most responsibility for the riot that took place that day. It was the president, not his lawyer, who decided to launch an effort to mislead the public about the election results; who chose to divide the country almost for sport; who crossed countless legal and moral lines.

Giuliani's role was to enable the president, feed him lies, encourage his worst impulses, and lead his most malevolent battles. He did so enthusiastically, because Trump had made him relevant again, years after he'd foolishly squandered the love and respect of millions.

The failed effort to overturn the 2020 election damaged Trump politically—he was impeached for a second time—but he still emerged from the debacle as his party's unquestioned leader.

Giuliani, on the other hand, was finished in every conceivable way.

Epilogue

The twentieth anniversary of the World Trade Center attacks arrived eight months after the January 6 insurrection. For Giuliani, the emotional high point of the commemoration each year was the reunion dinner he threw for his old City Hall and Giuliani Partners staff.

The election and Covid prevented him from throwing the event in 2020, and the fallout from the riots and Trump's loss were proving too draining for him to focus on it in 2021. But twenty years was a huge milestone, and Bernie Kerik offered to organize the event and even foot the bill.

It was held underneath the seventy-foot ceiling and Wedgwood dome of Cipriani, a glitzy Wall Street catering hall that hosted many of the city's prestige charity dinners. Not everyone from the old days was there. Some, like Peter Powers, had passed away, while others had either drifted apart from Giuliani or were so upset by his work for Trump that they stayed away.

It turned out to be a poignant affair. Speakers paid tribute to those who died in the towers that horrible morning, and those who risked their lives to save them. Kerik invited a host of new faces—military men who served their country after the attacks by joining the hunt for al-Qaeda in Afghanistan. A large audience bathed them in applause.

No one received a warmer ovation than Giuliani. When he lumbered up to the stage the crowd jumped to its feet. It wasn't lost on anyone how much had gone wrong for him. But as wayward as their old boss had gone, and as unrecognizable as he'd become, his old friends and employees all had stories to tell about acts of kindness he'd shown them or their family members over the years. Many were deeply grateful for his giving them the most meaningful years of their lives during his mayoralty.

The twenty-year milestone should have been a major moment in Giuliani's storied career. But much had changed for both New York and him over those two decades. The city no longer came to a standstill on the anniversary of 9/11 the way it once did; a generation had been born and raised since the tragedy, while many of those old enough to remember it filed it away as a long-ago event. The meaning of September 11 had also evolved; once a symbol of the nation's strength and unity in the face of adversity, its legacy was far more mixed now, as the attacks had been twisted into a rationale for two wars that left America less respected, and less unified.

Giuliani's meaning to the city, and to the country, had also changed. New Yorkers' feelings about him always careened back and forth from love to hate, but at seventy-seven years old he was less a lightning rod than a tragic figure.

Soon after the January 6 riot, Dominion Voting Systems and Smartmatic, the voting machine companies he maligned on Trump's behalf, filed defamation suits against him for his reckless allegations that they had engaged in a conspiracy to elect Biden. His co-defendants variously included Fox News and Sidney Powell.

He claimed in the sworn deposition of a related case that he "didn't have time" to vet some of the claims of voting fraud that he had made in court and publicly. The Dominion suit alone was for over a billion dollars.

In late April, FBI agents had knocked on the doors of his Madison Avenue apartment and Park Avenue office with search warrants. The Southern District of New York had sent the agents to collect cell phones, computers, and records in its investigation into his dealings in Ukraine (no charges were filed). The Justice Department subsequently opened a separate investigation into the creation of alternate elector slates, with a focus on Giuliani's role.

He was staring at millions of dollars in legal bills, a cash drain so serious that he feared bankruptcy. Donald Trump, for whom he had sacrificed so much, was not offering to return the favor.

So desperate for money was he that he began hawking video greetings for $400 a pop on the online service Cameo. That was dignified compared to his popping out of a jack-in-the-box dressed as a giant rooster in 2022 on *The Masked Singer*, a nationally televised entertainment show.

The most searing news of all came in the summer of 2021. His legal practice was "the love of my life," he told his listeners earlier in the year. "I'll be working until the day I die." But on June 24 the New York State Appellate Court, citing his efforts to mislead the judicial system and the public in the 2020 election, suspended his law license. A few weeks later, Washington, D.C., followed suit. The bedrock of his professional life disintegrated.

He was not one for self-pity; he was more angered by his predicament than depressed. Each time reporters called him for a comment on his latest setback, he answered with well-worn attack lines from the Trump days. The Southern District case against him, he said, represented a "corrupt double standard" by the Justice Department, which looked the other way at "blatant crimes" by Biden and even Hillary Clinton.

So radioactive was he from the election debacle, and the debacles before it, that the television networks declined to interview him on September 11. Burned by his on-air rants about Dominion and Smartmatic, and the lawsuits that followed, even Fox axed him from its 9/11 programming, an insult by an organization that once served as a second home.

According to *Politico*, Fox had banished Giuliani several months before 9/11. *Deadline*, the entertainment website, took issue with *Politico*'s reporting, but its take was even more brutal. "The mayor has a long and distinguished career," it quoted a Fox source as saying, "but in terms of recent coverage, he simply isn't relevant."

He was still in demand by New York's local stations, though, and conducted an outdoor interview with Melissa Russo, WNBC-TV's political reporter, on location at the Trade Center. He was never as thoughtful and soft-spoken as when he talked about September 11, and his bellicosity melted when she asked him about it.

"I don't come here a lot," he told her. "In many ways it's too painful. . . . Every once in a while I get a nightmare, or a bad dream about it."

She brought up his run of bad fortune, asking how he felt about the status of his reputation. "I'm very comfortable with it," he said calmly. "I just do what I think is right. I can't control the reaction of people."

Russo concluded her segment with a chat with her anchor about his erratic behavior. "He also is well aware that people think he's gone off the rails," she said. "But he attributes the damage to his legacy to what he calls an irrational hatred of his former client, President Donald Trump."

Speaking to the crowd at Cipriani that September night, the former mayor spoke movingly about the day of the attacks twenty years earlier, about the strength it took for the people in the room to get New Yorkers through the nightmare—and to get through it themselves. Many in the crowd were moved to tears.

He tried to lighten the mood, performing a terrible impersonation of Queen Elizabeth bestowing his honorary knighthood, and throwing in a tasteless joke about Prince Andrew, who was being sued for sexual assault.

Then he changed subjects and abruptly grew angry, bringing up a recent comment by General Mark Milley, chairman of the Joint Chiefs of Staff, about closing Bagram Air Base in Afghanistan during the U.S. evacuation.

"I wanted to grab his stars, shove it down his throat, and say, 'It's four hundred miles from China, asshole!'" he yelled, almost at the top of his voice.

"China is going to be our enemy for the next forty years! You have an airbase four hundred miles from them and you're giving it up? Idiot!

"What the hell is wrong with you? Who pays you? CHRIST that is crazy!"

Someone captured the strange tirade on a cell phone and circulated it to the press the next day, fueling a new round of speculation about his drinking (he said he'd had one scotch). Late-night comics played the tape on national television.

The country got one more chuckle out of him, and viewers wondered once more what had happened to America's Mayor.

The person who could best answer the question was Giuliani himself, and he offered it up again and again without anyone noticing. He had all but screamed out the answer the night of his on-air blowout with Piers Morgan in the early morning hours of June 4, 2020.

"What happened to me is the same thing that always happens to me. I happen to be in favor of truth and justice, and you people are in favor of a phony political narrative."

Somewhere early in life Giuliani developed a moral certitude that protected him from fear and self-doubt. He was infatuated with his sense of virtue, and viewed those who opposed him as either moronic or corrupt.

That belief in his convictions shielded him like armor from pressures that would cripple other leaders, and helped him stick to his decisions when thousands, even tens of thousands, united to oppose him. It drove his greatest crusades, from his mission to eradicate the mob, to his determination to clean up New York City. It made him clear-eyed and decisive when so many others were paralyzed with fear on September 11.

But the almost fanatical sense of righteousness that propelled his rise also presaged his catastrophic fall. His unshakable belief in his own moral code shielded him from shame, and contrition, and gave him comfort when committing horrible acts. The disasters he inflicted upon the country would not have been possible if he hadn't been so capable of justifying each bad decision.

Releasing Patrick Dorismond's juvenile record, smearing Marie Yovanovitch, accusing Joe Biden of dementia, and attempting to upend a fair election were immoral acts that he saw as his duty.

Christianné Allen, his young assistant, left Giuliani in September for another job after spending two years watching her brilliant but troubled mentor manage to get a United States president impeached twice in a little over a year. Never once did he utter a word of regret.

A Christian conservative, she left Giuliani's employ believing in what he did for Trump. She was deeply impressed by the strength of his convictions, and the importance he placed on morality. It was his belief in what he was doing, she said, that got him through his toughest days.

"He believed what he was doing was right," she said. "That's all the motivation he needed."

Acknowledgments

Capturing the sweep of Rudy Giuliani's tumultuous life was a mammoth undertaking, and it was only possible because so many people were generous with their time, insight, and support.

My deepest thanks to Jonathan Karp at Simon & Schuster for envisioning this project and entrusting me to realize it. Likewise, Bob Bender, my editor, encouraged me every step of the way, and kept me focused on what was most important. And thank you to Flip Brophy, my agent, friend, advisor, and on-call therapist—this was our third book together, a journey I wouldn't have missed for the world.

Thank you to Tanya Kozyreva, our freelancer in Ukraine, and to Kelsey Carolan and Abby Geluso, our researchers, for their wonderful contributions.

A special thank-you to Claire Brinberg, Patrick Healy, Paul Lombardi, and Adam Nagourney for being there when I most needed them in this adventure. Thank you with all my heart to Dan Goldberg, Andrew Miller, Brian Donnellan, Jack Stephenson, Justin Blake, David Goodhand, Ben Kushner, David Chalian, Jeff Soref, Ray Delgado, Seth Weissman, Joseph Altuzarra, Karen Avrich, Melissa Russo, Tracy Vale, Bill Goldstein, Jed Rothstein, Sarit Work, Paul Polansky, Chris Coad, Jody Hotchkiss, and Mike Cruz.

Much of this book was written in Fire Island Pines in the dead of winter, which was made possible only because of the support and friendship of Karen and Walter Boss (we'll always have Chapter 14). And my eternal gratitude to the great Robert Weber.

Thank you to all the journalists whose reporting on Giuliani over the decades revealed so much about him. They include Jim Dwyer, Maggie Haberman, Michael Schmidt, Kevin Flynn, Michael Shear, and Ken Vogel of the *New York Times*; Paul Schwartzman, Josh Dawsey, Phil Rucker, and Carol Leonnig of the *Washington Post*; and Jeffrey Toobin, Adam Entous, and Dexter Filkins of the *New Yorker*. A special thanks to Mark Halperin, Michael Wolff, and Maggie for their assistance and encouragement.

Above all, thank you to my friend Wayne Barrett, who left us far too early, and with whom I communed throughout this project. His body of work on Giuliani is extraordinary.

Several books were invaluable to my understanding of different aspects of the Giuliani story. They were: *102 Minutes* by Jim Dwyer and Kevin Flynn; *The Prince of the City* by Fred Siegel; *Rudy!* by Wayne Barrett and *Grand Illusion* by Wayne Barrett and Dan Collins; *Five Families* by Selwyn Raab; *I Alone Can Fix It*, by Carol Leonnig and Philip Rucker; and *Too Famous* by Michael Wolff.

My deepest thanks to David Weiner, my colleague and friend, for his patience and generosity during this project.

Thank you to my family: Jesse, Steven, and Elissa Kirtzman, and Anthony Autovino and Kurt, Sally, Debbi Jo, and all the Fromans. And to the memory of my late parents, Marvin Friedman and Doris Kirtzman, who encouraged me from the moment I woke up as a teenager and realized I was a journalist.

And finally, and again, and forever, thank you to my husband, Kyle Froman, who makes everything worth it.

Acknowledgments

From David Holley:

I am so deeply grateful to have Raquel Gordian as a partner and best friend—she has been patient, loving, and unceasingly supportive during 2.5 years of stress and endless discussions about one person.

I also can't thank Andrew Kirtzman enough for bringing me on to partner with him for this project, and for being a supportive, fun, and engaging collaborator and friend. I can't imagine having done this with anyone else.

Thank you to my friends and family: Ed Johnson, Tom Adams, Tucker Miller, Meredith Holley, and Carmelo and Sherry Gordian. And thank you, in addition to those Andrew has named, to the archivists and researchers who aided us on this project at the New York City Municipal Archives and the Dolph Briscoe Center for American History.

Notes

PREFACE

xvii *and that he needed to "work through privileges" [and four subsequent messages]:*
Text exchange between Andrew Kirtzman and Rudy Giuliani.

INTRODUCTION

1 *"For me it is particularly significant... Great Britain":* "Rudy Flies to Knighthood,"
Pittsburgh Post-Gazette, February 13, 2002.

2 *Nathan and Giuliani had their game faces on:* Numerous confidential interviews
with Giuliani aides.

2 *"For services after the September... Mayor of New York":* Julie McCarthy, "Rudy
Giuliani Given an Honorary Knighthood by Queen Elizabeth," *All Things Considered*, NPR, February 13, 2002.

2 *spent an unusual amount of time chatting ("maybe two minutes":* Ibid.

2 *"She congratulated me . . . her admiration":* "Giuliani Receives Knighthood,"
Giuliani press conference, February 13, 2002.

2 *"I said I was receiving it on behalf... I told her I was":* Ibid.

3 *"What's important in all . . . the man to do it":* Paula Zahn and Walter Rodgers,
"Former New York City Mayor Rudy Giuliani Knighted by Queen Elizabeth,"
American Morning with Paula Zahn, CNN, February 13, 2002.

4 *determined to capitalize on it:* Numerous confidential interviews with former
Giuliani aides and staff members.

4 *he had registered a new company... named Giuliani Partners:* New York Secretary
of State online database, retrieved 11/25/2019.

4 *"the city's most important politician of his generation":* Barry Bearak and Ian Fisher,
"The Republican Candidate; A Mercurial Mayor's Confident Journey," *New York
Times*, October 19, 1997.

Notes

6 *"I got about five friends left"*: Chris Sommerfeldt, "Rudy Giuliani Complains He Only Has 'Five Friends Left' After Forgetting to Hang Up on Daily News Reporter," New York *Daily News*, February 26, 2020.

6 *"Those mail-in ballots . . . voted here twice since he died"*: Transcript, "Rudy Giuliani Trump Campaign Philadelphia Press Conference at Four Seasons Total Landscaping," Rev.com, November 7, 2020.

7 *"We don't know if people were voting twice or three times"*: Ibid.

7 *Daryl Brooks turned out to be a convicted sex offender*: "Convicted Sex Offender Can Stay on Ballot," Associated Press, October 22, 2004; Interview with Brooks.

7 *"Giuliani wrecks Trump campaign's well-laid legal plans"*: Alex Isenstadt, "Giuliani Wrecks Trump Campaign's Well-Laid Legal Plans," *Politico*, November 14, 2020.

7 *"This will be a very, very strong case . . . try thinking rationally"*: Transcript, "Rudy Giuliani Trump Campaign Philadelphia Press Conference at Four Seasons Total Landscaping."

7 *"I will be fine . . . from the ceiling"*: Kate McKinnon and Colin Jost, "Weekend Update: Rudy Giuliani on Trump's Election Lawsuits," *Saturday Night Live*, November 7, 2020.

CHAPTER 1: MORALITY

11 *"In 1960 the people say yes to progress"*: Peter Kihss, "Big Crowds Here Acclaim Kennedy and Mob His Car," *New York Times*, October 20, 1960.

12 *"Jack! Jack! Jack!" [and subsequent quotation]*: John Maceli interview.

13 *"The brothers were real authority figures"*: Joseph Centrella interview prior to his passing.

14 *"If you didn't have his same beliefs, there was something wrong with you"*: Edwin Betz interview.

14 *"I'm going to tell you how I conduct myself . . . when you're shaving. And I do."*: *Rudy Giuliani Show*, 77 WABC Radio, January 18, 2021.

15 *"Three cousins killed . . . protecting the mob uncle"*: Wayne Barrett and Adam Fifield, *Rudy! An Investigative Biography of Rudolph Giuliani* (New York: Basic Books, 2000), p. 65.

15 *On April 2, 1934, a milkman named Harold Hall*: Harold Hall statement, April 19, 1934, Wayne Barrett archives.

15 *"As I started up the stairway I saw the gun stare me in the face"*: Ibid.

16 *"He is egocentric to an extent . . . dependence on his parents"*: Psychiatric evaluation by Benjamin Apfelberg, M.D., May 18, 1934, Wayne Barrett archives.

16 *"People in the neighborhood were terrified of him"*: Barrett and Fifield, *Rudy!*, p. 26.

16 *"He would say over and over, 'You can't take anything that's not yours'"*: Giuliani interview with Eric Pooley, "Mayor of the World," *Time*, December 31, 2001.

17 *"I had a very healthy relationship with him" [and three subsequent quotations]:* Giuliani interview with Nancy Collins, "Gotcha! Nancy Collins Cross-Examines Crime Buster Rudolph Giuliani," *New York*, May 25, 1987, pp. 32–33.

17 *"My mom pressured me to succeed":* Rudy Giuliani Show, 77 WABC Radio, February 24, 2021.

18 *"She was pretty domineering":* Confidential interview with a Giuliani friend.

18 *"She was the one who gave him the support that he needed":* Joan D'Avanzo interview.

19 *"He pretty much kind of kept to himself":* John Connor interview.

19 *"If you're saying these guys have too many activities, what about yourself?":* Interviews with Anthony Shanley, George Schneider, and Joe Centrella prior to his passing. The story was first reported by Paul Schwartzman in "Driven From the Start," New York *Daily News,* May 11, 1997.

20 *"He's bluffing" [and three subsequent quotations]:* Peter Powers interview prior to his passing.

20 *arrested for allegedly loitering for "immoral purposes":* Michael Leahy, "Pledging Allegiance," *Washington Post,* December 16, 2007.

21 *Unemployed, he drifted back to Leo's bar:* Barrett and Fifield, *Rudy!,* p. 47.

21 *"Our glorious political history abounds with payoffs":* Copies of the *Manhattan Quadrangle* obtained by the author.

21 *"budding interest in the opposite sex":* Giuliani interview with Alexandra Marks, "Rudolph Giuliani: Faith in Work, God, and Himself," *Christian Science Monitor,* October 3, 2007.

22 *"We spent all our time reading" [and subsequent quotation]:* Bernard McElhone interview.

23 *"open the windows [of the Church] and let in some fresh air":* Maureen Fielder, "Vatican II: It's About That 'Fresh Air,'" *National Catholic Reporter,* October 8, 2012.

23 *"He was too opinionated":* Paul Schwartzman, "Politics over Priesthood," New York *Daily News,* May 12, 1997.

23 *traveling to train stations near his Long Island home at 5:30 a.m.:* Tony Mauro interview.

23 *Giuliani and Placa had plastered his car:* Peter Powers interview.

23 *"He told me he wanted to become the first Italian-Catholic President":* Paul Schwartzman, "Love and the Law," New York *Daily News,* May 13, 1997.

23 *"Down at the bottom of the hill at Manhattan was the Pinewood" [and subsequent quotation]:* Gene Hart interview.

24 *he was on campus, dressed in an ROTC uniform:* Rudy Giuliani Show, 77 WABC Radio, February 12, 2021.

24 *"The first time I attended a class in which a prayer wasn't said . . . people were staring at me":* Transcript, "Former Mayor Rudolph W. Giuliani Delivers Remarks

at the Family Research Council Action Washington Briefing 2007: Voter Values Summit," October 22, 2007.

25 *"It was the most politically organized, sophisticated, activist class" [and subsequent quotation]*: Sylvia Law interview.

25 *"There was a change in the atmosphere from '65 to '68" [and subsequent quotation]*: Norman Siegel interview.

25 *"Rudy was never into changing the law"*: David Finkelstein interview.

26 *"Just exactly how I missed it, I can't describe"*: Giuliani interview with Barry Bearak and Ian Fisher, "The Republican Candidate; A Mercurial Mayor's Confident Journey," *New York Times*, October 19, 1997.

26 *"I began to view my love of debate as pointing toward a new calling"*: Rudolph W. Giuliani with Ken Kurson, *Leadership* (New York: Hyperion, 2002), p. 173.

CHAPTER 2: JUSTICE

28 *"Did you introduce yourself as Congressman" [and four subsequent quotations of Giuliani and Bertram Podell]*: Courtroom transcripts.

29 *"badge of honor to be known as public enemy number one"*: Arnold H. Lubasch, "Podell Indicted on Charge of Taking Airline Bribes," *New York Times*, July 13, 1974.

29 *"kept telling himself how bad it was what this guy had done"*: Howard Kurtz, "Giuliani and His New York Appeal," *Washington Post*, June 20, 1989.

30 *"a boxer closing in on a battered opponent"*: Arnold H. Lubasch, "Podell Enters Guilty Plea, Ending Conspiracy Trial," *New York Times*, October 2, 1974.

30 *"knowingly and intentionally"*: Ibid.

31 *"It gives you a chance to do only what's right"*: Video, "Rudy Giuliani on the 2012 Presidential Election," U.S. Chamber of Commerce's annual legal issues summit, October 24, 2012.

31 *"He seemed not to know his way around" [and two subsequent quotations]*: Fredrick Lowther interview.

32 *"shy and too nice a guy" [and two subsequent quotations by Giuliani and Peter King]*: Gail Sheehy, "When Hillary Clinton and Rudy Giuliani Did Battle for a Senate Seat," *Vanity Fair*, June 2000.

33 *"He worshipped her" [and subsequent quotation]*: Pat Rufino interview.

34 *"He was offended and upset when lawyers were not prepared"*: Craig Wolff, "Lloyd F. MacMahon, a Federal Judge, Dies at 76," *New York Times*, April 9, 1989.

34 *"He said from the beginning that Rudy was the best law clerk he ever had" [and subsequent quotation]*: Jon Sale interview.

34 *He was fortunate enough to have found a powerful federal judge*: Rudolph W. Giuliani Vulnerability Study, 1993.

35 *"He used to work really, really late" [and subsequent quotation]*: Pat Rufino interview.

35 *"He hit on everybody"*: Barrett and Fifield, *Rudy!*, p. 84.

Notes

37 *"My father used to say, 'The first thing that's important'"*: Giuliani interview with Michael Winerip, "High-Profile Prosecutor," *New York Times*, June 9, 1985.

38 *"There is not a problem, a major problem, a systematic problem of political repression in Haiti"*: Giuliani testimony, 1982.

39 *"A situation of political repression does not exist, at least in general, in Haiti"*: Ibid.

39 *"would show these pathetic people sort of holding hands and kissing each other" [and subsequent quotation]*: Giuliani interview with *Barron's National Business and Financial Weekly* in 1983, cited in "The Long, Cruel Career of Rudy Giuliani," *Jacobin*, December 13, 2016.

40 *"His secretary called me up and said"*: Donna Hanover interview, "Negative Ads?; Crimebuster; Debating Implants," *The MacNeil/Lehrer NewsHour*, PBS, September 10, 1985.

41 *"For many years, we have tolerated in America" [and two subsequent quotations]*: Transcripts, Ronald Reagan, "Remarks Announcing Federal Initiatives Against Drug Trafficking and Organized Crime," the Great Hall at the Department of Justice, October 14, 1982.

41 *Hundreds of FBI agents and prosecutors were deployed*: My narrative about Giuliani's role in the commission case is based on interviews with thirteen former Southern District prosecutors and Selwyn Raab, *Five Families: The Rise, Decline, and Resurgence of America's Most Powerful Mafia Empires* (New York: Thomas Dunne Books, 2005).

41 *"I think we can end traditional organized crime"*: Giuliani interview with Arnold Lubasch, "U.S. Attorney to Stress Fight Against Heroin," *New York Times*, July 3, 1983.

42 *As Giuliani tells the story, he experienced a eureka moment . . . [and three subsequent quotations]*: Rudolph W. Giuliani with Ken Kurson, *Leadership* (New York: Hyperion, 2002), pp. 214–15.

43 *"It causes you to focus" [and three subsequent quotations]*: Walter Mack interview.

44 *"A Real-Life Perry Mason"*: Kim Foltz with Connie Leslie, "A Real-Life Perry Mason," *Newsweek*, December 5, 1983.

45 *"He was just always there, totally into the law"*: Daniel Richman interview.

46 *"This is a bad day, probably the worst ever, for the Mafia"*: Giuliani press conference, February 26, 1985.

47 *"Every era has a law-enforcement figure" [and two subsequent quotations]*: Michael Winerip, "High-Profile Prosecutor," *New York Times*, June 9, 1985.

49 *"When you are sitting on a case where the correspondent"*: Howard Kurtz, "Bess Myerson Indicted on Bribery Charges," *Washington Post*, October 8, 1987.

50 *"Giuliani tried to bury the people under the avalanche of prejudicial publicity" [and subsequent quotation]*: Jay Goldberg interview.

50 *"This is a case that had to be tried"*: Giuliani press conference, December 22, 1988.

50 *"I should have slowed it down"*: Giuliani interview with William Glaberson, "Giuliani's Powerful Image Under Campaign Scrutiny," *New York Times*, July 11, 1989.

51 *"I hope the legacy we leave is the continued emphasis on the need to reform"*: Andrew Kirtzman, *Rudy Giuliani: Emperor of the City* (New York: HarperCollins World, 2001), p. 3.

CHAPTER 3: COMBAT

53 *"like Moses"*: Interview with Ken Frydman.

53 *"The mayor doesn't know why the morale . . . is so low"*: Giuliani speech at police rally, September 16, 1992.

54 *Jimmy Breslin, the tabloid columnist, would paint . . . [and two subsequent paragraphs]*: Jimmy Breslin, "Cops Show True Colors," *Newsday*, September 17, 1992.

55 *"November 7, 1989, is a date that will live in history"*: Dinkins election night speech, November 7, 1989.

55 *The bottom was falling out from the city's economy*: Fred Siegel, *The Prince of the City: Giuliani, New York, and the Genius of American Life* (San Francisco: Encounter Books, 2005), pp. 29, 74, 80.

56 *"We must never, never abandon the compassion"*: Ibid., p. 47.

56 *"Even the basic rudiments of civil behavior" [and subsequent quote]*: Joelle Attinger, "The Decline of New York," *Time*, September 17, 1990.

58 *"We have a city to save"*: Giuliani 1993 fundraiser.

58 *"Too many of us are . . . than we are"*: Bill Clinton speech at Dinkins fundraiser, September 26, 1993.

59 *"My administration will be universal in its concern"*: Giuliani election night speech, November 2, 1993.

60 *"As last night's terrible murder . . . confronting urban America"*: "Urban Crime" panel, C-SPAN recording, March 16, 1994.

60 *Giuliani, dressed in a gray suit and gray tie, was the first to speak . . . [and four subsequent quotations]*: Ibid.

61 *Eschewing standard platitudes about crime . . . [and two subsequent quotations]*: " 'Freedom Is About Authority': Excerpts from Giuliani Speech on Crime," *New York Times*, March 20, 1994.

62 *"I want arrests"*: William Bratton with Peter Knobler, *Turnaround*, New York Times, "Books on the Web," 1998.

62 *"it was better to have Sharpton pissing in your tent than pissing on it"*: Bill Lynch interview in 1999.

63 *"We're not going to go back to being disregarded and disrespected"*: Andrew Kirtzman, *Rudy Giuliani: Emperor of the City* (New York: HarperCollins World, 2001), p. 72.

Notes

63 *"I want to reach out to all of the communities in the city"* [and subsequent quotation]: Giuliani press conference, January 17, 1994.

63 *"Maybe you should ask yourself some questions"*: Giuliani radio show, July 16, 1999.

64 *"He would recall every number on that page to a decimal point"*: Joe Lhota interview.

66 *"The election this year presents a fundamental dilemma"* [and four subsequent quotations]: Ibid., pp. 131–32.

68 *"We will fight for every house in the city"*: Bill Bratton press conference, December 2, 1993.

69 *"Basically, where you saw the dots, that's where you wanted to put the cops"* [and subsequent quotation]: Jack Maple interview in 1999.

70 *"would throw herself in front of a truck to protect her boss"*: Interview with Phil McConkey in 1999.

71 *"Commissioners would line up like planes on a runway"*: Confidential interview with a senior official in the administration.

71 *"She brought out the worst in Rudy"*: Confidential interview with Giuliani aide.

72 *"Nine people would agree on something in a meeting"*: Confidential interview with a senior official in the administration.

72 *the Department of Environmental Protection was ordered to run the daily reservoir levels by the City Hall press office*: Interview with DEP official.

72 *The streets grew safer*: Statistics from Citizens Crime Commission.

73 *"The mayor really wanted to be the police commissioner"* [and two subsequent quotations]: Author interviews with Bill Bratton in 1999 and 2022.

74 *"out of control"*: Giuliani press conference, February 23, 1995.

74 *"He'd be down in the office watching* The Godfather *with Cristyne"*: Confidential interview with Giuliani aide.

74 *"THE WOMAN BEHIND THE MAYOR"* [and two subsequent quotations]: Craig Horowitz, "The Woman Behind the Mayor," *New York*, September 25, 1995.

75 *"I was the press gal"*: Cristyne Lategano interview with author in 1999; she declined to cooperate for this book.

77 *"Don't tell me there are only six or seven hundred useless bureaucrats at 110 Livingston Street"*: Giuliani press conference, April 6, 1994.

77 *"My integrity is not for sale"* [and subsequent Cortines quotation]: "Turmoil in the Schools; 'My Integrity Is Not for Sale,' Cortines Says in His Statement," *New York Times*, April 9, 1994.

78 *"He's made it very clear that no matter what I do or say"* [and two subsequent Cortines quotations]: Ibid., pp. 124–25.

78 *"He shouldn't be so sensitive about it"* [and subsequent Giuliani quotation]: Ibid., p. 125.

78 *"I don't have any hard feelings"* [and two subsequent Cortines quotations]: Ramon Cortines interview in 2022.

Notes

CHAPTER 4: TROUBLE

80 *Organizers sold one thousand tickets . . . the most famous woman in America:* Author was in attendance.

80 *"looking like Cleopatra in full regalia":* Gail Sheehy, "Cheer and Loathing in New York," *Vanity Fair*, June 2000.

81 *"Good evening, Mr. Mayor":* Andrea Peyser, "Hizzoner Gets Fair Shake—But Real Joke's on First Lady," *New York Post*, March 12, 2000.

81 *"I can't wait to get to Shea Stadium" [and seven subsequent song quotations]:* "2000 Inner Circle Show: Livin' La Rudy Loca," YouTube, December 19, 2013.

82 *"Well, I hear you're the real star" [and three subsequent quotations in conversation between Clinton and Giuliani]:* Sheehy, "Cheer and Loathing in New York."

82 *"My main problem is with anger" [and eight subsequent quotations in Inner Circle performance]:* "2000 Inner Circle Show: Livin' La Rudy Loca," YouTube, December 19, 2013.

84 *Sitting quietly at his table in place of Donna Hanover . . . was the woman with whom he was having an affair:* Andrew Kirtzman, *Rudy Giuliani: Emperor of the City* (New York: HarperCollins World, 2001), p. 279.

85 *"This is a chief executive who is out of control":* Abby Goodnough, "Mayor Threatens Council on Homeless," *New York Times*, December 17, 1998.

85 *his job approval rating was at 60 percent:* "Mayor Giuliani Belongs in Senate, Not White House, New York City Voters Tell Quinnipiac College Poll; No Clear Choice to Replace Him," Quinnipiac/Poll, November 18, 1998.

86 *"Certainly there is no hunting like the hunting of man":* David Kocieniewski, "Success of Elite Police Unit Exacts a Toll on the Streets," *New York Times*, February 15, 1999.

87 *Half of them were Black:* New York State Attorney General report, 1999.

87 *"He was standing on the stoop" [and five subsequent quotations]:* Jeffrey Toobin, "The Unasked Question," *New Yorker*, February 27, 2000; Kirtzman, *Rudy Giuliani*, p. 228; Transcript, "Police Officers Testify in Amadou Diallo Trial," February 14, 2000.

88 "OH GOD! COPS KEEP KILLING 'R' BABIES": Kirtzman, *Rudy Giuliani*, p. 232.

88 *"It would be very unfair to jump from this incident":* Giuliani press conference, February 6, 1999.

89 *"Giuliani is on the run":* Peter Noel, "Father of the Movement," *The Village Voice*, March 30, 1999.

89 *"I don't like to define people this way, typically":* David Freedlander, "'They Saw the World in This Dog-Eat-Dog, Manichaean Way': The Ugly '90s Roots of Rudy's Bond with Donald Trump," *Vanity Fair*, November 10, 2019.

90 *"This is a great publicity stunt":* Giuliani press conference, March 16, 1999.

90 *"This is a waste of time" [and subsequent quotation]:* Confidential interviews with mayoral aides, July 20, 1999.

Notes

90 *"The Fall of Supermayor"*: Craig Horowitz, "The Fall of Supermayor," *New York*, April 19, 1999.

91 *"I already have the footprint on my back"*: Kirtzman, *Rudy Giuliani*, p. 255.

91 *Meyers was treating Giuliani's mother, Helen, for a diabetes-related problem*: Judith Giuliani interviews.

91 *Wearing a Yankees jacket ... he began to flirt with her*: Ibid.

91 *"one of those moments you remember forever" [and two subsequent quotations]*: Confidential interview with source close to Judith Nathan.

91 *"It was the thunderbolt"*: Giuliani press conference, May 24, 2003.

92 *"I have a bad feeling" [and subsequent quotation by Giuliani]*: Matt Mahoney interview.

92 *Nathan says he told her he loved her on their third date ... [and four subsequent quotations]*: Confidential interview with source close to Judith Nathan.

92 *"It was just like one day she was kind of on the scene" [and two subsequent quotations]*: Confidential interviews with numerous City Hall employees.

93 *All of their favorite spots seemed to have a connection*: Confidential interview with source close to Nathan.

94 *"Unlike my wife, I was not a social climber" [and subsequent quotations]*: Bruce Nathan divorce papers in Wayne Barrett archives; Lloyd Grove, "The Thunderbolt," *New York*, May 10, 2007.

94 *Judith accused Bruce of spousal abuse*: Judith Nathan in divorce papers in Wayne Barrett archives; Grove, "The Thunderbolt."

95 *"I knew he was going to be an adversary" [and six subsequent quotations in conversation with Tony Carbonetti]*: Confidential interview with source close to Judith Nathan.

96 *his "Alibi Squad"*: Manny Papir interview.

96 *"She's a horrible human being"*: Tony Carbonetti interview.

CHAPTER 5: PALS

97 *"Tonight: Donald Trump! Need we say more?" [and seven subsequent quotations in interview between Larry King and Donald Trump]*: Transcript, "Donald Trump Announces Plans to Form Presidential Exploratory Committee," *Larry King Live*, October 7, 1999.

98 *"the tallest and most luxurious residential tower in the world"*: Charles V Bagli, "Trump Starts a New Tower Near the U.N.," *New York Times*, October 16, 1998.

99 *"most people"*: Devin Leonard, "Dug In, Trump Battles Walter Cronkite Group over His Big, Big Tower," *The Observer*, July 12, 1999.

99 *"peculiar" Buildings department decision ... [and two subsequent quotations]*: Correspondence and internal memos from Giuliani administration archives.

100 *"a very complicated legal question"*: David M. Herszenhorn, "Giuliani Declines to Join Fight over Trump Tower Near U.N.," *New York Times*, August 19, 1999.

Notes

100 *"Fred Trump was a very big man, a giant"*: K. C. Baker, "Farewell to Fred Trump," New York *Daily News*, June 30, 1999.

100 *Donald, who told a biographer that he considered it a sign of weakness for a man to cry:* Tim O'Brien, 4:01 p.m., February 9, 2021, Twitter.com.

100 *a hero who contributed incalculably to the city's greatness:* Angela Mosconi, "Trump Patriarch Eulogized as Great Builder," *New York Post*, June 30, 1999.

101 *Trump typically scrawled a note on the invitations, and directed them to "Randy L":* Giuliani administration archives. In an interview with the author, Randy Levine said, "I just think Rudy was pro development, and we thought that this was not in my neighborhood, a bunch of rich guys and women who just didn't want their views being blocked."

101 *"Randy L Not nice" [and four subsequent quotations of Giuliani and Donald Trump]:* All correspondences and internal memos from Giuliani administration archives.

102 *"Every time a New Yorker, or anyone else, for that matter, passes by this monstrosity":* Eric Herman and Helen Peterson, "Trump's Tower Gets Court OK," New York *Daily News*, November 22, 2000.

103 *"The Mayor's aides insist that in the last few months they have seen a New Rudy emerge":* James Traub, "Introducing Mr. Nice Guy," *New York Times Magazine*, August 1999.

103 *"Speaking of marlin, Mayor Rudolph W. Giuliani and a friend seemed to be enjoying dinner at the Johnny Marlin restaurant":* Russell Drumm, "October Fish Takes Tournament," *East Hampton Star*, December 2, 1999.

105 *"The idea of, in the name of art . . . of the Virgin Mary is sick":* Giuliani press conference, September 22, 1999.

105 *Polls showed New Yorkers opposed his move two to one:* Dave Goldiner, "Sour on Rudy," New York *Daily News*, October 1, 1999.

105 *"The left-wing elite opposes me":* Wayne Barrett, "Romancing the Right," *The Village Voice*, February 8, 2000.

106 *"I don't want any money coming out . . . psychological problems":* Giuliani press conference, October 1, 1999.

106 *"RUDY—This is great!":* Giuliani mayoral archives.

107 *the past six weeks had seen a neck-and-neck race turn:* Marjorie Connelly, "Polls Show Dorismond Shooting Is Influencing Senate Race in New York," *New York Times*, April 13, 2000.

107 *"As we eliminate drug gangs and drug criminals":* Howard Safir City Council testimony, March 13, 2000.

108 *"Have any krills?":* C. J. Chivers, "Grand Jury Clears Detective in Killing of Unarmed Guard," *New York Times*, July 28, 2000.

108 *Dorismond took offense, flew into a rage, and threw a punch:* Dorismond grand jury report.

109 *"I would urge everyone not to jump to conclusions"*: Giuliani press conference, March 16, 2000.

110 *"People do act in conformity very often with their prior behavior"*: Giuliani *Fox News Sunday* interview, March 19, 2000; Andrew Kirtzman, *Rudy Giuliani: Emperor of the City* (New York: HarperCollins World, 2001), p. 274.

110 *"That Mr. Dorismond spent a good deal of his adult life punching people was a fact"*: Ibid., p. 275.

110 the New York Times *poll couldn't even measure it*: Adam Nagourney with Marjorie Connelly, "Giuliani's Ratings Drop over Actions in Dorismond Case," *New York Times*, April 7, 2000.

111 *waking up in the middle of the night with anxieties about his health*: Rudolph W. Giuliani with Ken Kurson, *Leadership* (New York: Hyperion, 2002), p. 138.

111 *"I was diagnosed yesterday with a—prostate cancer" [and two subsequent quotations]*: Author attended press conference; transcript, "Giuliani Announces He Has Prostate Cancer," CNN, April 27, 2000.

112 *"Will you be a nicer guy now" [and subsequent quotation of Giuliani]*: Video, "New York Mayor News Conference," C-SPAN, April 27, 2000.

112 *"Rudy & Friend Dine & Dine" [and three subsequent quotes]*: Mitchell Fink, "Rudy & Friend Dine & Dine," New York *Daily News*, May 2, 2000.

113 *"Here's the first look at the mystery woman"*: Richard Johnson, "Rudy's Mystery Brunch Pal Is Upper East Side Divorcee," *New York Post*, May 3, 2000.

113 *"a very good friend"*: Giuliani press conference, May 3, 2000.

114 *"I'm hoping they can reconcile their differences"*: Fredric U. Dicker, "Bruno to Rudy: Deal with It!—Concerns for Senate Campaign," *New York Post*, May 10, 2000.

114 *"This is very, very painful" [and six subsequent quotations from Giuliani and Donna Hanover]*: Giuliani and Hanover press conferences on May 10, 2000.

116 *"They tried to reconcile for a period"*: Confidential interview with Giuliani aide.

116 *"Rudy, there are a lot of sharks in the water"*: Kirtzman, *Rudy Giuliani*, p. 282.

116 *Withdrawing would confirm to his Republican critics . . . that he didn't care about the party*: Confidential interview with campaign aide.

117 *"involves thinking about your life, mortality, the quality of your life" [and subsequent quotation]*: Andrea Mitchell, *Decision 2000: N.Y. Senate Race & Conversation with N.Y. Mayor Rudy Giuliani*, MSNBC Special, May 18, 2000.

117 *gave him a standing ovation*: Author was present at the speech.

117 *"I'm a very fortunate man, and this is one demonstration of why" [and five subsequent quotations]*: Video, "Giuliani Withdrawal," C-SPAN, May 19, 2000; transcript, "Rudolph Giuliani Holds News Conference," FDCH Political Transcripts, May 19, 2000.

CHAPTER 6: MISTAKES

121 *"It's a State of the City speech ... I was going to give" [and four subsequent quotations]:* Rudy Giuliani, "Transcript of State of the City Address," archives of Rudolph W. Giuliani, January 8, 2001.

121 *The count was down to less than a third of that:* "Restoring Accountability to Government," Mayor's Office, December 19, 2001; "Seven Major Felony Offenses," New York City crime statistics 2000–2020; NYPD CompStat Unit, "CompStat Report Covering the Week 3/28/2022 Through 4/3/2022," Police Department City of New York.

122 *more than compensating for the exodus:* U.S. Census figures; Mayor's management report fiscal 2001 supplement, *Reengineering Municipal Services 1994–2001*, City of New York, pp. 255–56.

122 *"This is America in the 21st century":* James Traub, "Giuliani Internalized," *New York Times*, February 11, 2001.

123 *"New Yorkers don't talk about crime":* Ibid.

124 *"MAYDAY, MAYDAY, MAYDAY!":* Luke Healy interview.

124 *that killed six people and injured more than a thousand:* Anthony L. Fusco, "Report from Chief of Department," FDNY Chief, February 1993, pp. 1–7.

125 *the two departments' radios literally operated on different wavelengths:* Numerous internal City Hall memos, including September 5, 1997, memorandum from Ralph Balzano to Mayor Rudolph Giuliani.

125 *"FDNY recalls new models after firefighter's close call":* William Murphy and Melanie Lefkowitz, "Static over Radios; FDNY Recalls New Models After Firefighter's Close Call," *Newsday*, March 22, 2001.

125 *Almost immediately, reports ... failed to deliver:* Giuliani mayoral archives; Wayne Barrett archives; Letter from Alan G. Hevesi to Thomas Von Essen, Commissioner of the New York City Fire Department, April 3, 2001; "Committee on Fire and Criminal Justice Services," April 10, 2001, report.

125 *"This isn't about reality":* Herbert Lowe, "Mayor Backs FDNY's Use of Radios," *Newsday*, March 26, 2001.

126 *"Sending firefighters into burning buildings with radios that have not been properly field-tested is irresponsible and dangerous":* QNS News Team, "Hevesi Probe Calls Fire Department Radios Dangerous," *QNS News*, April 5, 2001.

126 *"There are better ways to get their endorsement than to kind of roll over for them":* Kevin Flynn, "Hevesi Says Fire Dept. Broke City Rules in Buying Radios," *New York Times*, April 4, 2001.

126 *Little known at City Hall was that her sister:* Confidential interview with a source familiar with the situation. The potential conflict of interest was first reported by Wayne Barrett and Dan Collins, *Grand Illusion: The Untold Story of Rudy Giuliani and 9/11* (New York: Harper, 2006), pp. 230–33; Marian Barell declined to comment for this book.

127 *"If Giuliani wants to build a bunker only for the people he trusts":* Blaine Harden,

"'Rudy's Bunker' Keeps New York's Giuliani in the Line of Fire," *Washington Post*, June 21, 1998.

128 *"The building is secure and not as visible a target"*: Internal City Hall memo.

128 *"This group's finding is that the security of the proposed O.E.M.":* William Rashbaum, "Memo Details Objections to Command Center Site," *New York Times*, January 26, 2008.

129 *"We knew that the area was still a target"*: Jerry Hauer interview.

129 *"When I did actually sit down and unburden myself" [and subsequent quotation]:* Rudolph W. Giuliani with Ken Kurson, *Leadership* (New York: Hyperion, 2002), p. 140.

130 *"They really disliked each other"*: Confidential interview with Giuliani aide.

130 *"trying to cling to a marriage that has been dead for years" [and two subsequent quotations]:* Raoul Felder press conference, May 11, 2001.

131 *"In light of the quite public parting of the ways" [and subsequent paragraph]:* Internal City Hall memo from Tony Carbonetti to Donna Hanover and Irene Halligan, archives of Rudolph W. Giuliani, January 8, 2001.

132 *"I think the best thing for you to do would be to sit down with each other"*: Donald Trump, "The Art of the Deal," *New York*, June 4, 2001.

132 *"I don't know how much longer I can stay here" [and subsequent quotation in conversation with Howard Koeppel]:* Interview with Howard Koeppel and Mark Hsiao.

CHAPTER 7: CATASTROPHE

135 *"I see water. I see buildings. I see buildings"*: 9/11 Memorial and Museum.

135 *Pfeifer jumped into his car and radioed just twelve seconds later:* Pfeifer's story is based upon an interview with him; his testimony before the 9/11 Commission; his testimony to NYFD investigators; and a conversation conducted on a West Point radio program. His movements that morning were also recorded on film by French documentary makers for their film *9/11*.

135 *"We just had a plane crash into upper floors of the World Trade Center"*: Joseph Pfeifer, *Ordinary Heroes: A Memoir of 9/11* (New York: Portfolio/Penguin, 2021), p. 12.

136 *providing a sickening soundtrack as the commanders tried to make decisions:* Pfeifer interview, and oral testimony by Fire Marshal Steven Mosiello to World Trade Center Task Force interview, October 23, 2001.

136 *Eight years of efforts to improve communications:* Kean et al., *The 9/11 Commission Report: Final Report of the National Commission on Terrorist Attacks Upon the United States*, 2004, pp. 280–300; Wayne Barrett and Dan Collins, *Grand Illusion: The Untold Story of Rudy Giuliani and 9/11* (New York: Harper, 2006), p. 50.

137 *The plane crash into the North Tower ... so most commanders didn't bother to carry them: The 9/11 Commission Report*, pp. 314–15; Jim Dwyer and Kevin Flynn, *102*

Minutes: The Untold Story of the Fight to Survive Inside the Twin Towers (New York: Times Books, 2004), p. 204.

137 *Eight years after the old Saber I radios failed them:* Ibid., p. 283.

138 *"I was in heaven, sitting between Ralph Branca and Joe Black":* Amanda Griscom, "Man Behind the Mayor," *New York*, October 15, 2001; Stephanie Slepian, "Richie Sheirer, a Rock on 9/11, Dead at 65," *Staten Island Advance*, January 3, 2019.

139 *"Don't worry, Rudy isn't that crazy" [and subsequent quotes]:* Jerry Hauer interview.

140 *There were going to be terrible losses:* Richard Sheirer, 9/11 Commission testimony, May 18, 2004.

142 *"How near are you to the mayor?":* Rudolph W. Giuliani with Ken Kurson, *Leadership* (New York: Hyperion, 2002), p. 4.

143 *"Can we get helicopters up to the roof and help any of those people" [and six subsequent quotations]:* Transcript, "Former NYC Mayor Testifies Before 9/11 Commission," CNN, May 19, 2004; Giuliani, *Leadership*, pp. 8–9.

144 *"You're not supposed to be here" [and subsequent quotation]:* Pfeifer, *Ordinary Heroes*, p. 36.

144 *"There should be a representative from the Police Department there":* Jim Dwyer and Kevin Flynn, "Fatal Confusion: A Troubled Emergency Response; 9/11 Exposed Deadly Flaws in Rescue Plan," *New York Times*, July 7, 2002; Wayne Barrett and Dan Collins, "Rudy's Grand Illusion," *The Village Voice*, August 22, 2006.

144 *Giuliani would argue the opposite:* Transcript, "Former NYC Mayor Testifies Before 9/11 Commission," CNN, May 19, 2004.

145 *"You see Chief Ganci and Chief Ganci only" [and four subsequent quotations]:* Dwyer and Flynn, *102 Minutes*, p. 108.

146 *He felt something at his feet:* Interview with Pfeifer.

146 *"About 15 floors down from the top" [and subsequent quotation]:* The 9/11 Commission Report, p. 309; Dwyer and Flynn, *102 Minutes*, p. 223.

147 *"Had I known the full picture":* Pfiefer, *Ordinary Heroes*, p. 207.

147 *"It's coming down, everybody down!" [and two subsequent quotations]:* Giuliani, *Leadership*, pp. 11–12.

149 *"It's going to blow!" [and three subsequent quotations]:* Author experience.

152 *"The first thing I'd like to do is to take this opportunity":* Andrew Kirtzman, *Rudy Giuliani: Emperor of the City* (New York: HarperCollins World, 2001), p. 301.

153 *They arrived to find a small army of police:* Tom Von Essen with Matt Murray, *Strong of Heart: Life and Death in the Fire Department of New York* (New York: ReganBooks, 2002), p. 508.

153 *"Today is obviously one of the most difficult days in the history of the city" [and five subsequent quotations]:* Kirtzman, *Rudy Giuliani: Emperor of the City*, pp. 303–4.

155 *"I just had to see it one more time":* Interview with Bernie Kerik.

155 *"I can't make sense of this incident." [and three subsequent quotations]:* Transcription of Giuliani eulogy at Ganci funeral.

Notes

156 *"Rudolph Giuliani is the personification of courage"*: Transcript, "Rudolph Giuliani: Guiding New York City's Transformation, Recovery," CNN, November 10, 2001.

156 *"He moves about the stricken city like a god" [and subsequent quotation]*: Bob Herbert, "In America; The Right Answer," *New York Times*, September 20, 2001.

156 *But his administration's ineptitude:* Jim Dwyer and Kevin Flynn, "Fatal Confusion: A Troubled Emergency Response; 9/11 Exposed Deadly Flaws in Rescue Plan," *New York Times*, July 7, 2002.

157 *"a preponderance of the evidence indicate[d] that emergency responder lives":* J. Randall Lawson and Robert L. Vettori, *Federal Building and Fire Safety Investigation of the World Trade Center Disaster: The Emergency Response Operations*, National Institute of Standards and Technology, September 2005, p. 228.

157 *The tragedy of the radios was hammered home:* Barrett and Collins, *Grand Illusion*, pp. 230–33; confidential interviews with sources familiar with the matter.

157 *Years after the Trade Center attacks: The 9/11 Commission Report*, pp. 321–23.

CHAPTER 8: EXPERTS

158 *"Why didn't anyone else say anything about this" [and three subsequent quotations]:* Interview with Manny Papir.

159 *"He was extremely powerful" [and subsequent quotation]:* Judith Giuliani interview.

160 *an accused pedophile priest: Richard Tollner v. Diocese of Rockville Centre, St. Pius X Preparatory Seminary, and Alan Placa*, Supreme Court of the State of New York, County of Nassau, Index No. 900001/2019; David W. Chen, "Scandals in the Church: A New York Case; Priest from Sex Abuse Panel Is Suspended over Allegations," *New York Times*, June 15, 2002.

160 *"Well, my wife came home last night" [and subsequent quotation]:* Thomas Von Essen interview.

161 *"bullshit":* George Pataki, *Beyond the Great Divide: How a Nation Became a Neighborhood* (Brentwood, TN: Post Hill Press, 2020); Carl Campanile and Bruce Golding, "Giuliani Denies Asking Pataki to Cancel 2001 Election, Cries 'It's Bulls-T,'" *New York Post*, February 26, 2020.

161 *"maintain the unity that exist[ed] in the city":* Giuliani press conference, September 27, 2001.

162 *"If you do that, you're done":* Jerry Hauer interview.

162 *"The idea of going our separate ways was really kind of traumatic":* Janna Mancini interview.

162 *A handful of aides were dispatched to put together the financing:* Numerous confidential interviews with senior officials at City Hall and Giuliani Partners.

163 *"I'm going to do the best I can to keep my personal life as personal as possible":* Author was present.

Notes

163 *"find[ing] companies and operations we can expand and assist"*: Giuliani press conference, December 31, 2001.

163 *Two years earlier, he had handed Ernst & Young*: Charles V. Bagli, "Ernst & Young Gets Breaks to Stay in New York City," *New York Times*, July 23, 1999.

164 *"I'm going to play some golf in Florida" [and subsequent quotation in conversation with Bernie Kerik]*: Matt Mahoney interview.

165 *But it wasn't clear what Giuliani Partners actually was*: Confidential interviews with numerous employees.

165 *"I didn't understand what they were going to do"*: Joe Lhota interview.

165 *"this was their moment to cash in"*: Janna Mancini interview.

166 *"Is this really happening?"*: Bernie Kerik and Matt Mahoney interviews.

166 *"He could sell used cars easily—"[Sessions and Roy Bailey quotations]*: John Kirkpatrick, "Giuliani Relies on Dallasite; Former NYC Mayor Chooses Roy Bailey to Manage Partnership," *Dallas Morning News*, April 8, 2002.

167 *"They had great chemistry" [and two subsequent quotations]*: Confidential interviews with partners at Giuliani's consulting firm.

167 *He was also a priest accused of being a pedophile*: Richard Tollner v. Diocese of Rockville Centre, St. Pius X Preparatory Seminary, and Alan Placa, Supreme Court of the State of New York, County of Nassau, Index No. 900001/2019; Chen, "Scandals in the Church."

168 *The Suffolk County District Attorney opened a grand jury investigation*: Dan Barry, Daniel J. Wakin, and Elissa Gootman, "L.I. Monsignor Scorns Jury, Insisting He Is No 'Monster,'" *New York Times*, February 20, 2003.

168 *"He did nothing"*: Confidential interview with senior partner at Giuliani's consulting firm.

168 *"cautious but relentless in pursuing his victims"*: Ibid.

168 *"I'm not even a human being"*: Ibid. Alan Placa declined to comment for this book.

168 *Vatican court cleared him of the charges six years later*: Avni Patel, "Sex Abuse Victims' Groups Outraged by Vatican Decision to Clear Accused Priest," ABC News, December, 7 2009. Two lawsuits filed in 2019 alleging abuse named Placa: *Richard Tollner v. Diocese of Rockville Centre, St. Pius X Preparatory Seminary, and Alan Placa*, Supreme Court of the State of New York, County of Nassau, Index No. 900001/2019; *Christopher Fernan v. Diocese of Rockville Centre, St. Pius X Preparatory Seminary, and Alan Placa*, Supreme Court of the State of New York, County of Nassau, Index No. 900037/2019.

168 *It was a conceit, barely fleshed out*: Confidential interviews with numerous senior partners at Giuliani Partners.

169 *No company was more brazen about its intentions than Purdue Pharma*: Press release, "Purdue Pharma Engages Giuliani Partners as External Advisor," Purdue Pharma, May 28, 2002; Beth Macy, "They Were All Lawyered Up and Rudy Giuliani'd Up," *Politico*, August 5, 2018.

169 *"We believe that government officials are more comfortable knowing that Giuliani is advising Purdue Pharma"*: Ibid.

169 *They argued that investigators should give Purdue time to fix its issues. Hutchinson asked his investigators to keep him briefed*: Barry Meier and Eric Lipton, "Under Attack, Drug Maker Turned to Giuliani for Help," *New York Times*, December 28, 2007.

170 *"I understand the pain and distress that accompanies illness"*: Ibid.

170 *it turned to Giuliani Partners to give its good name a thorough rinse ... [and subsequent Giuliani quotation]*: Press release, "NTRA Hires Giuliani Partners LLC to Lead Review Process; Expands Process to Include Past Wagers," Business Wire, November 20, 2002.

170 *"It's not clear what anyone will be getting for his money other than the current credibility of the Giuliani name"*: Steven Crist column, *Daily Racing Form*, November 25, 2002.

171 *he was making $1 million per month*: Samuel Maull, "Lawyers for Giuliani, Hanover Exchange Barbs over Money," Associated Press, April 16, 2002.

172 *His Washington Speakers Bureau standard contract*: "Rudy Giuliani: No Free Speech," *The Smoking Gun*, February 16, 2007.

172 *"People started treating him like a king, and I think he liked it"*: Confidential interview with longtime Giuliani aide.

172 *He accompanied her daughter and her to debutante balls*: Bill Cunningham, "Evening Hours; Fanfare," *New York Times*, January 2, 2005.

172 *"He wouldn't spit on these people once"*: Confidential interview with former Giuliani aide.

173 *The five biggest music companies had joined forces ... "It's going to require a legal mind" [and two subsequent quotations]*: Confidential interview with partner at Giuliani Partners. Tommy Mottola declined an interview request.

173 *The opportunity evaporated in a haze of greed*: Confidential interview with partner at Giuliani Partners.

174 *"Our enemies insanely commit suicide to serve some irrational purpose" [and two subsequent quotations]*: Transcript, "Giuliani Farewell Speech," CNN, December 27, 2001.

174 *"The first principle of leadership" [and two subsequent quotations]*: Donna Longenecker, "Giuliani Outlines Principles of Leadership," *UB Reporter*, November 14, 2002.

175 *His speaking-fee haul in 2002 was estimated at $8 million*: Joyce Wadler, "Giuliani Marriage Ends with $6.8 Million Deal," *New York Times*, July 11, 2002.

176 *"It was the quintessential ugly Americans"*: Confidential interview with· person who visited England with Giuliani.

176 *"Manny used to love it when I would play piano" [and nine subsequent quotations]*: Judith Giuliani interview; Kate Anson, Sunny Mindel, and Manny Papir declined to comment about her description of them as "the triad of evil."

Notes

177 *His two children . . . she bragged that she removed their contact information*: Confidential interviews with friends of Judith Giuliani and the Giuliani children. Judith Giuliani has denied it.

177 *"It was a power struggle from day one"*: Confidential interview with Giuliani friend.

178 *"She treated him like an indentured servant" [and four subsequent quotations]*: Confidential interviews with Giuliani aides.

179 *"It had, like, red feathers meant to look like horns" [and four subsequent quotations]*: Judith Nathan interview.

179 *"the spark that lit the flame" [and four subsequent quotations]*: Manny Papir interview.

CHAPTER 9: RAMBO

181 *"Where are you" [and nine subsequent quotations]*: Bernie Kerik interview.

183 *"I believe that the skill I developed better than any other was surrounding myself with great people"*: Rudolph W. Giuliani with Ken Kurson, *Leadership* (New York: Hyperion, 2002), p. 98.

184 *"the most single-minded brilliant person"*: Craig Horowitz, "Tears of a Cop," *New York*, March 25, 2005.

184 *Giuliani referred to him . . . Kerik's daughters*: Bernard B. Kerik, *From Jailer to Jailed: My Journey from Correction and Police Commissioner to Inmate #84888-054* (New York: Threshold Editions, 2015), p. 139.

184 *sent homicide detectives to question and fingerprint Fox News employee*: William K. Rashbaum, "Kerik Accused of Abusing His Authority for Publisher," *New York Times*, March 11, 2002.

185 *"Our grief has turned to anger, and anger to resolution" [and subsequent quotation]*: Transcript, "President George W. Bush Addressed a Joint Session of Congress on the Subject of the War on Terrorism," September 20, 2001.

186 *"Look at that destruction, that massive, senseless, cruel loss of human life"*: Transcript, "Opening Remarks to the United Nations General Assembly Special Session on Terrorism," United Nations Assembly, October 1, 2001.

187 *"We sometimes repeat our mistakes" [and subsequent quotation]*: Randi F. Marshall, "Giuliani: Action Needed Against Iraq," *Newsday*, September 21, 2002.

187 *"I see Iraq as part of the overall effort to remove"*: Transcript, "Showdown: Iraq," *CNN Late Edition with Wolf Blitzer*, CNN, December 29, 2002.

187 *"purely social visit[s]"*: Associated Press, "Giuliani visits the White House but says it's not about a job," July 31, 2002.

188 *"Welcome to a free Iraq"*: Kerik, *From Jailer to Jailed*, p. 111.

189 *The decision proved catastrophic*: James Dobbins et al., *Occupying Iraq: A History of the Coalition Provisional Authority* (RAND Corporation, 2009), Summary, pp. xv, xxvi, xxxiii; Stuart Bowen, *Hard Lessons: The Iraq Reconstruction Experience* (Special Inspector General for Iraq Reconstruction, 2009), p. 75.

412

Notes

189 *Kerik inherited a shambles . . . "There was no vetting process"*: Bernie Kerik interview.

190 *"I was fucking excited" [and four subsequent quotations]*: Kerik, *From Jailer to Jailed*, p. 108.

191 *"They'd get tips and they'd go and actually raid a whorehouse" [and subsequent quotation]*: Stephanie Gaskell, "Former Iraq Commander: Bernard Kerik Was 'a Waste of Time' in Iraq," New York *Daily News*, May 5, 2008.

191 *Kerik—who denied raiding houses of prostitution*: Bernie Kerik interview.

191 *"I'm here to bring more media attention" [and subsequent quotation]*: Rajiv Chandrasekaran, *Imperial Life in the Emerald City: Inside Iraq's Green Zone* (New York: Vintage, 2007), p. 97.

191 *Kerik called Gifford's account "completely ludicrous"*: Bernie Kerik interview.

191 *But there was no question that Kerik was soaking up . . . "a 100 percent change" [and two subsequent quotations]*: Romesh Ratnesar, "Can a New York Cop Tame Baghdad?," *Time*, June 9, 2003.

192 *"Kerik has been roundly criticized by senior and junior CPA officials" [and three subsequent quotations, including by Clayton McManaway and Fred Smith]*: Dobbins et al., *Occupying Iraq*, pp. 76–77.

192 *"When he came into the office he didn't sit down with me . . ."*: Interview with General Ahmad Albayati.

193 *"Because of his leadership, his knowledge, and his experience" [and two subsequent quotations by Bush and Kerik]*: Transcript, "President Bush, Police Commissioner Kerik Discuss Police Force in Iraq," White House, October 3, 2003.

194 *"not worthy of the Boy Scouts" [and subsequent quotation by Von Essen]*: Transcript, "National Commission on Terrorist Attacks Upon the United States," Eleventh Public Hearing, Wednesday, May 19, 2004; Richard Schwartz, "Shameful Showboating: Ex–Navy Secretary Insulted Heroes to Raise His Own Profile," New York *Daily News*, May 20, 2004.

195 *"Memo to 9/11 Commission"*: "INSULT: Brass Defends City's Honor: Memo to 9/11 Commission: This Man Is a New York Hero. He Is Not a 'Boy Scout,'" *New York Post*, May 19, 2004.

195 *"get down on his hands and knees"*: Schwartz, "Shameful Showboating."

195 *"we're all hurt" [and ten subsequent quotations, including from Richard Ben-Veniste, John Lehman, Tom Kean, and audience members]*: Transcript and video, "September 11 Commission Hearing," C-SPAN, May 19, 2004; transcript, "National Commission on Terrorist Attacks Upon the United States," Eleventh Public Hearing, May 19, 2004.

197 *"We did not ask tough questions"*: Thomas H. Kean and Lee H. Hamilton with Benjamin Rhodes, *Without Precedent: The Inside Story of the 9/11 Commission* (New York: Vintage, 2007), p. 231.

197 *"every day for about two years"*: Tony Carbonetti interview.

198 *"All that was lacking was the horse-drawn coach"*: Ruth La Ferla, "Vows; Judith Nathan and Rudolph W. Giuliani," *New York Times*, May 25, 2003.

198 *"It was sad that it was at Gracie Mansion" [and three subsequent quotations, including from Judith Giuliani]*: Mindy Levine interview.

198 *"Wearing that sparkling tiara was a former-mistress-now-wife's equivalent"*: Robin Givhan, "Graceless at Gracie," *Washington Post*, May 30, 2003.

198 *"I would like to introduce my wife"*: Ibid.

199 *"Honey, notice how nice I leave house"*: Handwritten note from Giuliani viewed by author.

200 *Bernie Kerik kicked off the proceedings ... [and two subsequent quotations]*: Author was in attendance.

201 *"I've never seen so many Republicans in New York City" [and six subsequent quotations]*: Transcript and video, "Republican National Convention, Day 1 Evening," C-SPAN, August 30, 2004.

202 *who was widely seen as an ineffective leader*: John J. Miller, "The Impossible Position of Tom Ridge: Director of Homeland Security—Or Something," *National Review*, June 17, 2002.

202 *"The president is looking for a replacement for Tom Ridge" [and three subsequent quotations in conversation with George W. Bush]*: Bernie Kerik interview.

203 *"flabbergasted"*: Ibid.

203 *"He said no"*: Tony Carbonetti interview.

204 *"dedicated, innovative reformer who insists on getting results"*: Transcript, "Remarks on the Nomination of Bernard B. Kerik to Be Secretary of Homeland Security," December 3, 2004.

204 *Kerik was fired as chief of investigations*: John Mintz and Lucy Shackelford, "Kerik's Surveillance Activity in Saudi Arabia Is Disputed," *Washington Post*, December 8, 2004.

204 *Taser had sold stun guns to the agency he was about to lead*: Larry Margasak, "Kerik Made Millions from Agency Contractor," Associated Press Online, December 9, 2004.

204 *why multiple homicide detectives had been assigned to find Judith Regan's cell phone*: Richard Cohen, "The Commish of Homeland Insecurity," *Washington Post*, December 9, 2004.

204 *Kerik had ties to an alleged mob-connected company through a close friend, Larry Ray*: Russ Buettner, "Bernard Kerik's Troubling Ties: Links to Company in Mobster Probe," New York *Daily News*, December 12, 2004.

204 *background check informed him that his nanny was an illegal immigrant*: Bernie Kerik interview

204 *Giuliani gave Kerik a tearful hug*: Ibid.

205 *"I know you've been around, but take my word for it"*: Ibid.

205 *a warrant was issued for his arrest*: Mark Hosenball, Charles Gasparino, and

Michael Isikoff with Evan Thomas and Kathryn Williams, "A Tough Guy Tumbles," *Newsweek*, December 20, 2004.

205 *"Bernard Kerik's Double Affair Laid Bare" [and four subsequent quotations]*: Russ Buettner, "Bernard Kerik's Double Affair Laid Bare," New York *Daily News*, December 13, 2004.

206 *"The two of them had an infatuation with him"*: Tony Carbonetti interview.

CHAPTER 10: FRONTRUNNER

208 *"I thought you'd be president by now"*: Confidential interviews with Giuliani advisors.

208 *"Someday, I will see him sworn in as president"*: Michael Cooper, "Helen Giuliani, 92, Mother of Former New York Mayor," *New York Times*, September 9, 2002.

208 *"[They felt] that he just had to put his name up and remind people"*: Adam Goodman interview.

209 *Giuliani traveled to New Orleans and held some meetings there, but passed on the offer*: Confidential interview with Giuliani aide.

210 *"how it is to play in the bigs"*: Bennett Roth, "Houston-Based Firm Adds a Power Partner: Giuliani; And the Newest Lawyer at Bracewell & Patterson Has His Own Reasons to Join," *Houston Chronicle*, March 30, 2005.

211 *"People who know me are not surprised"*: Giuliani press conference, March 31, 2005.

211 *Bracewell agreed to pay Giuliani Partners $10 million, and an annual salary*: Michael Shnayerson, "A Tale of Two Giulianis," *Vanity Fair*, January 2008.

211 *"He felt that voters should have the opportunity to give him the job"*: Confidential interview with Giuliani advisor.

212 *"You watch"*: Mike DuHaime interview.

213 *After dining with him at a downtown Houston restaurant*: Bennett Roth, "GOP Hopefuls Cast Eye on Texas Cash," *Houston Chronicle*, December 19, 2006.

213 *Ed Goeas, his pollster . . . declared it hopeless . . . [and subsequent quotation]*: Ed Goeas interview.

214 *In November 2006, he was ranked the most popular politician in the nation*: "Poll: Giuliani Is Most Popular Politician," CBS News, November 28, 2006.

214 *"RUDY LOSES PREZ PLANS" [and five subsequent quotations]*: Ben Smith, "Rudy Loses Prez Plans," New York *Daily News*, January 2, 2007; Ben Smith, "The Giuliani Dossier: A Brief Tour," *Politico*, April 19, 2007.

214 *"sympathetic to one of Giuliani's rivals for the White House"*: Ben Smith interview.

215 *"Bow to Mecca, shithead"*: Ibid.

216 *The local fire chief's wife asked him to sign a book . . . [and subsequent quotation]*: Stephen Rodrick, "Rudy Tuesday," *New York*, February 23, 2007.

216 *"The single most important part of leadership"*: Susan Page, "Giuliani: Can Hero

of 9/11 Win over His Own Party? Views on Social Issues Could Cost Him Republican Party's Nomination," *USA Today*, February 1, 2007.

217 *"Yes, I'm running" [and twelve subsequent quotations in conversation with Larry
King]:* Larry King, "Interview with Rudy Giuliani," CNN, February 14, 2007.

218 *"Would the day that Roe v. Wade is repealed be a good day for America" [and eight
subsequent quotations]:* Transcript, "The Republicans' First Presidential Candidates Debate," *New York Times*, May 3, 2008.

219 *"We all panicked and said how do we get him to check all the boxes" [and subsequent quotation]:* Tony Carbonetti interview.

219 *"We can kick your city's ass":* Transcript, *CBS This Morning*, CBS News, April 17, 1995.

219 *He told an aide he didn't want to be known for that anymore:* Confidential interview with Giuliani campaign official.

219 *"That righteous anger wasn't coming out":* Matt Mahoney interview.

219 *"He was running almost not because he wanted it":* Mike DuHaime interview.

220 *"He wasn't that plugged in" [and subsequent quotation]:* Confidential interview
with longtime advisor.

221 *"We want you to get Judith to call him less" [and two subsequent quotations, as
well as forty-call estimate]:* Confidential interview with person familiar with the
conversation.

221 *"It's really not where you want his mindset to be during a debate":* Confidential
interview with a campaign strategist.

221 *"She would purposely do it to get him off his game":* Confidential interview with
advisor to Giuliani.

222 *"You're going to make the most beautiful First Lady since Jackie Onassis":* Confidential interview with Judith Giuliani confidante.

222 *"They were so ridiculously incapable":* Interview with Judith Nathan.

222 *met with her at an Upper East Side coffee shop:* Confidential interview with person
familiar with the events.

222 *revealed she had discovered a 1974 wedding certificate that suggested Judith had
misled the press:* David Saltonstall and Heidi Evans, "First Hubby a 'Terrific' Guy,"
New York *Daily News*, March 22, 2007.

223 *"I'm aware of it" [and subsequent quotation]:* Confidential interview with person
aware of the conversation.

223 *"We appreciate the value of marriage":* Ibid.

223 *"She is a positive force for Rudy":* Dan Janison, "Team Rudy Wants Judi; Claims
That Judith Is Overly Involved in Hubby's Bid for Prez Won't Dim Role Within
Campaign, Staff Says," *Newsday*, March 24, 2007.

223 *In preparation for the Barbara Walters interview:* Confidential interview with
campaign aide.

224 *"It was a rocky road" [and eight subsequent quotations in conversation with Barbara Walters]:* Transcript, "The Next First Lady? Rudy Giuliani Wants Judith in
Cabinet Meetings," ABC News, March 30, 2007.

Notes

225 *she "obviously" would not be a cabinet member . . . "promoting overall health"*: "Giuliani; Making It Official," *The Hotline*, April 2, 2007.

225 *"Judi's Job with Pup-Killer Firm"*: Dan Mangan, "Judi's Job with Pup-Killer Firm," *New York Post*, April 2, 2007.

225 *"Attack me all you want"*: Giuliani press conference, April 3, 2007.

225 *the entire high command of the campaign was summoned*: Confidential interviews with multiple people who attended; Judith Giuliani interview; Ed Goeas interview.

225 *"If you don't want me in the meeting" [and two subsequent quotations]*: Confidential interviews with multiple people who attended.

226 *But Judith and her advisors wanted specific goals . . . wanted a plan to promote that*: Confidential interviews with multiple people who attended; Judith Giuliani denies she wanted to compare herself and Giuliani to Bill and Hillary Clinton.

226 *"If he is elected, the first lady picks a charity that she makes her focus" [and five subsequent quotations]*: Ed Goeas interview; Judith Giuliani didn't deny potentially wanting to champion an issue.

226 *"He didn't want to fight with her, but he didn't want to shut her down either" [and subsequent quotation]*: Ed Goeas interview.

227 *"18 points ahead in mid-July"*: ABC-*Washington Post* Poll, July 18–21, 2007.

227 *"He promised the endorsement"*: Mike DuHaime interview.

228 *"He sat there and said he would endorse Rudy"*: Judith Giuliani interview; John Heilemann and Mark Halperin, *Game Change* (New York: HarperCollins, 2010).

228 *threatening to support a third-party candidate if Republicans nominated him*: David Kirkpatrick, "Giuliani Inspires Threat of a Third-Party Run," *New York Times*, October 1, 2007.

228 *"There's obviously a little problem that exists between me and his wife"*: Niles Lathem, "Son-Burned Rudy's Toughest Test," *New York Post*, March 4, 2007.

228 *"I play golf with Andrew, and Andrew is a very, very good golfer, by the way"*: Transcript, *Situation Room with Wolf Blitzer*, CNN, September 24, 2007.

229 *"September 11 casts somewhat of a different light" [and six subsequent quotations]*: Transcript, "Former Mayor Rudolph W. Giuliani Delivers Remarks at National Rifle Association Conference," September 21, 2007.

230 *On November 9, Bernie Kerik was indicted on fourteen counts*: William K. Rashbaum and Maria Newman, "Grand Jury Indicts Kerik on Corruption Charges," *New York Times*, November 9, 2007.

230 *the* Village Voice *unloaded an exposé of Giuliani Partners' work for the government of Qatar*: Wayne Barrett, "Rudy's Ties to a Terror Sheikh," *The Village Voice*, November 28, 2007.

230 *Ben Smith reported that City Hall had found obscure pockets of the city budget*: Ben Smith, "Giuliani Billed Obscure Agencies for Trips," *Politico*, November 28, 2007.

230 *In 2006, Purdue Pharma, the maker of the addictive painkiller OxyContin . . . with deadly results*: Barry Meier and Eric Lipton, "Under Attack, Drug Maker Turned to Giuliani for Help," *New York Times*, December 28, 2007.

231 *"There's only three things he mentions in a sentence":* Joe Biden, Democratic debate, October 30, 2007.

232 *"Mr. Mayor, this is not what we all thought about" [and three subsequent quotations in conversation with Giuliani]:* Mike DuHaime interview.

232 *"They were just spending money hand over fist":* Anne Dunsmore interview.

233 *"Aggressive fighting for the right is the noblest sport the world affords" [and four subsequent quotations]:* Transcript, "Florida Votes," CNN Live, January 29, 2008.

CHAPTER 11: RELEVANCE

234 *"Looking forward to your tax refund? So are identity thieves" [and two subsequent quotations]:* Video, "Rudy Giuliani Commercial for LifeLock," YouTube user Lachlan Markay, November 5, 2019.

235 *perpetuating the deception:* "LifeLock to Pay $100 Million to Consumers to Settle FTC Charges It Violated 2010 Order," Federal Trade Commission, December 17, 2015.

235 *"rode up to the grandstand and fell off his horse":* Skip Hollandsworth, "There Will Be Boone," *Texas Monthly*, September 2008.

235 *"I think we've got to get ready for the debate":* Transcript and video, "Giuliani Endorsement of McCain," C-SPAN, January 30, 2008.

235 *"decompress":* "Giuliani Set to Return to His Houston-Based Law Firm," Law.com, February 12, 2008.

236 *Business at Giuliani Partners plunged 50 percent:* Michael Crowley, "The Indecider," *New York*, October 23, 2009.

236 *The campaign had burned through more than $60 million and ended up $4 million in debt:* John Gross, "Debt Settlement Plan for the Rudy Giuliani Presidential Committee," June 12, 2013.

236 *"I think I should've fought Iowa harder":* Crowley, "The Indecider."

236 *"I couldn't get him out of bed" [and three subsequent quotations]:* Judith Giuliani interview.

237 *She said he started to drink more heavily:* Ibid.

238 *"We moved into Mar-a-Lago and Donald kept our secret" [and one subsequent quotation]:* Judith Giuliani interview.

238 *Trump provided them with a hideaway:* Judith Giuliani interview.

239 *"During the period of time that we did that it was constant counseling" [and three subsequent quotations]:* Ibid.

239 *"kind of went into a cave" [and subsequent quotation]:* Joe Lhota interview.

239 *"There was a period where it was just the two of them for two or three months":* Tony Carbonetti interview.

241 *"When Trump saw the photos . . .":* interview with Judith Nathan confidante. A

spokesperson for Trump informed us that the former president wished to accept our interview request pending a conversation with Giuliani; he did not respond to our messages after that.

241 *"... spent a month at Mar-a-Lago, relaxing"*: Dan Barry, Benjamin Weiser, and Alan Feuer, "In Defending Trump, Is Giuliani a Shrewd Tactician or 'Untethered'?" *New York Times*, Aug. 27, 2018.

242 *"They need a leader like you, who can deal with corruption"*: Sewell Chan, "Giuliani Weighs In on Distant Mayoral Race," *New York Times*, May 8, 2008.

242 *As it happened, Klitschko was a client who was supposedly relying on Giuliani's*: Rosalind S. Helderman, Paul Sonne, David L. Stern, and Josh Dawsey, "Giuliani Discussed Interests of a Former Ukrainian Client During Summer Meeting with Top Zelensky Aide," *Washington Post*, January 31, 2020.

243 *it was he who introduced Giuliani to Vitali Klitschko, among others*: Press release, "Former Mayor of New York Rudolph Giuliani Met with Vitali Klitschko at a Nasdaq Studio in Times Square," TriGlobal Strategic Ventures, May 7, 2008; press release, "Vitali Klitschko's Press Conference at the Nasdaq Studio in Times Square, New York City," TriGlobal Strategic Ventures, October 12, 2017.

243 *Giuliani flew to Kyiv for a ceremony unveiling a monument*: Press release, "TGSV Participated in a Ceremony Unveiling the Monument Erected in Honor of IGOR Sikorsky, Aircraft and Helicopter Designer, in Kiev," TriGlobal Strategic Ventures, May 15, 2008.

243 *Klitschko sponsored the event*: Andrew Roth, "Unravelling Rudolph Giuliani's Labyrinthine Ties to Ukraine," *The Guardian*, October 30, 2019.

243 *"When we decided to put the fund together in my family"*: Marc Santora, "Giuliani Firm Plans Real Estate Investment Fund," *New York Times*, July 20, 2008.

244 *"I wonder if Rudy Giuliani might get a call to get vetted for VP" [and two subsequent quotations]*: Transcript, "Obama VP Vetter Resigns over Finances," Fox News, June 11, 2008.

244 *"In any meeting I was in"*: Correspondences with Bill McInturff.

244 *Giuliani was hurt by McCain's treatment of him*: Confidential interview with former aide.

245 *Bracewell & Giuliani helped broker a deal*: Press release, "Firm Represents Ukraine's SigmaBleyzer in Merger with Volia Cable," Bracewell & Giuliani, August 7, 2008.

245 *"This already has been the longest presidential campaign in history" [and six subsequent quotations]*: Transcript and video, "Rudy Giuliani 2008 Convention Speech," C-SPAN, September 3, 2008.

246 *costing the networks millions in lost advertising revenue*: Ed Goeas interview.

247 *"It's a big honor for me to have you here" [and two subsequent quotations]*: Video, "Rudi Rudolf Djulijani kod Ivana Ivanovica (Rudy Giuliani interview for Serbian television)," YouTube user snimi8, April 20, 2012.

Notes

247 *His client, Aleksandar Vucic, was running for office on a ticket with Tomislav Niko-lic:* Andrew Kirtzman, "Serbia's Mayor," *The New Republic,* July 12, 2012.

247 *Clinton fumed in a memo that his work for Vucic was "outrageous":* Stephen Braun and Chad Day, "Giuliani's Foreign Work Complicates Candidacy for Top Post," Associated Press, November 16, 2016.

248 *"I'm not here to get involved in the politics of Peru, but if she gets elected, I'd be very happy to help her":* Ibid.

248 *rebranding itself as a pro-U.S. freedom-fighting group:* Jeremiah Goulka, Lydia Hansell, Elizabeth Wilke, and Judith Larson, *The Mujahedin-e Khalq in Iraq: A Policy Conundrum* (RAND Corporation, Sponsored by the Office of the Secretary of Defense, 2009), pp. 3, 39, 40.

249 *"'America's Mayor' has presented himself as a centurion in the fight against 'radical Islamic terrorism'":* Daniel Benjamin, "Giuliani Took Money from a Group That Killed Americans. Does Trump Care?," *Politico,* November 23, 2016.

249 *"You are the heroes":* Matin Karim, "Iranian Opposition Holds Annual 'Free Iran' Conference, Ashraf 3—Albania," PMOI website, July 13, 2019.

251 *"The police force is not to be an occupying force" [and seventeen subsequent quota-tions]:* Transcript, *Meet the Press,* NBC News, November 23, 2014.

253 *"Burn this bitch down!":* Ray Sanchez, "Michael Brown's Stepfather at Rally: 'Burn This Bitch Down!,'" CNN, November 24, 2014.

253 *Giuliani went on CNN the next morning:* Transcript, "News Conference with St. Louis Mayor; Rudy Giuliani's Views on Ferguson; Ferguson Erupts Following Grand Jury Decision," CNN, November 25, 2014.

254 *"I do not believe, and I know this is a horrible thing to say":* Darren Samuelsohn, "Obama Doesn't Love America," *Politico,* February 18, 2015.

254 *"America has been treated to a spectacle that New Yorkers":* Errol Louis, "Rudy Giuliani's Obama Outburst Is Ugly, Divisive," CNN, February 20, 2015.

254 *"Do you think Rudy Giuliani has lost it" [and subsequent quotation]:* Transcript, "Press Briefing by Press Secretary Josh Earnest," White House Documents and Publications, February 20, 2015.

254 *"because he experienced so much pain":* Transcript, "Giuliani Versus Obama; Fac-ing Criticism; CBS Releases Falklands Video," Fox News, February 23, 2015.

254 *"Some people thought it was racist":* Maggie Haberman and Nicholas Confessore, "Giuliani: Obama Had a White Mother, So I'm Not a Racist," *New York Times,* February 19, 2015.

255 *"Over my years as mayor of New York and as a federal prosecutor":* Rudolph Giuliani, "Rudy Giuliani: My Bluntness Overshadowed My Message," *Wall Street Journal,* February 22, 2015.

255 *"Since Giuliani's disastrous run for the Republican Presidential nomination, in 2008, he has become a national embarrassment" [and two subsequent quotations]:* Jeffrey Toobin, "The Paranoid Style of Rudy Giuliani," *New Yorker,* February 20, 2015.

255 *"There's something wrong with the guy":* Ibid.

Notes

CHAPTER 12: GUARDRAILS

256 *"You get what you inspect, not what you expect"*: Author's copy of "Peter Principles."

257 *"He took ushering my father out of this world as seriously as any other job" [and three subsequent quotations]*: Heather McBride interview.

257 *"He took the Peter Powers death harder"*: Confidential interview with Giuliani confidant.

257 *"He was in bad shape"*: Confidential interview with Giuliani confidant.

257 *the constant advice from his friends to leave her*: Confidential interviews with numerous Giuliani confidants.

258 *"Bernie Kerik is history"*: Transcript, "Press Conference with Former New York City Mayor Rudy Giuliani (R) and Former Representative Rick Lazio," Federal News Service, December 22, 2009.

258 *"He was like family to me, someone I could never have abandoned"*: Bernard B. Kerik, *From Jailer to Jailed: My Journey from Correction and Police Commissioner to Inmate #84888-054* (New York: Threshold Editions, 2015), p. 212.

258 *"He was torn up" [and four subsequent quotations]*: Bernie Kerik interview.

260 *"Your father had a dying wish"*: Interviews with numerous people who attended and heard the eulogy.

260 *"Who's on Rudy Giuliani's radar in terms of" [and ten subsequent quotations]*: Transcript, "Democratic Party's History of Racism; Using the N Word; Interview with Former New York City Mayor Rudy Giuliani," *Sean Hannity*, Fox News, June 24, 2015.

261 *"How long have they been friends of yours" [and seven subsequent quotations]*: Video and typed transcript, *Rudy Giuliani's Common Sense*, Episode 74 (since removed), YouTube user Rudy W. Giuliani, October 2, 2020.

261 *"Tony, he's serious" [and two subsequent quotations]*: Ibid.; Tony Carbonetti interview.

261 *"carnival barker"*: Confidential interview with former Giuliani aide.

262 *"sending people that have lots of problems"*: Transcript, "Here's Donald Trump's Presidential Announcement Speech," *Time*, June 16, 2015.

262 *the law firm's revenue shot up from $200 million to $300 million*: Ibid.; Bracewell partner and Giuliani advisor Dan Connelly in *New York* magazine.

262 *"He was a good partner for a while"*: Confidential interview with a former partner at Bracewell.

262 *"I remember him walking into the room and the energy of this person"*: Confidential interview with a former Bracewell employee.

262 *"He was perfectly personable" [and three subsequent quotations]*: Confidential interview with a former partner at Bracewell.

263 *Lawyers were coming back from New York with stories about his boozy dinners*: Confidential interviews with former Bracewell employees; Bracewell & Giuliani declined to comment about multiple subjects.

Notes

263 *"in parts of the world where I spend a lot of time"*: "The Decision: Rudy Giuliani Speaks on His Big Move to Greenberg Traurig," Bloomberg Law, January 19, 2016.

264 *"We begged him not to do it"*: Confidential interview with Giuliani confidant.

265 *"It doesn't make sense to me that you are going to vote for Trump" [and three subsequent quotations in conversation with Chris Cuomo]*: Transcript, "Interview with Rudy Giuliani," CNN, April 19, 2016.

265 *"If it doesn't show up, it's going to make him look really bad"*: Transcript, "Interview with Washington Congressman Adam Smith; Trump Taunts; Chicago Police Superintendent Fired; Terror Fears," CNN, December 1, 2015.

265 *"if he doesn't blow it"*: Yonah Jeremy Bob, "Giuliani to 'Post': US Is Ready to Vote for Trump if He Doesn't Blow It," *Jerusalem Post*, June 23, 2016.

265 *"more so probably than any other political figure"*: Jason Miller interview.

266 *they resented his close relationship with the boss*: Confidential interview with senior aide to Trump.

266 *"He got into it full-bore because his life was empty at that point"*: Confidential interview with Giuliani confidant.

267 *And as he sat in the Green Room, he grew angry watching a speaker*: Marc Santora, "We're Coming to Get You! It's Vintage Giuliani at G.O.P. Convention," *New York Times*, July 19, 2016.

267 *"I am here to speak to you about a very serious subject" [and ten subsequent quotations]*: Transcript and video, "Rudy Giuliani Delivers Remarks at Republican National Convention," C-SPAN, July 18, 2016.

269 *"Is he okay?"*: Michael Wolff, *Too Famous: The Rich, the Powerful, the Wishful, the Notorious, the Damned* (New York: Henry Holt, 2021), p. 36.

269 *"Is Rudy Giuliani Losing His Mind?"*: Kevin Baker, "Is Rudy Giuliani Losing His Mind?," *Politico*, September 4, 2016.

270 *"Go online and put down 'Hillary Clinton illness'"*: Transcript, "Shannon Bream, Fox News Hosts Fox News Sunday," August 21, 2016.

270 *"Giuliani: Press Ignores Signs of Clinton's Illness"*: Rebecca Morin and Nick Gass, "Giuliani: Press Ignores Signs of Clinton's Illness," *Politico*, August 21, 2016.

270 *"Giuliani Fuels Clinton Health Rumors Again . . . and Again"*: Anna Brand, "Giuliani Fuels Clinton Health Rumors Again . . . and Again," NBC News, August 22, 2016.

270 *"Rudy Giuliani Stokes Rumors About Clinton's Health"*: Video, "Rudy Giuliani Stokes Rumors About Clinton's Health," Bloomberg Politics, August 23, 2016.

270 *"Recently, Fox News' Sean Hannity and the Drudge Report have openly discussed Secretary Clinton's series of falls" [and subsequent quotation]*: Rudy Giuliani, "Rudy Giuliani: I'm Performing a Public Service," *USA Today*, August 29, 2016.

270 *He became a minister without portfolio . . . no one but the boss*: Confidential interviews with Trump advisors and news accounts, including Philip Rucker and Robert Costa, "Rudy Giuliani Gets the Street Brawl with Hillary Clinton That He's Always Wanted," *Washington Post*, August 22, 2016.

Notes

271 *"We could tell that this was one of the biggest national security trainwrecks" [and subsequent two quotations]:* We interviewed multiple sources familiar with the Russian interference discussion.

272 *"It's fine to emphasize the importance of protecting a company's digital information" [and two subsequent quotations]:* Confidential interview with former Greenberg shareholder who attended the meeting.

273 *"Rudy has always been a loyal soldier":* Jason Miller interview.

273 *"I moved on her, actually" [and seven subsequent quotations]:* Paul Farhi, "A Caller Had a Lewd Tape of Donald Trump. Then the Race to Break the Story Was On," *Washington Post,* October 7, 2016.

274 *"repugnant":* "Growing Number of Republicans Rebuke Trump," CBS News, October 8, 2016.

274 *"locker room banter":* David A. Fahrenthold, "Trump Recorded Having Extremely Lewd Conversation About Women in 2005," *Washington Post,* October 8, 2016.

275 *"This tape, which was recorded in 2005, on it, we hear Donald Trump behaving in, I think it's fair to say, a vile and disgusting way" [and seven subsequent quotations]:* Transcript, "Jake Tapper, CNN Hosts CNN's State of the Union," CNN, October 9, 2016.

276 *Triumphantly, he sat down in a seat across from Trump:* Multiple news accounts and books, including: Corey Lewandowski and David Bossie, *Let Trump Be Trump: The Inside Story of His Rise to the Presidency* (New York: Hachette, 2017), p. 205; and Jim Dwyer, Jo Becker, Kenneth P. Vogel, Maggie Haberman, and Sarah Maslin Nir, "The Indispensable Man: How Giuliani Led Trump to the Brink of Impeachment," *New York Times,* December 8, 2019.

276 *"Man, Rudy, you sucked":* Ibid.

276 *"We got a couple of surprises left":* Video, "Giuliani on Trump Rallies: Never Seen Enthusiasm Like This," Fox News, October 25, 2016.

277 *"We've got a bunch of things up our sleeves that should turn this around":* Video, "Rudy Giuliani hinted at Comey Letter 2 Days Before Release," YouTube user REWINDTHENEWS, November 4, 2016.

277 *Comey was particularly concerned about the behavior of Rudy Giuliani:* Byron Tau and Natalie Andrews, "Comey Tells House Panel He Suspected Giuliani Was Leaking FBI Information to Media," *Wall Street Journal,* December 8, 2018; Justice Department Inspector General's Report on the 2016 election.

277 *"The other rumor that I get is that there's a kind of revolution going on":* Nathaniel Meyersohn, Rudy Giuliani interview with Lars Larson, uploaded to SoundCloud by *BuzzFeed News,* 2017; Dareh Gregorian, "Investigation into Alleged FBI Leaks to Giuliani During 2016 Campaign Is Ongoing, DOJ Watchdog Says," NBC News, December 11, 2019.

278 *"I want to give a special thanks to our former mayor, Rudy Giuliani" [and subsequent quotation]:* Transcript, "Here's the Full Text of Donald Trump's Victory Speech," CNN, November 9, 2016.

278 *Rudy and Judith were the only people to join the Trump family*: Judith Giuliani interview.

278 *"What do you have to say now" [and three subsequent quotations]*: Tony Carbonetti interview.

CHAPTER 13: WASHINGTON

281 *"We are going to make this decision now" [and two subsequent quotations]*: Video, "Fox News—Election Night 2016 (11-8-2016) (6:23 P.M E.T.—3:07 A.M. E.T)," YouTube User DANNOTCH'S NEWSVIDEOS, November 24, 2016.

281 *"Congratulations, Mr. Secretary" [and three subsequent quotations]*: John Bolton, *The Room Where It Happened* (New York: Simon & Schuster, 2020), p. 10.

281 *Giuliani was making no secret of his interest in the job*: This account of the contest for secretary of state is based on interviews with John Bolton; numerous advisors to both Trump and Giuliani; Bolton, *The Room Where It Happened*; and Michael Kranish, Anne Gearan, Dan Balz, and Philip Rucker, "Trump Wasn't Happy with his State Department Finalists. Then He Heard a New Name," *Washington Post*, December 13, 2016.

282 *"Why did your candidate, and you yourself, refer to Hillary Clinton as sick and almost dying" [and three subsequent quotations]*: Video, "Chris Matthews vs. Rudy Giuliani, Election Night 2016," YouTube user Jack Coleman, November 9, 2016.

282 *pause about awarding him the most prestigious cabinet position*: Jeremy W. Peters and Maggie Haberman, "Republicans Divided Between Romney and Giuliani for Secretary of State," *New York Times*, November 24, 2016.

283 *"People who were on the plane said to me"*: Tony Carbonetti interview.

283 *found so many client conflicts that it took twenty-five pages to list them*: The transition report was obtained and published by *Axios*: "Full list: The Leaked Trump Transition Vetting Documents," *Axios*, June 24, 2019.

283 *"central casting"*: Ashley Parker and Maggie Haberman, "High in Tower, Trump Reads, Tweets and Plans," *New York Times*, November 19, 2016.

283 *"phony" and a "fraud"*: Eric Bradner and Catherine Treyz, "Romney Implores: Bring Down Trump," CNN, March 3, 2016.

284 *Forever casting about for one more opinion, Trump polled his guests at Mar-a-Lago*: Emily Smith, "Trump Spent Thanksgiving Asking: Mitt or Rudy," *New York Post*, November 26, 2016.

284 *"I probably have traveled in the last 13 years as much as Hillary" [and subsequent quotation]*: Mara Gay and Felicia Schwartz, "Rudy Giuliani Lobbies to Be Secretary of State," *Wall Street Journal*, November 25, 2016.

284 *The campaigning backfired*: Peters and Haberman, "Republicans Divided Between Romney and Giuliani for Secretary of State."

285 *"He loves it when the losers have to come and beg" [and five subsequent quotations about meeting in Trump Tower]*: Jason Miller interview.

Notes

285 *"had never heard anything like that before"*: Ibid.; John Bolton interview.

286 *"Donald was not going to like that mustache"*: Philip Rucker and Karen Tumulty, "Donald Trump Is Holding a Government Casting Call. He's Seeking 'the Look,'" *Washington Post*, December 22, 2016.

286 *"You know it's not my fault, right?"*: Tony Carbonetti interview.

287 *a metric ton of gold each day, worth billions of dollars:* Much of this account of Zarrab's case and Giuliani's role in it comes from court documents in the Zarrab case. Dexter Filkins of the *New Yorker* provided a compelling narrative of Zarrab's journey: Dexter Filkins, "A Mysterious Case Involving Turkey, Iran, and Rudy Giuliani," *New Yorker*, April 14, 2017. The account of the Oval Office conversation comes from numerous media accounts: Josh Dawsey, Carol Leonnig, and Matt Zapotosky, "Trump Asked Tillerson to Help Broker Deal to End U.S. Prosecution of Turkish Trader Represented by Giuliani," *Washington Post*, October 10, 2019; Jo Becker, Maggie Haberman, and Eric Lipton, "Giuliani Pressed for Turkish Prisoner Swap in Oval Office Meeting," *New York Times*, October 10, 2019. The story of the Oval Office conversation was originally reported by *Bloomberg News*: Nick Wadhams, Saleha Moshin, Stephanie Baker, and Jennifer Jacobs, "Trump Urged Top Aide to Help Giuliani Client Facing DOJ Charges," *Bloomberg News*, October 9, 2019.

288 *"Guys, give Rex your pitch" ... Tillerson called the proposition highly inappropriate:* Ibid.

289 *"It happened to be a good trade"*: Becker, Haberman, and Lipton, "Giuliani Pressed for Turkish Prisoner Swap in Oval Office Meeting."

289 *Rumors of his drinking were spreading:* Numerous confidential interviews with Hamptons socialites, as well as Giuliani aides and confidants.

290 *"I was a catcher from a very young age" [and two subsequent quotations]:* Emily Smith, "Rudy Giuliani Rushed to the Hospital After Falling," *New York Post*, August 15, 2017.

290 *"He was shitfaced" [and one subsequent quotation]:* Interview with Judith Giuliani.

290 *"massive depression" [and two subsequent quotations]:* Judith Giuliani interview.

291 *"bullshit"*: Bernie Kerik interview.

291 *"If you spent an extensive amount of time with that woman you'd drink a lot"*: Tony Carbonetti interview.

291 *"He asked me if I thought Rudy was drinking too much"*: Confidential interviews with numerous Giuliani friends and former aides.

291 *"Donald Trump said during the transition that Rudy Giuliani was losing it"*: Ken Meyer, "Scarborough Suggests Giuliani's 'Drinking Too Much': 'Monkey Throwing Poo Against the Wall,'" *Mediaite*, May 8, 2018.

291 *"We became really close again then"*: Judith Giuliani interview.

291 *"They were very passionate, and very loving together"*: Laura O'Reilly interview.

292 *slurring his words so badly it was hard for her to understand him:* Judith Giuliani interview.

292 *denying it to the press despite mounting evidence to the contrary:* Julia Marsh, Reuven Fenton, and Gabrielle Fonrouge, "Rudy Giuliani's Wife Filed for Divorce After His Affair with Married Woman," "Page Six," *New York Post*, June 12, 2018; Jose Lamiet, "Giuliani Defends His Personal Assistant in Broward Insurance Fraud Case," *Miami Herald*, May 14, 2018.

292 *"In these divorce situations, you cannot place blame":* Emily Smith and Julia Marsh, "Rudy and Judith Giuliani to Divorce," "Page Six," *New York Post*, April 4, 2018.

292 *"When the marriage fell apart, he drank heavily":* Confidential interview with former Giuliani aide.

292 *"I wouldn't say that alcohol ruined the marriage" [and subsequent quotation]:* Judith Giuliani interview.

293 *"Where's my Roy Cohn?":* Michael S. Schmidt, "Obstruction Inquiry Shows Trump's Struggle to Keep Grip on Russia Investigation," *New York Times*, January 4, 2018.

293 *"He's going to get you into trouble":* Jay Goldberg interview.

293 *"There would be frequent conversations at the end of the day at Kelly's office":* Confidential interview with senior Trump White House official.

293 *Kelly let the idea die on the vine:* Confidential interview with senior Trump White House aide.

294 *"I don't know yet what's outstanding" [and subsequent quotation]:* Bob Fredericks, "Rudy Giuliani Joins Trump Legal Team, Hopes to End Russia Probe in 'a Week or Two,'" *New York Post*, April 19, 2018.

295 *"Mr. Giuliani . . . is coming on board as a short-timer":* Maggie Haberman and Michael S. Schmidt, "Giuliani to Join Trump's Legal Team," *New York Times*, April 19, 2018.

296 *"I would get on my charger and go right into their offices with a lance" [and eight subsequent quotations in conversation with Sean Hannity]:* Video, "Rudy Giuliani: I'm Sorry Hillary, but You're a Criminal," Fox News, May 2, 2018; transcript, "Exclusive Interview with Rudy Giuliani," Fox News, May 2, 2018.

297 *"We'll cover your expenses out of personal funds":* Chris Geidner, "Rudy Giuliani Says Trump Repaid Michael Cohen for the Stormy Daniels Hush Money," *BuzzFeed News*, May 2, 2018.

297 *"He's learning the subject matter" [and subsequent quotation]:* Jordan Fabian, "Trump on Giuliani: He'll Get His Facts Straight," *The Hill*, May 4, 2018.

298 *"The other day you . . . told BuzzFeed . . . that at some point" [and nine subsequent quotations in conversation with George Stephanopoulos]:* Transcript, *ABC This Week*, ABC News, May 6, 2018.

299 *"Giuliani's conduct since joining the Trump legal team has been the subject of sev-*

eral private conversations" [and subsequent quotation]: Samuelsohn and Schreckinger, "'It's extremely insulting': Giuliani Fires Back at Allegations of Erratic Behavior."

299 a $6 million per year shareholder, claimed: Victoria Bekiempis, "Millionaire Rudy Giuliani Cries Poor in Divorce Court After Spending Big on Alleged Mistress," The Daily Beast, November 7, 2018.

299 "The last year and a half, I haven't been on television": Maggie Haberman and Michael Schmidt, "Giuliani's Law Firm Undercuts His Statements as They Part Ways," New York Times, May 10, 2018.

300 "And when you tell me that, 'You know, he should testify'" [and two subsequent quotations]: Video, "Rudy Giuliani: 'Truth Isn't Truth,'" Meet the Press, NBC News, August 19, 2018.

300 "Headline: MUELLER OFFICIAL DELETES": @RudyGiuliani, "Headline: MUELLER OFFICIAL DELETES 19,000 TEXTS OF TRUMP HATING AGENTS . . . as part of DOJ evidence destruction program. Where's the media outrage at destroying relevant evidence. You can violate any right, obstruct justice and prosecute by innuendo and NYT hero worships you," December 17, 2018, Twitter.com.

301 falsely, that Mueller's appointment was illegal . . . proposed he name one of Giuliani's closest friends to the job: @RudyGiuliani, "To my friend Jeff Sessions: Appoint an Independent Counsel like Louis Freeh or Judge Mukasey to investigate the 'investigation and investigators.' Also unlike the illegal Mueller appointment you will be able to cite, as law requires, alleged crimes," August 13, 2018, Twitter.com.

301 to "frame" the president: Rajaa Elidrissi, "Rudy Giuliani Says Special Counsel Robert Mueller's Team Is Trying to Frame President Trump," CNBC, June 6, 2018.

301 "sneaky, unethical leakers" and "rabid Democrats": Tom Porter, "Rudy Giuliani Called Mueller's Staff 'Rabid Democrats' and 'Sneaky, Unethical Leakers' After a New Report Said the Special Counsel's Findings Are Worse than Trump Claims," Business Insider, August 4, 2019.

301 with an approval rating of 77 percent in 2006, was now a figure of derision, down to a dismal 32 percent: Justin McCarthy, "Rudy Giuliani's Favorable Ratings Hit New Low," Gallup, June 26, 2018.

301 "I don't care about my legacy": Jeffrey Toobin, "How Rudy Giuliani Turned into Trump's Clown," New Yorker, September 10, 2018.

CHAPTER 14: JOYRIDE

302 "I hesitate to tell this story because people think I dreamed the whole thing" [and two subsequent quotations]: Rudolph W. Giuliani with Ken Kurson, Leadership (New York: Hyperion, 2002), p. 208.

Notes

303 *He wore Yankees jerseys, decorated his office with Yankees memorabilia:* Rudy Giuliani, "My Love Affair with the Yankees," ESPN, November 10, 2009.

303 *"Rudy Giuliani—devoted father, loyal friend" [and seven subsequent quotations in conversations with Giuliani and Lev Parnas]:* Mindy Levine interview.

303 *In truth, many of them were bitter at him for ruining his brand:* Confidential interviews with numerous Giuliani friends, confidants, and former aides.

305 *"my brother":* WhatsApp message between Parnas and Giuliani, December 7, 2018, disclosed during the 2020 impeachment proceedings.

305 *"I loved his family, and probably him":* Steve Inskeep and Ryan Lucas, "Transcript: NPR's Full Interview with Trump Lawyer Rudy Giuliani," *Morning Edition*, NPR, February 5, 2020.

306 *Parnas was a born salesman . . . including an energy business and a financial services company:* Michael Rothfeld, Ben Protess, William K. Rashbaum, Kenneth P. Vogel, and Andrew E. Kramer, "How 2 Soviet Émigrés Fueled the Trump Impeachment Flames," *New York Times*, December 19, 2019.

307 *He committed over $1 million for contributions:* Superseding indictment, *United States of America v. Lev Parnas and Andrey Kushkin,* S3 19 Cr. 725 (JPO), filed August 26, 2021.

307 *"Everything is great!!":* Court documents cited in Rothfeld et al., "How 2 Soviet Émigrés Fueled the Trump Impeachment Flames."

308 *"would give you such a boost in the midterm with a lot of the millennials" [and eight subsequent quotations]:* Video of Trump dinner; Kenneth P. Vogel and Ben Protess, "Tape Made Public of Trump Discussing Ukraine with Donors," *New York Times*, January 25, 2020

309 *"If this seems a bit complicated, think of the company 'LifeLock'" [and subsequent quotation]:* Letter from Fraud Guarantee to investors, September 12, 2018.

310 *The assertion was provably false:* Scott Shane, "How a Fringe Theory About Ukraine Took Root in the White House," *New York Times*, October 3, 2019.

310 *"They were perfect":* Ibid.

310 *He told Parnas and Fruman they'd had a great meeting . . . [and subsequent quotation]:* Aaron Parnas interview.

311 *"Thank you for everything you're doing":* Transcript, "The Lev Parnas Interview; Lev Parnas Unloaded a Whole Lot of Evidence Against President Trump," *Anderson Cooper 360*, CNN, January 17, 2020.

311 *The experience only deepened [and three subsequent quotations]:* Text exchange between Giuliani and Parnas December 6, 2008, submitted by Parnas to congressional investigators.

312 *believed that Viktor Shokin, the prosecutor general from 2015 to 2016, was turning a blind eye to government malfeasance:* Adam Entous, "The Ukrainian Prosecutor Behind Trump's Impeachment," *New Yorker*, December 16, 2019.

312 *In December 2015, then–Vice President Joe Biden paid a trip to the country*: Ibid.; transcript, "Remarks by Vice President Joe Biden to the Ukrainian Rada," Office of the Vice President, December 9, 2015.

312 *Parnas and Fruman set up an introductory call in December 2018 . . . He said Biden had him fired before he could crack the case*: House impeachment report, impeachment proceedings, and numerous news reports.

314 *"like a subordinate, trying to get a job" [and subsequent quotation]*: Confidential interviews with others who were present at the meeting.

314 *paid $1 million by Burisma to lobby the vice president. The material was inconclusive, however*: Entous, "The Ukrainian Prosecutor Behind Trump's Impeachment."

315 *"Can you initiate proceedings against him on these grounds" [and four subsequent quotations in conversation between Lutsenko and Giuliani]*: Yuriy Lutsenko interview.

316 *"I've got nothing"*: Giuliani text exchange on March 12, 2019, submitted by Parnas to congressional investigators.

316 *"Originally, I thought I would do it"*: Ben Protess, William K. Rashbaum, and Michael Rothfeld, "Giuliani Pursued Business in Ukraine While Pushing for Inquiries for Trump," *New York Times*, November 27, 2019.

317 *"I thought that, after this interview, they would immediately open the Burisma case"*: Entous, "The Ukrainian Prosecutor Behind Trump's Impeachment."

318 *confounded by his "fantasies" [and four subsequent quotations]*: John Bolton interview; John Bolton, *The Room Where It Happened* (New York: Simon & Schuster, 2020), pp. 409–10, 413, 420–23.

318 *"human hand grenade who is going to blow everybody up"*: Fiona Hill testimony.

318 *"look at the date" [and subsequent quotation]*: Bolton, *The Room Where It Happened*, p. 411.

319 *"He fired her again" [and three subsequent quotations]*: Giuliani and Parnas text exchanges, April 23, 2019 (first two), and May 3, 2019.

319 *"I believed that I needed Yovanovitch out of the way"*: Entous, "The Ukrainian Prosecutor Behind Trump's Impeachment."

319 *"We're not meddling in an election"*: Kenneth P. Vogel, "Rudy Giuliani Plans Ukraine Trip to Push for Inquiries That Could Help Trump," *New York Times*, May 9, 2019.

319 *private letter to Zelensky requesting a meeting [and two subsequent quotations]*: Giuliani's letter to Ukrainian president Volodymyr Zelensky, made public during 2020 impeachment proceedings.

320 *"enemies of the president"*: Transcript, "Giuliani to Urge Ukraine Officials to Investigate Biden; Work of Biden's Son Emerges as Potential 2020 Pitfall; Giuliani No Longer Going to Ukraine," Fox News, May 10, 2019.

320 *"I was told to give it to him in a very harsh way" [and subsequent quotation by Giuliani]*: Transcript, Parnas interview on *The Rachel Maddow Show*.

321 *"Hunter Biden did not violate any Ukrainian laws"*: Daryna Krasnolutska, Kateryna Choursina, and Stephanie Baker, "Ukraine Prosecutor Says No Evidence of Wrongdoing by Bidens," *Bloomberg News*, May 16, 2019.

321 *"Have you ever read your goddamn bribery statute" [and two subsequent quotations]*: Entous, "The Ukrainian Prosecutor Behind Trump's Impeachment."

321 *"I don't want to have any fucking thing to do with Ukraine" [and three subsequent quotations]*: The conversation was described to Bolton by a participant in the meeting; Bolton, *The Room Where It Happened*, p. 416.

323 *"Donald Trump is convinced . . . complete investigation of corruption cases"*: Transcript, "Volodymyr Zelenskyy Had a Phone Conversation with President of the United States," Office of the President of Ukraine, July 25, 2019.

324 *"We were sitting there reading through it"*: Daniel Goldman interview.

324 *"In the course of my official duties" [and subsequent quotation]*: Full text, "Document: Read the Whistle-Blower Complaint," *New York Times*, September 26, 2019.

324 *"We are ready to continue to cooperate for the next steps" [and five subsequent paragraphs]*: Transcript, "Read Trump's Phone Conversation with Volodymyr Zelensky," CNN, September 25, 2019.

325 *"The best way I could describe the Trump Hotel is as a cesspool of Trump officials" [and two subsequent paragraphs]*: Aaron Parnas interview.

326 *"I don't know those gentlemen"*: Brett Samuels and Morgan Chalfant, "Trump Distances Himself from Indicted Giuliani Associates," *The Hill*, October 10, 2019.

326 *"I felt like my family left me"*: Betsy Swan, "Lev Parnas Reveals Why He Turned on Trumpworld," *The Daily Beast*, January 17, 2020.

CHAPTER 15: SMEARED

328 *"Rudy Giuliani, on behalf of President Trump, led a smear campaign"*: The U.S. House of Representatives, "The Trump-Ukraine Impeachment Report," December 2019, pp. 38–40.

329 *"so somebody knew where I was"*: Christianné Allen interview.

329 *"I have no other way to protect my reputation"*: Adam Entous, "The Ukrainian Prosecutor Behind Trump's Impeachment," *New Yorker*, December 16, 2019.

330 *He and Rion resumed their interviews inside a private room*: Video, "One America News Investigates: Ukrainian Witnesses Destroy Schiff's Case (Part 3)," One America News Network, December 16, 2019.

330 *"I wish I'd met you earlier"*: Ibid.

330 *smoked cigars, drank whiskey, and snacked on horsemeat sausages*: Andrii Telizhenko interview.

331 *"human Dobermans in little black Mercedes"*: @ChanelRion, "It was flattering to have George Soros and Viktor Pinchuk personally waiting for us at the airport

last night in Kiev—with their entourage of human Dobermans in little black Mercedes," December 19, 2019, Twitter.com.

331 *"What did you get?" [and subsequent quotation]:* Rebecca Ballhaus and Julie Bykowicz in Washington and Thomas Grove in Kyiv, "'Just Having Fun': Giuliani Doubles Down on Ukraine Probes," *Wall Street Journal*, December 13, 2019.

331 *"He's going to make a report":* Amanda Becker, "Democrats Huddle to Draft Impeachment Charges Against Trump," Reuters, December 7, 2019.

331 *"That's Rudy":* Shane Harris, Ellen Nakashima, Greg Miller, and Josh Dawsey, "White House Was Warned Giuliani Was Target of Russian Intelligence Operation to Feed Misinformation to Trump," *Washington Post*, October 15, 2020.

331 *"a devastating pile of smoking guns" [and two subsequent quotations]:* "One America News Investigates: Ukrainian Witnesses Destroy Schiff's Case (Part 3)," YouTube user One America News Network, December 16, 2019; Aaron Blake, "One America News's Ukraine-Rudy Giuliani Exposé is a Stunning Piece of Propaganda," *Washington Post*, December 16, 2019.

332 *"I feel betrayed by a man that I supported":* Sarah Maslin Nir, "Giuliani Divorce: It's Ugly, It's Operatic. What Did You Expect?," *New York Times*, September 13, 2019.

332 *"Judith is vindictive":* Emily Smith, "Rudy Giuliani Claims 'Vindictive' Ex Is Trying to 'Extort' Him out of Millions," *New York Post*, March 14, 2019.

332 *"We both cried" [and four subsequent quotations, including by Giuliani]:* Judith Giuliani interview.

333 *"I never understood why your very existence...":* Letter from Ken Kurson to Judith Nathan obtained by author.

334 *"SUCH ATROCIOUS LIES BY THE RADICAL LEFT":* Quint Forgey, "Impeachment: As Impeachment Vote Nears, Trump Accuses Democrats of an 'Assault on America,'" *Politico*, December 18, 2019.

334 *"I don't know if you could have found anyone who could have been a real Rudy ally":* Confidential interview with Trump senior advisor.

334 *"He was happy to see the mayor":* Christianné Allen interview.

334 *"They just kind of made the whole thing a big swirl":* Jason Miller interview.

334 *"Secretary of Deflection":* Anthony Scaramucci interview.

334 *"very, very good insurance":* Stephanie Kirchgaessner, "Rudy Giuliani says Trump will stay loyal to him but jokes that he has 'insurance,'" *Guardian,* November 14, 2019.

335 *"Rudy was there when a lot of you guys weren't":* Jason Miller interview.

335 *"The thing about Rudy that he doesn't understand now is that Trump has hung him out to dry already":* Transcript, *CNN Tonight*, CNN, January 15, 2020.

336 *"Fuck Trump!":* Christianné Allen interview.

336 *"The need to begin defending our God-given freedoms":* anne.allen.165, "Honored to announce my Ambassadorship with the new think tank Falkirk Center! Co-Founded by my home university's (Liberty University) President, Jerry Falwell Jr.

and Turning Point USA founder Charlie Kirk. The need to begin defending our God-given freedoms in America has never been greater! Our center's mission will be to 'equip courageous champions to proclaim the Truth of Jesus Christ, to advance His Kingdom, and renew American ideals.' We are CHAMPIONS of Christ for America!," November 30, 2019, Facebook.com.

337 *"The Democrats would call it impeachment" [and subsequent quotation]*: Video, *"Rudy Giuliani's Common Sense*: Since No Crimes Exist, It Must Be Dismissed," Episode 1, YouTube user Rudy Giuliani, January 24, 2020.

338 *"I have very definite opinions on the best cigars for the right time and the right place"*: Video, *"Rudy Giuliani's Common Sense*: The Trial: Opening Statement Bombshell Documents," Episode 2, YouTube user Rudy Giuliani, January 29, 2020.

338 *"Acquitted for life!"*: @RudyGiuliani, "Acquitted for life," February 5, 2020, Twitter.com.

338 *"Right now, as we're speaking, I'm signing your presidential pardon"*: Larry Celona, "Bernie Kerik Details the Trump Pardon Phone Call That Changed His Life," *New York Post*, February 18, 2020.

339 *"and not even in order" [and two subsequent quotations]*: Christianné Allen interview.

340 *"Biden can't complete a sentence"*: @RudyGiuliani, "In addition Biden can't complete a sentence. Imagine if you could cross examine him about the millions and millions the Biden Family Enterprise made selling his office?," March 2, 2020, Twitter.com.

340 *"Do we have to diagnose"*: @RudyGiuliani, "Do we have to diagnose what is wrong with him? It's obvious. However, like his corrupt pattern of selling his office for millions since he was a Senator, the Swamp Media covers it up. They hate DJT so much, they don't care about the damage done to our country," March 8, 2020, Twitter.com.

340 *"The Democrat party must think we"*: @RudyGiuliani, "The Democrat party must think we, the American people, are idiots. In a year this man may not know his own name," March 9, 2020, Twitter.com.

340 *that the candidate had dementia*: Transcript, "Rudy Giuliani, President Trump's Personal Attorney Is Interviewed on Fox News' 'Watters' World,'" Fox News, August 16, 2020.

340 *"WOW! Sleepy Joe doesn't know"*: Marty Johnson, "Trump: Biden 'Doesn't Know Where He Is, or What He's Doing,'" *The Hill*, March 3, 2020.

340 *hit #3 on a ratings chart at one point*: December 29, 2020, weekly update from Chartable for *Rudy Giuliani's Common Sense*.

341 *"Now with 7 days of Mob rule of cities"*: @rudygiuliani, "Now with 7 days of Mob rule of cities with mostly DEMOCRAT MAYORS, it is obvious that these Mayors are incapable of protecting their citizens. They enable the rioters by abandoning police precincts for burning and ordering police to stand down and be assaulted without arrest," June 1, 2020, Twitter.com.

Notes

341 *"Put 1,000 people in prison": Bernie & Sid in the Morning,* 77 WABC Radio, June 2, 2020.

341 *"WAKE UP!":* @rudygiuliani, "WAKE UP! Black Lives Matter wants to destroy law enforcement, end bail, empty the prisons (including drug dealers as well as users), provide themselves with reparations, AND a full-time government income without the necessity of work," June 23, 2020, Twitter.com.

341 *"To support BLM":* @rudygiuliani, "To support BLM is to support:- Violence - Anarchy - Obliteration of history - Destruction of much of our Constitution - Common ownership of property - Destruction of Israel - The elimination of our American way of life People are being fooled by Black Lives Matter," June 25, 2020, Twitter.com.

342 *"That is an accurate statement, an accurate warning" [and twenty subsequent quotations in interview with Piers Morgan]:* Video and typed transcript, "Piers and Rudy Giuliani Clash over Donald Trump's Tweets | Good Morning Britain," *Good Morning Britain,* June 4, 2020.

344 *"So, you did ask Ukraine to look":* Transcript, "Rudy Giuliani, Attorney for President Trump, Interviewed on CNN 'Cuomo Prime Time,'" CQ Transcriptions, September 19, 2019.

344 *"Shut up, moron!":* Transcript, "Rudy Giuliani on His Role in Ukraine Issue, Discusses Trip to Ukraine; Fox News Network Ingraham Angle," Fox News, September 24, 2019.

344 *"phony":* Ken Meyer, "Out-of-Control Giuliani Blows Up Bloomberg TV Interview with Wild Rant over Hunter Biden, Joe's 'Dementia,'" *Mediaite,* October 7, 2020.

344 *"defamation":* Giuliani interview with Lisa Montgomery on Fox Business, October 28, 2020.

344 *"What happened to you?":* Transcript, "MSNBC's Jonathan Capehart Cuts Right to Chase in Hot Mess Interview with Rudy Giuliani: 'What Happened to You?,'" MSNBC, September 12, 2020.

344 *"Soros is hardly a Jew" [and five subsequent quotations]:* Olivia Nuzzi, "A Conversation with Rudy Giuliani over Bloody Marys at the Mark Hotel," *New York,* December 23, 2019.

345 *"I'm the president, I already know how to do this":* Confidential interview with a campaign official.

345 *Donald Trump sat by himself with an ice bucket, three Diet Cokes, and a bottle of hand sanitizer:* The account of the debate session comes from confidential interviews with two senior aides to the president; Chris Christie, *Republican Rescue* (New York: Simon & Schuster, 2021), pp. 68–74; and Carol Leonnig and Philip Rucker, *I Alone Can Fix It: Donald J. Trump's Catastrophic Final Year* (New York: Penguin, 2021), 293.

346 *"Go to Hunter...go to Ukraine...go to the Biden family grift" [and five subsequent quotations]:* Confidential interviews with multiple senior aides to Trump.

433

Notes

347 *"a hot mess inside a dumpster fire inside a trainwreck" [and subsequent quotation]:* Transcript, "Trump-Biden Chaotic Presidential Debate Analysis," CNN, September 29, 2020.

347 *"Would you shut up, man?":* Presidential debate, September 29, 2020.

347 *"Smoking-gun email reveals how Hunter Biden introduced Ukrainian businessman to VP dad" [and subsequent quotation]:* Emma-Jo Morris and Gabrielle Fonrouge, "Smoking-Gun Email Reveals How Hunter Biden Introduced Ukrainian Businessman to VP Dad," *New York Post*, October 14, 2020.

348 *could not say whether the customer was Hunter Biden:* Jordan Howell and Erin Banco, "Man Who Reportedly Gave Hunter's Laptop to Rudy Speaks Out in Bizarre Interview," *The Daily Beast*, October 14, 2020.

348 *The previous month, the Treasury Department outed Andriy Derkach, whom Giuliani interviewed in Ukraine, as an active Russian agent:* "Treasury Sanctions Russia-Linked Election Interference Actors," United States Department of Treasury, September 10, 2020.

348 *"foreign element":* Joel Gehrke, "Pompeo Hints at 'Foreign Element' Behind Hunter Biden Leaks," *Washington Examiner*, October 15, 2020.

348 *"deeply suspicious that the Russian government":* "Public Statement on the Hunter Biden Emails," letter, October 19, 2020.

349 *"It is completely unverified and frankly, Rudy Giuliani is not the most reliable source anymore":* Colby Hall, "Exclusive: Fox News Passed on Hunter Biden Laptop Story over Credibility Concerns," *Mediaite*, October 19, 2020.

349 *"Let's say, just not sugarcoat it":* Reed Richardson, "Bret Baier Calls Out Dubious Sourcing of Alleged Hunter Biden Emails: Let's 'Not Sugarcoat It, This Whole Thing Is Sketchy,'" *Mediaite*, October 15, 2020.

349 *"The Pentagon Papers were stolen, but the press had no problem printing it":* Rudy Giuliani Show, 77 WABC Radio, October 15, 2020.

349 *he authenticated two emails from the laptop:* Ryan Lizza, Rachael Bade, Tara Palmeri, and Eugene Daniels, "Politico Playbook: Double Trouble for Biden," *Politico*, September 21, 2021.

349 *The* New York Times *concurred months later:* Katie Benner, Kenneth P. Vogel, and Michael S. Schmidt, "Hunter Biden Paid Tax Bill, but Broad Federal Investigation Continues," *New York Times*, March 16, 2022.

349 *"They checked every box" [and subsequent quotation]:* Christianné Allen interview.

350 *Cohen deliberately timed the film to debut a few weeks before Election Day:* Eric Kohn, "Giuliani with His Hands Down His Pants: An Oral History of the 'Borat 2' Scene That Shocked the Nation," *IndieWire*, December 22, 2020.

350 *"You are one of my greatest heroes" [and sixteen subsequent quotations]: Borat Subsequent Moviefilm: Delivery of Prodigious Bribe to American Regime for Make Benefit Once Glorious Nation of Kazakhstan,* Jason Woliner, New Line Cinema, 2020.

351 *After she pulled out the wiring he lay down on the bed, face up, and dug far into his pants to tuck his shirt back in:* Ibid.

352 *"a complete fabrication":* Emily Smith, "Rudy Giuliani Says 'Borat' Sting Is 'Complete Fabrication,'" *New York Post*, October 21, 2020.

352 *"I take off a mic every night":* Annabel Nugent, "Stephen Colbert Lampoons Rudy Giuliani's Borat Defense: 'I Would Buy That, but I've Watched the Footage,'" *The Independent*, October, 23, 2020.

352 *"love-hate relationship with conspiracies":* Matt Flegenheimer, "Joe Rogan Is Too Big to Cancel," *New York Times*, July 1, 2021.

352 *"gross":* Johnell Gipson, "Joe Rogan Shares His Thoughts on Rudy Giuliani's Embarrassing 'Borat 2' Scene—'Did He Know That She Was Supposed to Be 15?,'" *CheatSheet*, October 27, 2020.

352 *"'Borat Subsequent Moviefilm' captured Giuliani in a private, un-vetted, scotch-filled meeting at a critical moment in our country's history":* Chris O'Falt, "'Borat 2': The Real News Is Rudy Giuliani's Staggering Lack of Judgment," *IndieWire*, October 22, 2020.

353 *"There's only one reason [Hunter] has that drug problem":* "'Any Time They Want': If Biden Wins, Democrats Themselves Could Oust Him at Whim, Trump's Lawyer Giuliani Tells RT," RT, November 3, 2020.

354 *"We should assume if he has a credible lead":* "Rudy Giuliani: Trump Should Declare Victory 'as Early as Possible,'" *MediaMatters*, November 3, 2020.

354 *Giuliani spent his evening at a desk in the Red Room with his son, Andrew:* Reporting on Giuliani's actions at the White House on election night is based on interviews with senior administration officials who were present at the time. Many details were first reported by Carol Leonnig and Philip Rucker, *I Alone Can Fix It: Donald J. Trump's Catastrophic Final Year* (New York: Penguin, 2021).

355 *"There were a lot more important things to do than talk to Rudy" [and nine subsequent quotations in conversation between Giuliani and others]:* Confidential interviews with senior administration officials.

356 *"This is a fraud on the American public":* Leonnig and Rucker, *I Alone Can Fix It*, p. 346.

CHAPTER 16: CONSPIRACY

358 *"Dear Mr. President," she wrote on January 10, "I tried to call you yesterday to talk about business" [and six subsequent paragraphs, including bullet points from the letter]:* Author viewed the letter. Maria Ryan did not respond to numerous requests for an interview.

360 *"Guys, this is fraud" [and eleven subsequent quotations, including from others at the press conference]:* Transcript, "Trump Campaign Press Conference," November 4, 2020.

360 *"Obviously a political hack"*: Ibid.

361 *"something out of a Coen brothers film"*: Transcript, "Biden on Cusp of 270, with Only AK, AZ, GA, NC, NV and PA to Be Called; Presidential Race Tightens in Georgia," CNN, November 4, 2020.

361 *"I talked to the president" [and four subsequent quotations]*: Bernie Kerik interview.

362 *"People didn't want to be associated with him"*: Confidential interview with senior campaign official.

362 *"STOP THE COUNT!"*: Aaron Rupar, "Trump's desperate 'STOP THE COUNT!' tweet, briefly explained," *Vox*, November, 5 2020.

363 *"They had no plan" [and four subsequent quotations]*: Confidential interviews with senior campaign officials.

364 *"Lawyers Press Conference Four Seasons, Philadelphia" [and three subsequent tweets]*: Video of press conference; Jose Martinez, "Donald Trump's Lawyers Hold Press Conference at Wrong Four Seasons in Philadelphia," *Yahoo*, November 7, 2020.

365 *"Are they coming to you or are they coming to me?" [and subsequent quotation]*: Interview with Marie Siravo.

365 *"This is the guy from 9/11"*: Interview with Daryl Brooks.

365 *Brooks had served over three years in prison for allegedly exposing himself to two young girls*: Interview with Daryl Brooks; Dave Goldiner, "Giuliani Shrugs Off GOP Poll Watcher's Sex Conviction and Compares Trump Volunteer to Hunter Biden," New York *Daily News*, November 9, 2020.

366 *"How can they call an election" [and two subsequent quotations]*: Transcript and video, "Trump Campaign Pennsylvania News Conference," C-SPAN, November 7, 2020.

366 *"It's not looking good" [and subsequent quotation]*: Confidential interviews with senior campaign officials.

367 *"All the networks" [and subsequent quotations]*: Transcript and video, "Trump Campaign Pennsylvania News Conference," C-SPAN, November 7, 2020.

367 *the others waited while the president changed*: Confidential interviews with senior campaign officials.

368 *"This was a dishonest election" [and four subsequent quotations]*: *Uncovering the Truth with Rudy Giuliani & Dr. Maria Ryan*, 77 WABC Radio, November 8, 2020.

368 *"He had zero regard for whether something was factual or not" [and subsequent quotation]*: Confidential interview with a senior aide to Trump.

369 *"Why isn't he looking into all the stuff that we're finding" [and eight subsequent quotations]*: Bernie Kerik interview.

369 *"bullshit," and referred to his team as a "clown show"*: William Barr, *One Damn Thing After Another: Memoirs of an Attorney General* (New York: William Morrow, 2022).

370 *"100 percent within his rights"*: Dareh Gregorian and Julie Tsirkin, "McConnell Shrugs Off Trump Concession Delay," NBC News, November 9, 2020.

370 *"They're letting you down" [and two subsequent quotations]*: Confidential interviews with people who witnessed the Oval Office confrontation; Carol Leonnig and Philip Rucker, *I Alone Can Fix It: Donald J. Trump's Catastrophic Final Year* (New York: Penguin, 2021), p. 346; Jonathan Swan, "Off the Rails," *Axios*, January 17, 2021.

370 *"It's actually mind-boggling when you look at it" [and two subsequent quotations]*: Rudy Giuliani Show, 77 WABC Radio, November 13, 2020.

371 *the president had just named him the new head of his legal team*: Christianné Allen interview.

372 *But Clark's team had edited it heavily*: Bernie Kerik interview; confidential interviews with campaign officials.

372 *"The best description of the situation is widespread nationwide voter fraud" [and three subsequent quotations]*: Transcript and video, "Clip of Donald J. Trump for President, Inc. v. Boockvar Oral Argument," User clip, C-SPAN, November 20, 2020.

373 *"One might expect that when seeking such a startling outcome" [and two subsequent quotations]*: Memorandum Opinion, *Donald J. Trump for President, Inc., et al. v. Kathy Boockvar, et al.*, No. 4:20-CV-02078, November 21, 2020.

374 *"thousands and thousands" [and subsequent quotation]*: Transcript and video, "Trump Campaign News Conference on Legal Challenges," C-SPAN, November 19, 2020.

374 *"There were just thousands of clicks happening"*: Christianné Allen interview.

374 *"Nobody's going to pay attention to the fucking fraud"*: Bernie Kerik interview.

375 *"What we are really dealing with here and uncovering" [and two subsequent quotations]*: Transcript and video, "Trump Campaign News Conference on Legal Challenges," C-SPAN, November 19, 2020.

375 *"We'll own her and all of her craziness"*: Jason Miller interview.

375 *"I've seen all of you taking pictures right now"*: Transcript and video, "Trump Campaign News Conference on Legal Challenges," C-SPAN, November 19, 2020.

376 *"a grotesque embarrassment"*: Ibid.

376 *"a complete embarrassment"*: Confidential interview with a campaign official.

376 *"a national embarrassment"*: Video, "'The Conduct of the President's Legal Team Is a National Embarrassment': Christie," ABC News, November 22, 2020.

376 *"the most dangerous one hour and 45 minutes of television in American history"*: Transcript, *The ReidOut*, MSNBC, November 19, 2020.

376 *"He didn't focus on it for more than thirty seconds" [and subsequent quotation]*: Bernie Kerik and Christianné Allen interviews.

376 *"Look, the people who certified your election" [and seven subsequent quotations in conversation between Carone and Johnson]*: Transcript, "Trump Lawyers Rudy

Giuliani & Jenna Ellis Testify Before Michigan House Oversight Committee: Full Transcript," Rev.com, December 3, 2020.

377 *sending lewd videos of her fiancé and her to his former wife:* Violet Ikonomova, "Giuliani's Michigan Witness Mellissa Carone Harassed, Sent Sex Videos to Boyfriend's Ex," *Deadline Detroit*, December 4, 2020.

377 *"... as if they're vials of cocaine":* Giuliani testimony to Georgia legislators, December 10, 2020.

377 *"We've got lots of theories":* testimony of Rusty Bowers before House January 7 hearings, June 21, 2022.

377 *"The White House physician helped a lot":* Geoff Earle Rachel Sharp, "I Got Ultra-Rare Regeneron to Cure My COVID, Rudy Giuliani Says—After Admitting He Got Better Treatment Because He Is 'a Celebrity,' " *Daily Mail*, December 11, 2020.

378 *"Rudy Giuliani is a horrible human being":* Dana Milbank, "As Americans Die by the Thousands, Trump Cronies Cut in Line for Coronavirus Treatments and Vaccines," *Washington Post*, December 14, 2020.

378 *Jared Kushner ... checked out of the situation:* Peter Baker and Susan Glasser, *The Divider: Trump in the White House, 2017–2021* (New York: Simon & Schuster, 2022).

379 *he called a contact at the Department of Homeland Security, Ken Cuccinelli ... Giuliani stopped Trump before it was set in motion, and helped prevent a historic disaster ... Trump told Giuliani he didn't want to see her back in the White House:* Interview with Bernie Kerik; Maggie Haberman and Zolan Kanno-Youngs, "Trump Weighed Naming Election Conspiracy Theorist as Special Counsel," *New York Times*, December 19, 2020; Jonathan Swan, "Off the Rails: Inside the Craziest Meeting of the Trump Presidency," *Axios*, February 2, 2021; Alan Feuer, Maggie Haberman, Michael S. Schmidt, and Luke Broadwater, "Trump Had Role in Weighing Proposals to Seize Voting Machines," *New York Times*, January 31, 2022.

380 *"We are in the eve of a day that will live in history" [and subsequent quotation]:* Rudy Giuliani Show, 77 WABC Radio, January 5, 2021.

380 *who sent fake certifications to Congress hoping to delay the January 6 count:* Luke Broadwater and Alan Feuer, "Jan. 6 Committee Subpoenas Fake Trump Electors," *New York Times*, January 28, 2022.

380 *"What they're saying is not just a cover-up":* The Rudy Giuliani show, 77 WABC Radio, January 5, 2021.

381 *took a drive that turned into a crawl:* Bernie Kerik interview.

381 *"Every single thing that has been outlined as the plan for today is perfectly legal" [and two subsequent quotations]:* Transcript, "Rudy Giuliani Speech Transcript at Trump's Washington, D.C. Rally: Wants 'Trial by Combat,' " Rev.com, January 6, 2021.

382 *head back to the Willard with him twenty minutes into the president's speech:* Bernie Kerik interview.

Notes

382 *"fight like hell"*: Brian Naylor, "Read Trump's Jan. 6 Speech, A Key Part of Impeachment Trial," NPR, February 10, 2021.

383 *"I'm not there at Capitol Hill, but I'm watching it right across the street" [and two subsequent quotations]: Rudy Giuliani Show*, 77 WABC Radio, January 6, 2021.

EPILOGUE

386 *"didn't have time" [and subsequent quotation]*: Eric Coomer, Ph.D., *Plaintiff v. Donald J. Trump for President, Inc., et al., Defendants*, "Videotaped Deposition of Rudolph Giuliani," Case Number 2020CV34319, August 14, 2021.

387 *a cash drain so serious that he feared bankruptcy*: Inae Oh, "Rudy Giuliani Is Reportedly Close to Broke—And Donald Trump Isn't Taking His Calls," *Mother Jones*, August 1, 2021.

387 *"the love of my life"*: *Rudy Giuliani Show*, 77 WABC Radio, January 21, 2021.

387 *"corrupt double standard"*: William K. Rashbaum, Ben Protess, Maggie Haberman, and Kenneth P. Vogel, "F.B.I. Searches Giuliani's Home and Office, Seizing Phones and Computers," *New York Times*, April 28, 2021.

387 *even Fox axed him from its 9/11 programming*: Tara Palmeri, "Politico Playbook: Scoop: Fox to Rudy: You're Banned," *Politico*, September 24, 2021.

388 *"The mayor has a long and distinguished career"*: Dominic Patten, "Rudy Giuliani Not Banned from Fox News, Just Not 'Relevant,'" *Deadline*, September 24, 2021.

388 *"I don't come here a lot"*: Melissa Russo, "Rudy Giuliani: 'If You Think I Committed a Crime, You're Probably Really Stupid,'" NBC News, July 31, 2021.

388 *"I'm very comfortable with it"*: Melissa Russo, "Rudy Giuliani Denies Alcohol Problem, Sounds Off on FBI in Exclusive Interview," NBC News, August 27, 2021.

388 *"He also is well aware that people think he's gone off the rails"*: Melissa Russo, "Rudy Giuliani Reflects on Sept. 11 Attacks and on His Legacy," NBC New York, September 10, 2021.

389 *"I wanted to grab his stars, shove it down his throat" [and two subsequent quotations]*: Video, "Twitter—Rudy Giuliani Drunk Speech at the 9/11 Dinner (12th September 2021)," YouTube user Walthero Thor, September 12, 2021.

389 *"What happened to me is the same thing"*: Video and typed transcripts, "Piers and Rudy Giuliani Clash over Donald Trump's Tweets," *Good Morning Britain*, June 4, 2020.

390 *"He believed what he was doing was right"*: Christianné Allen interview.

Index

441

Index

Index

Index

Index

awards and honors, *see* awards and honors of RG

birth (1944), 12–13, 16

George W. Bush and, 160–61, 169, 200–202, 206, 209

Catholic priesthood and, 21, 22, 26, 31, 45, 167–68

chemistry with Donald Trump, 83, 239–41, 255, 265–66, 270–71, 300, 334–35

children, *see* Giuliani, Andrew (son); Giuliani, Caroline (daughter)

conservative resentment politics and, 250–55, 266–69, 339–40

education, *see* education of RG

family background, 12–18, 20–21, 32–33, 36–37, 52–53, 95, 198–99

financial challenges, 306, 357–59, 387–88

full name of, 23

health issues, *see* health issues of RG

homes of, *see* homes of RG

law enforcement as mayor, *see* law enforcement and RG as mayor

Leadership, 42, 174, 183, 196, 216, 302

legal career, *see* legal career of RG

long-term presidential aspirations, 12, 23, 33, 207–9, 233

marriages and relationships, *see* Hanover, Donna (wife); Lategano, Cristyne; Nathan, Judith Stish (companion and wife); Peruggi, Regina "Gina" (wife); Ryan, Maria

mayoral campaigns, *see entries beginning with* "mayoral election"

mayoralty of New York City, *see* mayoralty of RG

media relations, *see* media relations of RG

moral compass of, *see* moral compass of RG

opera and, 14, 33, 34, 121, 256, 344

political affiliations, *see* political affiliations of RG

presidential campaign (2008), *see* presidential campaign of RG (2008)

Senate campaign, *see* U.S. Senate campaign of RG (2000)

seventy-fifth birthday, 303–5, 322

Donald Trump and, *see* Trump, Donald; Trump and presidential election of 2016; Trump and presidential election of 2020; Trump presidency

Vietnam War draft deferment, 34–35

Washington Speakers Bureau engagements, 4, 171, 172, 173–75

Giuliani, Rudy (uncle), 175

Giuliani Capital Advisors, 199

Giuliani Communications, 357

Giuliani-Kerik (later named Giuliani Security & Safety), 199

Giuliani Partners LLC, 4, 162–74, 199, 209–10, 385

decline of, 262–63, 306

Ernst & Young and, 162–66, 175, 241–42

Keiko Fujimori (Peru) and, 248

income of, 171–75, 211, 242–43

Kerik resigns from, 206

Vitali Klitschko (Ukraine) and, 242–43

Lifelock and, 234–35, 249, 272, 309

Mujahedin-e Khalq/"People's Holy Warriors of Iran" (MEK) and, 248–49

National Thoroughbred Racing Association (NTRA) and, 170–71

Manny Papir leaves, 179–80

Purdue Pharma/OxyContin and, 169–70, 230, 249

Qatar and, 230

RG presidential campaign (2008) and, 234–36, 241–43, 306

Sony Music Entertainment and, 172–73

Aleksandar Vucic (Serbia) and, 246–47

Reza Zarrab (Turkey) and, 286–89

Giuliani Security & Safety Asia, 199

Giuliani-Von Essen, 199

Givhan, Robin, 198

Goeas, Ed, 213, 226–27, 232

Goldberg, Jay, 50, 293

Goldman, Daniel, 322–23

Index

Index

Index

Index

Index

Index

Index

Index

Index

Index

Index